Developmental/Adapted Physical Education

Making Ability Count

FIFTH EDITION

Michael Horvat Ed.D.
University of Georgia

Leonard Kalakian Ph.D.
Emeritus, Minnesota State University–Mankato

Ron Croce Ph.D.
University of New Hampshire

Virginia Dahlstrom

Benjamin Cummings

Boston   Columbus   Indianapolis   New York   San Francisco   Upper Saddle River
Amsterdam   Cape Town   Dubai   London   Madrid   Milan   Munich   Paris   Montreal   Toronto
Delhi   Mexico City   Sao Paulo   Sydney   Hong Kong   Seoul   Singapore   Taipei   Tokyo

Acquisitions Editor: *Sandra Lindelof*
Editorial Assistant: *Brianna Paulson*
Project Editor: *Katie Cook*
Production Supervisor: *David Chavez*
Cover Design: *tani hasegawa*
Manufacturing Buyer: *Jeff Sargent*
Marketing Manager: *Neena Bali*
Production Management and Composition: *Elm Street Publishing Services/Integra Software Services Pvt. Ltd.*

Library of Congress Cataloging-in-Publication Data
Developmental/adapted physical education /
    Michael Horvat . . . [et al.],. —5th ed.
        p. cm.
Includes bibliographical references and index.
ISBN-13: 978-0-321-67827-0
ISBN-10: 0-321-67827-3
    1. Physical education for people with disabilities—United States.   2. Mainstreaming in education—United States.
I. Horvat, Michael A., 1947-
    GV445.E34 2011
    796.04'56–dc22

                                                                            2009045208

1 2 3 4 5 6 7 8 9 10—QWD—14 13 12 11 10

Benjamin Cummings
is an imprint of

www.pearsonhighered.com

ISBN-13: 978-0-321-67827-0
ISBN-10:   0-321-67827-3

To my brother, mom (in memory), and dad (in memory), who taught me the importance of self-respect and the imperative of hard work and doing what is right; and to my wife (Lisa) and children (Ryan and Morgan). I love you all.

—Ron Croce

I acknowledge my husband, Len Kalakian, for his inspiration, wonderful spirit, and continual support.

—Virginia Dahlstrom

This book is dedicated to John and Adaline Horvat who taught me the value of hard work and believing in myself; and to my children Ian, Kala, and Michael.

—Michael Horvat

Contents

Preface

Developmental/Adapted Physical Education: Making Ability Count serves not only as the title of this book but also as an underlying statement of philosophy. The fifth edition was undertaken in an effort to provide a conscientiously updated and reliable resource focusing on the ever-expanding world of physical activity for individuals with disabilities. Since 2003, when the fourth edition of our text published, extensive changes have occurred in methodologies, teaching techniques, and legal requirements for teaching individuals with disabilities. These changes have evolved from both empirical and experimental research as well as from changes in federal and state legislation.

All human beings, particularly with regard to acquisition of fundamental motor skills, climb a universal developmental ladder. The climb up this developmental ladder is characterized by an orderly, sequential achievement of developmental motor milestones (hence, the text's title). While genetic endowment, relative ability/disability, and individual experience (nature and nurture) impact the rate at which one progresses from one developmental milestone to another, they *do not* have a material impact on the orderly sequence of developmental milestone achievements.

Adapted physical educators must understand typical human development as their benchmark reference for understanding and recognizing when, where, how, and why development departs from that which is typical. When a child's unique interweaving of nature and nurture are found to impede typical development, the teacher must seek alternative approaches to teaching/learning to better accommodate the child's unique circumstances. In effect, the teacher seeks to adapt curriculum; with the primary goal to minimize, to the extent possible, the gap between the child's present developmental status and his or her developmental potential.

Too often, the task of teaching children who have disabilities is perceived in a negative context; one that tends to focus on what the child *cannot* do. Our approach throughout the text is one that focuses on ability first; on what the child *can* do. The *making ability count* approach celebrates that which the child brings to the table, and builds from there. It accentuates the child's positives, and, in turn, facilitates development of educational goals whose primary focus is not disability; but, rather, the child's potential. Emphasis is on the child's development of functional abilities and independence.

As authors, teachers, and educational administrators we have regular occasion to field questions from physical education (adapted and general), special education, and elementary classroom teachers regarding how certain activities should be taught and/or which types of activities might be suitable for students who have certain disabilities.

Some of these questions include:

- What can I do to help?
- What sorts of activities are indicated/contraindicated for my student with _____ (fill in condition name)?
- Where can I go to find information about children who have _____ (fill in condition name)?
- Are there special safety precautions about which I must be aware?
- What are some of the ways physical education activities can be modified to accommodate my students who have disabilities?
- How and when can children with disabilities be included in general physical education classes?
- What do I need to know when teaching children whose disabilities stem from health disorders?
- I believe one of my students could benefit from a switch, at least part time, into segregated, adapted physical education. Where do I go, now?

Answers to such questions will be unique to the individual child, whose individual situation prompts a call for an individual answer. This text has been designed to help readers answer the questions above and a range of similar questions according to individual student circumstances.

Today's physical educator must be able to teach all children, including those with disabilities. Both general and adapted specialists must be knowledgeable with regard to (1) administration and interpretation of a range of test results, (2) writing individualized physical and motor fitness/skill programs, (3) determining criteria for educational placement (regular or adapted), and (4) selection and application of teaching strategies unique to individual children, often in the same class, who present with a range of learning styles and abilities.

We continually emphasize using the team approach; incorporating special educators, physicians, administrators, therapists, parents, and children into a smoothly functioning unit. The physical educator must be able to use the vocabulary of the other professionals on the team. Without a thorough background in, and understanding of, various conditions, the physical educator risks being excluded (overtly or covertly) from the important opportunity to make important recommendations and decisions regarding educational placement.

Our years as public school physical education teachers, adapted physical education teachers, and coaches; in addition to our experience in higher education, has prepared us to write a text that is knowledge-based and field tested. In addition, we have taught adapted physical education courses, have supervised clinical and practicum experiences, and have an understanding of what the teacher needs to be successful in teaching or coaching children with disabilities. We have upgraded all aspects of the text especially the chapters on autism, head injuries, and teaching methodologies (pedagogy), and believe that even teachers with limited experience can formulate meaningful curricula for virtually all children with disabilities. Case studies and learning activities are embedded in every chapter of the fifth edition; we encourage instructors to use these to implement learning strategies in a school environment.

Finally, physical educators must never lose sight of the overall role they play in the total development of each child who comes under their guidance. The physical, emotional, social, and cognitive benefits that accrue from positive experiences of physical activity should never be underestimated. Sometime around the 1st and 2nd century A.D., the Roman poet Juvinal wrote, *"Sit mens sana in corpore sano."* A sound mind in a sound body. The translated full text of the passage advises that, 'a sound mind in a sound body is a thing to be prayed for.' This advice is as sound today as it was two millennia ago. No child should ever be excluded from meaningful participation in physical education and sport.

Acknowledgments

This textbook could not have been written without the insights and encouragement from many individuals whom the authors count as professional colleagues and friends. We are especially grateful to colleagues who provided editorial comments throughout the project from whom we received encouragement to continue. We are also indebted to the pioneer efforts of teachers, coaches, students, and athletes (all with and without disabilities) who have taught us about individual differences and who have taken ideas about the achievement of human potential to unprecedented new heights.

We offer sincere thanks to the following reviewers who forced us to think about and explain things more clearly: Carol Barnes, Mississippi College; Luis Columna, State University of New York, Cortland; Mary Lou Baranowski Drews, San Diego State University; Sherry Folsom-Meek, Minnesota State University, Mankato; Jason Langley, West Virginia University; Everette McAnally, Freed-Hardeman University; Scott Modell, California State University, Sacramento; and Dennis Vacante, University of Maryland.

We extend special thanks to Steve Butterfield and Anne Gruzladi for their comments and suggestions; to Dr. Larry Verity for his input on the diabetes chapter, and to Chris Ray for his suggestions to the chapter that addresses visual impairments.

Thank you to organizations and individuals who provided photos including:

- Parents and children of the Pediatric Exercise and Motor Development Clinic, University of Georgia
- Wadena-Deer Creek, MN public school students, parents, teachers, Terry Olson, and administrators
- Miracle Softball League
- U. S. Paralympics
- Courage Center, Golden Valley, MN.

We count it a privilege to be able to share this textbook with our colleagues in adapted physical education, and are especially appreciative of colleagues for whom *Developmental/Adapted Physical Education: Making Ability Count* has remained the text of choice. Were it not for you, this text would not have survived the first edition.

We would be egregiously remiss were we not to acknowledge, gratefully, Dr. Carl Eichstaedt who began this process more than 20 years ago. His extensive contributions to this project's previous four editions are pillars in the platform upon which this text stands today. We thank Carl for setting the bar so high in the beginning and hope to continue to build upon the tradition that he has been so instrumental in establishing.

Finally, we thank the publishing team at Benjamin Cummings; including a very special thanks to Project Editor, Katie Cook for everything she has done to make an extraordinarily difficult task doable.

Michael Horvat

Leonard Kalakian

Ron Croce

Virginia Dahlstrom

Introduction: Physical Education for Children With Disabilities

The chapters in this section provide information concerning legal mandates and the placement of children with disabilities into physical education. The initial steps in providing services for children with disabilities are described in chapters that address the collaborative programming team; the parent-teacher team; assessment and evaluation; cognitive and perceptual development; and development of physical fitness. With this information, you should be able to

1. understand the basis for physical education services at the federal, state, and local level

2. understand how to develop an individualized education plan (IEP) and what it means to place children with disabilities in the least restrictive learning environment or the most appropriate environment

3. understand the roles of parents and various professionals in the educational process

4. understand the process of evaluation and assessment in program planning and implementation

5. understand and apply the concepts of physical fitness, perceptual development, and motor development when teaching children with disabilities.

But First I Have Some Questions, Professor

CASE STUDY

The professor looked at her watch and put away her notes. The students had picked up their backpacks and stored their course outlines and notes from today's lecture. The first day was over. She felt this was going to be a good group. Several students had volunteered. Others had asked insightful questions. One student told of his experience as a volunteer for a local Special Olympics team. Another shared that she had a brother who had died from Duchenne muscular dystrophy. One student expressed concern about the impact of teaching physical education in a full inclusion setting and wondered whether she would really be able to effectively teach children with disabilities. The class wasn't hesitant to ask questions such as these:

- You mean children with disabilities haven't always been in school? Why and when did this come about?
- How will I know whether a condition qualifies as a disability? Who decides?
- If I'm teaching regular physical education, what kinds of disabilities might some of my children have?
- What are some causes of disability?
- Is physical education really required for ALL children with ALL types of disabilities?
- Who decides whether a child with a disability is going to be in my physical education class?
- How will I determine children with disabilities' physical education needs?
- What if one of my children is blind? Can I say things like, "See you later?"
- Is there a difference between "disability" and "handicap"?
- What is "person first" language and why is it important?
- Sometimes kids (and adults) can be insensitive, even cruel. Will children in my regular class (and my colleagues) be accepting of children they perceive as "different"? What can I do?

After returning to the office, the professor thought that, yes, there were many questions to answer regarding individuals with disabilities and their ability to participate in physical activity, sports, and recreation. When these students graduate, they may be faced with the challenge to provide meaningful physical activity opportunities for individuals with disabilities in a variety of settings. From there, the professor's thoughts turned to fine-tuning the next day's lecture and discussion for the Adapted Physical Education class.

This chapter focuses on questions you may want to ask, or are thinking about, as you start your experience in adapted physical education. When confronted by new and challenging situations, you need to know where any given new situation might lead.

We tend to want to ask questions when faced with situations that seem relatively removed from our previous experiences. However, the more we need to know, the more fearful we may be about exposing our self-perceived naiveties. As a physical education teacher, you may be particularly concerned about your responsibility to develop and implement programs for children with disabilities.

Let us consider some important initial questions. As concerns arise in the course of your class experience, we anticipate that your questions will be encouraged and welcomed. Be assured there is far less risk in asking a question than in allowing a possible harmful situation to develop because your question may have gone unasked.

You Mean Children With Disabilities Haven't Always Been in School? Why and When Did All This Come About?

Until relatively recently, many children with disabilities were not merely isolated from regular school programs—in many cases, they were excluded from school entirely. Parents of children with disabilities became accustomed to "Sorry, but" excuses for their child's ineligibility for public education: "Sorry, but . . .

- Your child has too many behavior issues
- Our buildings are not designed to accommodate children who use wheelchairs
- We are not equipped to provide services to children with severe intellectual disabilities
- Your child has multiple disabilities. Her deafness disqualifies her for services for our students who are blind, and her blindness disqualifies her for services for our students who are deaf."

Until recently, parents had little recourse but to accept these explanations. Whereas more well-to-do parents may have had opportunity to seek expensive private educational services, parents of modest means often had no choice but to see their children go without educational services.

Not too long ago, when children with disabilities were afforded public education, they would be grouped (i.e. segregated) categorically according to disability. For example, children with a range of intellectual disabilities would be placed in one program, while children with a range of physical disabilities would be placed in a separate program. In such situations, the disability label dictated educational placement, and curriculums within such programs tended to be of a disability-specific "one size fits all" nature.

Categorical groupings, however well-intentioned, often did little more than promote preconceived notions and negative stereotypes among education professionals (and the public) about disability labels, including the children to whom labels were applied (i.e., if you've seen one, you've seen them all). Preconceived notions about disability labels in education tend to drive curriculum decisions and delivery. Categorical approaches tend to prompt questions like: "What are the educational needs of children with cerebral palsy?" Current approaches

ask the question: "What are the education needs of this individual child who happens to have cerebral palsy?" Here, individual need trumps label. The nature of the latter question acknowledges that children who share a disability label often may have little in common beyond their shared disability label.

Today, children with a range of disabilities identified in laws, both federal and state, are fully entitled to a free, public education. That education is required to be individually designed when necessary, and take place to the degree reasonably possible in regular education settings (i.e., the least restrictive environment).

How Will I Know Whether a Condition Qualifies as a Disability? Who Decides?

To be eligible to receive special education services, according to federal special education law, a child must first be diagnosed with a condition recognized by law as disabling. Although having a law-specified disability is a precondition to be eligible for special education services, the disability, by itself, does not automatically warrant education apart from regular curriculums. Once a child is deemed eligible for special education by virtue of having a recognized disability, that disability, for educational programming purposes, becomes subordinate to the child's assessment-determined, individual educational needs.

Federal special education law recognizes the following conditions as disabilities. (Please note that the terms below are federal classifications and do not represent the most current terminology.)

Autism—is a developmental disability significantly affecting verbal and nonverbal communication and social interaction that adversely affects a child's educational performance. Generally evident before age three, other characteristics associated with autism are engagement in repetitive activities and stereotyped movements, resistance to environmental change or change in daily routines, and unusual responses to sensory experiences.

Deaf-blindness—means concomitant hearing and visual impairment, the combination of which causes such severe communication and other developmental and educational needs that they cannot be accommodated in special education programs solely for children with deafness or children with blindness.

Deafness—is a hearing impairment that is so severe that the child is impaired in processing linguistic information through hearing, with or without amplification that adversely affects a child's educational performance.

Hearing impairment—is an impairment in hearing, whether permanent or fluctuating, which adversely affects a child's educational performance but is not included under the definition of deafness.

Emotional disturbance—(the term includes schizophrenia) means a condition exhibiting one or more of the following characteristics over a long period of time and to a marked degree that adversely affects a child's educational performance:

- An inability to learn that cannot be explained by intellectual, sensory, or health factors.
- An inability to build or maintain satisfactory interpersonal relationships with peers and teachers.
- Inappropriate types of behavior or feelings under normal circumstances.
- A general pervasive mood of unhappiness or depression.
- A tendency to develop physical symptoms or fears associated with personal or school problems.

Mental retardation—means significantly sub-average general intellectual functioning, existing concurrently with deficits in adaptive behavior and manifested during the developmental period that adversely affects a child's educational performance.

Multiple disabilities—means concomitant impairments (such as mental retardation-blindness or mental retardation-orthopedic impairment), the combination of which causes such severe educational needs that the students cannot be accommodated in special education programs solely for one of the impairments. Multiple disabilities does not include deaf-blindness.

Orthopedic impairment—is a severe orthopedic impairment that adversely affects a child's educational performance. The term includes impairments caused by a congenital anomaly, impairments caused by disease (e.g., poliomyelitis, bone tuberculosis), and impairments from other causes (e.g., cerebral palsy, amputations, and fractures or burns that cause contractures).

Other health impairment—means having limited strength, vitality, or alertness, including a heightened alertness to environmental stimuli that results in limited alertness with respect to the educational environment, that:

- Is due to chronic or acute health problems such as asthma, attention deficit disorder or attention deficit hyperactivity disorder, diabetes, epilepsy, a heart condition, hemophilia, lead poisoning, leukemia, nephritis, rheumatic fever, sickle cell anemia, and Tourette syndrome; and
- Adversely affects a child's educational performance.

Specific learning disability—means a disorder in one or more of the basic psychological processes involved in understanding or in using language, spoken or written, that may manifest itself in the imperfect ability to listen, think, speak, read, write, spell, or do mathematical calculations, including conditions such as perceptual disabilities, brain injury, minimal brain dysfunction, dyslexia, and developmental aphasia.

Specific learning disability does not include learning problems that are primarily the result of visual, hearing, or motor disabilities, mental retardation, emotional disturbance, or environmental, cultural, or economic disadvantage.

Speech or language impairment—means a communication disorder, such as stuttering, impaired articulation, language impairment, or a voice impairment, which adversely affects a child's educational performance.

Traumatic brain injury—is an acquired injury to the brain caused by an external physical force, resulting in total or partial functional disability, psychosocial impairment, or both, that adversely affects a child's educational performance. Traumatic brain injury applies to open or closed head injuries resulting in impairments in one or more areas, such as cognition; language; memory; attention; reasoning; abstract thinking; judgment; problem solving; sensory, perceptual, and motor abilities; psychosocial behavior; physical functions; information processing; and speech. Traumatic brain injury does not apply to brain injuries that are congenital or degenerative, or to brain injuries induced by birth trauma.

Visual impairment including blindness—is impairment in vision that, even with correction, adversely affects a child's educational performance. The term includes both partial sight and blindness (34 CFR 300.8, July 2007).

Having one of these disabilities serves predominately to determine that a child qualifies for consideration for special education services; it does not automatically mean a child will receive special education. That determination is to be based on need, not on label. Determination of a child's need for special education services, including adapted physical education, typically is made at the local level with direction or assistance from state and federal laws and guidelines.

If I'm Teaching Regular Physical Education, What Kinds of Disabilities Will I See in My Class?

Refer to the above list of disability categories. You may expect to see children from any category in a regular physical education class. Three decades ago, Julien Stein (1979) stated, "The success and effectiveness of programs, activities, and efforts should be based upon numbers of children screened out of—not into—special programs." He suggested that there is a potential to successfully integrate 90–95% of children with disabilities into regular physical education programs. His prediction has largely come to fruition. Over the years, more and more children with disabilities have been placed safely and successfully in regular physical education settings and served by regular physical education teachers. Increasingly, adapted physical education specialists primarily serve children whose disabilities preempt meaningful participation in regular physical education classes. Alternately, adapted physical education specialists serve as consultants to physical education teachers in inclusion settings.

What Are Some Causes Of Disability?

Disabilities may be congenital or acquired. A congenital disability is one that comes with and is generally, but not always, apparent at birth. An acquired disability is one that can occur anytime in life following birth. Certain congenital disabilities may not clinically manifest themselves or be diagnosed until sometime after birth, (e.g. Duchenne muscular dystrophy). Nonetheless, such conditions are considered congenital.

Congenital disabilities can be caused by genetic abnormalities. Down syndrome, a condition that among other manifestations causes intellectual deficiency, is one familiar example. Congenital disabilities can be caused by certain maternal infections during pregnancy. Rubella (German measles) during the first trimester is known to cause cerebral palsy. Ingesting certain intoxicants during pregnancy, including drugs (both legal and illicit), tobacco, and alcohol, can result in birth defects. These are but a few examples.

Acquired disabilities can result from causes ranging from obvious (e.g., illness or injury) to unknown. Someone might acquire a heart condition from rheumatic fever (disease) or sustain spinal cord damage in a fall (injury). Yet another might develop asthma (cause unknown).

Is Physical Education Really Required for All Children With All Types of Disabilities?

The answer is a qualified yes, and derives predominately from special education law enacted by Congress in the mid-1970s. Today's qualified "yes" answer was at one time less equivocal.

The original law, Public Law 94-142 (Education for All Handicapped Act of 1975), mandated for the first time in history that children with disabilities, who fell within the law's age range, were fully entitled to a free public education, individually designed if necessary, in the least restrictive environment. Of particular and lasting importance to

physical educators, physical education was explicitly included in the law's definition of special education. Despite three major revisions of PL 94-142, physical education remains integral to each revision's definition of special education.

Prior to PL 94-142's most recent revision (entitled Individuals with Disabilities Education Improvement Act of 2004 [IDEIA 2004] or [IDEA 2004]), physical education generally was understood to be an entitlement for all students with disabilities, regardless of whether physical education was provided to students without disabilities. The final regulation pursuant to IDEA 2004, as it presently affects physical education, reads as follows:

> . . . the public agency has no obligation to provide children with disabilities physical education if it does not provide physical education to nondisabled children attending their schools (Federal Register, 2006).

Hence, the answer is yes, *provided* physical education is otherwise a requirement for similar students without disabilities. If a school requires no physical education for students without disabilities, it cannot be compelled to provide physical education for a student in that school who has a disability. If a student with a disability were in the eleventh grade in a school *and the school required physical education only through grade ten*, the school would not need to provide physical education to the eleventh grader with a disability. Finally, while a school cannot be compelled to provide physical education in either of the above cases, according to IDEA 2004, nothing in the law would appear to prevent a school from providing the physical education to a student with a disability according to the school's discretion.

Children who have conditions that do not qualify as disabilities under IDEA may be entitled to individualized programming under Section 504 of the Rehabilitation Act of 1973. Section 504 specifies that no person by reason of disability alone "shall . . . be excluded from participation in, denied the benefits of, or be subjected to discrimination under any program receiving Federal financial assistance." Section 504, unlike IDEA, does not rely on disability labels to determine eligibility for special services. Instead, Section 504 specifies that anyone with significant limitations in one or more major life activities is eligible to be considered for special services. Therefore, for example, a person with obesity who is not associated with any special-education law recognized disability could be eligible for individualized education (including physical education) under Section 504 if the obesity significantly limited the person in any recognized major life activity (e.g., mobility, education, work).

Who Decides Whether a Child With a Disability Is Going to be in My Physical Education Class?

Anyone, in any given educational setting, can make a referral to initiate an inquiry as to what type of physical education, regular or adapted, a child with a disability should receive. You, as a physical education teacher, whether you teach regular or adapted physical education, may be a part of this decision-making process.

Once a child is referred and assessed to identify his or her unique educational needs, IDEA 2004 designates who shall be part of the needs assessment and placement determination process. Designees include the following:

- someone representing regular education
- someone representing special education
- someone representing school administration
- parent or guardian
- child (when appropriate)
- a person qualified to interpret results of assessment to determine individual needs.
- any additional person mutually agreed on by the above parties (e.g., school nurse, school psychologist, physical therapist) (CFR 300.34, 2007)

Although IDEA 2004 does not specify that someone representing physical education, regular or adapted, must be a member of the above team, the law clearly intends that persons with special expertise in educational areas being assessed are to be integral to the decision-making process. Even though the intent of the law is clear, parents and teachers need to be vigilant to ensure that physical education is represented whenever the child's physical education is being considered.

How Will I Know What a Child With a Disability Needs in Physical Education?

If you are a regular physical education teacher, keep in mind that children with disabilities are children who first and foremost are children, but who happen to have disabilities. Quite generally, children and youth with disabilities and those without disabilities tend to be more alike than different. The vast majority of what good teachers know about educating children and youth without disabilities is directly applicable to children with disabilities. Whenever one allows disability to inordinately stand at the forefront of relationships with persons who have disabilities, one risks losing sight of the reality that people typically are much more alike than different.

If you are an adapted physical education teacher, you will have specialized in the education of persons who have disabilities, and you will be knowledgeable across a spectrum of situations and conditions that may affect a person's physical education attitudes, aptitudes, and experience. You may well be the person to whom the regular physical education teacher comes for consultation about a question concerning a child. When you, as an adapted physical education specialist, have questions, you might consult with a college or university colleague specializing in adapted physical education. Additionally, you will be able to access recent professional journal articles and research.

Finally, whenever a child with a disability has physical education needs that are different from those met within the context of the regular curriculum, an individualized education plan (IEP), as mandated in IDEA 2004, will be developed. The IEP, where it addresses physical education, will give the physical education teacher direction in meeting the child's unique physical education needs.

What if One of My Students Happens to be Blind? Can I Say Things Like, "See You Later?"

Generally, yes. "See you later" quite typically is construed as nothing more than an acknowledgment that two or more people are temporarily parting company. Likewise, generally it is fine to go out for a "run" with a friend who trains in a wheelchair or to say to your friend who is deaf, "I hear you're having a good football season this year." Whenever you are in doubt about something you believe a person with a disability might be sensitive about, just ask. Most persons with disabilities will respond readily and frankly and empathize with your need to know.

Is There a Difference Between "Disability" and "Handicap"?

Yes, although dictionaries oftentimes do not make the distinction. Throughout this text, one may be considered to have a disability when an organ or body part does not function in accordance with standard expectations. A disability may be considered to have become a handicap when the condition that disables limits the individual's ability to do what he/she wants to do. In essence, a disability may or may not be handicapping. Much depends, first, on the individuals' relationship with his/her disability and, second, on the particular situation in which the individual finds him/herself.

It is important to note that the term disability is objective (i.e. a statement of fact), while the term handicap is subjective (i.e. a statement of opinion). A disability may or may not be handicapping. One need understand that, to say a person's disability is handicapping is to make a subjective judgment about that person's relationship with his/her disability. Such determination is often best left to the individual whenever he/she has the capacity and maturity to reason.

Disability Versus Handicap

One can objectively note that a person has an amputation. South African runner Oscar Pistorius runs 400 meters in 46:25. The world record is 43:18. Oscar Pistorius has two below-the-knee amputations; he runs with prostheses (Michaelis, 2008). Oscar has a disability, but does Oscar have a handicap?

One can objectively note that a person has diabetes. Steve Chop, an athlete with insulin-dependent diabetes, competes in ironman triathlons (2.4 mile swim, 112 mile bike, 26.2 mile run) (Peterson, 2008). Steve Chop, as a triathlete, has a disability, but does he have a handicap?

One can objectively note that a person has paraplegia. Charles Krauthammer, a Pulitzer Prize winner, syndicated columnist, and cable news commentator has paraplegia. Does Charles, as a writer and news commentator, have a handicap?

According to the scenarios above, answers to the disability versus handicap question might tend to fall into the "no" handicap category. However, one should not make decisions without knowing the individual. The authors prefer disability over handicap unless one can be reasonably sure that the disability in question rises to the level of a handicap.

What Is The Meaning of Person First Language, and Why Is It Important?

"The guiding principle for 'non-handicapping' language is to maintain the integrity of individuals as human beings. Avoid language that equates persons with their condition..." (Publication Manual of the American Psychological Association, 2001).

Person first language serves to ensure that acknowledgement and recognition of a person with a disability always remains first and foremost on the person and always second on the person's disability label. Examples: He is not an autistic child. He is a child with autism (i.e. a child who happens to have autism). She is not a diabetic. She is a person with diabetes. The man is not epileptic. He is a man who has epilepsy. Avoid thinking, "the disabled." Instead, think in terms of "persons who have disabilities." In a similar vein, guard against referring to a group with like disabilities by the disability label group members share (e.g. the epileptics).

Too often when the label comes before the person (e.g. he's autistic), the person becomes the label. The label essentially becomes the person's identity. The person becomes reduced to his/her disability label, and labels all too generally focus attention on the aspect of one's personhood that is negatively stereotyping. Too often labels bring into the forefront how the person is different and implicitly somehow inferior to people not so-labeled.

Begin by using person-first language if you are not already doing so, and sensitively support others who have yet to recognize the often devaluing reality that we reduce people to labels when, however unwittingly, we allow labels to come before people. The above is not fairly dismissible as political correctness, as some might allege. It is a matter of dignity and treating people with respect.

LEARNING ACTIVITY

Having read this chapter's questions and answers, what additional questions come to mind which you would like answered? Discuss your questions with your classmates and then, present your questions (and answers) to your professor.

Sometimes Kids (and Adults) Can Be Insensitive, Even Cruel. Will My Children Without Disabilities (and My Colleagues) Be Accepting of Children They Perceive as "Different?" What Can I Do?

Be the best example possible, avoiding any inclination toward self-righteousness. People would likely, and perhaps rightly, perceive such an attitude as condescending.

Be positive in efforts to promote an environment that is fair for all. Try not to look the other way when your intervention might make a positive difference. Try to avoid laughing at remarks or jokes made at another's expense. Indeed, try thoughtfully to intervene. Intervention can be particularly trying when colleagues are the source of questionable remarks and jokes. When you hear remarks and behaviors directed at others, ask yourself, "Is this the way I would want to be thought of, spoken about, or treated"?

Avoid refering to children with disabilities as "special." Many persons with disabilities do not want or appreciate the "special" designation. "Special" has a habit of pushing to the forefront that one part of the person's being which sets her or him apart, obscuring the many more things the person may have in common with others.

Do not be overly indulgent toward or accepting of behaviors among children who have disabilities that, were it not for disability, you might find irritating or unacceptable. Such a double standard is not helpful to the person in question and serves only to perpetuate the objectionable behavior. The presence of disability, by itself, is not grounds for expecting less from your child.

CHAPTER SUMMARY

1. Questions that appear in this chapter are representative of those asked in the authors' classes by students who are new to adapted physical education. They are real questions from real people. More questions will arise as the term progresses, and you are encouraged to ask. Know that your questions can contribute positively to class dynamics. Classes tend to be most satisfying, from both the students' and teacher's perspective, when students proactively take part in the learning process.

2. Many people, including some students and their teachers, unwittingly perpetuate disability labels and stereotypes about people who have disabilities and, in so doing, deny persons with disability dignity, individuality, and opportunity to achieve in accordance to potential.

3. Physical education teachers, regular and adapted, must become familiar with the origin, duration, and severity range of many disabling conditions, but even more important, physical educators must learn to look beyond the disability so as to develop meaningful learning experiences designed to maximize each individual's unique potential.

4. Quite generally, children with and without disabilities are more alike than different. Recognizing this reality can become an important part of the rationale to include, whenever reasonably possible, children with disabilities in regular education settings.

5. A major trend over the past three decades has been to include more students with disabilities in regular education settings. There are at least two explanations, one negative and one positive. Negative: increasingly tight budgets, particularly during tight economic times, mitigate against placing students with disabilities, when educationally necessary, in relatively more restrictive educational settings. Positive: progress with regard to teacher preparation, both pre-service and in-service, enables teachers today, perhaps more than ever before, to meaningfully integrate students with disabilities into regular classroom settings.

6. IDEA 2004 is the latest revision of blockbuster federal special education legislation that first appeared in 1975 (Education for All Handicapped Children Act of 1975). Of particular significance to physical educators is that physical education is explicitly mentioned by name in the law's definition of special education. Physical education, by virtue of its explicit inclusion in the definition, is integral to special education, and, therefore, must be made available to children with disabilities, wherever such opportunities are available to children without disabilities.

REFERENCES

34 CFR, Section 300.8. Child with a Disability. Ch III, p. 12. (2007, July 1).

American Psychological Association. (2001). *Publication Manual of the American Psychological Association* (5th ed.). Washington DC.

Assistance to States for the Education of Children with Disabilities and Preschool Grants for Children with Disabilities; Final Rule. Federal Register, 34 CFR, parts 300 and 301. Department of Education. (2006, August 14).

IDEIA. (2004). Individuals with Disabilities Education Improvement Act of 2004 (IDEIA 2004 or IDEA 2004), Pub. L. No. 108–446.

Michaelis, V. (2008, April 28). Double-amputee sprinter takes case to court. *USA Today*.

Peterson, L. (2008, March 12). Diabetic triathlete prepares for Wisconsin competition. *The Advocate of Eldersburg and Sykesville*.

Rehabilitation Act of 1973, Pub. L. No. 93–112 §504, Title V.

Shalock, R.L., et.al. (2007). The renaming of mental retardation: Understanding the change to the term Intellectual Disability. *Intellectual and Developmental Disabilities, 2*, 116–124.

Stein, J.U. (1979, June). The mission and mandate: Physical Education, the not so sleeping giant. *Education Limited*, 27–29.

CHAPTER 2

Legal Mandates

Eric is an 11th grade boy with Down syndrome. As with many students with Down syndrome, Eric is overweight. If Eric's propensity to gain weight gain does not become the focus of continued intervention, he most certainly will become obese in early adulthood.

Physical education in Eric's state is required of all students through the 10th grade. Given Eric's IDEA 2004-recognized disability, he has, through grade 10, qualified for both regular and adapted physical education, and his IEP has focused helping him maintain a healthy lean body mass to fat ratio. Now that Eric is an 11th grader, his school, according to new language in IDEA 2004, is no longer required to provide him physical education, adapted or otherwise. New language in IDEA 2004 essentially states that adapted physical education is required only if physical education is a requirement at the student's grade level.

Eric's parents have asked his school district's director of special education about what the school can and should do to ensure Eric continues to benefit from activity levels to help him maintain healthy body composition. They have suggested that, if federal special education laws no longer apply, perhaps one or more federal civil rights laws applicable to education might. The special education director has agreed to research the matter. The parents have indicated their intent to consult with the state's primary special education advocacy group and, if necessary, a civil rights attorney for answers to ensure that all bases have been covered.

Compulsory education laws have been in effect nationwide since 1918. That being said, students with disabilities were routinely excluded from opportunity for a public education throughout the majority of the twentieth century. When students with disabilities were accepted, they typically received the barest curriculum adaptations, and their eventual dropping out of school was the rule rather than the exception.

Although advocacy organizations for persons with disabilities had been in existence for decades throughout the twentieth century, some dating back to the late nineteenth century, their impact on public education remained limited. Advocacy organizations heightened public awareness, strived to persuade, and appealed to senses of moral obligation, but schools and a range of agencies, both public and private, quite generally were not legally obliged to respond.

Today, schools are obliged by both federal and state civil rights and special education mandates to educate students with disabilities. Providing special education services is no longer an option. It is the law, federal law.

To facilitate an appreciation for how far special education, including adapted physical education as an integral part of special education, has come in a relatively short period, this chapter chronicles ground breaking court decisions and federal mandates that have brought us where we are today.

Civil rights laws presented herein remain intact and in force. The predominate federal special education law that drives the practice of special education today, including the practice of adapted physical education, is PL 108-446, Individuals with Disabilities Education Improvement Act of 2004 (IDEIA 2004 or IDEA 2004). IDEA 2004 is the fourth, and most recent, revision of the act that began as PL 94-142, Education for All Handicapped Children Act of 1975.

Readers should be aware that each state will have its own set of special education laws, and said laws will impact the practice of physical education for students with disabilities in unique ways. State laws, however, while they may add to or build upon requirements imposed by federal laws, cannot in any way diminish the rights granted by federal laws. While reviewing state laws clearly transcends the scope of this text, readers are advised to become aware of relevant education law in the states where they practice.

Brown v. Board of Education

The beginning of the end of unresponsiveness to advocacy for persons with disabilities in and out of schools occurred, however unintentional the result, in 1954 with the historic U.S. Supreme Court case *Brown v. Board of Education* in Topeka, Kansas. Prior to this court decision, African-Americans received programs/services (when services were provided), including education, apart (i.e. segregated) from those offered to the majority White community. Segregation had long been legitimized according to the premise that segregation was legal as long as separate programs/services were deemed, according to the majority community, to be equal. The policy historically had been referred to as *separate but equal*. Reality was that separate but equal was always separate, but seldom, if ever, equal.

The *Brown v. Board of Education* decision signaled the beginning of the end of race-based segregation in public schools. The court wrote: "In these days, it is doubtful that any child may reasonably be expected to succeed in life if he is denied the opportunity for an education. Such opportunity, where the state has undertaken to provide it, is a right and must be available on equal terms." The effect of the court's ruling was that separate was inherently unequal and, therefore, in violation of the U.S. Constitutional guarantee of equal protection under the law.

Disability Advocacy Groups See Disability Civil Rights Parallels

Relying on legal principles of the Brown decision and, later, the Civil Rights Act of 1964 (which explicitly outlawed discrimination based on race), parents of children with disabilities began to demand equal constitutional rights for their children. Parents of children with disabilities and their advocates argued that persons with disabilities, like persons of color (both groups had been historically disenfranchised from the mainstream of the American experience), were entitled to equal protection under the law.

Parents of children with disabilities and their advocates asserted that equal protection under the law called for education for children with disabilities that must be both free and appropriate.

The first major breakthrough resulting from such advocacy came in 1965 with Title IV of the Elementary and Secondary Education Act (Public Law 89-750). This act authorized grants to states to initiate, expand, and improve educational programs for children with disabilities and created a Bureau of Education for the Handicapped.[1]

Although PL 89-750 was designed to provide educational opportunities for children with disabilities, many schools circumvented its directives. At that point, advocacy groups through the courts began to exert even more pressure. What was to become a national phenomenon began in 1971 when the Pennsylvania Association for Retarded Children filed suit *(PARC v. Commonwealth of Pennsylvania)* on behalf of 13 citizens in that state with intellectual disabilities. Citing the U.S. Constitution's guarantees of equal protection under the law, the suit argued that these children's access to public education should be equal to that afforded children without disabilities. In a consent agreement, the court ruled in favor of PARC.

One year later (1972), the federal court in the District of Columbia issued a similar ruling involving not only children with intellectual disabilities, but also those with the full range of conditions causing disability. All children, said U.S. District Judge Joseph Waddy *(Mills v. Board of Education)*, have a right to suitable publicly supported education, regardless of the degree of the child's mental, physical, or emotional disability. In response to arguments that this position would impose an intolerable financial burden on the community, Judge Waddy added the following: "If sufficient funds are not available to finance all of the services and programs needed and desirable in the system, then the available funds must be expended equitably in such a manner that no child is entirely excluded from a publicly supported education" (p. 1728).

---

[1] The term *handicap* appeared in federal language as a descriptor of federal choice until passage of Public Law 101-476. (Individuals with Disabilities Education Act [IDEA], 1990). Passage of this law marked the end of *handicap* as a descriptor in federal language. With passage of Public Law 101-476, the word *disability* in federal language replaced *handicap*. Rationale for this change appears elsewhere in this text. Throughout the remainder of this chapter, where the term *handicap* or other terms or phrases no longer considered current continue to be used, the authors' purpose is to remain true to the text of language as written at the time.

Section 504 Of The Rehabilitation Act Of 1973 (PL 93-112)

In September 1973, Congress enacted legislation prohibiting agencies receiving federal funding from discriminating on the basis of disability. Section 504 of the Rehabilitation Act of 1973 (PL 93-112) states: "No otherwise qualified handicapped individual in the United States . . . shall, solely by reason of his handicap, be excluded from the participation in, be denied the benefits of, or be subjected to discrimination under any program or activity receiving Federal financial assistance."

Section 504 requires that programs offered by institutions that accept federal funds must be *physically* accessible to persons with disabilities. The physical accessibility mandates in Section 504 specifically address architectural barriers affecting persons with disabilities. The law, at the time of passage, did not require that all of an institution's structures be accessible to persons with disabilities. Rather, it required that entire programs be accessible. In the case of schools, entire programs in many cases could be made accessible through reasonable reassignment to alternate classes, rooms, and/or buildings. Building modifications became required only when reasonable accommodations could not otherwise be made. For example, remodeling would be necessary if a student using a wheelchair were required to be on the second floor of her school building to take the only section of a required class. Remodeling might take the form of an elevator or disability accessible lift retrofitted to the stairs. Since June 3, 1977, all buildings belonging to institutions covered under Section 504 are required to have been constructed according to Section 504's minimum accessibility requirements.

LEARNING ACTIVITY

Explore your campus and/or community. Identify at least 10 accommodations that have been made in your environment specifically designed to make physical space more accessible to persons who have disabilities (e.g. Brailed elevator buttons, curb cuts at corners, curb cuts with bumps, drinking fountains accessible to persons who use wheelchairs).

Section 504 asserts that all programs must be conducted in the least restrictive and most integrated settings feasible. In other words, a student may not be categorically assigned to a special program or segregated activity (e.g., adapted swimming) simply because the student has hearing loss. To be compliant, an institution cannot solely on the basis of disability (1) *categorically separate* groups of individuals with disabilities from groups of individuals without disabilities, or (2) *indiscriminately place* an individual with disabilities in special or segregated programs and/or activities. For example, a student (or group of students), who is legally blind may not be assigned arbitrarily to a special program or segregated activity (e.g. swimming) purely based on legal blindness.

Regarding Section 504's impact specific to physical education and activity-centered co-curriculums, the implications become exceedingly clear. Section 504 mandates that disability alone as justification for exclusion does not satisfy intent of the law. Guarantees of protection against discrimination and equal protection under the law are afforded in all aspects of school offerings. This includes, if not explicitly, then clearly implicitly, physical education, intramural sports, and interscholastic sports, all of which are to be suitably modified as necessary.

Compliance with Section 504 is federal law and is applicable nationwide. Publically funded institutions nationwide, including schools, need remain compliant with the law to ensure continuing eligibility to receive federal funding.

Education for All Handicapped Children Act of 1975 (PL 94-142)

Public Law 94-142 clearly became a law of blockbuster proportions. This law, was singularly responsible for setting in motion the kind and quality of education for children with disabilities that we see, and sometimes take for granted, today. To this day, PL 94-142 remains widely regarded as a major turning point in special education, including physical education, for person's with disabilities in the United States.

Unlike previous federal special education initiatives, PL 94-142 had no expiration date and was regarded as a permanent instrument. The law addressed special education needs of children with disabilities ages 3 through 21. This law did not simply mark another expression of federal interest in special education. Rather, it provided a specific educational commitment to all children with disabilities. Public Law 94-142 clearly set forth as national policy the proposition that meaningful education must be extended as a fundamental right to individuals with disabilities. Public Law 94-142 became a lightning rod for both positive and negative reaction from all branches of education. Regardless of individual perceptions of the propriety of this law, its provisions since passage have had far-reaching affects on the education of virtually every child with a disability.

Although not a new term in federal language, PL 94-142 made clear reference to *child find*. The child find provision of PL 94-142 required that all children in a state who need special education, regardless of severity of disability, must be located, identified, and evaluated. This mandate was born of the premise that all children have value and can learn if given appropriate educational opportunity and that society can no longer excuse its failure to provide that opportunity by claiming lack of funds and/or unawareness of the existence of children with disabilities. Youngsters with disabilities were now to be brought out of the educational shadows and accounted for by local school districts. Public Law 94-142 called for education in the *least restrictive environment* (LRE). LRE, in the original law and subsequent revisions, refers to the place in school where the child is to be assigned educationally; it must be the most beneficial teaching and learning environment for the child. To the maximum extent possible, children with disabilities are to be educated alongside children without disabilities. Although there is nothing in the mandate requiring that children with disabilities be educated alongside children without disabilities, clearly the mandate is that such educational placements occur to the maximum extent whenever reasonably possible.

LRE emphasizes identification of the individual child's unique educational needs. Recognizing individual needs *before* considering the most appropriate placement (i.e., LRE) is of utmost importance. These placements (note the plural, because often the child benefits most from more than a single placement) can be in different groupings and/or at different sites, but all must be identified and justified as necessary to adequately address the child's individual needs.

To ensure that the education of a child with a disability was indeed appropriate, each child whose educational needs could not be met within the context of the regular curriculum became entitled to an individualized education plan (IEP). The IEP in its inception and as it exists today is a written document developed cooperatively by parents and the school (and the child, when appropriate). This document specifies what unique or special programs and/or services will be provided to meet the child's unique educational needs. Not all children with disabilities necessarily need IEPs. However, any child with a disability is entitled to an IEP (and by law, one must be in place) whenever any special program or service apart from the regular curriculum is provided specifically to meet the child's unique educational needs.

Public Law 94-142 mandated that all expenses incurred by the school to educate a child with a disability occur at no cost to the parent. The district within which the child with disability resides must either provide a free, appropriate education in the least restrict environment or contract for and stand the cost of educating the child in some alternative setting. Regardless of where the education transpires and costs incurred, parents incur no educational costs for educating their child with a disability beyond paying taxes earmarked to support public education.

Explicit Inclusion of Physical Education

Physical education's prominence within PL 94-142, including its explicit inclusion within the law's definition of special education, was no coincidence. Support for physical education as being integral to special education was steadfast within the congressional committee that authored the bill. The committee's position on physical education, which became part of the law's final language, read as follows:

> Special education as set forth in the Committee bill includes instruction in physical education, which is provided as a matter of course to all nonhandicapped children enrolled in public elementary and secondary schools. The Committee is concerned that although these services are available to and required of all children in our schools, they are often viewed as a luxury for handicapped children. The Committee expects the Commissioner of Education to take whatever action is necessary to assure that physical education services are available to all handicapped children and has specifically included physical education within the definition of special education to make clear that the Committee expects such service, specially designed when necessary, to be provided as an integral part of the educational program of every handicapped child. (1977, p. 42, 489)

Beginning with 94-142 in 1975 and through three subsequent major revisions (IDEA 1990, IDEA 1997, and IDEA 2004), physical education has been explicitly included in the law's definition of special education. Specifically, note (ii) immediately below: "Special education means specially designed instruction, at no cost to the parents, to meet the unique needs of a child with a disability, including... (ii) Instruction in physical education" (34 CFR 300.39, Ch. III, 1 July 2007).

Physical education services must be provided according to the law. Language reads as follows:

a. "Physical education services, specially designed if necessary, must be made available to every child with a disability receiving free appropriate public education (FAPE), unless the public agency enrolls children without disabilities and does not provide physical education to children without disabilities in the same grades.

b. Regular physical education. Each child with a disability must be afforded the opportunity to participate in the regular physical education program available to nondisabled children unless—

1. The child is enrolled full time in a separate facility; or
2. The child needs specially designed physical education, as prescribed in the child's IEP.

c. Special physical education. If specially designed physical education is prescribed in a child's IEP, the public agency responsible for the education of that child must provide the services directly or make arrangements for those services to be provided through other public or private programs.

d. Education in separate facilities. The public agency responsible for the education of a child with a disability who is enrolled in a separate facility must ensure that the child receives appropriate physical education services in compliance with this section" (34 CFR 300.108, Ch. III, 1 July 2007).

The law defines special education as follows:

(2) Physical education means—
(i) The development of—
A. Physical and motor fitness;
B. Fundamental motor skills and patterns; and
C. Skills in aquatics, dance, and individual and group games and sports (including intramural and lifetime sports); and
(ii) Includes special physical education, adapted physical education, movement education, and motor development (Source: 34 CFR 300.39, Ch. III, 1 July 2007).

> ### LEARNING ACTIVITY
>
> Consider physical education environments with which you are familiar. How would you rate for accessibility on a one to 10 scale these physical education facilities (1=poor, 10=exemplary)? Offer specifics when explaining reasons for your rating(s). For the physical education facilities that you rated low, how could these spaces be retrofitted to make the facilities more reasonably accessible?

Education for All Handicapped Children Act Amendments of 1986 (PL 99-457)

Although PL 94-142 addressed educating children with disabilities ages 3 through 21, the language of the law contained a loophole that resulted in the law's failure to be applied evenly across all 50 states.

Specifically, in some states, children ages 3 and 4 were not covered, because states in question, as a matter of policy, did not educate 3 and 4 year olds. This circumstance was remedied with passage of PL 99-457, wherein education of children with disabilities ages 3 and 4 became an across-the-board requirement throughout the United States. This component of the law was termed *mandatory*. Additionally, this law included a *discretionary component* calling on states to address the early intervention needs of infants and toddlers with disabilities ages 0–2. *Discretionary* meant that provision of such services was not required. However, with passage of PL 99-457, the federal government offered attractive financial incentives to states willing to mount and undertake early intervention initiatives for children with disabilities ages 0–2.

Serving a purpose similar in intent to the IEP, PL 99-457 called for development of an individualized family service plan (IFSP) for each child aged 0–2 with a disability. The purpose of the plan is to give parents insights and guidance regarding their child's education-related needs and how such needs might be met. The IFSP specifies services designed to meet the young child's unique needs. Further, the IFSP development process is one that actively solicits family involvement in both the development and implementation of the IFSP (Hallahan, Kauffman, & Pullen, 2009).

Americans with Disabilities Act (ADA) of 1990 (PL 101-336)

The Americans with Disabilities Act (ADA), like Section 504, a civil rights law, passed in 1990, became operational on June 26, 1992. The law states in essence that individuals with disabilities *must* be provided equal opportunities in all aspects of life. ADA defines an individual with a disability as one who:

- Has a physical or mental impairment that substantially limits one or more major life activities;
- Has a record of such an impairment; or
- Is regarded as having such an impairment.

In practice this act prohibits the private sector and agencies that do not receive financial assistance from discriminating against individuals with disabilities. (Section 504 of the Rehabilitation Act of 1973 had limited this prohibition to agencies that received federal financial assistance.) Communities, schools, public and private community service providers, and employers are now required to comply with mandates of ADA. Buildings, restrooms, drinking fountains, ramps, elevators, telephones, parking lots, parks, swimming pools (including health spas), and schools are now required to be disability accessible.

Title I of this law pertains to employment policies affecting individuals with disabilities. Business owners must meet the following requirements:

- Existing facilities used by employees must be made readily accessible and usable by persons with disabilities.
- Job restructuring, modification of work schedules, and reassignment to a vacant position must be utilized.
- Equipment, devices, examinations, training materials, and policies must be acquired or modified, and qualified readers or interpreters must be provided.

Although the ADA does not specifically identify public school physical education, individuals with disabilities can no longer be denied access to classes or activities solely on the basis of disability. School administrators, teachers, or coaches cannot prevent persons with disabilities from participating in an activity simply because the person may not be able to participate in *all* activities. When the person is able to participate in any part of a given activity, reasonable accommodations and adaptations must be made to enable the individual to participate meaningfully in the activity. For example, a person who does not walk may wish to bowl. An ADA case can be made to require a school or bowling establishment to provide a ramp from which the person can deliver the ball while sitting.

Violations of ADA may result in litigation and fines. Public entities, including schools, that continue to be in violation of ADA requirements risk loss of funds emanating from both state and federal government.

Individuals with Disabilities Education Act (IDEA) Of 1990 (PL 101-476)

The Individuals with Disabilities Education Act of 1990 (IDEA) became federal law on October 30, 1990. However, much of what became law with IDEA's passage already had been mandated by Congress with two previously passed federal laws, PL 94-142 (Education for All Handicapped Children Act, 1975) and PL 99-457 (Education for All Handicapped Children Act Amendments, 1986). Passage of PL 101-476

- combined Public Laws 94-142 and 99-457 under one umbrella law.
- marked the beginning of removal of the word *handicap* from federal language in favor of *disability*. The term *disability* is believed to be less judgmental, subjective, and devaluing than is *handicap*. The rationale is that a disability may or may not be handicapping, depending on how

one relates to one's disability. To label a disability as handicapping tends to promote the notion that all disabilities in general are handicapping and that a given individual's disability is handicapping to that individual. Language that promotes preconceived notions about disability, particularly words and phrases that might be arbitrarily judgmental or devaluing, need be avoided, hence the impetus for the language change.

- provided that at age 16, individualized education for a child with a disability must include an individualized transition plan (ITP) designed to better enable the child to make the transition from life in school to life in the community.

Individuals with Disabilities Education Act Amendments Of 1997 (PL 105-17)

Public Law 105-17 (IDEA 97) marked a significant review and revision of its antecedent, PL 101-476 (IDEA 1990). Several motivations prompted Congress' review. Certain discretionary programs under the original IDEA 1990 had expired and were in need of reconsideration and reauthorization. During the ensuing years, school discipline and safety had increasingly become issues that needed to be addressed. Parents, teachers, and administrators had become critical of the lack of achievement by children with disabilities under the original IDEA, and strategies needed to be adopted in the new law to address these concerns. Special education funding, in the view of special education advocates, had reached crisis proportions because of increasing costs and, in part, because of backlash from some advocates of children *without* disabilities. Advocates for the latter argued that special education funding was increasingly taking a toll on the total education budget, and education of children without disabilities had long since begun to suffer.

Congress responded to criticisms of the then existing law. Major changes that appeared in IDEA 1997 germane to the focus of this text are as follows:

- Achievement expectations for children with disabilities were heightened, to bridge the gap between what children with and without disabilities learn. The new law required that regular progress reports be made to parents of students with disabilities.
- Schools became required to include results of students with disabilities in state and district assessments and to set performance goals for students who have disabilities as they did for students without disabilities.
- Parents became more fully enfranchised in the planning of their child's education. Previously, some

states provided only for parent involvement with regard to educational decisions for their child. The revised law required that parents be integral to the process of determining eligibility for special education services, including placement decisions.

• The new law was designed to remove financial incentives for placing children in separate settings when they could be better served in a regular classroom. This was accomplished by the easing of restrictions on how IDEA funding could be used for children with disabilities in regular classroom settings, even when students without disabilities might benefit as well.

• Regular education teachers became more directly part of the team that developed the child with a disability's IEP. Such involvement became essential as the law removed barriers to placing children with disabilities into regular education settings.

• For the first time, states became required to gather data to ensure that school districts were not disproportionally, and without otherwise cause, placing children from minority or limited English proficiency backgrounds in special education. The law further required that data be gathered to determine whether children from the above groups were being disproportionally disciplined, suspended, or expelled.

• The new law was designed to enhance school safety and discipline. For the first time, IDEA 1997 clarified how school disciplinary rules and the obligation to provide a free, appropriate education to children with disabilities needed to interface. The law explicitly required that children with disabilities receive instruction and services, as needed, to help them follow rules and get along in school. Prior to disciplining a student, the school became obliged to determine if the student's behavior had been caused in whole or part by his/her disability. School officials became limited in their ability to discipline students whose unacceptable behaviors were determined to be disability related, because to do so would have been to punish the child because she/he had a disability (likewise prohibited under PL 93-112, ADA, 1990).

• The new law did recognize that certain disability-related behavior issues would require prompt intervention by school officials, specifically when the child with a disability was deemed likely by school officials to put himself/herself and/or other children at substantial risk (i.e. bringing a weapon or illegal drugs to school).

• The new law enabled the school to request from a hearing officer a suspension of up to 45 days. If the suspension was approved, the school would still be required to ensure that the child continued to receive special education services wherever she/he might be placed during the suspension period.

• IDEA 1997 was designed to reduce the potential for conflict between parents and school. The law more fully enfranchised parents in the decision making processes that affected their child's educational placement and the curriculum he/she received. The revised law further was designed to proactively report to parents on their child's educational progress.

PL 108-446, The Individuals With Disabilities Education Improvement Act of 2004 (IDEIA or IDEA 2004)

IDEA 2004 is the most recent revision of blockbuster federal special education legislation that began with PL 94-142, the Education for All Handicapped Children Act of 1975. IDEA 2004 is the fourth major revision of this non-expiring federal special education law. Earlier, we presented a synopsis of the original law, including summaries of how each revision differed from its predecessor. This brings us to the most recent revision, IDEA 2004, and a summary of how new language in this revision will impact the practice of special education, including physical education (regular and adapted), throughout IDEA 2004's lifetime. Prominent changes in IDEA 2004 have tended to focus on three general areas; the IEP process, due process, and discipline (Families and Advocates Partnership for Education/Parents Advocacy Coalition for Educational Rights, 2004, 2005).

IEP Process

Short term instructional objectives For all but a very small percentage of students who have IEPs, short term instructional objectives are no longer required. PL 94-142, including revisions up through IDEA 1997, required that IEP-stated *annual goals* be supported by companion short term instructional objectives. Short term instructional objectives, where they have appeared and where they will continue to appear, can be likened to successive steps on a skill development ladder, where the annual goal occupies the top rung. Short term instructional objectives need be written in behavioral terms, so that their achievement is clearly measurable. For example, one short term objective might state, "Using a kickboard, Len will flutter kick the entire width of the pool one time, without assistance." This objective supports the annual goal; "Len will develop a functional front crawl." Critics of deleting short term instructional objectives from IEPs cite that such objectives identify essential, behaviorally measurable, stepping stones toward achieving important IEP-stated annual goals, and as such, should remain integral to *every* IEP.

While IDEA 2004 no longer requires short term instructional objectives for the majority of students with IEPs, nothing in the new revision prevents parents and/or teachers from supporting their continued inclusion. Teachers can benefit from the continuing inclusion of short term instructional objectives, because they offer stated guides to goal achievements, including lesson plan development. Parents can benefit, because short term instructional objectives offer a measurable way to determine their student's progress from Point A to Point B, through to the achievement of an annual goal.

Grade level and alternate achievement standards for students with disabilities

The No Child Left Behind Act (PL 107-110, NCLBA or NCLB), signed into law by President George W. Bush on January 8, 2002, requires school achievement among the majority of students with disabilities to be measured according to state standards for students enrolled in the regular curriculum. For students with the most significant disabilities, achievement of alternate state achievement standards is acceptable. For all students who have an IEP, the IEP must demonstrate that state achievement standards, regular or alternate are being addressed. IDEA 2004's required alignment with NCLB, including a summary of potential pitfalls in striving to achieve alignment, appears later in this chapter.

IEP progress reports

Many advocates for students with disabilities see the IDEA 2004 change in progress reporting requirements as a weakening of the law. IDEA 1997 stated that progress reports must spell out "the extent to which progress is sufficient to *attain the goal by the end of the year.*" Progress must still be reported, but is no longer required to be reported with the precision called for in the (now deleted) quote above. Progress reporting as previously required has generally been seen as valuable information in determining the degree to which set standards were being met. Given 2004 progress reporting language, parents will be informed of their student's progress throughout the year. However, there may be heightened risk that some parents only at year's end will realize that progress has not been sufficient to achieve goals.

Transition from school to community life

Prior to IDEA 2004, IDEA required that the IEP specify a plan to help high school age students adjust from school to community living. IDEA 2004 now requires that actual transition activity, not merely a plan for activity, must begin at age 16. Successful transition ensures that when the student leaves school she/he will, in accordance with potential, function purposefully and independently within the community at large. By way of transition example applicable to physical education, a student with a disability who learns to ski in a school should, upon leaving school, be able, to the maximum extent possible, independently access opportunities to ski in the community-at-large.

IEP meeting attendance and participation options

IDEA 2004 now allows IEP team members to be excused from attendance if their area is not being discussed. It also allows for alternate means of meeting participation when actual attendance is not possible (i.e. conference calls). The new provision is viewed as having pros and cons. On one side, busy professionals are now afforded options for effective time management when meetings are called. On the other side, when professionals from across disciplines meet face-to-face, they tend to see problems/address issues from different points of view, and this sort of cross pollination risks becoming diminished when team members are absent, because their subject areas are not on the agenda.

Pilot program for multi-year IEPs

IDEA 2004 authorizes the Secretary of Education to allow school districts within certain states to offer an IEP whose lifespan is 3 years. This pilot initiative is offered to a maximum of 15 states. This initiative is seen as having pros and cons. On the con side, there is concern that 3-year IEPs, with their multi-year goals, will become less specific, and more vague than goals that appear in single year IEPs. The potential for vagueness could become further exacerbated by the IDEA 2004 provision that short term instructional objectives for the majority of students with IEPs need no longer accompany long term goals. On the pro side, professionals with primary responsibilities to serve children directly (e.g. teaching, counseling, therapy) may now be spending less time in IEP meetings and more time providing direct service to students.

Transfers between school districts

School districts that receive a new student who already has an IEP must continue providing service according to that IEP, at least temporarily. Service must be continued until that IEP is formally adopted by the receiving school or a new one has been implemented. This provision is intended to help parents know, at least in the interim, what services they can expect from the new school.

Due Process

Statute of limitations IDEA 2004 sets forth the range of services schools are obliged by law to provide. When parents believe their child's school is in violation of the law, they have a statute of limitation of two years in which to exercise due process rights. The statute of limitation clock starts once parents know or *should have known* that an alleged IDEA 2004 infraction has occurred. Interpretation of "should have known" will be critical, because the nature of that decision will determine whether a right to challenge may still be exercised.

Due process complaint notice Parents who file a due process complaint must (1) support their complaint with facts and (2) propose a solution. The school must (1) respond to the parent within 10 days or (2) within 15 days notify a state hearing officer that it is challenging the complaint. A state hearing officer upon receipt of the intent to challenge has 5 days to render a decision. The new complaint resolution process affords the school the advantage of knowing that the complaint issue at hand will be resolved within a prescribed period of time. The process is seen by critics as complex, one that intimidates parents, and in the end, may dissuade some parents from asserting their rights.

Who pays when attorneys become involved? Under certain conditions, attorneys' fees may be reimbursable to parents who prevail in due process complaints. On the other hand, parents may be obliged to pay the school's attorneys fees if their case is determined to be frivolous, unreasonable, or without foundation. Parents may become liable for a school's attorneys' fees if the parent's action is judged harassing, unnecessarily delaying, or needlessly increasing the cost of litigation.

Discipline

Stay put Students with disabilities, whose alleged violations of school rules justify more than a 10 day removal from the current educational setting, no longer have the right to remain in the current setting pending appeal. Prior to IDEA 2004, denial of the right to stay put, pending appeal, applied only to students who brought weapons or illegal drugs to school. With the advent of IDEA 2004, schools may now immediately remove students for 45 days who inflict or who are at substantial risk for inflicting "serious bodily injury." Substantial bodily injury includes death; extreme physical pain; protracted and obvious disfigurement; or protracted loss or impairment of a bodily part, organ, or mental faculty.

Services to be received in interim alternative educational settings A student removed from his/her educational setting, while remanded to an alternative or interim setting, remains fully entitled to a free, appropriate education consistent with IDEA 2004 rules. Alternative settings include, but are not limited to, placement in a more restrictive environment within the school, in a special school, at home, in a treatment center, or in a detention center.

Manifestation determination review The purpose of a manifestation review is to determine the cause of problematic behavior under review. The school may not discipline a student with a disability (the same as it would if the student did not have a disability) if misbehavior is determined to be disability related. Prior to IDEA 2004, the burden fell upon the school to show that a child with disability's misbehavior was not a manifestation of disability. That burden of proof is now shifted to parents.

45 day limit for removal from current educational settings The 45 calendar day limit on the removal for these offenses has been changed from 45 calendar days to 45 school days.

When Physical Education Is Not Required for Students With Disabilities

Prior to enactment of IDEA 2004, physical education as an integral part of special education was required of all children with disabilities whenever the child with a disability was determined to have physical education needs. This right applied to children with disabilities irrespective of whether physical education was required of children without disabilities. With enactment of IDEA 2004, the requirement that physical education be provided to children with disabilities has been abridged such that physical education must now be made available to children with disabilities only when it is required of children without disabilities in the same grade (34 CFR 300.108, 14 August 2006).

No Child Left Behind Act of 2001, PL 107-110: Implications for IDEA 2004

The stated purpose of the No Child Left Behind Act (NCLB, or NCLBA), which was signed into law in 2002, reads in part as follows:

> . . . to insure that all children have a fair, equal, and significant opportunity to obtain a high-quality education and reach, at a minimum, proficiency on

challenging state academic achievement standards and state academic assessments (PL 107-110, Section 1001).

Despite U.S. Department of Education regulations intended to align IDEA 2004 with requirements of NCLB (2007), there remain questions regarding whether these two laws can be truly compatible. According to Ratcliffe and Willard (2006),

> ... IDEA's focus (is) on the individual learner and the development and implementation of an IEP to ensure that instruction will be delivered at the child's level of academic and functional performance. But NCLBA assumes that all students can be instructed at grade level and mandates that all but those with the most severe cognitive disabilities can be assessed against grade-level standards. The conflicting laws create a situation in which a child is instructed at a level that is consistent with his or her academic and functional performance but is tested at a level that may include content and concepts well beyond those in which the child has had no instruction (p. 3).

Educators across the board generally applaud initiatives that support establishment of high expectations for *all* students. Concern arises among advocates for students with disabilities when high expectations according to NCLB become perceived as one size fits all standards for all students, including the majority of students with disabilities.

On the positive side, expecting high standard achievements by students with disabilities reinforces the IDEA 1997 expectation that standards for students with disabilities were in need of rethinking (i.e. heightening). Achievement in accordance with potential, including achievement of standards that underpin functional behaviors and skills beyond school years, provides the foundation for all learners to achieve, to the extent possible, purposeful, independent citizenship in society-at-large.

On the negative side, NCLB could become a detriment to meeting individual needs as set forth in IDEA 2004 (Ratcliff and Willard, 2006). Directing disproportionate attention upon students with disabilities to achieve regular state standards, critics say, mitigates many students with disabilities from achieving full potential. Attention focused toward NCLB may translate into attention focused away from IDEA, including IDEA's provision that every child with a disability, when necessary, is entitled to an appropriate, individually designed education.

NCLB specifies core subject areas wherein students must be tested to determine whether students within states are achieving state standards. Core areas, at the time of publication, include English, reading or language arts, mathematics, science, foreign languages, civics and government, economics, arts, history, and geography. Across education in general, there is growing concern that, in the rush to satisfy NCLB achievement standards in core subject areas, curriculums will become narrowed and teachers will become obliged to teach to tests. Physical education's absence from among core subject areas gives rise to concern that, in the rush to achieve state standards in NCLB-prescribed core subject areas, resources and focus will be drawn away from physical education, including adapted physical education for students with disabilities.

NCLB, like IDEA, is subject to periodic revision. In 2004, the American Association of Health, Physical Education, Recreation, and Dance (AAHPERD) hosted a national conference to heighten awareness of need to develop lobbying strategies for health and physical education to be included among NCLB core subject areas (AAHPERD 2004). Emphasis on revision to include physical education has come from some members of the U.S. Senate and House of Representatives.

CHAPTER SUMMARY

1. Special education legislation is complex and continues to evolve. Federal legislation centered on special education and civil rights has made a significant impact on instruction in physical education.

2. Two general categories of federal law, civil rights, and special education, impact the practice of special education nationwide, including the practice of adapted physical education.

3. The *Brown v. Board of Education* U.S. Supreme Court decision and federal civil rights legislation intended to end racial segregation served as a model for disability advocates pursuing similar rights for persons with disabilities. Basis for arguments in each instance was, and remains, the U.S. Constitution guarantee of equal protection under the law.

4. In addition to federal civil rights and special education laws that impact special education, state laws also have impact unique to each state. In all instances, state mandates "are in addition to," they do not diminish federal mandates.

5. PL 94-142, the Education of All Handicapped Children Act of 1975 is considered to be the original

blockbuster legislation that set special education, including adapted physical education, on the path that brings the practice of special education where it is today.

6. PL 94-142, the Education of All Handicapped Children Act of 1975 has seen four revisions. The Individuals with Disabilities Education Improvement Act of 2004 (IDEIA 2004 or IDEA 2004) is the most recent. Much from previous revisions remains in the current law. Major changes appearing in the most current revision have been addressed in this chapter.

7. Physical education continues to be explicitly included in IDEA's definition of special education. Significance of this inclusion is that, by virtue of the law's definition of special education, physical education, specially designed if necessary, *is* special education.

8. Education delivered according to IDEA 2004 is required to be in alignment with PL 107-110, the No Child Left Behind Act of 2001. Despite federal regulations that delivery of special education services according to IDEA 2004 be aligned with NCLB requirements, some view these laws as being contradictory to one another. (NCLB requires that most students with disabilities achieve regular state education standards, while IDEA 2004 requires that all students with disabilities are entitled to an appropriate education, individually designed, when necessary.)

9. It remains incumbent on physical education teachers, regular and adapted, to know and advocate for compliance with all applicable laws. Laws presented in this chapter determine the context within which physical education services are to be provided to students who have disabilities.

REFERENCES

_____. (2004). IDEA 2004 Summary. Minneapolis, MN: Families and Advocates Partnership for Education/ Parents Advocacy Coalition for Educational Rights. Retrieved from http://www.fape.org/idea/2004/ summary.htm.

_____. (2004). Physical Education and Health Education Professionals from Across the Country Address No Child Left Behind. Reston, VA: AAHPERD. Retrieved from http://www.csuchico.edu/cjhp/2/1/vi-x-aahenews.pdf.

Americans with Disabilities Act of 1990. Pub. L. No. 101-336. (1990 July 26).

Brown v. Board of Education. 347 U.S. 486, 74 Ct. 686, 98L. Ed. 873. (1954).

Bruder, M.B. (December 2000). The Individual Family Service Plan (IFSP). *ERIC Digest* #E605. The Eric Clearinghouse on Disabilities and Gifted Education. Arlington, VA: The Council on Exceptional Children.

Code of Federal Regulations. Title 34. U.S. Government Printing Office. 14 August 2006, 1 July 2007, 1 January 2008.

Education Amendments of 1974, Pub L. No. 93-380. (1977 august 21) No Child Left Behind Act of 2001, Pub L. No. 107-110. (2002 January 8).

Education for All Handicapped Children Act of 1975, Pub. L. No. 94-142, s.6 20 UU.S.C Section 1401. (1975 November 29).

Education of the Handicapped Act of 1986, Pub L. No. 99-457. (1986 October 6)

Education of the Handicapped Amendments of 1983, Pub. L. No. 98-199. (1983 December 2).

Horvat, M. (1990). *Physical Education and Sport for Exceptional Students.* Dubuque, IA: Wm. C. Brown.

Hallahan, D., Kauffman, J., & Pullen, P. (2009). *Exceptional Learners: Introduction to Special Education,* 11th ed. Boston: Pearson Education.

Individuals with Disabilities Education Act, Pub. L. No. 101-476. (1990 October 30).

Individuals with Disabilities Education Act, Pub. L. No. 105-17. (1997 June 4).

Mills v. Board of Education of the District of Columbia, 348 F. Supp. 866. (D.D.C., 1972).

No Child Left Behind Act of 2001, Pub. L. No. 107-110. Title I: Improving the Academic Achievement of the Disadvantaged. Section 1001. Statement of Purpose.

PARC v. Commonwealth of Pennsylvania, 334 F. Supp. 1257 (E.D. Pa. 1971) and F. Supp. 279 (E.D., Pa. 1972)

Ratcliffe, K.G., & Willard, D.T. (November 2006). NCLB and IDEA: Perspectives from the Field. *Focus on Exceptional Children.* Vol. 39, Issue 3, p. 1–14.

Rehabilitation Act of 1973, Pub. L. 93-112, Section 534, Title V. (1973 April 23).

U.S. Department of Education, Office of Special Education Programs. (2007 February 2). Alignment of IDEA and NCLB.

U.S. Department of Health, Education, and Welfare, Office of Education (April 1977). Rules and Regulations, Section 504.42 (65) Fed. Reg. Section 84.34, Participation of Students, P. 22, 682.

U.S. Department of Health, Education, and Welfare, Office of Education (April 1977). Final Regulations of Education of Handicapped Children, Implementation of Part B of the Education of the Handicapped Act. 42 (163) Fed. Reg. Part II, Section 121a302, Residential Placement, p. 42, 488. Section 121a301b, Free Appropriate Publication Education- Methods and Payments, p. 42, 488. Section 121a307. Physical Education. Section 121a14, Special Education, p. 42, 489.

Continuum of Placements and Program Planning

Sam is a 13 year old boy eligible for special education services under a disability diagnosis of emotional disturbance. He frequently interrupts and acts out in class to the extent that his classroom teachers have difficulty teaching and his peers have difficulty learning. In regular physical education, Sam has levels of physical fitness and motor skill development that fall well within normal parameters. He is a good swimmer and is not a wall flower when his middle school has a school dance. Because he is aggressive, he has no trouble making baskets and scoring touchdowns. In effect, when one looks at IDEA 2004's definition of physical education, Sam's disability, emotional disturbance, does not fit the physical education deficits according to IDEA 2004.

Historically, one of physical education's cardinal objectives has been social development. Noting this, Sam's classroom teachers, and his regular physical education teacher, are advocating for Sam to be placed into adapted physical education where he might work on improving his social skills. The school's adapted physical education teacher, Mr. Rodgers, however, reminds his colleagues that IDEA 2004's definition of physical education makes no mention of adapted physical education having responsibility for social development. Mr. Rodgers, argues that because Sam is not deficient in any aspect of physical education as defined in IDEA 2004; proper placement is with a behavior management specialist or school psychologist.

Everyone agrees that Sam's behavior issues are in immediate need of being addressed. His behaviors, after all, are making a shambles out of regular class settings. The question is not whether Sam is in need of social development, but, rather, where, *according to the law* and *the most effective assignment of professional resources*, Sam should be placed.

Continuum of Placements

Each public agency shall ensure (1) That to the maximum extent appropriate, children with disabilities, including children in public or private institutions or other care facilities, are educated with children who are nondisabled; and (2) That special classes, separate schooling or other removal of children with disabilities from the regular educational environment occurs only if the nature or severity of the disability is such that education in regular classes with the use of supplementary aids and services cannot be achieved satisfactorily (34 CFR 300.550, 2005).

The language of IDEA 2004 is clear with regard to states' obligations, not simply to educate students with disabilities, but to educate whenever reasonably possible in general (i.e. integrated) education settings. The rule applies universally to all states. Individual states' rules may add to or supplement federal rules; however, none may in any way diminish federal rules or withhold federally granted rights.

Placement Options

Federal law requires, at minimum, the following continuum of placements to be available:

- Regular classes
- Special classes
- Special schools
- Home instruction
- Instruction in hospitals and institutions

To ensure achievement of potential in regular class setting placements, children with disabilities must be afforded, as needed, supplementary services including, but not necessarily limited to, resource room access and itinerant instruction (34 CFR 300.551, 2005).

Regarding supplementary services, the student may be assigned to a resource room for instructional support so that when the student returns to the general classroom setting, she/he is better prepared to achieve in the regular class setting.

Itinerant instruction may be provided by teachers who travel from school to school. In adapted physical education, the itinerant teacher may serve students across a school district or educational cooperative. She/he may teach students with disabilities in pull-out settings away from the regular class or assist the student's regular teacher (physical education or classroom), in the regular class setting.

Paraprofessionals, variously titled teacher aides or educational assistants, may help the teacher (adapted physical education, regular physical education, or classroom) with instruction of an entire class or provide individualized attention to a given student.

The Placement Process Applicable to All School Subjects

IDEA 2004 spells out how educational placement decisions are to be made, including who will be party to the decision making process. Placement decisions are to be made by persons knowledgeable about (1) the child, (2) the meaning of evaluation data, and (3) placement options. With specific regard to physical education, whenever physical education is addressed, whether the issue is interpretation of physical education test results or delivery of physical education services in a regular or adapted setting, physical education personnel, regular and/or adapted, need be included.

Persons knowledgeable about the child include:

- The parent of the child with a disability
- At least one regular education teacher if the child is, or may be placed in a regular education setting
- At least one special education teacher or, if appropriate, a special education provider of the child who represents the local education agency (LEA) (e.g. school administrator, including, but not limited to school principal, special education director)

- Individual who can interpret the educational implications of evaluation results
- At the discretion of parents or the school, other individuals who have special knowledge or expertise about the child (e.g. related service providers including, but not limited to, physical therapists, occupational therapists, recreational therapists, speech therapists, orientation and mobility specialists)
- Whenever appropriate, the child with a disability (34 CFR 300.344, 2005)

Factors to be considered when making placement decisions are as follows:

- Placement must be determined according to the IDEA 2004-designated IEP process
- Placement must be as close as possible to the child's home
- Unless the IEP specifies some other arrangement, the child will be educated in the school he/she would attend if she/he did not have a disability
- In selecting the least restrictive environment (LRE), consideration must be given to potential harmful effect on the child or determent to the quality of services she/he needs
- The child cannot be removed from age-appropriate regular classrooms solely because of needed modifications in the general curriculum (34 CFR 300.552, 2005)

Extracurricular Placements

Public agencies, including schools, must take steps as necessary to provide students with disabilities equal opportunity to participate in extracurricular programs, including but not limited to athletics, recreation, and special interest clubs (e.g. hiking, band, choir, skiing/snowboarding, fitness) (IDEA 2004, 3 December 2004, Section 300.107 (a)(b)). Participation should be integrated whenever reasonably possible or separate according to the student's individual needs.

Placement Trends

The following trends are representative of those currently impacting placement and program planning for children who have disabilities. Emphasis is on *representative*, as an exhaustive list transcends the scope of this text. Trends included herein are selected with a view to their relevance for inclusion in physical education and related physical activity settings.

Increased placement of students with disabilities in general education settings Since passage of PL 94-142, the Education for All Handicapped Children Act of 1975, social and political pressure has been mounted by parents, advocates for persons who have disabilities, and law makers to integrate students with disabilities into regular education settings. Educating students with disabilities in regular settings as opposed to in special (i.e. segregated) settings is alleged to afford the following advantages:

- Opportunity for students to attend their neighborhood school
- Higher expectations
- Families become more integrated into communities
- Greater social opportunities
- Greater academic achievement
- Higher self-esteem
- Greater opportunity for normalizing experiences (i.e. anticipatory experience as preparation for life in the community-at-large) (http://www.kidstogether.org).

Critics of including students with disabilities in general education settings see the practice as too often being driven by needs to cut costs. They suggest that the rush to include students with a wide range of disabilities, in fact, disadvantages the very children that inclusion is alleged to help. Some parents of children without disabilities assert that inclusion settings disadvantage children without disabilities, because the teacher is forced to teach to the middle or below (Hitchinger, 2007).

Collaborative team approaches to assessment, program planning, and instruction

Collaborative team approaches to assessment, program planning, and instruction offer the benefit of bringing a wide range of expertise to the design and delivery of curriculum. For example, physical educators, physical therapists, and occupational therapists each operate according to respective expertise in the psycho-motor domain. However, when they work collaboratively, collective contributions to the learning process have the potential to transcend anything that one professional working singularly might accomplish. The occupational therapist may help in the development of manipulative skills. The physical therapist may help in the development of strength and range of motion. The student, having had the benefit of physical and occupational therapy may then be best positioned to benefit from the physical educator's teaching the mechanics of overhand throwing.

Functionally based curriculums

A curriculum is deemed functional when its contents prepare learners to functionally integrate into life activities involving work, family, social interaction, and pursuit of leisure in the community-at-large. A functional curriculum is one that prepares the learner for life beyond school hours and beyond school years.

The individualized transition plan (ITP) is integral to the trend toward functionally based education. The ITP, required by IDEA 2004 to be implemented by age 16, helps the student make the transition from life in school to life in the community. The ITP helps functionalize the student's in-school learning so that knowledge and skills learned in school effectively generalize to living as an adult in the community-at-large.

A functionally based curriculum in physical education prepares the learner for meaningful work, independent living, and leisure. Functionally based physical education provides the knowledge and motivation that promotes the lifelong pursuit of health and overall well being. Skills learned in physical education, particularly skills of the lifelong variety, open doors to lifelong positive social interactions with family and friends. Indeed, physical education skills (e.g. golf, tennis, swimming, skiing, basketball, softball, volleyball) become social skills whenever people socially interact (i.e. integrate) based upon common interests and skills in leisure pursuits.

Focus on independence

Arguably, the primary goal of education is to enable the learner to become independent. Independent does not mean aloof or isolated. Rather, it means being able to engage in major life activities (e.g. numeracy, literacy, community membership, work, personal care, family, leisure) without need of assistance or oversight.

Independent movement is a pillar in the platform of independent living. Among the goals of physical education for all persons and particularly for persons whose disabilities challenge mobility independence is to maximize the potential to negotiate physical space without need of assistance.

Community-based instruction

Increasingly, community-based sports programs and recreation providers are responding to the active lifestyle interests of people with disabilities. Such programs offer both instruction and participation opportunities. For physical education, this means emphasis on learning experiences that prepare students to recreate in integrated, community-based settings.

Opportunities to learn and participate in community-based settings are becoming increasingly abundant. For example, integrated wilderness experience learning and participation opportunities are accessible to persons with a range of disabilities (http://www.wildernessinquiry.org). Bowling alleys offer instruction and provide ramps and other assistive devices, to roll the ball for bowlers with limited mobility (http://www.ncpad.org/). Ski areas are becoming disability accessible, including offering adapted equipment rental services and instruction (http://www.aspensnowmass.com/schools/challenge.cfm).

Cooperative teaching, cooperative learning, and peer and cross-age teaching

Cooperative teaching generally involves two teachers teaching in the same class setting. For cooperative teaching to be effective, teachers need to share the common belief that teaching together has greater potential than teaching separately. In physical education, an adapted physical education teacher may cooperatively teach alongside the regular physical education teacher in the regular setting so that the student with a disability will learn along side his/her peers without disabilities.

Cooperative learning occurs when a group of two or more students work together to achieve a common goal. Johnson and Johnson (1999) summarize the advantages of cooperative learning over competition and individual learning as follows:

> Structuring situations cooperatively results in students interacting in ways that promote each other's success. Structuring situations competitively results in students interacting in ways that oppose each other's success, and structuring situations individualistically results in no interaction among students (p. 67).

Unlike competition that often occurs in physical education settings where there is only one winner (individual or team), cooperative learning is alleged to promote maximum learning for all group members, because all share equally in the group's accomplishments. Cooperative learning may be particularly beneficial and motivating among students with disabilities who are not experienced in competition and/or who have yet to be successful in competitive, negative-sum (i.e., one winner, many losers) activities.

Peer and cross-age teaching Peer and cross-age teaching refers to students, under teacher supervision, teaching students. This can occur when more advanced students assist the teacher by giving less advanced students individual attention. When such instruction occurs within the context of a same-grade class, the applicable term is *peer teaching*. *Cross-age* teaching occurs when students, generally older, teach younger students in the younger students' class setting.

Assessment

IDEA 2004 first and foremost is about education, individually designed when necessary, in the least restrictive environment. In order to individualize instruction, one must first know the individual. To know the individual, one must assess. Assessment needs to be designed to reveal (1) the student's present level of educational development, (2) factors influencing the student's present level of educational development, (3) the kinds of educational strategies that will best enable future learning in accordance with potential, and (4) where, according to IDEA 2004's continuum of educational placements, the child will most readily learn.

Medical Assessments

A thorough medical evaluation should be performed by the physician to determine the individual's level of functioning. Ideally, this evaluation will include the physician's judgment as to how the student's disability might potentially affect educational placement, programming, and outcomes.

Medical files will be stored in a central, secure place. The teacher who accesses medical files must recognize that information contained therein is strictly privileged and is to be held in strictest confidence.

Requirements of All Education-related Tests

Test results are only as good as the quality of tests from which results come. The phrase from computer science, *garbage in, garbage out*, is applicable here. That is, flawed tests will always yield flawed results. Teachers should not accept as an article of faith that test results are good unless the teacher has good reason to believe the test itself is technically adequate. At minimum, the teacher must be confident that the test:

- Is valid. To be valid, test/test item must measure what it purports to measure (e.g. If an item purports to measure throwing accuracy, does it truly measure throwing accuracy?).
- Is reliable. To be reliable, test/test item must yield consistent results across trials (e.g. Will a test item, consistently performed across multiple administrations, yield consistent scores from the same examiner?).
- Is objective. To be objective, a test/test item scored by two or more qualified observers must produce identical or very near identical scores for the same performance (e.g. judges scoring a dance routine).
- Has been used only for the purpose for which it was intended (e.g. specific motor skills tests cannot be properly used to assess physical fitness).

Test Selection and Administration

When we think of assessment for adapted physical education purposes, we must recall the IDEA 2004 definition of physical education. Pursuant to IDEA 2004, physical education means the development of:

- Physical and motor fitness
- Fundamental motor skills and patterns
- Skills in aquatics, dance, and individual and group games and sports (including intramural and lifetime sports)

Physical fitness includes the following (President's Council of Physical Fitness and Sport 2009).

- Muscular strength
- Muscular endurance
- Flexibility
- Cardiovascular endurance
- Body composition

Motor fitness includes the following (President's Council of Physical Fitness and Sport 2009).

- Speed
- Balance
- Coordination
- Power (Explosive strength)
- Reaction time

Skills in aquatics, dance, and individual and group games and sports (including lifetime sports) are self-explanatory. Physical education teachers are obliged to address the above-bulleted areas in accordance with the IDEA 2004 definition of physical education. This is not to suggest that teachers are bound only to address the above areas to the exclusion of possible others. It means only that, to be in compliance with IDEA 2004, the above areas, at minimum, must be covered.

Purpose of Assessment Determines the Type of Assessment Instrument Chosen

Assessments for adapted physical education purposes are conducted, at minimum, for the following reasons:

- Screening
- To determine qualification for adapted physical education services
- To determine individual physical education needs
- To make placement decisions according to the placement continuum
- To determine student learning
- To determine curriculum effectiveness
- Accountability

Screening   Screening tests are utilized when there is need to assess a large number of students in a short period of time. The role of a screening test is to identify students, typically a relatively small percentage, whose performances depart sufficiently from the norm to be considered candidates for special services. Emphasis is on *considered*. Screening tests alone, while they may heighten suspicion that a student needs special programming, are not sufficiently precise to support that judgment unequivocally. A student identified through screening should be subsequently referred for in-depth assessment to determine the existence of educational needs, if any,

that cannot be met by participation in the general curriculum (Horvat, Block, and Kelly, 2007).

Tests to determine qualification for special services
Tests to determine qualification for special services, including adapted physical education, ideally are *standardized* and *norm-referenced*. A test is standardized when procedures for administering the test are spelled out such that it can be administered in precisely the same manner from one student to the next and from one tester to the next. Norm-referenced means that results from the student tested can be measured directly against those of the student's peers, for example according to age and gender (e.g. ten year old Ginny scored at the 85th percentile in the Motor Domain of the Battelle Developmental Inventory) (BDI-2, 2005).

Standardized, norm-referenced tests, provided such test's norms can be fairly applied to students with disabilities, are instruments of choice to qualify students for special education, including adapted physical education programs and services. When the student's score deviates from the test mean score by a predetermined amount, that student can be considered eligible for special education programming and/or placement.

Tests to determine individual physical education needs   Once it is determined that the student has special needs, the next step is to determine which special needs exist. Here, direct observation, check lists, rating scales, criterion-referenced instruments, and task analyses become helpful.

Direct observation is an informal technique that enables the teacher to gather information specific to the student's present performance or behavior characteristics. Teachers may compile information from observations related to physical functioning (e.g. coughing or wheezing following six minutes of activity), motor characteristics (e.g. tripping, falling, running into others), or behaviors (e.g. willingness to participate, passiveness, aggressiveness). Documented, informal observations can indicate the number of times characteristics and behaviors occur that have potential to affect teaching and learning.

Check lists can provide valuable initial information about the student's functional level with regard to physical fitness, motor skills, transition to and from physical education class, response to the teacher, peer interactions, interaction with equipment, effort and self-acceptance, and cognitive levels (Block, 2000).

Rating scales enable teachers to express opinions and judgments across a range of student performances and behaviors (e.g. 5 = very good, 4 = good, 3 = average, 2 = fair, 1 = poor, 0 = performance/behavior not observable).

Criterion-referenced instruments take individual skills (e.g. overhand throw) and reduce them to sequential steps through which the student progresses from entry level through mature adult-level skill execution. Statements identifying skill performance are stated in behavioral terms for each skill level in the sequence. If a given skill has been broken down, for example, into five developmentally sequenced steps from entry level through to mature adult-level skill execution and the student executes skill in accordance with criterion-referenced statement three, then instruction can focus on skill development in accordance with criterion-referenced statement four.

The Brigance Inventory of Early Development II (2004) is one example of a long-standing, criterion-referenced test that, among other sectors, measures gross and fine motor development in children from birth through 7 years.

While the I CAN (Kelly & Wessel, 1990) program is considered more curriculum than a test, I CAN offers numerous examples of criterion-referenced skills taught in physical education settings, virtually all of which have utility in active living settings beyond school.

Task analysis identifies the step-by-step sequence of discrete tasks necessary for a motoric or behavioral task to be performed successfully (Blunt, 2005). An example of task analysis in fishing:

1. Remove bait from box
2. Carefully grasp hook with pointed tip exposed
3. Affix bait to hook
4. Place thumb on reel button to keep line from unwinding
5. Draw arm into overhand throw (casting) position
6. Begin casting motion
7. Immediately release thumb from button
8. Follow through with casting motion
9. When bait strikes water, rewind reel to tighten line
10. Stop rewinding when excess slack in line has been removed

Note that the end result can only be achieved if individual task components unfold in the proper sequence. Task analysis can be valuable when assessing students' skills at their present levels of proficiency and for developing sequentially based skill instruction.

Teacher-developed tests   In some instances, published tests may be inappropriate for use with some students who have disabilities. This may be particularly true with norm-referenced tests when students with disabilities, as is often the case, are not represented in the group when the test's norms were developed.

Whenever the teacher self-develops a test, she/he, as with published tests, must always be cognizant of the need for validity, reliability, and objectivity. The teacher should be certain that content of the test accurately reflects content of the curriculum. That is, the percent of time spent on any given activity during instruction should be mirrored by the percent of items/points measuring proficiency in that activity on the test (e.g. If 20 percent of instruction has been fitness-related; then, 20 percent of test items should measure fitness-related improvement/learning).

Authentic assessment   Schools are entrusted with the responsibility to prepare students to become functional, productive citizens in the world beyond school. As such, assessments in school should measure the extent to which the student has developed knowledge and skills essential for successful living in the community-at-large.

Functional assessment in golf, for example, should require more than a paper and pencil test. It should also require skill testing using a range of clubs, and, ideally, at least part of the assessment protocol would require the student to demonstrate what she/he has learned on an actual golf course. **Table 3.1** provides an example of authentic assessment of skills in basketball.

Functional assessment that is future employment related might include demonstration of fitness sufficient for one to engage successfully in a physical occupation. If future employment were to be piecework related, functional assessment might include a battery of manipulative fine-motor coordination items likely to be encountered in piecework assembly employment settings.

Assessment Instruments for Consideration in Physical Education

Assessment instruments in **Table 3.2** (on page 30) are grouped according to instrument focus as follows:

- Motor behavior
- Posture/gait
- Perceptual-motor
- Fitness
- Self-concept/attitude

Table 3.1 Sample Authentic Assessment for Selected Basketball Skills

	Simple ◄──► Complex				
Environment	Individualized instruction in APE class	Combinations of skills into patterns	General skills in drills and lead-up activities	Play in recess and after school	Community and recreation participation in competitive settings
Skill Performance	Dribbles/passes with prompts and guided assistance	Dribbles/passes, but with hesitant and slow responses	Dribbles/passes with verbal cue	Dribbles/passes independently	Dribbles/passes independently to correct player
Game Performance	Dribbles/passes inappropriately	Dribbles/passes but does not look for teammate	Moves independently and looks for teammate	Independently dribbles and passes to teammate	Moves with dribble and passes in game setting

The list of tests in Table 3.2 is not exhaustive; however, we believe it to be representative of what is worthy of consideration. Remember, when considering any test from this table, ask, "Is it valid? Is it reliable? Is it objective? Will it be used for the purpose for which it was intended?"

Program Planning

Central to IDEA 2004 is the individualized family service plan (IFSP), individualized education plan (IEP), and individualized transition plan (ITP). We also include leisure services as integral to the IEP and ITP to emphasize importance of community integration that includes worthy use of leisure time after school and beyond school years.

Some students have conditions that disable; however, their conditions are not recognized as disabilities under IDEA 2004. They, therefore, do not qualify for individualized instruction under IDEA. Such students, however, are eligible for individualized programming via a *504 Plan*. Eligibility for a 504 plan is addressed according to Section 504 of the Rehabilitation Act of 1973 and in the Americans with Disabilities Act of 1990. (See heading entitled The 504 Plan later in this chapter.)

The IFSP

The IFSP, in its present form, has evolved from earlier revisions of IDEA that required states to provide a free, appropriate education for children with disabilities ages 3–5. Part C of IDEA 2004, today, calls upon states to provide early intervention IFSP services, when necessary, for infants and toddlers, age birth through two.

IFSP eligibility Regarding meeting eligibility criteria for an IFSP under IDEA 2004, Shakelford (2006) cites inconsistencies in states' eligibility definitions:

The task of defining the eligible population has been a challenge for states. Eligibility requirements influence the numbers and types of children needing or receiving services, the types of services provided, and ultimately the cost of the early intervention system. Over the years, several states have revised their definitions: some have narrowed their eligibility criteria and others have expanded them (page 1).

The message is that practitioners who provide early intervention services to infants and toddlers need to remain current with regard to infant and toddler service eligibility in their respective states, and that eligibility requirements are subject to change.

Components of the IFSP Services including special instruction, diagnostic testing and services, assistive technology, and health services are to be provided to infants and toddlers as determined by provisions set forth in the IFSP. Required IFSP components are as follows (IDEA 2004, Section 636 (d)):

- Child's present level of development
- Statement of the family's resources, priorities, and concerns relating to the child's development
- Statement of measurable results expected for both child and family
- A statement of the environments (natural and/or otherwise) for early intervention services
- The projected dates for initiation of services and the anticipated length, duration, and frequency of the services
- The identification of the service coordinator from the profession most immediately relevant to the infant's, toddler's, or family's needs
- The steps to be taken to support the transition of the toddler with a disability to preschool or other appropriate services

Table 3.2 Assessments for Consideration

Test	Ages	Components	Comments
Motor Behavior			
Bayley III Scales of Infant Development (Bayley, 2005)	1–42 months	Mental scale, motor scale, behavior rating scale	Screening for psychomotor development; Bayley Infant Neurological Screener (BINS) measures basic neurological function
Brigance Diagnostic Inventory of Early Development (Brigance, 1978)	Birth to 7 years	Gross and fine motor movements, language, comprehension skills, self-help	Flexible criterion-referenced instrument based on developmental sequences
Denver Developmental Screening Test II (Frankenburg, Dodds, & Archer, 1990)	Birth to 6 years	Gross motor, fine motor, personal–social, language development	Screening for developmental delays in early childhood through primary ages
Bruininks-Oseretsky Test of Motor Proficiency II (Bruininks & Bruininks, 2005)	4–21 years	Fine motor precision, fine motor integration, manual dexterity, bilateral coordination, balance, running speed and agility, upper-limb coordination, strength	Assesses gross and fine motor functioning; eight sub-tests, 53 items
Peabody Developmental Motor Scales II (Folio & Felwell, 2000)	Birth to 7 years	Gross and fine motor skills including; reflexes, balance, locomotor, non-locomotor, manual dexterity, hand–eye coordination	Norm-referenced developmental screening of skill development at various ages
Movement Assessment Battery for Children-2 (Henderson, Sugden, & Barnett, 2007)	3–12 years	Balance, control, coordination, throwing, kinesthetic awareness	Norm-referenced assessment for functional or neurological difficulties
Test of Gross Motor Development II (Ulrich, 2000)	3–10 years	12 locomotor skills plus throwing, catching, kicking, striking, bounding	Norm- and criterion-referenced locomotor and object control skills
Perceived Physical Competence in Children with Mental Retardation (Ulrich & Collie, 1990)	7–12 years	Perceived physical competence	Shown contrasting pictures of children performing motor skills. Child points to pictures that represent how she/he feels on a 4-point scale
Fundamental Movement Checklist (McClenaghan & Gallahue, 1978)	2–7 years	Locomotor and object control skills	Criterion-referenced checklist of patterns at initial, elementary, and mature levels
Fundamental Motor Patterns (Wickstrom, 1983)	2–7 years	Locomotor and object control skills	Criterion-referenced checklist of locomotor and object control skills
Special Olympics Sport Skill Guides (2000–2003)	All	Assessments for 34 Special Olympics sport events	Record whether skill is performed with physical assistance, physical prompt, demonstration, verbal cue, or visual cue
Assessment, Evaluation, and Programming Systems (AEPS) for Infants and Children (Bricker, 2002)	Birth to 6 years	Fine motor adaptive, gross motor, communication, cognitive, social	Six developmental levels for children at risk for developmental delays (Scoring: 0 = does not pass, 1 = inconsistent, 2 = pass)
Adapted Physical Education Assessment Scale-II (American Association for Physical Activity and Recreation, 2002)	4.5–17 years	Perceptual motor, object control, locomotor skills, adaptive behavior	Test based on scores from general population. Designed to identify students in need of special education services in adapted physical education

Table 3.2 Assessments for Consideration (*continued*)

Test	Ages	Components	Comments
Everyone Can (Kelly, Dummer, & Sampson, 2002)	K–grade 5	Instructional materials for 70 physical education objectives, plus assessment score sheets	Rooted in I CAN criterion-referenced assessment developed by Wessel (1976)
Posture/Gait			
New York Posture Screening (New York State Department of Education, 1966)	10 years and above	Shoulder girdle, back, foot placement, body alignment	Criterion–referenced posture screening for 13 areas of the body
San Diego State University Posture Evaluation (Lasko & Aufsesser, n.d.)	10 years and above	Strength, flexibility, orthopedic evaluation, posture	Criterion-referenced screening of orthopedic deviations and improper gait and body mechanics
Rancho Amigos Observational Gait Analysis (Gronley & Perry, 2001)	10 years and above	Range of motion in trunk, pelvis, hip, knee, ankles, and toes during gait	Range of motion during gait, cycle on weight acceptance, single limb support and swing, limb advancement
Fitness			
Eurofit (Skowronski et. al., 2009)	6 years and above	Long jump, sit and reach, 25 meter dash, medicine ball throw, balance walk, sit-ups	Modification of Eurofit Test Battery for individuals with intellectual disabilities
Kansas Adapted/Special Physical Education Test Manual (Johnson & Lavay, 1988)	5–21 years	Flexibility, upper body strength/endurance, aerobic movement and endurance	Adaptations to accommodate most children with special needs in health-related fitness
Fitnessgram/Activitygram (Cooper Institute for Aerobic Research, 2007)	Kindergarten–college	Aerobic capacity, body composition, muscular strength, endurance, flexibility	Currently used by 6,000 schools; accompanied by *Physical Best*, 2nd ed.
Brockport Physical Fitness Test (Winnick & Short, 1999)	10–17 years	Musculoskeletal functioning, trunk lift, grasp strength, bench press, isometric push-up, dumbbell press, reverse curl, pull-up, wheel chair ramp test, body composition skinfold, BMI	Flexibility, back saver sit and reach, stretch activity, Apley test, Thomas test
Self-concept Attitude			
Manual for Self-Perception Profile for Children (Harter, 1988)	Grades 3–6	Assesses cognitive, social, physical and general self-worth domains	28-item scale on child's perception of competencies in sports and outdoor games
Psychological Skills Inventory for Sports (Mahoney, Gabriel, & Perkins, 1987)	Athletes	Assesses psychological skills consistent with elite performance	Used with athletes with disabilities
Piers-Harris-2 Children's Self-Concept Scale (Piers, Harris, & Hersberg, 2002)	Grades 3–12	Measures behavior, intellectual and school status, physical appearance, anxiety, popularity, happiness	60 statements with "yes" or "no" responses based on children's perceptions
Martinek-Zaichkowsky Self-Concept Scale (Martinek & Zaichkowsky, 1977)	Grades 1-8	Measures satisfaction and happiness, home and family relationships, ability in sports, games, behavior and personality traits	Child points to a picture (total: 25) and responds to how she/he feels

The IFSP is similar in intent to the IEP. Its specific purpose is to maximize potential for development during infant and toddler years when intervention is known to have the most impact. Early years are critical times for physical, motor, social, and cognitive development, given such development is largely hierarchical.

The IEP

The IEP is a written document delineating specifics of the comprehensive education plan for the student with a disability. However, not all students with disabilities are required to have an IEP. An IEP is required when the student with disability's needs cannot be met within the context of the regular curriculum. The IEP is developed in meetings that include teachers, parents, school administrators, therapists, the child (when appropriate), and others who may have special knowledge about the child.

The IEP gives direction to providers of the child's education. It is a legal document, and, as such, the school is obliged to comply with its directives. The IEP, however, does not rise to the level of a guarantee that a student will achieve all IEP-specified education goals (Hyatt, 2004)

Because physical education is a primary service according to IDEA 2004, it must be included in the IEP of every student with a disability whose physical education needs cannot be met within the context of the general curriculum. Every child is entitled to the opportunity to participate in physical education and achieve the same program goals as his/her peers. Pursuant to IDEA 2004, the IEP team is obliged to consider the following.

General factors: The IEP team must be mindful of:

- The strengths of the child
- Parents, concerns for enhancing their child's education
- Results of initial or most recent evaluations of the child
- Academic, developmental, and functional needs of the child

Special factors:

- In the case of a child whose behavior impedes the child's learning or that of others, the IEP team should consider the use of positive behavioral interventions and supports, and other strategies, to address that behavior.
- In the case of a child with limited English proficiency, the IEP team should consider the language needs of the child as those needs relate to the child's IEP.
- In the case of a child who is blind or visually impaired, the IEP team should provide for instruction in Braille or the use of Braille unless the IEP

team, after an evaluation, determines that this is not appropriate for the child.
- Consider the communication needs of the child
- Consider whether the child needs assistive technology devices or services

Components of the IEP IEP forms will differ from state to state and from school districts within a state. However, all IEP documents must include all components required according to IDEA 2004. To assist in the development of IEP forms that comply with IDEA 2004, the US Department of Education has developed a model form (http://idea.ed.gov/). Contents of the form, with minor adaptations, are shown in **Table 3.3** on page 33.

Physical education and the IEP Because physical education is a primary service by virtue of its inclusion in the law's definition of special education, physical education should appear on the IEP of any student with a disability whose physical education needs cannot be met entirely and without modification in the general curriculum. A physical educator should be an IEP team member and present whenever a child's physical education is being considered. If the possibility exists that a child will be in regular and adapted physical education, a physical education teacher representing each setting should be present. The following is a description of physical education placements on a continuum ranging from least to most restrictive:

1. Regular physical education (ability to meet regular program goals): In this setting the student with a disability participates without program modifications alongside peers without disabilities and partakes of the same curriculum. Children with mild disabilities are commonly placed with good results in this setting.

2. Regular physical education, but with resource support to teacher and/or student: The student with a disability participates alongside peers without disabilities; with resource support to ensure the student's success. Examples of resource support include a paraprofessional to provide individualized attention to a student with attention deficit hyperactive disorder, a flexion mitt for a student with cerebral palsy for assistance in grasping a racquet, a wheelchair for a student with paraplegia, phonic ear for a student with a hearing impairment, instructions in Braille for a student who is blind, and someone to sign for a student who is deaf.

3. Part-time placement in regular physical education/part-time placement in segregated setting: Depending on the student's disability, there

Table 3.3   Individualized Education Program

A statement of the child's present levels of academic achievement and functional performance including:

- How the child's disability affects the child's involvement in the general education curriculum (i.e., the same curriculum as for nondisabled children) or for preschool children, as appropriate, how the disability affects the child's participation in appropriate activities.

A statement of measurable annual goals, including academic and functional goals designed to:

- Meet the child's needs that result from the child's disability to enable the child to be involved in and make progress in the general education curriculum.
- Meet each of the child's other educational needs that result from the child's disability.

For children with disabilities who take alternate assessments aligned to alternate achievement standards (in addition to annual goals), a description of benchmarks or short-term objectives.

A description of:

- How the child's progress toward meeting the annual goals will be measured
- When periodic reports on the progress the child is making toward meeting the annual goals will be provided such as through the use of quarterly or other reports, concurrent with the issuance of report cards.

A statement of the special education and related services and supplementary aids and services, based on peer-reviewed research to the extent practicable, to be provided to the child, or on behalf of the child, and a statement of the program modifications or supports for school personnel that will be provided to enable the child:

- To advance appropriately toward attaining the annual goals
- To be involved in and make progress in the general education curriculum to participate in extracurricular and other nonacademic activities.
- To be educated and participate with other children with disabilities and non disabled children in extra curricular and other nonacademic activities.

An explanation of the extent, if any, to which the child will not participate with non disabled children in the regular classroom and in extracurricular and other nonacademic activities.

(continued)

Table 3.3 Individualized Education Program (*continued*)

A statement of any individual appropriate accommodations necessary to measure the academic achievement and functional performance for the child on State and districtwide assessments.

If the IEP Team determines that the child must take an alternate assessment instead of a regular State or districtwide assessment of student achievement, a statement of why:

• The child cannot participate in the regular assessment

• The particular alternate assessment selected is appropriate for the child.

The projected date for the beginning of the services and modifications and the anticipated frequency, location, and duration of <u>special education and related services</u> and <u>supplementary aids and services</u> and <u>modifications and supports.</u>

Service, Aid, or Modification	Frequency	Location	Beginning Date	Duration

Transition Services

Beginning not later than the first IEP to be in effect <u>when the child turns 16, or younger if determined appropriate by the IEP Team</u>, and updated annually thereafter, the IEP must include:

• Appropriate measurable postsecondary goals based upon age-appropriate transition assessments related to training, education, employment, and where appropriate, independent living skills

• The transition services (including courses of study) needed to assist the child in reaching these goals.

Transition (Including Courses of Study)

Rights That Transfer at The Age of Majority

• Beginning no later than one year before the child reaches the age of majority under State law, the IEP must include a statement that the child has been informed of rights, if any, that will transfer to the child on reaching the age of majority.

may be times when a student with a disability taking physical education in the regular setting is not appropriate. Generally, placement in the regular physical education setting is indicated whenever the student safely *and* successfully participates, including reasonable likelihood of achieving the lesson's objectives for everyone, alongside peers without disabilities. For example, correct placement during a volleyball unit would involve the student with a disability safely and successfully playing as part of a volleyball team. Incorrect placement would have the student with a disability sitting on the sideline keeping score.

4. Full-time adapted physical education in a regular school. Here, for safe, successful participation to be ensured, the student's physical education is required to be taken apart from an inclusion setting. While the setting is segregated, instruction takes place in a regular school that serves students without disabilities. Segregated settings are reserved for students who, were they to be placed in the inclusion setting that included all reasonable accommodations, could not reasonably be expected to succeed.

5. Full-time placement in adapted physical education in a special school (non-residential): Placement at this level is indicated for students who, according to type and degree of disability, must be served in a specially designed facility, both in terms of architectural design and specialized programming.

6. Placement hospitals or full-time residential settings: Here, students with the most severe disabilities are served, much as in level 5, but in the most restrictive of settings.

LEARNING ACTIVITY

When might students with mild, moderate, and severe disabilities be best served in integrated classes? When might students with disabilities be best served in segregated classes? Offer examples, including rationale for your decisions. Also, consider and explain how students without disabilities' learning might be affected positively and negatively by including students with disabilities (mild, moderate, and severe) in regular physical education class settings.

Example physical education portion of an IEP Figure 3.1 provides an example of what the physical education portion of an IEP might look like. Ron is a

12-year old with a non-progressive orthopedic disability. He uses a manual wheelchair. Beyond the disability that affects his lower extremities, his primary issue with regard to physical education is low fitness. Physical education appears on Ron's IEP, because modifications, although minimal, are needed to ensure successful participation. Modifications include, but would not be limited to, use of the wheelchair in class, and fitness exercises designed specifically to meet Ron's unique fitness needs. Although Ron's mode of ambulation differs from that of his peers and his exercise regimen has been individually designed to accommodate his specific fitness needs, he can safely participate in the regular physical education class and be reasonably expected to achieve fitness objectives set out for the entire class.

The ITP

The individualized transition plan (ITP) is a component of the IEP that spells out services required for successful transition from secondary school life to life in the community-at-large. Actual transition activity, not merely having a plan in place, according to IDEA 2004, must begin by age 16.

Transition planning must be designed to be results oriented and based on the individual's needs, taking into account the individual's strengths, preferences, and interests. Transition plans are to address post-secondary education options, employment options, adult living objectives, and participation in a range of social and leisure activities appropriate for the student. Successful transition will facilitate, to the maximum extent possible, productive, satisfying, independent living in the adult world beyond school years (34 CFR 300.43, 2008).

Wehman (1996) recommends seven steps to facilitating a successful ITP. They include:

1. Organization of the ITP team

2. Organizing a circle of support for the ITP process

3. Identifying key transition activities upon which the ITP process will focus

4. Conducting ITP meetings in conjunction with IEP meetings

5. Implementing the ITP

6. Updating the ITP annually and providing quarterly progress reports to principal parties

7. Via an exit meeting and follow-up inquiry, ensure that employment, and integrated community living, including participation in integrated recreation, have become meaningful realities.

Figure 3.1 IEP Physical Education Portion Sample.

Child's Name: Ron

Birth Date: September 6, 19XX

Chronological Age: 12 years, 6 months

Classification: Orthopedically impaired

Present Level of Performance
Ron's overall level of physical and motor fitness is below average for boys at 12 years of age. Ron demonstrated deficiencies in range of motion in the shoulder and elbow and weakness in his arms and trunk. He scored below the 40th percentile on the long-distance run and isometric strength items.

Annual Goals
1. Develop and maintain a functional level of cardiorespiratory endurance.
2. Increase and maintain a functional level of upper body strength and conditioning.
3. Increase flexibility of his upper body.

Short-Term Objectives (Fall)
Goal 1: Ron will demonstrate
1. the ability to propel his wheelchair for 100 yds. in one minute
2. the ability to run continuously for 20 minutes

Goal 2: Ron will
1. perform the flexed arm hang for 2 seconds
2. increase his isometric strength to 17 kg with each hand; 30 kg in shoulder, flexion and extension
3. complete a 6-station circuit training program
4. increase his ROM in the shoulder areas to 30°

Evaluation Criteria (Criteria, Procedures, Scheduling)
Criteria: Levels of performance as specified in the short-term objectives

Procedures: Use of dynamometers, resistance equipment (Dumbbells, surgical tubing)

Scheduling: Fitness testing will be administered during class time at the end of the semester. Corresponding teacher observations and checklists of performance will be required.

Services Provided, Initiation, and Duration
1. instruction in the regular physical education program
2. consultant services with the educational service unit's special physical education teacher
3. services to be initiated September 12, 20XX, with instruction in regular physical education 4 days per week, 30 minutes per day for the calendar year

Participation in the Regular Program
The child will be integrated into regular physical education resistance training and body-conditioning classes. He will have the use of the wheelchair for running activities.

Support systems, including tracking to monitor progress, need to be in place to ensure that ITP goals come to fruition. Cooperation among parties principal to the ITP process, including school personnel, parents, the student, and community service providers is essential to successful transition.

Physical education and the ITP Physical education on the ITP should address, but not be limited to, developing physical and motor proficiencies that support meaningful,

independent adult living and employment, and facilitating meaningful access to community-based social and leisure-time activities. Portions of two ITPs that would involve physical education; one work-related, one leisure-related, appear respectively in **Figures 3.2** and **3.3**.

The 504 Plan

IDEA 2004 is a special education law. As such, only children who have disabilities *as defined by IDEA*

Figure 3.2

Individualized Transition Plan
(Physical Education)

Student:_____   Meeting Date:_____

School:_____   School Principal:_____

Parent/Guardian:_____   Special Education Teacher:_____

Teacher:_____   Adapted Physical Education Teacher:_____

ITP Coordinator:_____   Vocational Teacher:_____

Assessment: Manual testing: 1 repetition maximum on weight machines. Flexibility. Job analysis in community setting.

Transition Goal: To develop sufficient muscular strength and flexibility to improve work productivity on the following tasks:

> Stacking boxes
> Carrying weighted objects
> Propelling a weighted dolly

Desired Outcomes:

1. Improve overall level of muscular strength and flexibility through participation in a community-based weight training program
2. Improve ability to perform job-related tasks without interruption over a 4-hour period.

Support Activities	Personnel	Date
Analyze skills needed for work experience	Vocational teacher	
Determine physical functioning skills needed to perform tasks	Adapted physical education teacher	
Identify community facility for exercise program	Adapted physical education teacher	
Schedule and implement exercise program	Adapted physical education teacher and special education teacher	
Select appropriate work experience	Student, parents, in consultation with vocational teacher	
Complete work application	Student and parents	
Begin work program	Special education teacher, vocational teacher, and job supervisor	
Evaluate progress	Collaborative ITP Team	Ongoing

2004 are eligible to receive special education according the IFSP, IEP, and ITP. However, many students with disabling conditions are not eligible for IDEA services, because their conditions are not recognized as disabilities according to IDEA's definition of disability. One example would be a student who is simply obese, a condition that disables, but one not recognized under IDEA 2004 as a disability. Although such students are not protected under IDEA, they are protected under civil rights legislation (Section 504 of the Rehabilitation Act of 1973, Americans with Disabilities Act of 1990). These acts, unlike IDEA, do not specify disability categories (e.g. intellectual deficit, orthopedic impairment, emotional disturbance). Rather, they define disability broadly as "any physical or mental impairment which substantially limits one or more major life activities."

A 504 plan for a qualifying student is similar in intent and design to individualized plans required by IDEA 2004. The major distinction between an IEP and a 504 plan is that the latter is driven by civil rights, rather than special education, law. Often, 504 plans, for a range of explanations often including absence of funding, tend not to be as forthcoming as IFSPs, IEPs, and ITPs. They are, however, no less a requirement of law and are required to be implemented, as needed.

Figure 3.3

Individualized Transition Plan
(Physical Education)

Student:_____ Meeting Date:_____

School:_____ School Principal:_____

Parent/Guardian:_____ Special Education Teacher:_____

Teacher:_____ Adapted Physical Education Teacher:_____

ITP Coordinator:_____ Recreation Therapist:_____

Assessment: Front crawl swimming skill, muscular endurance, cardiovascular endurance, flexibility. Determine accessibility requirements for suitable swimming facility. Determine skills necessary to travel independently from home to swimming facility and back.

Transition Goal: To develop

- swimming skill sufficient to support transition
- fitness to support swimming activity
- ability to travel independently to and from facility
- ability to independently access swimming facility
- interest in activity that supports weekly participation in integrated community swim

Desired Outcomes:

1. Develop swimming skill to a level that supports ongoing interest in continuing participation beyond school years.
2. To develop the range of skills contained herein to support independent access to swimming in integrated community settings.

Support Activities	Personnel	Date
Determine swimming skills and related fitness needed to support activity	Adapted Physical Education Teacher	
Determine travel and facility access skills needed to support activity	Special Education Teacher, Adapted Physical Education Teacher, Therapeutic Recreation Specialist	
Determine social functioning skills needed to support activity	Adapted Physical Education Teacher, Special Education Teacher, Therapeutic Recreation Specialist	
Address identified swimming and related fitness needs	Adapted Physical Education Teacher	
Address identified travel and facility access needs	Special Education Teacher, Physical Education Teacher, Therapeutic Recreation Specialist	
Address identified social functioning skills needed	Adapted Physical Education Teacher, Special Education Teacher, Therapeutic Recreation Specialist	
Identify accessible swimming facility	Therapeutic Recreation Specialist	
Schedule initial swim at community-based facility	Therapeutic Recreation Specialist	
Student initially accesses swimming facility with family support	Adapted Physical Education teacher, Therapeutic Recreation Specialist in consultation with family	
Student independently accesses swimming facility by herself/himself, with family, or with friends	Therapeutic Recreation Specialist	Himself/herself:: With family: With friends:
Evaluate progress	Collaborative Program Team	Ongoing

CHAPTER SUMMARY

1. To the maximum extent possible children with disabilities are to be educated with peers who do not have disabilities.

2. When children cannot reasonably be expected to succeed in the regular curriculum, they are entitled to education, individualized as needed, in as close to the regular curriculum as is reasonably possible.

3. Assessment is integral to developing the individualized education plan. One cannot individualize unless one knows the individual. One cannot know the individual without assessment.

4. Assessment is essential for determining what the curriculum should be, tracking the student's progress, and evaluating the effectiveness of instruction.

5. An individualized education program is required for every child with a disability whose educational needs cannot be met without modification in the regular curriculum setting.

6. Parents of children with disabilities must be included in the development of their child's individualized education plan.

7. Assessments must be (1) valid, (2) reliable, (3) objective, and (4) used only for the purposes for which they are intended.

8. Norm-referenced tests, because they compare student performances to one another, tend to be helpful in making educational placement decisions.

9. Criterion-referenced tests, which break skills down into developmental sequences (e.g., overhand throw, jump, hop), tend to be helpful in tracking individual learner progress once placement has been made.

10. Teacher developed tests may be used for assessment when commercially developed or otherwise published tests are not available or appropriate. When teacher developed tests are used, they must adhere to the standards enumerated in #7.

11. Assessment needs to be authentic; that is, tests should measure skills according to how effectively they can be meaningfully executed in the real world environment.

12. Schools must take necessary steps to ensure students with disabilities have equal opportunity to participate in extracurricular activities.

13. Pre-schoolers are entitled to an individualized family service plan (IFSP). The IFSP is similar in intent to the IEP. Its purpose is to facilitate and promote maximum child development prior to entry into kindergarten, when intervention is known to have the greatest impact.

14. An individualized transition plan must have been activated for students with disabilities who have reached the age of 16. The purpose of the ITP is to help ensure as smooth a transition as possible from young adult high school life to adult life in the community.

15. Section 504 plans are to be developed for students who do not have disabilities as defined in IDEA 2004, but who, nevertheless, manifest physical or mental impairments that substantially limit one or more major life functions.

REFERENCES

_____. Special Olympics Sports Guides (2000–2003). Washington, DC: Special Olympics.

American Association for Physical Activity and Recreation. Adapted Physical Education Assessment Scale-II. (2002). Reston, VA: American Association for Physical Activity and Recreation.

Americans with Disabilities Act of 1990, Pub. L. No. 101-336. (26 July, 1990).

Aspen Snowmass: http://www.aspensnowmass.com/schools/challenge.cfm. Retrieved: 21 April, 2009.

Battelle Developmental Inventory (BDI-2) (2005). Meadows, IL: Riverside Publishing.

Bayley, N. A. (2005). *Bayley scales of infant and toddler development (Bayley III)*. Sanantonio, TX: Pearson.

Block, M. (2000). *A teacher's guide to including students with disabilities in general physical education*. Baltimore, MN: Paul H. Brooks Publishing Co.

Blunt, M. (January 2005). *Essential skills and task analysis*. Staff Highlights. Missouri Schools for Severely Handicapped.

Bricker, D. (2002). *Assessment, evaluation, and programming systems (AEPS) for infants and children* (2nd ed.). Baltimore, MD: Brookes.

Brigance Inventory of Early Development II. (2004). North Billerica, MA: Curriculum Associates.

Bruininks, R. H., & Bruininks, B. D. (2005). *Bruininks test of motor proficiency II*. San Francisco: Pearson.

Code of Federal Regulations. 34 CFR, Section 300.334 300.550 300.551 300.552. (30 December, 2005).

Code of Federal Regulations. 34 CFR, Section 300.43 (1 January, 2008)

Education for All Handicapped Children Act of 1975, Pub. L. 94-142. (29 November, 1975).

Folio, M. R. & Felwell, R. (2000). *Peabody developmental motor scales* (2nd ed.) Austin, TX: Pro-Ed.

Frankenburg, W. K., Dodds, J. B., & Archer, P. (1990). *Denver developmental screening test II*. Denver: Denver Developmental Materials.

Gronley, J. K., & Perry, J. (December 1984). *Gait analysis techniques: Observational gait analysis*. Downey, CA: Los Amigos Research and Education Institute.

Harter, S. (1988). *Manual for self-perception profile for children*. Denver: Author.

Henderson, S., Sugden, D., & Barnett, A. (2007). *Movement assessment: Battery for children*. London: Pearson

Hitchinger, J. (December 14, 2007). Schools accused of pushing mainstreaming to cut costs. *Wall Street Journal Online*, p. A1. Retrieved: 17 April, 2009

Horvat, M., Block, M., & Kelly, L. (2007). *Developmental and adapted physical activity assessment*. Champaign, IL: Human Kinetics.

Hyatt, K. (2004). *IEP meetings: A guide to participation for parents*. National Association of School Psychiatrists: Bethesda, MD (http://www.nasponline.org/families/iep. pdf. Retrieved: 21 April, 2009)

Individuals with Disabilities Improvement Education Act of 2004, Pub. No. L 108-446, Section 300.107 (a)(b). (3 December, 2004).

Individuals with Disabilities Improvement Education Act of 2004, Pub. L No. 108-446, Section 636 (d). (3 December, 2004).

Johnson, D., & Johnson, R. (Spring99). Making cooperative learning work. *Theory Into Practice*; Vol. 38 Issue 2, p67, 7p.

Johnson, R. E., & Lavay, B. (1988). *Kansas adapted/special education test manual*. Topeka, KS: Kansas State Department of Education.

Kelly, L., Dummer, G., & Sampson, T. (2002). *Everyone can*. Champaign, IL: Human Kinetics.

Kelly, L., & Wessel, J. (1990). *I CAN: Primary skills*. Pro-Ed: Austin, TX: Pro-Ed.

Kidstogether.org: http://www.kidstogether.org/inclusion/ benefitsofinclusion.htm. Retrieved: 17 April, 2009.

Lasko, P., & Aufsesser, P. (n.d.). *San Diego state posture evaluation*. San Diego, CA: Authors.

Mahoney, M. J., Gabriel, T. J., & Perkins, T. S. (1987). Psychological skills and exceptional athletic performance. *The Sport Psychologist, 1*, 181–199.

Martinek, T., & Zaichkowsky, L. (1977). *Manual for the Martinek-Zaichkowsky self-concept scale for children*. Jacksonville, FL: Psychologists and Educators.

McClehaghan, B., & Gallahue, D. (1978). *Fundamental movement*. Philadelphia: Saunders.

Meredith, M. D., & Welk, G. J., editors. Fitnessgram/ Activitygram: Test Administration Manual (2007). Dallas, TX: Cooper Institute for Aerobic Research/Champaign, IL: Human Kinetics.

Model IEP Form. US Department of Education: Office of Special Education and Rehabilitative Services, Office of special Education Programs: http://idea.ed.gov/ download/modelform_1IEP.pdf. Retrieved: 24 April, 2009.

National Association for Sport and Physical Education. (2005). *Physical best* (2nd ed.). Champaign, IL: Human Kinetics.

The National Center on Physical Activity and Disability (NCPAD): http://www.ncpad.org/. Retrieved: 20 April, 2009

New York Department of Education (1966). *New York posture screening*. Albany, NY: Author.

Piers, E.V., Harris, D. B., & Hersberg, D. S. (2002). *Piers-Harris children's self-concept scale*, 2nd ed. Los Angeles: Western Psychological Services.

President's Council of Physical Fitness and Sport. (2009). http://www.fitness.gov/digestmar2000.htm. Retrieved 20 April, 2009.

Rehabilitation Act of 1973, Pub. L. No. 93-112, Section 504, Title V.

Shakelford, J. State and Jurisdictional Eligibility Definitions for Infants and Toddlers with Disabilities under IDEA. National Early Childhood Technical Assistance Center. NECTAC Notes, Issue No. 21, page 1. (July 2006). http://www.nectac.org/~pdfs/ pubs/nnotes21.pdf. Retrieved: 21 April, 2009.

Skowronski, W., Horvat, M., Nocera, J., Roswal, G., & Croce, R. (2009). Eurofit Special: European Fitness Battery Score Variation Among Individuals with Intellectual Disabilities. *Adapted Physical Activity Quarterly, 26*, 54–67.

Ulrich, D. (2000). Test of Gross Motor Development II. Austin, TX: Pro-Ed.

Ulrich, D. A., & Collier, D. H. (1990). Perceived physical competence in children with mental retardation: Modification of a pictorial scale. *Adapted Physical Activity Quarterly, 7*, 338–350.

Wehman, P. (2006). *Life beyond the classroom: Transition strategies for young people with disabilities*, (4th ed.). Baltimore: Paul Brooks Publishing co.

Wickstrtom, R. (1983). *Fundamental movement patterns* (3 rd ed.). Philadelphia: Lea and Febiger.

Wilderness Inquiry: http://www.wildernessinquiry.org. Retrieved: 19 April, 2009).

Winnick, J., & Short, F. (1999). *Brockport physical fitness test*. Champaign, IL: Human Kinetics.

Psychosocial Aspects of Disability

I am America's child, a spastic slogging on demented limbs drooling I'll trade my PhD for a telephone voice.

Bart Lanier Safford III, *An Obscured Radiance*

CASE STUDY

Sarah is a 13 year old with spastic cerebral palsy. The condition, right hemiplegia, causes hyper tonicity and hyper reflexia on her body's right side. Sarah's cerebral palsy is not accompanied by intellectual defecit.

Sarah, as the result of poor self-esteem and well-meaning, but misguided, overprotection, is reticent to do things for herself; things that she is quite capable of doing. In physical education (regular and adapted- she participates in both), she expects teachers or classmates to retrieve the ball for her when it has fallen beyond her reach. Likewise, she is unwilling to help bring out and put away equipment used in the day's lesson. In the absence of repeated prompting from her teacher, she will sit-out rather than participate in the day's activity.

Sarah avoids use of her right side extremities, because (1) her right side is difficult to manage and movements are imprecise and (2) right side use, related to self-esteem issues, draws unwanted attention her disability. As a result, she slowly, but steadily, is losing strength and range of motion to her right side that may well become irreversible, and she is increasingly becoming unnecessarily dependent on others to do things for her that she is perfectly capable of doing for herself.

Sarah is in need of modifications to her IEP that (1) will help mitigate her poor self-esteem and (2) motivate her to become independent in accordance with her true potential.

Sarah's family and the professionals responsible for her education are challenged to: (1) design strategies for Sarah to improve her self-esteem and (2) incorporate behavior management interventions to prompt Sarah to want to become as independent as possible. How might the two challenges above be interrelated?

This chapter addresses a range of psychosocial and behavioral phenomena often observed among children in general, with particular focus on children who have disabilities. At the outset, it is important to note that children who have disabilities are first and foremost children; that disability in and of itself certainly has potential to impact self-perception and behavior, but does not automatically translate into difficulty with adjustment.

The extent of disability's impact on any individual is in large measure a function of the significance that the disability holds for the person. How the person perceives her/his disability largely depends on life events that have contributed to the formulation of values. Values impact how the individual views the world and his/her place in it (Best, Bigge, & Sirvis, 1990).

Self-Concept

Baldwin and Hoffman (2002) define self-concept as;

> self-evaluation or self-perception, and it represents the sum of an individual's beliefs about his or her own attributes. Self-concept reflects how a (person) evaluates himself or herself in domains (or circumstances) in which he or she considers success important.

Having a positive self-concept has been linked to positive social and emotional development in young people; while having a negative self-concept has been associated with development of maladaptive behaviors and emotions (Hadley, Hair, and Moore, 2008). Research in social psychology consistently reveals that arousal levels, motivation to achieve, and quality of interpersonal relationships are closely related to strength of self-concept. Researchers further assert that the strength of self-concept is mediated by one's understanding of how she/he is perceived by others. This implies that if an individual's feeling of self-worth is not shared by others, it is of little positive value to the individual. Simply stated, "What I think about me depends largely on what I think you think about me."

While young people in general are challenged to develop functional, positive self-concepts, students with disabilities often face greater challenges.

Harter (1999) identifies eight domains considered important by adolescents as they form concepts of themselves. They include:

- Scholastic competence
- Athletic competence
- Physical appearance
- Peer acceptance
- Close friendships
- Romantic relationships
- Job competence
- Conduct/morality

With the exception of romantic relationships and job competence, perceived competence in all of the above domains becomes increasingly applicable to positive self-concept formation in young people as they develop.

Researchers have determined that self-concept is multi-factorial (Byrne, 1996; Marsh, Papiaoannou, & Theodorakis, 2006). For example, having a high athletic self-concept with regard to athletic competence tends to correlate with high athletic achievement. However, a high self-concept with regard to athletic competence would not necessarily affect academic achievement, if the person manifests low self-concept with regard to scholastic competence. As such, a person who holds a positive self-concept with regard to one domain will not necessarily hold a positive self-concept in other domains. According

to Cheng & Ferhnam (2004), the more domains in which a person holds a positive self-concept, the more likely that person will be to report overall happiness.

Body Image

The image of one's body and the value one places on that image are significant factors in the formulation of self-concept. Body concept and the esteem in which that concept is held is central to personal identity.

Dissatisfaction with body image is prevalent in the society-at-large irrespective of ability/disability. Media attention heaped on *size zero* models, for example, impact women and girls who perceive that less is more. Many teenage girls with healthy weights believe themselves to be overweight (http://www.womenshealth.gov/bodyimage/kids/). Many men and boys link masculinity with muscularity (Kimmel & Mahalik, 2004). Often, the extremes to which girls, women, boys, and men aspire become wholly unrealistic. By way of example, if the current GI Joe figure, a perennially favorite action figure among preadolescent males, were extrapolated to life size, the figure's biceps would be larger than those of any body builder in history (Pope, et al, 1999).

Individuals with disabilities can be especially challenged in regard to achieving positive body image. This observation is confirmed by Best, Biggie, and Sirvis (1990) who report that social adjustment correlates negatively with self-concept when disability is visible.

Defense mechanisms

Everyone at one time or another has relied on defense mechanisms to deal with stress. One who relies consistently on defense mechanisms, however consciously or subconsciously, tends not to deal adequately with the source of the stress. Reliance on defense mechanisms is akin to trying to get rid of dandelions in the lawn by pulling-up the yellow flowers. The problem keeps coming back, because the roots remain. Defense mechanisms include the following:

- Regression — Confronted by a threatening situation, the person returns to an earlier level of maturity or adjustment (Example: Bed wetting as a response to stress long after child has toilet trained).

- Repression — The person purposefully, but subconsciously, forgets (obliterates from memory) events with which is unable to cope. (Example: A child abused by adults who does not remember the abuse, but subsequently has difficulty forming relationships with non-abusive adults.)

- Denial — The person refuses to acknowledge the existence of real situations and circumstances. In repression the person obliterates stressful situations and circumstances from memory. In denial, the person may acknowledge stressful situations and circumstances, but denies they have consequence or significance. (Example: "I couldn't be having a heart attack. It's probably just the pizza.")

- Rationalization — A person creates "acceptable" reasons for events or circumstances, because the true reasons are emotionally unacceptable. (Example: A person continues to smoke and justifies it by saying, "If I try to quit, I'll just gain weight.")

- Resignation — The person gives up when confronted by seemingly insurmountable circumstances. (Example: "I'm not tall enough to play basketball.")

- Becoming dependent or demanding — A person requires unnecessary assistance to get attention, affection, and care from important others. (Example: An otherwise able bodied child expecting to be pushed down the hall in his/her wheelchair.)

Overreliance on defense mechanisms is not compatible with development of healthy attitudes to support stress management. Fostering realistic attitudes about one's disability helps avoid reliance on self-defeating behaviors and inordinate reliance on symptom-treating defense mechanisms. Developing healthy, adaptive strategies to deal with adversity facilitates getting at the root causes of stress, including the ability to set goals that, in the long run, support independent living.

Striving for Acceptance and the Price It Extracts

Virtually everyone strives to be accepted and to count in the lives of other people. People with *and* without disabilities alike can become entrapped in the effort to develop false fronts that in the individual's own eyes make her/him appear more acceptable to others. This kind of striving, however, particularly among persons with disabilities, has potential to become self-defeating when the false front is contrived to cover up traits perceived by the person to be undesirable. According to Wright (1960) in her now classic text on physical disability (as cited by Dunn & Elliot, 2005):

> The price of trying above all to hide and forget is high. It is high because the effort is futile. A person cannot forget when reality requires him to take his disability into account time and time again. The vigilance required for covering up leads to strain, not only physically but also in interpersonal relations, for one must maintain a certain distance (social as well as physical) in order to fend off the frightening topic of the disability ... Trying to forget is the best way of remembering. (p. 24)

Wright points out that acting like a normal person is not the same as feeling like a normal person (i.e. a worthy human being). Wright concludes that "all too often, one pays a price for the apparent success when the motivation is to prove that one is 'as good as

anybody else.'" Any attempt to hide, forget, or cover up traits considered by the person to be unacceptable likely will have a negative impact on the person's self-concept. Implication is that the person wishing to obscure a disability by acting "normal" often ends up without associates. On one hand, the person may resist associating with people who are similar or have similar levels of disability for fear of drawing attention to her/his own disability. On the other hand, the person may avoid association with persons who do not have disabilities for fear of having the differences become even more obvious. The person threatened by contact may avoid contact with either group. Given the need to feel "at home" with one's self, such a person may become self-rendered virtually homeless.

Severity of Disability, Adjustment, and Self-Concept

Empirical evidence strongly suggests that severe disability does not go hand in hand with maladjustment. Conversely, mild disability offers no guarantee of positive adjustment.

Some persons with mild disability, that is relatively easily obscured, recognize greater potential for hiding their disability. The hiding process can prompt denial and thwart positive adjustment, because the person has already engaged in self-devaluation. Self-devaluation, in turn, diminishes self-concept.

Persons with more severe, undeniable disabilities may see little recourse but to accept themselves as persons with disability. In either case, the person who positively

---

LEARNING ACTIVITY

Enter the following phrases into any online search engine:

"the 'r' word"

"end the 'r' word"

In the process you will learn or learn more about the controversy over continuing use of the term 'retarded' in everyday language. The Special Olympics organization currently invites individuals to publically pledge to end their use of the 'r' word on the Special Olympics' website (http://www.r-word.org/). Note at the same time, however, that P. L., 108-446, Idea 2004 uses "mental retardation" to denote one of the conditions that qualifies as a disability for legal eligibility to receive special education services.

Do you think the word *retarded* should continue to be used? Enter into a discussion with members of your class regarding this issue. Can your group reach a consensus on this issue?

adjusts may need to cling temporarily to the "normal ideal." It may be necessary to temporarily embrace that ideal before finding satisfaction with being oneself.

The foregoing discussion is not intended to minimize the significance of adjustment issues that challenge persons with severe disabilities. Persons with severe *congenital* disabilities sometimes are accorded the least status in social communities. Persons with severe acquired disabilities, on the other hand, sometimes are accorded higher social status in the community, by themselves and the community at large. It is hypothesized that a severe congenital disability, because it is present from birth, greatly limits experiences that ensure status in the community. Conversely, the person with an acquired disability may have had greater opportunity for normalizing social experiences in society-at-large prior to acquiring her/his disability.

Empathy, Sympathy, and Pity

The terms *empathy* and *sympathy* are often treated as synonyms; yet, however subtle, the words have different meanings. With empathy, the person feels or at least strives to share in the emotions of another (e.g. "I feel your pain."). Truax (1970), in an opinion that remains virtually unchallenged to this day, posits that without empathy, there is little basis for helping.

Empathy While empathy is an essential emotion in the helping professions, it also has risks. When one empathizes, one assumes some level of emotional involvement in the life circumstances of another. Emotional involvement, in turn, harbors potential to cloud objectivity when the teacher/therapist/helper opens his/her heart to circumstances affecting the person in her/his care. This is not to dissuade caregivers from empathy, but to alert caretakers in the range of helping professions to the potential risks of emotional involvement.

Sympathy Pure sympathy differs from empathy in that it conveys compassion of another's circumstances without empathy's level of emotional involvement (e.g. "I appreciate your circumstances, and I am concerned for you.") (Slote, 2007; Lazarus & Lazarus, 1994). While empathy and sympathy each evoke subjective feelings of emotion, the latter tends to be more objective than the former.

Empathy and sympathy have their place and time in teaching-learning environments and, when thoughtfully expressed and acted upon, add humanity to lives and environments that often are remediation and treatment centered.

Pity Pity has no place in helping relationships. Quite universally, pity is among the most unwelcome emotions among persons who are the objects of pity. Pity essentially says, "You poor, unfortunate fellow. I cannot imagine how anyone would want to be or live like you." Pity is hurtful; it devalues worth, and devalued worth causes additional suffering. Pity adds insult to injury. People generally wish for understanding (i.e. empathy, sympathy), not pity.

Anecdotes extolling outstanding achievements by persons with disabilities often, however unintentionally, evoke pity. The time honored story of one Pete Gray provides a case in point. Gray, who at the age of six lost an arm in a truck accident, went on to become a major league baseball player. One newspaper account (Rusk & Taylor, 1946) of Gray's achievement read as follows. Pay particular attention to the last sentence:

> Gray is an inspiration … The mere fact that a one-armed ball player has crashed the big league opens up new and electrifying vistas for each of them [similarly handicapped persons]. If one can overcome his handicap in such fashion, there is hope for them all. (p.140)

Reference to "them," however unintentional the devaluing, effectively promotes a we-they dichotomy; one based on disability *alone* that sets the individual with a disability apart from persons without disabilities. The final phrase, "there is hope for them all," drives home the stigma, particularly to the reader with a disability (i.e. "Poor fellow, Pete Gray. But don't worry. Even for people like you there is hope.")

Inspirational messages should not be eliminated. They should, however, be tempered by recognition that a message's undertones can perpetuate hurtful stereotypes that devalue the self-worth of persons for whom the message may have been intended.

Terminal Illness in Children

Perhaps life's ultimate reality is death, yet death remains a reality with which many are unable to functionally cope. Children in school settings can be terminally ill from conditions including, but certainly not limited to, Duchenne muscular dystrophy, cystic fibrosis, and cancer.

Anxieties surrounding the imminent death of a terminally ill child are perplexing for everyone. People tend to accept death in older persons, but a child's death assaults reason.

The dying child (if she/he is mature enough to grasp death's significance) and those affected by the child's death experience, provided time permits, change in attitude as death approaches. Elisabeth Kubler-Ross (2008), in her classic text on death and dying, describes five discrete stages which people experience as they come to grips with death and tragedy. They are as follows:

1. Denial ("This can't be happening to me.")

2. Anger (misplaced feelings of rage or envy toward anything/anyone that symbolizes life and energy)

3. Bargaining (often with one's concept of the super-natural for more time)

4. Depression ("What is the point? Why go on?")

5. Acceptance ("It's going to be okay.")

Kubler-Ross says that the dying child will often single out one adult with whom to communicate feelings about death. That person is often not a parent but a teacher or therapist. The child tends to choose someone other than the parent, because the child, sensitive to the parent's grief, does not wish to compound that grief. The person selected must be willing to accept the child's feelings, otherwise the child will experience profound loneliness.

When children die, there is no less need to support friends and classmates who will remain after their friend or classmate has died. Dyer (2009) recommends eight strategies to help surviving children grieve well:

1. When talking to a child about a loss, find out first what the child knows and what she/he thinks has happened. Children may be aware of more than you think.

2. Answer any question simply and honestly, but only offer the details that the child can absorb. Do not give the child more information than is requested.

3. Let the child have time to grieve, be upset, and talk about fears.

4. Give the child a chance to talk. Listen, validate feelings, and then provide reassurance.

5. Encourage the child to draw, read, write letters or poetry, sing, tell stories, and play with clay. Creative means of expression are all helpful ways for a child to express grief.

6. Let the child go outside to play and be active; activity is a good way to cope with anxiety.

7. Try and keep regular routines. Children can even grieve a change in behavior and mourn the environment and the predictability of a schedule that existed before the loss or death.

8. Be patient and flexible. Children grieve intermittently. The child can cry one moment and then play normally the next.

The Helping Relationship

According to Christ & Blacker (2006):

> The helping relationship is complex and dynamic and is the core of how we are able to provide care. It is founded on the remarkable trust that persons who are helped place in the helper. The helping relationship is always inherently based on some degree of imbalance in power that comes from the helper's status because of the knowledge s/he possesses, and his/her control over access to resources (pp. 181-182).

In a helping relationship, the person helped is often assumed to be unable, in the absence of external assistance, to help himself/herself. The act of helping another can easily be interpreted as helplessness on the part of the person receiving help. Judgment that the person helped is helpless can be made by the helper, the person being helped, or by persons observing. Because helping suggests that the relationship is one-sided, value judgments often are made about the recipient. The recipient, particularly when need for help is prolonged, may be judged inferior to others who appear self-reliant and independent.

Virtually everyone needs help at one time or another, and one's sensitivity to need for help is highly individual. Most people respond positively to assistance when it is genuinely needed and is *not* offered to satisfy the helper's ego. The latter is likely to be dismissed as condescending.

Persons with disabilities in need of assistance generally desire the minimum assistance necessary and only when necessary. Before helping, obtain consent (when consent can be meaningfully given or refused) from the person involved. Do not assume that help is needed or wanted. Assistance, particularly if unsolicited, can be interpreted as denial of the person's independence. When a person desires to help but is uncertain about what exactly to do, she/he should simply ask. The helper should focus on assistance with the task at hand, not on the helping relationship itself. Fuss and emotional display by the helper suggests ego feeding at the expense of the person receiving assistance.

This Chapter opened with a line of poetry by Bart Lanier Safford III. We close this section with another of Safford's poems. Safford, who has cerebral palsy, has earned three degrees in higher education. In the opening excerpt, however, he placed his academic achievements in perspective in fewer than 20 words. For Safford and those for whom he speaks, the psychosocial aspect of disability is not pristine, abstract theory but an enduring fact of life. Safford, whose gift with words enables him to say in a few words what some say in volumes, has written the following poem, which might well have been directed to physical education teachers and those who coach persons with disabilities. His poem is titled, "The Baseball Manager and the Warm-up Jacket":

In high school in Brooklyn
I was the baseball manager,
proud as I could be
I chased baseballs,
gathered thrown bats,
handed out the towels
It was very important work
for a small spastic kid,
but I was a team member
When the team got
their warm-up jackets

I didn't get one
Only the regular team
got these jackets, and
surely not a manager
Eventually, I bought my own
but it was dark blue while
the official ones were green
Nobody ever said anything
to me about my blue jacket;
the guys were my friends
Yet it hurt me all year
to wear that blue jacket
among all those green ones
Even now, forty years after,
I still recall that jacket
and the memory goes on hurting.

Bart Lanier Safford III

Behavior Management

Teachers have many responsibilities. Among them, one of the most important is behavior management. Effective teaching and learning cannot occur in a poorly managed class. The result of a mismanaged class is disrespect for teacher and peers and general disorder. Here, teachers quite generally cannot teach, and students, as a consequence, quite generally do not learn. In a mismanaged class, both teachers and students suffer. (Marzano, 2003).

According to Wright, Horn, and Sanders (1997) in a study involving some 60,000 students, the teacher is the most important variable in student achievement. Teacher effectiveness is the single most important factor in student achievement, and class management is critical to student achievement. Managing students and student behavior warrants top priority from all teachers, novice and veteran alike, who aspire to teaching excellence.

Marzano (2003) has studied factors that, when employed effectively, decrease disruptive student behaviors in class settings. Factors include (1) establishment of class rules and procedures, (2) disciplinary interventions, (3) establishment of teacher-student relationships, and (4) establishment of a mental set (i.e., mindfulness of the importance of what is being taught and learned). Marzano cites that when these factors are applied consistently, disruptive student behaviors diminish, from 28 to 40 percent. Marzano devotes a chapter to each factor and includes *action steps* to help ensure each factor's potential to effectively manage student behavior and, as a consequence, promote class order and learning.

The All Important First Day

There is a time-honored saying, "You never get a second chance to make a first impression." This certainly applies to meeting students the first day of class.

Emmer, Evertson, and Worsham (2003) and Marzano (2003), combined, offer theses suggestions:

With younger students:

- Prepare name tags
- Greet students at the door. Help them with name tags and where to stand or be seated (e.g. name tag on a desk or activity room floor).
- Don't allow students to wander around and be confused about what/what not to do.
- Tell students about yourself.
- Have students tell their name and a favorite activity.
- Talk about class rules, procedures and, as needed, disciplinary interventions.

With older students:

- Stand at doorway, and monitor general activity inside and outside as they first enter the room or activity area.
- Greet students as they enter.
- Take care of administrative tasks at very beginning of class (e.g. take roll, fill out cards/forms, as needed and collect them).
- Tell students your name, and offer background information about yourself (e.g. background, teaching experience, hobbies/interests related/ unrelated to your teaching).
- If students do not know one another, provide a brief opportunity for students in small groups to become acquainted with one another.
- Orient students to class content and the types of activities in which they will participate. Consider distributing a questionnaire to determine students' activity interests.
- Distribute a course outline and briefly address your expectations for the class.
- Provide students a written copy of class rules, procedures, assignments, and grading criteria. Explain to students that they may be offered an opportunity to participate in the modification of rules and procedures.
- Go over your system of consequences for good and unacceptable behavior.
- Allow time for questions.
- End class with a routine that allows for orderly culmination and exit.

The First Few Days: Setting the Tone

Successful teachers are successful, in part, because they have established ways to set the tone for their classes during the first few days. The quality of the teaching/learning experience for both teacher and students throughout the remainder of the school year can be determined in large measure by the tone set by the teacher early on. A tone not set by the teacher will likely be set by the students, the consequences of which may be risky at best. Beyond aforementioned activities undertaken during the all important first day, tone setting during the early days of class can include the following. The list is not exhaustive, but rather exemplifies strategies that, in the writers' collective experience, have proven effective:

- Establish class routines and make sure students understand them, understand their purpose, and can execute them without confusion according to the spirit in which they are intended.
- Let students know how you wish to be addressed (e.g. Mr., Ms., Mrs., Doctor, Professor, Coach).
- Engage students in 'getting to know you' activities.
- Introduce new students to class members, so that the new student feels a sense of belonging and welcome.
- Continue to go over class rules and procedures to ensure thorough understanding of such, including their rationale; while recognizing need, at times, for modifications according to the uniqueness of each class.
- Be neither passive nor aggressive in your demeanor; but, rather, be constructively assertive and confident in front of the class (e.g. through eye contact, body language, vocalizations and facial expressions appropriate to the message, clear and unambiguous statements).
- Act early on with consistency to positively encourage individual and class behavior compatible with effective teaching/learning and civility and, positively and consistently discourage conduct that disrupts.
- Establish and consistently apply constructive consequences, positive and negative, for civil and unacceptable behavior.
- Maintain a respectful distance from students. Be friendly and approachable. But remember, you are the student's teacher, not the student's pal.
- By example, establish the clear expectation that everyone, teacher and student alike, is to be treated with dignity and respect.

Managing Behavior on a Day to Day Basis Throughout the Year

All behavior has consequences and the consequences for behavior can be positive or negative. Positive consequences emanating from the teacher are intended to result in an increase in the frequency of behaviors that produce positive consequences. The reverse is true with negative consequences. For a dissenting opinion, see Choice Theory (Glasser, 1998) later in this chapter.

Consequences can be imposed externally by another person or entity and/or self-imposed (i.e. experienced internally). Example of an external consequence would be teacher-imposed rewards or discipline for good or unacceptable behavior. Example of internal consequences would be feelings one experiences following participation in a self-valued activity where the performance has been either satisfying or disappointing.

While consequences for behavior can be externally or internally imposed, they do not often exist mutually exclusive of one another. For example, if I perform below my teacher's expectations *and* my own self-imposed expectations, I end up dealing with my teacher's disappointment and my own self-imposed disappointment combined; perhaps even compounded.

Importance of identifying determinants of behavior, good and bad   Good students are good students for a variety of reasons. Likewise, students who misbehave do so for a variety of reasons. Precisely because *all* behavior has purpose, it behooves the teacher who wishes to manage behavior, to determine the purpose underlying the behavior in question. Regarding managing behavior that is unacceptable, DeBruyn & Larson (2009) state:

> In maintaining a professional approach to changing unacceptable behavior to acceptable behavior, we must never forget that the first step to a solution lies in discovering the purpose of the misbehavior . . . The student who arrives habitually late is different from the student who talks back to the teacher . . . We cannot treat any misbehavior effectively until we know the reason for it. (p. xii)

It is likewise important to note that the same misbehavior (e.g. the foul mouth, the disrupter, the day dreamer), observed in seemingly similar students, can stem from a variety of disparate causes. According to Gossen (1997), every time something is not the way we want it to be, we behave to change it. Why we behave as we do, according to Gossen, depends on why we seek to change our circumstances. Wilson (1993), as cited by Gossen, cites motivation to change one's circumstances on three levels:

> Level One: to avoid pain, physical and/or emotional. Essentially, the person is asking himself/herself, "What will happen to me if I don't do it?"
>
> Level Two: to gain approval or a reward from significant others whose approval is valued. Essentially, this person is asking herself/himself, "What do I get if I do it?"
>
> Level Three: for self-respect. Essentially, the person is asking himself/herself, "Who will I be if I do it?"

At any given time, a person may behave on all three levels depending on which circumstance among a constellation of circumstances she/he is trying to change. Behavior at levels one and two are driven by factors *external* to the person, while motivations for behavior at level three tend to be *internal* or *intrinsic* (i.e., driven by need for respect for oneself). Desires for positive change that are intrinsically motivated, in the long run, are the changes, that when achieved, persist over time. This is true; because the desire for change that comes from within requires little or no extrinsic payback.

According to DeBruyn & Larson, while there are many reasons for misbehavior, the vast majority stem from (1) lack of attention, (2) lack of power, (3) desire for revenge, and (4) lack of self-confidence. Other needs at the root of misbehavior, many of which are subsumed under Wilson's three levels and DeBruyn & Larson's four reasons are as follows:

- Hunger (poverty, poor diet)
- Thirst (underlying medical condition e.g. diabetes)
- Sex/sexuality (loss of boyfriend or girlfriend, parents breaking up)
- Rest (student may have an after school job, after which she/he must do homework; parents not enforcing adequate sleep time, parents fighting late at night)
- Gregariousness (motivation to be part of a clique or "inner circle.")
- Aggression (mismanaged need to be assertive, manifesting itself as aggression or bullying)
- Affiliation (need to feel close to and safe with someone who can be trusted. That "someone" can be a teacher, classmate, or a gang outside of school)
- Inquisitiveness (need to know what is going on, usually for purposes of gaining and maintaining control over one's life)
- Achievement (desire to succeed and to be recognized. Students who cannot succeed in school in acceptable ways may resort to behavior that is uncivil and unacceptable. The underlying mentality, conscious or subconscious, is that attention for negative behavior is better than no attention.)
- Power/Status (Fulfillment of this need can manifest itself both positively and negatively. Negative: bullying, gang affiliation; job, if it detracts from education. Positive: teacher assistant, class officer, team captain.)
- Autonomy (need to be one's own boss and to have control over one's life).

The message here is that the student will strive to have his/her above needs met, one way or another, positively or negatively. Effective behavior management calls for (1) acknowledging the need (unfulfilled or fulfilled)

behind a behavior being manifested, (2) acknowledging and reinforcing positive strategies for achieving need fulfillment; and, (3) as needed, finding, implementing, and reinforcing alternative, positive ways for and with the student to achieve fulfillment in civil, self-empowering ways.

General behavior management strategies A host of strategies are available to the teacher to help manage individual student and class behavior. Not all strategies will work in all situations, and some teachers will use certain strategies more effectively than others. Suffice it to say the right teacher using the right strategy at the right time has potential to be an effective class manager. General behavior management strategies found to be effective include:

- Clear behavioral expectations: Students, especially students who manifest challenging behaviors, need to know exactly what behaviors are expected of them. Students with challenging behaviors especially need to be reminded of behavior expectations on a regular or, as needed, day to day basis. Provided students operate at a threshold cognitive level, they may be asked individually and as a class to state those expectations. Consequences for meeting and failing to meet expectations should be unambiguous and applied consistently and fairly.
- Class procedures predictability: Students, especially students with challenging behaviors stemming from information processing disabilities, tend to behave better when class procedures do not vary from day to day. For students who do not handle change well, consistency and repetition, to the extent that it does not get in the way of teaching and learning, can generally be quite helpful. Change in class routine should be well thought out in advance and structured in its execution.
- Attention to class structure: Structure is about the teacher consciously determining which decisions students will and will not be able to make as the class transpires. Students should be neither allowed nor expected to make decisions beyond their abilities to see and respect consequences. In a tightly structured class, the teacher, to ensure order, will make the majority, if not all, decisions regarding student activity and conduct. Structure can and generally should be relaxed as students demonstrate motivation and maturity to act on their own in ways conducive to effective teaching and learning.
- Praise an individual student publically for good work/behavior (but not effusively so as to embarrass the student); however, when reprimanding a student, if reasonably possible, reprimand in private (so as not to humiliate).

- Monitor *your own* responses to challenging student behavior. Ask yourself, "What messages are my actions sending to the student and to the class."
- Proximity management of disruptive behavior: This can include, but is not limited to, direct eye contact with the student, moving to stand near the student, anticipating problem areas with a particular activity and moving to that area as the activity begins, quietly asking the student, "Do you need help?," arranging the class such that students with challenging behaviors are not in a convenient position to be provoked by others in who, then, become party to the misbehavior. A quiet, often non-verbal, reprimand; particularly when only one or two students are involved is usually a more effective and less disruptive strategy than a verbal reprimand that draws the entire class' attention.
- Group contingencies: Peer pressure can be powerful and effective when applied sensitively. For example, the teacher might say to the class, "We can't start our activity until everyone is in his/her place." This strategy addresses the entire group and does not draw unnecessary attention to the student or students who may be being inattentive or slow getting into place.
- If students talk inappropriately amongst themselves while you are talking, resist the urge to raise your voice, so as to over power the volume of students' disruptive conversations. The teacher, talking louder as a reaction to disruptive student conversation, often does little more than raise the volume of everyone's voice. Instead, sit or stand still, stop talking, make expressionless eye contact with the class in general and with the offending student(s) in particular. Quite generally, the class, including the offending student(s) will quickly sense your silence and the class will become silent. At that point, with the class' attention reestablished, you may commence speaking in your normal tone.
- The Premack principle: Attributable to psychologist David Premack, relies on the prospect of participation in a highly preferred activity to reinforce participation in a lesser preferred activity. The Premack principle, sometimes known as Grandma's rule, essentially says, "You must do what I want you to do (e.g. eat your vegetables) before you get to do what you want to do (e.g. eat your ice cream)." In an activity setting, the teacher might say, "We can have free activity if we finish today's lesson on time."

Praise given should be praise earned
According to Dowling, Keating, & Bennett (2005):

> Any use of reinforcement procedures must be highly contingent on the demonstration of appropriate behaviors. There is nothing that can damage the potential value of reinforcement faster than reinforcing students who have not put forth genuine effort. Be sincere when doling out reinforcement. The students will only value your praise or any other type of positive reinforcement if the reinforcement follows behavior that requires some effort on their part. Reinforcing mediocre or minimal behaviors will never affect a child's ability to develop either chronic, long-lasting behaviorchanges, or any meaningful level of intrinsic motivation.

This statement clearly has merit; however, when teaching students who have disabilities, there may be need to take a closer look at the sentence, "Reinforcing mediocre or minimal behaviorswill never affect a child's ability todevelop either chronic, long-lasting behaviorchanges, or any meaningful level of intrinsic motivation." With some, students who have disabilities, what might appear to be little effort on the student's part may, in fact, be a major accomplishment for the student in question. Sometimes a student's response to instruction seemingly as minimal as achieving eye contact with the teacher, may, in context, be a major accomplishment for both teacher and student. And, reinforcement must be forthcoming. The message here is that, sometimes, to ensure we do not lose the learner's interest in the process; we are obliged to recognize the need to measure (and reward) progress in proverbial inches rather than in feet; ounces rather than pounds. Requirements for reinforcement should not be so minimal so as to render the activity valueless. Conversely, and equally important; the requirements for reinforcement should not be so great so as to cause the learner to simply give up in frustration and /or abandon interest.

Choice theory
Much of what continues to be written about behavior management suggests that the peoples' behavior is best modified through a system of externally imposed (usually by a higher power) punishments and rewards. Psychiatrist, William Glasser (1998), takes exception. He posits that, on the contrary, all behavior, including the choices that drive behavior, is, *internally, not externally*, motivated; that people make *internal choices* to behave based upon internal need (1) to be loved and connected, (2) to achieve a sense of competence and personal power; (3) to act with a degree of freedom and autonomy; (4) to experience joy and fun; and (5) to survive.

Glasser believes that punishments and rewards, externally imposed by people with power on people without power (to the end that the latter behave "correctly") is destructive of relationships; that external systems of control harm everyone, including the controllers and the controlled. External motivators, he posits are coercive, and concedes coercion will, in fact, yield obedience for the moment. However, because all behavior, he alleges, is internally driven, coercion from without is little more than badgering and does little in the long run to win hearts and minds.

Glasser posits that each person has in his/her own mind a unique picture of his/her quality world. He states, "For each of us, this world is our personal Shangra-la" (p. 45). When our quality world pictures and real world circumstances are in synch, we are happy. When they are not, we are in conflict. He believes school behavior management strategies of the sort that elicit "correct" behavior through systems of punishments and rewards simply rate, berate and, manipulate students into submission until school ceases to be part of the student's quality world picture. As a consequence, the school and teachers that may once have been in the student's quality world picture begin to be replaced by anti-school and antisocial pictures; including disrespect for self and others, rebellion, apathy, violence, drugs, and dysfunctional relationships.

Central to Choice Theory is the premise that the only person whose behavior we can control is our own. All we can give another person is information. How can we give information to others that offers the prospect of being received with the good intentions in which it was offered? According to Glasser (1998), by building positive relationships we become part of the student's quality world picture. To earn a place in the student's quality world, he suggests striving to become a "lead teacher" as opposed to a "boss teacher." A parallel in the business world is the manager who leads/inspires, in contrast to the boss who intimidates. Happy [students], Glasser says, at minimum, always have at least one trusted person, someone who believes in them, in their quality world. In some children's lives; regrettably, but far better than no one, that 'at minimum' person may be the child's teacher. What can a teacher do? Glasser advises the following:

> As long as the people we want to help have only antisocial pleasure pictures in their quality world, all we can do that has any chance of succeeding is to build relationships with them and get into their quality worlds. Punishment, which is used mainly with students, especially with those who come from poor homes and don't like school, does just the opposite. The more we do what we think is right — punish—the further we get from what we want.

He concludes:

> "It is a wonder that our schools are doing as well as they are, considering how much we punish and how many students do not have teachers and schoolwork in their quality lives." (p. 50)

CHAPTER SUMMARY

1. The psychosocial implications of disability can extend further than the direct impact of the disability itself.

2. When difficulties in adjustment become apparent, persons with and without disabilities may turn to defense mechanisms in order to cope. These may include regression, repression, denial, rationalization, resignation, and becoming dependent or demanding.

3. Empathy and sympathy are reasonable emotions to feel and express in helping relationships. Pity is not acceptable. The person who pities, wittingly or unwittingly, places himself/herself in a position of feeling superior to the person toward whom pity is directed. Pitying creates a power imbalance between one who pities and one who is pitied. Pity is disempowering, hurtful, and, quite generally, unwelcome.

4. Teachers may encounter children who have terminal illness. In such circumstances, the teacher should be prepared to provide support to the dying child and to the child's peers. Both the dying child and the child's peers may rely heavily on the teacher for emotional support. The teacher must understand her/his own responses to death and must be prepared to cope with the children's responses.

5. In adapted physical education settings, teachers become involved in helping relationships. These relationships, however they transpire, must preserve the dignity and self-worth of the person receiving help. Help should be offered only when needed. Offering help too quickly, where help is not really necessary (or appreciated), may deny the recipient the opportunity to achieve independence. The teacher, uncertain of whether to help or how much help is needed, should simply ask the person to whom help is being offered.

6. All persons, irrespective of ability/disability, have psychosocial needs. How individual needs are met impact, both positively and negatively, on the individual's adjustment to personal circumstances.

7. Teacher effectiveness is the single most important variable in student achievement, and behavior management is essential to effective teaching.

8. Regarding behavior management, setting the tone for behavior expectations during the first few days of class will affect, positively or negatively, the tone of student behavior in class through the remainder of the school year.

9. Strategies for managing behavior cited in this chapter stem from two behavior management premises. One school of thought is that behavior is better managed through a system of externally imposed rewards and punishments. The other is that all behavior is internally motivated by the individual's internal drive to have internal needs satisfied.

REFERENCES

Baldwin, S. A., & Hoffman, J. P. (April 2002). The dynamics of self-esteem: A growth-curve analysis. *Journal of Youth and Adolescence*, v. 31, n2, 101–113.

Best, S.J., Carpignano, J.L., Sirvis, B., & Bigge, J.L. (1991). Psychosocial aspects of disability. In J.L. Bigge, *Teaching individuals with physical and multiple disabilities*, 3rd ed. (pp. 110–137). New York: Merrill/Macmillan.

Byrne, B. M. (1996). *Academic self-concept: A developmental perspective*. New York: The Guilford Press.

Cheng, H., & Furnham, A. (2004). Perceived parental rearing style, self-esteem and self-criticism as predictors of happiness, *Journal of Happiness Studies*, v. 5, n1, 1–21.

Christ, G., & Blacker, S. (February 2006). Helping Relationship: Beyond the best of intentions. *Journal of Palliative Medicine*, Vol. 9, n1, p182–182.

DeBruyn, R., & Larson, J. (2009). *You Can Handle Them All*. Manhattan, KS: The Master Teacher.

Dunn, D. S., & Timoth, E. R. Revisiting a Constructive Classic: Wright's *Physical Disability: A Psychosocial Approach*. Rehabilitative Psychology. Rehabilitation Psychology, 2005 May; 50(2): 183–189.

Dyer, K. (2009). Ways to Help a Child Cope with a Loss: Advice for Parents, Teachers and Caregivers. http://www.squidoo.com/children-grief. Retrieved: 07, July, 2009.

Emmer, E. T., Evertson, C. M., & Worsham, M. E. (2003). *Classroom management for secondary teachers* (6th ed.). Boston: Allyn & Bacon.

Glasser, W. (1998). *Choice theory in the classroom*. New York: HarperCollins.

Gossen, D. (1997). *Restitution: Restructuring School Discipline*. Chapel Hill, NC: New View Publications.

Hadley, A. M., Hair, E. C., & Moore, K. A. (August 2008). What kids think about themselves: A guide to adolescent self-concept for out-of-school program practitioners. Research to Results. Washington, DC: Child Trends. Publication # 2008-32.

Harter, S. (1999). *The construction of the self: A developmental perspective*. New York: The Guilford Press.

Kimmel, S. B., & Mahalik, J. R. (March 2009). Measuring masculine body ideal distress: Development of a measure. *International Journal of Men's Health*, v. 3, 1–10.

Kubler-Ross, E. (2008). *On death and dying*. London: Routledge,

Lazarus, R. S., & Lazarus, B. N. (1994). *Passion and reason: Making sense of emotions*. New York: Oxford University Press.

Marsh, H. W., Papiaoannou, A., & Theodorakis, Y. (2006). Causal ordering of physical self-concept and exercise behavior: Reciprocal effects model and the influence of physical education teachers. *Health Psychology*, v. 25, n3, 313–328.

Marzano, R.J. (2003). *Classroom management that works: Research-based strategies for every teacher*. Alexandria, VA: Association for Supervision and Curriculum Development.

Pope, H. G., Olivardia, R., Gruber, A., & Borowiecki, J. (May 1999). Evolving ideals of male body image as seen through action toys. *International Journal of Eating Disorders*, v. 26, n1, 65–72.

Rusk, H. A., & Taylor, E. J. (1996). *New hope for the handicapped*. New York: Harper & Row.

Safford, B. L III. An obscured radiance. El Paso, TX: Endeavors of Humanity Press. n.d.

Safford, B. L III. (1978) The baseball manager and the warm-up jacket. *Disabled USA*. 2(2).

Slote, M. (2007). *The ethics of care and empathy*. New York: Routledge.

Truax, C. (1970). Length of therapist response, accurate empathy and patient improvement. *Journal of Clinical Psychology* v. 26, n4, 539–541

Wright B. A. (1960). *Physical disability: A psychological approach*. New York: Harper & Row.

Wright, S. P., Horn, S. P., & Sanders, W. L. (1997). Teacher and classroom context effects on student achievement: Implications for teacher evaluation. *Journal of Personnel Evaluation in Education* vol. 11, n1, 57–67.

Parents and the Collaborative Team Approach

Javier is a nine year old boy whose family recently immigrated to the U.S. from Costa Rica. He is newly enrolled at Monroe Elementary School. Initial screening tests across the curriculum have revealed that Javier exhibits a range of developmental delays, both in the classroom and in physical education. He has since been referred for in-depth assessment by a child study team to determine whether his delays might be socio-cultural- and/or IDEA 2004-related.

Because physical education is where Javier has demonstrated significant delay, the physical education teacher assigned to Javier's child study team will be required, according to IDEA 2004, to become proactive in establishing a positive working relationship with Javier's parents who, at this point among other challenges faced by Javier's parents, speak little English. Pursuant to IDEA 2004, it is the responsibility of the school court to initiate contact and establish a collaborative relationship with parents when it has been determined that the child has a disability. The challenge before the child study team, of which the physical education teacher is an integral part, is to craft a strategy for parent involvement in Javier's education that satisfies both the letter and spirit of IDEA 2004.

Place yourself in the role of physical educator on the child study team. What would *you* do to help the team establish and nurture a collaborative relationship with Javier's parents? What strategies would you recommend to the team as a whole to develop a positive parent-child study team relationship (unique to Javier's family's circumstances) in keeping with both the letter and spirit of IDEA 2004?

To develop appropriate educational and service plans that achieve educational objectives; teachers, physicians, therapists, and families must collaborate. Cooperation from home, community, and school is necessary to ensure informed decisions are made according to the child's educational needs.

The legal background and justification for collaborative team approaches to special education, including adapted physical education, is set forth in the most recent reauthorization of the Individuals with Disabilities Education Act of 2004 (IDEA 2004). In accordance with IDEA 2004, evaluation, placement, and program planning for children with disabilities must be carried out by a group of individuals, or a collaborative team, that relies on input from a variety of sources. In school settings, teams consist of teachers, administrators and consultants who bring their skills together to conceive and implement an appropriate education for the child. Collaborative teams in school settings are termed multidisciplinary, trans-disciplinary, interdisciplinary, or cross-disciplinary.

Definitions in the literature of the terms multi, trans-, inter, and cross-disciplinary in reference to teaming often appear to be in conflict. Even when terms are defined according to a single source, distinctions may not appear clear-cut. Salmons and Wilson (2007) define these terms in **Table 5.1**.

The common thread among each of the team types is that each, in its unique way, is a collaborative enterprise. Depending upon where the reader is in his/her career, she/he has been or will become involved in one or more of the above collaborative team types. Important things to take

Table 5.1 Team Types

Team Type	Team Nature
Multidisciplinary	Relating to or making use of several disciplines at once. Members of multidisciplinary team, "make recommendations specific to their areas of expertise" (Salmons and Wilson, 2007). Multidisciplinary teams are reasonably analogous to discussion panels where each panel member offers facts/opinions from the perspective of her/his discipline, leaving a third party responsible for integrating information provided.
Trans-disciplinary	Approaches that transcend boundaries of traditional disciplines (Salmons and Wilson, 2007). Trans-disciplinary approaches to teaming blur the boundaries between traditional disciplines. Trans-disciplinary approaches tend to be founded in the belief that "knowledge cannot be singularly claimed as belonging to or originating in any one discipline" (Ausberg, 2006). Example: health and physical education.
Interdisciplinary	Process of combining two or more disciplines, fields of study, or professions (Salmons and Wilson, 2007). Where trans-disciplinary approaches to teaming tend to blur boundaries between disciplines, interdisciplinary approaches tend to dissolve them. The result often is, for all intents and purposes, two or more discrete disciplines morphing into one. Example: social psychology.
Cross-disciplinary	Coordinated effort involving two or more academic disciplines (Salmons and Wilson, 2007).Cross-disciplinary approaches to problem solving tend to cross traditional disciplinary boundaries to shed light on some phenomenon, behavior, or circumstance. Example: the psychology of obesity.

away from the immediate discussion of team types is that team members regardless of team type label, in order for the team to be functional, must (1) honestly believe in team approaches in general and (2) be accepting of the specific team's disciplinary approach (i.e. multi, trans, inter, or cross) to answering questions/solving problems.

Potential Team Members and Services

Members of collaborative teams uniquely contribute to the team effort according to each member's expertise and training. Examples of expertise contributed according to discipline and training appear in **Table 5.2**.

Regular Physical Education Teacher

Although the regular physical education teacher is not trained in-depth to teach children with disabilities, this teacher will have direct contact with children on a daily basis and is responsible not only for including individuals with disabilities into the regular physical education program, but also for implementing the educational program. The physical education teacher often provides screening or diagnostic information concerning the individual's functional ability through observation or assessment in the regular instructional setting. Once input from the programming team is gathered and assessed, the regular physical education teacher becomes responsible for planning and implementing the physical activity program with or without support services or equipment. The teacher is also charged with implementing the instructional objectives for all children in regular classes to ensure that program goals and objectives for all children are achieved.

A regular physical education teacher who teaches a number of children with disabilities in regular education settings should consult on an intermittent or continual basis with other team members.

Adapted Physical Educator

Traditionally, the adapted physical educator has been trained to provide special, developmental, or adapted physical education services consistent with the definition of physical education in IDEA 2004. This professional is usually a full-time specialist who may teach, be a consultant to an entire school district, or consult from school site to school site across school districts on an itinerant basis. The adapted physical education specialist should be the professional who provides primary assessment of physical and motor function that leads to informed adapted physical education program planning. Recently, the adapted physical education specialist's role has evolved from one of providing direct teaching services to students with disabilities to one of consulting with regular physical educators who increasingly are being called upon to teach children with disabilities integrated into their regular class settings.

Additionally, the adapted physical educator will be knowledgeable in appropriate evaluation instruments to assess physical fitness, motor development, perceptual motor functioning, posture, and gait analysis. For school districts that do not have direct access to adapted physical educators, these services may be provided by state departments of education, regional resource centers, or universities on a consultant basis for both regular and special education teachers who have the responsibility of implementing the physical education activity program.

Table 5.2 Collaborative Educational Programming Team Members and Services

Team Members	Role/Services
Regular physical educator	Provides screening or diagnostic information Provides referral for exceptional services Engages in planning and implementation of instructional program Ensures that all children meet program objectives Consults with programming team Records progress and achievement Interacts with parents Ensures/encourages social-emotional interactions among all children Fosters fitness and motor skill development Provides behavior management
Adapted physical educator	Fosters fitness and motor skill development Provides for/consults on behavior management Fosters sports skill development Assesses nutritional status and provides dietary consultation Provides screening and assessment of physical functioning Provides program development and implementation Consults with parents Develops after-school program Fosters social-emotional development Consults with regular physical education teacher
Special educator	Provides educational diagnosis Observes and screens for learning problems Records functional ability and progress Designs appropriate instructional program materials Aids regular education teacher in determining special needs, including attention maintenance strategies, behavior management Provides ongoing consultation with team members Provides additional physical activity opportunities
Physical therapist	Aids in planning, conducting, and evaluating program Consults with programming team Provides muscle testing and posture evaluation Provides gait analysis Provides information on primitive reflexes and reactions Provides ambulation training Carries out sports classification
Occupational therapist	Restores daily living skills Implements self-help skills Helps develop vocational skills Helps with sensory integration Evaluates reflex behavior and postural reactions, play, muscle tone Consults with programming team members
Recreational therapist	Promotes social, emotional, and physical development Assesses play and recreation skills Aids in integration between school and community Provides after-school program
Administrators	Budgetary control Assigns staff and class schedules Aids in securing equipment and makes decisions on accessibility of environment Develops programming team Establishes class times and facilitates program implementation Serve as liaison between school and community
Physicians	Provides primary care of child with disability Provides data concerning functional ability Evaluates levels of performance Reassesses and consults on an ongoing basis with programming team Provides information on medical history and changes in condition Provides information on medication Provides specialized information needed to implement program

(continued)

Table 5.2 Collaborative Educational Programming Team Members and Services (*continued*)

Team Members	Role/Services
School nurse	Collects and interprets medical information Provides postural, vision, and auditory screening Provides record keeping and treatment information Provides in-service training Interprets effects of medication Provide temporary health care
Parents	Participate in initial referral and planning of IEP Provides medical and developmental history Reports changes in condition or medication Advocates for child Communicates with other members of the team
School psychologist	Assesses and interprets educational, psychological, and behavioral instruments Evaluates suspected area of deficit Consults with the classroom teacher Provides Information on medication and exceptionality Interprets assessment information to parents Aids in program planning and implementation between home and school Aids in behavior and environmental management Aids in developing social-emotional interaction
Nutritionist	Recommends dietary program Provides consultation on allergies, additives, and their effects on functioning Provides in-service training and counseling on dietary intake and exercise for specific exceptionalities Provides nutritional guidance and counseling
Athletic coach	Encourages active participation Supervises training and extent of participation Provides opportunities to participate with peers Promotes social and psychological interaction

Special Educator

The special education teacher is commonly located in a self-contained classroom or resource room to accommodate children with physical or learning disorders (Hallahan, Kauffman, & Pullen, 2009). Services that this professional can offer to regular teachers might include educational diagnoses, perceptual-motor assessments, assessment of behavior and attention disorders, and behavior and environmental management consultations. One or more of these services can aid the physical educator in developing instructional units that include students with disabilities. For example, a child who experiences difficulty with visual-motor perception may have difficulty catching a ball. The child may, however, begin to experience success in catching when the color of the ball is made to contrast with a plain-colored background out of which the ball is coming. The interaction of both professionals through ongoing consultation, communication, and record keeping can contribute immensely to improving the physical and motor development of children with disabilities.

Furthermore, if special education teachers provide a portion of the physical activity program, children benefit from the added practice, individual attention, and additional expertise available in the regular classroom setting.

Physical Therapist

The physical therapist (PT) is responsible for planning, conducting, and evaluating an individualized program for medically referred children. Services provided by this professional are designed to increase functional abilities of children with neurological, musculoskeletal, and physical impairments. Although physical therapy is *not* an alternative to physical education, this professional can be critical to enabling the physical education teacher to adequately address specific needs.

The PT can help the teacher evaluate the functioning and strength of muscles; provide screening to evaluate postural deficiency and/or weakened muscles; conduct gait analysis to identify improper body or foot placements or inappropriate postural compensations;

assess range of motion to determine the flexibility of joints and muscles or the effect of contractures; and assess neuromotor coordination to determine functional ability of muscle groups and muscle tone. Physical therapists may also provide information on the presence of primitive reflexes and their influence in motor development as well as sensorimotor and/or perceptual motor functioning. Physical therapists are frequently responsible for ambulation training and the fitting and/or modification of ambulatory aids, such as crutches.

Physical therapists may also provide information on the sports classification of children through an evaluation of their remaining neuromuscular functional ability. Information from physical therapists can be helpful in planning the program and providing appropriate services through a cooperative effort with other teachers. For example, the use of range-of-motion exercises in a therapeutic setting can easily be implemented by physical education teachers in a resistance training program. In this manner the cooperative effort of two or more professionals can provide a more comprehensive physical activity program for the child. Another important role of the PT is to encourage parents to provide more opportunities for developing motor skills and increasing strength. Although the services of a physical therapist may be sporadic or nonexistent in some school districts, even ongoing consultation on a limited basis can effectively enable parents, teachers, and therapists to accomplish common goals.

Occupational Therapist

The occupational therapist (OT) is another professional who may be available to the school on a part-time basis. An occupational therapist formulates and administers activity programs designed to restore or develop skills of daily living. As part of the restoration of functional ability, the OT will focus therapeutic interventions on fine motor muscle activity that can aid children in managing implements or eating utensils.

The OT may also contribute to enhancing sensory and vestibular functioning and developing higher neural functioning based on the work and training in sensory motor integration pioneered by Dr. Jean Ayres. These services should be coordinated by the physical education teacher and delivered in conjunction with the child's developmental physical education program. Emphasis should be on development of balance and coordination skills to provide the child with a sound movement base that will aid in developing functional self-help skills.

Other responsibilities of the OT may include evaluating reflex behavior, postural adjustment reactions, muscle tone, play, and social interaction skills. The OT should also provide ongoing consultation with other teachers, therapists, and parents to increase the child's ability to self-initiate movement and develop self-care and vocational skills.

Recreational Therapist

The recreational therapist (RT) is a professional who is not generally available in the school setting. However, services of the recreational therapist in a community-based recreational setting can contribute to increasing social, emotional, and physical functioning. The RT can provide experiences that are nonexistent in the school setting, such as camping, hiking, or skiing, which aid in integrating children within the community and peer group. A recreational therapist can also provide services such as leisure assessments for play or recreation and the selection of recreation activities to achieve program objectives. Community-based recreational organizations provide additional opportunities to develop and practice skills learned in the school instructional program. The more success children experience, the more adaptable they become to their home, community, and school environments. Because recreation therapy has not been designated a primary service under IDEA 2004, recreation therapy, by law, may not substitute for a child with disability's physical education. Nevertheless, recreation therapy offers unique benefits for children who have disabilities, and collaboration with RT professionals is encouraged.

Administrators

The administrative makeup of the educational programming team can include a variety of professionals. The school principal or vice principal, superintendent, and director of special education all contribute to the delivery of services. Administrators will coordinate the school instructional program and assign staff and supportive services to the programming unit. These professionals act as liaisons between school and home by coordinating meetings, interpreting test results, and securing services that are requested by team members.

Each of these professionals must interact with other team members to adequately channel appropriate funding and equipment needed for children with disabilities. A primary responsibility of the administrative unit is to arrange flexible schedules to accommodate special needs. For example, children with diabetes may function more appropriately if their physical activity program is scheduled after lunch to ensure the proper balance of food intake and insulin prior to activity.

Administrators also make decisions regarding the accessibility of the building and classrooms as well as the interpretation and evaluation of the overall program. A thoroughly informed administrator can often generate funds to offset the lack of facilities and equipment; and secure alternative services or other professionals needed to provide the best available instructional program.

Physicians

The physician often provides an essential component of the integration process. For many children with physical disabilities, the physician provides primary care and is responsible for information concerning the student's functional ability. Rather than confining children to inactivity, physicians can evaluate levels of performance that are within a medical margin of safety.

As children improve in functional ability, physicians can reassess and collaborate with teachers on appropriate types and levels of activity. For example, children with respiratory disorders may be under the care of a pulmonary physician who recommends periodic rest intervals during periods of physical activity to prevent exercise-induced bronchospasm.

Other physicians may provide information on the medical history and changes in the child's condition. If medication is indicated, physicians will prescribe the medication and provide information related to usage as well as potential side effects. Teachers should be aware of the types of medication prescribed, their purpose, and any changes in dosage or type used by children.

If a specialist is available, such as a neurologist, this professional may provide the specialized information needed for placement or for determining the child's level of functioning. When physicians are not associated with the school district, the family physician or specialist may provide the information on the child's functioning required to develop the individual program.

School Nurse

The school nurse is a health care professional who collects and interprets relevant medical information for the programming team. This information may include postural, visual, and auditory screening. The school nurse may also maintain medical records and update the treatment information for children.

In addition, the school nurse may provide in-service training on the onset of disease, dietary concerns and/or nutritional disorders, and on the referral process for specific services. When a child experiences respiratory distress or seizures, the school nurse provides intervening health care until the child recovers or more extensive

medical supervision is provided. In other instances, school nurses will dispense or interpret the effects of medication and consult with teachers when children are excused from physical activity for reasons associated with their condition.

Parents

The cooperation of parents or guardians is essential for effective programming. Parents will be involved, at the very least, in the initial referral and planning stages of the IEP. They can also provide the medical and developmental history as well as any recent changes in the child's condition or medication. Parents are also the primary advocates for children and ensure that a proper placement and instructional program is provided. Parents should be viewed not as adversaries but as allies who provide useful input when team members formulate an appropriate instructional program. Parents may be called upon to conduct a structured home learning program to supplement the school's instructional program.

School Psychologist

The school psychologist can provide additional information that is outside the realm of the physical education teacher or special educator. The psychologist may assess, diagnose, and design appropriate interaction techniques in areas where physical education teachers require assistance. Through intensive evaluations, school psychologists may determine the suspected cause of the child's behavior or learning deficiency. This will enable physical education teachers to plan more appropriately for the child's special needs. The school psychologist can also provide continuous monitoring and follow-up observations to rule out intervening causes of learning or behavior problems. For example, they can substantiate suspected soft neurological signs and sensory or perceptual problems. School psychologists may also interpret assessment information for parents, coordinate efforts to determine appropriate educational placement, and assist in planning and implementing educational programs for use in the home and school.

Nutritionist

The nutritionist is not a common addition to the programming team but can provide essential information for successful integration. Children with nutritional disorders, for example, require a sound dietary program as well as an appropriate exercise regimen to control weight gain or loss. Additionally, children with learning deficiencies may be required to adhere to a diet exclusive of sugar or food additives that may contribute to learning or attention disorders. Children requiring insulin or dietary supplements will benefit from counseling on proper dietary intake and exercise. Finally, some children fast unduly or partake in eating binges and then regurgitate the food to lose weight. Nutritional guidance and counseling may be essential for individuals with eating disorders.

Coach

The coach of an athletic team or the intramural sports director may have a significant impact on successful integration. Rather than relegating children to the sidelines away from active participation, allowing them to participate in sports under proper supervision can strengthen them physiologically and psychologically. Children with disabilities often can participate in sports and in the training that is required for sports competition at a level equal to that of peers without disabilities. After-school training programs provide the skills necessary for sports participation, and contribute to positive psychological adjustments for many children with disabilities (Horvat, Henschen & French, 1986).

Putting Theory Into Practice

In the ideal setting, cooperation and interaction among all professional groups would ultimately aid in developing the best educational program available for children with disabilities. However, in many school districts little information is shared among professionals for a variety of reasons, including conflict over who should assume what role. Ideally, all team members will recognize the roles of other team members and function according to their assignments. As indicated earlier, therapists and educators can and should cooperate to achieve common goals whenever expertise intersects.

Part of the conflict of roles among allied professionals comes from the inclusion of physical education as a primary service and therapy as a related service under IDEA. This practice does not need to be detrimental to effective programming if lines of communication remain open and there is mutual respect among professionals.

Another reason for a lack of appropriate services for children with disabilities is the attitude of some school districts toward compliance. Minimal compliance means providing the fewest services required under the law. Even though such school districts may satisfy the letter of the law, they may not address the intent of the law: to provide the best educational atmosphere. Many school districts are faced with budgetary constraints that prohibit buying equipment or

providing appropriate access to programs and services. However, lack of funds should not affect the *commitment* of school districts to develop sound educational programs based on individual needs.

The school district or local educational system may also be hindered by a lack of trained professionals in one or more areas. This state of affairs is more the rule than the exception. Lack of professional expertise can severely detract from the planning of an appropriate individualized education program; however, support from administration and existing professionals sometimes can overcome this deficiency. Requested assistance may take several years of planning and negotiation before appropriate services are rendered. This is especially true in the training of personnel in physical education who may not have expertise to teach children with disabilities. The teaching load in many school districts may preclude the hiring of a full-time specialist even on an itinerant or consulting basis. However, with the help of additional funds, in-service education or physical education consultants can be made available to school districts.

Time constraints can also present a problem. Staff conferences, professional meetings, planning, and class contact hours can burden even the most well-meaning teacher. For teachers in regular physical education, staff meetings may seem most important, but the placement and programming needs of children with disabilities will also require significant teacher input. If such input does not occur the school's unique blend of talents is not being used to the greatest extent possible.

Finally, all members of the team should be treated as professionals who can contribute meaningfully to the physical activity program. For the most part, physicians and administrators are regarded with professional esteem because of their professional status or experience. Regular and special physical education teachers, however, as well as therapists and school nurses, are also professionally trained and can contribute immensely to the programming team. Finally parents, although they may possess no formal educational background or training, are virtual professionals. The valuable insights they can contribute from their intimate knowledge of, and love for, the child render them professionals in their own right.

In spite of the potential conflicts and lack of adequate resources in some situations, the programming team can be a viable aid in developing and planning the educational program. Although not all elements of the team may be included, or different terminology may be used to describe different roles, the nature of the interaction among professionals will ultimately determine the effectiveness of the program.

Regular physical education teachers, adapted physical education teachers, physical therapists and occupational therapists all work in the psycho-motor domain with students who have disabilities. Whenever professionals work in areas where professional boundaries, lines of responsibility, and service provider roles are not always clear-cut, there is potential for duplications in service, gaps in service, and disagreement over who is to provide which service. If you are the physical education teacher, what strategies would you suggest when meeting with physical and occupational therapists to ensure there will be neither duplication, nor gaps in service; and that disagreements over who provides which service might be kept to a minimum.

Developing the Parent-Teacher Team

Parents generally wish to be active in supporting and promoting legislation enacted on behalf of children with disabilities and to work as team members alongside education professionals in development of the individualized family service plan (IFSP), individualized education plan (IEP), and/or individualized transition plan (ITP). Precisely because parents were the child's first teachers, they already will have exerted significant influence on their child's growth and development. In the process, they will have developed valuable insights into the child's unique characteristics and needs. According to Mandel (2008):

> Only 15 to 20 percent of the child's waking hours are spent in school. Therefore, the majority of the child's school-age life comes under the eyes and supervision of the parents, not the teacher. Not to include the parent in the child's education ignores the tremendous influence parents hold over the child.

Regrettably, according to Mandel, collaboration between the teacher and parents sometimes becomes stifled when one side perceives the other "as the enemy rather than as a partner" (page viii-ix).

From the perspective of the teacher:

- A passive parent may be perceived as one who doesn't care about the child's education.

- An active parent may be seen as aggressive and/or a troublemaker.

From the perspective of the parent:

- A teacher's actions perceived by the parent as negative can be viewed as a result of "not liking my child."

- A teacher who does not excuse the child for some outside-of-school activity may be perceived as giving no consideration to the child's outside-of-school life.

Both perspectives, according to Mandel, quite generally are inaccurate and derive from stereotypes and preconceived notions. For teacher and parents to become a team, each party must be able to develop respect for and trust in the other. The teacher's strength in the partnership will derive from formal university training and subsequent years of practical teaching experience. The parent's strength in the partnership will derive from intimate knowledge of child's strengths, limitations, personality, and home environment. When each party acknowledges the other's strengths, a foundation has been laid for building a successful partnership. Quite generally, the more meaningfully parents become involved with teachers in their child's education, the greater the child's overall achievement (Epstein 2008).

Strategies to Encourage Collaborative Team Building

While teacher, parents, and ultimately the child mutually benefit from collaborative teamwork between parent and school, it is primarily the responsibility of the school to ensure that parents are made to feel valued as team partners. And, because parent-school collaboration is mandated by IDEA 2004, positive and functional collaboration is in the best interests of the school, parent, and child. Given that parent-school collaboration is integral to IDEA 2004 regulations, it is imperative that both school and parent share a mutual understanding of the law in regard to school-parent teaming. With specific regard to parent's right to participation in development of the child's education program, IDEA 2004 requires that:

- Parents be members of the IEP team.

- Parents be afforded access to all records related to determining and monitoring the child's educational program.

- The school takes steps to ensure a parent is present at all IEP meetings or has been afforded opportunity to attend.

- Meeting times and places are clearly communicated and parents know they are allowed to invite persons to the meeting whom they believe will help present their concerns for their child's education.

- When transition is at issue, the child must, when appropriate, be extended an invitation to attend; also, representatives from agencies to be involved in the transition plan.

- If neither parent can be personally present at a meeting, parent(s) must be offered an alternative means to participate (e.g. conference call).
- Meetings can be conducted in parent's absence; however, when parents are not present there must be clear, recorded documentation of parent's refusal to participate.
- School must ensure that parents understand meeting proceedings (i.e. interpreter for person with deafness, translator for non-English speaker). (34 CFR 300.345, 34 CFR 300.501, 2005)

School-parent collaboration is required. It needs to be decided how collaboration takes place such that (1) there is mutual respect among principal parties, (2) both the letter and spirit of the law are respected, (3) the process remains child-centered, and, in the end, (4) the child emerges the primary beneficiary.

Initial Contact With Parents and the Importance of First Impressions

Often, parents need to be made to feel welcome by the school. Teachers can make parents feel welcome by initiating contact with the parent when the student first enters the teacher's class. Contact can come in the form of a letter, email, phone call, or invitation to meet with the teacher at school. Written communications offer the advantage of having what one would like to communicate reduced to writing, and this helps ensure mutual understanding. Letters, however, are monologs. Phone and/or one-on-one conversations with parents, on the other hand, are dialogs, and while one-on-one dialogs can be time consuming from the teacher's perspective, they have potential to be perceived by parents as more welcoming and personal.

Promoting Collaboration From the Parent's Perspective

Rice (2006) suggests a range of strategies for parents who wish to become meaningful partners in their child's education. Teachers should become familiar with strategies to help parents fulfill their potential as collaborative team members. Rice first and foremost advises parents to "do your homework." Rice advises:

- Learn all you can about your child's school by seeking out people in the know. This includes, but would not necessarily be limited to, other parents, nurses, teachers, administrators, therapists, parent organizations, and advocacy groups.
- Be positive.
- Become familiar with what goes on during your child's class experience, including class routine, rules, and goals.

- See yourself as a team leader, one who is likely most well informed regarding your child's educational, medical, and family history.
- Provide all special education team members with your contact information, including when you can best be reached.
- Request contact information from all special education team members, including times when each member can be reached.
- Indicate to the teacher how often you would like to communicate; daily, weekly, monthly, quarterly.
- Always respond to notes sent home from school to ensure that team members know you are in the loop.
- Create and maintain a communications journal between you and your child's teacher that travels back and forth between you and your child's teacher. Communications journals are commercially available or one can be tailored by the team, including parents, to best serve the team's and child's unique needs.
- Be sure the method(s) of communication you and the team decide upon is included in your child's IEP.
- Finally, strive to fulfill all requests made of you as a parent, so that you can reasonably expect other team members to fulfill requests emanating from home.

Promoting Collaboration From the Teacher's and Team's Perspective

Teachers and team members can support collaborative team building by supporting parents with regard to becoming effective team members as per Rice's (2005) suggestions. Additionally, teachers and team members can support collaborative team building as follows (ARC of New Jersey, 2005):

- Seek out training on collaboration and invite parents to participate.
- Create an action plan with parents as equal partners to address how communication can be increased and improved.
- Encourage parents to seek out advocates and the advice of advocacy groups.
- Assign one team member to be the liaison or 'go-to' person to ensure the parent has reasonable and meaningful access to all team members.
- Make certain parents have ample opportunity to raise and discuss issues and express concerns.
- Be flexible with regard to parent visitations at school, including observation of the class environment.

- Conduct team meetings at a round table. Change seating arrangements regularly. Offer refreshments if feasible.
- To help keep conversations student-focused, have the child present, if appropriate.
- Just as parents attend school and team meetings, strive to, when appropriate, attend parent meetings.
- Provide written agendas for each meeting. Be certain parents have meeting agendas sufficiently in advance so as to enable parents to proactively offer feedback.
- Be sure to address parent concerns at meetings.

Parent Education

Parent education involves more than providing information in the traditional parent-teacher conference. These conferences are just the starting point in parent education. In parent-teacher conferences, teachers can provide more specific information to parents about developmental deficiencies, behavior disorders, or learning or information processing problems. Parent education meetings are then implemented to promote understanding and knowledge of issues that affect physical fitness and recreational or motor skill development. These meetings can be conducted periodically throughout the school year to cover topics of interest, or several meetings can be held to provide greater depth in one area. Teachers may also arrange for speakers or demonstrations on a particular topic. For example, one session could involve the use of motor training for individuals deficient in balance; another might address more general areas, such as recreation activities, recreational program availability, programs, or summer camps.

By matching program goals with parent concerns, teachers can impart to parents a more thorough knowledge of physical activity programs and program availability. Common areas of concern can be addressed, and parents can gain a better understanding of the importance of physical activity. Constructive communication can evolve as parents voice their needs and teachers respond in a professional manner.

Parent Training

Parent training extends the education of parents a step beyond the information or understanding phase of the parent-teacher relationship. The primary reasons for conducting parent-teacher sessions are to inform parents about specific teaching or behavior management techniques and to develop home-based activity programs designed to improve the child's functional ability.

Training sessions can be conducted at schools, parent-teacher association (PTA) meetings, mental health centers, or in informal group settings. The length of the parent-training session may vary according to parental interest and need. Most sessions will require follow-up communication, specifically with at least one parent in the home. Because most parents are not able to develop their own educational resources even with the help from parent-training sessions, teachers play an essential role in the development of resources for home use.

Teachers can also direct parents to commercial products that have been developed for implementing home programs. Many products include guides, instructional manuals, and sequenced tasks that require a minimum amount of equipment, supplies, and training.

Helping Parents Keep Children Active Outside of School

Immediate and long range goals of physical education are to develop physical and motor fitness, motor skills, social skills, and positive attitudes toward participation that carry over into life outside of school and beyond school years. With regard to the latter, parents of children with disabilities are the most important members of the collaborative team who will make regular physical activity as a part of life happen. Many parents, however, will need assistance in learning what kinds of activity opportunities are available and how such activities might best be accessed. Here, the physical educator can be the primary team member to help identify available activity opportunities in her/his community/region.

An important goal in seeking activity opportunities for children with disabilities outside of school is to search out programs that offer meaningful participation opportunities where need for special accommodations can be kept at a minimum. Keeping accommodations to a minimum helps ensure that the broadest range of activities possible become and remain available. Quite generally, the greater the need for special accommodations to ensure meaningful participation, the less available and accessible that activity is likely to be.

Another goal for parents seeking out activities for their children is to consider activities in which family members can participate together. This is in no way to suggest avoidance of activities absent of direct family involvement; but rather, that if assistance becomes required for meaningful participation, a family member might be in the best position to provide informed assistance.

Table 5.3 provides a few examples of outside of school activities for children with disabilities. Example activity opportunities may not be available in all regions, but they exemplify the kinds of active lifestyle opportunities that exist throughout the country.

Table 5.3 Sample Community-Based Activity Opportunities for Children and Youth with Disabilities

Organization	Description
Miracle League Baseball	Offers opportunities to participate in baseball to children and youths with a range of physical and intellectual disabilities. There are Miracle League chapters throughout the U.S. and Puerto Rico serving 80,000 participants. http://www.miracleleague.com
I can do it— You can do it	The program goal is to improve the health of six million American children who have disabilities by encouraging increased physical activity and healthy nutritional behaviors. Mentees with physical and/or cognitive disabilities who have comprehension abilities 5.5 years and above are engaged by mentors ages 18 and over with and without disabilities in health promoting physical activity and nutrition education. http://cdd.unm.edu/ICanDoIt/learnmore
The President's Challenge	The President's Challenge, offered by the President's Council on Physical Fitness and Sport helps people ages six and above, including people with disabilities, make and keep commitments to physical activity. Participants have the opportunity to win President's Active Lifestyle Award (PALA). Participants choose from over 100 activities, log their participation time on paper or online, and earn points based on the intensity of the activity and the amount of time spent being active. www.presidentschallenge.org
Courage Alpine Skiers and Snowboard	Courage Alpine Skiers and Snowboard offers opportunities for winter sports participation and instruction for persons who have a range of disabilities. Participation categories include: stand up-two track; stand up-three track; stand up-four track; stand up-visual impaired; bi-ski; dual ski, mono ski; and snowboard. Courage Center offers 26 additional active recreation and sports activities throughout each season of the year. Participation levels range from beginner to elite level competition. www.courageskiers.com
Accessible Trails	Throughout the U.S. wilderness trails are increasingly becoming accessible. The American Disabilities Act of 1990 requires trails be constructed with persons who have mobility impairments in mind. Local community recreation and park departments and state departments of natural resources are good resources for locating disability accessible trails. Pacific Northwest Trail Information for the Disabled (http://accessibletrails.com) lists accessible trails on a regional basis.
Access Leisure	The city of Sacramento, CA Department of Parks and Recreation offers a wide range of active leisure opportunities for youth and adults with physical, sensory, and intellectual disabilities (www.accessleisuresac.org). Among the activities offered are camps and outdoor recreation, power soccer, handcycling, goal ball, sled hockey, fitness development, and wheelchair/quad rugby. Sacramento is one of a number of cities in the U.S. that partner with U.S. Paralympics (http://usparalympics.org/) to offer programs in a range of activities designed for beginners through competitors.
Blaze Sports	In partnership with the National Recreation and Park Association and operating in 25 states and Washington, DC, Blaze Sports offers sports, sports training, competitions, summer camps, and recreational opportunities for youth and adults with disabilities. Activity opportunities include: wheelchair basketball, goal ball, wheelchair tennis, cycling, track and field, soccer, scuba, and boccia. www.blazesports.org.

Home Programs

Initially, designing home programs may appear burdensome and time consuming for teachers. However, the extra practice at home can help remediate a child's motor deficiency and enhance the teaching process. Physical education teachers may be limited by time, number of children, and/or space requirements that hamper their ability to provide individualized instruction. Therefore, children who require additional instruction may lag behind their peers in developing physical fitness and motor skills. A home learning program can be implemented in such instances to provide extra practice and enhance effectiveness of the school program (Bishop & Horvat, 1984; Horvat, 1991). Home programs can be completed outside of class on an individual or family basis and range from developing task cards to long-term learning programs.

A task card is a developmentally sequenced set of skills prepared on an individual basis. Each card should contain a clear explanation of the task, the amount of time to spend on the task, safety precautions, and an evaluation procedure. Task cards can be used to accomplish short-term objectives, or they can be incorporated into a comprehensive home learning program to satisfy long-term goals.

A home learning program is developmentally sequenced, accompanied by a series of task cards, and designed to be implemented by parents to help in their child's achievement of long term educational goals. Because more time, equipment, and knowledge are needed to implement long-term assignments, the parent and teacher require a complete understanding of the home learning program. Included in this chapter is an example of a home learning program that has been used to enhance the balance performance of elementary-school-aged children with learning disabilities.

Developing Homework Materials

The key to providing a positive learning experience is to devise a structured home program based on needs and/or interests. To be successful, any home learning program should include the following components: (a) a clear explanation of the task; (b) specific teaching directions, including modeling and prompting procedures; (c) equipment needed; (d) safety factors; (e) time for each teaching session; (f) recording procedures; and (g) a specific amount of time needed to complete the assignment. By including all these program components, the teacher leaves nothing to chance and ensures that each task is divided into segments that are appropriate for the child's individual needs and can be easily understood by the parents. Throughout implementation of a home program, parents can acquire additional clarification of teaching skills through visits or phone contacts from the teacher.

In many cases, a short-term assignment will enable children to learn a motor task. However, long-term assignments are sometimes necessary for the child to attain goals over a period of time. For such occasions, teachers should design comprehensive developmental progressions of motor skills or physical fitness activities. The following sample includes one segment of a balance program—the locomotor balance skill of hopping. The same procedure can be used to teach additional physical fitness or motor tasks.

How To Use the Home Learning Program

This program is designed to provide children with opportunities to develop balance and gross motor ability. The teacher demonstrates the use of all materials in a parent-training session before the parent introduces the program to his/her child.

Teaching Directions

Length   Sessions should last approximately 30 minutes three times weekly. Skills may be taught anytime during playtime but should be limited to one session per day.

Place   Sessions may be conducted inside or outdoors. A level area is needed for balance activities.

Preparation   An effective way to become familiar with this parent program is to administer it to another person outside of the parent-training session. Instruct the person acting as the child to make mistakes so that you can practice the prompting procedures.

Pace   Additional skill assignments will be sent home each week, depending on the student's rate of improvement. A child who has difficulty completing a skill may need several sessions to learn or master the skill. Also, if the child becomes bored, utilize the games included in each section to renew interest and supplement the instructional technique.

Proceeding to the next level   Because each skill level is based on the preceding skill, each skill is to be completed before progressing to the next skill level. If children have difficulty, utilize another skill in the progression. Utilize only the skills that children have not mastered. Mastery consists of the child performing at the "What to Say" level. Send new activities home weekly, according to the child's progress, to be inserted into the parent's program.

Program Segment

The following is an example of a home program segment.

Timing   Use a wristwatch with a second hand to time children on activities that require a time sequence, or count 1001, 1002, 1003, keeping pace constant.

Dynamic Balance—Hopping

Skill Level 1:   Hop on preferred and then the nonpreferred foot (**Figure 5.1**).

What to Say

Parent: "Hop on your preferred [or nonpreferred] foot, landing on the same foot at least three times."

Child: Hops on preferred/nonpreferred foot three times.

Parent: "Wow! That was really good."

What to Do   If the child has difficulty with the skill, show (model) the correct method, emphasizing bending the nonsupported leg at the knee and taking off and landing on the same foot.

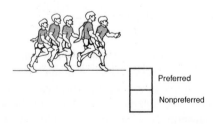

Figure 5.1 Skill level 1: Hop on preferred/nonpreferred foot.

Prompt If the child still has difficulty, place the child in the proper position, bending the nonsupported leg at the knee. If the child still has difficulty, support the child by the hand. Then allow the child to attempt the skill, and remember to praise.

Praise Remember to praise the child for any improvement or accomplishment, including honest effort.

Skill Level 2: Hop for distance. (Figure 5.2).

What to Say

Parent: "Hop forward, taking off and landing on the same foot as far as you can."

Child: Hops forward on the preferred/nonpreferred foot ___ feet.

Parent: "Good hopping."

What to Do If the child has difficulty, show (model) the correct method. Then let the child try the skill, and give praise for any accomplishment.

Prompt If the child still has difficulty, return to Skill Level 1 and try again.

Praise Remember to praise the child for any improvement or accomplishment.

Skill Level 3: Hop forward/backward/sideways over a line (Figure 5.3).

What to Say

Parent: "Hop forward/backward/sideways over the line, taking off and landing on the same foot." (Give just one command.)

Child: Hops on preferred/nonpreferred foot forward/backward/sideways over a line.

What to Do If the child has difficulty, show (model) the correct method of hopping. (Remember to give only one command at a time.) Then let the child try the skill, and give praise for any accomplishment.

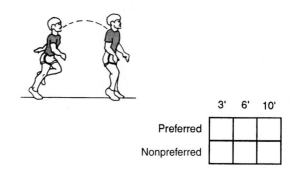

Figure 5.2 Skill level 2: Hop for distance.

Skill Level 4: Hop forward/backward in succession over lines (Figure 5.4).

What to Say

Parent: "Hop on your preferred or [nonpreferred] foot, taking off and landing on the same foot forward/backward over these lines."

Child: Hops forward/backward over four lines in succession on the preferred/nonpreferred foot.

Parent: "That was really hard! Good job."

What to Do If the child has difficulty with the skill, show (model) the correct procedure. Then let the child try the skill, and give praise for any accomplishment.

Prompt If the child still has difficulty, return to Skill Level 1 and Skill Level 2 for more practice.

Praise Remember to praise the child for any improvement or accomplishment.

In addition to basic motor skills, other skills and physical activities (such as sports skills and recreational activities) can be included in a home program to solidify effectiveness of the parent-teacher team

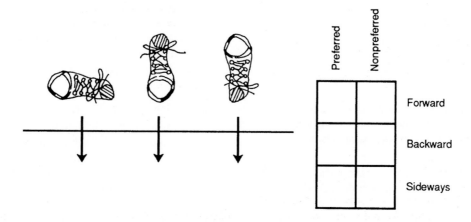

Figure 5.3 Skill level 3: Hop forward/backward/sideways over a line.

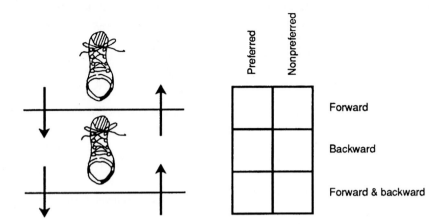

Figure 5.4 Skill level 4: Hop forward/backward in succession over lines.

(return to Table 5.3 for examples). A structured home program can benefit all stakeholders, first and foremost the child, and foster a positive relationship between the teachers and parents. Children can develop the skills that are common to their age group, parents can assume a larger role in the educational process, and teachers can provide individualized instruction outside the classroom to reinforce and support in-school learning. Additional opportunities can then be afforded on a short-term or long-term basis, depending on the responsiveness of the child and/or parent(s). Most important, a home learning program can initiate and foster communication between parents and teachers and, thereby, serve as a means by which the parents can become a vital resource in the educational process.

CHAPTER SUMMARY

1. The purpose of the collaborative team is to help children achieve established educational objectives. The team is responsible for making informed decisions on evaluation, placement, and program planning.

2. The makeup of the team is determined according to individual needs and the services required. Information should be gathered from as many sources as possible, including the student, to develop an appropriate program.

3. Communication and cooperation are essential in developing the most appropriate education for the child. All team members, including parents, should be treated as professionals who can contribute equally to the process.

4. Lack of interaction and cooperation among team members can result from a number of circumstances, including conflict over professional roles, the prevailing attitude of school district regarding compliance, with mandates, a lack of trained professionals in one or more areas, time factors related to scheduling team conferences, and unequal regard for the professional role of each team member.

5. Many educators view parents as a threat to their educational leadership. However, because parents are the child's first teachers, a relationship between parents and teacher should be developed to ensure development of the most appropriate educational program.

6. When parents become part of a partnership in the educational process; goals, expectations for, and progress of children are more easily communicated. Parents can take an active part in the educational process by reinforcing many of the concepts and objectives of the school program in the home environment.

7. Interaction and communication between educators and parents can be helpful to the overall educational process and the total development of the child. Parents can provide additional background information that contributes to formal assessments. The child becomes the primary beneficiary of the close

working relationship between teachers and parents. Benefits to the child include learning new skills, opportunity for additional practice, more opportunity for individualized instruction, positive interactions with family, and reinforcement of desired behaviors both in and out of school.

9. Parent training goes beyond the information-gathering and understanding phase of the parent-teacher relationship. Through parent training, the teacher informs parents about specific teaching or behavior management techniques and works with them to develop a home learning program based on individual needs.

10. Homework is an often neglected strategy in physical education. Task cards and home learning programs are two examples of strategies that provide further practice for children who require additional assistance.

11. Home learning programs not only provide additional opportunities for practice but also allow parents to become actively involved in the educational process. Through home learning programs, educators can utilize parents as vital resources in the education of children and bridge the gap between home and school.

REFERENCES

The ARC of New Jersey. (March 2005). Parent-teacher collaboration: Assigning roles. http://www.arcnj.org/pdfs/parent-teachercollaboration.pdf. Retrieved: 06 July 2009.

Bishop, P., & Horvat, M. (1984). Effects of home instruction on the physical and motor performance of a clumsy child. *American Corrective Therapy Journal, 15,* 34–38.

Code of Federal Regulations. CFR 300.345.300.501. (December 2005)

Epstein, J.L. (February 2008). Improving family and community involvement in community schools. *Education Digest,.* Vol. 73, Issue 6.

Hallahan, D.P., Kauffman, J.M., & Pullen, P.C. (2009). *Exceptional learners: Introduction to special education.* Princeton, NC: Merrill.

Horvat, M. (1991). *Home learning program for developing gross motor skills.* Kearney, NE: Educational Systems Associates.

Horvat, M., Henschen, K., & Grench, R. (1986). A Comparison of the psychological characteristics of male and female able-bodied and wheelchair athletes. *Paraplegia,* 24, 115–22.

I can do it- You can do it. http://www.cdd.umn.edu/ICanDoIt/learnmore.htm. Retrieved: 22 June 2009

Macdonald, S. (2007). National Trails Training Partnership: http://www.americantrails.org/resources/accessible/ADASummFeb00.html. Retrieved: 25 June 2009.

Mandel, S. (2008). *The parent-teacher partnership: How to work together for student achievement.* Chicago: Zephyr Press.

Miracle League Baseball. http://www.miracleleague.com Retrieved: 22 June 2009.

Pacific Northwest Trail Information for the Disabled. http://www.accessibletrails.com/. Retrieved: 25 June 2009.

Rice, M. (June 2006). The parent teacher team: Establishing communication between home and school. *Exceptional Parent,* v36 n6 p49.

Sacramento Department of Parks and Recreation. http://www.accessleisuresac.org/index.html#sports. Retrieved: 06 July 2009

Salmons, J., & Wilson, L. (2007). Crossing the line: An interdisciplinary conversation about working across disciplines. A Trainerspod Webinar, 23 August 2007. http://www.vision2lead.com/Crossing.pdf. Retrieved: 11 June 2009

The President's Challenge. http://www.thepresidentschallenge.org. Retrieved: 07 July 2009.

U.S. Paralympics. http://www.usparalympics.org. Retrieved: 06 July 2009.

CHAPTER 6

Motor Development and Postural Control

CASE STUDY

Several children in Mr. Sosa's third grade class lag behind the other children in physical and motor functioning. One child with a visual impairment has difficulty tracking and catching or striking objects, while other children try to avoid thrown objects rather than trying to catch the object. Several children are clumsy and awkward which affects their stability and locomotor skills.

Because some children have more opportunities to play and learn motor skills, they may be more proficient than others. While developing his instructional lesson plans, Mr. Sosa devises strategies to accommodate various physical characteristics, motivation, and prior movement experiences. Initially, he works on specific movement patterns so children learn basic movements and then integrate and execute the movement. Some children require physical and visual prompts but generally improve with opportunities to practice. Later he challenges his class to modify their movements in changing environments. Therefore, running encompasses proper arm movements, foot placement, and stride length that later is used in games with stopping, turning, and running in various directions. His catching tasks learn the proper hand positions, posture, and visual tracking procedures. Since some children are fearful of the ball he progresses from soft nerf balls to larger balls and frisbees as well as running and catching. For children with limitations he also uses brightly colored objects for catching; physical prompting, footprints, and running downhill to develop the running pattern. For some children, he has also developed a home program utilizing task cards of specific skills that need to be developed. Task cards provide modifications and allow children to practice at home and progress at their own pace.

Motor skills develop in a predictable sequence from basic skills to more complex movement patterns, beginning at the head and proceeding to the feet, and beginning from the midline of the body and proceeding to the extremities. The head develops initially and has the greatest degree of control in the upper extremities. During the process of maturation, the arms will develop in mass and control before the lower extremities. Similarly, control of the large muscles of the trunk and shoulder girdle develops before control of the hands and fingers.

This sequence of motor development and postural control is orderly, although not all abilities will be mastered at a specific age. On the contrary, innate potential is not a guarantee of appropriate development unless one receives appropriate sensory and environmental stimulation that is necessary to facilitate development (Haywood, & Getchell, 2009). Children will possess a variety of physical characteristics, genetic factors, levels of motivation, and opportunities to practice that will either foster or restrict their developmental progress.

As individuals progress through development, teachers should ascertain individual needs before proceeding to the next level of development. Therefore, programming for special needs must be implemented at the appropriate functioning level, with age providing a general guideline of expected skill development. If children can overcome or compensate for deficiencies, they will attain similar levels of functional ability. For children with movement disorders, the more completely we understand the stages of development and underlying mechanisms of disease or injury, the more likely we can develop an instructional program based on individual needs. With this premise in mind, we will provide an overview of the developmental system of movement, motor control, and physical fitness from anatomical and motor control perspectives.

Random and Reflexive Movement

A newborn infant will move the head, arms, and legs when it is awake and alert, producing some apparently disorganized movement. The movements of kicking the legs, waving the arms, and rocking the body appear to be more spontaneous rather than goal directed or reflexive in the developing infant. Although these movements appear spontaneous and unorganized, they are actually coordinated (Sugden & Keogh, 1990). From the recordings of infants' muscular activity, we see that supine kicking movements are rhythmic and have a coordinated pattern. Although disorganized, the hip, ankle, and knee move cooperatively rather than independently and may be the infant's first attempts to produce some purposeful movement (Gabbard, 2008; Haywood, & Getchell, 2009). These movements are considered normal in healthy babies, whereas persistence in older children may be indicative of developmental or motor delay.

The earliest movements of newborns are reflexive. These reflexes are involuntary, subcortical movements that are exhibited as responses to the external environment and provide various functions, such as protection, information gathering, and nourishment. Internally, infants also respond involuntarily to sensory stimulation of touch, pressure, and sound.

These initial involuntary movements are spontaneous and stereotypical but serve as the foundation for future motor development. With the development of the central nervous system, primitive reflexes are relegated to the lower areas of the brain (medulla and spinal cord). Primitive reflexes are innate and generally will persist for a specific number of weeks or until the brain develops sufficiently to achieve control. They will gradually decrease in strength and are inhibited as voluntary control is assumed. Although reflexes are involuntary, they can be used to evaluate the soundness of the neurological system. When a reflex cannot be elicited, is uneven in strength, or persists too long, a dysfunction of the nervous system is suspected.

The earliest reflexes are indicative of the undeveloped nervous system. With maturation, the control of these reflexes extends from the spinal cord to the brain stem and midbrain control. The highest level of nervous system development is achieved when the reflexes become inhibited and voluntary control of movements is initiated (**Table 6.1**) (Gabbard, 2008; Haywood & Getchell, 2009; O'Sullivan & Schmitz, 2006).

Additional reflexes will also appear at birth and become assimilated into the voluntary response system. Swallowing, blinking, pupillary response, sweating, stretch response, and the pattern jerk function initially as reflexes and will continue to function in the voluntary response system.

In the early stages of development, reflexes under control of the spinal cord are necessary for motor development. These include the stretch reflex, flexion reflex, crossed extension reflex, and extensor thrust reflex. The flexion reflex is a contraction of the flexor muscles while the extensor muscles are inhibited or relaxed. Commonly this is exhibited as withdrawal from a painful or hot stimulus and is achieved through the reciprocal reactions of flexing and extending opposing muscle groups.

The crossed extension reflex will function in conjunction with the flexion reflex, allowing the stimulated limb to extend and push itself away from the source of heat or pain. In a motor pattern, this reflex is used to maintain posture; stimulation of a leg will result in flexion, while the opposite limb provides stability and postural adjustments. In jumping patterns, persistence of the reflex will not allow both legs to extend independently. If only one leg flexes while the other extends because of persistence of the reflex, the individual is restricted in movement ability. Additionally, standing posture is initiated by the extensor thrust reflex, allowing the leg muscles to make necessary postural adjustments for support when the feet are stimulated.

For more sophisticated motor development, reciprocal intervention is required to alternately flex and extend muscles involved in coordinated movement patterns. If reflexes are not inhibited—as often seen in cerebral palsy—stability, muscle tone, and movement ability will obviously be impeded.

Righting Reflexes

The brain stem signals the emergence of the ability to control muscle tone and posture, as well as several equilibrium reactions, including the righting reflexes. The righting reflexes are concerned with maintaining the position of the body through the input of sensory information into the vestibular apparatus. Sensory information is then sent to the brain stem, which controls contraction of the appropriate postural muscles necessary to maintain an upright posture. The brain stem also controls the visual muscles that fixate the eyes while the head is moving. Four righting reflexes that are under brain stem control are the labyrinthine-righting, neck righting, body righting, and the optic-righting reflex. The labyrinthine-righting reflex is concerned with the infant's ability to lift the head and maintain an upright head position when the body is turned. The neck-righting reflex is concerned with the alignment of the neck to the head. While the labyrinthine reflex keeps the head upright when the body is turned, the neck-righting reflex will allow the neck to follow the head to an upright position, leading to segmental rolling. The body-righting reflex is responsible for stimulation of one side of the

Table 6.1 Common Reflexes Used to Identify Motor Problems

Reflex (Reaction)	Stimulus	Response	Persistence
Brain Stem Reflexes			
Asymmetrical tonic neck reflex (ATNR)	Rotation or lateral flexion of the head.	Increased extension on chin side with accompanying flexion of limbs on head side.	Difficulty in rolling because of extended arm; interferes with holding the head in midline, resulting in problems with tracking and fixating on objects. Evident in catching and throwing when one elbow is bent while the other extends because head position rotates or tilts to track a ball.
Symmetrical tonic neck reflex (STNR)	Flexion or extension of the head and neck.	With head flexion, flexes arms and upper extremities with extension of the legs. Backward extension of head results in extension of arms and flexion of legs.	Prevents creeping because head controls position of arms and legs. Retention prohibits infants from flexing and extending legs in creeping patterns. Also interferes with catching, kicking, and throwing because changes in head position affect muscle tone and reciprocation of muscle groups.
Tonic labyrinthine reflex (TLR) (prone and supine)	Stimulation of vestibular apparatus by tilting or changes in head position.	In prone position, increased flexion in the limbs; in supine position. extension occurs in limbs.	Affects muscle tone and ability to move body segments independently Into various positions, such as propping the body up in a support position prior to crawling or rolling.
Positive support	Stimulation when the balls of the feet touch a firm surface in an upright position.	Extension of the legs to support individual's weight in a standing position.	Disruption of muscle tone needed to support weight, or adduction and internal rotation of the hips that interfere with standing and locomotion.
Spinal Reflexes			
Grasping reflex (palmar and plantar grasping)	Pressure on palm of hand or hypertension of wrist. Plantar grasping: stroking the sole of foot will initiate contraction of toes.	Flexion of fingers to grasp then extension to release. In foot, toes contract around object stroking foot.	In hand, causes difficulty in releasing objects, in throwing and striking, and in reception of tactile stimuli. In foot, interferes with static and dynamic balance while standing and walking.
Crossed extension reflex	Stimulation to ball of foot.	Flexion followed by extension and adduction of opposite leg.	Coordination of leg movements in creeping and walking impeded by stiffness and lack of reciprocal leg movement.
Extensor thrust reflex	Sudden pressure or prick to sole of foot in sitting or supine position.	Toes extend, foot dorsiflexes with increased extensor tone.	Balance between flexion and extension impeded, often seen as stiffness of body in sitting position.
Moro reflex	Change in head position; drop backward in a sitting position.	Arms and legs extend, fingers spread; then arms flex and adduct across chest.	Interferes with ability to sit unsupported and with locomotor patterns or sports skills involving sudden movements (e.g., abduction of arms and legs during gymnastics interferes with balance).
Body righting	Rotate upper or lower trunk.	Body segment that is not rotated allows to align body.	Interferes with ability to right itself when head is held in a lateral position.

(continued)

Table 6.1   Common Reflexes Used to Identify Motor Problems (*continued*)

Reflex (Reaction)	Stimulus	Response	Persistence
Spinal Reflexes			
Neck righting	Turn head sideways.	Body follows head in rotation.	Cannot align head with neck when body is turned. Impeded segmental rolling.
Labyrinthine righting	Limit vision or tilt body in various directions.	Head will move to maintain upright position.	Unable to reorient head in proper body alignment and position. Interferes with head control in movement.
Optic righting	Tilt body in various directions.	Allows head to achieve upright position.	Unable to reorient head In proper body alignment and body posture. Interferes with head control in movement.
Parachute reactions	Lower infant forward rapidly or tilt forward to prone position.	Legs and arms extend and abduct to protect from fall.	Lack of support to prevent body from failing.
Tilting reactions	Display center of gravity by tilting or moving support surface.	Protective extension and muscle tone on downward side. Upward side has curvature of trunk and extension and abduction of extremities.	Clumsiness and awkwardness resulting In loss of balance, muscle tone, and falling.

body and subsequent ability of the infant to right itself even when the head is held in a lateral position. The optic-righting reflex allows the infant to alter and attain positions necessary to achieve an upright posture and head position (Shumway-Cook & Woollacott, 2006).

In the horizontal position, head control is achieved through reliance on vision; the righting reflexes in combination allow the infant to assume and maintain an appropriate upright body and head position. When the body is reoriented or a position is changed, the head assumes control by interacting with the labyrinthine and optic reflexes. The upper body assumes a proper alignment in conjunction with the head by mediating the neck-righting reflexes, while alignment of the lower extremities generally follows alignment of the upper body. Increased control of upright posture is achieved by providing infants with an increasing amount of visual, vestibular, and tactile stimulation from the environment.

If the righting reflexes persist, infants experience difficulty with posture and muscle tone. They will be unable to run, change directions, and maintain body alignment in movements requiring proper head control. Without the persistence of these reflexes or any maturational delays, the reflex movements are replaced by equilibrium reactions. Reactions are automatic responses that proceed from reflexes as the individual's central nervous system matures. These reactions allow individuals to maintain body support and to develop posture and balance control. Problems encountered in this stage of development include the inability to establish basic stability, body positioning, and muscle tone necessary for movement.

Other reflexes necessary for postural control are also mediated by the brain stem. The symmetrical tonic neck reflex (STNR) and the asymmetrical tonic neck reflex (ATNR) appear during the first 6 months of life and are elicited by a rotation of the head and stimulation of joint receptors in the neck (**Figure 6.1**). The STNR is elicited by forward flexion of the neck, resulting in flexion of the arms and upper extremities and extension of the legs. A backward extension of the head results in extension of the arms and upper torso and flexion of the legs and lower extremities. The persistence of the STNR reflex prevents assuming a four-point creeping pattern, because the head position controls the movements of the arms and legs. Retention of the reflex will prohibit infants from appropriately flexing and extending their arms and legs to complete the creeping pattern. This reflex also interferes with catching, kicking, throwing, and tumbling,

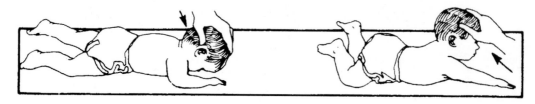

Figure 6.1 Symmetrical tonic neck reflex.

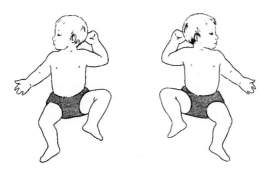

Figure 6.2 Asymmetrical tonic neck reflex (fencing position).

because the changes in head position may affect muscle tone and reciprocation of muscle groups.

The asymmetrical tonic neck reflex (ATNR) in a supine position is elicited by rotation or lateral flexion (tilt) of the head leading to increased extension of the limbs on the chin side with accompanying flexion of limbs on the head side (**Figure 6.2**). Persistence of the reflex will cause difficulty in rolling, because the extended arm impedes rolling. Furthermore, the reflex interferes with holding the head in the midline, resulting in visual perceptual problems commonly associated with tracking or fixating on objects. The reflex is also evident in skills such as catching and throwing, where one elbow is bent while the other extends because the head position is rotated or tilted to track a ball. In sports such as tennis or baseball, rotation of the head will interfere with crossing the midline and smooth integration of the movement.

Another tonic reflex concerned with body position is the tonic labyrinthine reflex (TNR) (**Figure 6.3**), which is elicited from stimulation of the vestibular apparatus during the first 4 months. In a prone position, the TLR is elicited by changes in head position, causing increased flexion in the limbs, while in the supine position extension occurs in all limbs. Persistence of this reflex affects the infant's muscle tone and ability to move body segments independently into various positions required for purposeful movement. For example, the infant's ability to prop itself into a support position prior to crawling or rolling will be affected.

The blending and inhibition of the tonic reflexes by the righting reflexes can ensure proper head and body positioning, whereas retention of these reflexes will adversely affect overall motor development. In a prone position, difficulties may be evident in raising the head or placing the hands under the body to achieve and maintain support, as in a kneeling position. Infants placed in the supine position may experience difficulties lifting the head and turning from the back to the side or performing a sit-up. Some activities, however, such as archery, baseball, and fencing, actively demonstrate the continued influence of reflexes on movements. For example, during periods of stressful activity and fatigue, sustained muscular contractions and endurance needed to perform the skill may be reinforced by reflexes (Sage, 1984). Furthermore, these reflex patterns are often basic components of skilled motor acts. This phenomenon is evident in the baseball player who jumps and stretches the glove hand overhead to catch a ball, with the head turned to the left, extension on the left side, and flexion on the right side that is similar to the motion elicited by the tonic neck reflex.

Grasp Reflex

The grasp reflex is elicited by pressure on the palm of the hand or hyperextension of the wrist, causing infants to grasp and then release. This reflex will become inhibited at approximately the 6th month. Persistence of this reflex causes difficulty in releasing objects used in throwing and striking and interferes with the reception of tactile stimuli.

In the lower extremities, the foot grasp reflex is persistent until 9 months and is elicited by stimulating the sole of the foot, resulting a curling of the toes. Persistence of this reflex results in difficulties achieving both static and dynamic balance, especially while standing and walking.

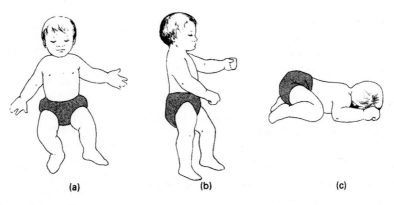

(a) (b) (c)

Figure 6.3 Tonic labyrinthine reflex.

Moro Reflex

The Moro reflex is elicited by a sudden noise, tapping of the abdomen, or insecure position of support. Infants will first extend the fingers, abduct the arms and legs, and then adduct the limbs and flex the fingers. Persistence of the Moro reflex after 9 months interferes with the ability to sit unsupported, to assume a four-point crawling position, or to stand unsupported in a two-point position. This reflex can also interfere with locomotor patterns and sport skills requiring sudden movement. For example, in gymnastics a fast movement may cause a loss of equilibrium while the individual performs a skill. The influence of the Moro reflexes would be apparent as the arms and legs abduct, causing the loss of balance.

Rudimentary Movement

Rudimentary movements are some of the first voluntary movements demonstrated by infants. They generally occur from birth to 2 years of age in a predictable sequence as the individual matures and receives sensory stimulation from the environment. These movements are often uncoordinated and hesitant because infants are limited in using any external perceptual information for any purposeful movement. At this stage, a primary accomplishment is to maintain an upright posture and control of the head and neck muscles.

Control of later movement is difficult if the infant cannot achieve postural and head control. In addition the initiation and mastery of manipulative tasks, such as reaching, grasping, and releasing, are additional milestones. The infant processes a great deal of information by moving to and exploring objects in the environment that are necessary for social, cognitive, and motor development. Simplistic locomotor patterns, such as creeping, crawling, and walking, also develop, progressing from the position of full contact with the ground, to an upright position on all fours, to an upright kneeling position, and finally to a standing upright posture.

Gallahue and Ozmun (2006) have indicated that rudimentary movements can be divided into two substages to represent an increased amount of motor control as a basis for the further movement development. The first substage includes the inhibition of primitive postural reflexes and the initiation of voluntary control. Voluntary movements are initiated but still lack the refinement necessary for skilled movement patterns. This lack of precision is evident in children who initiate a voluntary movement to grasp an object yet still move the entire hand, wrist, arm, and shoulder while attempting the movement. The second substage incorporates an increasing amount of perceptual awareness of the environment and more precise control of movement. Children need not rely solely on sensory information for movement responses but will begin to make perceptual judgments by integrating sensory and motor information for more precise movement decisions (French & Horvat, 1986), such as incorporating visual sensory information with tactile sensory information when grasping and releasing an object. This process becomes quite evident as children achieve more control of movement sequences.

These rudimentary movements are further refined when reflexes are inhibited and higher neurological control is achieved. The rudimentary skills that are commonly developed during this stage include rolling, sitting, standing, walking, grasping, and releasing (Wickstrom, 1983).

Rolling

In learning how to roll, infants are required to develop control of the head and neck. The skill occurs at approximately 4 months beginning from a back-lying position. Initially infants turn the head to focus on an object, inhibiting the body-righting reflex and allowing the body to turn in the same direction as the head. At times infants roll to the side after turning the head. With maturation, segmental rolling will improve as the hips and shoulders turn while the other body parts follow. The initial attempts at voluntary control of rolling occur from a front-to back-lying position and later from the back to stomach.

Sitting

The achievement of the sitting position generally will follow rolling. Initially, when infants are pulled into a sitting position, the head sags backward and then forward on the chest. At approximately 5 months the ability to hold the head upright is developed; by $6^{1}/_{2}$ months the baby will be sitting without support; and at 9 months the baby voluntarily assumes a sitting position.

Crawling and Creeping

The ability to crawl is demonstrated by dragging the body, using the arms and legs, with the abdomen in contact with a supporting surface. (Creeping uses the arms and legs for propulsion without the chest and abdomen in contact with the floor.) Crawling occurs at approximately 7 months as infants attempt to reach for an object and then, following the reach, move the head and chest forward. Creeping develops after a supporting position on the hands and knees has been achieved. Development of creeping proceeds from moving one arm and then one leg, to homolateral movements, and finally to crossed-extension patterns, which appear at 10–11 months.

Standing and Walking

The ability to maintain a standing position is achieved at approximately 9 months with the assistance of a table or railing. When upright, infants can move around furniture or the play area with assistance. After unsupported standing is developed, walking develops as infants move from one area to another. A variety of individual differences are apparent in walking patterns between 8 and 18 months, depending on stability, strength, and motivation.

The initial patterns of walking are awkward; precise control is achieved with more opportunities to practice. Refinements in the walking pattern are demonstrated by an increase in speed and length of step, a decrease in the base of support, the ability to position the feet forward, and finally the synchronized coordination of the arms and legs. Further maturation and practice refine the walking pattern, while the ability to walk backward occurs at 19 months and ascending stairs at approximately 21 months.

Reaching and Grasping

The manipulative skills of reaching and grasping will appear at approximately 4 months. Grasping develops from palm grabbing at 5 months to a pincher-type movement using the thumb and forefinger at 13 months. Releasing is more difficult for infants because the ability to relax the hand muscles is not usually developed until 18 months. Reaching and grasping skills illustrate that proximodistal development is occurring, with movement sequences uncoordinated and slow until motor development is further advanced.

Fundamental Movement

The fundamental movement stage continues the expansion of motor development and progress from rudimentary movements. In this stage, more voluntary control and active movement within the environment are possible. Movements become more predictable as the ability to move, the combining of movements into patterns, and the modification of movements according to task and environmental demands are achieved. For children this stage reflects the integration of cerebellum, basal ganglia, and motor cortex as the child begins to plan and execute appropriate movements.

From the stable upright position of the rudimentary stage, locomotor patterns such as running, jumping, hopping, galloping, and skipping can be developed. Object control or manipulation patterns such as throwing, catching, and kicking also proceed from the rudimentary skills of grasping and releasing, while stability movements such as static (standing on one foot) and dynamic (beam walking) balance movements develop after achieving an upright stable position. In this stage of development, the child must rely on visual, auditory, and tactile-kinesthetic (haptic) perceptual skills in the environment to incorporate play and movement patterns into sequences, such as combining a locomotor (running) and ball-control (catching) skill. These environmental influences create the need for executing movement patterns in reaction to stimuli in stable and changing environments. For example, the pattern of running must first be developed with a smooth integration of stride and upper body movements. As a mature pattern is developed, the movement is incorporated into games that require children to use and modify movements on situational demand, such as stopping, starting, or running backward. As stated earlier, breakdown in coordinating these stimuli or breakdown in the feedback loops results in a motor dysfunction.

The emphasis in this stage of development should be placed on the individuals' ability to incorporate a wide variety of movements into their learning repertoire. The appearance and sophistication of these skills will develop from the initial appearance of the patterns, to moderate control, and finally to a highly efficient, coordinated, mature pattern that can be used in a variety of movement settings.

Skills in the fundamental movement stage will develop in stages or levels. Substage 1 constitutes the initial attempts to perform the movement pattern. Movement may be poorly coordinated and may include improper sequences or restricted use of the body, a lack of spatial and/or temporal awareness, and a nonfluid integration of the movement. This is evident in the skill of throwing, when the initial attempts may be characterized by a step with the improper foot, a lack of hip rotation and follow-through, and an exaggerated use of the upper body when releasing the ball. At this time the schema or pattern is not fully developed and will require practice and feedback on the appropriate technique.

Substage 2 incorporates more coordination and control of the pattern. When the child throws an object, a proper cross-step, initial follow-through, and less restriction of movement may be apparent. McClenahan and Gallahue (1978) have indicated that with maturation, most individuals will achieve this stage of physical functioning if they have the proper opportunities for practice and instruction. Children with disabilities may be restricted in their opportunities for practice or opportunity for specific instruction or feedback on their performance. Additional practice and instruction are required to reach this level of functioning to enable children to develop their movement schema and adjust to using feedback information.

As children mature and receive instruction and opportunities to practice (substage 3), all the elements of a proficient pattern should be evident as well as increased control of the movement. Throwing will consist of a proper stride, upper rotation of body and hip, overarm release, and follow-through. In order to complete the skill and to be successful at throwing, the learner requires practice, instruction, and an interest in or motivation for the activity. Practice should vary, and learners must adapt to various amounts and situations in order to be flexible in generating their movement sequences. A sound developmental foundation, or schema, in motor development is needed for children to control movements required in complex movement patterns such as sport and recreational activities. A lack of development in this stage restricts future success because fundamental skills are the foundation for more precise control and development. Skills commonly developed in this stage are running, jumping, hopping, galloping and skipping, throwing, catching, and kicking (Gabbard, 2008; McClenahan & Gallahue, 1978; Sugden & Keogh, 1990; Wickstrom, 1983).

Running

Running originates from the development of a proficient walking pattern. Initially the feet are turned out, while the arms are held away from the body. The first attempts at running are unstable and uncoordinated because children do not have appropriate balance or leg strength to achieve a period of nonsupport. Between 2 and 3 years of age, they gain the ability to attain balance and development of strength, enabling them to leave the ground in a nonsupport position. In general, a mature running pattern is achieved by 6 years of age when the stride and flight phase are lengthened, the trailing foot is swung forward during recovery, arms are used in opposition with a forward lean of the body, and a pronounced period of nonsupport is evident.

Jumping

Jumping develops after proficient walking and running patterns are achieved. Initial jumping occurs at approximately 18 months, beginning with an exaggerated motion such as walking down a step. Although this is not a true jumping pattern, it seems to be a preliminary step to jumping with two feet. Next, children become able to jump up and down in a stationary position while development of leg strength and coordination allows them to elevate the body from the ground. At about 2 years of age, children will be able to push off with two feet and land without losing balance. By 5 years of age, adequate leg strength enables developing children to achieve a mature jumping pattern.

The vertical jump and horizontal jump each have common characteristics, such as a preparatory crouch, a forward and upward swing of the arms to initiate action, a rapid extension of the legs to propel the body, flight time when the body is extended, and flexion of the hips, knees, and ankles to absorb the landing. The extra dimension of the horizontal jump requires a forward and upward movement rather than just an upward movement. This slight variation is more complex because a momentary loss of balance allows the legs to move forward in preparation for the landing.

Hopping

The ability to hop requires more stability and strength than jumping because the takeoff and landing are on one foot. The first attempts at hopping (stationary and moving) involve uncoordinated movements and a minimal amount of flexion and extension of the support leg, with a corresponding lack of height and a flat-footed landing. Children also do not use the arms effectively, while the nonhopping leg is often rigid and may touch the floor. As balance and coordination are developed, the nonsupport leg is more controlled, does not touch the floor, and arm action while hopping is less extraneous.

Initial stages of hopping are prevalent by the age of 4, while proficiency is achieved at the age of 6 with both preferred and nonpreferred legs. Girls are generally more proficient because of their physical maturity and a social and play environment that provides them with more opportunities to practice hopping.

Galloping and Skipping

The skills of galloping and skipping are learned when basic skills in other locomotor movement patterns are developed. Galloping is a combination of walking and leaping that occurs when the transfer of weight from one foot to the other is achieved. Initially, at about 3 years of age, children demonstrate a slight leap coupled with a run. From this initial sequence the gallop is mastered with a transfer of weight to the forward foot on the same side, incorporating a step-leap pattern. By 5 or 6 years of age, a mature pattern will develop by coordinating arm movements and a momentary elevation of the feet.

Galloping seems to be favored by boys, whereas girls prefer skipping. Skipping is a step-hop pattern, with the step longer than the hop before the pattern is repeated on the opposite side of the body. For a mature pattern, precise timing and control is essential because the transfer of weight and the shift to step-hop on the opposite side is intricate. Skipping occurs at 6 or 7 years from a mature hopping pattern. As hopping proficiency increases, the movement adds a step on one side of the body. With the improvement of balance, the step-hop pattern becomes an ingrained movement on the opposite side of the body. Final development of skipping includes the refinement of both the arms and legs as well as elevation and control of the movement.

Throwing

The pattern of throwing can be seen as early as 6 months, when infants are first able to grasp and release an object. At this substage, the action is initiated from a sitting position primarily with the arms because infants are still unable to assume an upright position.

With the development of stability and other locomotor movements, the throwing action will begin to appear. Initially, at approximately 2 years, an object is released with a forearm extension and no body rotation. The feet remain stationary throughout the action except for a slight flexion of the trunk when the ball is released. At approximately 3–5 years, children begin to rotate the hips and spine, although the feet remain in a stationary position. Prior to the throw, the object is brought backward and momentarily held with a cocked wrist before the child initiates a forward horizontal movement. The elementary substage at 6 years is more proficient because a transfer of weight forward is evident on the same side of the body as the throwing arm. Also evident are trunk rotation and overarm movement, with the elbow leading and the beginning of a follow-through. In the mature pattern at 6 to 7 years of age, a more complete transfer to the foot opposite the throwing arm, trunk rotation, and follow-through are demonstrated. Children can achieve greater control in both speed and precision when integrating both sides of the body and can achieve a wider base of support.

Catching

Catching is a fundamental skill that requires the ability to control a thrown object. Initial attempts at catching are characterized by avoidance of the thrown object or a tendency to extend the arms and allow the ball to bounce off them. Children also attempt to trap balls against their chest, turn their head, or close their eyes when objects approach.

During the elementary substage at 4 years, children visually track the ball yet may still blink before catching it. At this substage, the arms are outstretched with the palms perpendicular, although the coordination of the movement is poor. The hands unevenly grasp the ball and pull it to the chest. At approximately 6 years, a mature pattern is evident as the individual tracks the released ball until task completion, prepares the arms for catching, and controls the ball with the hands and fingers while "giving" with the arms to absorb the ball's momentum.

Other factors also affect the ability to catch, including the size and velocity of the ball. Although a large ball is easier to catch, more precise control is difficult. A larger ball will result in more elementary catching patterns, such as trapping, because the hands and fingers are needed for precise control. In contrast, a smaller object such as a tennis ball is also difficult to

control until the mature catching pattern is achieved. The most appropriate ball size is one that allows children to cup with the hands but does not require precise fine motor control to throw (Gallahue & Ozmun, 2006; Williams, 1983).

Speed and angle of release will also affect catching. Children experience difficulty judging the speed of an object, and performance deteriorates as speed is increased. As they mature perceptually and receive training and experience in catching at different speeds, children will not require as much time to track the ball before making decisions.

Another factor that affects catching patterns is the individual's position. A stationary position, with the ball tossed directly at children, is initially the best position to assume when learning to catch. Moving to catch an object will disrupt performance until students are able to master the catching pattern as well as sideways, forward, or backward movements.

Kicking

Kicking is a fundamental pattern that requires the use of the feet to propel an object. The kicking pattern (directed at a stationary ball) originates at 24 months, beginning with an initial step with a straight leg and little accompanying movement of the arms and upper body. While the kicking leg is swung forward with a minimal amount of force and no follow-through, the opposite foot assumes a position of stability and support.

During the elementary substage of the pattern, the trunk leans slightly forward while the arms are held out at the side for balance. Children take several approach steps and begin to flex the kicking leg at the knee, swinging the leg backward and then forward in a striking motion. The children also initiate extension of the leg on follow-through.

The mature kicking pattern incorporates the arms swinging in opposition while kicking, a forceful leg swing, increased flexion, and extension action at the hip and knee to generate a more pronounced backswing, follow-through, and impact with the ball. The development of strength, stability, and practice in the mature pattern allows more force to be generated in the kick. As with catching, children find control of the ball in games such as soccer or kickball more difficult because it requires coordination of the hands and eyes as well as the extremities.

Sport and Recreational Movement

The final stage of motor development and control occurs at approximately age 7 and is characterized by the attainment of specific goals and changes in the external environment. Games, sports, and recreational activities require children to constantly alter and match their movements with a more skilled pattern. The basic locomotor, manipulation, and stability movements must then be more elaborate and coordinated as the demands of a particular sport or recreational activity require more intricate and combined movements. For example, the sport of softball would involve the execution of overhand and underhand throws; the catching of ground balls and fly balls; striking a ball; running the bases and fielding fly balls; stability movements for batting, pitching, and fielding; and dynamic movements to change levels and directions.

At this stage, more immediate and accurate decisions are needed about movements. Children also need to remember previous experiences and compare new information to what was previously learned. Likewise, children become more adept at modifying movement behaviors according to the changing environment and meeting a variety of movement challenges.

Movements become more automatic as the demand for more sophistication requires responses to the environment and the development of more complex patterns. Combining cognitive and affective attributes refines these skills.

Within this substage there are three separate but overlapping transitional stages that lead to the development of highly skilled performance. As previously stated, teaching should emphasize cognitive development, physical abilities, and motivation of children rather than conform to specific age guidelines. Furthermore, the ability to reach the pinnacle of motor development and control will depend on how much time is allocated for instruction, practice, and competition.

Most experts combine the sport and recreational skill phase into a series of substages or skill levels. In most instances the child first attempts to refine and combine mature movement patterns into total body movement as he or she adds range and complexity to a previously learned fundamental task. Children are limited in overall skill and proficiency at this stage and usually possess an interest in a wide variety of activities. This provides the first opportunity for competition and testing one's skills against others' (and is commonly integrated into lead-up activities), while the teacher emphasizes accuracy and skill in performing movement patterns to achieve proficiency.

The child attains some proficiency through practice of selected activities and movement experiences. The child may focus on a select number of activities limited by personal preference and physical attributes. An increasing emphasis on form, skill, and accuracy is needed for the child to control intricate movements for sports competition and recreational pursuits. As the perceptual process is developed, the child can incorporate external information into playing strategies that are needed for developing skill and accuracy and that

can be repeated consistently. It is also important to emphasize the proper technique and practice opportunities for children to improve. Often a child whose play or movement opportunities are limited will be restricted in skill development.

At the highest level of motor development and control, movements are sophisticated and automatic. Children who reach this level of development practice and continually refine their skills to achieve the highest level of performance. All aspects of development, including genetic endowment, fitness, motivation, and instructional opportunities, must be present to attain this level of functioning. Conscious involvement of movement is minimal, and the cognitive appraisal of information must be sophisticated and precise, because optimal performance depends on prior experience and strategy. Children are more precise and can make distinctions among different kinds of intersensory information, while the control mechanism related to postural stability and body movement is highly developed, thus enabling them to complete the motor action accurately and consistently.

Functional Movement

In addition to movement skills, changes in development contribute to the functional development of children. In this context, functional development relates to the development of those skills that are required to perform many activities of play, daily living, or self-care needed to function in home and community-based settings (Horvat & Croce 1995). These skills may be related to reaching or grasping to play with a toy, eating a meal, or brushing their teeth. In other contexts, functional skill development is related to work-specific tasks.

Postural Control Development

Development of skilled, goal-directed movements requires complex and subtle postural adjustments involving the head, trunk, and limbs so as to maintain the body over its center of gravity. Overall, the postural control system has two primary functions: to develop an orientation of body segments against gravity and to ensure that balance is maintained, and to fix body orientation and body segment positions that serve as a reference for perception and action relative to the external world. These functions of postural control occur because of multisensory inputs regulating orientation and stabilization of body segments, flexible postural reactions for balance recovery after disturbances, and anticipatory body segment positioning during voluntary movements. The development and application of postural control mechanisms is dependent on spinal reflex activity (e.g., stretch reflex) and higher order adaptive mechanisms involving vestibular, visual, somatosensory (proprioceptive and touch/pressure) systems, as well as information processing in the cerebral cortex.

Development of postural control mechanisms is an essential aspect for developing goal-directed movements such as locomotion and object manipulation. According to Shumway-Cooke & Woollacott (2006), the emergence of postural control can be characterized by the following principles. First, it appears that the development of postural control is best characterized by a cephalo-caudal (head-to-tail) progression of control, with first sense involved with head control being vision. As infants begin to develop independent sitting, they slowly learn to coordinate sensory-motor information relating to the head and trunk. This extends the rules for head control to trunk control. Secondly, the ability to use individual senses to control posture precedes the ability to integrate multiple senses to control posture (see Chapter 7, Information Processing and Perceptual Development).

Lastly, postural control development can be best characterized as a discontinuous, step-like process of integrating multiple sensory and motor systems, and the ability to incorporate new strategies into the repertoire for postural control. Hence, postural control development involves three components—perception (integrating sensory information); cognition (attention, motivation, information processing, and developing appropriate movement strategies); and action (generating muscular forces to control body position). The ability to modify both sensory and motor strategies to changing task and environmental conditions develops in late childhood, thereby reducing the child's ability to adapt to the environment until this time.

The postural control system of children with disabilities is often compromised. These postural problems have serious consequences for movement, as adequate postural control is a prerequisite for adequate mobility. Goals for adapted physical education should be to develop effective task-specific sensory and motor strategies for postural control, and to increase the child's ability to perform functional skills, such as walking up a flight of stairs or kicking a ball, under varying environmental contexts (Debu, 2004).

When designing the program, the physical educator must first determine the constraints to normal postural control. Is the abnormal postural control the result of a sensory impairment(s) (problems with visual, vestibular, and/or somatosensory systems), the result of deficits in sensory organization processes, the result of musculoskeletal restrictions, or the result of cognitive impairments (Montgomery and Connolly, 2002)? For example, somatosensory feedback is essential for all locomotor activities as this feedback informs the individual about body position relative to the supporting surface, especially whether the individual is on uneven or sloped ground. This information, in turn, evokes specific ankle strategies, which allows the individual to adapt appropriately to surface conditions and to perform the particular task. If the child has diminished or inadequate somatosensory feedback, then an inappropriate ankle strategy will be evoked and postural instability will be the end result. At this point the physical educator might devise a learning strategy whereby the child is instructed to rely more on visual information to evoke the appropriate postural motor strategy. Similarly, if the primary reason for poor balance and postural control is a visual impairment that cannot be corrected medically, then the child might be instructed to use other sensory modalities such as the tactile use of the cane when walking or the kinesthetic use of leg position when ascending/decending stairs, as well as relying on other senses for the necessary feedback to control posture.

It is important for the physical educator to also realize that musculoskeletal limitations can lead to problems in postural control. Any limitation in strength or joint range of motion in the upper or lower extremities and trunk can have a negative impact on postural control. For example, if the inappropriate postural control response is due to insufficient range of motion and strength at the ankle joint, the physical educator can initiate an aggressive range of motion and muscle strengthening program for the ankle. Finally, impairments in cognition—such as attention, memory, spatial relations, body schema, and praxis—are challenges that also can compromise postural functioning.

To improve overall postural control, balance challenges ought to be progressive. As the child improves in performing a task under a specific environmental condition, the challenge of the task or the type of environment in which the task is performed should be increased or changed. The adapted physical educator should always take into consideration the postural demands of the task (e.g., how one system or multiple systems impact performance), and incrementally add balancing challenges over time.

LEARNING ACTIVITY

What muscles are involved in maintaining posture? How can these muscles be strengthened?

Putting it all Together in the Learning Environment

When applying the information discussed in this chapter it is important to recognize how a number of systems—the individual, the environment, and the task—interact to facilitate coordinated, goal-directed movements. According to Garcia and Garcia (2006), the individual is represented by anatomical and physiological components and such intrinsic factors such as perception, attention, and developmental level. The teacher cannot change the characteristics that the individual brings to the physical education, sport, and recreational setting, but these are things for which the teacher can accommodate. Each individual brings a unique subset of abilities and a unique developmental level to the setting, which will have a bearing on how well and to what extent the child can participate in the activity. Given the unique characteristics of the child, the content to be taught, and the activities in which the child will be engaged, the teacher must decide on what adaptations to the environment are needed and the best and most appropriate learning opportunities.

The environment provides the context for the experience or movement and is influenced by a number of factors, including the teacher and his/her expertise, previous experiences (motor memories) the child brings to the situation, motivation of the individual, and the equipment used in the task. Equipment is the one aspect on which the teacher has the greatest impact and can manipulate the most. For example, it is within the environmental constraints where the teacher can adapt the equipment used and the rules to fit the needs of the student. It is here where the teacher can also provide the necessary positive feedback that individual performers need to improve their performances. Teachers represent the "extrinsic information source for students," which allows the performer to focus on the area of the body or part of the skill to which they need to pay attention

(Garcia & Garcia, 2006). In essence, the teacher provides a learning environment that is nurturing and flexible to the individual's developmental and skill level.

The task provides its own unique components, including task demands (strength, endurance, and flexibility needed to perform the task); level of difficulty (task complexity); and mechanical factors and forces acting on the body such as range of motion, balance, and center of gravity manipulation. Task difficulty is another aspect that can be easily modified by the teacher to meet the unique developmental and skill level of the performer. For example, a combination task involving running, catching, and throwing, which uses concepts of space, direction, hand-eye coordination, and object manipulation, may be appropriate for some individuals while not being appropriate for others. Some individuals might not have sufficiently mature levels of motor development to participate adequately, and, therefore, can benefit significantly from modification of the task. For instance, the teacher could adapt equipment so as to make it easier for less-skilled individuals to catch, and modify the rules to allow for variations in throwing.

To summarize, all goal-directed movements are the product of the interaction of multiple systems composed of multiple subsystems (factors) that are constantly interacting with one another and constantly changing based on task demands. It is these systems and subsystems that the teacher must take into account and manipulate to maximize the physical education experience and skill development, especially when working with individuals with disabilities.

CHAPTER SUMMARY

1. Children enter school with a variety of needs, interests, and ability levels. All children will develop at their own rate. However, all children follow a similar sequential order of motor development. This process can be identified by the stages and patterns apparent in the developmental sequence that is commonly age related.

2. Although using these age-related guidelines for most children is beneficial, their use with exceptional students may be less effective. A knowledge and understanding of basic principles of motor development are necessary to assess functional ability adequately.

3. Motor skills develop in a sequence from basic skills to more complex motor patterns. The sequence is fairly predictable, although not all abilities will be mastered at a specific age.

4. Programming for children with disabilities must be implemented at the appropriate functioning level, with age providing a general guideline of expected skill development. Children with a disability will still progress through similar stages of motor development and control if they can overcome or compensate for the deficiency.

5. Stages of development proceed from primitive reflexive movements to specialized skill development and control.

6. Reflexes are subcortical in nature and present at birth. These serve as the foundation for future motor development. Reflexes usually persist until the brain develops sufficiently to achieve control. At this point, the reflexes do not disappear but rather become inhibited.

7. As neurological development proceeds to the higher areas of the brain, movement control is possible. The cerebral cortex, basal ganglia, cerebellum, and brain stem are important in the control of movements. Each provides a varying influence on motor control, which is reflective of higher neural control.

8. Rudimentary movements are some of the first voluntary movements demonstrated by young children. These usually occur from birth to 2 years of age. These rudimentary movements are refined when reflexes become inhibited and higher neurological control is achieved.

9. Fundamental movements develop after rudimentary movements. Movements at this stage become more predictable, and more complex patterns of movements can be observed. Some examples of fundamental movements include running, hopping, throwing, and kicking.

10. The final stage of motor development and control occurs at approximately age 7 and is characterized by the attainment of specific goals and changes in the external environment. Games, sports, and recreational activities require children to change and match their movements constantly when a more skilled pattern is required.

11. Motor control is analyzed by the study of isolated tasks under specific conditions. The development of motor control is closely aligned to motor development.

12. For children with disabilities, the process of motor control may be adversely affected; that is, they may experience difficulty achieving precise control. Neurological or muscular deficiencies contribute to spatial and temporal awareness problems. Sensory deficits result in a lack of specific cues within the environment, while students with learning problems may be weak in input and decision making, as well as in judgment about changing demands and stimuli.

13. The teacher should strive to provide instruction at the appropriate level of development and control for all children. Each child may have special needs or may possess certain characteristics that influence his or her functional ability. To implement a program, the cooperation of other support personnel may be required to develop the awareness of the student's ability. Additionally, teachers should incorporate the following basic factors into their programs: instruction based on developmental principles and the functional ability of the child; the most appropriate method of learning for the child (e.g., auditory, visual) based on assessment information; individualized instruction and opportunities for the student to practice at school and/or at home; and the attempt to develop form and precision as well as performance measures of distance or height.

14. With the incorporation of these basic principles, the teacher should then select activities to enhance or develop the child's functional ability. Furthermore, a more thorough assessment and evaluation may be indicated before a specific activity program or individualized educational plan is begun. The input from the educational team and specific evaluation information can then be used to develop the child's abilities at his or her functional level.

15. Postural control development is best characterized as a discontinuous, step-like process of integrating multiple sensory and motor systems. Postural control is often compromised in children with disabilities. Postural problems have serious consequences for movement and therefore, ought to be addressed by adapted physical educators.

REFERENCES

Debu., B. (2004). Postural control: A limiting factor for the motor development of individuals with down syndrome. *European Bulletin of Adapted Physical Activity, 3*(31). www.bulletin-apa.com.

French, R., & Horvat, M. A. (1986). The acquisition of perceptual skills by motorically awkward children. *Motor skills: Theory into practice, 8*, 27–38.

Gabbard, C. P. (2008). *Lifelong motor development* (5th ed.), San Francisco, CA: Pearson/Benjamin Cummings.

Gallahue, D. L., & Ozmun, J. C. (2006). *Understanding motor development: Infants, children, adolescents, adults* (6th ed.). Dubuque, IA: McGraw-Hill.

Garcia, C., & Garcia, L. (2006). Moving and learning in physical education: A motor-development and motor learning perspective. *JOPERD, 77*(8), 31–33.

Haywood, K. M., & Getchell, M. (2009). *Life span motor development* (5th ed.). Champaign, IL: Human Kinetics.

Horvat, M., & Croce, R. (1995). Physical rehabilitation of individuals with mental retardation: Physical fitness and information processing. *Critical Reviews in Physical and Rehabilitation Medicine, 1*(3), 233–252.

Keogh, J., & Sugden, D. (1985). *Movement skill development.* New York: MacMillan.

McClenahan, B. A., & Gallahue, D. L. (1978). *Fundamental movement: A development and remedial approach.* Philadelphia: Saunders.

Montgomery, P. C. & Connolly, B. H. (2002). *Clinical application for motor control.* Thorofare, NJ: Slack Incorporated.

O'Sullivan, S. B., & Schmitz, T. J. (2006). *Physical rehabilitation: Assessment and treatment* (6th ed.). Philadelphia: Davis.

Sage, G. H. (1984). *Motor learning and control: A neuropsychological approach.* Dubuque, IA: Wm. C. Brown.

Shumway-Cook, A., & Woollacott, M. H. (2006). *Motor control: Translating research into clinical practice* (3rd ed.). Philadelphia: Lippincott, Williams, & Wilkins.

Sugden, D., & Keogh, J. (1990). Problems in Movement Skill Development (Growth, Motor Development and Physical Activity Across the Life Span). South Carolina: University of South Carolina Press.

Wickstrom, R. L. (1983). *Fundamental motor patterns* (3rd ed.). Philadelphia: Lea and Febiger.

Williams, H. G. (1983). *Perceptual and motor development.* Englewood Cliffs, NJ: Prentice-Hall.

Information Processing and Perceptual Development

CASE STUDY

Fran has difficulty processing information and, as a consequence, often does not accurately understand what tasks she needs to perform. Mr. Croce, her teacher, has worked diligently with her by providing her with sensory feedback in "small chunks" and providing physical prompts along with his instructions. In this context, instead of describing the tennis swing he models the appropriate swing motion and physically moves her through the desired movement. He also pairs children together so that they can mimic their swing and practice in small groups. Although Fran still has difficulty performing the tennis swing, her skill level has improved significantly and she is far more proficient than she was initially. Mr. Croce makes sure that he works with all of his students at their ability levels and incorporates verbal feedback in his teaching methodology. In his feedback to students, Mr. Croce eliminates all but the most relevant information so as not to over load them with too much information at any one time.

Motor performance is based on the ability to receive and interpret sensory information prior to executing a movement task or sequence. This sensory information informs the brain of the body's position in space, positions of different body parts in relation to each other, environmental changes, and various movement parameters that will be needed to perform the skill correctly (e.g., force, speed, duration, and direction of the movement in question). Perception is the means by which we receive and interpret sensory information from the environment. The body is constantly bombarded with sensory information (tactile, kinesthetic, auditory, visual) that is gathered by sensory receptors and sent to higher brain areas for analysis and integration before movement execution (Schmidt & Lee, 2005).

When a child has difficulty learning or performing a new skill, often teachers erroneously look solely at the child's motor output. Rather than focus only on the motor output, teachers should take into account all aspects of information processing and perceptual development. In this context, when teaching a skill the teacher views motor performance as encompassing all aspects of sensory input, decision making, motor output, and feedback as points of emphasis (**Figure 7.1**). With this in mind, teachers should use the following steps to understand information processing and how children use perceptual skills in the learning process:

1. stimulus reception (input)

2. sensory integration and processing

3. motor output

4. feedback

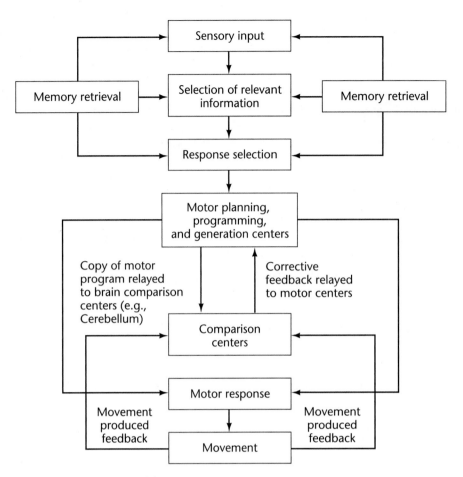

Figure 7.1 Information processing model.

Step 1—Stimulus Reception (Input) The first step focuses on the ability to gather relevant features of the task, such as the speed, direction, and trajectory of a Frisbee, while positioning the body for stability (kinesthetic) and moving the arms and hands to a position (kinesthetic) to catch (tactile) the object. For children, and especially for those children with cognitive and attention deficits, selecting pertinent information becomes difficult if they cannot detect the relevant features of the task or if they become distracted by irrelevant information. Children also have difficulty retaining sensory information. Williams (1983) indicated that children lose up to 60% of all sensory information within 1–5 seconds after being presented with the stimulus. For children with cognitive and attentional difficulties, this may result in the loss of 80–90% of the stimulus. More importantly, when a sensory stimulus is presented to a child with disability, the child may not be able to select pertinent task-related information and may retain even less in short-term memory (STM) before analysis. In this case inefficient or inadequate use of sensory input will directly impact the child's ability to make a decision when selecting the most appropriate motor output. Developmentally, it appears that STM ability improves markedly up to early adolescence, with

the largest changes taking place between 3 and 7 years of age. For some children, the ability to use STM will be effected by disability. For others, the rapid increase in STM during childhood has been attributed to increased speed in identifying stimuli and in search and recall strategies (Gabbard, 2008).

For example, some children frequently have problems receiving information from the environment because of concomitant sensory impairments. As a result, these children do not have sufficient information to adequately develop correct motor responses, such as initiating walking for children with visual impairments. It is important for teachers to understand that the movement responses are predicated on large quantities of sensory input from numerous sources located throughout the body. This information is then processed, and an appropriate response is selected, programmed, and executed. Each sensory system additionally provides the performer with constantly updated information regarding the quality of the movement (feedback). A loss of input from one sensory system can significantly affect a child's motor performance. To offset this loss or delay of input, teachers can assist these children by maximizing sensory input through those sensory systems which are functioning properly.

In contrast, some children will not cope well with vast amounts of sensory input. When working with these children, teachers should limit the amount of stimuli presented at one time. This allows the children to attend to smaller amounts of information, which they then can process and integrate more efficiently. Teachers must ensure that these "sensory defensive" children are not overwhelmed with sensory information.

Moreover, the inability to attend selectively to relevant information can have serious consequences on the performance of a skill, especially during the early stages of learning. This fact is compounded in children with developmental disorders or attention deficits because they have limitations in information processing. For these children, even selectively attending to small amounts of performance-generated information takes a considerable amount of their total information processing capacity and makes it very doubtful that additional information can be attended to and digested adequately.

Step 2—Sensory Integration and Processing The next step in the process involves the integration and analysis of sensory information. Processing mechanisms receive sensory stimuli, process and integrate the stimuli, and decide on the most appropriate plan of action. This decision mechanism is important because it can restrict the amount of information processed both before and during performance. Naturally, if more sensory information can be processed, the child can make a more appropriate decision concerning the desired motor output. For children with some prior experience with the task, the ability to use and process sensory information becomes more efficient as they become better able to use previously learned skills and experiences to execute the proper movement. They may also access long-term memory (LTM) to compare present and past experiences related to the task. As with STM, LTM also improves significantly during childhood, enabling children to recall and retrieve information as well as improving decision-making capabilities (Gabbard, 2008). In addition, the child is better able to adjust the motor output to the new situations or changes in the environment because of a greater repository of motor experiences from which to choose an appropriate motor response.

If the learner is able to gather and decipher incoming sensory information, a decision concerning the correct motor output can be selected and executed. If a child has problems deciphering incoming sensory information, then the amount of stimuli must be restricted. For example, if a child cannot track a pitched ball and has difficulty judging when to swing, to practice swinging at pitched balls may be unwise. In this case, the teacher may start with the ball on a tee to eliminate

the need to track the speed and direction of the ball and enable the child to concentrate on the swing mechanics and making contact. In essence, the teacher simplifies the task and allows the child to concentrate on a more limited amount of sensory information. As the child becomes more proficient at hitting the stationary ball and develops skill, the teacher can have the child swing at a tossed ball from a close distance, eventually adding a greater distance to the toss. The key here is manipulating the context in which the child must perform. Often, the context must be simplified so that the child can experience success. When the child masters the skill in this simplified context, then the teacher can incorporate increasingly greater complexity to the situation.

Children with cognitive and/or attention difficulties have particular problems with processing information and developing appropriate motor responses. Children may not have sufficient prior sensory and motor experiences, to attend to appropriate sensory cues, or be capable of recalling experiences from LTM to aid in the integration and analysis of new sensory information. The more we place these children in situations where they have to focus on and analyze appropriate sensory stimuli, the more proficient they will become in the process and, hence, better at choosing the most appropriate motor response for the environmental context in which they must respond.

Step 3—Motor Output Once all sensory information is processed and analyzed, the performer selects the most appropriate motor response given the particular environmental constraints. At this point, a certain motor response is desired, and a central processor (motor areas in the brain) is commanded to execute the movement. The brain triggers movement by way of messages to the body's muscles. Motor skills are acquired when an individual practices a new skill. Over time, this repetition creates new "motor memories," or engrams, which essentially produce automatization of the newly learned skill. The ability to learn new skills is based on the ability to perform more simple subskills (often referred to as subroutines).

Most children routinely progress through motor development milestones and learn the prerequisite subroutines needed to learn more complex skills. However, children with disabilities may not have the necessary prerequisite skills or motor patterns to learn and perform a new skill. Frequently, children with disabilities have delayed motor development and lack basic motor patterns that are essential to performing complex motor behaviors (see Chapter 6). In order for these children to learn more complex skills, they first must learn basic motor patterns and develop the appropriate level of physical functioning to execute the movement. For children with motor delays, learning begins at a much lower organizational level and needs to be emphasized to promote not only learning but also retention of the movement.

Step 4—Feedback   When the learner executes the movement, some feedback is available while the task is being performed via proprioceptive, tactile, kinesthetic, auditory, and visual information. Often, movement-produced feedback may not be processed appropriately by children with disabilities. However, feedback concerning the movement can also be represented after the movement is completed, when the child is better able to process the information. This type of feedback is called augmented feedback and usually takes the form of verbal or visual instructions after the task is completed. For example, if the child missed a target when throwing a ball, the teacher can use feedback to help the child readjust his or her body position and release so that on the next attempt the child will throw the ball more accurately. Because feedback provides information, motivation, and reinforcement to the learner, it is extremely important for promoting successful motor skill acquisition. In conjunction with providing ample opportunity to practice the skill, the teacher should offer feedback to enable the child to process the information concerning his or her performance.

As we relate teaching and learning to information processing, we see that if the amount of sensory information is inadequate or not retained, the child will have difficulty making a precise decision concerning the appropriate motor output. Likewise, if the decision-making capabilities or past experiences (LTM) are compromised, the child again is placed at a disadvantage in selecting the appropriate motor output. By determining where in the input–processing–output–feedback sequence the breakdown in skill development occurs, the teacher can devise the most appropriate motor remediation program. Then, the teacher can teach to the specific area of deficit or compensate by providing a more appropriate input modality that may be more efficient for the child. In either case, the ability to process information and the extent of perceptual development is essential for learning to occur. We cannot assume that the child is processing all the information that is being presented and using all of feedback appropriately. Teachers must be aware of the most efficient modality of learning and present information that the child can assimilate to properly execute the intended task.

Perception

As the central nervous system develops and the child comes to rely on sensory information, we see that the child develops an increasing reliance on perceptual information. The ability to integrate sensory information (process whereby the individual collects information) and perceptual information (process whereby the child associates meaning to this information) is integral for skilled motor behavior. According to Keogh and Sugden (1985), sensory information is paramount for children to understand how the body moves alone or in relation to the environment. As movers, we must have information regarding what our body can do and what it is doing during movement. This allows us to develop a body knowledge system and a means to select, plan, execute, evaluate, and modify our movements. Therefore, it is paramount that teachers (a) understand the preferred sensory modality the child uses to process sensory information and feedback and then (b) use that modality as the conduit for providing sensory input.

The primary sensory systems children use in learning situations include the visual, auditory, and tactile-kinesthetic systems. At birth, the perceptual systems are intact and functioning, although the infant is still relying on primitive reflexes for information, protection, and nourishment. As the child develops, there is a gradual change in the perceptual system as reflexes are inhibited and more information is obtained through sensory modalities to make decisions.

The first major change in sensory-perceptual processing involves a shift in reliance on information from the tactile-kinesthetic system to the visual system. The second major change involves a refinement or improvement in the discriminatory ability of each sensory system. This is often referred to as *intrasensory development*. This leads to an increase in the capacity of each sensory system to handle more information and to a refinement in the discriminatory abilities of each sensory system. This rapid increase in intrasensory development occurs from the ages of 3 to 6 years. As a result, the child is better able to process available sensory information and to control motor processes. The final major change centers around improved *intersensory processing and integration*; that is, the developing child is better able to integrate simultaneously information from multiple sensory systems. This process overlaps intrasensory develop, so that both intrasensory and intersensory development are often occurring simultaneously (Gabbard, 2008; Williams, 1983).

Visual-Perceptual Development

By the time a child reaches the age of 2, the ocular apparatus is fully mature (Gallahue & Ozmun, 2006). Although the ocular apparatus is physically mature, visual-perceptual abilities lag behind in development; while children may be able to fixate on objects and track them, refinements in visual-perception still need to occur. For example, a young child has extreme difficulty in intercepting a tossed ball with any appreciable degree of control, because the perception of moving objects, perception of distance, and anticipatory timing skills are not yet developed (Gallahue & Ozmun, 2006).

The relationship between movement and visual-perceptual development has been debated for many years. Many researchers adhere to the hypothesis that movement is integral for visual-perceptual development in children (Gallahue & Ozmun, 2006; Payne & Issacs, 2008). Further, without volitional movements, visual-perceptual adjustments to environmental changes will not occur, or at least will be delayed. Although this hypothesis is an intriguing one, research in this area is speculative at best. According to Gallahue and Ozmun (2006), movement is in all likelihood effective for promoting perceptual abilities in children; whether it is a necessary condition is doubtful. Although volitional movement may not be a necessary condition for developing visual-perceptual abilities, the level of a child's perceptual skills will affect a child's ability to learn and perform a motor skill (Gallahue & Ozmun, 2005).

Visual perception is often broken down into visual acuity, depth and movement perception, figure-ground perception, spatial orientation and perception of spatial relationships, and visual-motor coordination. *Visual acuity* is defined as the ability of the visual system to discern detail in objects and may be measured both statically and dynamically. Static visual acuity encompasses the ability to distinguish detail when both the individual and object are stationary. Dynamic visual acuity encompasses the ability to distinguish detail when the object is moving. Overall, dynamic visual acuity appears to develop somewhat later than does static visual acuity (Gallahue & Ozmun, 2006; Williams, 1983).

Depth perception is defined as the ability to judge how near or far away one or more objects are from a person. Depth perception also allows an individual to see three-dimensionally. *Movement perception* involves the ability to perceive that an object is moving. Together, depth perception and movement perception constitute two of the more important visual-perceptual abilities in children.

Our sense of depth perception is derived from many visual cues, such as the relative sizes of objects, the observed size of objects of known height, shadows and lighting, and movement parallax. *Parallax* refers to the geometrical phenomenon that the direction of a stationary object from an observer changes if the observer changes location and that the direction of an object changes less for a distant than for a near object. Also, as we all well know, objects closer to an observer that are in motion seem to move faster than distant objects (movement parallax).

Stereopsis (seeing in three dimensions) requires that the brain recognize that objects at various distances have images on the two retinas, which do not fall on exactly corresponding locations; that is, the image has disparity. For example, suppose that you are fixating (converging) on an object 1 meter away. Images of an object 2 meters away will lie somewhat nasally on both retinas; the images of an object 0.5 meters away will lie somewhat temporally. Thus, some retinal cells will be responding to near objects, some to far objects, and others to in-between distances—the neural basis for stereopsis. Finally, another visual cue for distance and depth is *optical expansion* (or retraction). This occurs whenever the distance between an individual (the perceiver) and another person or object changes. If an object's retinal size increases, say, by one-half when the object moves toward the individual, then the brain will perceive that the object is one-half the distance closer. Both optical expansion and retraction specify proportional changes from a starting point rather than distance in more absolute terms (Keogh & Sugden, 1985).

Figure-ground perception is the ability to extract relevant detail from contexts (object of visual regard) that contain irrelevant or distracting information (visual surroundings). Often, visually-oriented combinations containing a maximum amount of blending and distraction are the most disruptive when the individual attempts to distinguish a figure from its background. Moreover, according to Gallahue and Ozmun (2006), maturity in this ability also involves elements of attention. In conjunction with visual acuity, visual figure-ground perception enables a performer to clearly distinguish an object and to separate it from its surroundings. Clearly, such a skill is integral not only for performing physical skills, but also for obtaining vital feedback on performance.

Spatial orientation refers to the ability to recognize an object's arrangement in space. *Perception of spatial relationships* involves the relationship between the self and objects in the environment. Many motor tasks are performed in environments in which objects are oriented in specific ways or in environments whereby performance is defined by particular spatial dimensions. Together, spatial orientation and perception of spatial relationships allow us to move freely through our environment safely and proficiently. Very early in life, by about age 4, children can learn and distinguish between directional extremes (e.g., high–low, over–under, front–back, etc.), and can learn and distinguish vertical from horizontal positions; they still have problems with oblique or diagonal orientations. By age 8, most children can differentiate oblique and diagonal orientations but may still confuse left and right (Haywood & Getchell, 2009). Based on this information, teachers should be cognizant of how young children respond to directional orientations and how feedback given in these terms might be misconstrued.

Visual-motor coordination is often defined as the ability to integrate eyes and hands for object tracking, manipulation, and interception (Gallahue & Ozmun, 2006). According to Payne and Issacs (2008), as dynamic visual acuity improves so does the ability to track fast-moving objects. Williams (1983) has stated that accurate perception of movement matures at about 10 to 12 years of age. The ability to accurately intercept objects is often termed *object interception* or, more accurately, as *coincidence-anticipation timing*. This involves the ability to match the final location of a moving object with a specific motor response (e.g., catching or striking the object). This ability improves throughout childhood and, according to Gallahue and Ozmun (2006), it is difficult to establish a concrete developmental model for this behavior. Whatever the age when this skill becomes fully mature, the ability to perform a coincidence-anticipation timing skill is a cornerstone of performance in many sport-oriented skills. **Table 7.1** summarizes the basic visual-perceptual abilities and the approximate age

Table 7.1 Intrasensory Development in Young Children

Sensory Modality/Behavior	Age
VISUAL-PERCEPTUAL DEVELOPMENT	
Visual acuity (capacity to distinguish detail in objects in static and dynamic situations)	Improves rapidly between ages 5 and 7 and again between 9 and 10; static visual acuity matures prior to dynamic visual acuity (about age 10 and 11, respectively).
Depth perception (capacity to judge how near or far an object is from oneself)	Improves rapidly between ages 7 and 11; matures by age 12.
Movement perception (capacity to judge movement of an object)	Improves rapidly between ages 8 and 12; by age 9 can make accurate Judgments regarding moving objects; by age 12 can make quick and accurate judgments regarding moving objects.
Figure-ground perception (capacity to distinguish an object from its surroundings)	Improves rapidly between ages 4 and 6; matures between ages 8 and 12.
Spatial orientation/relationships	Spatial orientation improves rapidly between ages 5 and 7; by age 4 can learn directional extremes and vertical from horizontal positions; by age 8 may still confuse left and right directions. Success with Increasingly more difficult spatial relationships shows a progressive improvement throughout early childhood.
Visual-motor coordination (capacity to integrate eyes and hands for object tracking, manipulation, and interception)	Improves rapidly between ages 3 and 7; matures between ages 10 and 12. Object Interception improves significantly throughout childhood.
Processing of visual informatlon	Children process information more slowly than do adults; this ability improves rapidly between ages 6 and 10, maturing shortly thereafter.
AUDITORY-PERCEPTUAL DEVELOPMENT	
Auditory acuity (ability to discern presence or absence of sound)	By 6 months adult-like hearing; one does see improvement throughout childhood, but this may be attributed to improved attention.
Auditory discrimination (capacity to differentiate between two acoustic stimuli)	Improves from 3 to 5 years of age; continued refinement until approximately 13 years of age.
Sound localization (capacity to localize sounds emanating from different spatial locations)	Although the ability to localize sounds is present early in infancy, refinement in the ability to localize the general direction of sound well occurs at about age 3.
Auditory figure-ground (capacity to select relevant auditory stimuli from irrelevant ones)	Many children have difficulty selecting relevant sounds from irrelevant ones. Although an Important skill, little is known regarding age changes in ability.
TACTILE-KINESTHETIC DEVELOPMENT	
One-point touch localization (ability to discern one point of contact on the skin)	Appears to be well developed by age 5.
Multiple-point touch localization (ability to discern two or more points of contact on the skin)	Dramatic improvement between ages 4 and 6, maturing shortly thereafter.
Tactile-kinesthetic recognition (haptic memory-recognition of objects through manipulation)	Haptic memory for forms improves rapidly between ages 6 and 8, with the most dramatic changes occurring between 4 and 5.
Spatial Orientation (knowledge of body in space)	Rapid improvement between ages 6 and 8.

equivalences for developing these abilities (Gallahue & Ozmun, 2006; Williams, 1983).

Auditory-Perceptual Development

Although not quite as important as visual-perceptual and tactile-kinesthetic development, auditory-perceptual development is nonetheless exceedingly important for skilled motor behavior in children. In addition to the act of hearing, children must learn to judge the particular characteristics of the sounds heard. Auditory perception is often broken down into auditory acuity, sound localization, and auditory figure-ground (see **Table 7.1**). *Auditory acuity* is defined as the ability of the auditory system to discern the presence or absence of sound. Auditory acuity improves progressively throughout childhood and even into adolescence, although improvements in late childhood and adolescence may be attributed to improved attention level and the ability to follow directions on auditory tests more closely (Haywood & Getchell, 2005).

Sound localization refers to the ability to recognize the direction from which a sound emanates. Sound localization is important for the child's overall motor development insofar as it allows the child to visually link sounds with their sources and helps the child to establish associations between specific sounds and objects and events within the environment (Williams, 1983). The ability to localize sounds is enhanced by the child's ability to select relevant sounds from irrelevant ones (*auditory figure-ground*). Children continue to improve in sound localization and by age 3 can localize the general direction of distant sounds. Little is known regarding developmental changes in auditory figure-ground in children (Haywood & Getchell, 2009).

Tactile-Kinesthetic Perceptual Development

Tactile-kinesthetic perception can be considered a combination of the following "subsystems" or "sub-senses": (1) cutaneous or touch, which provides information regarding stimulation of the skin and/or deeper tissues; (2) kinesthetic, which provides information regarding joint movement and position and muscle stretch and tension (touch and kinesthetic receptors are often collectively termed proprioceptors); and (3) vestibular, which provides information about linear and angular acceleration and deceleration and/or position of the head relative to the body. Some authors also include the haptic subsystem, which is a unique combination of information from touch and kinesthetic subsystems and from dynamic touch, which integrates information from muscular, kinesthetic, and touch subsystems (Gibson, 1996). Other authors, such as Warren, Yezierski, and Capra (1997a, 1997b), separate the touch-tactile system into the sub-

modalities of discriminative touch, vibratory touch, proprioception (position sense), crude nondiscriminitive touch, thermal (hot and cold) sensations, and nociception (pain). Regardless of the number of subsystems used to describe tactile-kinesthetic perception, this system as a whole is important for supplying information about the external environment, such as shape, size, angle, and texture of objects, and about the relative position of the body in space (Williams, 1983).

It is apparent that the tactile-kinesthetic system is not a single sensory system, as are the visual and auditory systems. The tactile-kinesthetic system is made up of quite a number of different sensory receptors that collectively provide vital information about the external environment (exteroceptive sensations) impinging on the body (tactile-touch) and the internal environment (proprioceptive sensations), as well as about the body's position in space (vestibular receptors and proprioceptors). Also, unlike the visual and auditory systems, receptors from this sensory system are found throughout the body, rather than in a more clearly defined area (i.e., eyes for seeing and ears for hearing).

The primary exteroceptors found in the cutaneous and subcutaneous tissues can be broken down into three major groups: mechanoreceptors (touch and pressure receptors), nociceptors (pain receptors), and thermoceptors (hot and cold detectors). Only mechanoreceptors will be discussed here, because these receptors have the most to do with movement and sensory feedback during movement.

Mechanoreceptors are specialized cells that provide information to the central nervous system (CNS) regarding touch, pressure, vibration, and skin tension. They include the following receptors (**Table 7.2**): Meissner's corpuscles, Pacini's corpuscles, Ruffini's corpuscles, Merkel's disks, and hair follicle receptors. Each of these receptors respond to different types of mechanical stimuli and have both varying threshold levels for activation (either high or low levels of sensitive to stimulation) and varying rates of adaptation to stimuli (i.e., rapidly adapting, so that they respond maximally but their response levels decrease if the stimulus is maintained; or slowly adapting, so that they keep transmitting information for as long as the stimulus is applied). Also, these receptors tend to be found in different places within the skin and deeper tissues (**Figure 7.2**).

Whereas cutaneous mechanoreceptors provide detailed information about external stimuli impinging on the body proper, there is another major class of receptors providing information about mechanical forces arising from within the body. These are called proprioceptors (meaning "receptors for self"). The primary purpose of proprioceptors is to provide continuous information about position of the limbs in space and forms the basis of our kinesthetic

Table 7.2   Tactile, Kinesthetic, and Vestibular Receptors and Their Stimuli and Locations

Receptor(s)/Location	Stimulus
MECHANORECEPTORS IN SKIN AND DEEPER TISSUES	
Meissner's corpuscles	Detect low-frequency vibration, touch, and pressure on skin
Hair follicle receptors	Motion detection and direction
Pacini's corpuscles	Detect high-frequency vibration and deep pressure
Merkel's disks	Skin displacement—localize touch and pressure over skin
Ruffini's corpuscles (endings)	Skin displacement and stretching
PROPRIOCEPTORS IN MUSCLE, TENDON, AND JOINTS	
Muscle spindles	Detect length (stretch) and rate of change of stretch of muscle tissue
Golgi tendon organs	Detect tension at musculotendinous junction; protect from overstretching or excessive tension
Joint receptors (Ruffini endings, modified Pacini corpuscles, and Golgi-type receptors)	Joint movement and pressure; detect limb position
VESTIBULAR RECEPTORS	
Hair cells in semicircular canals in membranous labyrinth inner ear	Detect angular acceleration motions of the head
Hair cells in saccule and utricle in membranous labyrinth	Detect gravitational forces and linear acceleration motions of the head

awareness. Kinesthesis is defined as a person's awareness, without the use of vision, of positions and movements of the body and its parts and the person's ability to identify the agent (itself or externally generated) causing the movement. Another type of proprioceptive feedback that is important for motor control is vestibular input. Although vestibular input is considered a proprioceptive source of information and is paramount for controlled movement, information from the vestibular system is not consciously perceived. In total, development of

kinesthesis is crucial to movement skill production and feedback analysis.

There are numerous proprioceptive receptors located in the muscles, joints, and tendons, which when taken together contribute to our sense of kinesthesis. These proprioceptors are involved with coding the parameters of joint movement and position—direction, rate, and duration—and providing information about muscle length (how much and how fast it changes) and tension (Keogh & Sugden, 1985). Although researchers cannot document the developmental progress of these

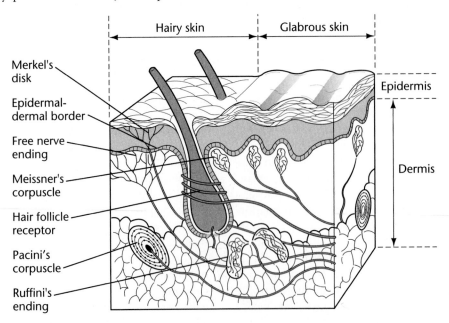

Figure 7.2 Sensory receptors in the skin.

Source: Reprinted by permission from M. F. Bear, B. W. Connors, and M. A. Paradiso, in *Neuroscience: Exploring the brain* by T. S. Satterfiled (Ed.). Copyright © 1996 Lippincott, Williams and Wilkins, Balitmore.

proprioceptors precisely, their importance in providing information about muscle, joint, and tendon position is crucial for an individual's ability to move and process feedback.

Muscle spindles (**Figure 7.3**) are one type of proprioceptor and are located parallel to the skeletal muscle fibers (cells). The muscle spindle is a morphologically extremely complex sensory receptor and is made up of a number of small muscle fibers enclosed in a connective tissue capsule. These smaller muscle fibers are referred to as intrafusal fibers (within capsule); those muscle fibers outside the muscle spindle are called extrafusal fibers (outside capsule). Sensory axons innervate muscle spindles by encircling the intrafusal fibers (often termed *spindle afferents*). Also, these intrafusal fibers are innervated by a special class of motor neurons called gamma motor neurons (alpha motor neurons are the class of motor neurons that innervate the actual muscle fibers). The function of these gamma motor neurons is to reset the spindle once it has been stretched. They do not function directly in overall muscle contraction (Enoka, 2008).

Because muscle spindles are parallel to the extrafusal fibers (muscle fibers), stretching of the muscle causes a stretch on the intrafusal fibers of the muscle spindle. This action displaces the spindle afferents, producing spindle afferent discharge. This discharge is coded in such a way that the CNS is informed of how much and how quickly the muscle is being stretched. Contraction of the muscle produces the opposite effect: the spindles are silent, and there is no spindle afferent discharge. The muscle spindle is reset by the gamma motor neurons, whereupon the muscle spindle is ready once again to detect stretch in the muscle tissue.

How is information from the muscle spindle used during movement? At the lowest levels, information is involved in the reflexive activation of muscles (stretch reflex). As information ascends the central nervous system, it provides important feedback to the brain regarding muscle position and contributes to our perception of body position in space. Moreover, the muscle spindles are extremely important in maintaining the body in an upright posture.

The muscle spindle is the cornerstone of a very important physiological reflex called the myotatic reflex (**Figure 7.4**). This reflex is also referred to as the deep tendon reflex (DTR) or stretch reflex. This reflex involves the contraction of a muscle when it is rapidly stretched and relaxation of its antagonist muscles. To elicit this reflex, the muscle spindle is activated by either quickly stretching the muscle or by briskly tapping either the muscle directly or its tendon with a reflex hammer (e.g., knee-jerk reflex). Clinically one may observe a hyperactive stretch reflex in individuals with various types of brain damage (e.g., cerebral

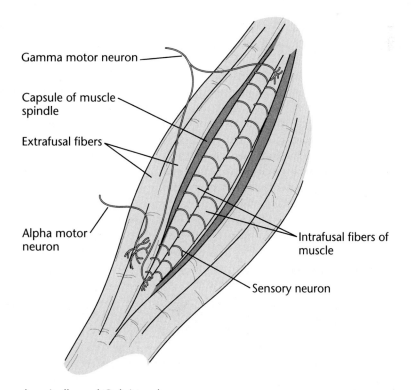

Gamma motor neuron

Capsule of muscle spindle

Extrafusal fibers

Alpha motor neuron

Intrafusal fibers of muscle

Sensory neuron

Figure 7.3 Anatomy of the muscle spindle and Golgi tendon organ.

Source: J. H. Wilmore and D. L. Costill, *Physiology of sport and exercise*, 2nd ed., Human Kinetics, Champaign, Il, 1999.

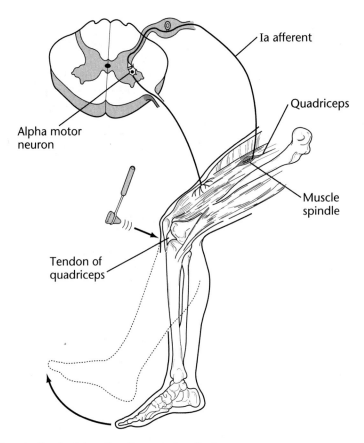

Figure 7.4 The muscle spindle stretch reflex (knee-jerk reflex).

Source: Reprinted by permission from M. F. Bear, B. W. Connors, and M. A. Paradiso, in *Neuroscience: Exploring the brain* by T. S. Satterfiled (Ed.). Copyright ©1996 Lippincott, Williams and Wilkins, Balitmore.

palsy, stroke, or head trauma). This is often referred to as hyperactive or increased muscle tone and is manifested by an increased resistance to passive stretch. It is especially pronounced in the antigravity muscles, that is, flexors of the arm and fingers, and extensors of the leg.

A second type of proprioceptor is the *Golgi tendon organ (GTO)* (**Figure 7.3**). Unlike the muscle spindle, the GTO is a relatively simple sensory receptor made up of a single afferent (sensory) connection and no efferent (motor) connections. The GTO is arranged in series with the muscle and tendon. Whether a muscle is stretched or contracted, tension is developed within the tissue, and forces are applied to the GTO. Hence, the GTO acts as a tension detector. This is in contrast to the aforementioned parallel-arranged muscle spindle, which detects length and rate of length change of the muscle (Enoka, 2008).

The GTOs function in the following way. The GTO is sensitive to tension changes resulting from either stretch or contraction of the muscle. This elicits a reflex called the GTO or inverse myotatic reflex, whose primary function is to protect the muscle tendon from injury that would result from too much tension. The GTO reflex is an inhibitory reflex, inhibiting its own

muscle (that is, inhibiting the muscle having the tension) and exciting antagonists.

Teachers may witness an abnormal reaction of the GTO reflex in children who have overly tight or spastic muscles. A characteristic of the increased resistance seen in spastic muscles is the clasp-knife reflex. This response reflects a sudden collapse of all resistance when a spastic muscle is aggressively stretched. The clasp-knife response is due to increased GTO activity, resulting from increased tension levels within the muscle stretched. Motor neurons responsible for the hypertonicity are quickly inhibited, thereby reducing the dangerously high tension levels within the muscle. As a result of this reflex, the muscle relaxes extremely fast, often resembling the quick opening of a pocket knife: hence, the term *clasp-knife reflex* (**Figure 7.5**). Together, the muscle spindles and GTOs reciprocally control force (GTO) and unit length (muscle spindle) of the muscle.

In conjunction with the muscle spindle and GTO, joint receptors provide information about limb position in space. However, in contrast to the muscle spindle and GTO, joint receptors are not a single, well-defined entity. More readily what one finds are various types of receptors (e.g., Golgi-type endings, pacinian corpuscles,

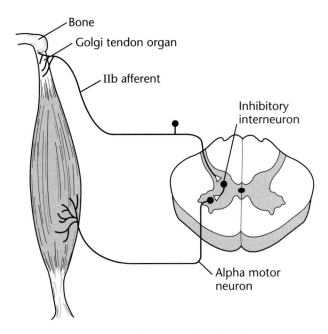

Figure 7.5 Circuitry of the clasp-knife reflex.

Source: Reprinted by permission from M. F. Bear, B. W. Connors, M. A. Paradiso, and M. A. Paradiso, in *Neuroscience: Exploring the brain* by T. S. Satterfield (Ed.). Copyright © 1996 Lippincott Williams and Wilkins, Baltimore.

and Ruffini's endings), in various locations surrounding and within the joint proper (e.g., joint capsule, ligaments, and loose connective tissue). These joint receptors provide the CNS with information about joint velocity, acceleration, displacement, and position of limbs during movement (Enoka, 2008).

Finally, the vestibular system (**Figure 7.6**) is involved in kinesthesis by detecting acceleration movements of the head and using this information to orient the head and eyes during movement and to control posture. Receptor cells found within the inner ear detect linear and angular acceleration movements of the head and through an intricate and complex network influence eye and body movements. The primary receptors for the vestibular system are tiny hair cells that are found within the semicircular canals (detecting angular acceleration of the head), and the saccule and utricle (detecting linear acceleration of the head). In total, vestibular receptors are sensitive to (1) head position in space (i.e., whether the head is upright, upside down, or in some other position) and (2) sudden changes in direction of the body.

Tactile-kinesthetic perceptual development is often broken down into the following functional abilities: one-point touch localization, or discrimination, multiple-point touch localization, tactile-kinesthetic recognition, and spatial orientation (**Table 7.1**). *One-point touch localization or discrimination* involves the ability to discern whether a single stimulus is in contact with the body independent of vision. Based on limited research, perception of a single point of the hands and arms appears to be mature by age 5 (Haywood & Getchell, 2009). In *multiple-point touch localization* testing, the minimal interstimulus distance required to perceive two simultaneously applied skin indentations as distinct is measured. The accuracy with which more than one stimulus can be sensed on the body varies from region to region of the body, such that in the fingertips stimuli can be perceived if they are only 2 mm apart. In contrast, stimuli applied to the forearm are not perceived as distinct until they are minimally 40 mm apart (Warren et al., 1997b). Based on limited data, it appears that this ability is developed by age 7.

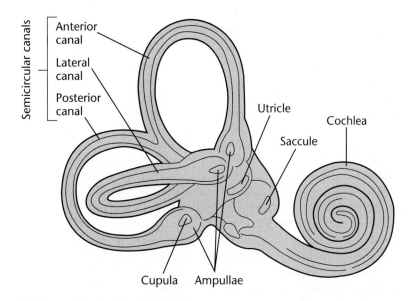

Figure 7.6 Anatomy of the vestibular apparatus in the inner ear.

Tactile-kinesthetic recognition has to do with the ability to recognize objects and their characteristics by tactile-kinesthetic manipulation alone (Williams, 1983). Finally, *spatial orientation* is a more global or all-inclusive tactile-kinesthetic ability that deals with perception of the body's location and orientation in space independent of vision. Usually, this ability is tested by having the child walk a straight line while blindfolded and measuring the deviation from the straight path (Haywood & Getchell, 2009). One sees significant improvement in the skill between the ages of 6 and 8.

Intrasensory and Intersensory Development

With a general understanding of the major sensory-perceptual systems, we now can investigate what is meant by intersensory and intrasensory integration. *Intrasensory* integration refers to the ability to integrate sensory information within one sensory system, whereas *intersensory* integration refers to the ability to integrate or use multiple sources of information simultaneously to solve problems and/or to adapt to the environment. Intersensory integration involves the transfer of ideas or concepts across different modalities (Williams, 1983).

Intersensory integration has been further distinguished between cross-modal (or intermodal) equivalence (CME) and cross-modal concepts (CMC) (Blank & Bridger, 1974; Sugden & Keogh, 1990). Cross-modal equivalence involves recognizing a particular set of stimulus features as the same or equivalent when they appear in two different sensory modalities. Cross-modal concepts encompass the ability to utilize a concept or principle to solve problems that are associated with distinct yet equivalent information presented through more than one sensory modality (Williams, 1983). As one can see, intersensory integration is a much more complex phenomenon involving widespread areas within the CNS where sensory information from multiple sensory modalities converge (e.g., multimodal areas in frontal, parietal, and temporal lobes). Intersensory development and function thus represent an advanced form of brain development and processing.

The ability to function in a multiple sensory mode is believed to involve the gradual integration of all available stimuli by the child into a more complex sensory picture of the environment. Therefore, the ability to integrate several sources of information simultaneously into one map or picture is not something that is performed discretely at visual, auditory, and tactile-kinesthetic levels, but rather is performed intermodally and multidimensionally (Williams, 1983). According to Williams, there are three levels of intersensory functioning: (1) a low, more automatic level of integration, which is prewired into the nervous system and which appears to be present at birth; (2) a higher level of integration, which involves analyzing perceptual features and which occurs at a more conscious, thinking level; and (3) a cognitive-conceptual level of integration, which involves transferring ideas and concepts across different sensory modalities. As children move up through these levels of intersensory development, they become more efficient at using multiple sources of sensory information. This allows for much more adaptive behaviors and a higher level of neural functioning.

It is important to note that refinement of both intrasensory and intersensory functions occurs simultaneously and that at any given age of development, certain intrasensory abilities may be more advanced than selected intersensory functions. Further, a disruption in the organization and interaction of multiple sensory systems can lead to developmental delays that may have serious deleterious effects on motor functioning. For example, Williams, Temple, and Bateman (1978) found that children (approximately 6 years old and younger) with advanced intersensory integration ability were superior in learning performance than children with less advanced intersensory development. According to these authors, it appears that at younger ages, the level of intersensory integration directly affects a child's ability to perform a gross perceptual-motor task involving the sequencing of a series of simple motor tasks into one, smooth movement chain of greater complexity. As the child increases in age, the ability to use multiple sensory cues appears to have little effect on learning and mastery of such motor skills. **Table 7.3** summarizes intersensory abilities and the approximate age equivalences for developing these abilities (Williams, 1983).

When a child embarks on learning a new physical skill or changes the way he or she is already performing a skill, intimate cooperation between body and brain is required. No one knows for sure just how and where memories are stored in the brain, but scientists are learning more about the subject every day. Neuroscientists have found that the frontal lobe—the conscious, verbal, problem-solving, hard-thinking area of the brain—is most active when you learn a skill. This makes intuitive sense, because during skill practice the performer is thinking about the information the teacher is imparting as well as analyzing the feedback being generated by the movement. The performer is analyzing instructions and thinking about where various body parts need to be during every part of the movement.

Also, the brain stays active for several hours after a practice session has ended, actively processing

Table 7.3   Timeline for Intersensory Development in Young Children

Sensory Modalities/Behaviors
VISUAL-AUDITORY INTEGRATION
Children 5 years and younger have problems performing auditory-visual integration tasks.
Rapid development in performing auditory-visual integration occurs between ages 5 and 7,
with 6- and 7-year-olds significantly better than 5-year-olds.
Eight-year-olds perform at a similar level on auditory-visual, visual-auditory, visual-visual, and auditory-auditory tasks.
Rapid improvement in auditory-visual integration between ages 8 and 10.
Auditory-visual integration improves until approximately age 12.
Intersensory integration of auditory and visual information is more efficient when task is presented visually first.
VISUAL-TACTILE/KINESTHETIC INTEGRATION
Three-year-olds perform poorly in tasks involving visual-tactile/kinesthetic integration.
Visual-tactile/kinesthetic integration abilities involving shape recognition are almost mature by age 5.
Significant refinement of visual-tactile/kinesthetic integration abilities occur between ages 5 and 7, plateauing thereafter.
A second period of improvement in visual-tactile/kinesthetic integration abilities occurs between ages 9 and 11; integration is more effective when presented visually first, which appears not to be the case in younger children.
AUDITORY-TACTILE/KINESTHETIC INTEGRATION
Although not supported by some researchers, it appears that the child's awareness of tactile stimulation is more accurate when accompanied by auditory stimulation.
Auditory-tactile/kinesthetic integration abilities show improvement throughout childhood. Also, there appears to be a more natural connection between these two modalities compared to visual-tactile/kinesthetic integration abilities.
Overall, intersensory integration is extremely important in developing skilled motor behavior. It appears that this is particularly so in the early development of both gross and fine motor skills.

all of this new information and building what is often called an "internal model" of the skill. As the skill is progressively learned, activity shifts to deeper parts of the brain—to areas that handle automatic, nonconscious activity. This shift in processing allows the skill to be recalled and "run" quickly, without much thinking. A novice might have to consciously think through over a dozen distinct steps to get a skill right. For the expert, the skill is automatic, with little thinking required. The degree of practice required to automate a particular skill can range well into the hundreds of thousands of repetitions (Kottke, 1980). Often individuals with cognitive and/or attention deficits have problems developing this internal model and have problems developing appropriate strategies that facilitate skill acquisition and retention.

Without a doubt, teaching children with developmental and other disabilities is hard work. Adapted physical educators are often teaching new, novel tasks in a relatively short time period to a moderately large group of students. So, how can adapted physical educators maximize skill acquisition in children with delays in postural control, information processing, and perceptual-motor development? The answer lies in a basic understanding of motor learning principles and their application to the pediatric population with disabilities.

Although issues of motor control and learning might be somewhat different in the pediatric population with disabilities compared to the pediatric population without disabilities, many of the basic tenants are similar to those found with the general population (Croce, Horvat, & Roswal, 1996). Because many of the skills we want children with disabilities to perform require a combination of information processing and motor control abilities, applying basic motor learning principles to the teaching of these children is essential.

As a general rule, teachers should teach both specific tasks and the underlying movement patterns and strategies. Focusing on teaching broad-based movement patterns that can be generalized to other situations will improve learning, whereas teaching solely specific tasks will enhance performance of that specific task but not generalize to a broader spectrum of skills. Teachers can promote skill by making learning meaningful and exciting and by motivating students by teaching the most relevant tasks and establishing realistic goals.

Another key teaching concept is modeling. Modeling is the process of replicating a task that has been demonstrated by another person. By accurately demonstrating a skill, the child learns by replicating this model through visual and information processing and putting that model into action. It appears that modeling allows children to recognize errors earlier in the learning process and helps reduce anxiety in the learner when faced with a novel task. Observational practice also provides the child with an image of the goal movement. This is especially effective for the learning of complex skills where it can provide a "picture" of how the various components of the task fit together (Schmidt & Lee, 2005).

Feedback might be the most important variable in skill acquisition. Feedback can be given verbally, nonverbally, and visually; and when accurately applied, feedback enhances practice and allows the child to self-correct. While it is often assumed that feedback given concurrently with the movement is effective, this is generally not the case. In reality, concurrent feedback is less effective to learning compared to feedback provided after the movement, especially when delayed for a few seconds. This effect has been attributed to learners' spontaneously evaluating the movement based on the processing of their own intrinsic feedback before the augmented (instructor supplied) feedback is presented. The effect of diminished feedback frequency and timing on skill acquisition has been interpreted in terms of the "guidance hypothesis" (Schmidt & Lee, 2005).

According to the guidance hypothesis, when feedback is provided too often learners tend to become dependent on it and they minimally process their own intrinsic feedback. This effect is particularly pronounced when feedback is provided concurrently with the movement or immediately afterwards. As a consequence, learners fail to develop their own internal error-detection-and-correction mechanisms, which would allow them to perform effectively when the augmented feedback is withdrawn. It should be mentioned, however, that the effects of feedback frequency depend to some extent on skill complexity (Wulf & Shea, 2004). Simple skills benefit from reducing feedback, whereas more frequent feedback might be required for learning more complex skills or when teaching young children (Sullivan et al., 2008). Nonetheless, effective teaching strategies ought to use both reduced and delayed feedback. Using feedback sparingly and providing it only after the learner has had a chance to process his or her own intrinsic feedback results in more effective learning.

We've all heard the saying "practice makes perfect," and to retain what we have learned, we need practice! However, conditions under which one practices has a profound impact on learning. If a skill is practiced incorrectly, then one will end up learning that skill perfectly incorrectly. Also, if practice is not efficient and does not incorporate the most appropriate perceptual information, then the contextually related aspects of skill retention will suffer significantly. Surprisingly, individuals learn better if practice is mixed up a bit rather than being very similar. This is called blocked practice vs. random practice. With blocked practice, one initially sees enhanced performance (not learning), but

long-term retention and learning is best achieved when skills are practiced randomly. Moreover, in some instances individuals tend to do well initially with blocked practice and then better with random practice as skill improves.

For example, we can address practicing shooting a basketball in a set of short-distance shots, then in a set of medium-distance shots, and finally in a set of long-distance shots (blocked practice). Or, we can practice in sets that combine all three distances (or more) or even practice layups with distance shooting (random practice). As a primary teaching rule randomization improves learning, especially when we randomize tasks with similar movement patterns (Schmidt & Lee, 2005).

Several hypotheses have been put forward to explain the learning effects of random versus blocked practice (often referred to as the contextual interference effect). The most prominent one is the elaboration hypothesis (another one is the reconstruction hypothesis). According to this view, random practice promotes the use of multiple and variable information-processing strategies. This, in turn, leads to more distinctive and elaborate memory representations, with the different tasks learned residing together in short-term memory where they can be compared (which is not possible under blocked conditions). Also, the use of different encoding strategies presumably leads to a more elaborate memory representation than the impoverished encoding under blocked conditions, which is assumed to be the reason for the learning advantages (Schmidt & Lee, 2005). Overall, teachers of children with information processing problems or perceptual-motor delays may find that applying practice schedules that alternate between blocked units (in some cases more appropriate initially) and random practice works best.

Lastly, another technique used by teachers and therapists is to have children practice components of the skill before attempting to practice the entire skill (i.e., part-whole transfer). This is often seen when adapted physical educators or therapists first work on postural control mechanisms used in a particular task and then progress to working on other components of the skill. This type of skill training is debatable, however. One problem associated with this type of learning is that practicing parts of a skill in isolation rather than learning the whole skill may change the motor programming of the individual skill part rather than the whole skill (Schmidt & Lee, 2005). Therefore, practicing only a part of a skill (say part of a spiking motion in volleyball), and then asking the child to somehow process that into the entire motion of the skill within the context of what actually occurs during game situations is extremely difficult and contrary to the way in which learning actually occurs.

Accepting the fact that cognition, information processing, and developmental level all play a critical role in acquiring motor skills, the adapted physical educator must determine the best way to teach motor skills to children who have deficiencies in these areas. Teachers should provide children with appropriate perceptual information regarding their performance, use the most efficient modality to provide appropriate feedback, and organize the learning environment to maximize skill retention and transfer (Horvat, Croce, & Zagrodnik, in press).

CHAPTER SUMMARY

1. At birth the perceptual systems are intact and functioning although the infant still relies on primitive reflexes.

2. The first major change in sensory-perceptual processing involves a shift in reliance on the tactile-kinesthetic system to reliance on the visual system for modifying motor behavior.

3. Visual acuity is the ability to discern detail in objects, statically and dynamically; depth perception is the ability to judge how far away or near objects are from a person; and movement perception is the ability to perceive an object while moving.

4. Stereopsis, or three-dimensional vision, requires the brain to recognize objects at various distances.

5. Figure-ground perception is the ability to extract relevant detail from contexts.

6. Spatial orientation refers to the ability to recognize an object's orientation or arrangement.

7. Visual-motor coordination is the ability to integrate the eyes and hands.

8. Auditory acuity is the ability of the auditory system to discern sound; sound localization is the ability to recognize the direction of the sound.

9. The tactile-kinesthetic system is not a single sensory system, as are the visual and auditory systems. This system is made up of sensory receptors that provide information from the environment (exteroceptive sensations), sensations impending on the body (tactile) and the internal environment (proprioceptive), and position in space (vestibular and proprioceptors).

REFERENCES

Blank, M., & Bridger, W. (1974). Cross modal transfer in nursery school children. *Journal of Experimental Psychology, 58,* 277–282.

Croce, R., Horvat, M., & Roswal, G. (1996). Augmented feedback for enhanced skill acquisition in individuals with traumatic brain injury. *Perceptual and Motor Skills, 82,* 507–514.

Enoka, R. M. (2008). *Neuromechanics of Human Movement,* (5th ed.). Champaign, IL: Human Kinetics.

Gabbard, C. P. (2008). *Lifelong motor development* (5th ed.). San Francisco, CA: Pearson / Benjamin Cummings.

Gallahue, D. L., & Ozmun, J. C. (2006). *Understanding motor development: Infants, children, adolescents, adults* (6th ed.). Dubuque, IA: McGraw-Hill.

Gibson, J. (1996). *The senses considered as perceptual systems.* New York: Houghton Mifflin.

Haywood, K. M., & Getchell, M. (2009). *Life span motor development* (5th ed.). Champaign, IL: Human Kinetics.

Horvat, M., Croce, R., & Zagrodnik, M. (in press). Utilization of sensory information in intellectual disabilities. *Journal of Developmental and Physical Disabilities.*

Keogh, J., & Sugden, D. (1985). *Movement skill development.* New York: MacMillan.

Kottke, F. J. (1980). From reflex to skill: The training of coordination. *Archives of Physical Medicine and Rehabilitation, 59,* 551–561.

Payne, V. G., & Issacs, L.D. (2008). *Human motor development: A life span approach* (7th ed.). Mountain View, CA: Mayfield.

Rock, I. (1975). *An introduction to perception.* New York: Macmillan.

Schmidt, R. A., & Lee, T. D. (2005). *Motor control and learning: A behavioral emphasis* (4th ed.). Champaign, IL: Human Kinetics.

Sugden, D., & Keogh, J. (1990). *Problems in movement skill development* (Growth, motor development, and physical activity across the lifespan). South Carolina: University of South Carolina Press.

Sullivan, K. J., Kantak, S. S., & Burtner, P. A. (2006). Motor learning in children: Feedback effects on skill acquisition. *Physical Therapy, 89*(6), 720–732.

Warren, S., Yezierski, R. P., & Capra, N. F. (1977a). The somatosensory system I: Discriminative touch and position. In D. E. Haines (Ed.), *Fundamental neuroscience* (pp. 219–235). New York: Churchill Livingstone.

Warren, S., Yezierski, R. P., & Capra, N. F. (1977b). The somatosensory system II: Nondiscriminative touch, temperature and nociception. In D. E. Haines (Ed.),

Fundamental neuroscience (pp. 237–253). New York: Churchill Livingstone.

Williams, H. G. (1983). *Perceptual and motor development.* Englewood Cliffs, NJ: Prentice-Hall.

Williams, H., Temple, I., & Bateman, J. (1978). Perceptual-motor and cognitive learning in young children. In *Psychology of motor behavior and sport.* Champaign, IL: Human Kinetics.

Wulf, G., & Shea, C. H. (2004). *Understanding the role of augmented feedback: The good, the bad, and the ugly.* In A. M. Williams & N. J. Hodges (Eds.). *Skill acquisition in sport, research, theory, and practice* (pp. 121–144). London: Routledge

Physical Fitness Development

CASE STUDY

Bill is a middle school student who had a liver transplant when he was in elementary school. His teacher, Mr. Kalakian, has noticed that, although Bill is healthy, his fitness is developmentally 2–3 years behind his age group. In addition, Bill is not as strong or flexible as his classmates and seems to fatigue easily. Mr. Kalakian has consulted with Bill's physician and based on his input has designed a program of strengthening exercises; which includes strengthening Bill's core and upper and lower limbs through a well-designed circuit-training program. Bill seems eager to participate but is unsure of his capabilities and is timid in many responses. Mr. Kalakian constantly praises Bill's efforts and encourages Bill to record his progress as he becomes more comfortable with his ability to exert himself safely in physical activity.

There are many definitions for the term *physical fitness*, which reflects its multidimensional and hierarchical nature. Physical fitness is defined by most professionals as a set of attributes, which either people have or acquire, relating to their ability to perform physical activity. Additionally, one may view physical fitness as a state of well-being, characterized by a low risk of premature development of hypokinetic disease (conditions related to inactivity, such as obesity and cardiovascular disease) and by having the energy to participate in a variety of activities (Physical Fitness and Sports Research Digest, 2000). Because of the multifaceted nature of physical fitness, professionals often view fitness as being made up of several subcomponents; most often including the health-related and skill-related components of fitness.

Health-related fitness consists of those components of physical fitness that are most directly related to good health and well being. The health-related components are commonly defined as cardiovascular fitness, body composition, flexibility, and muscular strength and endurance. Skill-related fitness is comprised of the components of physical fitness most directly related to enhanced performance in sports and motor skills. The skill-related components are commonly defined as power, speed, agility, balance, coordination, and reaction time. Because this text is concerned more with the ameliorative effects of exercise to counteract the detrimental effects of inactivity and to optimize the child's functional capacity within the physiological limitations of his or her disability, we will be concerned chiefly with the components of health-related fitness.

Much of our survival depends on the development of physical fitness. Independent movement implies ability, to the extent possible, to initiate movement independently to fulfill life's most basic and not-so-basic needs. Persons who, for whatever reason, cannot move to meet requirements (and beyond) of daily living must rely on others for mobility and are rendered relatively dependent on them for survival.

Physical fitness is essential for independence of movement and for maintaining or developing functional skills. Fitness development is also important for play, sports participation, and job-related skills that rely on high levels of physical development (Seaman, 1999). Not all individuals may achieve total independence of movement, but everyone should be afforded the full opportunity to achieve independence in accordance with his or her potential. Likewise, individuals with disabilities and those without disabilities can gain similar benefits from physical activity programs.

Physical fitness development takes on even greater importance in today's society. Childhood obesity levels are rising with estimates suggesting that one in three children in Western countries are overweight. People from lower socio-economic status and ethnic minority backgrounds are at higher risk of obesity and subsequent cardiovascular disorders and diabetes, as are individuals with disabilities. The nationwide epidemic of obesity may be due, in part, to declining levels of physical activity, raising the possibility that other components of health-related physical fitness may also be in rapid decline (Rees et al., 2009). Thus, fitness development should be one of the priorities of any adapted physical education program.

Fitness Is Fitness, Regardless of Ability or Disability

We believe it difficult to overstate the case that fitness for persons with disabilities is, first and foremost, simply fitness. From this perspective, there is a need to demystify some of the folklore about providing physical education opportunities for persons with disabilities. When one looks at each specific fitness component under the comprehensive fitness umbrella, the label "disability" by itself, does not redefine fitness. All people, as individuals, have individual fitness needs. Some people have labels, and some labels are disability labels (e.g., cerebral palsy, spina bifida, mental retardation). However, any given label does not redefine fitness for the individual, nor does it neccessarily redefine that individual's fitness needs or requirements. Aerobic capacity, muscular fitness, body composition, and body mass index (BMI) all impact a child's growth and development. It is suggested that training volume, training equipment, age suitability of the physical activity, and motor skill proficiency are among the factors that should be considered in the prescription of pediatric exercise programs for individuals with disabilities (Fisher, 2009). The individual's unique needs remain the defining factors for developing and maintaining physical functioning.

Prioritizing Fitness Needs

While we need to recognize the uniqueness of each person's fitness needs, there is also a need to recognize that certain kinds of fitness, for most people, likely are more important than others. Instead of focusing on cardiovascular or aerobic fitness, there is a growing consensus that health-related fitness is more essential for children during development (Bar-Or & Rowland, 2004). In this context, fitness is related not only to cardiovascular functioning but also to muscular strength/endurance, caloric expenditure and body composition, and flexibility (Bar-Or & Rowland, 2004). Rationale for this growing consensus is that health factors are everyone's concern, and, in fact, health-related fitness promotes good health and independent functioning. For example, by successfully engaging in health-related fitness activities, an individual is likely to enjoy benefits of lower cholesterol, lower blood pressure, normal-range blood glucose levels, and an optimal level of lean muscle tissue (i.e., better health). Perhaps the bottom-line rationale for prioritizing health-related fitness is that fitness is essential for independent living and for developing functional skills.

Winnick and Short (2000) emphasize that health entails two constructs: physiological health and functional health. Physiological health is viewed as capacities associated with well-being, such as appropriate levels of body fat and aerobic functioning, whereas functional health is related to physical capability, such as activities of daily living and leisure skill participation. Certainly, as physical educators we would like everyone to share our enthusiasm for an active lifestyle; however, physical educators need to recognize and respect that being athletic, for whatever reason, may not be particularly crucial in some people's constellation of lifestyle choices and one need not be athletic as a prerequisite to being healthy. Likewise, we emphasize the concept of functional skill development in physical fitness. In this context, the term *functional* or *functional skills* is the ability to perform those activities of daily living or self-care activities that are essential for promoting independence required in home and community settings. In addition, *functional* relates to work-specific tasks, sports, or play activities that promote independent functioning (Horvat & Croce, 1995).

The potential health benefits of exercise in children can be summarized as follows: Regular physical training is beneficial in preventing cardiovascular disease, respiratory disease, and certain metabolic disorders (Bar-Or & Rowland, 2004). In addition, by controlling those risk factors specific to disease (e.g., coronary artery disease), exercise can protect against developing diseases in the future. Thus, a program of intensified physical activity favors wellness and also promotes overall functioning in children. Regular physical activity is an important factor in regulating and maintaining body weight and generally results in an increase in lean body mass and fat-free mass (FFM), with a corresponding decrease in body fat. Exercise can also help children with disabilities develop motor skills and promote or restore functioning from an acquired disability. Further, fitness can be functional and help individuals with disabilities maintain independent living, perform work-related tasks, and maintain attention.

Challenges to Physical Fitness Development

Seaman (1999) has indicated that people with disabilities face many challenges that impede their progress to become physically active. Horvat and Croce (1995), and Winnick and Short (2000) have identified the following challenges to fitness development faced by individuals with disabilities:

- Architectural barriers may require an inordinate amount of energy expenditure and impede independent movement.
- Many people with disabilities are overprotected, fostering an inactive lifestyle and the potential for obesity and other health concerns.
- Inefficient movement patterns and poor body alignment increase energy expenditure required to perform everyday tasks. Fatigue occurs easily, reducing job efficiency and the desire to participate in leisure activities.
- Restricted sensory input, abnormal reflex activity, spasticity, and/or paralysis reduces mechanical efficiency and functioning, which in turn fosters inactivity.
- The use of prosthetic and orthotic devices contributes to a loss of functional muscle mass, reduces neuromuscular efficiency, and contributes to excessive fatigue.
- Depression or anger often results from an accident, disease, or acquired disability, often leading to reduced participation in physical activities.
- Individuals with cognitive or attention deficits require behavior intervention and prompting to sustain a sufficient level of fitness.
- Motivation to complete a task or sustain an effort to induce a training effect is often lacking.
- Children with disabilities often do not develop age-appropriate play skills, which further decreases their physical functioning and social interaction.
- Attitudinal barriers often focus on what the individual cannot do instead of what the individual can accomplish.

Development of Fitness

Basically, physiological responses to exercise during acute (single-bout) or chronic (repeated) exercise sessions are similar in children of all ages, and there are no underlying physiological factors that make children with disabilities less suitable for prolonged, intense exercise (Bar-Or & Rowland, 2004). Likewise, children with disabilities respond to training interventions in a manner similar to that of their able-bodied counterparts in stereotypical ways (specificity of training). Developmentally, Bar-Or (1989a) concluded that the research indicates that aerobic power, muscle strength, and anaerobic muscle power are trainable in children, although the degree of trainability of aerobic power is somewhat lower in prepubescents than in older age groups. Likewise, we see that children and adults with disabilities will respond to exercise challenges similarly and will display many of the same physiological adaptations as their nondisabled peers. For instance, children with disabilities will respond to both intensity and duration of the training stimulus in a similar manner to that of their nondisabled peers. For the teacher and coach it is essential to understand that exercise interventions that improve aerobic functioning, muscular strength and endurance, flexibility, and body composition should be emphasized to promote functional health in children with disabilities. Winnick and Short (2000) recommend identifying health-related concerns and establishing a fitness profile for children as the first step in the assessment process. Variations from typical development can then be addressed by the teacher to ensure that children can attain the same functional level as their peers.

Aerobic and Anaerobic Capacities

From basic physiology, you will recall that metabolism increases proportionally to increases in workload. However, when faced with increasingly higher energy demands, the body ultimately reaches a limit for oxygen consumption. At this point, oxygen consumption peaks and remains constant even with increasing workloads. This peak value is often referred to as maximal oxygen uptake (VO_2max), maximal aerobic power (capacity), or simply cardiorespiratory endurance capacity. This value is often regarded as the best single measure of cardiorespiratory endurance and aerobic fitness.

When VO_2max is used as a criterion measure, maximal aerobic capacity in children is lower than that found in the adult population during physical activities, such as pushing a wheelchair, that require sustained energy utilization (**Figure 8.1**). As a child grows, there is a concomitant increase in aerobic capacity; aerobic capacity of boys increases until about age 18, whereas in girls it hardly increases beyond age 14 (Bar-Or, 1993; Rowland, 1996). This rise in aerobic capacity is due primarily to increases in the size of the heart, lungs, and skeletal muscle. One must note, however, that a child's need for energy is related to body size, so aerobic capacity, or VO_2max, is more appropriately expressed relative to body weight in milliliters of oxygen consumed per kilogram of body

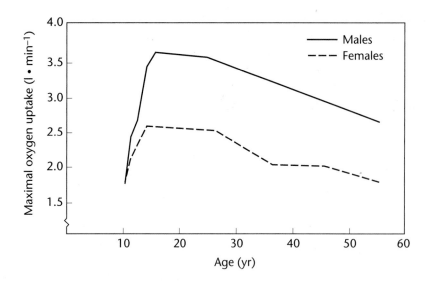

Figure 8.1 Maximal oxygen uptake as a function of age.

Source: Reprinted by permission from Carl P. Gabbard, Lifelong motor development, 5th ed. Copyright © 2008 Pearson Education, San Francisco.

weight, or by fat-free weight. When one expresses VO_2max in relative rather than absolute terms (e.g., body weight or lean body mass), there is hardly any age-related change in the VO_2max of boys, whereas there is a continual decline in the VO_2max of girls. This decline in VO_2max in girls is most likely due to the increase in body fat and the decrease in lean body mass that occur in girls during adolescence (Bar-Or, 1993; Rowland, 1996). One must also note that training increases observed in growing children may reflect activity levels as well as growth-related factors. For example, Rowland (1996) indicated that a 6-year-old boy whose activity is sedentary until the age of 12 will improve his VO_2max by over 100 percent.

Therefore, maximal aerobic capacity, when using VO_2max per kilogram of body weight as the criterion, is not deficient in most children. Although the aerobic capacity of children might not be deficient, one must note that the metabolic cost of running and walking (and possibly in other activities) at a given intensity is greater in children (and far greater in some children with disabilities) due to a biomechanically wasteful locomotion style (Bar-Or, 1993; Rowland, 1990). This leaves children with a lower energy reserve, which may be evident if they have to perform a maximal effort. If one considers the fact that many children with disabilities, in particular those children with physical disabilities, are more inefficient than their nondisabled peers, this lower energy reserve may be even more extensive. During growth, improvements in endurance capacity occur primarily from improved gait mechanics, qualitative changes in oxygen delivery, and/or increases in speed and strength (Rowland, 1990). In contrast, children with disabilities generally are less efficient and possess lower levels of strength, which will then affect their overall functioning.

As a rule, children can generally perform endurance tasks reasonably well but fatigue more quickly in high-intensity anaerobic activities. This is not surprising, for if we observe children playing, we seldom see them performing high-intensity activities for extended time periods. Moreover, children with disabilities often demonstrate lower levels of functioning at each age level and consistently underperform when compared to their nondisabled peers. Whether this is due to a lack of activity, overprotection, or lack of motivation, the end result may be a lower level of physical functioning.

A child's anaerobic capacity (ability to perform supramaximal tasks of 1 minute or less in duration), is lower than that of an adult (Bar-Or, 1993). Thus, an 8-year-old boy produces about 45–50 percent of the mechanical power produced by a 14-year-old boy, and even when adjusted for body weight, this amount is still only about 65–70 percent. In girls the trend is similar, although performance per kilogram of body weight plateaus at about ages 11 to 12 (Bar-Or, 1993). Compared to adults, children display a lower tolerance for anaerobic activity, yet, through maturation, anaerobic capacity will improve with age (Rowland, 1996). The reasons for this improvement appear to be related to the concentration and rate of utilization of muscle glycogen (Pfitzinger & Freedson, 1997). Glycogen is the form of carbohydrate stored in muscle tissue, which can be broken down rapidly in the cell and used as an energy source. Without this essential energy server, children cannot sustain high levels of anaerobic activity and will fatigue more easily.

In summary, maximal aerobic power does not change (in boys) or even decreases (in girls) with age.

This is not found with anaerobic performance, which is lower in children, whether expressed in absolute or relative terms (i.e., whether scaled to body weight or lean body mass). Consequently, children—and, especially, children with disabilities—are at a functional disadvantage when performing activities lasting between 10 and 60 seconds.

Cardiovascular Function

From the beginning of growth as a single tube in utero to the detection of a heartbeat during the fifth prenatal month, the heart undergoes some rather dramatic changes. The size of the heart will increase in a similar manner as body weight, its weight will double during the first year, quadruple by 5 years, and increase six times by the age of 9. From the ages 9–18, heart growth parallels the general growth curve and functionally has all the mechanisms that are essential to the adult heart. Heart volumes also increase from approximately 40 ml at birth, to 80 ml at 6 months, to 160 ml at 2 years of age.

Basal heart rates or beats per minute (bpm) decrease progressively during childhood. At birth, higher heart rates are present because of the smaller dimensions of the heart but fall approximately 10–20 bpm during the ages of 5–15 (Rowland, 1996). Gender differences are apparent, with females manifesting a rate 5 bpm higher than males. However, maximal heart rate remains constant, independent of age or body dimensions. In terms of efficiency, the preadolescent heart rate is 30–40 bpm higher than a young adult while engaged in the same task (Gabbard, 2008).

Heart rate and stroke volume in children vary because stroke volume is related to heart size; the larger the heart, the more blood can be pumped during each beat. At birth, stroke volume is 3–4 ml, as opposed to 40 ml in the preadolescent and 60 ml in the young adult. As a way of compensating for the smaller stroke volume, children will elicit higher average heart rates: 120–140 bpm in newborns, 100 bpm by age 4, 90 bpm by age 6, and 80 bpm by age 14 (Gabbard, 2008). Blood pressure changes are also apparent: Average blood pressure is 70/55 in the newborn, 100/62 by age 10, and 115/65 by age 15 (Rowland, 1996).

Children have particular hemodynamic characteristics, which may be rate limiting under certain exercise conditions (see the *Cardiovascular Terminology* box for definitions of key terms). The primary cardiovascular limitations in children include the following. First, children have a lower concentration of hemoglobin, the oxygen carrying molecules in the blood. These levels increase slowly during childhood for both genders until puberty from 10 g/dl at 6 months to adult levels of 16 g/dl (men) and 14 g/dl (women) (Malina Bouchard, & Bar-Or, 2004). This, in and of itself, can limit exercise capacity in children. At puberty, one sees a significant rise in boys' hemoglobin concentrations due to bone marrow stimulation by testosterone and a plateau in girls' concentrations. Secondly, children have a lower stroke volume (SV) at rest and during submaximal exercise compared to adults, but a higher heart rate (HR) and a greater capacity to extract oxygen from the blood (termed arteriovenous oxygen difference, or AVD-O_2). The end result is that children have a much lower cardiac output (the amount of blood pumped by the heart per minute) than that found in adults at any given level of oxygen consumption (Bar-Or, 1993). Individuals with disabilities will vary from this typical developmental scenario, impacting their ability to engage in strenuous activity. For example, children with Down syndrome may be limited in their cardiac output because of cardiac insufficiency or damage to the heart. Likewise, an individual with a spinal injury will be affected because of differences in autonomic responses from the central nervous system. Further, children with cardiovascular diseases, such as aortic stenosis or pulmonary stenosis, will have reduced stroke volume and cardiac output, thus limiting their capacity to perform aerobically.

Cardiovascular Terminology

- Heart rate (HR)—the number of times the heart beats per minute.
- Stroke volume (SV)—the amount of blood ejected from the left ventricle during contraction of the heart musculature.
- Arteriovenous oxygen difference (AVD-O_2)—the difference in oxygen content found in arterial and mixed-venous blood. This difference reflects the amount of oxygen removed by the tissues and increases with increased workloads.
- Cardiac output—the volume of blood pumped by the heart per minute; represented by the formula:

Cardiac output = heart rate (HR) x stroke volume (SV).

Children with disabilities also tend to be at a disadvantage during maximal exercise, when oxygen extraction can no longer keep pace with the exercise workload or when exposed to the combined stresses of intense exercise and extreme heat. Consequently, teachers should use caution when exercising children in hot, humid environments. As a general rule, teachers must be aware that when children with disabilities exercise at high intensity levels under hot, humid conditions, they will have greater difficulty trying to maintain their exercise performance. Moreover, if children have poor mechanical efficiency when engaged in physical activity (e.g., children having neuromuscular or orthopedic disabilities), a specific workload will require a greater energy expenditure than in children whose techniques are more biomechanically correct. The combination of a "wasteful" biomechanical style and performing activities under hot, humid conditions makes for a situation that can be quite dangerous for any child, and for children with disabilities even more so.

Muscular Strength

Muscular strength is the ability of the muscle tissue to apply force and refers to a maximal or near-maximal muscular exertion of brief duration. Often we define strength as the maximal force that can be exerted in a single voluntary contraction. An example of muscular strength is lifting oneself from the ground onto a wheelchair or transferring from a wheelchair to the driver's seat of an automobile. In regard to a functional task, strength may, for example, be the ability to lift and carry an object in the home or a work-related setting. Virtually any activity meeting the criteria of brief duration and maximal or near-maximal exertion would require strength to perform.

Strength development is important for all children, regardless of ability or disability, because a certain amount of strength is required to perform virtually all activities. Even the seemingly simplest activities are strength activities for the person who is strength deficient. Indeed, minimum levels of strength must be achieved before minimal skill levels can be achieved. For example, one cannot become proficient using crutches until minimum levels of grip, arm, and shoulder girdle strength have been developed. Without strength, even the simplest activities are difficult.

Developmentally, the growth of the muscle occurs by hypertrophy (size). The number of muscle fibers is fixed at birth or within the first year of life. Increases in muscle fiber size during the growth process reflect an increase in total muscle mass and increases linearly with age (Beunen & Thomis, 2000).

Muscular strength increases with age in both sexes, reaching a peak at about 29 years of age. Increases for males are much greater than for females (**Figures 8.2** and **8.3**). Increases in strength are influenced by a variety of factors, of which the most important are serum testosterone concentrations in male adolescents—the point at which specific adult hormonal profiles start to emerge—and neural adaptations (Falk & Tenenbaum, 1996; Kraemer & Fleck, 2005). Motor unit activation is also essential to developing force within the muscle, and some of the increases in strength observed in children, especially in prepubescents and postpubescent girls, are attributed to this phenomenon. Blimkie (1989) states that "training-induced neural adaptation refers to increased ability to activate prime mover muscles

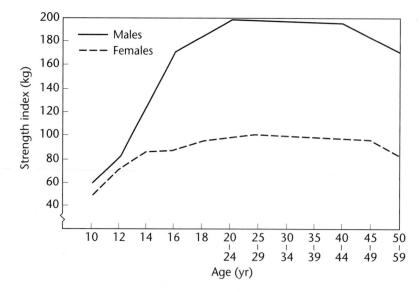

Figure 8.2 Strength index (means) of right and left grip of arm.

Source: Reprinted by permission from Carl P. Gabbard, *Lifelong motor development*, 5th ed. Copyright © 2008 Pearson Education, San Francisco.

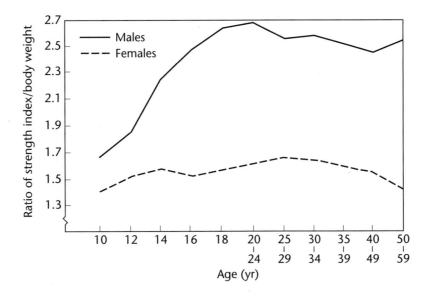

Figure 8.3 Ratio of strength index to body weight.

Source: Reprinted by permission from Carl P. Gabbard, *Lifelong motor development,* 5th ed. Copyright © 2008 Pearson Education, San Francisco.

and/or the improved coordination of synergists and antagonists". This results in an increased ability to apply a greater force in the intended direction of movement by way of increased motor unit activation. For some children with disabilities the ability to recruit motor units may be diminished and affect the ability to produce age-appropriate levels of strength. For example, children with intellectual disabilities have demonstrated a reduced capacity in motor unit activation during controlled movement (Horvat et al., 2003).

Muscular Endurance

Muscular endurance means the ability to persist and refers to a submaximal muscular effort repeated for a relatively long period of time. It is often defined and measured as the repetition of submaximal contractions or the holding of a submaximal contraction. Unlike strength activities, muscular endurance activities do not involve brief, all-out exertions. Rather, they require persistent, submaximal effort. Many activities in school, home, and physical education require muscular endurance. Lifting medium-heavy weights or meeting medium-heavy resistance over an extended period involves muscular endurance. Insofar as repetition leads to skill, and repetition requires endurance, endurance is extremely important for skill and sport performance; hence, muscular endurance is often the key to success in sport.

Pure muscular endurance and pure muscular strength may be thought of as extremes on a continuum. Many activities that enhance strength can, with modest alteration, be used to enhance muscular endurance. Because of the intensity of a strength-developing activity, duration of that activity becomes limited by rapid onset of fatigue. The same activity could be used to develop muscular endurance by simultaneously reducing resistance, thereby increasing potential for duration. When muscles are fatigued gradually, as is the case in endurance exercise, they experience a training effect characterized by an increased muscular capacity to sustain a submaximal, protracted effort.

We would like to spend a moment comparing muscular strength and endurance. Endurance is achieved by many repetitive contractions of a portion of the available muscle fibers. These repetitive contractions require a continuous supply of energy; hence, the types of muscle fibers best suited for muscular endurance are those having aerobic characteristics: a good oxygen supply, numerous mitochondria, and sufficient amounts of aerobic enzymes needed to supply the cell's energy needs (i.e., adenosine triphosphate, or ATP). Strength, in contrast, requires a greater cross-sectional area or bulk of the muscle tissue, because a greater cross-sectional area contains more protein filaments within the tissue with which to produce force. One should keep these points in mind when designing muscular strength and endurance training programs.

To develop muscular endurance, three sets of 30-plus repetitions of any given exercise are recommended. Further, for a maximal training effect, the person should engage in such exercise approximately three times weekly. Such recommendations, though appearing frequently in the literature, are offered as rules of thumb only and in certain settings may need to be modified based on individual need or capacity.

Flexibility

Flexibility refers to the ability of body segments to move through typical ranges of motion. One must realize that the range of motion about various joints may differ; therefore, flexibility can be limited in some joints, while in other joints it may be well within normal ranges. For most joints, limitations in range of motion are due to one or more of the following factors: (1) bony structure anomalies, (2) muscle bulk, (3) tightness in the muscle and its fascial sheaths, and (4) tightness within the connective tissue proper (i.e., tightness within the tendons, ligaments, and joint capsule). For the most part, the more active the child, the more flexible he or she will be. Second, flexibility is influenced by temperature: Local warming increases flexibility, whereas local cooling reduces flexibility. This factor becomes extremely important when conducting a stretching program for children with slight, spastic muscles.

Like strength, flexibility can be a major determinant of success in many physical and motor activities. Virtually all activities require a minimum degree of flexibility before the activity can be executed comfortably, correctly, and safely. Developmentally, Malina Bouchard, and Bar-Or (2004) indicated that flexibility scores using the sit-and-reach test are stable from 5–8 years in boys, decline with age to approximately 12–13 years, and then increase up to 18 years of age; in girls, scores are stable from 5–11 years of age, increase up to 16 years, and then plateau (Gabbard, 2008; Malina Bouchard, & Bar-Or, 2004). In contrast, Payne and Issacs (2008), citing data from the NCYFS (National Children and Youth Fitness Study) I and II studies, show an increase in flexibility for children 6–18 years of age, with girls demonstrating higher scores at all ages (**Figure 8.4**).

Unexpected muscle stretching beyond typical motion range may cause strain, ranging from mild strain to strain so severe that surgical repair is needed. The range of motion through which a body can move comfortably, even when disability affects flexibility (e.g., spastic cerebral palsy), is largely a function of the muscle stretching to which an individual is accustomed.

Maintaining flexibility is a lifelong need. Without flexibility, one's capacity to enjoy movement may become greatly diminished. For example, diminished flexibility in the shoulder may inhibit the individual's ability to push a wheelchair. Flexibility is also essential to maintaining fitness, preventing injury, and facilitating motor skill performance. Gabbard (2008) indicates that flexibility research has produced the following conclusions:

1. Flexibility is joint specific.

2. Flexibility is not related to limb length.

3. Strength development is compatible to range of motion.

4. Activity levels are better indicators of flexibility than age.

5. Females generally are more flexible than males.

We commonly see a loss of flexibility as a function of disability as well as the aging process. Although some flexibility potential might be lost as a function of disability, a large part may be attributable to changes in activity patterns and use of the muscle. This is especially important for children with disabilities, who are

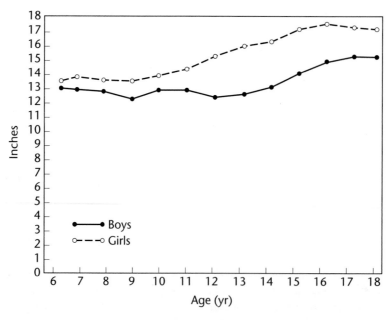

Figure 8.4 Average sit-and-reach scores for ages 6–18. The zero point was located at 12 inches.

Source: Ross, J. G., Dotson, C. O., Gilbert, G. G., & Katz, S. J. (1985). New standards for fitness measurement. *Journal of Physical Education, Recreation & Dance,* 56(1), 62–66.

often inactive and lose flexibility as a result of disuse rather than their disability. In other cases, such as muscular dystrophy, the resulting loss of muscle function is often accompanied by loss of flexibility, further complicating the ability to move.

Although some children may have more muscle flexibility potential than others, virtually everyone should strive to develop and maintain flexibility in accordance with her or his own potential. There may be exceptions to every rule, but it is doubtful that activity designed to develop flexibility would ever render one too flexible.

When developing flexibility, muscles must be stretched only to, but not through, the individual's threshold of discomfort. To be sure, stretching to the point of discomfort is essential to increasing a muscle's range of motion; however, it is equally true that stretching beyond that point risks injury. Should a muscle have been injured for any reason (i.e., strained), the general rule is to avoid stretching that muscle until it has healed. Stretching an already strained muscle will likely reinjure muscle fibers that have not yet fully healed.

Stretching for flexibility development should always be slow and deliberate. Rapid stretching, particularly bouncing (ballistic stretching) is undesirable, because it activates the muscle's myotatic (stretch) reflex. When this reflex is activated, the muscle actually resists the attempt to stretch by eliciting the reflex that actually causes the muscle to contract. As long as reflex contractions are being provoked, in this case due to ballistic-type stretching, flexibility exercise will be to no avail. In fact, stretching activity of this nature may actually cause muscle injury ranging from soreness to actual muscle strain (i.e., torn muscle fiber).

Typically, the person might stretch a given muscle or muscle group for a duration of between 15 seconds minimum and 45 seconds maximum. Fifteen seconds may be the point at which the muscle experiences sufficient stretch to become more pliable. Forty-five seconds may be the point past which the individual experiences diminished returns.

Body Composition

Body composition refers to the relative proportions of fat to lean body mass. Body composition data are valuable because weight alone does not reveal what sort of tissue comprises the weight showing on the scale. Two people who weigh the same can have remarkably different body compositions.

Placing priority on body composition, despite its potential contribution to fitness development, sometimes becomes the focus of controversy. Body composition has yet to be widely studied in children and youth. For this reason, applying body composition norms taken from adults to children and youth is of questionable validity. Where body composition measures are applied to children and youth, results usually are reported in terms of percentiles derived from children and youth rather than in percentages of body fat derived from adult studies. Also, there is some concern that overconsciousness about being thin does not promote health and may provoke some children to eat improperly. There is additional concern that skinfold measures (i.e., telling a child he or she is fat), tell the child nothing she or he does not already know. Putting a number to the percentage of fatness with what one sees in the mirror may do little more than add insult to injury (Chapter 19).

Developmentally, adipose tissue plays a vital role in energy storage, insulation, and protection of the newborn (Malina Bouchard, & Bar-Or, 2004). Essential fat makes up 3.5 percent of body weight in males and 8–12 percent in females and is used as energy for disposition of new tissue in children 3–10 years of age. Adipose tissue first appears in the fetus and at birth is generally well distributed, accounting for approximately 16 percent of body weight at birth, 24–30 percent during the first year, and 14 percent of body weight by 6 years of age. Some children will also experience a midgrowth increase at approximately 5½ to 7 years (Gabbard, 2008).

Body fat will increase during the first 6 months and then taper off from 1 to 7 years of age. During this period, no gender differences are evident. However, at age 7 the proportion of body fat increases and continues to increase in girls, whereas in boys it may continue to develop or actually decrease (Payne & Issacs, 2008). This difference may account for a body fat content that is 50 percent greater in females than in males of the same age (Rowland, 1996). For children with disabilities, an inordinate amount of body fat may be present, which restricts their overall functional performance. Inactivity and a high-fat diet will contribute to further difficulties in stimulating activity and motor performance (**Figure 8.5**).

Effect of Training

As interest in developing resistance training programs for children increases, especially for prepubescent children, guidelines for such programs are needed. Aside from the strength benefits of resistance training, a major goal of the program should be to teach children about their bodies, promote lifetime fitness, and provide them with a positive attitude about strength training and exercise in general. Also, teachers must keep in mind that children are not only physiologically different from adults, but also emotionally different. Therefore, children should not be treated as "little" adults, but rather as uniquely distinct individuals.

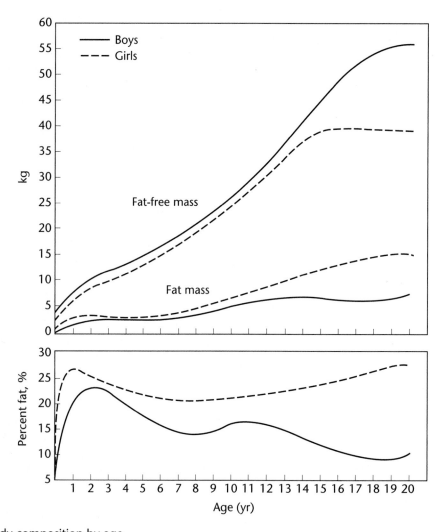

Figure 8.5 Body composition by age.

Source: Reprinted by permission from Carl P. Gabbard, *Lifelong motor development*, 5th ed. Copyright © 2008 Pearson Education, San Francisco.

Rather than encouraging them to compete, teachers should instead encourage children to feel good about themselves and their performance and to concentrate on self-improvement (Faigenbaum & McFarland, 2008). For children with disabilities, performance should be related to improving functional skills needed for independence and the development of motor skills that will encourage an active lifestyle.

In addition, resistance training programs have been found not only to be relatively safe (Faigenbaum & McFarland, 2008; Kraemer & Fleck, 2005; Williams, 1991), but also may prevent certain types of injuries in young athletes. It appears that the potential for injury during resistance training programs is no greater, and may even be less, than those risks associated with participation in organized sports and recreational activities (Faigenbaum & McFarland, 2008). Both the National Strength and Conditioning Association (Faigenbaum et al., 2009) and the American Academy of Pediatrics (2008) stress that children can benefit from properly

supervised and properly prescribed resistance training programs. Major benefits cited were (1) increased muscular strength and muscular endurance, (2) decreased injuries during sport and recreational activities, and (3) improved skill performance.

Resistance training has had a positive effect on children who are overweight or obese (Sgro et al., 2009). The increased rate of obesity in children is an international epidemic. The World Health Organization (2006) estimates that at least 20 million children under the age of 5 are overweight. One major cause of this problem is suboptimal levels of physical activity in children (the other major factor being diet and caloric intake). This has led to a number of evidence-based exercise strategies that might be appealing, safe, and effective in addressing this problem. Resistance training has been shown to reduce adiposity, improve insulin sensitivity, improve glucose control, and reduce other adverse health problems such as coronary artery disease and Type II diabetes (Benson et al., 2008).

Position statements from various national organizations strongly advocate using supervised resistance-training programs with children and adolescence (Faigenbaum et al., 2009; Lavallee, 2002).

Teachers should note that regular physical training is not necessarily the same as physical activity. Although physical activity involves some training, regular physical training refers to the habitual and orderly practice of physical activities, such as calisthenics, resistance exercises, running, and games/sports performed at specific intensities and for distinctive durations (Malina, Bouchard, & Bar-Or, 2004). Therefore, training programs vary in kind or type (e.g., endurance training, strength training, and skill training), and the effects of such programs are generally specific to the type of training stimulus (Saltin & Rowell, 1980).

Interpreting research on the effects of training during childhood on growth and maturation is exceptionally difficult because of problems associated with partitioning training-induced effects from changes associated with normal growth, maturation, and genetics. Also of importance is the fact that measures or estimates of "normal" activity are based primarily on surveys of adolescent sport participation, with little data for preadolescents (Malina, Bouchard, & Bar-Or, 2004). Even with these limitations, there is a consensus that regular physical activity is an important factor in regulating and maintaining body weight, increasing lean body mass, improving cardiovascular functioning, and improving blood cholesterol levels (Dobbins et al., 2009). Moreover, researchers have found that exercise can improve health, fitness, and coordination levels in children with a wide range of disabilities (Halvorson, 2009; Johnson, 2009).

An important question for physical educators is that given the favorable impact of physical activity on fitness, how might a regular program of physical activity and exercise impact a child with disabilities? The answer to this question is not a simple one. Nevertheless, if we look at some of the research on exercise and disability over the last decade, the possibility that a combination of physical activity and prudent caloric intake throughout life may help to improve physical functioning in children with disabilities.

The implications for physical education are enormous: Early intervention may prevent obesity by way of promoting a sensible diet and substantial levels of physical activity. In addition, regular physical training is beneficial in preventing cardiovascular disease, respiratory disease, and certain metabolic disorders (Bar-Or & Rowland, 2004). Sallis and Patrick (1994) have suggested that all adolescents be active daily and engage in physical activities that last for 20 minutes minimally per session and require moderate to vigorous exertion levels. Horvat and Franklin (2001) report that play at recess can promote greater heart rate and activity counts than sedentary settings. By controlling those risk factors specific to disease (e.g., coronary artery disease), exercise can protect against developing diseases in the future. Thus, given the sedentary lifestyle currently displayed by children and youth, all children—and in particular children with disabilities—require daily physical education that stresses a habitual and orderly practice of physical activities, such as calisthenics, resistance exercises, running, and games/sports performed at specific intensities and for distinctive durations.

CHAPTER SUMMARY

1. The degree to which children and youth respond to exercise depends on maturation and the exercise stimulus encountered during the activity program. In many ways, children respond to exercise in much the same way as their adult counterparts. Nevertheless, there are several age-dependent and gender differences in the response to exercise.

2. Maximal aerobic capacity, when using VO_2max per kilogram of body weight as the criterion, is not deficient in children; however, because of inefficient biomechanics during the performance of various activities, the metabolic cost of performing these activities is greater in children than in adults. Thus, when the total spectrum of exercise conditions are considered, children perform inferiorly to adults in aerobic activities. As the child grows, one sees a dramatic improvement in endurance fitness. Sufficient evidence suggests that children can adapt physiologically to endurance training.

3. Children perform inferiorly to adults in anaerobic activities (activities lasting between 10 and 60 seconds) and often display a lower tolerance for these types of activities than do adults. As the child matures, however, anaerobic capacity improves greatly with age. The primary reasons for this improvement appear to be the concentration and rate of utilization of muscle glycogen.

4. Recent research clearly demonstrates that following several weeks of resistance training, children with disabilities display increases in strength, increases in lean body mass, and improvement in skilled motor performance.

5. Childhood obesity and inactivity have increased substantially over the past decade. There is a consensus that regular physical activity is an important factor in regulating and maintaining body weight and generally results in an increase in lean body mass, with a corresponding decrease in body fat. A sensible diet and moderate to substantial levels of physical activity are the most efficacious way to mitigate the high levels of obesity found currently in our children and youth. Teachers should work in conjunction with medical professionals for advice on the dietary and exercise needs of the child participating in the physical education program.

REFERENCES

American Academy of Pediatrics. (2008). Strength training by children and adolescents. *Pediatrics, 107*(6), 1470–1472.

Bar-Or, O. (1989a). Trainability of the prepubescent child. *The Physician and Sports Medicine, 17*(5), 65–82.

Bar-Or, O. (1989b). Temperature regulation during exercise in children and adolescents. In C. V. Gisolfi & D. R. Lamb (Eds.), *Perspectives in exercise science and sports medicine: Volume 2: Youth, exercise, and sport* (pp. 335–367). Indianapolis: Benchmark Press.

Bar-Or, O. (1993). Importance of differences between children and adults for exercise testing and exercise prescription. In J. S. Skinner (Ed.), *Exercise testing and exercise prescription for special cases: Theoretical basis and scientific application* (pp. 57–74). Philadelphia: Lea & Febiger.

Bar-Or, O., & Rowland, T. W. (2004). *Pediatric Exercise Medicine.* Champaign, IL: Human Kinetics.

Benson, A., Torode, M., & Singh, M. (2008). The effect of high-intensity progressive resistance training on adiposity in children: A randomized control trial. *International Journal of Obesity, 32*, 1016–1027.

Beunen, G., & Thomis, M. (2000). Muscular strength development in children and adolescents. *Pediatric Exercise Science, 12*, 174–197.

Blimkie, C. J. R. (1989). Age- and sex-associated variation in strength during childhood: Anthropometric, morphologic, neurologic, biomechanical, endocrinologic, genetic, and physical correlates. In C. V. Gisolfi & D. R. Lamb (Eds.), *Perspectives in exercise and sports medicine: Volume 2: Youth, exercise and sport* (pp. 99–163). Indianapolis: Benchmark Press.

Dobbins, M., DeCorby, K., Robeson, P., Husson, H., & Tirilis, D. (2009). School-based physical activity programs for promoting physical activity and fitness in children and adolescents aged 6–18. *Cochrane Database of Systematic Reviews*, Medline PMID: 19160341.

Faigenbaum, A., Kraemer, W., Blimke, C., Jeffreys, I., Micheli, L., Nitka, M., & Rowland, T. (2009). Youth resistance training: Updated position statement paper from the National Strength and Conditioning Association. *Journal of Strength and Conditioning Research.*

Faigenbaum, A., & McFarland, J. (2008). Relative safety of weightlifting movements for youth. *Strength and Conditioning Journal, 30*(6), 23–25.

Falk, B., & Tenenbaum, G. (1996). The effectiveness of resistance training in children. *Sports Medicine, 22*, 176–186.

Fisher, M. (2009). Children and exercise-appropriate practices for grades K-6. *JOPERD, 80*(4), 187.

Gabbard, C. P. (2008). *Lifelong motor development* (5th ed.). San Francisco, CA: Pearson/Benjamin Cummings.

Halvorson, R. (2009). Exercise Benefits Developmentally Disabled Kids. *IDEA Fitness Journal, 6*(4), 121–124.

Horvat, M., & Croce, R. (1995). Physical rehabilitation of individuals with mental retardation: Physical fitness and information processing. *Critical Reviews in Physical and Rehabilitation Medicine, 7*(3), 233–252.

Horvat, M., & Franklin, C. (2001). The effects of the environment on physical activity patterns of children with mental retardation. *Research Quarterly for Exercise and Sport, 72*, 189–195.

Horvat, M., Ramsey, V., Amestoy, R., & Croce, R. (2003). Movement response variability, in youth with and without mental retardation. *Research Quarterly for Exercise and Sport 74*(3), 319–323.

Johnson, C. (2009). The benefits of physical activity for youth with developmental disabilities. *American Journal of Health Promotion, 23*(3), 157–167.

Kraemer, W. J., & Fleck, S. J. (2005). *Strength training for young athletes.* (2nd ed.) Champaign, IL: Human Kinetics.

Lavallee, M. (2002). Strength training in children and adolescents. American College of Sports Medicine. www.acsm.org

McGuigan, M., Tatasciore, M., Newton, R., & Pettigrew, S. (2009). Eight weeks of resistance training can significantly alter body composition in children who are overweight or obese. *Journal of Strength and Conditioning Research, 23*(1), 80–85.

Malina, R. M., Bouchard, C., & Bar-Or, O. (2004). *Growth, maturation, and physical activity.* (2nd ed.) Champaign, IL: Human Kinetics.

Payne, V. G, & Issacs, L. D. (2008). *Human movement development* (7th ed.). Mountain View, CA: Mayfield.

Pfitzinger, P., & Freedson, P. (1997). Blood lactate responses to exercise in children: Part 1, Peak lactate concentration. *Pediatric Exercise Science, 9,* 210–222.

Physical Fitness and Sports Research Digest. (2000). Definitions: Health, fitness, and physical activity, Series 3 (9), 1–6.

Rees, A., Thomas, N., Brophy, S. Knox, G., & Willimas, R. (2009). Cross sectional study of obesity and prevalence of risk factors for cardiovascular disease and diabetes in children aged 11–13. *BMC Public Health.* PubMed PMID: 19317914.

Rowland, T. W. (1990). *Exercise and children's health.* Champaign, IL: Human Kinetics.

Rowland, T. W. (1996). *Developmental exercise physiology.* Champaign, IL: Human Kinetics.

Sallis, J. F., & Patrick, K. (1994). Physical activity guidelines for adolescents: Consensus statement. *Pediatric Exercise Science, 6,* 302–314.

Saltin, B., & Rowell, L. B. (1980). Functional adaptations to physical activity and inactivity. *Federation Proceedings, 39,* 1506–1513.

Seaman, J. (1999). Physical activity and fitness for persons with disabilities. *Research Digest, 3,* (5). Washington, DC: President Council on Physical Fitness and Sports.

Sgro, M., McGuigan, M., Pettigrew, S., & Newton, R. (2009). The effect of duration of resistance training intervention in children who are overweight or obese. *Journal of Strength and Conditioning Research, 23*(4), 1263–1270.

Williams, D. (1991). The effect of weight training performance in selected motor activities for preadolescents (abstract). *Journal of Applied Sport Sciences Research, 5*(3), 170.

Winnick, J. P., & Short, F. X. (2000). The Brockport physical fitness test. *PALAESTRA, 16,* 20–25, 46–47.

World Health Organization. (2006). *Obesity and overweight.* Fact Sheet No. 311, September 2006.

Teaching Individuals With Learning and Behavior Disabilities

Section II focuses on disabilities that affect learning or behavior and, in turn, performance. For children who have learning and/or behavioral difficulties, characteristics and teaching suggestions are provided to develop and implement the physical education program.

This section is designed to

1. provide information regarding the characteristics and physical/motor functioning of children with learning, attention, or behavior exceptionalities and/or autism.

2. provide instructional methods to develop and implement appropriate programs that meet the needs of individual learners.

3. provide teaching strategies and management systems that are appropriate to facilitate instruction in physical education.

CHAPTER 9

Intellectual Disabilities

CASE STUDY

Duane is an adapted physical education teacher who works with his school's special education and vocational rehabilitation teachers on transition plans. Duane has several individuals who are transitioning from school to work and to the community. He has found that one of the difficulties in placing individuals with intellectual disabilities (ID) in a work setting is the individual's lack of physical functioning abilities requisite for effective integration in a range of work and community living environments. In collaboration with the other teachers, Duane has analyzed the work environments and physical attributes needed to perform the transition-related tasks. Based on these analyses, Duane has structured physical education classes such that his transition students will better develop physical strength and balance necessary for lifting, carrying, performing work tasks, and, no less, independent community living.

To help determine efficacy of restructured physical education curriculums, Duane and his transition teacher colleagues have arranged for their transition individuals with ID to trial-perform essential tasks in community agency environments where they will be employed. Duane and his special and vocational education colleagues are pooling their expertise to make sure that their transition curriculum helps ensure meaningful employment and independent community living for their participants with ID.

The general public's conception of individuals with intellectual disabilities (ID) is that they are incapable of learning or caring for themselves. Most of this sentiment probably stems from the medical definitions of ID, which stress the pathology, disease, genetic orientations, and/or incurable aspects of the condition. Although the accomplishments of individuals with intellectual disabilities and public awareness of those accomplishments, are increasing, it is still difficult to separate superstition and oversimplification from facts when it comes to children with ID.

Clearly, the range of cognitive deficits found in individuals with ID is indicative of functioning and potential. Individuals with less severe intellectual deficits are capable of independent functioning, employment, and social relationships, including marriage and children. Most are capable of independent functioning with limited and less pervasive supports. In contrast, individuals with more severe cognitive deficits are limited not only by intelligence quotients (IQ) but also by the ability to relate socially to individuals in the community, to focus on goals, and to complete tasks. Individuals with less self-sufficiency or with accompanying motor deficits require more extensive supports on a continual basis. Contemporary thinking reflects the premise that the individual is capable of achieving basic functional skills, and it broadens preexisting definitions to encompass the individual's actual functioning in daily living and community settings. For this population, the ability to perform physically and process information adequately is essential to ensure independent functioning.

According to the classification and terminology from the American Association on Intellectual and Developmental Disabilities (AAIDD) (2002), individuals with ID will demonstrate primary cognitive deficits that are determined from an assessment of intellectual functioning and adaptive skills. The term *intellectual disabilities* (ID), replaces *mental retardation* and refers to significantly subaverage intellectual functioning existing concurrently with deficits in adaptive skills and documented as occurring from birth to 18 years of age. Intellectual levels are based on an IQ score below 70 to 75 on a standardized intelligence scale. Because there is such variability in determining intelligence, a second component dealing with adaptive skills was added. Adaptive skills refers to the effectiveness or degree with which the individual meets standards of personal independence and social responsibility for age and cultural group. Pitetti and colleagues (1993) have indicated that these attributes fall under three categories: maturation, learning capacity, and social adjustment. In addition, the AAIDD definition specifically requires documentation on a standardized test within the context of community environments that are typical of individuals in their peer group and indexed to the need for supports.

In this context, limitations in practical and social intelligence are addressed. Practical intelligence relates to managing activities of daily living and using physical abilities for personal independence that are crucial for adaptive functioning in such skills as self-care, safety, leisure, or work. Social intelligence is the ability to understand social expectations, including the behavior of others and acting in a socially acceptable manner. The interdependence of practical and social intelligence to adaptive skill functioning is closely linked and is a useful predictor of what the individual may actually accomplish within the community environment. Hence, the individual with a low IQ score may function appropriately in the community, while another person may record a greater IQ score yet not adjust to community living. In this definition, these dimensions are clearly intercorrelated and require standardized testing areas.

One should note that previous terminology of mild, moderate, severe, and profound mental retardation was directly linked to IQ testing and is no longer applicable. Heward (2009) indicated that the AAIDD 2002 definition provides conceptual procedures in classification by the supports that are needed by the individual. This constitutes a change from the intellectual classification to the supports needed to improve functioning in school, home, community, and work-related setting. According to the AAIDD definition, diagnosis may reflect a person with ID who needs limited support in communication and social skills. The premise of needed supports relates to the ability to predict independence and integration into the community for the individual and will replace levels of retardation. Supports may be intermittent (short-term during periods of transition); limited (short-term, restricted basis, e.g., job training); extensive (long-term consistent involvement, in work or home support); and pervasive (long-term, constant, potentially life-sustaining). The system of supports links the concept of functional capabilities or limitations that are specific to each individual and his or her capabilities. Finally, the age of onset is documented as the condition occurring from birth to 18 years of age, or what was conceptualized as the developmental age, that is specifically related to cognitive growth and the level of cognitive functioning achieved.

It should be noted that the definition is still under considerable debate, but seems to be heading to focusing on functional behaviors and providing supports in a social-ecological context (Heward, 2009). The definition by Luckasson et al. (2002) will probably remain the updated classification system and is as follows: intellectual disability is characterized as significant limitations in intellectual functioning and in adaptive behavior as expressed in conceptual, social, and practical adaptive skills and originates before 18 years of age. Schalock et al. (2007) indicated that the following assumptions are integral to the term intellectual disability:

1. Limitations in present functioning must be considered within the context of community environments typical of the individual's age, peers, and culture.

2. Valid assessment considers cultural and linguistic diversity as well as differences in communication, sensory, motor, and behavior factors.

3. Within an individual, limitations co-exist with strengths.

4. An important purpose of describing limitations is to develop a profile of needed supports.

5. With appropriate personalized supports over a sustained period, the life functioning of the person with intellectual disabilities generally will improve (Luckasson et al., 2002).

Etiology and Incidence

The causes of intellectual disability are not easily determined and are partly responsible for some of the misconceptions related to the disorder. Some causes may be organic, hereditary, or as in most cases, idiopathic; they may affect children at various stages of their development. **Table 9.1** describes causes of ID during different periods of development.

Prenatal Period

If infants do not have sufficient time in the womb (prematurity) or exceed the normal time by more than 7 days (postmaturity), deficits may occur. Likewise, infants with low birth weight (5½ pounds or less) are

Table 9.1 Intellectual Disabilities Etiology by Periods of Development

Prenatal Period (Before Birth)	Perinatal Period (At Birth)	Postnatal Period (After Birth)	Combined Periods
1. Chromosomal anomaly, Down syndrome, Turner's syndrome, Klinefelter's syndrome 2. Unknown prenatal influences (hydrocephalus; microcephaly) 3. Disorder of metabolism (phenylketonuria, PKU) 4. Maternal disease (rubella) 5. Blood incompatibility (Rh factor) 6. Maternal care (nicotine, alcohol, drug addiction)	1. Prematurity; postmaturity 2. Low birth weight 3. Difficult labor and delivery 4. Birth Injury	1. Disease (meningitis, encephalitis) 2. Brain Injury 3. Toxic substances (lead, mercury) 4. Disorders of metabolism (galactosemia, endocrine or growth dysfunctions, diabetes) 5. Malnutrition 6. Degenerative Disorders	1. Brain Trauma 2. Anoxia to the brain 3. Tumors/lesions 4. Syphilis 5. Idiopathic conditions

at risk, as well as those who experience trauma, such as difficult deliveries from breech birth or cesarean section or unnecessary physical contact during the birth process.

Chromosome anomaly, or Down syndrome, is a common form of ID in which an extra chromosome is present in each cell or the structure of chromosomes is affected. Other chromosomal abnormalities include fragile X syndrome, Klinefelter's syndrome, and Turner's syndrome.

Unknown prenatal influences may exist, resulting in abnormalities with no definite cause. Among those conditions with unknown influences are hydrocephalus, an accumulation of cerebrospinal fluid on the brain; microcephaly, a lack of development of the cranium; anencephaly, a malformation of the development or absence of the brain.

Disorders of metabolism may be present. An example is phenylketonuria (PKU), which is a condition caused by a lack of metabolic enzyme that prevents the building of protein and results in brain damage.

Maternal disease, such as rubella or German measles, can damage the developing embryo and subsequently damage the cerebral cortex, eyes, and ears.

Blood incompatibility between parents, in which the Rh factor is not contained in the mother's blood but is in the father's blood, will result in a high risk of blood incompatibility between mother and fetus.

Maternal care is also a primary consideration, especially in regard to the consumption of nicotine, alcohol, and drugs during pregnancy, which can damage the developing embryo.

Perinatal Period

During, or immediately after birth the brain can be compromised by a difficult delivery, bleeding, or low birth weight.

Postnatal Period

Diseases that interfere with the development of the brain or infections of the cranium (meningitis) or the brain (encephalitis) contribute to abnormal development. Environmental influences that interfere with the development of the brain may result from deprivation of sensory experiences or stimulation.

Furthermore, any toxic substances, such as lead, mercury, arsenic, or manganese, or metabolic disorders, such as diabetes and malnutrition, adversely affect the developing brain cells. Other disorders of metabolism, such as digestive, endocrine, or growth dysfunctions, also affect development. Included in these are galactosemia (a digestion disorder of the mother's milk), and hypothyroidism, in which growth hormones are not sufficiently produced.

Combined Periods

Intellectual disabilities are also caused by a variety of incidents that can occur before, during, and after birth. Trauma to the head, anoxia to the brain, tumors, lesions, syphilis or other sexually transmitted diseases, and psychological disorders are all possible causes of deficits. In addition, many forms of ID are idiopathic (i.e., have no known causes) or may be due to environmental influences, sensory deprivation, abuse, or neglect.

Approximately 13% of the school population is classified as having ID. The majority of children (90%) are mildly affected, require only limited supports, and are educated in regular classes. Approximately 5% are severely affected and require more extensive supports and assistance in their educational placement. ID will affect males and females in a similar manner, although some syndromes, such as Turner's syndrome (absence of X chromosome in females) and Klinefelter's syndrome (XXY sex chromosome in males) are sex linked.

Planning the Physical Activity Program

Most individuals will normally develop age-appropriate motor skills through maturation and observation of other children. Children with ID progress through the same sequence of motor development as their peers, although they are deficient in some areas and may require more specific instructions, time to practice, and additional opportunities to facilitate maturation and learning of motor skills. Development of physical and motor skills is essential for improving functional skills, community integration, and appropriate leisure and work experiences. In this context, the term *functional* or *functional skills* relates to activities of daily living or self-care activities needed to function in home and community-based environments.

Generally, most children with mild to moderate involvement, with intermittent supports, can be integrated into regular physical education classes and will closely resemble their peers in functional ability. In contrast, more involved children may function significantly lower in physical and motor development and possibly require more specific supports, intervention, and opportunities to facilitate development. Accordingly, teachers should match their instructional goals to the the individual child's developmental level in order to achieve program goals and objectives.

Assessing Level of Functioning

The level of physical and motor functioning should be ascertained before the IEP is developed and a physical education program implemented. Likewise, to facilitate learning and retention, teachers should strive to use the most efficient teaching techniques and appropriate cues (i.e., modeling) as well as needed supports for children to function in the educational environment. Norm- and criterion-referenced physical and motor assessments that are specifically designed for children with ID may provide the appropriate information to adequately assess the level of functioning and entry point for instruction. Additional information should be solicited from the collaborative programming team to develop behavioral goals and objectives that lead to increasing functional skill development and help in the transition plan.

Functional Ability

A primary consideration in developing a program for children with ID is their functional ability. Some children with mild involvement will function at a level that closely approximates their peers in physical fitness and motor development, although they may require more time or instruction to learn a skill. Clearly, the range of cognitive deficits found in individuals with ID is indicative of functioning and potential

(Horvat & Croce, 1995). The greater the severity of involvement, the less the individual is capable of independent functioning. Individuals with more severe cognitive deficits are limited not only by IQ but by the ability to relate socially to individuals in the community, to focus on goals, and to complete tasks. These individuals are less self-sufficient and may require more extensive supports on a continual basis to overcome deficits in physical functioning.

For children with more extensive involvement, deficiencies in motor development, as well as the social integration level, are more apparent. Younger children may require additional instruction and practice in focusing their attention to develop fundamental motor skills needed to facilitate movement, play, stability, and object control; older children may require instruction or observation of rules and strategies for group and team games, sports, and recreational activities that are common in their peer group and needed for community integration or work-specific skills. In addition, the overall growth and development may be affected by ID, although environmental constraints, such as nutrition, can be addressed to facilitate growth (Cronk, Puelzl-Quinn & Pueschel, 1996; Lindgren & Kotoda, 1993). In contrast, individuals with minimal cognitive deficits are more capable of independent functioning, rely less on pervasive supports, and are more easily integrated into community and home activities.

Appropriate Management and Rewards

Many times children with ID are prone to frustration, aggressive behaviors, or a lack of motivation, which can interfere with learning and achieving program goals. They may also demonstrate inappropriate behaviors when placed in stressful situations and when their instructional routine or environment is changed. Teachers and parents should try to facilitate an incentive system to eliminate inappropriate behavior and increase or maintain positive integrations and physical improvement. Controlling the environment may eliminate unnecessary and irrelevant stimuli that hinder the set routine for a particular activity. Teachers and parents should provide children with opportunities for appropriate emotional outlets for play and physical activity, as well as reinforcing acceptable behaviors to provide incentives for children to participate in physical activities. This may be as simple as using community recreational services to learn to play tennis or instruction in Tae Kwon Do.

Community-Based Programs

At times teachers can become discouraged with the child's level of progress or lack of progress during physical activity classes. Often a skill taught on Friday is lost over a weekend or vacation period, requiring teachers to begin teaching the skill again. Most teachers would probably say that children with ID require more opportunities to learn and practice their skill outside the classroom. In addition, the goal of any activity is to generalize the skill to community- or home-based settings, for example, developing play behaviors at home for young children. Several programs, such as Special Olympics or programs offered by recreational centers, provide opportunities for children to develop skills in sports and games as well as to gain exposure to the appropriate social development that is needed for optimal development. Although outside-the-school opportunities should not be substituted for physical education, it seems only logical that providing children with additional opportunities for participation will increase their physical and social functioning. Children should be encouraged to take advantage of organizations that provide sport or recreational experiences, and the development of strong parent-teacher teams should also be encouraged to facilitate community activities. Home-based programs developed by the teacher will allow parents to provide extra practice and instructional time needed to develop physical fitness, play skills, and social interaction. For older children, the development of physical fitness in community settings can be directly linked to increased work performance (Smail & Horvat, 2006; Seagraves et al., 2004). For teachers, who are limited by time and the number of children in their class, community and home-based programs can enhance their instructional program and also encourage the generalization of these skills outside the school setting (Carter, Horvat, & McCullick, in press).

Implementing the Physical Activity Program

Teachers who strive to develop truly comprehensive and effective physical education programs for children with ID should be mindful of those characteristics generally found to be unique to the population. The following analysis, and the outline of characteristics and instructional strategies in **Table 9.2**, can aid the instructor in tailoring a physical education program specifically to the needs of children.

Physical Fitness

Children with ID have a tendency toward low levels of physical fitness (Pitetti, Rimmer & Fernhall, 1993). Research indicates that children with ID lag behind their normal peers in static strength, dynamic strength, explosive strength, flexibility, cardiovascular endurance, and agility (Croce & Horvat, 1992; Pitetti & Fernhall, 1992; Horvat, Croce & McGhee, 1993). Fernhall (1992) has indicated that individuals with ID tend to have lower cardiovascular fitness, lower

maximal heart rates, inferior muscular development, and greater body fat than peers without ID. In addition, these children may be obese because of poor dietary habits and the lack of opportunities to participate in physical activities. Further, the impact of environmental factors such as nutrition may affect the growth status of children with ID (Cronk et al., 1996). The members of the collaborative programming team who can best develop a program of nutrition and physical activity include the nutritionist, parent, physician, and physical educator. These professionals should develop a broad base of physical fitness activities, behavior management, and appropriate dietary habits (Croce, 1990; Kelly, Rimmer & Ness, 1986; Whitt-Glover, O'Neill, & Stelter, 2006).

Because of the variability of physical and functional skill development, fitness levels of children may be variable. Based on previous work, it is evident that changes in functional level can be initiated with activity programs. Horvat and Croce (1995) consistently maintain that individuals with ID will respond to training interventions in a manner similar to that of their peers without ID. A critical element of most exercise programs is the ability to maintain intervention and generalize the activity to home, community, and work settings. A progressive activity program that gradually increases the duration, repetition, or time involved in an activity should be used. If appropriate, additional opportunities should be provided at home or in community and recreation settings. This was evident in several settings Zetts, Horvat, & Langone (1995) used circuit and vocational training in a community setting; Seagraves and Horvat (2004) implemented a resistance and vocational training program in a school-based setting; and Smail and Horvat (2006) implement their training program in school and community settings. Physical fitness activities, such as walking, jogging, aquatics, dance, aerobics, parachute activities, and stationary cycling, and progressive resistance exercises can be used with children with ID in regular physical education classes or community setting (Smail & Horvat, 2009). A circuit training program, as depicted in **Figure 9.1**, is an excellent way to help children increase physical fitness.

Learning-Memory Functions

Children with ID often have problems with complex thoughts and encounter problems conceptualizing a rule and/or strategy needed in a game. Because they also may possess a limited attention span, disrupted sensory and memory functions, instruction should be repeated and demonstrated on successive days to promote learning. The use of working memory or retaining information in short term memory is critical to recall and use of information in motor sequence or work-related tasks. Once the task is

Table 9.2 Characteristics and Instructional Strategies

Factor	Characteristics	Instructional Strategies	Physical Activity
Physical fitness	Tendency toward obesity; dynamic and explosive strength, flexibility, and cardiovascular endurance lag behind peers.	Provide a broad base of physical fitness activities based on the level of functioning and functional skill development. Gradually increase the duration and number of repetitions for each activity. Consult appropriate team members to develop diet and exercise program.	Aquatics, physical fitness and dance activities, aerobics, out side-the-school programs, walking, static stretching, yoga, parachute, jogging, and stationary cycling activities. Progressive resistance exercises (surgical tubing and weights).
Learning and memory functions	Difficulty with abstractions and problem solving, working memory, attention span, transfer of learning, and communication skills; unable to comprehend benefits of activity and difficulty with sensory information.	Use concrete examples and visual cues; provide opportunities to practice and demonstrate skill in a variety of settings; initiate activities that encourage verbalization; provide task-specific feedback.	Parachute, fundamental motor skills, activities coupled with modeling and visual cues, movement education activities, water exercises, stunts and games, swim skills, academic games and concepts, home and play activities.
Lack of opportunities	Sedentary lifestyle; restricted access to activity; lack of spontaneous play and opportunities to participate. Lack of generalization to home and community settings.	Encourage activity; use outside-the-school, community, sports, and recreational centers. Facilitate play with family members and peers.	Play activities; Special Olympics activities, community recreation, sports and fitness activities, including swimming, walking, cycling, and weight training.
Growth and motor development	Behind peers in balance, body perception, agility, locomotor skills, perception, and coordination; growth lags behind peers with insufficient nutrition; and variation in symmetry of movement.	Utilize a broad base of developmental motor skills based on functional skills, play behaviors, and balance.	Balance beam, board, line activities, gymnastics, tumbling stunts and routines, rhythms, movement education, homework activities, fundamental motor skill instruction, community recreation activities.
Social development	Poor self-image; tend to be imitators and followers. Lack of social interaction in play skills.	Provide appropriate social interaction activities with no failure concept; give praise for an accomplishment; utilize activities for appropriate level of functioning.	Social sequence activities, good behavior game, movement education, parachute, and play activities that require sharing and social interaction.
Inappropriate behavior and lack of motivation	Low frustration and poor performance under stress; aggressiveness; lack of motivation or ability to exert a sustained effort and comprehend benefits of activity.	Structure activities to ensure success; eliminate inappropriate responses and reinforce appropriate behaviors and any accomplishment; be an active model; utilize relaxation and activities that emphasize self-control and sustaining an activity.	Movement education activities, yoga, static stretching activities, community activities, recreation sports and fitness activities.
Play development	Inability to initiate play on an individual or group basis.	Provide numerous opportunities for solitary and structured play in school and after-school environment.	Manipulative toys, water play, balls in all variety of sizes and textures, sensory stimulation.

encoded in long-term memory, children with ID seem to retain information similar to their peers. This was evident in learning work-related skills as well as Tae Kwon Do forms (Smail & Horvat, 2006; Carter, Horvat, & McCullick, in press). Transfer of learning, which is often utilized when children learn similar skills, such as soccer and kickball, is not well developed and will necessitate repetitions of teaching instructions for each new skill. In addition Horvat,

Croce, and Zagrodnik (2010) indicated that children with ID including DS have difficulty utilizing sensory information to maintain stability. They recommend utilizing various feedback paradigms that use tactile-kinesthetic information in initial stages of learning and then accessing visual and vestibular sensory information. For example, when teaching Tae Kwon Do movement forms tactile prompts are used initially and later paired with visual prompts.

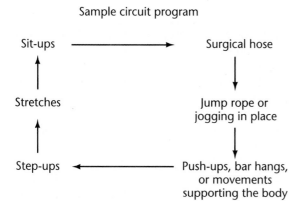

Sample circuit program

Figure 9.1 Sample cucuit program.

Teachers should also use concrete examples and prompts when teaching. A visual model of a person throwing a ball, as well as a poster depicting an appropriate throw, will reinforce the appropriate pattern in the early stages of learning. Once a throwing skill is learned, teachers should provide plenty of opportunities to practice. Throwing instructions can be followed by movement activities with balls, throwing at targets, or playing games that involve throwing, such as dodgeball. Teachers can also add a verbal response from the child during the activity to encourage appropriate verbalization and organization of movement information. As children learn about organizing relevant information, and they learn motor skills, they may become more efficient in retaining movement information (Horvat & Croce, 1995; Horgan, 1985). In addition, Croce, Horvat and Roswal (1994) have indicated that moderate levels of exercise increase the attention in children with ID and can possibly facilitate learning. Other activities that improve fitness include parachute games, fundamental motor skills, water exercises, and swim skills; academic games and homework activities can be added for the purpose of organizing and retaining information as well as completing the skill.

Motor Development

Children with ID are also deficient in their motor performance. Common development components of stability, body perception, gross agility, locomotor movement, and object control may be different because of motivation or difficulties in information processing (Horvat & Croce, 1995). Smail and Horvat (2005) also noted differences in symmetry and function on body sides that was alleviated with balance training. It is apparent that developmental and learning impairments restrict motor performance as well as opportunities to participate. Whitt-Glover, O'Neil, and Steltler (2006), reported that children with ID participate in less activity and have a tendency to be obese. In a manner similar to developing physical

fitness, children with ID will learn and develop motor skills. In order to facilitate development, a broad base of developmental physical education activities should be used to overcome motor deficits.

For preschool-aged or low-functioning children, activities should be provided that involve stability, object control, and locomotor movements that can be used in home and community settings, especially with peers. Developmental locomotor and object control skills that can be used in play settings should also be implemented outside the school to provide additional opportunities for practice and development.

Social Development

Children with ID tend to possess a low self-concept and may feel inferior to their peers in integrated classes. These children may not demonstrate appropriate social interactions with others or hesitate to join in any physical activity. In some instances, the low social interactions may occur from a lack of motivation or from lack of opportunities to participate in play-based activities (Horvat, Malone & Deener, 1993).

Teachers should arrange activities that involve intratask variation so that the task may be completed without failure and will ensure success. For example, children may take as much time as possible to swim across the pool, or they may use a kickboard for assistance. Activities can be modified to reflect the normal social-sequence development from solitary play to activities that foster group interaction. Activities that provide opportunities to share turns, that alternate responsibilities, and involve waiting for their turn are appropriate for this population and level of social development. In addition, the development of skills that facilitate play behaviors should be encouraged and implemented in the home if possible.

LEARNING ACTIVITY

Discuss the physical, motor, and social skills attributes often apparent among transition age children with ID. What skills will be needed to help ensure successful transition to independent living, work, social life, and active leisure?

Inappropriate Behaviors and Lack of Motivation

Inappropriate behaviors may be commonplace, especially when children are placed in stressful situations. To avoid completing a task, children may instead display inappropriate behavior. Children may also become frustrated because of their lack of understanding of a task, or they may display aggressive behavior when they cannot master a skill. Children with ID may also be hard to motivate, often not seeing the importance of the task, need to practice, or the importance of participating with sufficient intensity to produce changes in functional ability (Croce, 1990; Croce & Horvat, 1992; Montgomery, et al., 1988).

Most times teachers can ignore inappropriate behaviors and, in conjunction, can positively reinforce appropriate behaviors or participation and completion of tasks. Behavior games and activities that do not involve failure can provide teachers with opportunities to praise children for success. In addition, teachers can use activities such as relaxation, stretching, and yoga that not only increase flexibility, but also aid in developing and regaining control. Outside recreational or play settings, such as the community pool or fitness center, also provide opportunities for children to display appropriate social behaviors when coping with stressful situations and possibly increase their motivation for physical activity. In addition, a behavior-prompting program should be used to increase exercise or play behavior. Deener and Horvat (1995) used self-recording and social praise program to successfully increase running duration in children with ID. Others also have reported significant increases in participation with behavior management strategies (Eichstaedt & Lavay, 1994; Croce & Horvat, 1992; Smail & Horvat, 2006).

Play Development

Many times the importance of play for children with ID is overlooked. Participating in both solitary and cooperative play enhances the child's overall development and social, cognitive, and motor functioning, but such opportunities are not always available to children with ID (Horvat, Malone & Deener, 1993). By participating in activities during and after school that involve the use of manipulative toys, stuffed animals, balls, sand, and different textures, children can develop appropriate play experiences. Activities that incorporate music will also allow children to move and play. In addition, water play, such as blowing bubbles, kicking on an inner tube, and splashing, can be used when teaching aquatics and as a method to develop leisure-time activities and community-integration skills. Play at recess and after school can provide still more opportunities for physical activity. It has been reported that children with ID will display activity patterns similar to those of children without ID during play at recess. In each case, heart rate and activity counts were elevated during recess, supporting the contention that children with ID can benefit from play experiences (Horvat & Franklin, 2001; Lorenzi, Horvat & Pellegrini, 2000). Providing children with more opportunities to participate enables them to develop age-appropriate skills that will contribute to their overall development and integration into the school environment.

CHAPTER SUMMARY

1. Intellectual disabilities refers to significant limitation in intellectual functioning and adaptive skills that is evidenced during the developmental period.

2. Significantly subaverage intellectual functioning is specifically related to performance on a standardized intelligence test.

3. Adaptive behavior is expressed as conceptual, practical social skills that are expected of the individual's peer group.

4. The development period refers to the time from birth to 18 years of age.

5. The cause of ID is not easily determined. In a majority of the cases, the cause is idiopathic, or unknown. However, some cases may be due to chromosomal abnormalities, trauma, metabolism disorders, and a variety of other causes that can

be manifested in the prenatal, perinatal, postnatal, or combined periods.

6. Approximately 13 percent of the school population is classified as intellectually disabled. Of these, approximately 95 percent are mildly affected with limited supports and are in regular classes. Approximately 5 percent are more severely involved with more extensive supports.

7. Children with ID progress through the same sequence of motor development as their peers, who are not intellectually disabled only at a slower rate. Children with ID require more specific instruction time, practice, and additional learning opportunities.

8. It is essential to assess the physical and motor functioning of children with ID before developing the IEP and implementing a physical education program. Appropriate norm- and criterion-referenced physical fitness and motor assessments should

provide appropriate information to determine the child's functional ability.

9. Primary factors in developing the physical education program are the child's functional ability and level of functional skill development. Appropriate activities should be selected to enhance physical and motor functioning.

10. Opportunities outside of the school in community-based settings should be encouraged for additional practice, play, and socialization.

11. Children with ID are prone to low levels of physical fitness and require a broad base of physical fitness activities and appropriate dietary

habits that can be generalized to community and work settings.

12. Motor performance is also lacking and should reflect the development of balance, body perception, and locomotor and play skills that can be used in the home and community.

13. Appropriate social development and play should be included in the motor instructional program to facilitate appropriate behavior as well as developing skills.

14. Behavior management techniques eliminate inappropriate behavior and increase motivation and participation for children with ID.

REFERENCES

Carter, K., Horvat, M., & McCullick, B. (in press). Pedagogical approaches to learning Tae Kwon Do formas for an individual with and intellectual disability. *Journal of Physical Education and Dance.*

Croce, R. V. (1990). Effects of exercise and diet on body composition and cardiovascular fitness in adults with severe mental retardation. *Education and Training in Mental Retardation, 25,* 176–187.

Croce, R., & Horvat, M. (1992). Effects of reinforcement based exercise on fitness and work productivity in adults with mental retardation. *Adapted Physical Activities Quarterly, 9,* 148–178.

Croce, R., & Horvat, M. (1995). Exercise-induced activation and cognitive processing in individuals with mental retardation. In A. Vermeer (Ed.), *Medicine and sport science: Aspects of growth and sensorimotor development in mental retardation* (pp. 144–151). Basel, Switzerland: Karger.

Croce, R., Horvat, M., & Roswal, G. (1994). A preliminary investigation into the effects of exercise duration and fitness level on problem solving ability in individuals with mental retardation. *Clinical Kinesiology, 48,* 48–54.

Cronk, C. E., Puelzl-Quinn, H., & Pueschel, S. M. (1996). Growth standards in children with Down syndrome. *Developmental Brain Dysfunction, 9,* 59–71.

Deener, T., & Horvat, M. (1995). Effects of social reinforcement and self-recording on exercise duration in middle school students with moderate mental retardation. *Clinical Kinesiology, 49*(1), 28–33.

Dyer, S. M. (1994). Physiological effects of a 13-week physical fitness program on Down syndrome subjects. *Pediatric Exercise Science, 6,* 88–100.

Eichstaedt, C., & Lavay, B. (1994). *Physical activity for individuals with mental retardation.* Champaign, IL: Human Kinetics.

Fernhall, B. (1992). Physical fitness and exercise training of individuals with mental retardation. *Medicine and Science in Sports and Exercise, 25*(4), 442–450.

Fernhall, B., Tymesaon, G., & Webster G. (1988). Cardiovascular fitness of mentally retarded individuals. *Adapted Physical Activity Quarterly, 5,* 12–28.

Heward, W. L. (2009). *Exceptional Children* (9th ed.). Upper Saddle River, NJ: Pearson Education.

Horgan, J. S. (1983). Mnemonic strategy instruction in coding, processing, and recall of movement-related cues by mentally retarded children. *Perceptual and Motor Skills, 57,* 547–557.

Horgan, J. S. (1985). Issues in memory for movement with mentally retarded children. In J. Clark & J. H. Humphrey (Eds.), *Motor Development.* Princeton, NJ: Princeton Book Company.

Horvat, M., & Croce R. (1995). Physical rehabilitation of individuals with mental retardation: Physical fitness and information processing. *Critical Reviews in Physical and Rehabilitation Medicine, 7*(3), 233–252.

Horvat, M., Croce, R., & McGhee, T. (1993). Effects of a circuit training program on individuals with mental retardation. *Clinical Kinesiology, 47*(3), 71–77.

Horvat, M., & Franklin, C. (2001). The effect of the environment in physical activity patterns in children with mental retardation. *Research Quarterly for Exercise and Sport, 72,* 189–195.

Horvat, M., Malone, D. M., & Deener, T. (1993). Educational play: Preschool children with disabilities. In S. Grosse & D. Thompson (Eds.), *Play and recreation for individuals with disabilities: Practical pointers.* pp. 58–66. Reston, VA: American Alliance for Health, Physical Education, Recreation and Dance.

Horvat, M., Croce, R., & Zagrodnik, J. (2010). Sensory information to facilitate learning in intellectual disabilities. *Journal of Developmental and Physical Disabilities*.

Kelly, L. E., Rimmer, J. H., & Ness, R. A. (1986). Obesity levels in institutionalized mentally retarded adults. *Adapted Physical Activity Quarterly, 3*, 167–176.

Lindgren, G. W., & Kotoda, H. (1993). Maturational rate of Tokyo children with and without mental retardation. *American Journal of Mental Retardation, 98*, 125–134.

Lorenzi, D., Horvat, M., & Pellegrini, A. D. (2000). Physical activity of children with and without mental retardation in inclusive recess settings. *Education and Training in Mental Retardation and Developmental Disabilities, 35*, 160–167.

Luckasson, R., Borthwick-Duffy, S., Buntix, W. H., Coulter, D. L., Craig, E. M., & Reeve, A., et al. (2002). Mental retardation: Definition, In *Classification and systems of supports* (10th ed.). Washington, DC: American Association on Mental Retardation.

Montgomery, D. L., Reid, G., & Seidl, C. (1988). The effects of two physical fitness programs designed for mentally retarded adults. *Canadian Journal of Sport Science, 13*, 73–78.

Pitetti, K. H., & Fernhall, B. (1997). Aerobic capacity as related to leg strength in youths with mental retardation. Pediatric Exercise Science, 9, 223–232.

Pitetti, K. H., Rimmer, J. H., & Fernhall, B. (1993). Physical fitness and adults with mental retardation. *Sports Medicine, 16*(1), 23–56.

Pitetti, K. H., & Tan, D. M. (1991). Effects of minimally supervised exercise program for mentally retarded adults. *Medicine and Science in Sports and Exercise, 23*(5), 594–601.

Seagraves, F., Horvat, M., Franklin, C., & Jones, K. (2004). Effects of a school-based program on physical function and work productivity in individuals with mental retardation. *Clinical Kinesiology, 58*(2), 18–29.

Schalock, R. L., Luckasson, R. A., Shogren, K. A., et al. (2007). The naming of mental retardation: Understanding the term intellectual disability. *Intellectual and Developmental Disabilities, 45*(2), 116–124.

Smail, K. M., & Horvat, M. (2006). Relationship of muscular strength on work performance in high school students with mental retardation. *Education & Training in Developmental Disabilities, 41*(4), 410–419.

Smail, K. M., & Horvat, M. (2005). Effects of balance training on individuals with mental retardation. *Clinical Kinesiology, 59*, 43–47.

Smail, K. M., & Horvat, M. (2009). Resistance training for individuals with intellectual disabilities. *Clinical Kinesiology, 63*(2), 20–24.

Whitt-Glover, M. C., O'Neill, K. L., & Steltler, N. (2006). Physical activity patterns in children with and without down syndrome. *Pediatric Rehabilitation, 9*(2), 158–164.

Zagrodnik, J., & Horvat, M. (2009). Chronic exercise and developmental disabilities, In T. McMorris, P. Tomporowski, & M. Audiffen (Eds.), *Exercise and Cognition.* pp. 269–282. Hoboken, NJ: John Wiley and Sons.

Zetts, R., Horvat, M., & Langone, J. (1995). The effects of a community-based resistance training program on the work productivity of adolescents with moderate to severe intellectual disabilities. *Education Training in Mental Retardation and Developmental Disabilities, 30*, 166–178.

CHAPTER 10

Learning and Attention Deficit Disorders

CASE STUDY

Ron, a third grader, has difficulty paying attention, blurting out answers, and information processing. He tends to be disorganized and has difficulty maintaining attention sufficient for him to complete his work. In physical education, he has difficulty interacting with other children and prefers playing alone or going at his own pace. Ron's teacher is aware of his difficulties and tries to put Ron in situations where he is successful and does not have to process an inordinate amount of information at any given time.

Ron's teacher uses stations in class so that children can work at their own pace and relies on small-group instruction to facilitate effective skill instruction and promote positive interactions among children and between teacher and child. Ron's teacher has noticed that Ron is beginning to volunteer answers to questions, work cooperatively with peers, and praise peers for their efforts. The teacher also feels that increased physical activity levels have been helpful to Ron. Physical activity appears to have helped him to concentrate and to become more attentive. Ron's teacher has developed a home relaxation program for him and has encouraged him to be more active during out of school hours.

Learning disabilities are one of the most recently recognized and controversial of all exceptionalities. Until the 1960s a scarcity of information was available about learning disabilities; most children with such disabilities were grouped in classes designed for the intellectually disabled. To further complicate matters, a functional definition for identifying and placing learning-disabled students in special education was not available. There is no widespread agreement even today regarding terminology among academic disciplines. Psychology has used such terms as *perceptual disorders and hyperkinetic activity*, whereas the medical profession favors *brain injury or brain damage*, and language specialists prefer the terms *dyslexia* and *aphasia*.

In physical education, much of the work related to learning disabilities is based on the perceptual motor theories of Kephart, Barsch, and Cratty, the neurological development theories of Doman and Delacato, the sensory integration concept of Ayres, and the visual constructs of Getman and Frostig. Language disability theories concentrate on deficiencies in language and are generally based on the assumption that an intimate relationship exists between learning disabilities and deficits in language.

Recent attempts to define learning disabilities trace their origin to concepts of brain injury and minimal brain dysfunction. Children who were learning disabled originally were perceived as suffering from an infection or injury to the brain that caused deficiencies in perception, thinking, and emotional functioning. This idea was expanded with the concept of *minimal brain dysfunction* (MBD), which included children with deficiencies in language and motor development. In addition, the inclusion of minimal brain dysfunction in the definition of learning disabilities was an attempt to clearly differentiate learning disability from intellectual disability by using the concept of near-average intelligence to define the population. The term *specific learning disabilities* then evolved to describe children with language, speech, and communication problems.

In order to consolidate these concepts into a unified definition, the federal government offered the following definition in the Individuals with Disabilities Education Act (IDEA) rules and regulations:

> A disorder in one or more of the basic psychological processes involved in understanding or in using language, spoken or written, which may manifest itself in an imperfect ability to listen, think, speak, read, write, spell, or to do mathematical calculation. The term includes such conditions as perceptual handicaps, brain injury, minimal brain dysfunction, dyslexia, and development aphasia. The term does not include children who have learning problems which are the result of visual, hearing or motor handicaps, of mental retardation, or of environmental, cultural, or economic disadvantage.

In order to fully understand learning disabilities, one should note the differences in a child's capacity and actual achievement. Although the concept of discrepancy is not included in the IDEA definition, it can help us arrive at a more operational definition of learning disabilities. Discrepancy between capacity and achievement is assessed in one or more the following academic areas:

- Oral expression
- Listening comprehension
- Written expression
- Basic reading skills
- Reading comprehension
- Mathematical calculation
- Mathematical reasoning

Under the most recent IDEA regulation each state must develop criteria to identify children with learning disabilities. According to Heward (2009) most states use three criteria for a learning disabled diagnosis including (1) severe discrepancy between intellectual ability and academic achievement, (2) exclusion criteria that reflects differences that are not specific to another condition, and (3) learning problems that are evident despite standard educational efforts. An important part of this process is to employ scientific research-based intervention (SRBI) to determine eligibility for special education. Among the SRBI that can be employed are:

> Responsiveness to Intervention (RTI), a three-tiered approach that starts with primary (evidence based) intervention in the general education classroom that includes monitoring and assessing performance. Tier 2 (secondary intervention) includes students who are having difficulties in general education classes and require small-group instruction and additional tutoring. Children in this tier can be successful and return to the regular classroom, receive a second tier-2 intervention with some modifications or proceed to Tier-3 or instruction in special education (Heward, 2009).

Another intervention which may be more specific to physical and motor activity intervention is a Cognitive Processing Deficit Approach. This approach concentrates on identifying the processing deficits that are involved in learning disabilities (Flanagan et al., 2006). Processing problems and deficits are linked to the federal definition (a disorder in one or more of the basic psychological processes) and allow teachers the opportunity to develop interventions based on student needs (Florello, Hale, & Synder, 2006) and facilitate additional intervention planning based on the child's response to RTI (Flanagan et al., 2006).

Differentiated instruction is a technique to accommodate carrying levels of functioning within the same class. Initial assessment will help determine initial levels of functioning and academic problems or behavior difficulties. Because there is tremendous variability among children, one specific strategy may not work for everyone, requiring a variety of strategies such as cooperative learning or information processing strategies. The ability to adequately access and evaluate progress can be used to overcome variability including authentic assessment, rubrics, etc. (Horvat, Kelly, & Block, 2007). These teaching strategies are matched with learning styles to facilitate success and provide flexibility when dealing with learning problems. For example, the child who has difficulties with visual input information can receive instruction that is tactile or kinesthetic to feel (and learn) the correct pattern when swinging a tennis racket.

For teachers in physical education, a discrepancy is apparent if the child's performance level is one or two years behind the expected level of development. An individual who is functioning below the expected level of achievement will lag behind his or her peer group, and the discrepancy usually increases as the child gets older. Teachers must be aware, however, that discrepancies at various ages are not always comparable. Children who are deficient by one year in motor skill development at the age of 15 may not have as serious a problem as the 6-year-old who is deficient by one year in physical or motor development.

Recently, attention deficit disorder (ADD) or attention deficit hyperactive disorder (ADHD) have been applied to children with learning problems. According to the Center for Disease Control (CDC) survey, children 6–17 with ADHD (with and without LD) had increased with 5 percent having ADHD without LD, 5 percent had LD without ADHD, and 4 percent had both conditions (Pastor & Reuben, 2008). In addition, boys are more likely to demonstrate all conditions (ADHD without LD, LD without ADHD, and both ADHD and LD) than girls. Children with Medicaid are also more likely to demonstrate ADHD (Pastor & Reuben, 2008). Some other demographic data indicate children in mother-only households were also more likely to have each of the three diagnosis (Pastor & Reubern, 2008). Children with attention deficit disorders demonstrate academic difficulties as well as social problems (such as difficulty in working cooperatively), are impulsive, and have difficulty at sedentary tasks (Cunningham & Siegal, 1987; Pellegrini & Horvat, 1995). The diversity of school-related problems associated with attention deficit disorders and its relationship to learning disabilities resulted in the policy mandate by the United States Department of Education to clarify funding categories to provide service to children with ADHD under the following disability categories: learning disability, emotional disturbance, or other health impairment. In this chapter we choose to include attention deficits with and without hyperactivity with learning disabilities.

More specifically, the American Psychiatric Association (2000) included diagnostic criteria for attention deficit disorders in their recent guide (DSM–IV–TR, pp. 92–93). See the box on page 128. Because children may have a variety of characteristics it is important to thoroughly evaluate the child for potential problem areas and base program planning on the specific needs, developmental level, and interests of the child.

Etiology and Incidence

With such a broad interpretation of the definition of learning disabilities and attention deficit disorders, estimates of individuals who will qualify for special education services range from 1 to 40 percent of the entire school-aged population. It is interesting to note that more boys than girls are identified as learning disabled, with a ratio of approximately 2:1 of boys to girls. We should use caution with these statistics, however, because boys are sometimes more obvious in exhibiting overt behavioral and learning problems than are girls, who may be overlooked because their problems do not attract as much attention.

More children 12–17 years of age are identified with learning or attention deficits than children 6–11 years; although poverty and single-mother status may mitigate this prevalence of LD. Although educators do excellent jobs in remediating or compensating for learning difficulties, we should not assume that learning disabilities disappear or that children grow out of problems as they enter high school, college, or the work environment. The continuous evaluation and identification of children with learning deficiencies and attention deficits are a concern for all teachers and are evident at all ages.

Causes of Learning Disabilities and Attention Deficits

The causes of learning disabilities and attention deficits are generally unknown; rarely can the specific reason for a disorder be determined. One common speculation about learning disabilities is that they are *organically based*, and another is that they are *biochemically based*. The first theory holds that one of the primary reasons for learning disabilities is an injury to the brain that impedes the ability to receive and integrate sensory impulses. This is a widely accepted theory and is assessed by the administration of an electroencephalogram (EEG). The second theory posits that several biochemical factors, including a lack in amino acids, allergies, mineral and vitamin deficiencies, glandular disorders, hypoglycemia, and artificial foods and colors are related to learning difficulties. Theoretically, sensory input may be interrupted or stopped at synaptic junctions because of the breakdown of neurotransmitters, which interferes with the learning process. Finally, some researchers feel that the interaction between the biochemical and anatomical components of brain function disrupts the ability to receive, process, and retain sensory information. Some also believe that there is a genetic influence on whether learning disabilities run in families because children learn and mimic the actions of their parents.

Impact on Functional Development

Children with learning disabilities and attention disorders are often characterized by decreased physical functioning. Alexander (1990) indicated that whereas many academic concerns are addressed in the education literature, a scarcity of information is available on the physical and motor concerns of children with attention deficits and learning problems. Several concerns relate to movement, such as balance and awkwardness; others to perception, such as a disrupted feedback mechanism and memory disorders; and still others to lower physical work capacity. Each of these concerns posit that many of the child's early experiences with activity are not positive and should be addressed before an instructional program is implemented. In addition, children may also be diagnosed as having a developmental coordination disorder. According to the APA (2000), this diagnosis is made for a motor impairment that interferes with academic achievement or activities of daily living. Problems of developmental coordination disorder included delays in motor and nonmotor (language, etc.) abilities in children 5–11 years of age and are not associated with medical conditions or personality disorders.

Diagnostic Criteria for Attention Deficit Hyperactivity Disorder

A. Either (1) or (2):

(1) Six (or more) of the following symptoms of *inattention* have persisted for at least 6 months to a degree that is maladaptive and inconsistent with developmental level:

INATTENTION

(a) Often fails to give close attention to details or makes careless mistakes in schoolwork, work, or other activities.

(b) Often has difficulty sustaining attention in tasks or play activities.

(c) Often does not seem to listen when spoken to directly.

(d) Often does not follow through on instructions and fails to finish schoolwork, chores, or duties in the workplace (not due to oppositional behavior or failure to understand instructions).

(e) Often has difficulty organizing tasks and activities.

(f) Often avoids, dislikes, or is reluctant to engage in tasks that require sustained mental effort (such as schoolwork or homework).

(g) Often loses things necessary for tasks or activities (e.g., toys, school assignments, pencils, books, or tools).

(h) Is often easily distracted by extraneous stimuli.

(i) Is often forgetful in daily activities.

(2) Six (or more) of the following symptoms of *hyperactivity-impulsivity* have persisted for at least 6 months to a degree that is maladaptive and inconsistent with developmental level:

HYPERACTIVITY

(a) Often fidgets with hands or feet or squirms in seat.

(b) Often leaves seat in classroom or in other situations in which remaining seated is expected.

(c) Often runs about or climbs excessively in situations in which it is inappropriate (in adolescents or adults, may be limited to subjective feelings of restlessness).

(d) Often has difficulty playing or engaging in leisure activities quietly.

(e) Is often "on the go" or often acts as if "driven by a motor."

(f) Often talks excessively.

IMPULSIVITY

(g) Often blurts out answers before questions have been completed.

(h) Often has difficulty awaiting turn.

(i) Often interrupts or intrudes on others (e.g., butts into conversations or games).

B. Some hyperactive-impulsive or inattentive symptoms that caused impairment were present before age 7 years.

C. Some impairment from the symptoms is present in two or more settings (e.g., at school [or work] and at home).

D. There must be clear evidence of clinically significant impairment in social, academic, or occupational functioning.

E. The symptoms do not occur exclusively during the course of a pervasive developmental disorder, schizophrenia, or other psychotic disorder and are not better accounted for by another mental disorder (e.g., mood disorder, anxiety disorder, dissociative disorder, or a personality disorder).

Source: Adapted from the *Diagnostic and Statistical Manual of Mental Disorders* (4th ed.) (DSM–IV–TR), 2000, Washington, DC: Author.

Planning the Physical Activity Program

Because of the lack of understanding among disciplines, children with learning disabilities are often misunderstood. Often teachers subscribe to the view that these children are LD (lazy and dumb). Because the exceptionality is not obvious (as is, for example, the disability of a child sitting in a wheelchair), teachers often neglect or do not understand the needs of children with learning disabilities. The exceptionality does not render children incapable of learning but does require teachers to develop the physical education program and proper instructional methods according to their unique needs and functioning level of learning. With this in mind, teachers should consider the environment, social-sequence level of development, incentives, medication, relaxation, and remediation or compensation in planning and developing a comprehensive physical activity program.

Environment

Many times stimuli within the environment are sufficient to confuse, distort, or disrupt a child's ability to learn a motor skill. One preventive step for teachers is to control or adapt the teaching environment to best accommodate variations in learning. In rapidly changing environments beyond the control of teachers, teachers should take steps to prepare the child gradually to deal with distractions.

1. Physical educators can provide a highly structured program that establishes a routine for teaching procedures and arrangement of the physical education environment. Children should come to class in the same manner, at a designated location, before receiving instructions for the activity. Classes should always follow the same routine, moving from one station or group to another during the learning session. Teachers can minimize irrelevant stimuli at stations using cones, marking the specific area, or using mats as boundaries (Bishop & Beyer, 1995). Equipment should always be distributed and collected in the same manner, large equipment always positioned in the same location. By structuring the environment in this way, children may develop a sense of security and confidence that allows them to participate and develop age-appropriate motor skills.

2. Reducing stimuli (or intensity of stimuli) can help an instructor deal effectively with small groups (Hallahan, Kauffman, & Pullen, 2009), Although it is often difficult to reduce space without disrupting the activity, it may be possible to divide a gymnasium or pool, or to condense the teaching area by using cones as boundaries, and still conduct the activity according to program goals. Thus the instructor may reduce a wide-open space, which often interferes with learning, and provide the secure environment needed for children. Teachers can also remove external stimuli or reduce their effect on the activity in progress. For example, many times teachers bring too much equipment to a softball activity; all that is needed is two bats (one light, one heavier) and two balls (one held by the teacher). Additional equipment may distract children and may not be needed for the activity. Similarly, it is difficult to teach a basketball class while cheerleaders are practicing, or to teach a motor skill while another group is bouncing on the trampoline and may require facing away from the attractive stimulus. By reducing the outside stimuli (light, smell, sounds) during the activity, teachers can enhance children's ability to attend to teachers and/or class activities rather than to extraneous stimuli that disrupt the learning process.

3. Teachers should utilize an adequate number of teaching stations, audiovisual aids, and homework. Children may respond to such motivational devices as film loops, pictures, and posters, which may compensate for other deficiencies and which can reduce frustration by promoting an understanding of the activity. Teaching stations should be available to allow children appropriate time for instruction and practice, which is preferable to having the children wait in line, inadvertently attending to other stimuli. In addition, this procedure will provide concrete experiences and maximize the active learning time of all children in a class. Homework can also be effective for children with learning disabilities, providing additional practice opportunities and time to master a specific task. Horvat (1982) successfully used parents as tutors to overcome static and dynamic balance deficiencies with elementary school-aged children with learning disabilities.

4. Educators can enhance the stimulus value of instructional materials by using such devices as brightly colored balls or targets, which help children differentiate equipment from the background, or whistles and shrill sounds, which are easily discernible and can also be differentiated easily from background noises. Although teachers may not be able to control the environment completely in the initial stages of learning, some reduction of outside distractions is essential to alleviate additional problems. Because physical education settings may include rapidly changing tasks or environments, teachers should gradually prepare children to deal with distractions as part of the learning process.

Social-Sequence Level of Development

Children with learning disabilities may be socially immature and often reluctant to engage in activities because of their learning problems. They tend to withdraw from social relationships and may become the person no one wants on the team. Concerned teachers can provide an opportunity for a successful physical education experience by selecting activities at the functioning social level of each individual. This can be accomplished by following the social-sequence level of development.

The social-sequence level is the degree of social interaction that is involved in a particular activity. For example, the solitary kicking of a ball would be at the lowest level of a "ball-kicking sequence," whereas a kickball game would be at the highest level because more social interaction is required. The social-sequence levels are

1. Playing alone

2. Parallelling (two children playing with no interaction)

3. Onlooker

4. Two children in associative play, that is, informally playing together for brief periods

5. Cooperative play, or playing together in small groups

6. Cooperative play in which children play organized games in larger groups

Teachers can use these levels to help select an appropriate and socially acceptable activity for any given child. If children can function successfully at one level, they can progress to the next level with a minimum frustration and anxiety. In this manner teachers can facilitate social development by matching motor skills and providing appropriate learning experiences that encourage and develop social interaction.

Incentives and Rewards

Many times teachers can foster an appropriate behavior by utilizing an appropriate incentive and reward system. Social praise and incentives not only strengthen social acceptance but also reward children (who often are frustrated) for appropriate attempts or completion of a motor task. Trocki-Ables, French, and O'Connor (2001) used verbal praise and a token economy to facilitate performance on running fitness performance; while Horvat's (1982) home-based program used self-recording, stars, and hand-outs for coloring as incentives and performance awards. Teachers can also provide more tangible rewards in the form of stars, smiley faces, extra periods of activity, or free time on a piece of equipment initially for participation and later for task completion.

Finally, encouragement and goal setting can help children achieve their program goals. By actively participating and setting reachable goals, children can achieve success at their level of functioning and gradually move to more difficult tasks. As the children experience success, they become more motivated and can gradually take control of the pace for learning.

Medication

For children with learning disabilities, poor performance due to a short attention span may justify the use of medication. The physician and nurse will usually prescribe and dispense medication for such children; however, it is vital for teachers to recognize certain facts and reasons for using medication. Medication is used primarily to alter the neurological or biochemical makeup of children, rather than as a cure for a deficiency (e.g., short attention span). Teachers must be aware of each child's use of medication and of possible side effects that may contraindicate some activities, as well as periods of time the individual changes or is removed from medication (drug holiday). The four most commonly used medications for children and their side effects are listed below.

1. Methylphenidate (Ritalin, Methylin). Immediate (3–4 hours) and extended release (6–8 hours, 10–12 hours). Possible side effects include impaired coordination, loss of appetite, weight loss, insomnia, and nervousness.

2. Dextroamphetamine (Dexedrine, Denostrati). Possible side effects include psychic dependence, insomnia, restlessness, nervousness, dizziness, tremor, and dystonic movements of the head, neck, and extremities.

3. Dexmethylphenidate (Focalin). Immediate and extended release. Possible side effects include weight loss, irritability, tics, and sleep disturbances.

4. Amphetamine (Adderall). Immediate and extended release. Side effects can include appetite suppression, weight loss, and irritability.

Although teachers are not directly involved in dispensing medication, it is vital that they be aware of medication and its use to determine any detrimental effects on the individual's motor performance. Likewise, teachers should be aware of the possible benefits of medication and of any changes in dosage or termination of medication that might cause erratic behavior.

LEARNING ACTIVITY

Investigate and discuss the various types of medications, and their effects, used for treating learning disabilities and attention deficits.

Relaxation

One method that is not often used by teachers, but may be helpful, is relaxation training. The need for relaxation and stress reduction is common to most populations and perhaps should be used more frequently in all physical education classes. By incorporating relaxation activities, teachers can help children reduce anxiety and control tense muscles as well as improve concentration. Children can be taught to regain control especially after a period of highly excitable activities. In fact, relaxation exercises can be used to bring the class to a paced ending with a cool-down period and, more important, can help children regain their self-control. The following are examples of verbal instructions for several typical relaxation exercises.

> Bend the feet upward.... Pull hard!
> Harder! And let go.
> Push the feet down as far as you can....
> Push harder! And let go.
> Turn the feet farther, farther! And let them go.
> Straighten the knees as far as possible.... Now press your legs down into the mat, and let go.
> Straighten the knees again.... Press your legs together as tightly as you can... and let go.
> Straighten the fingers and pull back the wrist joints... and let go.
> Bend the fingers and wrist.... Now bend the joints of your elbows fully... more. And let go.
> Straighten the fingers and elbows, farther.... Squeeze shoulders forward and together. And let go.
> Close your eyes, and let your head fall to one side, return to middle, and fall to the other side. Repeat the movement again, and let go.
> Lift your head off the floor... and now drop back again and let go.
> Press your head back against the mat firmly, and then let go.
> Tighten the jaw, cheeks, face, and let go.
> Pull in the abdominal muscles, and let go.
> Push the legs forward until your back touches the mat, and let go.
> Sink into the mat, and breathe in and out as deeply as possible, and let go.
> Tighten the muscles of the shoulder girdle, and let go.
> Now tighten the fists, harder, and let go.

Other relaxation methods may be used, including the techniques of *Jacobson*, in which children learn to contract and relax muscles beginning with the extremities and proceeding to the head and neck and finally to the trunk. The child can tighten tense muscles and then concentrate on "letting go" and relaxing specific muscles or parts of the body. A similar technique developed by *Rathbone* uses static stretching for range of motion and breathing exercises to relax the diaphragm in conjunction with contracting and relaxing specific muscle groups. *Yoga* is a common activity that can aid in relaxation of muscles as well as control of breathing. Assuming specific postures—along with deep inhalation, retention of breath, and exhalation of breath—helps children develop flexibility and retain their emotional control and concentration. Other forms of exercise, such as *tai chi*, aid in increasing concentration and improving flexibility and balance for children and adults. Finally, an association set technique such as the *Yates relaxation technique* uses specific words to visualize a relaxed state. Words such as *melt* or *let go* are associated with relaxed or pleasant scenes that are anxiety free.

Cognitive Processing

Many teachers mistakenly believe that children with motor deficiencies simply require practice in the motor skill in which they are having problems, and so they direct all their instructional time to teaching these skills. No single approach to teaching, however, will always eliminate the deficit. Teaching to a deficit may result in success with time and practice, but it may also result in failure for the individual who can tolerate only a minimum of stimulation. Teaching to the deficit also neglects the information available to the other sense modalities. Teaching *around* the deficits, however, assumes that intersensory learning is occurring and that the individual can integrate auditory, visual, tactile, and kinesthetic sensory information (French & Horvat, 1986).

The model in **Figure 10.1** was developed from this source as a method for understanding various styles of learning and applying scientific research-based applications to learning. For example, some children may not be able to use visual input which necessitates using another modality to supply that information (i.e. tactile) to allow decision making and the appropriate motor output. Likewise, difficulty with decision making in any modality will also affect motor output, perhaps requiring the teacher to allow more time for processing or using a stimulus that is more distinguishable. The key is to match your instruction with the most appropriate method for the child to learn.

The instructor should always remember that children will learn and respond to instruction differently. If the deficiency cannot be overcome, it should be compensated for by appropriate teaching strategies at the individual's tolerance level for learning and with the most effective modality or modalities. In some instances, the teacher can cue the child prior to the task to allow more time to process the correct response. Other prompts may use visual models or physical guidance to cue the response. The initial concern is that the child learn and that we allow the child the opportunity to be successful. Specific learning styles may be determined in consultation with the special educator, school psychologist, occupational therapist, and/or adapted physical educator.

In addition, the teacher or parent should be aware of the severity level of the learning difficulty. Mild to moderate learning disabilities may necessitate practice in school and at home on balance and coordination, whereas severe learning disabilities may require a more extensive perceptual-motor learning program as well as many of the other measures discussed earlier. The severity level of the specific learning disability *must* be determined by the appropriate assessment process before the teacher plans the physical education program.

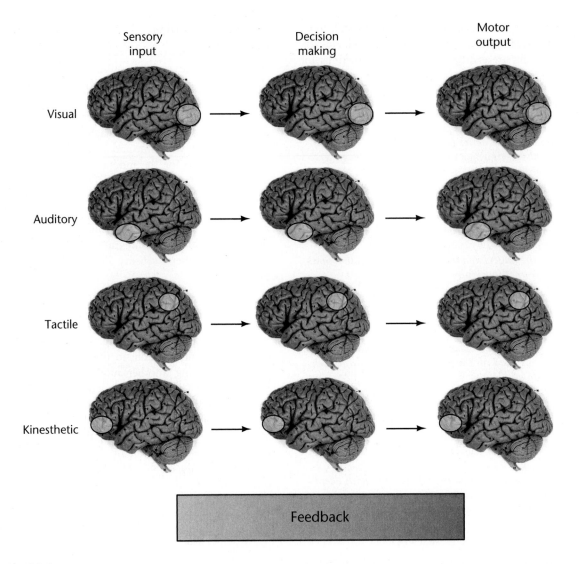

Figure 10.1

Implementing the Physical Activity Program

Motor dysfunctions that are usually associated with children with learning disabilities include dysrhythmia and deficits in coordination, balance, body image, haptic awareness, and motor planning (Harvey & Reid, 1997, 2003; Wharry, Kirkpatrick, & Stokes, 1987). For children who are unable to function adequately, a limited spectrum of movement has been developed. This is manifested in deficiencies in age-appropriate motor skills as well as poor social development and frustration that may be associated with the inability to perform motor activities.

It is especially important for teachers to plan the physical education program based on the individual learning characteristics. Most of the characteristics of children with learning disabilities have some effect on physical and motor performance. For example,

although hyperactivity is not a specific motor problem, it will be difficult for children to attend appropriately to the teacher and/or movement. The child who is hyperactive will attend to nothing, whereas the child who is distractible attends to everything in the environment. Deficits in the auditory, visual, or haptic modalities may also interfere with how the children receives, interprets, or finally performs a particular activity, while receptive, expressive language problems may manifest themselves in the inability to follow directions or execute movements requiring a vocal response. In addition, children may require additional time to process information. For example, children may still be responding to a verbal request and have difficulty understanding the task while the teacher inadvertently moves to the next skill. Allowing extra time to process the information or cueing the response may allow the child the necessary time to process the appropriate information and complete the task.

It is essential that children develop a sound movement base to ensure the development of age-appropriate skills. If a skill cannot be learned because of a deficit, teachers should compensate for the activity by using other strategies (modalities that may be more functionally appropriate for the child). The following sections describe some common characteristics of children with learning disabilities, along with specific teaching strategies and activities that can be implemented in a physical activity program. See also **Table 10.1**.

Hyperactivity

Children who are hyperactive are always in motion, constantly shuffling their feet, rocking, and manipulating objects. They attend to everything and often demonstrate the inability to sit or stand long enough to receive instructions for the activity. Physical activities should be aimed primarily at the problems caused by hyperactivity. Teachers should structure the environment by reducing the effect of outside stimuli to control the number of choices available and limit irrelevant stimuli to increase the chances for attending behavior. Medication may be used to promote attention and counter some of the symptoms of hyperactivity, but teachers should be aware of possible side effects, mood variations, or change in the dosage of or removal of medication that would result in changes in functioning. During the prekindergarten and kindergarten years, teachers are concerned primarily with social interactions and peer relationships, whereas primary grade children need to be taught to sit and attend to instructions. For the child who is hyperactive, this may signal the beginning of learning problems.

Teachers should also use methods that emphasize self-control, such as relaxation techniques or concentrating on how slowly an activity can be performed. Asking a child to walk as slowly as possible across the gym evokes interesting responses from children and requires them to focus on the task. Physical fitness skills that are structured, such as group exercises or training circuits, can be used successfully to counteract hyperactivity. Vigorous activities may be appropriate if they are followed by periods of relaxation that allow children an opportunity to regain control.

Perceptual-Motor Impairments

Perceptual-motor impairments can be auditory, visual, tactile, or kinesthetic (Chapter 7). Auditory perception refers to those functions that involve the ear's reception of sound and the integration of these signals. It involves discrimination of sound, locating the course or direction of sound, discriminating pitch and loudness, and selecting relevant from irrelevant auditory stimuli. This modality is very important in numerous physical activities, such as rhythmic movement and dance. Children

with an auditory perceptual deficit may also have difficulty following the physical educator's verbal instructions. They may be unable to sequence the words correctly or to determine the direction of the voice because of the numerous noises within the environment. Likewise, children who are unable to distinguish verbal cues concerning the correct way to grip a baseball bat would also be unable to complete the correct procedure or form in hitting a baseball. Of course, the child who needs and is given additional time to process this information may respond more appropriately.

Visual perception refers to the brain functions that involve the eyes' reception of signals and the integration of these signals. It involves making spatial relationships, discriminating dominant features in different objects, discriminating an object from its background, and identifying a figure when it can be only partially seen. For example, children with a figure-ground deficit may have a problem catching a ball or throwing a ball to a specific location or a teammate.

Haptic perception refers to the brain functions that interpret information received through the tactile (touch) and kinesthetic (movement of the body and muscles) senses and is essential for development and control of movement. Tactile perception involves the discrimination of geometric shapes, textures, object consistency, pain, and pressure. Kinesthetic perception includes balance skills and sensitivity to direction or position. Children with a tactile deficit may have problems manipulating objects because of the lack of meaningful information provided by the sense of touch, whereas a kinesthetic deficit could include problems with body image, balance skills, and tension in the muscles.

Individual learning differences and learning styles should influence selection of instructional strategies or alterations in the program that may be beneficial to ensure success. By determining the extent of the deficiency in the learning process, teachers can maximize the achievement movement potential for children with perceptual problems. The use of our earlier model will help the teacher develop the appropriate instructional technique.

Perceptual deficits that impede motor skill acquisition necessitate selecting meaningful teaching strategies to aid in distinguishing or enhancing auditory, visual, tactile, or kinesthetic cues. For example, a slight dysfunction in auditory perception may be overcome by using the hands, feet, sticks, or drums to create a rhythmic sequence used in dance activities and directing the child's attention to relevant input. Verbal cues, sounds made with implements (e.g., rattles), or recorded audio can also produce a variety of sounds, melodies, and/or pitches that may provide the appropriate auditory cues or prompts that help children select a proper response.

Table 10.1   Characteristics and Instructional Strategies

Behavior	Characteristics	Teaching Strategies	Physical Activity
Hyperactivity	Constant motion or rocking back and forth, tapping and/or shuffling while in a seated position, inability to focus attention.	Conduct activity in an area free of outside stimuli; carefully structure the entire program; simplify rules and use brief instructions, medication, reduction of space; enhance instructional stimulus (e.g., colored balls), operant conditioning.	Structured program beginning with vigorous activities (parachute, aquatics, running, hopping, jumping skills) and ending with a quiet activity (relaxation training). Emphasis on how slowly an activity can be done. Dance and rhythms.
Perceptual-motor impairments			
Auditory Figure-ground discrimination Sound localization Temporal perception	Deficiencies in: • distinguishing sounds from background • differentiating between sounds • determining direction of sounds • differentiating pitch	Use percussion instruments that will distinguish the figure or sound from the background; spoons; bells that form distinct sounds.	Auditory games that stress locations of objects and sounds, such as scavenger hunts; moving to and away from sounds.
Visual Figure-ground discrimination Spatial relationships Perceptual constancy Discrimination Visual-motor match	Deficiencies in: • differentiating object from background • assessing varying sizes and distances • determining balls of various sizes • differentiating between large and small • matching visual cue with motor output	Put masking tape on wall and floors, basketball backdrop, and goals that stand out; use colored footprints, brightly colored balls or beanbags.	Ball games with brightly colored balls; footprints for rhythmic movements and gross motor skills; stunts, tumbling, and trampoline activities. Activities that incorporate seeing (visual), feeling (haptic), manipulation (visual and haptic), hearing (auditory), and moving (visual and auditory).
Haptic Body awareness Body image Tactual perception	Deficiencies in: • determining laterality and directionality • identifying body parts • differentiating between objects and sizes • crossing the midline	Utilize activities emphasizing body parts on self and others; touch-and-move activities; activities based on functioning level and concepts using directions and directionality.	Tunnels, tires, mazes to move in, out, around, under; balance beams, boards, trampoline; activities of laterality. Discrimination and crossing the midline all pertain to balance and cross lateral movement patterns. Mirror exploration with body parts.
Gross motor deficits	Lack of balance, hand-eye, eye-foot coordination; awkwardness; dysrhythmia, poor motor planning.	Assess level of performance through direct observation. Use norm- and/or criterion-referenced tests. Provide program based on child's needs and most efficient modality for learning.	Utilize the part method or task analysis while teaching the skill. Introduce such activities as aquatics, rhythmic movements, balance progressions, parachute games, trampoline, group games, basic locomotor skills.
Attention Disorders			
Distractibility	Short attention span; inability to concentrate on appropriate tasks.	Use concise terms and/or demonstrations; use a single-task approach; do not keep children passively waiting; repeat instruction and activities to ensure retention; eliminate irrelevant stimuli; enhance stimulus value (mirrors, colors, etc.); use behavior management.	A variety of gross motor skills and simple activities; also parachute, aquatic skills/ games, and movement education activities.

Table 10.1 Characteristics and Instructional Strategies (*continued*)

Behavior	Characteristics	Teaching Strategies	Physical Activity
Disinhibition	Random shifts in attention, daydreaming, lack of inhibitory control.	Introduce activities that can be set into a routine; stop and start activity at the same time; practice; structure behavior management to focus attention.	A variety of gross motor skills and simple activities; also parachute games, aquatic skills/games, and movement education activities.
Perseveration	Inability to shift attention to succeeding task or spending too much time on one task.	Guide the students to another task, utilize a variety of tasks, rewarding only when one is completed; change activities frequently, with each being distinctly different from one another, e.g., formation, starting position, skills, rules, and strategies.	Activities that are not highly sequenced: ball skills, rhythmic movements, simple games, movement education, gross motor skills, parachute, trampoline, physical fitness activities, stunts and tumbling, circuit games, stop-go, green light.
Impulsivity	Unplanned, meaningless, inappropriate reactions to a variety of stimuli; lack of inhibitory control.	Devise a highly structured environment with no distractions; serve as an active model in all activities to increase attention.	Good-behavior game; structured progressions of gross motor activities including locomotion skills (running, jumping, hopping, balance progressions, stunts and tumbling).
Memory disorders	Failure to recall information or in proper sequence; hold onto information and use within seconds. Storage of new or previously learned material; retrieve as needed.	Utilize simple tasks; reinforce and select activities that can be sequenced; verbal rehearsal. Overlearning repetition; mnemonic activities; cues, feedback.	Dance activities and gymnastic routines, tumbling, parachute, low-instructional games; fitness activities, trampoline.
Dissociation	Inability to see the auditory, visual, or social whole.	Use whole-part-whole method with little verbalization; use activities that demand integrated working of body rather than activities with part of the body.	Social-sequence activities; whole, part/whole locomotor activities; tumbling, balance activities.
Specific learning disabilities	Disorders of mathematics, reading, writing.	Work with educational programming team to determine the level of functioning and most efficient modalities for learning. Enhance existing modality or compensate for deficiency.	Games and relays that reinforce academic concepts: number and letter grids; parachute activities stressing academic concepts; developmental physical education activities and games that involve counting or other responses.
Disorders of language	Problems with plural formation, articulation, expressive and receptive language.	Utilize visual cues with verbal instructions, demonstration, gestures, and haptic cues. Do not substitute words with similar meanings (big/large, etc.). Pair words with picture demonstration. Encourage verbal response before performing activity. Use concrete rather than abstract movement activities.	Academic games and relays that encourage verbal responses or response to visual cues; parachute activities and developmental physical education activities; games that involve counting.
Soft neurological signs	Neurological dysfunction, including brain damage.	Work with the educational programming team to determine the level of functioning and most efficient modality for learning. Enhance existing modality or compensate for deficiency.	Develop a sound program based on the needs and functioning of the individual. Utilize physical fitness, aquatics, dance, fundamental skills and patterns, sports, and games.

(continued)

Table 10.1 Characteristics and Instructional Strategies (*continued*)

Behavior	Characteristics	Teaching Strategies	Physical Activity
Behavior/ conduct	A wide range of behaviors, with the capacity to excel in one and the inability to comprehend another; low frustration tolerance; explosive behavior.	Work with the educational programming team to determine the level of functioning and most efficient modality for learning. Enhance existing modality or compensate for deficiency. Structure the program; ignore inappropriate behavior; be enthusiastic and consistent.	Develop a sound developmental physical education program based on the needs and functioning of the individual. Utilize physical fitness, aquatics, dance, fundamental skills and patterns, sports, and games and praise accomplishment.
Social skills	Antisocial behavior; lack of friends; being last one selected in games; inablity to cooperate with peers; low self-esteem.	Use a gradual approach to participation, and allow time for practice before group participation. Praise any achievement or accomplishment (using successive approximations).	Implement social-sequence games and activities that require cooperation; movement education activities that require two people; parachute activities, stunts, and tumbling. Conduct the program in a small area; use a good-behavior game and movement education technique in which everyone is correct.

Perceptual functioning in the visual modality may be enhanced by using posters, pictures, film loops, or slides to reinforce correct input information. Continually modeling the proper form or using distinguishable colors (such as optic orange) may help children match the correct visual information with a motor output. Visual input can be enhanced by providing a designated target or zone, such as a square on a basketball backboard, that cues the child to a specific or designated area. More important, the cues can be controlled by the child who has adequate time to process and use the information.

Kinesthetic perception may be enhanced by full or partial cues designed to increase awareness of proper position. For example, spotting belts allow the child to "feel" the correct location of his or her body in space. Lighter equipment, or a variety of textures and sizes of implements, can supplement input and decision-making data to ensure the proper position or the execution of the motor skill (output). In each use, the child is directed to the appropriate task specific information.

Gross Motor Deficits/Awkwardness

Often children with learning disabilities or developmental coordination disorders manifest awkwardness and are uncoordinated in their movements (Harvey & Reid, 1997). They may have problems running, throwing, catching, kicking, and balancing; as a result, they may stumble during games and activities. It is important to accurately assess the level of functioning through direct observation or appropriate assessment

instruments. In many cases, the stimulus may be too fast for the child to make a decision on the location of an object, such as a Frisbee. Slowing the stimulus or reducing the distance may allow the child to gauge the object route and catch the object. Likewise, in fitness activities like swimming and resistance activities, the child can control the timing of the movement without adjusting to the external environment, allowing the child to control the movement. Many times physical educators will need to consult with the appropriate school personnel to determine whether the deficiency can be overcome through a program designed to develop maturational skills or activities designed to compensate for perceptual or sensory deficiencies. The program should be designed according to the child's level of development and effective style of learning. Activities such as fitness, fundamental motor skills, aquatics, dance, and group games and sports all may be appropriate.

Attention Disorders

Disorders of attention include distractibility, disinhibition, and perseveration. Many children with the problem of distractibility are unable to block out irrelevant stimuli and concentrate on a task. For these children, nonessential equipment, bright light or colors, and extraneous sounds interfere with the ability to concentrate on an appropriate task. A structured environment designed to eliminate inappropriate external stimuli or to gradually introduce children to the teaching setting can be effectively developed. For example, activities should be conducted in a softly colored room without pictures, posters, or obvious attractive visual stimuli. An activity perhaps should not be performed outdoors if, for example, someone is mowing a lawn nearby or if cars are rushing by the playground. Space should be limited to what is needed for the activity, while auditory distractions or background noises should be eliminated if possible in the early stages of learning. In addition, selected stimulus enhancement, such as the use of brightly colored balls that do not blend into the background, will allow children to concentrate more readily on the task.

Teachers should also remember not to overuse praise with destractible children. Too much positive reinforcement may actually complicate the problem further. A low-keyed positive reinforcer is more appropriate for children who find it hard to concentrate on the task at hand.

Another tactic is to increase gradually the stimuli that children can handle. For example, if children can follow only verbal directions, do not model the movement and issue verbal directions at the same time. Likewise do not select an activity that requires children to attend to several stimuli at once to be successful; instead, gradually integrate such activities with higher-level skills. This is as a common mistake of beginning teachers and may interfere with the child's ability to learn effectively.

Disinhibition, or random shifts in attention and daydreaming, will often manifest itself as an attention problem. Lazarus (1994) described this as a lack of inhibitory control and the presence of associated movement or movement overflow. A highly structured routine, including requiring specific clothing for class, locating equipment in the same position and dispensing it in the same manner, and beginning and ending the class in the same way, will at best relieve much of the anxiety leading to disinhibition. Parachute activities and gymnastic stunts, as well as fitness or circuit courses, are useful activities in structuring the environment and circumventing the problem.

Another attention disorder that may affect children is perseveration, or having difficulty shifting attention to a succeeding task or spending too much time on one task. By guiding children to another task and rewarding only the tasks that are completed, teachers can direct children to another skill. For example, if a child perseverates on bouncing a ball, the teacher can urge the child to stop and shoot by modeling and/or performing the activity simultaneously and rewarding the child only when both sequences are completed. Likewise, the teacher can have the parachute shaken vigorously and change the activity to hopping in a circle, thereby making it impossible for children to perseverate without being dragged around the circle. It may also be helpful for teachers to select distinctly different activities that are not highly sequenced, such as circuit games, relays, and/or physical fitness activities.

Impulsivity

Children may respond impulsively, or in an unplanned, meaningless, or inappropriate reaction, to a variety of stimuli. Impulsivity is one of the behaviors reported by Lazarus (1994) that reflect inhibitory control. Often these children respond to a stimulus without thought or fear of the outcome. For example, children may jump into the swimming pool without regard to the depth of the water or to their swimming ability. By serving as an active role model to increase attention and structuring all activities to provide discernible instructions, the educator may eliminate many impulsive responses. Many teachers also use structured games and progressions as well as fitness circuit activities to deal effectively with inhibiting unplanned responses and directing attention to completing the activity.

Disorders of Memory

Children may be unable to recall information or to recall it in proper sequence. This is naturally disruptive and frustrating for children who are learning a motor skill. If they are given progressive tasks, children can link movements that can be processed more easily and successively built upon. Activities such as rhythmic movements, gymnastics skills, tumbling routines, parachute games, low-instructional games, trampoline, and aerobic fitness activities are all tasks that can be started simply, sequenced, and reinforced. For example, gymnastics skills can be taught separately and practiced in routines to enhance retention and to provide feedback on learning and additional opportunities for practicing motor skills. Likewise, modeling or guiding children through the response will help them remember the skill and/or sequence that is appropriate.

Dissociation

At times children will not be able to see the entire auditory or visual sequence. This is called *dissociation*. If something is missing that distorts the proper motion or sequence, it is apparent that children will not learn the motor skill. For example, not seeing all the movements in a swimming crawl stroke will prohibit the child from learning that particular swimming skill. By using activities that require little verbalization, and by using the whole-part-whole method of teaching a motor skill, teachers can integrate specific movements into a proper sequence of movement instead of just associating movements with parts of the body. Basic locomotor skills can be used to enable the child to see the visual whole. To create an auditory whole, the instructor should initiate activities that require little verbalization and that are paired with appropriate visual cues, such as a hand signal with the verbal command "Go." In addition, children who miss the point of a remark or the humor of a situation, should be involved in social-sequence and interaction activities appropriate for their own level of functioning.

Specific Learning Disabilities

Although physical educators are not directly concerned with specific learning disabilities, that is, disorders of math, reading, and writing, indirect benefits can be gained from a joint effort with academic instructors. By determining the most efficient method for learning, educators can enhance the existing functioning level or compensate for a deficiency. Academic games that reinforce number and letter concepts are appropriate for this joint effort. Physical education activities that involve counting or number and letter grids are useful to help children reinforce academic concepts, such as those in reading and mathematics. Instructors should not assume that academic learning is to be substituted for physical education; however, the joint effort of classroom and physical education teachers can enhance the overall development and self-concept of children with learning disabilities.

Disorders of Language

As in the case of specific learning disabilities, language disorders, such as difficulties in plural formation, articulation, and expressive and receptive languages, are not the primary responsibility of the physical educator. However, the physical educator can work with teachers on common concepts, such as integrating both sides of the body or tracking tasks that may facilitate academic behaviors. Teachers can also use appropriate visual and haptic cues to encourage movements. In general, teachers should use concrete rather than abstract activities and should avoid words with similar meanings.

Games that involve counting and that encourage verbal response are appropriate. Academic games, parachute activities, and developmental physical education activities are all appropriate for children with a language disorder (French & Horvat, 1983).

Soft Neurological Signs

The most important thing to remember about neurological dysfunction, or soft neurological signs, is that some damage has occurred to the brain. If teachers can address the specific problem area early in the child's development, other areas of the brain may take over impaired functions before the process of myelinization takes place. A joint effort with the collaborative team is essential to determine the child's level of functioning and the best ways for the teacher to present information. If children can learn through the existing modality, then enhancing their strengths with specific instructional methodology is essential. However, teachers may be forced to compensate for an existing deficiency by using other modalities, cueing children and presenting instruction in a way that aids in learning. However, teachers must ensure that they do not overestimate the capacities of children who can tolerate only a minimum amount of stimulation.

A sound developmental physical education program that is based on the child's needs and functional ability is essential for children with neurological dysfunctions. Older children, for instance, who fail miserably at games involving coordination and teamwork may do well in activities such as swimming and physical fitness. However, no aspect of physical education should be neglected in developing a comprehensive activity program.

Behavior/Conduct

One of the unique characteristics of children with learning disabilities is the wide range of behaviors they display, such as the capacity to excel in one area and their inability to comprehend another. Children who are whizzes in mathematics but cannot read are often frustrating to teachers, to parents, and especially to themselves. In addition, these frustrations may hinder acceptance by peer attitudes. By not functioning well in physical activities that require coordination or perception, children may be placed at a disadvantage in making friends and interacting with others in peer group games (Alexander, 1990). They may also become frustrated and demonstrate inappropriate behaviors because of their lack of success.

Social Skills

Many children have difficulties interacting with others and making friends. Heward (2009) indicated that not every child will have interaction difficulties, but children may interpret social situations based on their own experiences and difficulty perceiving non-verbal expressions. Other children with low self-esteem may have a history of disappointments and lack of success in academic, activity, and social settings (Heward, 2009).

It is important to utilize the team concept for ascertaining the level of functioning and the most effective learning strategy for the child. Physical educators can provide the sound developmental program that is essential for children to gain peer group acceptance and social interaction, while regular classroom teachers and educational specialists can combine efforts to teach new concepts, provide practice, or reinforce learned concepts for children (Zentall & Stormont-Spurgin, 1995).

CHAPTER SUMMARY

1. One operational definition for *learning disabilities* is a performance level of 1 or 2 years behind the expected level of achievement in one or more of the following academic areas: (a) oral expression; (b) listening comprehension; (c) written expression; (d) basic reading skills; (e) reading comprehension; (f) mathematical calculation; and (g) mathematical reasoning. Individual states can determine discrepancy by using scientific-based research interventions.

2. The causes of learning disabilities are unknown; however, speculations include an injury to the brain or possible biochemical factors, such as a lack in amino acids, vitamin and mineral deficiencies, allergies, and in some cases genetics.

3. Children with learning disabilities are often misunderstood and are considered lazy, mentally deficient, or considered to have behavior problems. Learning disabilities, however, do not render children incapable of learning but require the teacher to develop alternative instructional methods based on their specific learning characteristics and scientific-based interventions.

4. Teachers can enhance the learning process by structuring the environment to limit outside distractions and external stimuli.

5. Teachers should provide appropriate activities at the functioning social level of each child.

6. Appropriate incentive and reward techniques should be utilized to strengthen the occurrence of appropriate behavior.

7. Teachers should also be aware of any medications being used, their side effects, and any contraindicated activities.

8. Relaxation techniques can be incorporated into the physical education program to help reduce hyperactivity, control and tense muscles, and improve concentration.

9. Deficiencies can sometimes be overcome with practice. If not, the deficiency should be compensated for by appropriate teaching strategies at the child's tolerance level for learning and with the most effective learning modality.

10. Many of the characteristics of children with learning disabilities will affect physical and motor performance. Children with learning disabilities are often deficient in coordination, balance, body image, haptic awareness, and motor planning. The physical education program should be based on the unique learning characteristics of each child.

11. Teachers can deal with hyperactivity by structuring the environment and emphasizing self-control activities.

12. Teachers may also be required to select meaningful teaching strategies to aid in enhancing auditory, visual, or haptic cues.

13. Attention disorders are prevalent in this population, so distractions during the learning process should be kept to a minimum.

14. Children with learning disabilities display a wide range of behaviors. They may excel in one area but be unable to comprehend another. Therefore, behavior disparity is a classic example of the importance of the team concept in assessing level of functioning and developing effective learning strategies. Physical educators can provide a sound base for peer group acceptance and social interaction, as well as incorporate academic games and concepts into the physical education program to assist in the total education of children with learning disabilities.

REFERENCES

Alexander, J. L. (1990). Hyperactive children: Which sports have the right stuff? *The Physician and Sports Medicine, 18,* 105–108.

American Psychiatric Association. (2000). *Diagnostic and statistical manual of mental disorders* (4th ed.) (DSM-IV-TR). Washington, DC: Author.

Bishop, P. & Beyer, R. (1995). Attention Deficit Hyperactivity Disorder (ADHD) implications for physical educators. *Palaestra* 11, 39–46.

Cunningham, C., & Siegal, C. (1987). Peer interactions of normal and attention deficit disordered boys during free play, cooperative task, and simulated classroom situations. *Journal of Abnormal Child Psychology,* 15, 247–268.

Flanagan, D. P., Ortiz, S. O., Alfonzo, V. C. & Mascolo, J. T. (2006). *The achievement test desk reference: Guide to learning disability identification.* New York: John Wiley and Sons.

Flanagan, D. P., Ortiz, S. O., Alfonzo, V. C. & Dyndou, A. M. (2006). Integration of response to intervention and norm referenced tests in hearing disability identification. *Psychology in the Schools, 43,* 807–825.

Florello, C. A., Hale, J. B, & Synder, L. C. (2006). Cognitive hypothesis and response to intervention for children with reading problems. *Psychology in the Schools. 43,* 835–853.

French, R., & Horvat, M. (1983). *Parachute movement activities.* Bryon, CA: Front Row Experience.

French, R., & Horvat, M. (1986). The acquisition of perceptual skills by motorically awkward children. *Motor Skill Theory into Practice, 8,* 27–38.

Hallahan, D. P., Kauffman, J. M., & Pullen, P. C., (2009). *Exceptional learners: Introduction to special education,* (11th ed.). Boston: Pearson Education.

Harvey, W. J., & Reid, G. (1997). Motor performance of children with attention-deficit/hyperactivity disorder: A preliminary investigation. *Adapted Physical Activity Quarterly, 14,* 189–202.

Harvey, W. J. & Reid, G. (2003). Attention-deficity/hyperacticity disorder: A review of research on movement skill performance and physical fitness. *Adapted Physical Activity Quarterly,* 20, 1–25.

Heward, W. L. (2009). *Exceptional children* (9th ed.). Upper Saddle River, NJ: Pearson Education.

Horvat, M. (1982). Effects of a home learning program on learning disabled children's balance. *Perceptual and Motor Skills, 55,* 1158.

Horvat, M., Kelly, L., & Block, M. (2007). *Developmental and adapted physical activity assessment.* Champaign, IL: Human Kinetics.

Individuals with Disabilities Act of 1997, Pub. L. No 105-17. (1997, June 4).

Lazarus, J. L. (1994). Evidence of disinhibition in learning disabilities: The associated movement phenomenon. *Adapted Physical Activity Quarterly, 11,* 57–70.

Pastor, P. N., & Reuben, C. A. (2008). Diagnosed attention deficit hyperactivity disorder and learning disability. United States 2004–2006. National Center for Health Statistics. Vital Health Stat 10(237).

Pellegrini, A. D., & Horvat, M. (1995). A developmental contextualist critique of attention deficit hyperactivity disorder. *Educational Researcher, 24,* 13–19.

Trocki-Ables, P., French, R., & O'Connor, J. (2001). Use of primary and secondary reinforcers after performance of a 1-mile walk/run by boys with attention deficit hyperactivity disorder. *Perceptual and Motor Skills, 93,* 461–464.

Wharry, R.; Kirkpatrick, S. W., & Stokes, K. (1987). Motor training and precision performance with learning disabled children. *Perceptual and Motor Skills, 65,* 973.

Zentall, S. S., & Stormont-Spurgin, M. (1995). Educator preference of accommodations for students with attention deficit disorder. *Teacher Education and Special Education, 18,* 115–123.

CHAPTER 11

Autistic Spectrum Disorders

CASE STUDY

Michael is a 9-year-old boy with autism. He has difficulty communicating with his peers and frequently fails to respond when people speak to him. Michael never initiates conversations and rarely makes eye contact with others in the class. Periodically, Michael becomes upset and loses his temper throughout the school day. Despite these barriers, Michael makes a strong effort to succeed and is slowly becoming more integrated in the community.

Michael currently receives special education at Springdale Elementary School. Mrs. Smith, Michael's adapted physical education (APE) teacher, has been unable to find effective teaching strategies to work with Michael. He rarely listens to Mrs. Smith and he has difficulty interacting with the five other children in his APE class. In order to reassess strategies for working with Michael, Mrs. Smith schedules an IEP team meeting. At the IEP meeting it was suggested that Mrs. Smith incorporate the TEACCH model in her class to best meet Michael's needs. This model incorporates structured teaching methodologies and physical boundaries as a way of fostering student independence. After one month using TEACCH, Mrs. Smith finds a significant improvement in Michael's behavior and performance during class.

In the 1940s the term autism was used independently by Kanner (1943) and Asperger (1944) to described children who were socially isolated, had poor eye contact, and had limited expressive gestures (Wing, 1991). Moreover, Kanner and Asperger found these children to lack imaginary play, had an obsessive desire for sameness, and displayed a repetitive pattern of activities. At times, they also found their behaviors to be destructive and aggressive, with odd and/or extreme reactions to sensory stimuli. Currently, Autism is classified as a developmental disorder of unknown cause, having heterogeneous behavioral symptoms. Major behavioral symptoms are qualitative deficits in social interaction, communication, and behaviors and interests that are unusually restrictive and repetitive (American Psychiatric Association, 2000). Relative to the educational environment, individuals with autism can display profound attention deficits and have severe problems in learning.

Diagnoses and Classification

According to the Diagnostic and Statistical Manual of Mental Disorders (DSM-IV-TR) published by the American Psychiatric Association (2000), Autism is classified as one of the five Pervasive Developmental Disorders (PDD). Other classifications for PDD are Asperger's Disorder (AD), Rett's disorder (RD), Childhood Disintegrative Disorder (CDD), and Pervasive Developmental Disorder-Not Otherwise Specified (PDD-NOS). Because of difficulties with a definitive diagnosis for each subtype of PDD, as well as there being no overwhelming support for the uniqueness of subtypes, many scientists and clinicians advocate the use of the term autistic spectrum disorders

(ASD) to describe the variety of symptoms found in these children (Reid & Collier, 2002).

Based on the DSM-IV-TR, children with ASD are characterized by severe and pervasive impairment in (1) reciprocal social interaction, (2) communication, and (3) stereotypical behavior, activities, and interests. Moreover, impairments are described in qualitative terms and must be "distinctly deviant relative to the individuals developmental level or mental age" (p. 69). Problems that may accompany ASD include:

- Sensory—Many children with ASD are highly attuned or have painful sensitivity to certain sounds, textures, tastes and smells, indicating that in ASD the brain may not be able to balance sensory input appropriately.
- Intellectual disabilities—Many children with ASD have some degree of mental impairment.
- Seizures—One in four children with ASD develop seizures (National Institute of Mental Health, 2008). Autistic Spectrum Disorder can often be detected by age 3, and occasionally as early as 18 months.

Autism

The two most prevalent types of ASD, and hence, the two types most encountered in the educational environment, are autism and Asperger's disorder. Based on DSM-IV-TR, for a diagnosis of autism six criteria must be met, including at least two impairments in social interaction, one impairment in communication skills, and another impairment in restricted, repetitive and stereotyped behavior. The last two criteria can occur in any of the three stipulated areas (see **Table 11.1**). In addition other characteristics of autism frequently, but not universally, observed include:

- Varying levels of intellectual disability
- Hyperactivity
- Aggression
- Self-injurious behaviors
- Temper tantrums
- Sleep disturbances

All of these behaviors are evident particularly in young children. Although there are two instances where problems in motor behavior are mentioned as being a part of autism, they are not part of the diagnostic criteria. These motor behaviors include repetitive behaviors, such as hand flapping, and odd postures, such as walking on tip toes.

Individuals diagnosed as autistic can share a common diagnosis, yet have varying behaviors. As a result, when designing physical education, activity, sport, and recreational programs for individuals with autism, their physical needs will vary and cover a diverse spectrum of deficiencies. Because of the diversity in behavior, designing appropriate physical education and sport programs for individuals with autism may be quite difficult, and require teachers to match the needs of each child to the specific activity and necessitate the teacher to teach in imaginative and unique ways.

Asperger's Disorder (Asperger Syndrome)

A milder and more functional type of ASD, having its own unique specific diagnostic, is Asperger's disorder (AD) (see **Table 11.2**). In 1944 a Viennese physician, Hans Asperger, published a paper in which he described

Table 11.1 Diagnostic Criteria for Autism

Category One: Difficulties in Social Interaction	Category 2: Difficulties in Communication	Category 3: Restricted, Repetitive, and Stereotyped Patterns of Behavior, Interests, and Activities
• Marked difficulties in using multiple nonverbal behaviors such as eye contact, facial expression, body postures, and gestures. • Failure in developing peer relationships commensurate with developmental level. • Lack of spontaneous seeking behavior to share enjoyment, interests, or achievements with other individuals. • Lack of social or emotional reciprocity.	• Delay or lack of appropriate language skills. • In individuals having adequate speech, difficulties in initiating and sustaining conversation with others. • Stereotyped and repetitive use of language. • Lack of varied, spontaneous make-believe play or social imitative play commensurate with developmental level.	• Preoccupation with one or more stereotyped and restrictive patterns of interest that is atypical. • Inflexible adherence to specific, nonfunctional routines or rituals. • Stereotyped and repetitive motor mannerisms such as finger or hand flapping or twisting. • Continual preoccupation with parts of objects.

To diagnose autism six or more criteria must be met; including two criteria from category 1, one criteria from category 2 and one criteria from category 3.

Adapted from the Diagnostic and Statistical Manual of Mental Disorders [DSM-IV-TR], *American Psychiatric Association*, 2000.

Table 11.2 Diagnostic Criteria for Asperger's Disorder

Category 1: Difficulties in Social Interaction	Category 2: Restrictive, Repetitive, and Stereotyped Behavior Patterns, Interest, and Activities	Category 3: Other Symptoms
• Marked difficulties in using multiple nonverbal behaviors such as eye contact, facial expression, body postures, and gestures. • Failure in developing peer relationships commensurate with developmental level. • Lack of spontaneous seeking behavior to enjoyment, interests, or achievements with other individuals. • Lack of social or emotional reciprocity.	• Preoccupation with one or more stereotyped and restrictive patterns of interest that is atypical. • Inflexible adherence to specific, nonfunctional routines or rituals. • Stereotyped and repetitive motor mannerisms such as finger or hand flapping or twisting. • Continual preoccupation with parts of objects.	• The disturbance causes significant impairment in social, occupational, or other areas of functioning. • No significant delay in language abilities. • No significant delay in cognitive development, age-appropriate self-help skills, adaptive behavior (not including social interaction), and curiosity about the environment during childhood.

To diagnose Asperger's, the child must exhibit at least two of the criteria in category 1 and one criteria in category 2.

Adapted from the Diagnostic and Statistical Manual of Mental Disorders [DSM-IV-TR], *American Psychiatric Association*, 2000.

a pattern of behaviors observed in several young boys of normal intelligence and language development, but who displayed autistic-like behaviors and significant deficiencies in communication and social skills. Asperger's disorder was later added to the DSM-IV and only recently has AD been recognized as a major classification of ASD. Overall, individuals with AD exhibit a variety of characteristic behaviors, which range from mild-to-severe and include:

- Marked deficiencies in social skills, having particular difficulty with transitions.
- Obsessive behaviors, often adhering to specific routines, and may be preoccupied with a particular subject over time.
- Extreme difficulty reading nonverbal cues (body language).
- Difficulty determining proper body space.
- Overly sensitive to sounds, tastes, smells, and sights; and are bothered by sounds or lights others seem not to hear or see.

Overall, it's important to remember that the person with AD perceives the world quite differently from those individuals without AD. Consequently, behaviors that seem odd or unusual by professionals are, in fact, the result of neurological differences found within the individual and neither the result of intentional bad behavior nor the result of what many professionals originally perceived as improper parenting. One other important point to remember is that by definition individuals with AD have a normal IQ and many of these individuals exhibit exceptional skill or talent in a particular area.

Similar to autism, motor manifestations may or may not be inclusive of the diagnosis. However, unlike autism, motor behavior is listed as an associated feature of the disorder. According to the DSM-IV-TR, "motor clumsiness and awkwardness may be present but usually are mild, although motor difficulties may contribute to peer rejection and social isolation" (DSM-IV-TR, p. 81). Consequently, "clumsiness" is thought to be common in this group, yet, not necessary for a formal diagnosis.

It is worth mentioning that currently there is an intense debate as to where AD fits within the overall criteria of ASD. Some professionals consider AD as being the same as high functioning autism, while others feel it is best described as a nonverbal learning disability. Still others feel that AD shares many of the characteristics of PDD-NOS, and it is quite common that some individuals are given a dual diagnosis of AD and high functioning autism. Hence, specifically where AD fits within the spectrum of ASD is still under debate and far from being resolved (see Bock & Myles, 1999 for an excellent review on Asperger's Disorder.)

Rett's Disorder (Rett's Syndrome)

Dr. Andreas Rett, an Austrian physician, first described Rett's disorder (RD) in 1966. Rett's disorder occurs almost exclusively in females and is a childhood disorder characterized by normal early development followed by a loss of fine motor skills, slowed brain and head growth, gate abnormalities, seizures, and intellectual disability. Individuals with RD often exhibit autistic-like behaviors in the early stages. Early symptoms include hypotonia (loss of muscle tone), loss of purposeful hand movements followed by compulsive hand movements such as ringing and washing, problems crawling or walking, problems communicating, and diminished eye contact. Rett's disorder is caused by a structural alteration or defect in the MECP2 gene, which is found on the X chromosome. It is believed that this gene controls the activity of other genes, causing these genes to be abnormally expressed. This ultimately leads to the problems seen in RD. The course and severity of the disorder varies greatly across individuals.

There are four stages of RD. Stage one, often referred to as the **early onset stage**, generally begins between six and 18 months of age. The infant may begin to show less eye contact with others and have a reduced interest in toys. There may be delays in gross motor skills such as sitting or crawling, and hand wringing and decreased head growth may be observed. This stage usually lasts for a few months but can persist for more than a year.

Stage two, often referred to as the **rapid destructive stage**, usually begins between ages one and four and may last for weeks or months. It is during this stage that the characteristic hand movements begin to emerge and often include compulsive washing, wringing, clapping, or tapping, as well as repeatedly moving the hands to the mouth. The hands are sometimes clasped behind the back or held at the sides, with random touching, grasping, and releasing. Some girls also display autistic-like symptoms such as loss of social interaction, communication skills, and the ability to speak. Gait patterns are unsteady and initiating motor movements can be difficult. It is at this stage that the slowing of head growth is usually noticed.

Stage three, often referred to as the **plateau or pseudo—stationary stage**, usually begins between ages two and ten and can last for years. Apraxia, the inability to initiate functional movements, and seizures are both prominent during this stage. However, one may actually see improvements in some behaviors including attention span and communication skills, with less autistic-like characteristics. Children in stage three may show more interest in their surroundings, have a greater attention span, and have improved communication skills.

The last stage, stage four, is often referred to as the **late motor deterioration stage**. This stage can last for years or decades and is characterized by reduced mobility. An inability to walk, muscle weakness, rigidity (muscle stiffness), spasticity (muscle tightness), dystonia (increased muscle tone with abnormal posturing of the extremity or trunk), and/or scoliosis (slight deviation of the spine) are prominent features during this stage. During this stage, there are no further declines in hand, cognition, and communication skills.

Childhood Disintegrative Disorder

Childhood Disintegrative Disorder (CDD) is sometimes referred to as disintegrative psychosis or Heller's syndrome, the later name based on the Austrian educator who first described this disorder in 1908. The disorder is rare, less than 1 in 100,000 children have CDD, and often resembles autism but differs in the pattern of onset, progression, and outcome. After two-to-three years of normal development, children with CDD begin to display a deterioration of social and language functioning (both understanding and speech). Skill in the use of large and small muscles diminishes as the child starts to lose those skills acquired during the first years of development. The overall loss of these skills is rapid, usually occurring within six-to-nine months of onset. The transition often begins with unexplained changes in behavior, such as unprovoked anger or agitation. Children ultimately may stop communicating, withdraw into themselves, and lose bowel and/or bladder control. About half of the children diagnosed with CDD have abnormal electroencephalogram (EEG) brain waves, and a significant number of these children have seizures, which indicate some sort of central nervous system involvement.

Pervasive Developmental Disorder-Not Otherwise Specified

The Pervasive Developmental Disorder-Not Otherwise Specified (PDD-NOS) diagnostic category is provided in the DSM-IV-TR to account for individuals that present themselves with symptoms characteristic of ASD, but cannot be specifically identified as having a type of ASD relative to one of the four major subgroups previously described. This category of PDD has no specific guidelines for diagnosis. Also, while deficits in peer relations are typically noted, social skill problems in children with PDD-NOS are less severe than those found in children having classical autism.

Epidemiology and Causes of ASD

The Centers for Disease Control (CDC) estimate that 2-to-6 per 1,000 children have some type of ASD (National Institute of Mental Health, 2008). Compared to the prevalence of other childhood conditions, this rate is lower than that of intellectual disabilities (9.7 per 1,000), but higher than that for cerebral palsy (2.8 per 1,000), visual impairment (0.9 per 1,000), and hearing loss (1.1 per 1,000) (National Institute of Mental Health, 2008). Males are four times more likely than females to be diagnosed as having ASD, and cases can be found across all racial, ethnic, and socioeconomic groups. The number of children with ASD has grown significantly over the past decade (somewhere in the range of 10–17 percent). The varying symptoms associated with ASD, increased awareness, and diagnostic criteria of the disorder have led many scientists and clinicians to question rising incidence rates. Nonetheless, many experts feel that awareness and revised diagnostic criteria alone do not account for the higher rates seen recently.

There is also much uncertainty surrounding possible causes of ASD. There is no known single cause of ASD, although it is generally accepted that these disorders are caused by abnormalities in brain structure and function. Brain scans show differences in shape and structure of the brains of children with autism compared to children without autism. During the first three years of life, brain connections grow at an accelerated rate. In individuals with autism, neurons seem to connect haphazardly causing widespread abnormalities. This is seen most in the cerebellum (linking cognitive functions with movement) and the limbic system (integrating emotions with specific experiences and memories). Abnormalities in these two regions apparently inhibit interest in one's environment and in social interactions, two of the major characteristics of children with ASD.

In some families, there appears to be a link between heredity and genetics and developing autism. While no single gene has been identified as causative, researchers are probing for irregularities in the genetic code that children with autism may have inherited (National Institute of Mental Health, 2008). Some scientists believe that some children with autism are born with a susceptibility to autism, but researchers have not clearly identified what the environmental "trigger" may be. Some believe that environmental toxins such as heavy metals (mercury), which are more prevalent in today's society, may be the reason for the rise in incidence over the past decades (Minshew, Johnson, & Luna, 2001). To date, there is no scientific evidence that thimerosal, a mercury-based preservative in childhood vaccinations, is causative of ASD (Rabinovitz, 2009).

Motor Characteristics of Children with Autistic Spectrum Disorders

Although delays and deficits in motor functioning are mentioned in the diagnosis for several subtypes of autistic spectrum disorders, there is little literature on the motor behavior in these individuals. In his original description of autism Kanner (1943) mentioned little about the motor behavior of his subjects, and no specific comments were made that could be construed as portentous of delayed motor development. This viewpoint has been supported by some researchers (e.g., Sigman & Capps, 1997), while other researchers have provided some evidence that the motor performance of children with ASD is in fact different from children without autism.

For example, Ornitz, Guthrie, and Farley (1977) using parental reports showed that children with autism had significant delays in attaining motor milestones at 6 months, and that these delays increased during the second 6 months. DeMyers (1976) compared children with autism with those with intellectual disabilities on jumping, running, skipping, hopping, stair use, and ball skills and found that, except for activities involving ball skills, children in both groups had similar skill levels. When it came to ball skills, children with autism were found to have specific difficulty. Considering that children with intellectual disabilities have levels of motor performance below those of typically developing peers without disabilities, children with autism would likewise be performing below levels deemed sufficient for their age levels. Reid, Collier, and Morin (1983) found similar results when they compared the performance of children and adolescence with autism to norms of typically developing peers and peers with intellectual disabilities on several movement tasks. The authors found that both the children and adolescence with high functioning autism (HFA) performed below levels for children in the other groups. More recently, Berkeley et al., (2001), identified motor deficiencies in children with HFA when compared to norms reported for the Test of Gross Motor Development (TGMD).

With regard to Asperger's Disorder, there is general agreement that children with AD have motor performance deficiencies. In his original work, Asperger (1944) noted that there were deficiencies in posture, gait, and recreational activities among the four individuals he described. These, as well as other deficits, have been described more recently in literature. Wing (1991) indicated that that 90 percent of her sample of 34 individuals with AD were poor at games involving motor skills and had problems writing and drawing. Likewise, Provost et al. (2007) found that individuals with AD showed deficits in motor functioning and had varying levels of motor clumsiness. Taken as a whole, the literature supports the assertion that children with ASD show impairments in motor development and performance compared to children without ASD and, in some instances, shows deficits in motor development when compared to other children with developmental concerns.

More recently researchers have examined whether or not children with HFA and AD display deficits in motor planning and/or execution (Hughes, 1996; Rinehart et al., 2006; Vernazza-Martin et al., 2005). Results obtained from this research indicate that a child's success when performing simple activities such as grasping and then placing objects on targets depend on a number of specific processes of what is termed "executive control." Executive control requires that individuals anticipatorily monitor given situations, adjust movements in response to externally and internally generated feedback, and coordinate separate elements of a movement into a coherent, goal-directed sequence of movements. The performance of children with normal development suggest that significant gains in executive control occur between the ages of 2 and 4 years, whereas the executive control of children with HFA and AD is delayed. Results further suggest that individuals with HFA have more consistently impaired executive control than individuals with AD (Hughes, 1996; Rinehart et al., 2006; Vernazza-Martin et al., 2005).

Planning The Program: Motor Intervention Techniques

In general ASD is a life-long disability, however, with early intervention and treatment ASD symptoms can substantially improve, although results do vary. With early intervention, remarkable gains in motor, language, and behavior skills can be seen. Intervention strategies are usually multifaceted and often include behavior modification, focusing on social and language skills, and improving motor performance, often in combination with medications to handle symptoms.

As mentioned previously, many children with ASD experience a range of sensory and motor difficulties. These children often exhibit hyper- and/or hypo-responses to sensory stimuli, exhibit poor visual spatial skills, and exhibit auditory processing problems. Overall, these atypical sensory reactions are believed to reflect poor sensory integration and/or arousal modulation within the central nervous system (Baranek, 2002). As important as these sensory difficulties may be, of particular interest to physical educators are difficulties with aspects of praxis. For example, Rinehart et al. (2001) found that highly functioning children with ASD had atypical motor preparation; that is, children with ASD displayed a lack of anticipation or a slowness of anticipation during movement preparation phases.

Interventions for sensory and motor deficits in children with ASD are multifaceted and can be defined under three broad categories: (1) traditional behavioral modification and psychopharmacological treatments (these treatments will not be explained here); (2) remedial interventions targeting specific sensory and/or motor components per se, with broader outcomes resulting from the sensory-motor treatment programs (e.g., sensory integration therapy); and, (3) comprehensive educational models (e.g., TEACCH model).

Sensory-Motor Interventions for Children With ASD

Sensory-motor interventions are based on the assumption that central nervous system processing of sensory information is essential for all higher-order motor and academic learning and that disruptions in processing can be treated by providing controlled sensory experiences to elicit adaptive motor responses (Croce & DePaepe, 1989). The goals of sensory-motor interventions include improving the child's sensory processing to improve attention and behavioral control, and improving the child's ability to integrate sensory information so that he/she can develop better perceptual and motor schemas.

The theoretical strength of many of the sensory-motor integration programs currently in use rests on data that children with ASD have quantifiable deficits in sensory and motor functioning. However, many of the programs provide rather dubious rationale for their use with children with ASD and have no empirical data to substantiate their effectiveness. Moreover, many of these approaches are based on out-of-date neurological theories that have been disproven (Croce & DePaepe, 1989). According to Baranek (2002), one of the biggest limiting factors in the efficacy data is that many studies have failed to directly link changes in the purported dysfunctional mechanism (e.g., vestibular dysfunction or sensory sensitivity) to functional changes in behavior. Therefore, to date research does not substantiate the effectiveness of sensory-motor integration programs in the treatment of ASD (Dawson & Watling, 2000).

Motor Learning/Educational Approaches for Children With ASD

Despite considerable research on educational interventions for children with disabilities, little work has been compiled in the area of physical education programming for children with ASD. What is known, however, is that a systematic approach to teaching, incorporating visual, verbal, and physical prompts can yield positive effects (Collier & Reid, 1987). What is also known is that sound physical education programming ought to incorporate activities involving moderate-to-strenuous physical activity, as children with ASD have been found to be less active and in poorer condition than children without disabilities (Yu-Pan, 2008). Fortunately, researchers have found that children with ASD respond favorably to exercise and dietary interventions so as to increase their exercise capacity, improve their fitness, and reduce their body mass index (Pitetti et al., 2007). Therefore, moderate-to-vigorous physical activity programs should be a component of any physical education program for children with ASD.

ASD is a spectrum disorder, and as such some children have mild characteristics while others have more profound disturbances. Therefore, individual assessment is key for the physical education teacher to understand student strengths, weaknesses, and unique learning styles. The goal of assessment is twofold: first to determine what a child needs to learn and secondly how best to present and teach each child.

Physical education is essential for the overall well being of the child with ASD; the unique behaviors of these children often lend themselves to unique challenges for the teacher. For this reason, when it comes to teaching physical education to children with ASD, a structured approach is imperative. One of the more common structured teaching models currently available is the Treatment and Education of Autistic and related Communication Handicapped Children (commonly known as TEACCH) and its physical education counterpart Success in Physical Activity (SPA). Both approaches are multifaceted and create an instructional program based on each child's current level of functioning and interests, and use the child's strengths while accommodating his/her weaknesses to build on skills already possessed. These programs also stress modifying and restructuring the environment to accommodate the specific needs of the child (Mesibov, 2006; Schultheis, Boswell, & Decker, 2000).

The most recognizable feature of the TEACCH model, is structured teaching methodologies. This includes organizing the physical environment, schedules, and work systems; stating clear expectations; using visual materials; and relying on behavior modification techniques. Children with ASD have difficulty understanding their environment and often exhibit aberrant behaviors when confused or faced with changes in routine. TEACCH emphasizes the importance of structure and using physical boundaries as a way of fostering independence for students.

 TEACHING TIPS

INSTRUCTING YOUR STUDENTS

- Provide copious amounts of both verbal (simple and direct) and visual demonstrations.
- Be consistent in the activities chosen to begin (warm-up activities) and terminate (cool-down activities) each class.
- Do not allow, or at least minimize, interruptions during class time.

Establishing clear, visual boundaries can minimize confusion (Blubaugh & Kohlmann, 2006). Students with autism are more likely to identify with, and carry out, assigned tasks in physical education class when the physical layout of the setting provides the appropriate visual cues. The physical education environment (i.e., gymnasium) is set up in a way that communicates to the child where everything is for a particular activity. This is often accomplished by cordoning off specific

activity areas with tape markings or dividers, or color-coding specific play areas with different symbols. For example, the object manipulation play area might be cordoned off with brightly colored red tape showing the boundaries of the play space with a shelf or basket clearly marked with objects to be used in the activity; the kicking area might be cordoned off with blue tape with a shelf or basket clearly marked with different types of balls to be used in the activity. Other parts of the gym would be further divided into different play spaces, clearly delineated by colored tape or room dividers. By dividing the gymnasium is such a way, the child with ASD knows exactly where to go for a particular activity—the square area outlined in green is for throwing activities, the rectangular area outlined in blue tape is for kicking, the round area outlined in red tape is for object manipulation, etc (**Figure 11.1**).

 TEACHING TIPS

ORGANIZING THE ACTIVITY AREA

- Activity stations should be partitioned off and clearly marked either with brightly colored tape or room dividers.
- Use a timer to signal when children move on to the next activity station.
- Provide only the exact number and type of equipment pieces needed to complete the task at each station.

A second major component of the TEACCH model is predictability (Blubaugh & Kohlmann, 2006). Predictability involves a preplanned sequence of activity, often displayed as a visual schedule, which the student completes daily. This is often accomplished by having the child start with an activity that is familiar to him/her and easy to complete. This often will be a series of warm-up exercises that readies the child for the day's activities. Then, the teacher can progress into new activities that are more challenging. It is also often desirable to end the class with an activity that is again familiar to the child, such as cool-down activities that are the same for each class. This has the affect of cueing the child that the class is finished. Finally, it is advantageous to use a timer to indicate when the child needs to move on to the next activity

The use of visual schedules helps with predictability. Schedules, as used in the TEACCH method, present to the child the assigned activities for the day and indicate the order in which they are to be completed during the class. Blubaugh and Kohlmann (2006) point out that visual schedules have the following benefits: (1) schedules help overcome communication barriers

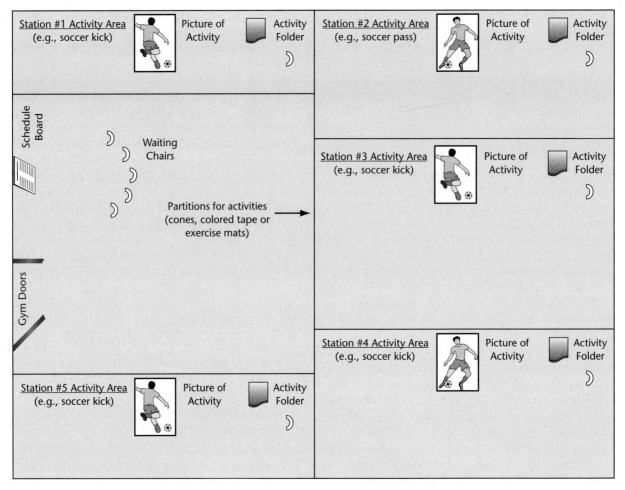

Figure 11.1 Gymnasium layout for teaching a soccer unit to children with autism. Room dividers or colored tape can be used to divide the activity area. Stations can also be color-coded to facilitate student movement from station-to-station.

Source: Modified from Schultheis et al. (2000).

that many children with ASD have; (2) schedules diminish problems created by impaired memory attention; (3) schedules facilitate class organization and lessen the time spent on class organization; (4) schedules foster student independence; (5) schedules make transitions to-and-from class components easier as they tend to deter abherrant behaviors; and (6) schedules increase student motivation.

There are many ways in which the physical education teacher can use visual schedules with children with ASD (Blubaugh & Kohlmann, 2006; Schultheis Boswell, & Decker, 2000). One way is to post each student's assigned activities on color-coded activity cards and place them on a large tack board or poster board located near the gymnasium entrance (the teacher can use tape, tacks, or Velcro to attach cards). Along with activity cards are photos of students and the order or sequence of participation for the scheduled activities. Pictures showing the activities (e.g., kicking a soccer ball) and equipment used in the activities (e.g., soccer ball) can also be

displayed, as can pictures of children actually participating in the various activities. Using pictures, words, colors, and/or number symbols for activity stations is also helpful. Other key points in teaching include: (1) making sure you have the child's attention when giving directions or demonstrating; (2) simplifying all verbal directions and supplement verbal directions with extra demonstrations and/or physical assistance: and (3) focusing on positive behaviors and reinforcing appropriate behaviors (**Figure 11.2**).

Upon entering the gymnasium, each student checks the tack board and his/her individualized schedule, removes the activity cards, and goes to the first station in the sequence of scheduled activities. This type of visual schedule fosters independence in the child, because the child learns to check the board, pull the activity cards, and go to the assigned area(s) to perform the specified activity (activities). Just as it is extremely important to have a specific routine in the beginning of class, it is equally important to have a

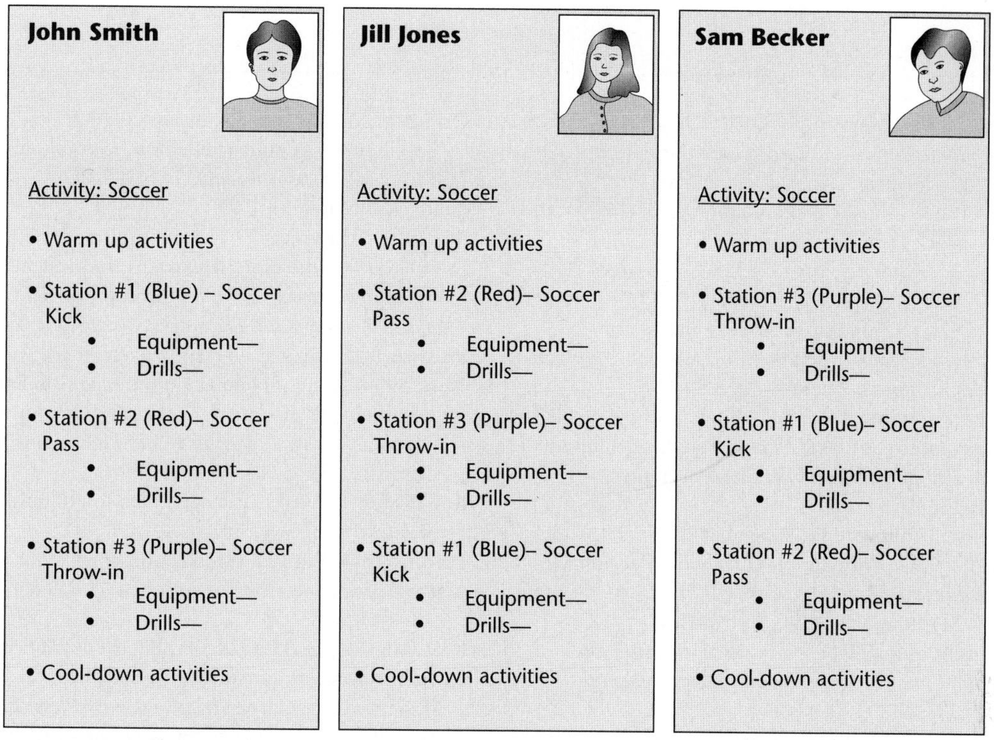

John Smith

Activity: Soccer

• Warm up activities

• Station #1 (Blue) – Soccer Kick
  • Equipment—
  • Drills—

• Station #2 (Red)– Soccer Pass
  • Equipment—
  • Drills—

• Station #3 (Purple)– Soccer Throw-in
  • Equipment—
  • Drills—

• Cool-down activities

Jill Jones

Activity: Soccer

• Warm up activities

• Station #2 (Red)– Soccer Pass
  • Equipment—
  • Drills—

• Station #3 (Purple)– Soccer Throw-in
  • Equipment—
  • Drills—

• Station #1 (Blue)– Soccer Kick
  • Equipment—
  • Drills—

• Cool-down activities

Sam Becker

Activity: Soccer

• Warm up activities

• Station #3 (Purple)– Soccer Throw-in
  • Equipment—
  • Drills—

• Station #1 (Blue)– Soccer Kick
  • Equipment—
  • Drills—

• Station #2 (Red)– Soccer Pass
  • Equipment—
  • Drills—

• Cool-down activities

Figure 11.2 Physical activity schedule for students as presented on a poster board layout. Schedules present the assigned activities for the day and indicate the order in which they are to be completed.
Source: Modified from Schultheis et al. (2000).

clear ending to the day's class. The same end-of-class routine should be incorporated each day. This assists the child with ASD to transition from physical education and succeed in academic classes. The more consistent the day-to-day routine is the less anxious the student is and the better able the child can participate in the day's activities (Blubaugh and Kohlmann, 2006; Schulthesis, Boswell, & Decker, 2000).

CHAPTER SUMMARY

1. Autism is classified as one of the five Pervasive Developmental Disorders (PDD.) Other classifications for PDD are Asperger's Disorder, Rett's Disorder, Childhood Disintegrative Disorder, and Pervasive Developmental Disorder-Not Otherwise Specified.

2. Because of difficulties diagnosing each subtype of PDD, as well as a lack of overwhelming support for the uniqueness of subtypes, many educators and clinicians advocate the use of the term autistic spectrum disorders (ASD) to describe the variety of symptoms found in children with PDD.

3. The number of children with ASD has grown 10–17 percent over the past decade.

4. There is much uncertainty surrounding possible causes of ASD, although it is generally accepted that these disorders are caused by some abnormalities in brain structure and function.

5. When teaching physical education to children with ASD, a structured approach is imperative. One of the more common structured teaching models available is the Treatment and Education of Autistic and related Communication Handicapped Children (TEACCH) and its physical education counterpart Success in Physical Activity (SPA).

6. Both TEACCH and SPA programs stress modifying and restructuring the environment to accommodate the specific needs of the child.

REFERENCES

American Psychiatric Association. (2000). *Diagnostic and statistical manual of mental disorders* (4th Ed-Text Revision). Washington, DC: Author.

Asperger, H. (1944). Autistic psychopathology in childhood. Translated by U. Frith. In U. Frith (Ed.). 1991. Autism and Asperger's Syndrome (pp. 37–92). Cambridge, England: Cambridge University Press.

Baranek, G. T. (2002). Efficacy of sensory and motor interventions for children with autism. *Journal of Autism and Developmental Disabilities*, 32, 397–421.

Berkeley, S. L., Zittel, L. L., Pitney, L. V., & Nichols, S. E. (2001). Locomotor and object control skills of children diagnosed with autism. *Adapted Physical Activity Quarterly*, 18, 405–416.

Blubaugh, N. & Kohlmann, J. (November 2006). TEACCH model and children with autism. *Teaching Elementary Physical Education*, 16–19.

Bock, S. J., & Myles, B. S. (1999). An overview of characteristics of Asperger syndrome. *Education and Training in Mental Retardation and Developmental Disabilities*, 34, 511–520.

Collier, D., & Reid, G. (1987). A comparison of two models designed to teach autistic children a motor task. *Adapted Physical Activity Quarterly*, 4, 226–236.

Croce, R., & DePaepe, J. (1989). A critique of therapeutic intervention programming with an alternative approach based on motor learning theory. *Physical and Occupational Therapy in Pediatrics*, 9(3), 5–33.

Dawson, G., & Watling, R. (2000). Interventions to facilitate auditory, visual, and motor integration in autism: A review of the evidence. *Journal of Autism and Developmental Disorders*, 30(5), 415–421.

DeMyers, M. K. (1976). Motor, perceptual-motor, intellectual disabilities of autistic children. In L. Wing (Ed.) *Early childhood autism*. NY: Pergamon Press.

Hughes, C. (1996). Brief report: Planning problems in autism at the level of motor control. *Journal of Autism and Developmental Disorders*, 26(1), 99–106.

Kanner, L. (1943). Autistic disturbance of affective contact. Nervous Learner 2: 217–250.

Mesibov, G. (2006). What is TEACCH? Retrieved July 1, 2009 from <http://teacch.com/mission.html>.

Minshew, N., Johnson, C., & Luna, B. (2001). The cognitive and neural basis of autism: A disorder of complex information processing and dysfunction of neocortical systems. In L. M. Glidden (Ed.), *International Review of Research in mental retardation* (Vol. 23, pp. 111–138). NY: Academic Press.

National Institute of Child Health and Human Development. (2001). *Fact sheet on autism*. Available at: http://www.cdc.gov/ncbddd/autism/.

National Institute of Mental Health. (2008). *Autism Spectrum Disorders*. Available at: http://www.nimh.nih.gov/health/topics/autism-spectrum-disorders-pervasive-developmental-disorders/index.shtml

Ornitz, E. M., Guthrie, D., & Farley, A. J. (1977). The early development of autistic children. *Journal of Autism and Childhood Schizophrenia*, 7, 207–229.

Pitetti, K. H., Rendoff, A. D., Grover, T., & Beets, M. W. (2007). The efficacy of a 9-month treadmill walking program on the exercise capacity and weight reduction for adolescence with severe autism. *Journal of Autism and Developmental Disorders*, 37, 997–1006.

Provost, B., Lopez, B., & Heimerl, S. (2007). A comparison of motor delays in young children: Autism Spectrum Disorders, developmental delay, and developmental concerns. *Journal of Autism and Developmental Disorders*, 37, 321–328.

Rabinovitz, J. (2009). The demonization of immunization. *Stanford Medicine*, spring, 8–18.

Reid, G., & Collier, D. (2002). Motor behavior and the Autism Spectrum Disorders. *PALESTRA*, 18(4), 20–44.

Reid, G., Collier, D., & Morin, B. (1983). The motor performance of autistic individuals. In R. Eason, T. Smith, & F. Caron (Eds.) *Adapted Physical Activity* (pp. 201–218). Champaign, IL: Human Kinetics.

Rinehart, N. J., Bellgrove, M. A., Tonge, B. J., Brerton, A. V., Howells-Rankin, D., & Bradshaw, J. L. (2006). An examination of human kinematics in young people with high-functioning autism and Asperger's disorder: Further evidence for a motor planning deficit. *Journal of Autism and Developmental Disorders*, 36, 757–767.

Rinehart, N. J., Bradshaw, J. L., Brereton, A.V., & Tonge, B. J. (2001). Movement preparation in high-functioning autism and Asperger disorder: A serial choice-reaction time task involving motor programming. *Journal of Autism and Developmental Disorders*, 31, 79–88.

Schultheis, S. F., Boswell, B. B., & Decker, J. (2000). Successful physical activity programming for students with Autism. *Focus on Autism and Other Developmental Disabilities*, 15(3), 159–162.

Sigman, M., & Capps, L. (1997). *Children with autism: A developmental perspective*. Cambridge, MA: Harvard University Press.

Vernazza-Martin, S., Martin, N., Vernazza, A., Lepellec-Muller, A., Rufo, M., Massion, J, & Assaiante, C. (2005). Goal directed locomotion and balance control in autistic child. *Journal of Autism and Developmental Disorders*, 35(1), 91–102.

Yu-Pan, C-Y. (2008). Objectively measured physical activity between children with autism spectrum disorders and children without disabilities during inclusive recess settings in Taiwan. *Journal of Autism and Developmental Disorders*, 38, 1292–1301.

Wing, L. (1991). The relationship between Asperger's syndrome and Kanner's autism. In U. Frith (Ed.) *Autism and Asperger's syndrome* (pp. 93–121). Cambridge, UK: Cambridge University Press.

Teaching Individuals With Sensory Impairments

Section III focuses on children with auditory and visual exceptionalities. Children with sensory impairments or loss may possess common characteristics that necessitate special considerations in order for them to participate in physical education.

This section is designed to

1. recognize the characteristics and physical/motor functioning of children with visual and hearing loss.

2. provide instructional strategies that are beneficial in facilitating teaching.

3. provide modifications, if necessary, for children with sensory loss.

4. provide examples of establishing communication to facilitate the instructional program.

CHAPTER 12

Visual Impairments

CASE STUDY

Ron is a 17-year-old boy who has been totally blind for ten years. He is hesitant when moving within the environment in general, with hesitance becoming especially noticeable when he negotiates stairs and otherwise uneven terrain. Ron's teacher, following observation in physical education, notes that Ron's step length in proportion to height is short, and his step width is disproportionately broad. He toes out and walks with arms held out to the side for balance. Unless prompted otherwise, Ron tends to be sedentary and seldom participates in physical activity.

To maximize Ron's potential for success in physical education, his teacher should consult with an orientation and mobility (O & M) specialist regarding strategies to address gait issues. Also, strategies should be sought from the O & M specialist that will help Ron learn to move through his general environment with greater confidence.

The physical education teacher also should test Ron for overall fitness. Because Ron is sedentary, the teacher may, as a result of Ron's fitness evaluation, recommend activity that emphasizes strength and conditioning to improve overall physical function and self-confidence. A mobility program should be considered to facilitate development gait mechanics that enhance ability to move through the general environment and, specifically, in activity settings.

In typical physical activity classes, most children rely primarily on vision to learn motor skills. They must be able to focus on different objects, such as balls and/or apparatus, determine the distance between near and far in changing situations, demonstrate eye-hand and eye-foot coordination, and discriminate between colors and background. In addition, children must remember what they see and be able to interpret visual sensations and react accordingly.

For children with visual impairments, proficiency in physical activity may depend on the amount of visual acuity they possess. Visual acuity is commonly measured with a Snellen test, which utilizes a chart of progressively smaller letters read at a distance of 20 feet. Normal, or 20/20, vision is the ability to read the selected criterion of symbols at a distance of 20 feet. As eyesight diminishes, the comparison with normal vision varies. For example, children with 20/100 vision will see at 20 feet what the normal eye can see at 100 feet. For children with visual impairment, the following classification system may be used for educational placement.

- *Legal blindness, 20/200.* The ability to see at 20 feet what the normal eye can see at 200 feet or a field of vision less than 20 degrees.
- *Travel vision, 5/200 to 10/200.* The ability to see at 5 to 10 feet what the normal eye can see at 200 feet, or enough sight to allow moving or walking without extreme difficulty.
- *Motion perception, 3/200 to 5/200.* The ability to see at 3 to 5 feet what the normal eye can see at 200 feet, or vision that can detect motion, but not a still object.
- *Light perception, less than 3/200.* The ability to distinguish a strong light at a distance of 3 feet that the normal eye can see at 200 feet, or to distinguish a bright light at 3 feet or less but no movement.

- *Total blindness.* The inability to recognize a strong light shone directly into the eye.
- *Tunnel vision.* A field of vision that is 20 degrees or less.

Besides the classification of vision, educational definitions based on the regulations of the Individuals with Disabilities Education Act (IDEA) define visual exceptionalities in the following manner: "Visually handicapped means a visual impairment which, even with correction, adversely affects a child's educational performance." The term includes both children who are partially sighted, low vision, and children who are blind. The use of the terms *partially sighted* and *blind* is directly related to educational placement. For individuals who are legally blind, the visual acuity is 20/200 or less in the better eye after correction, or the field of vision is limited to an angle of 20 degrees or less out of the normal 180-degree field of vision. In this condition, vision is severely limited, with practically no peripheral vision even if the central vision is 20/200 or greater. With a severely restricted field of vision, physical activity and mobility may be limited.

Partially sighted children possess a visual acuity of at least 20/200 but not greater than 20/70 in the better eye after correction. This represents approximately 10 to 30 percent of normal vision and is sometimes referred to as functional blindness. In addition, most children who are blind have some residual vision that allows them to read large print and/or see some portion of a shape or implement. To accommodate children and promote learning, children can be viewed on how vision affects learning and classified based on their residual vision.

- Low vision—children primarily use vision in learning
- Functionally blind—children use some vision for function but rely on other sensory modalities.
- Total blindness—children require compensatory use of tactile, kinesthetic, and auditory sensory information

Of specific interest for teachers is that in a survey of the activity limitations of visually impaired individuals, Kirchner (1985) indicated that 63 percent of these individuals have no major activity limitations, 20 percent have minor limitations depending on the nature of the activity, and only 17 percent have major restrictions on participation. Shepherd (1994) also indicated that the nature of the impairment and lack of residual vision is associated with developing motor skills as well as the incentive and ability to move proficiently.

Development and Structure of Vision

According to Holbrook (1996) one-tenth of 1 percent of all school-aged children are visually impaired, and approximately 85 percent of these children have some usable vision. The primary causes of visual impairment can be tracked to defects in development with the ocular mechanism, birth defects, disease, and injuries. Other causes cannot be traced and are classified as idiopathic. To understand the basic mechanism of vision, think of the eye as a camera that relays messages to the brain. Light enters the eye through the "camera's" outer layer (cornea) and passes through the pupil. The eye is protected by the eyelids and bony socket of the skull, which is filled with fat to absorb shock and allow eye movement. Four rectus muscles allow motion of the eye upward, downward, inward, and outward, while the two oblique muscles add upward and downward movement.

The eyeball consists of three layers. The first layer consists of a protective covering made up of the cornea and sclera (white). As light enters, it passes through the middle layer (uvea), which is responsible for transporting blood to the (1) iris (which gives color to the eye), (2) ciliary body (which produces fluid for aqueous humor) and allows vision to be adjusted (accommodation), and (3) the choroid, or the blood supply for the retina.

As the iris opens and closes to regulate the amount of light admitted, light next passes through the lens, a transparent biconvex structure that focuses light rays on the back wall of the retina to bring objects into focus. The retina, which is the third layer of the eyeball, contains receptor cells (rods and cones), which collect color and light images to the rear of the eyeball, that becomes the optic nerve. The optic nerve then conveys visual impulses to the brain (occipital lobe), where the stimuli are processed and interpreted and which results in vision. Visual acuity is approximately 20/400 at birth, 20/50 by 1 year of age and 20/20 by the age of 4. It should be noted that developmentally the eyes of the newborn are limited and not completely developed in contrast to the adult (**Figure 12.1**).

In addition to visual acuity, vision undergoes a developmental process that allows the child to use vision for reading as well as using visual information for learning. In the newborn, the muscles of the eye are weak, and vision is limited to focusing on near objects and responses to light. It could be said that we are born with sight but not vision. Vision will develop from several functions of the eye. For example, visual acuity is the ability to see objects clearly, as measured by performance on the Snellen test. In addition, the eyes must also demonstrate **visual fixation**, that is, the ability to gaze directly at an object; and **pursuant fixation**, by which they follow a moving object. Fixation of an object is pursuit at zero velocity, with the pursuit system correcting for small drifts off target. These movements are slower than the fast saccadic movements, (involuntary, abrupt, small movements, such as those made when the eye changes their point of fixation). The slower

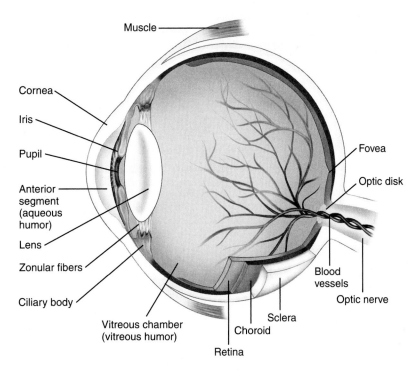

Figure 12.1 Anatomy of human eye as seen in a horizontal section.

eye movements go by a variety of names but are most commonly called smooth pursuit or tracking movement. The brain must allow the ability to process information and slowly track the object.

After fixation, the eye can then learn to focus. **Accommodation** is the ability to adjust the focus of the eyes to changing distances and is usually learned one side at a time. Commonly we use accommodation in sports as we track an object and in the classroom as we shift attention from the blackboard to the desk by bringing near objects into focus. **Binocular fusion** occurs at approximately 4 to 6 months as the two optic nerves at the back of the eye receive information from each eye and form a unified image. If the eyes are not aligned, the brain may suppress vision in one eye to avoid double vision. This results in poorer visual acuity, as occurs in amblyopia.

As the ability to use images emerges, the eyes, in order to examine close objects, must then turn together to keep images on each eye focused on the fovea of the retina. This is known as **convergence**. Likewise, *stereopsis* is a function of binocular fusion that allows us to judge distances between two or more objects. The brain recognizes that objects at various distances have images in the two retinas that do not fall at exactly corresponding locations (i.e., the image has disparity), and the brain adjusts accordingly. **Visual perception** or visual motor skills coordinate both eyes and the action stimulated by the eyes. The child must receive, organize, and interpret visual images that can be used in the learning process and stored in memory functions for later use.

Identifying Visual Problems

Most school districts require a preliminary visual screening that may detect some visual problems. Teachers have a greater opportunity to observe daily progress and may refer students for further screening or more appropriate educational placement if they suspect a visual impairment. In order to screen children, teachers should be aware of the symptoms of potential eye disorders, such as an inability of the eyes to work together (i.e., impaired eye coordination). Improper eye coordination may result from a lack of adequate development for vision or lack of control of the eye muscles. In addition, injury, disease, or trauma can affect the coordination of the eyes. Symptoms such as double vision, headaches, fatigue, dizziness, reading difficulties, inattention, clumsiness, poor reading, or avoiding tasks that require close work all may be symptomatic of poor eye coordination (**Table 12.1**).

The common visual abnormalities that may result in a deviation from this normal visual process include the following:

- *myopia*: nearsightedness, or the ability to see well up close; results when the eyeball is too long from front to back and light rays consequently fall in front of the retina
- *hyperopia*: farsightedness, or the ability to see well far away; results when the eyeball is too short from front to back and light rays consequently fall in back of the retina

Table 12.1 Symptoms of Vision Disorders

Physical Appearance	Motor Behavior	Complaints
Styes	Walks tentatively	Dizziness
Variation in pupil size	Excessive blinking	Headaches
Eyes in constant motion	Trips or stumbles frequently	Eye pain
Crossed eyes	Is sensitive to light	Blurred objects or symbols
Bloodshot eyes	Frowns or closes eyes to see objects	Double vision
Crusted eyelids	Has poor color discrimination and problems seeing objects from the side or background	Burning or itching
Holds objects up close or far away	Squints	Headaches

- *astigmatism*: distorted, blurred vision due to an irregularity of the lens or corneal surface, which results in light rays not being focused sharply on the retina
- *cataracts*: clouding or opaque condition occurring on the lens, resulting in blurred vision
- *retinitis pigmentosa*: progressive retinal rod detachment, beginning with night blindness and producing a gradual loss of the field of vision
- *amblyopia*: deviation or wandering of the eye, in which the "lazy eye" does not focus on the same object as the nonaffected eye
- *albinism*: hereditary condition in which there is a lack of pigment in the choroid and irises, which is manifested in sensitivity to light and refractive errors
- *strabismus*: crossing of the eyes caused by shortened or imbalanced internal rotators, or outward separation caused by shortened or imbalanced external rotators
- *nystagmus*: involuntary condition in which the eyeball moves side to side, up and down, or in a rotary motion as though the ocular muscles were twitching
- *heterophoria*: condition in which the muscles of the eye do not function in a coordinated manner; affects the use of binocular vision
- *glaucoma*: increase in pressure of the fluid inside the eye, which causes the eyeball to expand, resulting in gradual or sudden loss of vision beginning with decreasing peripheral vision
- *retrolental fibroplasia*: visual abnormality resulting from pure oxygen given to premature babies, in which scar tissue forms behind the lens
- *conjunctivitis*: inflammatory disease that involves infection of the conjunctiva.
- *keratitis*: inflammatory disease affecting the cornea
- *accidents*: trauma to the eyes resulting in puncture, retinal detachment, or lens dislocation

Planning the Physical Activity Program

Because vision is critical for motor development and physical functioning, a clear understanding of children's functioning is useful before planning and implementing the program. The following issues should be considered when planning the physical activity program for children with visual impairments.

Movement Skills/Gait

Fraiberg presents the most compelling evidence for movement difficulties in children with visual impairments (Adelson & Fraiberg, 1974; Fraiberg, 1977). Based on this work, we can see that children display inadequate movements during the developmental years. Movements are forced, repetitive, and stereotypical. Children are passive in seeking information and responding to interactions in the environment. Fraiberg (1977) indicated that children display developmental arrests or roadblocks to developing movement sequences. Sighted children will reach, grasp, and manipulate objects that they see and are active information seekers. Children with visual impairments are more passive and constrained unless they adapt to their environments. Hatton et al. (1997) indicated that some movement difficulties may be due to fear of movement, spatial disorientation, or parental overprotection.

Children with visual problems also demonstrate problems in extending basic reaching and grasping as a precursor to moving in the environment. Visual objects generally provide the lure to initiate movement in young children, whereas children with visual impairments must rely on sound to obtain directional and spatial information. This results in delays of self-initiated movements, such as rolling. Rettig's (1994) observations of interactions among children with visual impairments reveal that these children are lacking in play skills and spend most of their time playing alone unlike sighted children: 56 percent of blind children played alone, whereas sighted children spent only 14 percent of their time playing alone.

The absence of vision also predisposes the individual to gait difficulties and postural control (Ray, Horvat et al., 2008). Because of deficits in vestibular and visual input, specific reductions in gait speed, decreased stride length, and single-support stance time are evident which subsequently affects overall balance and initiation of movement. Individuals are more restrained and hesitant to move independently. For younger children this lack of movement confidence will affect the ability to engage in physical activities.

Health/Physical Fitness

Although limited information is available, the lack of physical activity in visual impairment is compromised and may facilitate chronic diseases such as diabetes, hypertension, and cardiovascular disease (Ray & Wolf, 2008). Fitness is generally lower in individuals who are visually impaired. (Lieberman, 2002) Any physical activity program should have as its aim the total development of children to encourage an active and productive lifestyle. Compared to their sighted peers, children are low in cardiovascular endurance, although performance on muscular strength and endurance tasks such as pull-ups, squat thrusts, flexed arm hangs, and standing high jumps is comparable to that of sighted children (Buell, 1983; Hopkins et al., 1987).

The lack of strength and power may be important in maintaining independent functioning in many functional tasks. Difficulties associated with climbing stairs or crossing the street in a certain time require the muscles to produce force to initiate movement (Ray & Wolf, 2008). Horvat et al. (2006) demonstrated that individuals with visual impairments are deficient in generating peak force and power which compromises their ability in many tasks and recommend training programs to promote strength and endurance.

Most children with visual impairment will not meet age-expected norms for peers with normal vision in running and throwing events if they are limited in the opportunity to practice and develop these activities. There is no specific reason to believe that sensory impairment leads to lower physical functioning. In a study by Kobberling, Jankowski, and Leger (1991), comparisons of habitual physical activity and aerobic capacity between sighted adolescents and adolescents who were blind indicated that the maximal oxygen consumption was higher among sighted subjects. The authors subsequently recommended that all adolescents, both the sighted and the blind, require a minimum of 30 minutes of daily activity to attain and maintain their age-predicated aerobic capacity. Shindo et al. (1987) reported that low physical work capacity in boys and young males with visual impairments is due to a lack of physical activity and that mild training accentuates physical functioning and cardiovascular fitness. Blessing et al. (1993) also reported significant increases in cardiovascular fitness and decreases in body composition after training in children with visual impairments, while Ponchillia et al. (1992) reported improved fitness in women who were blind after engaging in aerobic activities.

The overall lack of fitness seems to be related primarily to lack of physical activity and understanding of the capabilities of individuals with visual impairments. Skaggs and Hopper (1996) challenged teachers to provide opportunities to promote active lifestyle for children with visual impairments and indicated that specific strategies for improving motor skills are lacking. Sudgen and Keogh (1990) indicated that experience in physical activity among visually impaired children is limited by rhythmical stereotypes, such as body rocking and hand slapping, which are socially inappropriate and limit the opportunities for useful and functional movement experiences. Because many skills require externally paced movements, low scores among visually impaired children may not be so much an indication of physical capability as of the lack of opportunity to compensate for their inexperience.

Fundamental Movement Skills and Balance

The success of children with visual impairments in sport and games also depends on developing a sound movement base and providing opportunities to practice and refine skills (Richardson & Mastro, 1987). Because of the lack of visual feedback, self-corrections in form or movement patterns may not be as efficient as in sighted classmates. Children with visual impairments generally have more difficulty with postural control and greater instability after 10 to 12 years of age (Portfors-Yeomans & Riach, 1995). They also place greater demands on the somatosensory and vestibular information to establish movement patterns. Individuals with visual impairments use other sensory information to establish movement patterns, make movement corrections, and adapt to position in space (Horvat et al, 2003; Ray et al., 2007). Ribadi, Rider, and Toole (1987) also recommended balance training in developing adaptations to the nonverbal environment. Ray et al. (2005) have also had success in improving balance using auditory and tactile prompts to implement a tai chi intervention. To compensate for the lack of vision, specific cues and prompts can be used by the teacher to augment feedback for the following locomotor movement skills:

1. *Walking-running.* Stress proper placement of form, emphasizing leg and arm movements, development of efficient patterns, sound perception, and changes of speed and direction.

2. *Jumping-hopping.* Stress movements of legs and arms to emphasize proper form and efficient patterns, determining when to jump, sound perception, anticipation, and form preparatory to landing.

3. *Galloping-skipping.* Stress movements to coordinate legs, proper form, and integration of both sides of the body.

4. *Throwing/striking.* Stress movements of arms and legs to develop efficient patterns, direction, gauging speeds, and accuracy.

5. *Catching.* Stress proper position of arms and hands in efficient patterns anticipating ball, with sound perception and gauging speed.

6. *Kicking.* Stress foot placement and follow-through to develop efficient patterns, direction, gauging speeds, and accuracy.

Orientation and Mobility

For successful integration, children will require the ability to move about the environment safely and will require familiarity with their surroundings. They will need to commit a new environment to memory in order to determine positions and relationships to other persons or objects in the environment. Initially, these children have difficulty moving or traveling in the environment. This may be an extension of their early movement difficulties. Sudgen and Keogh (1990) indicated that individuals who are blind solve problems as they occur rather than preparing for what is happening. In contrast, sighted children recognize an object visually, whereas children with visual impairments recognize an object by touch. Orientation must prepare the children to understand

1. common objects in the environment (e.g., mail-box, tree)

2. fixed objects, such as stairs or pools

3. movable or moving objects, such as a ball or rope

4. positions of objects in space

5. nature of the terrain, such as hilly or straight

6. directions and paths of stationary or moving objects, as well as sound localization

Teachers should also strive to provide an awareness of the correct position or feel of an activity. By utilizing any remaining functional or residual vision, children can be taught to orient themselves to the instructional environment and make changes accordingly to enhance their movement efficiency. The following guidelines (Blasch, Wiener, & Welsh, 1997) have been used to orient children to inside and outside activity settings:

1. Utilize shape changes in playground settings as well as changes in texture (grass, sand, asphalt) to foster independent movements.

2. Emphasize the use of sound, such as (a) voice clusters (swings, merry-go-round); (b) radio in a window; (c) sound echoes from buildings (although not all students are capable of using this effectively); (d) sound echoes from walls in a gymnasium (echoes may aid totally blind children through recognition of a "closed-in feeling").

3. Take advantage of small sound sources that can be made by local Bell Telephone Pioneer Clubs and implanted into Nerf or foam balls or attached to goals or targets. Portable goal locaters are also available from commercial sources.

4. Utilize the sun early or late in the day for orientation, although children seldom use it during activity.

5. Use high contrast in colors for court markings; use cloth or nylon strip to lay out different courts instead of many lines. Make sure there is a contrast between uniforms and court or field.

6. Utilize different aspects of lighting to include

   a. vision adaptation from daylight to indoor

   b. vision adaptation from day, to dusk, to dark

   c. adequate lighting indoors

   d. curtains to shield sun

   e. reduced light for electronic games

   f. black light for electronic games

   g. sun glare (avoid running into sun, if possible)

   h. brightness (shadow adaptation)

7. Utilize the following for additional sources of orientation or guidance:

   a. natural cues in the court or competition area—net, goals, goalball court

   b. various sounds, such as beepers, crickets, calling (with paper tubes), bells, radios, tape players (for dance and gymnastics), speakers (at roller rinks), walkie-talkies, remote control transmitters, voice commands

   c. guide ropes for high jumping, safety ropes to locate targets, guide rails for bowling or to designate swimming or running lanes, or linking runners hand to hand or hand to upper arm

   d. boundary marking, alternate textures outdoors (sand and grass, dirt and grass, tall grass and short grass) and indoors (carpets, rubber mats, nylon or cloth, straps)

   e. foot placement guides, as in archery, shot, or discus; or arm placement guides, as in archery.

Modifying Activities and Equipment

For most activities, instruction and equipment need not be modified or adapted in order for children with visual impairments to participate with their sighted peers. The use of residual vision, tactile, kinesthetic awareness, and auditory awareness is generally sufficient to provide minor modifications that aid in the learning process and participation. The following sections, however, describe some examples of minor modifications that may be needed in the initial stages of learning.

Physical Fitness

In cardiovascular endurance events, children may require a sighted guide to lightly touch the arm, grasp the arm, or maintain contact with a short cord (**Figure 12.2**) (Sanka & Bina, 1978). Walking programs have proven beneficial to developing fitness (Weitzman, 1985). Harry Cordellos, one of the world's best blind athletes, utilizes a variety of positions to negotiate difficult terrains, such as hands on the sighted runner's hip, touch, and verbal commands to complete long-distance training. Because one technique may not be viable for all situations, all variations of residual vision, or all terrains, it is necessary to use the method that is most efficient and comfortable for runners. Generally, shorter races can be managed with a short cord tied to the sighted runner's belt. Specific lanes that are marked with the use of a guide wire or rope can be beneficial for sports. If physical guidance is not needed, verbal directions and safety hints can be provided for endurance races (Buell, 1983).

Cycling to develop strength and endurance can be performed with a stationary cycle, a tandem bicycle ridden with a sighted individual, or riding with a sighted partner. Skiing is accomplished with a sighted partner who gives verbal instructions concerning directions, changes in terrain, or the approach of other skiers.

Swimming is an excellent physical activity to develop cardiovascular fitness that requires few, if any, modifications. Depths are marked by raised letters on the side and deck of the pool, and swimming lanes can be separated with ropes and buoys to designate lanes, depths, and swimming areas. Auditory prompts, such as a metronome, or Adapt Tap can signal a swimmer's approach to the wall or can alert individuals to begin their turns. Diving boards usually contain a nonslip rough surface, hand rails can provide tactile information for the diver, and there are devices that spray water on the swimmer as they approach the wall. Finally, the use

Figure 12.2 A short cord is used to provide support in cardiovascular sports, such as track and field events.

of residual vision will enable children to develop a mental plan of the swimming environment, enhancing their ability to locate ladders and ramps to enter and exit the pool.

Games and Sports

Most children enjoy playing games, especially if those games provide additional opportunities to develop gross motor and physical fitness skills. For children with visual impairments, balls that are bright orange or yellow can be helpful and can encourage additional usage of residual vision. Guide wires, cut base paths, or sighted partners can help children determine the correct direction to run or move in games (**Figure 12.3**). For some children a batting tee can be used; in kickball, a stationary kick can initiate action. In dodgeball, players can also use sighted children to avoid a thrown ball.

To play volleyball and basketball requires assistance from teammates and acute concentration on the sound of the ball. Training in auditory perception for responding to and differentiating between sounds allows children to move in the direction of the ball or pass to the vocal cue of teammates. Many teachers will also use sound in the ball, or behind a goal, in soccer or basketball activities to provide continuous auditory cues.

Other Activities

Most children with visual impairments can participate in gymnastics, weight training, movement education, and hiking with minor modifications that help initiate the activity. In addition, sports such as wrestling, judo, and self-defense have been used with no modification in instruction or technique other than touching at the beginning and during the match (Mastro, 1985; Mastro, Montelione, & Hall, 1986). Other examples of activities that are suitable for children with visual impairments include throwing and jumping events in track and field that incorporate a minimum of verbal directions and positioning; bowling with a guide rail; archery with an audible goal locator; and relaxation and yoga activities (Krebs, 1979). Chin (1988) has used dance to initiate movements and develop spatial awareness in elementary school children with visual impairments. In addition, parachute activities that incorporate contact grasping of the parachute, and movement exploration and body image activities that incorporate verbal explanations can all provide movement cues and aid in positioning. Other resources are available in *Games for People with Sensory Impairments* (Leiberman & Cowart, 1996).

LEARNING ACTIVITY

Have students access the website for the U.S. Association of Blind Athletes (www.usaba.org) or the International Blind Sport Federation (www.ibsa.es/eng/) and discuss the various adaptations for sports.

Competition for the Visually Impaired

Since 1976 athletes have been competing in events sponsored by the United States Association for Blind Athletes (USABA). Opportunities are available in track and field, swimming, wrestling, goalball, gymnastics, archery, bowling, cycling, judo, powerlifting, football and downhill and cross-country skiing, according to the individual's functional classification (**Table 12.2**).

Figure 12.3 Technique used for running.

Table 12.2 Sports Classification for Individuals with Visual Impairments

Classification	Functional Ability
B_1	Ranging from no light perception in either eye to light perception, and inability to recognize the shape of a hand at any distance or in any direction.
B_2	From ability to recognize the shape of a hand to visual acuity of 20/600 and/or a visual field of less than 5 degrees in the best eye with the best practical eye correction.
B_3	From visual acuity above 20/600 and up to visual acuity of 22/200 and/or a visual field of less than 20 degrees and more than 5 degrees in the best eye with the best practical eye correction.
B_4	From visual acuity above 20/200 and up to visual acuity of 20/70 and a visual field larger than 20 degrees in the best eye with the best practical eye correction.

While many athletes are participating in the USABA, others are also competing, often with sighted peers, in clubs, schools, and universities. It is especially important for teachers to determine which opportunities may be available for children and direct them to the most suitable avenue for participation. As with sighted individuals, competition and sports may not be feasible. However, the opportunity to participate should be made available to everyone. In addition to events sponsored by the USABA, numerous opportunities may be available for children at every level of competition. One must only consider the many accomplishments by athletes with visual impairments to realize that individuals should be considered for competition strictly on their ability to participate in athletics. Some examples of athletes who are capable of outstanding performances include the following.

- Dr. Jim Mastro has won a gold medal in wrestling and in shot put, and a silver in the discus. He is also an avid goalball player, former president of the American Beep Baseball Association, and has participated in the Paralympics.
- In 1981, five blind climbers were members of the Pelion Expedition, which climbed the 14,410-foot peak of Mount Rainier.
- Harry Cordellos has run over 70 marathons, many under 3 hours, and completed the Hawaiian Iron Man Triathlon in 16 hours (swimming 2.4 miles, tandem biking for 112 miles, and running a marathon).
- Scott Moore was the first American to win a gold medal in the Paralympic games for Judo.

Implementing the Physical Activity Program

Children with visual impairments will possess a wide variation in visual functioning and residual vision. Teachers should consider the loss of vision and other prominent characteristics of children (**Table 12.3**) when implementing the physical education program. In order to integrate children into physical education classes properly, teachers should consider incorporating the instructional strategies described in the following sections into the physical education program.

Cognition

The cognitive ability of children with visual impairments will vary as much as it does among their sighted classmates. A visual impairment does not imply a lack of mental capacity. However, it is essential to realize that abstracts are sometimes difficult for children to grasp because of the lack of visual cues. Children will adapt more easily to their surroundings if they are aware of the specifications of their environment or memorize dimensions of a facility.

Because there is no loss of mental functioning, teachers should not lower their expectations for children with visual impairments. By reinforcing their cognitive strengths and providing activity interventions at an early age, children should be able to participate in a comprehensive physical education program of physical fitness, dance, aquatics, sports, and games. Teachers should emphasize parts of the task before completing the entire task, and they should pair auditory and tactile/kinesthetic training to emphasize abstract concepts.

Haptic Perception

Because the primary sensory apparatus of vision may be restricted at varying degrees of functional ability, teachers should utilize other sensory apparatus to compensate for the lack of vision in learning a skill. For example, all movements contain tactile sensations, muscular and proprioceptive sensations, and a kinesthetic sense of the activity. When planning and implementing the instructional program for children with visual impairments, teachers should incorporate an alternative modality to allow for compensation and, in turn, for learning to occur.

Children may observe a motor pattern or skill by placing their fingers on the performer's body during the activity. Likewise, dolls or mannequins can be used to demonstrate roles, stunts, and activities that may be difficult for children to comprehend by touching only the performer. In addition, teachers may manipulate

Table 12.3   Physical Activity Suggestions for Children With Visual Impairments

Behavior	Characteristics	Instructional Strategies	Physical Education Considerations
Cognition	Intelligence varies as much as with sighted peers. Adaptation by memorizing. Difficulty with abstracts.	Do not lower expectations because of visual deficiency. Reinforce strengths in memory to increase mobility, and to learn rules and strategies. Utilize visual efficiency training.	Appropriate physical education activities emphasizing whole-part-whole method of instruction, and auditory and haptic senses; opportunities to pair auditory and haptic senses.
Sensory awareness	Wide variety of useful vision. Proprioceptive awareness frequently poor. Lack of sensory lures to initiate movement.	Compensate for loss of vision by utilizing other senses. Use auditory, tactile, and kinesthetic training and residual vision.	Orientation and mobility training to learn the environment; activities using bright colors and contrast, whistles, other sounds; body image with mannequins and/or models.
Growth and maturation	Physical development often delayed because of inadequate movement opportunities. Poor physical fitness. Fatigues easily. Tendency toward obesity.	Provide opportunities and practice in variety of settings; physical education class should be based on individual needs; supplement movement activities and fitness activities at home in weekly program.	Activities that emphasize spatial orientation, body image, balance, coordination. Basic motor skills that deal with locomotor and fitness activities, including swimming, cycling, and jogging.
Body image	Problems identifying body parts on self and others. Difficulty understanding the relationships and uses of body parts.	Assess functioning related to the ability of individuals.	Activities that enhance body parts, such as throwing, kicking, gymnastics, tumbling, and trampoline activities; static and dynamic balances.
Spontaneous play	Spontaneous play limited; difficulty with creative movement and social development. Anxiety initiating movements.	Provide numerous social opportunities for interaction in a variety of settings.	Social-sequence activities, parachute, dance, rhythms, movement exploration.
Emotional expression	Shows little facial expression. Often unresponsive to needs of others and to nonverbal cues, gestures, facial expressions.	Provide opportunities for a variety of emotions and settings; make individual aware of different facial expressions.	Movement games; creative dramatics that utilize different emotions, facial expressions, and nonverbal reactions, such as shrugging shoulders; movement exploration.
Self-confidence	Lacks self-confidence; professes more vision than actually has. Sensitive about modifications. Wants to be as normal as possible.	Determine and emphasize strengths in programming; compensate for limitations.	Program based on the physical motor and social functioning of the individual; many opportunities to interact with peers; communication to compensate for deficiencies.
Gait	Stride length and speed reduced; hesitant, difficulty making correction.	Use tactile Kinesthetic training; orientation and mobility training.	Emphasize movement patterns and games that involve movement, sports and fitness activities.
Blindisms	Rocking back and forth; rubbing fingers into eyes, waving fingers in front of face; bending head forward; whirling around.	Encourage appropriate movements to replace blindisms; provide opportunities for movement; reinforce appropriate movement activity.	A menu of activities based on functioning that include fitness, motor development, dance, and aquatics.
Posture	Rigidity; forward bending and swaying.	Increase muscle tone and stretch tight muscles; actually inspect for appropriate postural cues; verbally reinforce correct posture.	Relaxation activities; yoga in static and dynamic position; postural exercises to develop inefficient areas and stretch tight muscles.

children to give them kinesthetic awareness of the activity. Ross, Lottes, and Glenn (1998) used a five-phase approach to teaching golf: (1) a hands-on approach to putting, using sounds as cues; (2) swinging a weighted swing trainer; (3) practice with balls of various sizes; (4) community-based instruction; (5) participating in a school tournament. Teachers can also use tactile awareness or encourage explanation of the space or boundaries in which children are participating. During the initial stages of learning, it may be beneficial for teachers to allow children to touch them while the skill is being demonstrated. By breaking a skill into small components in a whole-part-whole method of teaching, smaller segments of the activity can be paired with a tactile cue. Buell (1983) described a method of teaching a complex skill (jumping rope) by having children stand behind the teacher with their hands on the teacher's hips. The teacher and child initially would jump together without the rope; later teachers would turn the rope; and finally the child jumped and turned the rope. To ensure successful learning, teachers should actively encourage movement that involves various concepts of up and down, space, and the environment, as well as activities that provide children an opportunity to organize and move within their environment.

Auditory Perception

Besides haptic perception, many teaching cues and/or instructions can use a verbal explanation to help teach a specific activity. Because it is difficult to imitate something that cannot be seen, teachers should use concrete examples in their instructional methodology instead of concepts or abstracts. By pairing verbal instructions with haptic cues, teachers can augment the child's understanding of activities, which will in turn promote skill acquisition and understanding. Teachers may also wish to determine the location of sounds in a gymnasium or playground. A continuous sound is more appropriate than intermittent sounds. The source of the sound should be in front of children as they are moving toward it, or immediately behind children so they can move away from the sound (Mastro, 1985). Likewise, it is important for children to recognize a wide variety of sounds. For example, picking out a teammate's voice may indicate the direction to throw or pass a ball, while tracking a sound aids in determining the direction of the oncoming ball. Distinguishing one sound from a background of sounds can help the child concentrate or judge the position of a target, as in archery, basketball, or bowling. Finally, auditory cues can be used to signal a boundary area, as when the child approaches the wall in a swimming pool, or to discriminate between rhythms, tempos, and fast and slow movements used in dance and sports skills.

Growth and Maturation

Children with visual impairments may be delayed in their physical development, may be overweight, and may fatigue easily because of the overprotective nature of those around them. As a result, these children may have restricted movement and fewer play opportunities as well as a lack of motivation. Because these children may not have adequate opportunities to move and to learn physical and motor skills, their physical development should be encouraged.

Teachers should provide opportunities, instruction, and practice in a variety of gross motor and physical fitness skills and should cultivate a positive attitude toward activity that is based on the child's interest. Additional opportunities can be provided with after-school homework and sports activities.

Body Image

Because of the lack of visual cues, children often encounter problems identifying body parts and understanding the uses of the body in relationship to its parts. By assessing the functional and developmental level of vision, teachers can emphasize appropriate body image activities that use various parts of the body and movements to stimulate development. For example, balancing on the left foot, or throwing with the right hand, can provide practice in identifying specific body parts and their movements.

Poor posture and balance may also result from a lack of visual feedback. Without visual cues, children are often rigid or may exhibit a forward bend and sway. When provided cues on correct positions and reinforcement of appropriate postures, children can become more aware of changes in their body positions. Activities such as relaxation training, yoga, and postural exercises designed to stretch tight muscles and/or increase muscle tone can be implemented to aid in overcoming posture problems. More important, proper balance and posture are required to initiate and control movement.

Sensory Awareness

Children with visual impairments also display poor proprioceptive awareness of their bodies. To compensate for their lack of visual information, other sensory modalities, as well as residual vision, should be used to develop body awareness and changes in position. Activities with bright colors and sounds may provide contrasts needed to maneuver in their environment and can enhance teaching strategies. In addition, orientation and mobility training can help develop appropriate landmarks necessary to provide ongoing information and cues within the environment.

Spontaneous Play

Most sighted children will initiate self-play and develop smoothly through their social-sequence level of development (Rettig, 1994). In contrast, children with visual impairments may not initiate purposeful play and thus may encounter difficulty with creative movement and social development. When given opportunities to play alone and with groups in activities that require sharing and taking turns, children with visual impairments can experience appropriate play and development of social interaction (Swallow & Huebner, 1987). Play and movement awareness may be the crucial components to stimulating activity and spatial awareness in children with visual impairments. Several activities, such as the parachute, movement exploration, and rhythmic movements, are excellent for encouraging social interaction and development.

Emotional Expression

Without visual feedback, children with visual impairments often will demonstrate little facial expression and will be unresponsive to others because they do not see gestures, nonverbal cues, or others' facial expressions. Teachers should promote an awareness of facial expressions and emotions by allowing children to experience nonverbal actions, such as shrugging shoulders, smiling, frowning, and movement exploration activities.

Self-Confidence

All children should be allowed normal risk-taking experiences. Children with a visual impairment are often sensitive about activity modifications but may lack self-confidence if they are restricted in their opportunities for participation. In order to build their self-confidence and help them develop a positive attitude, teachers should develop the strengths of these children and should compensate for their limitations with sensory training.

Success in physical fitness, games, sports, and leisure activities will aid in physical and motor development as well as promote interaction and communication with peers that may lead to increased self-confidence and development of an appropriate social atmosphere. Robinson and Lieberman (2004) indicated that children with visual impairments have difficulties with self-control and making friends and that movement difficulties impede their self-perception.

Gait

As children develop their fitness and sensory awareness it is essential to develop the appropriate gait and stability. Independent living and being able to complete functional tasks is based on the ability to move the body into the environment. The absence of vision often restricts movement but stepping forward and supporting the shift of the body weight must be accomplished to allow initiation of movement, stepping, supporting the stance and increasing speed as needed. The ability to ascend and descend stairs and overall movement need to be taught and supported by increased sensory awareness and strength development.

Blindisms

To compensate for a lack of vision, many children will develop inappropriate movements (blindisms), such as rocking, rubbing fingers into eyes, waving fingers in front of the face, and whirling around. Much of the movement is inappropriate and often used to compensate for the lack of visual cues. Teachers should provide opportunities to replace these blindisms with more appropriate movements. The physical activity program consisting of physical fitness, dance, aquatics, and gross motor activities will allow children the opportunity for movement stimulation of the hands and bodies in an appropriate manner.

CHAPTER SUMMARY

1. In a typical physical education class, children rely primarily on vision to learn motor skills.

2. Children with visual impairments are individuals whose disability, even with correction, adversely affects their educational performance and ability to learn motor skills.

3. Instruction and teaching cues should be directed toward the haptic and auditory modalities of children to compensate for lack of vision.

4. Successful integration for some children with visual impairments depends on their ability to move efficiently and safely within the environment.

5. Orientation and mobility training may be helpful in acclimating children to outdoor and indoor settings.

6. Most activities, instruction, and equipment require few modifications for visually impaired students to participate successfully with sighted peers.

7. Athletes with visual impairments compete in events such as goalball, swimming, track and field, and downhill and cross-country skiing sponsored by the United States Association of Blind Athletes (USABA).

8. Children with visual impairments vary widely in visual functioning and residual vision. When selecting activities, the teacher should be aware of the child's cognition, sensory awareness, growth and maturation, body image, play level, emotional expression, self-confidence, blindisms, and posture.

REFERENCES

Adelson, E., & Fraiberg, S. (1974). Gross motor development in infants blind from birth. *Child Development, 45,* 114–126.

Blasch, B., Weiner, W., & Welsh, R. (1997). *Foundations of orientation and mobility* (2nd ed.). American Foundation for the Blind.

Blessing, D. L., McCrimmon, D., Stovall, J., & Williford, H. N. (1993). The effects of regular exercise programs for visually impaired and sighted schoolchildren. *Journal of Visual Impairment and Blindness, 87,* 50–51.

Buell, C. (1983). *Physical education for blind children.* (2nd ed.). Springfield, IL: Charles C. Thomas.

Chin, D. L. (1988). Dance movement instruction: Effects on spatial awareness in visually impaired elementary students. *Journal of Visual Impairment and Blindness, 81,* 188–192.

Fraiberg, S. (1977). *Insights from the blind: Comparative studies of blind and sighted.* New York: Basic Books.

Hatton, D., Bailey, D., Burchinal, M., & Ferrell, K. (1997). Developmental growth curves of preschool children with visual impairments. *Child Development, 68,* 788–806.

Holbrook, M. C. (1996). *Children with visual impairments: A parents guide.* Bethesda, MD: Woodine House.

Hopkins, W. G., Gaeta, H., Thomas, A. C., & Hill, P. (1987). Physical fitness of blind and sighted children. *European Journal of Applied Physiology, 56,* 69–73.

Horvat, M., Ray, C., Nocera, J. & Croce, R. (2006). Comparison of isokinetic peak force and power in adults with vision loss. *Perceptual and Motor Skills, 103*(1), 231–237.

Horvat, M., Ray, C., Croce, R., & Blasch, B. (2004). A comparison of isokinetic muscle strength and power in visually impaired and sighted individuals. *Isokinetics and Exercise Science, 12*(3) 179–183.

Horvat, M., Ray, C., Ramsey, V. K., Miszo, T., Keeny, R., & Blasch, B. (2003). Compensatory analysis and strategies for balance in individuals with visual impairments. *Journal of Visual Impairment and Blindness, 97*(11), 695–703.

Kirchner, C. (1985). *Data on blindness and visual impairments in the United States.* New York: American Foundation for the Blind.

Kobberling, G., Jankowski, L. W., & Leger, L. (1991). The relationship between aerobic capacity and physical activity in blind and sighted adolescents. *Journal of Visual Impairments and Blindness, 6,* 58–67.

Krebs, P. (1979). Hatha yoga for visually impaired students. *Journal of Visual Impairment and Blindness, 73,* 209–216.

Lieberman, L. (2002). Fitness for individuals who are visually impaired and deaf-blind. *Re:View, 1*(34), 13–23.

Mastro, J. V. (1985). Diamonds of the visually impaired athlete. *Palaestra, 1,* 43–46.

Mastro, J. V., Montelione, T. J., & Hall, M. M. (1986). Wrestling a viable sport for the visually impaired. *Journal of Physical Education, Recreation and Dance, 11,* 61–64.

Ponchillia, S. V., Powell, L. L., Felski, K. A., & Nicklawski, M. T. (1992). The effectiveness of aerobic exercise intervention for totally blind women. *Journal of Visual Impairment and Blindness, 86,* 174–177.

Portfors-Yeomans, C., & Riach, C. L. (1995). Frequency characteristics of postural control of children with and without visual impairment. *Developmental Medicine and Child Neurology, 37,* 456–463.

Ray, C. & Wolf, S. L. (2008). Review of instrinic factors related to fall risk in individuals with visual impairments. *Journal of Rehabilitation Research and Development, 45,* 1–7.

Ray, C. Horvat, M., Williams, M., & Blasch, B. (2007). Kinetic movement analysis in adults with vision loss. *Adapted Physical Activity Quarterly, 24*(3), 209–217.

Ray, C., Horvat, M., Keen, K., & Blasch, B. (2005). Using Tai Chi as an exercise intervention for improving balance in adults with visual impairments. *Re:View, 37*(1), 17–24.

Ray, C., Horvat, M., Croce, R., Mason, R. C., & Wolf, S.L. (2008). The impact of vision loss on postural stability and balance strategies in individuals with profound vision loss. *Gait and Posture, 16*(1), 1–14.

Rettig, M. (1994). The play of young children with visual impairments: Characteristics and interventions. *Journal of Visual Impairment and Blindness, 88,* 410–420.

Ribadi, H., Rider, R. A., & Toole, T. (1987). A comparison of static and dynamic balance in congenitally blind, sighted and sighted blind folded adolescents. *Adapted Physical Activity Quarterly, 4,* 220–225.

Richardson, M. J., & Mastro, J. V. (1987). So I can't see . . . I can play and I can learn. *Palaestra, 3*, 23–26.

Robinson, B. & Lieberman, L. (2004). Effects of level of visual impairment, gender, age on self-determination of children who are blind. *Journal of Visual Impairment and Blindness, 98*, 352–366.

Ross, D. B., Lottes, C. R., & Glenn, B. (1998). An adaptive physical education program teaching golf to students with visual impairment. *Journal of Visual Impairment and Blindness, 92*, 684–687.

Sanka, J. V., & Bina, M. J. (1978). Coming out ahead in the long run. *Journal of Physical Education and Recreation, 49*, 24–25.

Shepherd, R. J. (1994). Physiological aspects of physical activity for children with disabilities. *Physical Education Review, 7*(1), 33–44.

Shindo, M., Kumagau, S., & Tanaka, H. (1987). Physical work capacity and effort of endurance training in visually handicapped boys and young adult males. *European Journal of Applied Physiology, 56,* 501–507.

Skaggs, S. & Hopper, C. (1996). Individuals with visual impairments: A review of psychomotor behavior. *Adapted Physical Activity Quarterly, 13*, 16–26.

Sugden, D. A. & Keogh, J. F. (1990). *Problems in movement skill development.* Columbia, SC: University of South Carolina Press.

Swallow, R. & Huebner, K. (1987). *How to thrive, not just survive.* New York: American Foundation for the Blind.

Weitzman, D. M. (1985). An aerobic walking program to physical fitness in older blind adults. *Journal of Visual Impairment and Blindness, 79,* 97–99.

CHAPTER 13

Deafness/Hearing Loss

CASE STUDY

Several individuals with hearing loss participate in sports and physical education in our school system. Bill is a high school basketball player with moderate bilateral hearing loss. Generally, he wears hearing aids in practice and during games. He is an exceptional athlete and relies on lipreading and signing to communicate. His coach finds it difficult to speak slowly and, therefore, always ensures that Bill sees his face while speaking. On the court all the players use signs to call plays and defenses.

In contrast, Kayla is a softball player who, like Bill, wears hearing aids. She has some difficulty with the dirt and perspiration and sometimes will remove her aids. She signs and lipreads to communicate, but has some difficulty not being able to hear the sound of the ball hitting the bat. She adjusts by watching the position and movement of the bat and bat contact with the ball to guide her movements.

Another child, Michael, has a cochlear implant and is restricted from participation in contact sports like football or hockey. His teachers are concerned that blows to the head may deactivate the device and recommend the use of headgear or removal of the device prior to participation. It has also been suggested that the teachers consult with Michael and his parents regarding safety precautions and suitable activities for his participation.

Children with hearing loss may be categorized as either *deaf* or *hearing impaired*. Deaf children possess varying degrees of residual hearing and encounter problems receiving auditory stimuli and understanding speech even with the aid of amplification. The more informal term hard of hearing refers to varying degrees of hearing loss. Individuals who are *hard of hearing* are able to understand speech and respond to auditory stimuli, usually with the assistance of a hearing aid. In this context, many individuals favor the terms *deaf* and *hard of hearing* to describe hearing losses. Many in the deaf community do not classify themselves as disabled; they feel that the term hearing impaired designates something needs to be fixed and has a negative conotation because of the word impairment (Lieberman, 2005).

However, the federal government defines hearing losses, both *deafness* and *hearing impairments*, in the Individuals with Disabilities Education Act (IDEA) rules and regulations. *Deafness* means "a hearing impairment that is so severe that the child is impaired in processing linguistic information through hearing with or without amplification, that adversely affects a child's educational performance." *Hearing impairment* means "an impairment in hearing, whether permanent or fluctuating, that adversely affects a child's educational performance, but that is not included under the definition of *deafness*."

Any child with a hearing loss is unable to hear the quality of a sound, either partially or totally. The term *hearing impaired* was previously used to identify children who are hard of hearing and is currently still identified in the 2004 revision of IDEA. In either case, it is essential not to group everyone with a hearing loss together because they vary in residual hearing and language development, which are essential for inclusion in regular education classes.

Sound waves are produced by the alternate compression and refining of particles of matter to make up a cycle that occurs per second and is measured in a unit to designate cycles per second, or hertz (Hz). The human ear is sensitive to frequencies between 20 Hz and 20,000 Hz. When the frequency of a vibration changes, we perceive a change in pitch; the higher the frequency, the higher the pitch. Although individuals are sensitive to a wide range of pitches, the range between 500 and 2,000 Hz is of primary importance because the energy of speech sounds is concentrated in this region. The intensity of sound is measured in units called decibels (db). An increase or decrease in the loudness or softness is an increase in intensity of sound.

The normally functioning ear will accept sound waves and transform them into neural impulses that are decoded in the temporal lobes of the brain. A breakdown in hearing may occur in one or more of the transmission processes. Hearing losses may occur from a restriction in the range of frequencies received by the ear, the intensity of the perceived sound, or both. Of critical importance to the educational placement are three factors that impact the child's functional ability: (1) the site of the impairment, (2) age of onset, and (3) the extent of the hearing loss.

Site of Hearing Loss

The three types of hearing losses are conductive, sensorineural, and mixed. A conductive loss results from interference of sound impulses from the outer or middle ear to the inner ear (**Figure 13.1**). A dysfunction of the outer ear can prevent the transmission of sound impulses. The outer ear consists of the external ear (pinna) and the external acoustic meatus (auditory canal), a canal approximately one inch in length that extends from the external ear and ends at the eardrum (tympanic membrane). This is the separation point of the outer and middle ear.

Obstructions of the outer ear include accumulation of wax, foreign particles, or inflammation, which may cause problems with conducting or transmitting sound vibrations and which may result in temporary losses of hearing. These conditions are generally corrected by medication and/or drainage and do not usually require placement in special education, although even temporary losses of hearing can hinder the child's ability to follow directions.

The middle ear is a cavity approximately one to two cubic centimeters in volume that is connected to the nasopharynx by the eustachian tube. A dysfunction of the eustachian tube will affect hearing as well as result in enlarged adenoids, allergic congestion, and

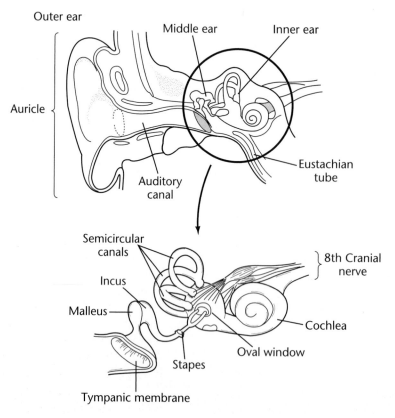

Figure 13.1 The human ear.

colds. Most middle-ear infections begin in the eustachian tube, resulting in unequal pressure on either side of the tympanic membrane that interferes with the vibration of sound waves and results in a conductive hearing loss. The middle ear contains three bones (incus, malleus, and stapes) that connect the tympanic membrane to the entrance of the inner ear (oval window). The bones transmit sound waves across the ossicular chain, with the last bone (stapes) being implanted in the oval window.

The most common conductive hearing loss in the middle ear is otitis media, or an inflammation of the middle ear. Chronic inflammations result in adhesions between the tympanic membrane and ossicular chain that may restrict the mobility of the ossicular chain and inhibit normal transmission of sound impulses. Another conductive hearing disorder that is bone conducted instead of air conducted may occur when new bony growths surround the capsule in the middle ear and affect sound conduction. In most cases, this condition can be corrected surgically, whereas inflammation of the middle ear is treated by medication. If the condition remains chronic, the use of amplification and speech training allows children to remain in regular classes. However, teachers should be concerned that losses of 15 db can affect educational performance.

In the inner ear the sound waves that have been transmitted are converted into neural impulses transported by the vestibular nerve and cochlear nerve and taken by the eighth cranial nerve to the temporal lobe of the brain for interpretation. Hearing losses in the inner ear are referred to as sensorineural. A large majority of children who possess sensorineural hearing losses have an impairment of the sensitive mechanisms of the inner ear or eighth cranial nerve. Unlike conductive hearing impairments, a sensorineural loss is resistant to amplification and generally cannot be corrected by surgery or medication. If a hearing loss results from an impairment of the neural mechanism, children may demonstrate a loss in the intensity of the sound, the sound may be distorted, or the sound may not reach the temporal lobe of the brain, a condition referred to as central deafness. Finally, hearing losses that occur in the outer, middle, and inner ear constitute mixed hearing losses and are part conductive and part neural. These hearing losses may involve variable amounts of residual hearing and range from difficulty understanding words to the inability to understand any speech sounds or language.

Age of Onset

The age at which hearing loss occurs is vitally important in establishing communication. Approximately 65 percent of all hearing losses occur before age 3

(Gallaudet Research Institute, 2001). Hearing losses that occur after children have acquired language (postlingual losses) have less severe implications for education than losses that occur before language had been acquired (prelingual losses). Because language development occurs in the first 5 years, children are at a severe disadvantage in responding to auditory stimuli if a problem occurs during this time. A postlingual loss may not interfere with educational development but may manifest itself in social and emotional frustrations because children miss portions of conversations or may not understand the actions of others, such as laughing at a humorous situation. Children may be deficient in motor functioning because they may not understand the rules and strategies of a particular game or sports activity.

Extent of Hearing Loss

Hearing losses can range in severity from slight to profound. Children with a 30 db loss are usually fitted with a hearing aid. Included in **Table 13.1** on page 172 are the general classifications of hearing loss.

Etiology of Hearing Losses

Of the 22 million reported individuals with hearing losses in the United States, approximately 3 to 5 percent are school-aged. Most children with hearing losses are educated in regular classrooms, with approximately 1 in 25 requiring extensive special education services. Among those individuals with hearing losses, approximately 40 percent are classified as mild, 20 percent as moderate, 20 percent as severe, and 20 percent as profound (Gallaudet Research Institute, 2001). Although only a small number of children will require special services, it should be noted that even slight hearing losses place the child at a disadvantage and affect incidental learning. The causes of hearing losses can often be determined from genetic or environmental factors. In the following list hearing losses are grouped by etiology.

1. The *hereditary*, or *endogenous, group* includes all deafness related to genetic causes. More than 50 genetic syndromes are associated with hearing loss, and approximately 50 percent of all profound hearing losses are genetically based. Deafness can be inherited as a dominant (14%), recessive (84%), or sex-linked (2%) disorder, whereas other hearing losses can be part of syndromes that produce other abnormalities (e.g., Treacher Collins syndrome).

2. The *prenatal group* includes those hearing losses caused by prenatal infections or trauma. Rubella, or German measles, may affect the developing fetus by causing hearing loss or other disabilities. Other

Table 13.1 Extent of Hearing Losses

Hearing Loss	Functioning and Educational Limitations
Slight, 16–25 db	Difficulty with faint or distant sounds but no significant difficulty with normal speech.
Mild, 6–40 db	Ability to interpret speech from a distance of 3–5 feet from the speaker, but approximately 50% of instruction may be distorted if the individual is not in the line of vision or distant from the speaker.
	Minor vocabulary and speech problems.
Moderate, 41–55 db	Faint conversations are misunderstood or distorted.
	Difficulty with group discussions and loud speech.
	Defective speech or tonal quality, receptive language problems.
Moderately Severe, 56–70 db	No speech at normal speaking level.
Severe, 71–90 db	Limited vocabulary.
	Problems discriminating vowels and consonants; understanding speech.
	Defective speech that deteriorates or does not develop spontaneously if occurring before 1 year of age.
Profound, 91 db or more	May decipher loud noises and vibrations.
	Visual and haptic perception are methods for receiving communication; cannot understand amplified speech.
	Speech and language will be resistant to spontaneous development and deteriorate if loss is prelingual.

prenatal infections include mumps, influenza, and toxemias. Prolonged labor, premature birth, difficult or injurious deliveries, or breathing failures (apnea) can also cause hearing losses.

3. The *postnatal* or *exogenous group* includes all deafness that is a result of postnatal illness or injury, such as viral infections (mumps, measles, or meningitis), chronic inflammation of the middle ear (otitis media), or, less often, trauma, accidents, and high fevers.

4. Acoustical trauma or exposure to high-decibel noise over an extended period of time can cause serious hearing loss. Acquired hearing loss is usually gradual, subtle, and cumulative. Exposure to the length and intensity of the sound can affect the sensory hair cells in the inner ear (**Figure 13.2**).

5. The remaining instances of hearing loss are of *undetermined etiology*. No specific environmental or genetic cause can be blamed for the hearing loss. Approximately 30 percent of all hearing loss cannot be traced to a specific cause.

About 15–18 million individuals have hearing losses, of which 3 million individuals are school-aged; 5 percent of all school-aged children have a hearing loss, with fewer than 19 percent of these children requiring special education services.

Symptoms of Hearing Loss

It is essential to detect any losses that may affect function. Teachers and parents have an opportunity to observe children and can refer them for more in-depth treatment. Teachers should especially be aware of the following which may indicate a hearing loss.

- Language/speech delayed
- Speech is not clear
- Volume is turned up
- Does not follow directions
- Does not respond
- Balance difficulties

Planning the Physical Activity Program

The development of communication is essential for integration into regular classes as well as for communicating in the deaf community (Stewart & Kluwin, 2001; Stewart, 1987). Although many professionals may disagree on the methods for improving communication, several methods are viable for physical education teachers. These include signing, amplification, and auditory training.

LEARNING ACTIVITY

Michael also is in weight training with Ron, our student with a visual impairment. How can we structure the learning environment to facilitate communication with Michael during the teaching process? What teaching strategies or safety precautions would be needed? How could you use sign language during class?

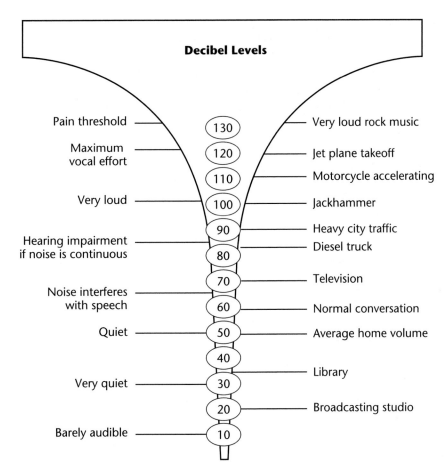

Figure 13.2 Comparative decibel levels.

Signing in Physical Education

Because communication is vital, sign language and fingerspelling are necessary instruction tools for physical education instruction. One of our previous authors, Carl Eichstaedt suggests that regular classroom teachers who deal with children with hearing impairments should be trained in signing and/or fingerspelling. Because signing is desirable, a workable composite of approximately 50 signs used commonly in physical education and athletics will assist the instructor of children with hearing loss (**Figure 13.3**).

Physical educators frequently use a single word or phrase to explain, encourage, correct, or control learning situations. Familiar expressions include: "Jump over, run to your left, come to me," "Good girl! Try again," "Crawl under. No, watch me," "Stop! Begin again," and "Sit down, stand up, run to boys." Such commonly used activity words are converted easily to signs, can be learned readily, and should become workable tools for every physical educator.

In many typical physical education situations, the child with a hearing loss should be placed directly in front of the instructor so that directions and commands will be understood. Many children with hearing losses can read lips, if the instructor is not too far away. When explaining new concepts, rules, or skills, the instructor should use simple terms and avoid unusual or complex idiomatic statements. Children with hearing losses will be unable to lip-read at far distances, such as from across the swimming pool or from the other end of the basketball floor. In such instances, the teacher may use signs and gestures that are consistent for all children.

The basic English alphabet can be learned in a short time. It is easier to fingerspell than to read fingerspelling. The dominant hand, held at shoulder level with palm out, spells the letters. Spelling slowly increases accuracy and eliminates confusion. If a letter is lost when the person is receiving the message, continue interpretation; the remaining letters may suggest the total word. Figure 13.3 shows the alphabet finger positions both as the receiver and the sender view them.

Most signs are for concept only—the idea, not the word, is stressed. The concept of *good* is signed in the following way: The left hand is open, palm up before the chest. The right hand, also open, touches the lips. The right hand is brought down so the back rests on the left palm (**Figure 13.3**).

Signing often requires shortening extraneous words or deleting word endings. "Go out to left field" is simply "Go"; the sender then points to left field. Common everyday gestures, such as pointing, motioning, demonstrating, and signaling, are acceptable because most children with hearing losses are familiar with them (Moores, 1987).

Many children use formal signing and fingerspelling, as set forth in a book and computer program titled *The Gallaudet Dictionary of American Sign Language.*

Also, when initially meeting a child, ask "Can you read my lips?" If the child says yes, continue the conversation in a normal voice; without shouting. Speak distinctly, but do not overenunciate your words; face the person, and do not turn your head while speaking. Also, try not cover your mouth or speak with something in your mouth. People with a

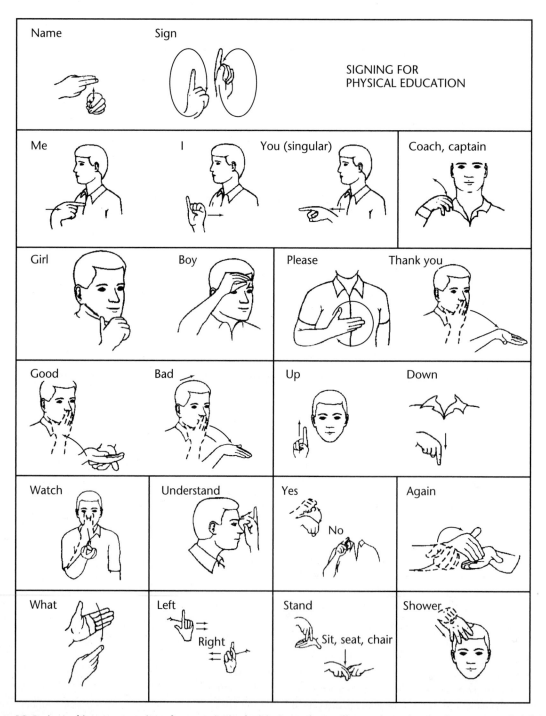

Figure 13.3 A working composite of approximately 50 signs that will greatly assist the instructor of children with hearing impairment.

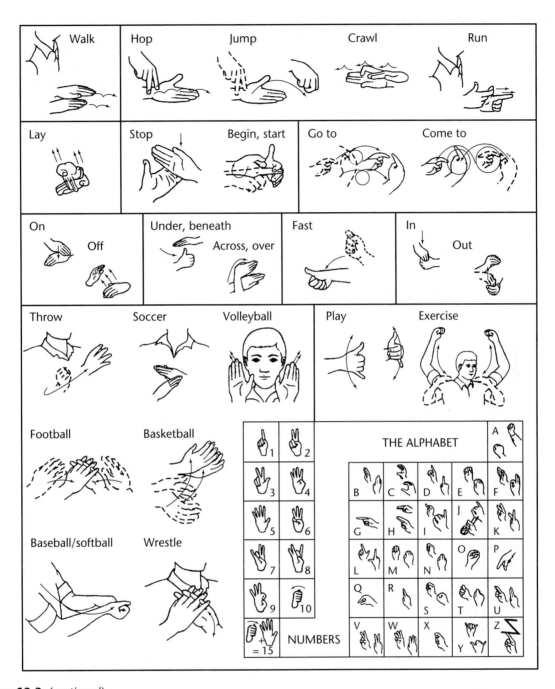

Figure 13.3 *(continued)*

mustache are also more difficult to understand because visual input may be distorted. If you do not understand what the child is trying to say, ask them to repeat the statements. Pretending to understand when you do not only leads to confusion and frustration. If either party still does not understand, use a paper and pencil to converse. Also, it is apparent that beyond a 90 db hearing loss, vision becomes the primary modality for communication. Without the proper visual input, children are placed at a disadvantage in social or learning settings that require communication (Nowell & Marshak, 1994).

Amplification and Auditory Training

Deafness does not always refer to a total lack of hearing. As previously indicated, hearing loss can vary in severity, and almost all children who are considered deaf have some residual hearing, especially those who have conductive disorders in the external or middle ear. Many children are also able to benefit from amplification, although it should be remembered that a hearing aid is not a panacea, and attempts to utilize residual hearing may be difficult. However, if amplification and auditory training enable children to learn a cognitive task, understand the strategies of a game, or interact socially, the use of such methods is more than justified.

Hearing aids are used to provide sound amplification within the residual hearing capacity of students. Ideally, the sound is magnified and can be distinguished from background noises or sounds. Amplification may enable the sound to become louder but does not necessarily mean the sound will be clearer. If the background sounds are confusing, children may not be able to discriminate or identify appropriate sounds in a noisy environment. The closer children are to the sound source, the more effective they will be in identifying sounds, although those with severe and profound losses must generally be within several feet to benefit from amplification.

Hearing aids are strapped to the body or behind the ear and can be worn on one ear (monaurally) or both (binaurally). For maximum effectiveness, children should wear the hearing aid throughout the day to effectively develop residual hearing. In this manner, children may learn to decipher and discriminate a variety of sounds necessary for communication. However, aids may be removed for physical reasons, such as earache, swimming, some contact sports, and excessive noise. At times, feedback in the amplified sound from the hearing aid is picked up by the aid microphone and goes through the system, creating a high-pitched sound that is extremely annoying. This generally occurs if the ear molds are not fitted properly and usually necessitates a new mold. It also occurs in closed in areas, such as a racquetball court.

The type of aid that is worn on the body consists of a small pocket unit containing a microphone, amplifier, volume control, and battery. The unit is connected to the ear by a cord, at the end of which is a loudspeaker. The body type contains all the basic components in a single unit set in an ear mold or eyeglass.

The hearing aid should be used in physical education, except during swimming or some contact sports, depending on the comfort level of the child. In addition, teachers should consider the following precautions in physical education for children with hearing aids:

1. Hearing aids should be securely fastened by means of a harness or tape.

2. Physical education teachers should have additional batteries if replacements are needed.

3. Clothing that causes annoying sounds to the wearer and distorts auditory discrimination and figure-ground should be avoided.

4. Perspiration should be wiped off the aid periodically.

Auditory training is another method to improve the use of residual hearing. Although the primary importance of auditory training may be for the classroom, physical education teachers must emphasize auditory training to aid in improving listening ability and communication. Awareness of a sound to start a race, signal a foul, or signal termination of play can be improved or taught. Teachers can also provide opportunities to help children distinguish a sound from a background, or they can set up games to help determine sound location or to discriminate between fast and slow tempos of music in dance activities. Many times sound distorations may confuse the child. Enclosed areas, such as a racquetball court or swimming pool, may initially confuse the child unless he or she can determine the location of the sound.

If children are able to recognize a sound, they should be able to match the sound with its meaning. In addition, information gathered from the visual and haptic senses will complement what children are able to hear and allow them to sort out information to distinguish and identify sounds.

Cochlear Implants According to the National Institute on Deafness and Communication Disorders a cochlear implant is an electronic device that provides a sense of sound for profoundly deaf individuals. The implant consists of an external portion that is placed behind the ear and an internal portion that is placed in the inner ear. An outer microphone will pick up external sounds that are sent to a speech processor that filters, amplifies, and arranges sounds picked up by the microphone. The transmitter and receiver/stimulator will receive signals from the processor and convert them into electrical impulses. Electrodes collect impulses from the stimulator to various regions of the auditory nerve. Cochlear implants are different from hearing aids in that the implants will bypass damaged portions of the ear and stimulate the auditory nerve to send signals to the brain that recognizes the signals as sounds. In contrast the hearing aid amplifies sound.

For children with cochlear implants, it is essential to care for the device and be aware of several safety precautions (Hilgenbrinck et al., 2004). For example the child should:

- Wear the processor in a carrier or pocket to prevent the processor from falling out.
- Tuck the cord into clothing during activity.
- Keep external parts, spare batteries, and cords available.
- Place the processor in a plastic bag to protect it from perspiration during exercise or while eating.
- Disengage or deactivate the processor if needed, such as in sports or in situations where static electricity is discharged.

Children will be encouraged to participate in most activities but should proceed with safety and protection.

Hilgenbrinck, et al, 2004 recommend that the device is deactivated and that other communication methods and strategies such as sign language or visual aids are used. Specific activities that could result in head injuries should require protective headgear or deactivation of the device. Participation may be restricted in contact sports such as football and hockey, but encouraged for baseball, basketball, and swimming as long as communication is established. (Hilgenbrinck et al., 2004).

Evaluation of Hearing Losses

The extent of hearing is usually evaluated by a physician who specializes in disorders of the ear, called an otologist, or by an audiologist, who specializes in the science of hearing. Most children with severe and profound hearing losses are identified during the first 3 years, whereas other losses are not evident until school age.

Most schools utilize a sweep test, in which the child is presented with a tone of 25 db at frequencies of 500 Hz, 1,000 Hz, 2,000 Hz, and 6,000 Hz. Other informal evaluations use a watch tick or coin click to observe the pupil's response to various sounds or observe children who complain of earaches or have movement problems.

Based on these informal assessments, a decision may be made to refer children for a more precise measurement of hearing. According to Blackman (1997), formal tests establish the type of hearing loss by assessing middle-ear air pressure and eardrum compliance with acoustic emmittance measures, such as tympanometry. Abnormal results indicate a conductive hearing loss, whereas normal results indicate a sensorineural loss (Blackman, 1997).

Air conduction testing may also be implemented to assess the sound waves that pass through the outer and middle ear to the inner ear. The audiologist can bypass the outer and middle ear and assess the air conduction through the skull directly into the inner ear. With a conductive hearing loss, the bone conduction threshold will be normal, while the level of air conduction will be higher. A hearing loss in the neural mechanism is reflected by air and bone conduction of equal levels. Another technique called *impedance audiometry* can be used to determine the condition of the tympanic membrane and middle ear without a voluntary response from the individual. Blackman (1997) has reported that several newer techniques can be used for young children or those with physical or cognitive impairments. Electrophysiologic tests, such as auditory brain stem response or evoked response audiometry, measure change in brain function as the child's response to auditory stimuli. Octoacoustic emissions also can provide mechanical vibrations that begin in the chochlea and are transmitted to the outer ear via the middle ear (Blackman, 1997).

Typical assessments of performance in physical education classes can be used with a minimum of modification. Hand signals, gestures, flags, and movements can signal the individual to initiate a prescribed physical education movement.

Modification and Adaptations

Most children will be participating in regular physical education classes and will require only minor modifications or adaptations to participate. The biggest problem facing teachers is to establish a system of communication (Stewart, 1987). This must be developed through the school's preferred method of total communication and may include lipreading, amplification, auditory training, and/or signing. Teachers should be aware that instructions should be given at a moderate rate, at face level, and, if outdoors, with the sun at the hearing-impaired child's back. In addition, preferred seating and/or changing positions should be encouraged to facilitate lipreading or residual hearing. When activities take place in an open area, communication signals to stop and start, such as snapping the lights on and off or waving flags, can be utilized.

Visual aids can be employed in demonstration. Cue cards, films, pictures, charts, and bulletin boards can take the place of detailed verbal explanations, and written instructions and rules can be provided to children prior to instruction (Schmidt, 1985).

In general, games or sports with a minimum of rules are easier to learn. Softball, volleyball, and kickball require little explanation, can be demonstrated easily, and proceed at a slower pace. Sports that are more intricate and that proceed at a faster pace over a large area, such as soccer and basketball, should begin with developmental drills and half-court or field games until children have mastered the fundamental motor skills. Once the game is spread out, appropriate signaling techniques can be used to move children into the proper position or sequence, as well as stopping or starting.

Teaching rhythmic activities requires some minor modifications. Auditory training and the use of vibrations can enable children to differentiate between sounds. Percussion instruments and/or blinking lights can also aid in establishing tempo or moving in conjunction with the beat.

Stunts and games that limit vision may be restricted. Because children have no visual feedback, the activity may be difficult and ultimately contraindicated. Lieberman and Cowart's (1996) book *Games for People with Sensory Impairments* should be consulted to aid in developing and modifying activities. Swimming is generally encouraged if water is not damaging to the ears; the teacher gives instructions when the child's head is out of the water or during a long drill.

In other cases, a minor modification of the stroke (backstroke or breaststroke) that will not obscure vision may be helpful. With gymnastics routines and movements, children should be allowed to use their vision and develop the kinesthetic awareness necessary to perform the activity correctly.

Implementing the Physical Activity Program

Children with hearing losses will display several characteristics that may hinder their motor performance, balance, and ability to interact with peers (Butterfield, 1988; Dummer, Haubenstricker, & Stewart, 1996). However, it should be remembered that children will vary in ability levels as well as in their ability to hear. Some children may have very low motor function, while others may perform at a high degree of skill. With this in mind, teachers should implement the physical activity program based on the characteristics, strategies, and physical education activities presented in **Table 13.2**.

Socialization

One of the most important elements of the educational plan for children is developing opportunities for socialization. Because of their distorted and fluctuating tonal quality and guttural speaking, children with hearing losses are often left out of play experiences. This may cause children to withdraw completely or to develop solitary play. In addition, their lack of social skills may restrict their interactions with other children and their ability to grasp team sports with complex rules.

Teachers should select activities that require the least amount of verbal communication and should integrate children with hearing peers. By utilizing individual sports and games, such as aquatics, tennis, badminton, and dance, teachers can create opportunities for success and acceptance that may promote feelings of self-worth and acceptance by the child's peers (Hopper, 1988). As children become more comfortable, they can progress to dual and team sports and games.

Language Development

Some children may experience difficulty expressing their thoughts and emotions as well as interpreting various expressions and gestures. Lyon (1997) indicated that language does not develop without play and indicated that play behaviors are similar to play behaviors of children who have not yet developed language. To aid children in language skill development, teachers can present guided discovery and manual guidance activities—pairing movements with descriptions to allow them to interpret concepts. Additionally, appropriate nonverbal communication, hand signals, or cues will enable children to understand concepts in play, dance, swimming, and creative movement that encourage emotions, gestures, and ideas. It is essential to remember that a hearing loss of more than 90 db will require more use of the visual system in a manner that is conducive for children to understand (Nowell & Marshak, 1994).

Hyperactivity

Children with hearing losses frequently manifest restlessness, wiggling, and active movements, probably because they are unable to receive auditory cues. Given an opportunity to position themselves to maintain visual contact and to use activities to control tension, children may perform in a more appropriate manner. Yoga, relaxation techniques, active games such as parachute play and relays, and dual sports and games can be incorporated to reduce hyperactivity.

Posture

At times children may lean forward and display abnormal tilts and rotation of the head to compensate for decreased hearing. Posture and balance should be encouraged to ensure stability for more intricate tasks. Teachers can model and reinforce appropriate postures that emphasize correct body alignment and movement positions. Activities that relate to overall development, such as cardiovascular fitness, flexibility, and muscular strength and endurance should be implemented to encourage appropriate body positions and development of key postural muscles.

Balance

Children who manifest static (stationary) or dynamic (moving) balance problems should compensate by using vision and haptic awareness. Siegel, Morchetti, and Tecclin (1991) indicate that children with sensory-neural losses are more inclined to have a balance disorder. Because balance is an integral component of all physical education activities, it is essential to select activities that provide for the child's development. Activities such as dance, gymnastics, and trampoline are all conducive to promoting static and dynamic balance. However, if children have inner-ear impairments that affect their ability to balance, compensation activities can be used to help children establish a broad base of support and lower their center of gravity.

Table 13.2 Characteristics of Children With Hearing Impairments

Behavior	Characteristics	Instructional Strategies	Physical Education Considerations
Socialization	Distorted tonal quality; guttural, highly fluctuating in pitch range; hard to understand; left out of spontaneous play and may withdraw and develop solitary play; difficulty grasping social situation, team games, and games with complex rules.	Use activities that require the least amount of verbal communication; socially integrate children on a hearing team, and create opportunities for success and acceptance by hearing peers; expand opportunities for deaf to interact with hearing peers (Dummer et al., 1996).	Individual sports and games, such as aquatics, tennis, badminton, dance; progression to dual and team sports.
Language	Expressive language difficulty; development of inner language delayed; difficulty expressing intense emotions; difficulty interpreting expressions and gestures.	Use guided discovery and manual guidance; pair movements with description of movement activities; stress nonverbal expression; establish appropriate communication system and visual stimuli (videos, posters).	Modern dance, aerobics, synchronized swimming, gymnastics, creative movement, movement exploration activities that encourage communicating emotions and ideas.
Cognition	Variable, based on ability to acquire language and read; decreased opportunities for incidental learning; language does not develop without play.	Present instruction in preferred method of communication, and use visual stimuli.	Emphasize active participation, play, and exploratory activities that reinforce academic concepts.
Hyperactivity	Restlessness; frequent wiggling, shuffling, and other active movements.	Allow children to position themselves to maintain visual contact; give praise for appropriate speaking attempts and motor behavior; intervene to extinguish inappropriate responses; use activities to control tension and promote relaxation.	Yoga, relaxation techniques to regain control; parachute, active games, gross motor skills, dual sports and games emphasizing active, rather than passive, activity.
Posture	Abnormal tilts and rotation of the head; forward lean.	Model appropriate static and dynamic postures; reinforce appropriate posture responses.	A variety of fitness activities, such as walking, jogging, cycling, flexibility exercises, resistance exercises that impact physical development, dance, and movement activities.
Balance	Static and dynamic balance deficits especially in sensory-neural losses.	Use vision and haptic awareness to compensate for poor balance; establish a broad base of support and lower center of gravity.	Dance, martial arts, tumbling, gymnastics, trampoline, perceptual motor activities in a developmental physical education program (Butterfield, 1988).
Motor speed	Distorted sense of time and temporalness; may be slow in accomplishing task.	Emphasize visual starting signals and activities that differentiate between fast and slow.	Dance, creative movement, and movement exploration; gymnastics and developmental locomotor skills.
Gait	Tendency to walk with a shuffling gait; dragging feet.	Reinforce and model correct walking pattern; utilize mirrors, visual and kinesthetic training.	Tap dance, rhythms, locomotor skills, and gymnastic activities.
Fitness and motor development	Overall motor development may lag behind peer group. Delays caused by environmental and experience factors (Butterfield, 1991). Tendency to be overweight (Dair et al., 2006).	Assess children and base program on individual functioning and capabilities. Provide quality instruction and stress participation.	Sound developmental physical education program of physical and motor fitness, fundamental skills and patterns, aquatics, dance, sports, and games.

Motor Speed

Often the motor speed of children with hearing loss is characterized by slow movements. Because children may manifest difficulties with the concepts of fast and slow, teachers should use signals or activities that emphasize differences in speed and time. Physical fitness, dance, and locomotor activities that contain temporal and speed elements should be implemented to differentiate between concepts of time and speed that are essential for optimal performance.

Gait

Children may also manifest a shuffling gait or a tendency to drag their feet. Because they may not receive auditory cues, teachers should reinforce and model correct motor patterns emphasizing form and precision. By using mirrors and visual and kinesthetic training, teachers can integrate rhythms, gross motor skills, and gymnastics to overcome gait-oriented problems.

Fitness and Motor Development

The overall motor development of children with hearing loss will vary in comparison to their peer group. This is evident in terms of physical fitness (Butterfield, 1988 in Ellis, Butterfield, & Lenhard, 2000) as well as motor development abilities (Dummer et al., 1996). Dair et al. (2006) indicate that the prevalence of overweight deaf children 6–11 years of age was above the national percentage. Because of the variability in physical and motor functioning among children with hearing losses, it is especially important to assess the individual's level of functioning and provide a developmental physical education program. This program should emphasize physical and motor fitness, fundamental skills and patterns, aquatics, dance, sports, and games (Lieberman, 2005).

CHAPTER SUMMARY

1. Children with hearing losses are classified as *deaf* or *hearing impaired*. Deaf children are restricted in hearing and understanding speech. There are varying degrees of hearing losses, and some children can understand speech with amplification.

2. Of critical importance to the teacher are three factors that describe the nature of a hearing loss: the site of the impairment, the age of onset, and the extent of hearing loss.

3. Establishing communication is vital in developing the physical education program and socialization process, as is the use of vision for a loss of more than 90 db.

4. Total communication should be established based on school policies. Elementary signing and manual communication can be used to communicate with deaf students. Amplification through the use of hearing devices and auditory training can also be effective tools in communication.

5. Most children with hearing losses can participate in the regular physical education program with little or no adaptations.

6. In developing teaching strategies and instruction, the educator should be aware of several factors that will influence the learning process. These include socialization skills, language skills, hyperactivity, posture, balance, speed, and gait.

7. Children with hearing losses will vary in physical fitness and motor development. It is important to assess the child's level of functioning and provide a developmental physical education program based on individual needs. Activities should be included that stress physical and motor fitness, fundamental skills and patterns, including aquatics, dance, sports, and games.

REFERENCES

Blackman, J. A. (1997). *Medical aspects of developmental disabilities in children birth to three* (3rd ed.). Gaithersburg, MD: Aspen Publications.

Butterfield, S. A. (1988). Deaf children in physical education. *Palaestra*, 6, 28–30, 52.

Butterfield, S. A. (1991). Physical and sport for the deaf: Rethinking the least restrictive environment. *Adapted Physical Activity Quarterly, 8*, 95–102.

Lieberman, L. (2005). Visual impairment and hearing losses. In Winnick, J. (Ed.) *Adapted physical education and sport*, (pp. 143–166). Champaign, IL: Human Kinetics.

Dair, J., Ellis, K. M., & Lieberman, L. J. (2006). Prevalence of overweight among deaf children. *American Annals of the Deaf, 151*(3), 318–326.

Dummer, G. M., Haubenstricker, J. L. & Stewart, D. L. (1996). Motor skill performances of children who are deaf. *Adapted Physical Activity Quarterly, 13*, 400–414.

Ellis, K., Butterfield, S., & Lenhard, R. A. (2000). Grip-Strength Performances by 6–19 year old Children With and Without Hearing Impairments. *Perceptual and Motor Skills, 90*, 279–282.

Gallaudet Research Institute. (2001). *Regional and national summary report of data from the annual survey of deaf and hard of hearing children and youth*. Washington, D.C.: GRI, Gallaudet University.

Heward, W. L. (2009). *Exceptional children* (9th ed.). New York: Merrill.

Hilgenbrinck L. C., Pyfer J., & Castle N. (2004). Students with cochlear implants teaching considerations for physical educators. *JOPERD 75*, 28–33.

Hopper, C. (1988). Self-concept and motor performance of hearing-impaired boys and girls. *Adapted Physical Activity Quarterly, 5*, 293–304.

Individuals with Disabilities Act of 1997, Pub. L. No 105–17. (1997, June 4).

Lieberman, L. L. & Cowart, J. F. (1996). *Games for people with sensory impairments*. Champaign, IL: Human Kinetics.

Lyon, M. E. (1997). Symbolic play and language development in young deaf children. *Deafness and Ed 21*(2), 10–20.

Moores, D. F. (2001). *Educating the deaf* (5th ed.). Boston: Cengage Learning.

National Information Center on Deafness. (1991). *Deafness: A fact sheet*. Washington, DC: Gallaudet University.

Nowell, R. C. & Marshak, L. E. (1994). *Understanding deafness and the rehabilitation process*. Boston: Allyn & Bacon.

Schmidt, S. (1985). Hearing impaired students in physical education. *Adapted Physical Activity Quarterly, 2*, 300–306.

Siegel, J., Marchetti, M., & Tecelin, J. (1991). Age related balance changes in hearing-impaired children. *Physical Therapy, 71*, 183–189.

Stewart, D. A. (1987). Social factors influencing participation in sport for the deaf. *Palaestra, 2*, 23–28.

Stewart, D. A., & Kluwin, T. N. (2001). *Teaching deaf and hard of hearing students: Content, strategies, and curriculum*. Boston: Allyn and Bacon.

Teaching Individuals With Congenital and Acquired Impairments

Section IV focuses on helping teachers incorporate into the physical education program children with posture and orthopedic impairments, neurological disorders, muscular dystrophy, and arthritis. Children with any of these impairments will benefit from physical education and require a thorough understanding of the condition.

This section is designed to help teachers

1. recognize the characteristics of children with impairments that affect movement or functional ability.

2. understand the concerns and the appropriate treatment, first aid, and medication that may be essential for these children.

3. to develop the expertise to design physical education programs based on the functional ability and needs of these children.

4. to understand the interaction with various disciplines in the treatment of these impairments.

5. to facilitate instruction in physical education for children with a breadth of impairments in the least restrictive environment.

Posture and Orthopedic Impairments

CASE STUDY

The children in Mrs. Blue's physical education class were undergoing posture and scoliosis screening. During screening, Mrs. Blue made note of the postural issues of several children, including slumping shoulders, not standing upright, weak abdominals, and sway in the lower back. She also noted that some children with sensory impairments and a boy who used a wheelchair leaned or slumped in ways that not only affected posture, but breathing as well. In response, Mrs. Blue modified the warm-up at the beginning of class to include stretches designed to emphasize proper alignment and to strengthen core muscles. For the child using a wheelchair, she introduced partner stretches and the use of a physioball to improve proper sitting posture and breathing. During the week of the screening, she reminded children to check their posture in a mirror to ensure proper alignment.

The primary focus of physical education classes is the development of physical fitness and motor skills. Only a minimal amount of time is designated to improving proper body mechanics. Instructional time designated for children with posture problems is relatively rare. Such children may not receive appropriate strengthening or flexibility exercises for postural deviations that ultimately contribute to back and/or knee strain, poor muscular development, and a restriction in motor skill development. More important, poor body mechanics generally exists concurrently with a poor body image and lack of self-esteem.

Children with disabilities have a greater incidence of postural defects than do the general school-aged population. For example, children with sensory impairments may exhibit faulty body mechanics or head tilts primarily due to the lack of feedback from the affected sensory apparatus that aids in maintaining and reinforcing appropriate postures. Likewise, nonambulatory children with amputations, spinal injuries, or neurological disorders may place undue pressure on their postural structure and must reassert their center of balance that was disrupted by injury or disability or compensate for remaining in a seated position. This chapter addresses the common posture and deviations that alter body mechanics, such as spinal injuries and amputations.

Posture

Posture is defined as the manner in which the body maintains alignment against gravity. Good posture involves the skeletal system, ligaments, muscles, fatigue, and the self-concept of the individual. Correct posture is achieved when all segments of the body are aligned properly over a base of support. Problems from poor posture may include back and shoulder pain, muscle imbalances, asymmetry in weight distribution, protruding abdomen, respiratory difficulties, and forward leans or positioning of the head.

Posture encompasses more than maintaining a static position, because movement requires children to assume and change positions of the body constantly. A sitting position with the back against the seat, feet on the floor, and thighs and back supported by the seat permits students to sit in a relaxed position while the chair provides support of the body. Additionally, when positioned at elbow height, the arms rest on the chair supports and relax the postural muscles while conserving energy. Improper sitting is characterized by failure to align the body with the chair back, slumping of the back and shoulders, and concentrating the majority of weight on one side of the body. Children in a wheelchair are especially susceptible to seated postural faults and resulting complications, such as pressure sores or respiratory dysfunctions from pressure on the rib cage, because their disability may restrict appropriate physical development that is necessary to maintain proper sitting posture.

Standing posture is characterized by an erect position with an elevated head and chest, posterior-tilted pelvis, slightly curved abdomen and lower back, slightly flexed knees, and feet parallel and spaced a comfortable distance apart to allow for an even weight distribution. Various body builds will affect standing postures, necessitating an appropriate knowledge of each body type as well as an awareness of sensory or orthopedic impairments that may affect the standing posture. Common standing postural problems include slumping the shoulders, improper tilts of the head, protruding abdomen, and improper foot placement.

Walking is a natural extension of the standing posture and should encompass the basic elements of standing while adding movement and supporting the body by alternately losing and regaining balance. The head and chest remain erect, while the chin is tucked. Arms will swing in opposition to the legs while the shoulders are level, and the feet will move in a forward direction, alternately striking the walking surface first with the heel, then rolling onto the balls of the feet. Each walking stride will vary according to the length of the stride and pace maintained by individual children.

Common problems associated with walking postures include slumping the shoulders, tilting the head, toeing the feet in or out, striking flat-footed, and/or dragging the feet. Children with prosthetic devices may face further complications in walking, such as difficulties in shifting weight or regaining balance, a lack of proper feedback (in the case of individuals with sensory impairments), and fatigue (in the case of children in a wheelchair). There is also a lack of symmetry and amount of force applied to each step in some conditions (Smail & Horvat, 2009).

Individual Differences in Posture

When analyzing proper posture, teachers should be aware of individual differences that are associated with age, body type, and exceptionality. Children in the primary grades will exhibit a slightly protruding abdomen and curvature of the spine that are common at this age and do not constitute a posture defect. However, the same occurrence in young adults indicates a marked defect and requires corrective measures.

Specific body types are more apt to assume a particular posture because of their build. Children may possess a mesomorphic, endomorphic, or ectomorphic body type, or any combination of the three body types. The upper torso may be the predominant characteristic of one body type classification, whereas the lower extremities may characterize another specific body type. The mix of body type classifications may lead to improper posture development, such as a muscular chest and back coupled with a slender abdomen and lower limbs, which may appear as a rounded upper back. In conjunction, orthopedic problems such as spinal injuries or amputations may also contribute to improper body alignment or posture because the disabilities may affect the remaining muscle mass, mechanics, or stability of the body in maintaining appropriate posture.

Because children may demonstrate postural deficiencies, it is necessary to develop good posture habits and to correct improper body alignments before they inhibit the development of age-appropriate motor skills or possible injury. If postural deficits are the direct result of a specific condition, proper strengthening exercises or procedures should be implemented to correct problems related to structural body alignment.

Postural Deviations—Etiology and Program Development

There is no single cause of posture deficits. Postural deviations can be either functional or structural. A functional condition can be overcome through corrective exercises or training in kinesthetic awareness of proper positions. Without proper maintenance of postural muscles and the use of corrective techniques, the deficiency may deteriorate, possibly become debilitating, and may either interfere with the physical performance capabilities of students or become a structural deviation. Structural deviations are due to abnormalities and/or deformities of the skeletal system resulting from disease or injury. Because of the severity of structural defects, most are treated by physicians with a combination of braces, casts, surgery, and prosthetic devices.

Teachers as well as the collaborative team members should constantly be aware of posture during the early school years, especially for those children whose condition may contribute to inappropriate posture. Reminders and reinforcement for proper sitting and standing posture may be the most effective way to eliminate postural defects. Posture deficiencies may also occur in a variety of positions and affect different areas of the body structure. Most teachers, coaches, and trainers will emphasize the development of the core muscles (postural) including abdominal, back (mid and lower), lumbar, spine, and pelvis. By strengthening these muscle groups the body is balanced, stable, and able to initiate stability and movement and avoid postural deviations and low back pain. The development of core muscles and stability movements can include a variety of exercises to stabilize and strengthen these muscle groups. Included in the following table are some specific exercises that can be included in strengthening core and stability muscles. In order for teachers to address posture problems effectively, appropriate exercises should be utilized for various parts of the body with consultation of the physician. Some of these exercises for specific body parts include the following (Kisner & Colby, 2007; Lasko & Knopf, 1992; Hislop & Montgomery, 2007; Dunn & Leitschuh, 2006; Wessel, 1976):

Postural Exercises: Head and Neck Deviations

The head and neck may have a tendency to droop forward, and in more severe cases this deviation may result in a rounding of the shoulders and back. A forward head occurs when the neck is extended forward and downward. Torticollis is a tilting of the head to one side caused by a shortening of the sternocleidomastoid muscle that attaches behind the ear and inserts into the clavicle and sternum.

Neck extension and round shoulders are primarily caused by functional problems and can be aided by proper exercise. Round shoulders may also be the result of a habit, requiring a need to reeducate the child to proper positions. Additionally, a lack of overall muscular development may be apparent and can be corrected by utilizing appropriate exercises, including the following:

1. In a standing or sitting position, rotate chin and touch each shoulder; hold and return.

2. In a standing or sitting position, touch ear to shoulder; hold and return. Place one hand on top of the head, and gently apply a little more pressure to help stretch the neck.

3. In a standing or sitting position, lower the chin toward the chest and apply light pressure, using the hands to press the head forward. Lift the head up, tilt the chin at an angle, and bring the head straight down toward the chest, again applying gentle pressure; repeat on the other side.

4. In a standing or sitting position, rotate the head slowly in a circle clockwise, and repeat in a counterclockwise direction, being careful not to hyperextend the neck in backward rotation.

5. In a standing or sitting position, apply resistance to the back of the head and attempt to push the head backward, on its own strength, against the resistance.

6. In a standing or sitting position, interlock hands behind the neck and pull hands forward while pushing against the hands with the neck muscles.

7. In a standing position, place a beanbag on the head while observing the proper posture in a mirror. Walk while balancing an object.

8. Lying supine, look up at the ceiling, bring the head and chin to the chest, and return (if lordosis is not present).

9. Lying prone, tuck chin, forehead against a mat, hold, and relax.

Trunk Deviations

Kyphosis is an abnormal increase in the flexion of the thoracic region of the spine and is sometimes called humpback. Kyphosis can also be structural and, if so, requires treatment by a physician. Functional kyphosis will commonly appear in conjunction with round shoulder and forward head. The more severe curvature or kyphosis is the result of weak back extensor muscles or fatigue as well as the shortening of the muscles of the chest and shoulder girdle. Stretching and strengthening the muscles involved in maintaining the spine, chest, and shoulder girdle allow more movement of the shoulders and rib cage and may correct kyphosis to some extent.

A lack of muscular development also contributes to a protrusion of the shoulder blades (winged scapula) from the spinal column. This occurs from the lack of shoulder girdle strength and may be corrected by stretching the muscles of the shoulder girdle while strengthening the muscle groups that align the scapula (trapezius and rhomboids).

Several exercises follow that may be used in overcoming trunk deviations.

1. In a standing position, use a bar or ladder and hang or climb for increasing periods of time.

2. In a standing or sitting position, pinch shoulders together while in front of a mirror and release. Bring shoulders up to the ears, contracting the muscles, and release the shoulders down.

3. In a standing position, clasp hands behind head and extend elbows forward, bringing elbows together in front of the face, and then extend elbows backward while straightening the spine erect.

4. In a standing or sitting position, raise elbows to shoulder level, clasp hands, and pull while providing resistance with each arm.

5. In a standing or sitting position, raise elbows to shoulder level in front of the body and cross one elbow over the other; then extend the elbows to sides.

6. In a standing or sitting position, raise elbows overhead, then touch elbows together behind the back.

7. In a standing position, grasp a towel or surgical tubing with hands spread, and raise arms overhead. Move the towel back as far as possible while maintaining straight arms, being careful not to hyperextend the back and keeping the head straight.

8. Lying prone, extend arms overhead. Raise the upper body from the floor and return several times, keeping the lower back straight.

9. Lying supine, place the hands on the lower abdominal area and press the lower back flat to the floor, making sure the knees bend and the pelvis tilts downward.

10. In a standing or sitting position, bring the shoulders up toward the ears, and move in a circular fashion forward and backward. Alternate bringing one shoulder up toward the ear and then the other shoulder. Press both shoulders forward and backward.

11. In a standing position, simulate the back crawl swimming movement, extending arm overhead and reaching backward as far as possible.

12. In a standing position in a door frame, press the hands against the door frame and apply force overhead and slightly behind the head.

13. In a standing position, with the small of the back against the corner of a wall or door, place the fists together in front of the chest, and pull the arms back as far as possible.

14. In a standing position in front of a table, place the hands on edge of table and press the chest toward the floor between the extended arms. Ensure that the motion is performed with the head raised.

Scoliosis is a deviation that requires early screening to circumvent serious problems. Scoliosis causes the spine to deviate abnormally to the side and is present in approximately 20 percent of the school-aged population, ranging from mild to severe deviations and occurring mostly in females. The frequency of scoliosis detected in young girls is due to rapid maturation and hormonal changes during adolescence. **Figure 14.1** illustrates four major types of scoliotic curves: thoracic, thoracolumbar, lumbar, and double major.

The *right thoracic* curve is most common and is indicated by a curve that deforms the ribs on the same side, causing a "rib hump" that will affect body alignment as well as the internal organs; the *thoracolumbar* curve is more gradual and less likely to cause a deformity, although it visibly affects the proper body alignment of the hips and is a primary cause of low back pain; the *lumbar* curve causes a deviation in the symmetry of the hips and is related to low back pain in the severe styles; and the *double major* curve includes two curves that are more balanced and less deforming, although the alignment of the ribs is primarily affected.

In scoliosis, the single curve will involve the entire spine and is commonly referred to as a "C" curve. Scoliosis with two or more curves is known as an "S" curve and results from the body's attempt to maintain balance. Functional scoliosis curves are approximately 90 percent genetic but may be accentuated by growth, abnormal posture, or overdevelopment of the back muscles.

Depending on the severity of the scoliotic condition and the physician's opinion concerning the effectiveness of exercise on scoliosis, the physician may prescribe exercises that may be conducted in a physical education or home setting to overcome functional

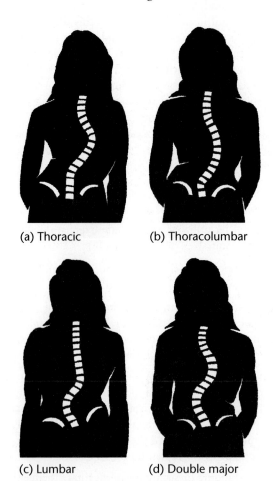

(a) Thoracic   (b) Thoracolumbar

(c) Lumbar   (d) Double major

Figure 14.1 Scoliotic spinal curves: (a) thoracic, (b) thoracolumbar, (c) lumbar, and (d) double major.

scoliosis. Several exercises for a left curvature (which may also be reversed for a right curvature) include the following:

1. In a standing position, hang from a bar or ladder with the arms extended, and flex the trunk to the left, raising the left hip and moving the feet to the left.

2. In a standing or supine position, extend the arms overhead with palms turned upward; hold and return.

3. In a standing position, face a wall and move the hands up the wall on the side of the curve. Return on the opposite side.

4. In a standing position, with hands on hips, raise the right arm overhead and left arm sideward to shoulder height. Raise the body on the tiptoes, and move the right leg sideward on the ground, stretching the body; hold and return.

5. In a standing position, place the hands at hips; then stretch the left arm downward without bending the left side of the body.

6. In a standing position, place the hands on hips; then stretch the right arm overhead while pressing left hand against ribs.

7. In a standing position, place the right hand behind the neck and left hand against the ribs, twisting to the left while rotating the right arm.

8. In a standing position, place the hands on hips and bend slowly forward while holding the head upright.

9. In a standing position, flex the trunk to the left while sliding the left hand down the left leg and extending the right arm overhead, hands stretched out.

10. In a kneeling position, extend the left leg sideward on the ground, and extend the right arm overhead while pressing left hand against the ribs. Flex the trunk to the left while moving right arm in an arc overhead continuing pressure of left hand on the ribs.

If the cause of scoliosis is structural or a severe deformity of the vertebrae, corrective exercises will have minimal, if any, effect. Severe curvatures are treated by an orthopedic surgeon and include bracing, surgery, fusion, casting, or electrical stimulation. In either case, the program should be developed in consultation with the physician and implemented within a medical margin of safety.

For example, a bracing is used on curves of less than 40 degrees and supports the body from the neck to the pelvic region with two metal rods to align the spine. Most activities are appropriate and should be implemented in consultation with the physician, because movements that incorporate flexion, extension, rotation, and high impact are contraindicated. Another support treatment is a molded cast that can be used when curves are more than 50 degrees and that consists of plaster enveloping the entire upper body. Noncontact activities should be utilized, with particular emphasis on strengthening the upper body when the cast is removed.

Surgery is indicated in rapidly progressing curves of 40 degrees or more and may involve the implementation of a steel rod next to the spine. Additionally, a technique using electrical stimulation in curvatures of 40 degrees or less has also been utilized. Electrostimulation at the rib area near the spine is used to contract specific muscle groups, applying pressure from these muscles to straighten the curve over a gradual period. This procedure is generally implemented primarily at night, freeing students from cumbersome braces and cast and allowing them to participate in physical activity during the day.

Lordosis, or hollow back, is an increase in the lumbar curve that causes a forward tilt of the pelvic girdle. The primary causes of the forward tilt are muscle shortening of the lower back and hip flexors in conjunction with tight hamstrings and weak gluteal muscles that contribute to the forward movement of the pelvis. A common cause of lordosis is also weak abdominal muscles. Several exercises that may be utilized to correct lordosis include the following:

1. On hands and knees, alternate rounding and flattening the back while tightening the abdominals when exhaling air (cat back).

2. In a sitting position, reach slowly to the feet; hold and return.

3. Lying prone, contract the buttocks muscles; hold and release.

4. In a standing or lying position, contract the buttocks muscles; hold and release.

5. In a standing or lying position, contract the abdominal muscles, and push the back against the floor or wall.

6. Lying supine, bring one leg up slowly; hold and return. Repeat with the other leg.

7. Lying supine, bring both knees to the chest; hold and return.

8. In a standing position, spread the feet and bend forward to reach one foot while keeping a slight bend in the knees; hold and return. Repeat with other foot.

9. With bent knee, lying supine, place feet flat on the floor and fold arms across chest raising shoulders from the floor; hold and return (curl-ups).

A condition called *ptosis* is often associated with lordosis and is caused by a weakness, sagging, or total collapse of the abdominal muscles. Muscle groups in the abdominal region should be strengthened to counteract this condition and alleviate some aspects of lordosis, using the following exercises:

1. In a sitting position, with bent knees, fold hands across the chest and curl up toward knees; hold and return. If muscle groups are extremely weak, lift the head and shoulders, leaving the small of the back on the floor to prevent back strain.

2. In a hanging or sitting position, bring both knees up slowly as far as possible and return.

3. Lying supine, flutter-kick legs, or flutter-kick in an aquatic setting.

Hip Deviations

Hip deviations generally occur concurrently with back deformities. A downward tilt of the pelvis over 50 degrees will constitute an abnormality called *anterior pelvic tilt.* Shortening of lower back and hip flexor muscles, in conjunction with sagging abdominal and tight hamstring muscles, pushes the pelvis forward. A pelvic tilt may also occur from improper body mechanics and often accompanies ptosis, lumbar lordosis, and a protruding buttocks. In order to correct the pelvic tilting, exercises that stretch both muscle groups and strengthen weakened areas should be implemented. Several of these exercises follow.

1. Lying supine, bend the knees and place feet flat on the floor, contracting abdominal muscles and tightening buttocks region.

2. Lying supine, bend the knees and place feet flat on the floor, contracting abdominal muscles and raising the buttocks from the floor; hold and return (pelvic tilt).

3. In a standing or sitting position, contract the abdominal and buttock muscles; hold and relax.

Knee Postural Deviations

Knock-knees and bowlegs are two common orthopedic deviations of the lower extremities that may require exercises prescribed by physicians. Knock-knees occur when the knees overlap or touch medially and result from the stretching of the medial knee ligaments in combination with weak external rotators. This imbalance causes the knees to come in contact and should be corrected by assuming proper postures and developing a proper balance in the primary muscle groups of the thigh and knee. The outward rotators of the thigh can be strengthened in combination with stretching the muscles of the lateral side of the thigh by using the following exercises in a standing position or standing with the support of a chair or bar.

1. With the feet parallel, attempt to turn the knees out while simultaneously pulling calves inward.

2. Bend the knees slightly and turn in an outward motion.

3. With heels apart and toes together, rotate the knees outward.

4. With heels apart and toes together, rotate the knees forward.

Bowlegs occur when the feet are together and the knees do not touch. Bowlegs are attributed to injury, poor diet, disease, poor sleeping habits, or anything that places undue pressure on the inner parts of the legs. Some bowing is prevalent in young children but should disappear during maturation, when the peroneals counteract the pull of the tibia (Dunn, 1997). If the knees are 5 inches or more apart, medical attention is required, and exercise will not be effective. With slight bowing, gymnastic and swimming activities are strongly recommended to increase peroneal development, as well as the following exercises:

1. In a standing position, with the heels together, flex the knees slightly and rotate knees inward, attempting to touch the insides of the knee.

2. In a sitting position, with the legs extended while sitting on the floor against a wall, roll the legs inward and turn the feet outward.

3. Lying supine, place a pillow between the ankles, spread the straightened legs, and close on the pillow.

Ankle and Foot Deviations

Flat feet occur when the longitudinal arch is lower than normal, contributing to a poor functional posture development by changing the stability of the foot. Although flat feet are not necessarily weak feet and are a minor postural deviation that generally does not hamper physical development, proper stability is required to prevent injury to other portions of the foot. Because of this, corrective exercises such as the following (to be performed in a sitting position) are encouraged to strengthen the transverse arch of the foot and provide stability.

1. Pick up pencils with the toes and feet.

2. Roll a tennis ball back and forth under the arch of the foot.

3. Roll a towel with the toes and feet.

4. Flex and extend toes and feet.

5. With feet flat on floor, flex toes into the floor, and pull the heel in toward the toes in an inchworm-type fashion; then reverse the action.

Other common foot deviations that may affect body mechanics include toeing in and toeing out. Toeing in, or pigeon toes, results from an inward position of the feet, while toeing out involves the feet pointing out while standing or moving. Toeing out can also cause pronation, which can lead to more serious body mechanics problems. Specific activities, such a walking a balance beam, roller skating, and ice skating, will aid in strengthening weakened muscle groups and correction of foot problems. In addition, teachers may also use the following exercises, which are to be performed in a sitting position:

1. Rotate and extend the foot clockwise and counterclockwise.

2. In a chair, push the inside of the foot against a barrier (for toeing out), and press the outer side of the foot against the reserve (for toeing in).

3. Repeat exercise 2, kicking a ball with the outside and inside of the foot.

4. With the feet on the floor, 24 inches apart, move the feet inward and outward, fanlike, without moving the heels.

5. With one foot on a towel, cross the opposite foot over the foot on the towel and apply pressure to the ankle area.

6. Use the same position as in exercise 5, rotating the foot laterally to drag the towel back and forth.

7. Pick up objects, such as marbles or pencils, with the feet.

Orthopedic Disorders

Children with orthopedic disorders will manifest chronic conditions and make lifelong adjustments to their disability. These conditions generally indicate a lengthy process of the disease and/or treatment and are permanent, resulting in a loss of functioning. Approximately 2 million individuals under the age of 21 are orthopedically impaired in the United States and are included in IDEA under the categories of "orthopedically impaired" or "other health impaired." Most are integrated into the regular school setting. Children with more severe impairments are placed in special schools or hospitals.

Increasing the physical functioning and motor development of these children is the major concern for teachers. Children with orthopedic impairments will progress in a manner of development similar to that of their nondisabled peers. The disability should not be the focus of the educator's programming. Instead, a process of development and rehabilitation should be implemented to maximize the child's physical and functional skill development potential. When children are enrolled in regular physical education classes, teachers should strive to encourage peer acceptance through active integration into classes, as well as encourage additional opportunities for sport and recreation outside the school. Two types of orthopedic disorders that are commonly integrated into regular physical education classes with minor modifications or adaptions are spinal cord injuries and limb deficiencies.

Spinal Cord Injuries

The spinal cord is made up of nervous tissue extending from the brain to the lower back encased by the vertebrae. It is approximately 18 inches in length, cylindrical in shape with the same general circumference, except for an enlargement in the cervical and lumbar areas where the nerves innervating the upper and lower extremities exit. The spinal cord provides a pathway for neural impulses to and from the brain and the nerves and muscles of the trunk and extremities.

The spinal cord is protected by the vertebral column, which consists of 33 vertebrae (**Figure 14.2**). The

---

CASE STUDY

Ken had no disability before diving from a boat into the shallow area of a lake. The compression of his spinal cord in the cervical region (although not complete) resulted in a loss of functioning in his extremities. Because his lesion was incomplete, he remains able to walk and to, otherwise, function adequately. His main challenge is with his gait; as he is unable to use accurate sensory information from his legs while walking up and down stairs and on uneven surfaces. Although he must constantly visually monitor *his* legs he is unable accurately to detect their position, which makes him hesitant and awkward when performing what would otherwise be a routine function.

His physical education teachers have developed a fitness and gait program to restore his physical strength. They also have worked with Ken to relearn the position of his legs during ambulation. Initially, Ken had to visually monitor his legs to see their location before stepping. By relearning how to interpret sensory feedback, Ken is now able to walk without looking at his feet and to navigate stairs and uneven terrain. Ken's strength program also helped him regain his physical function and control activities essential for independent daily living.

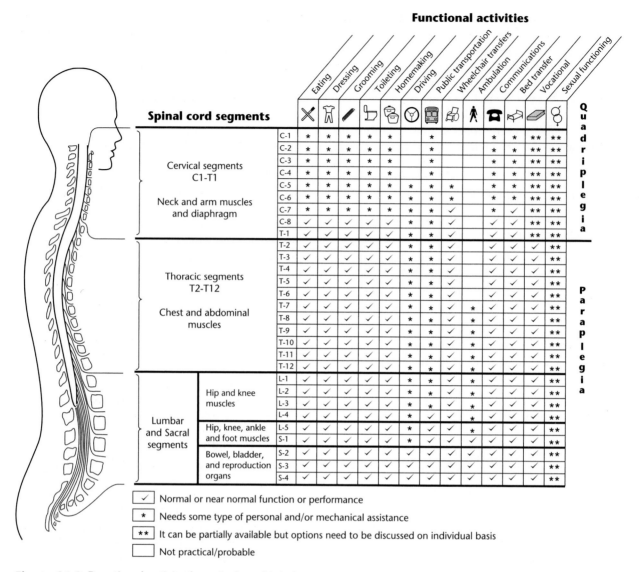

Figure 14.2 Functional activity for spinal cord injuries.
Source: Courtesy of the Health South Harmarville Rehabilitation Hospital.

7 cervical vertebrae are the bones that occupy the neck; the 12 thoracic vertebrae are located in the upper back behind the chest cavity; the 5 lumbar vertebrae comprise the lower back; and the 5 sacral and 4 coccygeal vertebrae comprise the tailbone.

Spinal nerves extend from the cord forming the peripheral nervous system and transmit messages from the brain and spinal cord to the working muscles. These spinal nerves include 8 cervical nerves (C_1–C_8), 12 thoracic nerves (T_1–T_{12}), 5 lumbar nerves (L_1–L_5), 5 sacral nerves (S_1–S_5), and one coccygeal nerve. The spinal cord itself is much shorter than the vertebral column and ends at the first or second lumbar vertebra. Spinal nerves of the lumbar and sacral regions comprise a group of long nerves referred to as the cauda equina.

Automobile, motorcycle, shooting, swimming, and diving accidents are responsible for a majority of spinal injuries, especially in the high school years. Approximately 55 percent of injuries occur within 16–30 years of age and most (80 percent) of those injured are male. When the spinal cord is injured, the transmission of impulses to the extremities will be disrupted. From a traumatic blow the vertebrae are fractured or dislocated causing damage from displaced bone fragments, discs, bruising, or tearing of the spinal cord (NIH, 2003; O'Sullivan & Schmitz, 2006). According to the NIH (2003), axons and neural cell membranes are damaged while bleeding may occur in the gray matter and spread to other areas of the spinal cord. Swelling, lack of oxygen, and lowering of blood pressure also occur, causing further damage to the neurons and axons (NIH, 2003). After the initial trauma, biochemical and cellular destruction that kills neurons strips axons of myelin and causes a response of the inflammatory immune system which causes additional damage and loss of functioning (NIH, 2003). In the preceding days/weeks secondary damage may occur that determines the extent of disability including:

- Changes in blood flow
- Excessive release of neurotransmitters which damage nerves
- Invasion of immune system cells causing inflammation
- Free radicals attack nerve cells and nerve cells self-destruct (NIH, 2003).

The remaining functioning ability will be determined by the extent and level of the spinal cord injury.

A complete spinal cord lesion (injury) results in absence of sensation and motor function below the level of that injury. An incomplete lesion, in which the cord is not completely transacted, results in varying amounts of sensation and motor functioning below the injury. Injuries may involve several levels, such as T_2–T_4 (interfering with functioning from the second thoracic to fourth thoracic vertebra). This type of injury will also be characterized by the availability of more functioning ability on one side of the body.

The higher the level of the spinal lesion, the more restricted the movement, because the spinal cord can no longer innervate the muscle below the site of the injury. An injury above the third cervical vertebra generally will result in death because the muscles of the diaphragm will be paralyzed, and life will not be maintained unless manual respiration is implemented. Furthermore, the site of the lesion will directly affect the remaining functional ability if lesions occur in the regions described in the following sections (NIH, 2003; Apple, 1996).

Fourth Cervical (C_4) Injuries at the fourth cervical vertebra generally will have control of the neck, including the sternocleidomastoid, trapezius, and upper paraspinal muscles and the diaphragm. The functioning of the upper limbs is impeded, and children have involvement of all four extremities, or quadriplegia. Assistance is required for transferring in and out of a wheelchair, and electrically powered assistive devices are used for upper limb functions.

Fifth Cervical (C_5) Injuries below the fifth cervical vertebra will allow functioning in the neck muscles, diaphragm, deltoid muscles of the shoulder, rhomboids, and biceps. Flexion of the elbow is possible as well as abduction of the shoulder, although shoulder extension relies on gravity to return to its original position. No functioning is available in the wrist and hand, necessitating manual supports on the wrist and arm as well as projections on the rims to maneuver a wheelchair.

Sixth Cervical (C_6) Injuries to children below the sixth cervical vertebra will allow the use of extensors of the wrist as well as more elbow flexion, shoulder flexion, and abduction. Children should be able to grasp lightweight and large objects, use an overhead bar for transfers, manipulate objects, and push a wheelchair.

Seventh Cervical (C_7) Injuries below the seventh cervical vertebra will allow functioning of the triceps, which permit extension of the elbow as well as flexion and extension of the fingers. Development of the triceps stabilizes the elbow and allows grasping and releasing activities. Children will be independent in maneuvering a wheelchair and transfers and can perform pull-ups, archery, and table-tennis–type activities.

Thoracic Level (T_1–T_5) Injuries to the first five thoracic vertebrae will allow movement in the upper extremities but not in the lower extremities (paraplegia). Children will be able to grasp and release and have total movement in the arms. Stability of the trunk will be lacking, necessitating a seat belt or brace for posture and body alignment. Transfers may be accomplished independently, and upper body strengthening and sport activities such as archery can be performed.

Thoracic Level (T_6–T_9) Injuries at the level below the sixth thoracic vertebra will allow more trunk stability because the muscles of the upper back, abdominal muscles, and muscles of the ribs are functioning. Upper extremity strength is much more apparent, providing opportunities for weight lifting and activities that require a strong grasping technique, such as bowling. Children should be able to completely control a wheelchair, eat and groom themselves independently, and stand with the aid of braces and forearm crutches.

Thoracic Level (T_{10}–T_{12}) Injuries at the level below the tenth thoracic vertebra will allow for complete abdominal control as well as use of the muscles of the upper back. Although the muscles of the lower back are weak, trunk control is available that allows participation in endurance activities such as swimming, propelling a wheelchair for moving, and weight training. Independent living can be achieved by children, and walking can be accomplished with the assistance of long leg braces.

Lumbar Levels (L_1–L_5) Injuries to the upper lumbar vertebrae (L_1–L_3) allow functioning in the muscles of the hip joint that flex the thigh; the fourth lumbar vertebra will allow flexion of the hip and, together with the fifth lumbar vertebra, controls movement in the lower leg and extension of the hip. Ambulation and independent living are possible, and children should be able to participate in most endurance wheelchair activities, such as track, basketball, and tennis.

Sacral Levels (S_1–S_5) Injuries in the sacral level will disrupt bladder and bowel control along with sexual functioning. The gastrocnemius and soleus muscles of the legs function if the injury occurs at S_2, whereas abduction and adduction of the lower leg is available if the injury occurs below sacral three (S_3). Maintenance of bladder and bowel control will involve a catheter until specific bowel and toilet training is implemented to regulate these functions. Sexual functioning will vary often, returning in lower spinal cord injuries after spinal shock is terminated. It is essential to remember that in a young individual with a spinal cord injury, sexual functioning may remain intact, with adequate potency and fertility available in both males and females. Children with sacral lesions have the highest level of motor functioning and can perform most endurance activities and sports that require intricate upper body movements.

LEARNING ACTIVITY

Research the anatomy and physiology of the spinal column and cord and determine what functions are controlled by nerves emanating at each level.

Planning the Physical Activity Program

The most obvious aspect of a spinal cord injury is the loss of movement and physical functioning in the extremities. In addition, there are other complications that affect the functional capacity of children and should be considered in developing an appropriate program. Some of the complications include the following:

1. *Contractures*, or a shortening of the muscles due to remaining in a stationary position or central nervous system involvement for an extended period of time. Active and passive stretching exercises as well as positioning techniques can be used to stretch shortened muscles.

2. *Spinal deformities*, including scoliosis and/or pelvic distortion, can occur from a lengthy confinement or poor posture in bed, standing, or in the wheelchair. Effective prevention must involve strengthening the weaker muscle groups, passive stretching of shortened muscles, posture training, weight training (progressive resistance exercises), and corrective sports, such as archery.

3. *Edema*, or a swelling in the feet, ankles, and lower legs, is due to poor vasomotor control and loss of muscle tone. To stimulate the vasomotor system, the legs are elevated or encased in elastic stockings. In the hands, elevation or passive movements of the joints are encouraged. In addition, upper-body exercise may have beneficial effects in promoting circulation and preventing blood from pooling in the lower extremities.

4. *Osteoporosis*, or problems associated with the absorption of minerals, leaves the bones below the lesion susceptible to fractures. General treatments are passive movements to stimulate circulation and a high-protein diet with vitamin D supplements.

5. *Pain* can be either consistent or periodic above or below the area of injury. Generally, mobilization, medication, and/or diversionary activities are utilized in the treatment of pain. For some individuals, arm exercise or overuse syndromes from using the arms to propel a wheelchair may aggravate shoulder pain (Figoni, 2009).

6. *Ossification* of bone in the connective tissue, usually in the hips, knees, and elbows, limits range of motion and subsequent movement. Surgery is usually the only alternative to removing the bone after the disease recedes.

7. *Spasms* occur when the spinal cord resumes some autonomous function below the injury, resulting in reflex muscle activity. Spasms may be mild or involve an intense response of the muscle, such as an alternating flexion and extension of the knee. Spasms greatly inhibit effective movement in limbs where partial control is available and should be treated with passive stretching, relaxation, cryotherapy, and medication.

8. *Decubitus ulcers* are pressure sores that occur from remaining in one position for extended periods of time. To treat pressure sores, pads and change of position can relieve pressure, while the pliability of the skin is maintained through massage and application of lanolin.

9. *Obesity and poor physical fitness* can be due to the lack of physical activity and inadequate caloric expenditure. Pulmonary deficiency may be diminished due to a lack of musculature in the abdominal region. Proper dietary habits and planned physical activity programs should be used to overcome the sedentary lifestyle often associated with physical disabilities.

10. *Temperature regulation* is difficult in higher level injuries as the thermoregulatory system is deficient. The ability to dissipate heat by perspiring in warm environments or to conserve heat by shivering is not as efficient because the counterregulatory effects of the sympathetic and parasympathetic nervous system are not present above T_6 injuries.

11. *Sensory information* is deficient regarding feel or position senses. Information going from the brain

to the spinal cord is affected, and the use of sensory and proprioception information from the limbs is deficient.

12. *Hypotension/hypertension* can affect resting blood pressure. Shifts in position from a supine to upright position may result in a decrease of blood pressure. Blood pooling in the viscera and lower extremities may necessitate wearing support stockings or postural supports. In contrast, hypertension or autonomic dysreflexia from vasconstriction of the visceral arteries may lead to an increase in blood pressure. Figoni (2009) stresses proper bowel and bladder management and discourages "boosting," or inducing autonomic dysreflexia, in an attempt to enhance performance.

13. Respiration is affected with injuries to the spinal cord at C_3, C_4, and C_5 or higher. These segments supply the phrenic nerves leading to the diaphragm and can cause breathing to cease without ventilator support (NIH, 2003). Injuries lower than C_5 will preserve breathing although it is shallow and pulmonary clearance will be affected.

14. Bowel and bladder problems are affected because the nerves that control these functions are near the termination of the cord. The use of intermittent catherization is used to aid in emptying the bladder while bowel movements are facilitated with a scheduled bowel emptying program (NIH, 2003).

As the child adapts to the stress of exercise and rehabilitation, the following complications may also become apparent (Rimmer, 1994):

1. *Spasticity.* To allow the muscles to work functionally and to alternately relax and contract, it is necessary to inhibit antagonist spasticity.

2. *Incomplete innervation.* In muscles that are partially paralyzed, weakness may occur from disuse atrophy and where muscle innervation is intact. Training can restore functioning to a point where it is approximately intact. In cases of partial muscle degeneration, training will restore functioning in only a portion of muscle.

3. *Muscle substitution.* In order to compensate for muscle weakness, muscle substitution or movements are implemented to complete a task. However, if muscle cannot be retrained or if adequate musculature is not available for muscle substitution, a brace may be used for support.

4. *Medication interactions.* Alcohol and steroids may cause muscle weakness and necrosis and affect the process that elicits muscle excitation. Generally, muscle recovery occurs from withdrawal from alcohol. However, some spasticity-inhibiting medications, such as dantrolene sodium, act directly on the muscle. Other medications, such as baclofen and diazepam, act directly on the cord.

5. *Muscle length changes.* Immobilization, muscle imbalance, and posture malalignment may result from spinal cord injury and elicit changes in muscle length. Active intervention, including stretching and strength training, is necessary to prevent length-associated changes.

Implementing the Physical Activity Program

A primary concern in selecting and implementing appropriate physical activities is the individual's functional ability. Because functional movement will depend on the level of the injury and the extent (incomplete or complete) of the injury, teachers should attempt to maximize the remaining movement potential. In most instances, physical activity programs will improve tolerance for activity and the daily demands of independent living. This is especially helpful after an injury, when it is essential to establish independent functioning as soon as possible.

The primary goal is to exercise all spared musculature activity using assisted free-active or resistance exercise. Upper-body exercises, including weights, pulleys, and surgical tubing, may increase range of motion and strength that is needed to develop and maintain positive and independent functioning (**Table 14.1**). The neuromuscular system should be developed and adapted to the stress of exercise by following the basic principles of strength and conditioning (Apple, 1996; Cambell, Vanderlinden, & Palisano, 2005):

1. *Overload.* The muscle should adapt to stress with resistance exercise designed to facilitate the frequency of muscle contraction.

2. *Progression.* For gains to occur, the muscle should be continually stressed by increasing the amount of weight, number of repetitions, or sets of exercises the individual accomplishes.

3. *Specificity.* Exercises should be selected according to the functional task. The exercise should duplicate the task to be performed by the muscle, including the movement pattern, range of the movement, and type or speed of contraction required. The exercise movement and strengthening activity should generalize to a specific movement or functional skill.

4. *Purpose.* The exercise should also be specific to the purpose of the movement. Exercises may be designed to promote endurance, increase resistance to fatigue, and increase oxidative capacity of the muscle fibers.

Table 14.1 Physical Activity Suggestions for Orthopedic Impairments

Complications	Physical Activity
Contractures	Active and passive stretching; surgical tubing and isometric or active resistance; water exercise and relaxation activities.
Sensory information	Body awareness and gait training. Emphasize postural stability and propriceptive and visual information to compensate for injury. Utilize body awareness and relaxation activities.
Spinal deformities	Upper-body strengthening with resistance exercises; water exercise, rowing, arm cycle, or archery. Strengthen weak muscles and emphasize postural training and breathing exercises.
Temperature regulation	Caution in hot and humid environments; ensure child is hydrated, and closely monitor spinal injuries T_6 and above.
Fitness	Encourage active participation to restore function and involvement. Utilize sports and recreational activities to promote lifestyle changes.
Psychological functioning	Emphasize independent functioning and training interventions to promote fitness, sports participation, activities of daily living (ADLs), and social interactions.
Locomotion	Lower body strengthening exercises; range of motion; locomotor training.

Many corrective activities, such as archery, can be used to develop the upper body as well as provide opportunities to actively participate. Fundamental skills such as running (rolling), throwing, catching, striking, and agility should be developed to ensure participation in team games and sports as well as outside-the-school competition. Parachute activities are also ideal to integrate young children with able-bodied peers as well as to develop upper-body functioning and posture and motor skill development (French & Horvat, 1983).

Lead-up games using targets, suspended balls, or rebound throwing may also aid in the development of fundamental skills for younger children and serve as the basis for more intricate sports and games, such as tennis, racquetball, basketball, and table tennis (Cratty, 1969).

Aquatic exercises and swimming are easily adaptable for individuals with spinal cord injuries. Because of buoyancy, children enjoy more freedom in the aquatic environment. Children should be able to assume a horizontal position and utilize swimming strokes with minor modifications, depending on the remaining muscle functioning. In this manner children can develop overall fitness, movement, and body awareness while being independent of their wheelchairs.

Dance is another activity that requires minor variations, such as expanding the formation to allow more room for movement. Movement sequence and tempos can be learned from performing dance activities, and skills and conditioning can be developed that may be useful in game, sports, and recreational activities.

Very little, if any, modification is needed for sports and games. At times the goal or standard may be lowered, if necessary, in volleyball or basketball. Court games may require allowing the ball to bounce more than once or picking up the dribble in basketball, while the large space required to play some games may be reduced to accommodate students with limited mobility. However, teachers should not disrupt a game to accommodate children in wheelchairs. Most individuals will desire to participate in a nonmodified atmosphere. For example, a child in a wheelchair may participate with his or her able-bodied classmates in basketball by following simple modifications:

1. Defender needs to guard child $1^1/_2$ steps away to allow the opportunity to shoot and pass.

2. Children with disabilities are allowed to pick up the dribble and push the wheelchair, but only twice, before passing or shooting.

3. Children in a wheelchair are not allowed to rebound inside the lane lines; this allows able-bodied individuals to jump without fear of landing on the wheelchair.

Modifications should be used only when necessary for the benefit of all individuals in the class, and the safety of all children should be emphasized. Some activities that were once not available for children with spinal cord injuries may now be made possible through the use of more extensive equipment and/or technique modifications. Activities such as white-water kayaking, skiing, and mountaineering have been made possible through the use of special equipment designed to alleviate the disability. A kayak may be modified to allow positioning and stability by removing the hard cockpit and building a form insert and room for the individual's legs. The paddling technique may be altered by changing the paddle, stroke, or release mechanism, depending on the functional ability of the child. For some children and school districts, the American Association of Adapted Sports Programs (AAASP) provide programs in handball, basketball, football, power soccer, power hockey, beep baseball, and track and field. For children who want to participate, this is a viable outlet. For other children, maintaining fitness and overall functioning may be the goal after injury. Each has its benefits and should be available for all participants.

Functional Skill Development

A primary factor in developing functional activities of daily living are gross motor skills, transfer skills, and muscle strengthening for ambulation or gait training. Many of these skills should be initiated in the clinical and rehabilitation setting. The educator should build upon and expand these skills in order for the child to continue to develop and enhance these skills. Ultimately many of these skills will generalize to play and sport and recreational skills that can be incorporated in the individual's lifestyle. In this context, the teacher can view these activities as developmental and essential to independent functioning.

Gross motor skills should concentrate on the lying and seated positions. For example, rolling will require the child to use the arms, head, neck, and upper torso to initiate movement to front, back, or side-lying positions. Depending on the remaining muscle function available, strengthening should occur to facilitate the movement. The task may be accomplished in segments (i.e., side-lying movements initially) or in unison if sufficient strength is maintained.

Muscle strength and endurance exercises can be passive or active or used in conjunction with the medium of the water. Once the prone lying position is established, the child can do push-ups, upper and lower back extensions and scapular retraction, incorporating prone on elbows or prone lying as a starting position and gradually using the standard pushup position (Kisner & Colby, 2007). Obviously, the lying positions should translate to a sitting position and necessitate establishing a level of balance using the upper torso to compensate for lack of lower extremity function. Exercises that use the upper body, such as stationary ergonmetry, activities using surgical tubing, or parachute activities, will assist in developing muscle function to maintain posture and can be supplemented with medicine ball activities, therabands, weighted ball throwing, weight shifting, and push-up activities as well as single or bilateral arm movements. Flexibility and range-of-motion exercises should be implemented on a daily basis to prevent contractures and facilitate functional movement (Lasko & Knopf, 1992; Hall & Brody, 2004; Figoni, 2009). In order to sit, the child will also need to develop strength and stability to move the legs. This may necessitate developing upper-body strength to be used in conjunction with balance movements. For example, the child may balance on one arm supporting the weight while using the other arm to move the legs to a particular position. Strength and balance are required and essential for continued development and self-sufficiency.

Limb Deficiency

The absence of a limb may be either congenital or acquired. In congenital amputations, a limb or a portion of a limb is not present at birth or is malformed. Congenital amputations may include absence of an entire limb; absence of all or a portion of the distal half of a limb; absence of the proximal portion of a limb, with hands or feet remaining attached by that portion of the bone.

Acquired amputations refer to the loss of a limb resulting from trauma, injury, disease, or surgery, which is generally linked with a malignant condition such as diabetes, circulatory problems, or cancer. The majority of amputations (27 percent) occur in people aged 61–70 and as a result of disease (**Figures 14.3** and **14.4**).

CASE STUDY

Martha has bi-lateral below the knee (BK) amputations. She has progressed to the level where she aspires to compete in a triathlon. Her teachers are working with her fitness levels to maximize her strength, flexibility, and aerobic conditioning such that she can perform aerobically for extended periods of time; while at the same time effectively managing her prostheses. Because her amputations are below the knee, her quadriceps, gluteus, and hamstring muscles need to be developed to manage the stress of both running and cycling. She is also going to the local YMCA to improve her swimming stroke and endurance and, to learn to ride a bicycle with adaptations and/or use her prostheses to facilitate movements required during cycling. Strength, flexibility, and technique for running, biking, and swimming are being matched to her needs for efficient use of her prostheses during the swim, bike, and run.

In school, her teachers are working to restore as much functional ability as possible in the affected limbs. Additionally, they are helping her with the training program that she uses outside the school setting. With the help of teachers and supportive adults and peers she is working very hard to accomplish her goal. She hopes to demonstrate to herself, peers, and adults that having an amputation, by itself, need not preclude enjoyment of active lifestyles; including participation in physical education and competitive sport.

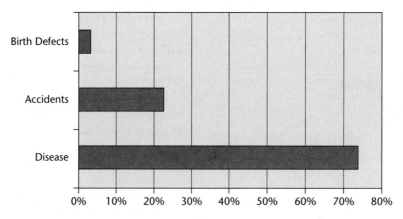

Figure 14.3 Distribution of congenital and acquired amputation cases.

The point of the amputation and portion of the limb remaining (**Figure 14.5**) will determine the child's functioning level. For example, a below-the-knee amputation will require a leg prosthesis for ambulation. However, because the knee is intact, flexion and extension are still possible. Children will possess developed quadriceps and some control of their lower extremities and the prosthetic device. Furthermore, the longer the stump, the easier it will be to fit a prosthesis while retaining as much original movement and strength in the extremity. When the amputation involves both legs, ambulation and functioning is significantly reduced; however, children should be able to manage a prosthetic device or use a wheelchair for movement. Comparisons of strength and flexibility of muscle and joints on both sides may reveal deficits in strength of as much as 50% on the affected side (Pitelti & Pedrolty, 2009). Flexibility is not as deficient but is typically lower in the affected side. These differences are more apparent in children than adults, making it more difficult to achieve muscle symmetry in muscle groups that move the prosthesis.

Upper-limb functioning is also affected by the site of the amputation. An above-the-elbow amputation will affect the movement of the arm because of lack of flexion and extension at the elbow. Attaching the prosthesis will also present a problem if a small portion of the limb is remaining. It is difficult to develop a prosthesis to simulate the numerous small muscles in the hand, and these devices are not as beneficial as those used with the lower limbs. Most upper-arm prostheses can be modified to manipulate rackets or other physical education equipment. More recent devices more closely approximate the human hand and may be effective in eliminating the need for extensive equipment modifications. However, it should be noted that the hand will not only perform grasp-and-release functions but also provides sensory information that cannot be duplicated by a prosthetic device. In most cases, the physician will preserve as much of the hand and wrist as possible to maintain functional capabilities. For example, the loss of each digit of the hand is based on an assigned value in relation to impairment of the hand: thumb (40%), second digit (20%), third digit (20%), fourth digit (10%), and fifth digit (10%). Likewise, amputations through the forearm not only affect hand function but also rotation of the arm depending on the length of the stump (**Figure 14.6**).

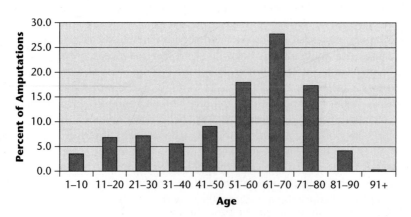

Figure 14.4 Amputation cases distributed by age.

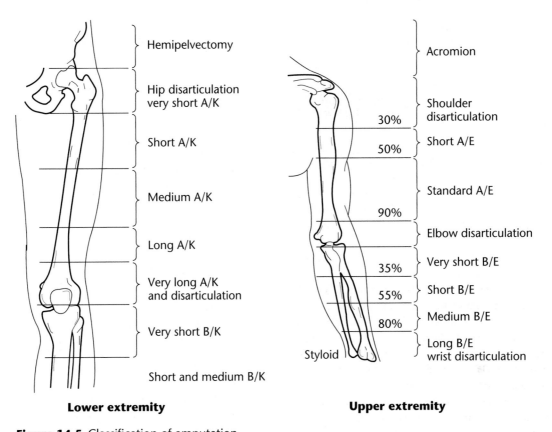

Lower extremity **Upper extremity**

Figure 14.5 Classification of amputation.

Source: National Academy of Sciences, National Research Council, *Artificial Limbs*, 1963.

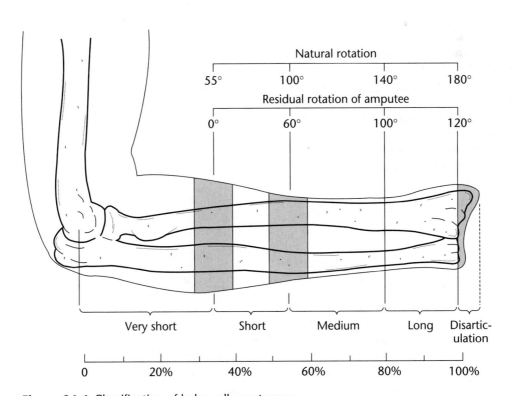

Figure 14.6 Classification of below-elbow stumps.

Source: National Academy of Sciences, National Research Council, *Artificial Limbs*, 1963.

Physical Limitations and Concerns

The loss of a limb is fairly obvious, but there are other limitations imposed by the amputation that may not be as obvious. First, standing and locomotion are affected. A lower leg amputation affects standing and locomotion without the assistance of an artificial limb or ambulatory device. Second, when an artificial limb is used, sensory information from the joints, proprioceptors, or muscle is absent. This lack affects the ability to sense position or feel the movement or force generated. For example, a child in a physical conditioning class relied on his prosthesis with hooks. When asked why he didn't select a newer, lighter prosthesis that was cosmetically more pleasing, he answered that it could not provide any sensory feedback and that because he had worn his device for some years he felt comfortable with it. Obviously the loss of touch is important, especially in a child with an upper limb amputation.

Third, support of the body is also affected in addition to postural and locomotor movements. The muscles that are attached to bones contract with a neural impulse and produce force that move the bone about a joint. Because muscles produce tension and allow a contraction, an opposing muscle group is required to allow relaxation of the muscle and movement in the opposite direction and to provide stability for the joint. The force generated by the muscle depends on its length and cross-sectional area. A full range of motion is needed to manage the prosthetic device and avoid contractures.

In addition, the loss of a limb will affect the center of gravity and balance until children compensate or adjust to a prosthetic device. An above-the-joint amputation, especially in the lower extremities, will generally restrict movement and development of motor skills more severely because of the lack of stability provided by a knee and/or elbow. Because muscles may pass over a joint, their ability to transmit force to the bone may be effected.

A fourth concern for children is temperature regulation. With the amount of cooling surface on the body reduced by the missing limb, the amputee will encounter difficulty with thermoregulation. Because the body has less surface area to perspire, warm and/or humid days can cause overheating problems, thereby creating a need for monitoring to ensure safe participation.

A fifth concern is skin care, especially of the stump area, to eliminate irritation. The stump requires periodic ventilation to remove perspiration and body secretions, which may cause irritation or infections. A major concern for the surgeon is to avoid scar tissue and crevices that may preclude keeping the stump clean.

Another concern is that children may not acquire age-appropriate motor skills because of their amputation and/or attitude toward participation, or because of overprotection by parents and educators. Likewise, children may demonstrate a low degree of fitness and obesity because of their sedentary activity patterns.

Although the loss of a limb may require compensation to learn a motor skill, teachers should encourage participation as well as alternative ways to move in the environment. Electrostimulation and exercise may also be used to strengthen the stump and corresponding muscles, to mobilize the joints, and to manage the prosthetic device properly.

Finally, children may possess a negative self-concept related to feelings of being different or inadequate. Many times children will avoid situations in which their condition is noticeable, such as the swimming pool. It is essential to educate other teachers and children about an amputee's condition and functioning of the prosthetic device to avoid any misconceptions about his or her condition and to facilitate as much active participation as possible.

LEARNING ACTIVITY

Discuss how an amputation above/below the joint (above/below the knee or elbow) can, but need not necessarily, affect potential to participate in and enjoy physical education, lifetime activity, and sport.

Physical Activities

The most important concept in the physical activity program is the development of confidence for the child with an amputation. Many times the limb deficiency causes a distortion of the child's body image. By selecting goals that are easily attainable, the child can achieve a measure of success designed to encourage participation and increase self-confidence. Increasing the amount of skill required and participation time can aid in building confidence levels and acceptance by other classmates. The Amputee Coalition of America (2002) has developed LLEAP (Limb Loss Education and Awareness Program) to help facilitate an understanding of losing a limb and ways to orient children back into the school environment. They have also developed the Youth Amputee ezine, a youth activities program (YAP) that allows children a chance to learn, read, and interact with other children with amputations. The YAP also sponsors a youth camp for children ages 10 to 16 from various parts of the country (Amputee Coalition of America, 2009).

In addition, young children will be periodically experiencing spurts in growth that necessitate refitting of the prosthesis and adjusting to the new demands of the device, such as accommodating balance and changing gaits. More important, it is necessary to allow children to make their own adjustments in an activity. For example, activities that require throwing may be mastered by catching and then throwing with the same arm.

Former major league pitcher Jim Abbott compensated for his loss of a right hand in this manner. Likewise, a lower-limb amputee may occupy a position in softball that does not require an excessive amount of running.

Many times teachers will overadapt or modify an activity solely on the basis of a disability. A common-sense approach for including upper- and lower-limb amputees in physical education is to assess the functional capabilities remaining before making any modification or adaptation. Pitetti and colleagues (2004, 2009) recommend the FITT&P principles of exercise:

F: Frequency or number of days per week.

I: Intensity or level of work.

T: Time in minutes or duration of the exercise program.

T: Type of exercise (swimming, weights, etc.).

P: Progression, frequency, or duration over a period of time.

Dr. Pitteti who has an amputation, believes that training can start at a minimal level and progress to 3–5 days a week at moderate to high intensity for 30–60 minutes. By reaching a desired level of fitness, the individual can be more functional, maintain weight control or participate in competitive sports (Pitetti & Manske, 2009; Pitetti & Manske, 2004). **Table 14.2** provides several strengthening exercises that can be implemented in class.

Children with an amputation can be successful in sports or recreational activities and can develop at a level similar to that of their able-bodied peers. Opportunities to participate in sporting events and to compete with able-bodied athletes may greatly enhance the psychological adjustment to disability (Horvat, French, & Henschen, 1986). Our case study of Martha demonstrates that individuals can participate in highly competitive events and achieve success. This may be apparent in local sporting events or the Ironman Triathlon. In addition, swimming activities are especially beneficial because of the lack of modifications and the overall benefits derived from the aquatic program. A recent publication emphasizes that aquatic therapy can alleviate pain while aiding movement without the prosthesis (Young, 2008). Other benefits such as improved circulation, respiratory function, range of motion, and motor control all may be evident in an environment that is enjoyable (Young, 2008).

Sports and recreational activities may also be valuable for the physical development of the child with an amputation. Kayaking or canoeing requires minor equipment or technique modifications to include all children, such as substituting a prosthetic device to balance the nose weight in a kayak. Most sports and games should be actively encouraged and are not outside the capabilities of the child with an amputation. Jogging, dance, golf, tennis, and weight training are examples of suitable activities for school-aged children with amputations that should be implemented to foster participation and functioning in an integrated environment.

Table 14.2 Sample Strength Training Exercises

Muscle Groups	Exercise	Equipment
General Core/Balance Performance	Knee Lift/Knee Extensions—sitting on ball and arms across chest or shift from one leg to another	Physioball
General Core/Balance	Roll-out on ball from sitting upright to walking out to 90 degree position.	Physioball
General Core/Balance	Back roll from sitting position to straightening arms and legs with back on the ball.	Physioball
Shoulders	Lie facedown with stomach on the ball; move arms and shoulders to 90 degrees.	Physioball
Shoulders/Chest	Sitting or standing, hug ball in arms with head up and release.	Physioball
Erector Spinal	Kneel in front of ball with stomach, hands and chest on the ball. Straighten legs and lift chest from the ball.	Physioball
Quads/Gluts	Place ball between the wall and participants back. Keep arms across the chest and slowly lower the body.	Physioball
Lower Back and Abdominals	Sit upright on ball with arms across the chest and move hips forward and back.	Physioball
Pelvic Muscles and Abdominals	Lie on your back with the legs bent. Tilt the pelvis; flatten your back and return.	On floor
Pelvic and Abdominal Muscles	Lie on your back, with arms at the side, tighten the stomach and push back against the floor.	On floor
Lumbar Spine/Pelvis	Lie on the stomach, hold weighted ball in front of the body. Lift the ball and chest.	Medicine Ball/Floor
Lumbar Spine	Kneel with upper body over the physioball and hand behind the head and perform back extension.	Physioball
Abdominals	Rest lower back on ball with head stable. Hold position on ball and vary by curling trunk forward with arms across the chest in crunch position.	Physioball

CHAPTER SUMMARY

1. Children with disabilities may be prone to a greater incidence of postural defects than the general school-aged population. Children with sensory impairments may exhibit poor postures and head tilts from lack of feedback; children who are nonambulatory may place undue pressure on their postural structure and must reassert their center of balance, which was affected by injury.

2. Posture is defined as the manner in which body alignment is maintained against gravity. Correct posture is achieved when all body segments are properly aligned over the base of support.

3. Specific body types are more apt to assume a particular posture because of their build. In analyzing proper posture, teachers must be aware of individual differences that are associated with age, body type, and exceptionality.

4. Posture deficiencies may occur in a variety of positions and affect different areas of the body structure. In order to effectively correct posture problems, the teacher should utilize appropriate exercises for various parts of the body.

5. Children with orthopedic disorders will manifest a chronic condition and lifelong adjustment process to their disability. These conditions generally indicate a lengthy process of the disease and/or treatment and are permanent, resulting in a loss of functioning.

6. The major concerns for teachers of children with orthopedic impairments are physical functioning and motor development.

7. When children are mainstreamed into regular physical education, teachers should strive to encourage peer understanding and acceptance through integration and should provide additional outside opportunities for sport and recreation.

8. The most obvious aspect of a spinal cord injury is the loss of movement and physical functioning in the extremities. Other complications, such as spasms, contractures, decubitus ulcers, ossification, pain, edema, and temperature regulation also can affect functional ability. A primary concern in selecting and implementing appropriate physical activities is the functional ability of the individual.

9. Appropriate physical activity programs can aid in the improvement of day-to-day functioning and tolerance for activity.

10. Amputations will restrict the mobility and physical functioning of children. Some concerns include temperature regulation, center of gravity and balance, overprotection by parents, motor skill deficiencies, and a negative self-concept.

11. Goals should be selected that are based on improving functional ability and ensuring success as well as increasing the child's level of self-confidence.

12. A commonsense approach for including children with upper- and lower-limb amputations in physical education is to assess the functional capabilities remaining before making any modification or adaptation.

REFERENCES

Amputee Coalition of America. (2009). Youth Amputee eZine. Knoxville, TN: Author.

Amputee Coalition of America. (2009). Youth Camp. Knoxville, TN: Author.

Amputee Coalition of America. (2002). Limb loss and awareness program LLEAD. Knoxville, TN: Author.

Apple, D. F. (1996). *Physical Fitness: A guide for individuals with SCI*. Washington, DC: Veterans Health Administration Research and Development.

Cambell, S. K., Vanderlinden, D. W., & Palisano, R. J. (2005). *Physical Therapy for Children* (3rd ed.). Elsevier Sciences.

Crafty, B. (1969). *Developmental games for physically handicapped children*. Palo Alto, CA: Peek Publications.

Dunn, J. (1997). *Special physical education* (7th ed.). Dubuque, IA: Wm. C. Brown.

Engstrom, B., & Van de Ven, C. (1993). *Physiotherapy for amputees* (2nd ed.). New York: Churchill Livingstone.

Figoni, S. (2009). Spinal cord disabilities: paraplegia and tetraplegia. In American College of Sports Medicine, *Exercise management for persons with chronic diseases and disabilities* (3rd ed.) Champaign, IL: Human Kinetics.

French, R., & Horvat, M. (1983). *Parachute movement activities*. Bryon, CA: Front Row Experience.

Hall, C. M., & Brody, L. T. (2004). *Therapeutic Exercise: Moving Toward Function*. Baltimore, MD: Lippincott, Williams, & Wilkins.

Haslop, H., & Montgomery, J. (2007). *Daniels and Worthingham's muscle testing and techniques of manual examination*. (8th ed.). New York: NY.

Horvat, M., French, R., & Henschen, K. (1986). A comparison of the psychological characteristics of male and female able-bodied and wheelchair athletes. *Paraplegia, 24,* 115–22.

Kisner, C., & Colby, L. A. (2007). *Therapeutic exercise: Foundations and techniques* (2nd ed.). Philadelphia: F. A. Davis.

Lasko, P., & Knopf, K. (1992). *Adapted and corrective exercise for the disabled adult* (5th ed.). Dubuque, IA: Eddie Bowers.

Lockette, K. F., & Keyes A. M. (1994). *Conditioning with physical disabilities.* Champaign, IL: Human Kinetics.

National Institute of Neurological disorders and Stroke. (2003). Spinal Cord Injury. Bethesda, MD: NIH.

O'Sullivan, S., & Schmitz, T. J. (2006). *Physical Rehabilitation* (5th ed.). Philadelphia, PA: F.A. Davis Co.

Pitetti, K. H., & Manske, R. C. (2004). Lower limb amputation In *LeMura & von Duvillard S. P. Clinical Exercise Physiology.* Baltimore, MD: Lippincott, Williams, & Wilkins.

Pitetti, K. H., & Pedrotty, M. H. (2009) Lower limb amputation In *American college of sport medicine: Exercise management for persons with chronic diseases and disabilities* (3rd ed.). Champaign, IL: Human Kinetics.

Rimmer, J. H. (1994). *Fitness and rehabilitation programs for special population.* Dubuque, IA: Brown and Benchmark.

Smail, K., & Horvat, M. (2009). Resistance Training For Individuals with Intellectual Disabilities. *Clinical Kinesiology.*

Visual Health Information. (2005a). Exercise Ideas for Conditioning on the Ball. Tacoma, WA: VHI.

Visual Health Information. (2005b). Exercise Ideas for Core Strengthening. Tacoma, WA: VHI.

Visual Health Information. (2005c). Exercise Ideas for Lower Body Strengthening. Tacoma, WA: VHI.

Visual Health Information. (2005d). Exercise Ideas for Upper Body Strengthening. Tacoma, WA: VHI.

Wessel, J. (1976). I Can: Posture. Northbrook, IL: Hubbard.

Williams, M., & Worthington, C. (1961). *Therapeutic exercise for body alignment and function.* Philadelphia: Saunders.

Young, E. (2008). Aquatic therapy is serious fun. *In Motion.* Vol. 18(6), 44–45.

Neurological Disorders

Mr. Peters has several children with cerebral palsy in his physical education classes. Two children seem to be affected with minimal involvement on one side of the body. Another child is more severely affected with involvement in the arms and legs and uses a wheelchair. Although there are some differences in functioning among his students, Mr. Peters has had success with resistance exercises to develop muscle strength and promoting range of motion. He has also worked with the district physical therapist to suppress reflexes and focus on exercises to help with ambulation, especially those that facilitate going up and down stairs and transferring.

Mr. Peters has also incorporated passive resistance activities to facilitate muscle function and mobility and is encouraged that his child with the most severe involvement can control her head, neck, and posture such that she effectively accesses a computer to complete her academic work. He has worked with the girl's father on a home intervention of aquatic activities and has noticed that some function in her arms and shoulders is becoming available. Mr. Peters is pleased with his students' progress and encourages them to participate in recreational and sports-related activities to maintain and enhance their motor functioning.

Children with neurological disorders have their own unique characteristics that may complicate developing physical fitness and motor skills. These children are often prohibited from physical activity because of their disorder. Many teachers and administrators maintain inappropriate attitudes and misconceptions about neurological disorders as well as about the child's ability to achieve age-appropriate physical and motor skills. This chapter stresses the importance of physical functioning as it relates to children with disorders of the nervous systems.

The nervous system consists of the brain, spinal cord, ganglia, and nerves that transmit and receive information from the working muscles. If this system is disrupted or injured, the movement process will be affected. Because the degree of remaining function varies greatly depending on the site and extent of the injury to the nervous system, children should be treated individually and actively encouraged to participate in regular physical activity classes.

Cerebral Palsy

Cerebral palsy is a motor impairment that results from a lesion in or trauma to the developing brain that affects the brain's ability to control movement and posture (National Institute of Neurological Disorders and Stroke (NINDS), 2006). This impairment is not contagious, fatal, inherited, or a disease; rather it is a term that describes manifestations of observed motor characteristics and movement control problems.

Approximately 800,000 individuals in the United States have cerebral palsy and 10,000 infants develop cerebral palsy each year. Of these, one-third are under 21 years of age, while 1,000 newborns and another 2,000 infants in their first year manifest cerebral palsy due to head injuries.

Cerebral palsy can be described as a group of conditions that originate in infancy and are characterized by weakness, paralysis, lack of coordination and motor functioning, and very poor muscle tone directly related to pathology of the motor control center of the brain. These conditions may also occur in different degrees of severity and extent of limb involvement (NINDS, 2006). Cerebral palsy is a nonprogressive disorder of the immature or developing brain. Although the disorder is nonprogressive, the neurological system typically develops so quickly that expectations are not consistent with typical development.

Abnormalities of motor tone or movement in the first several weeks or months after birth may gradually improve during the first year and eventually be "outgrown" as the child continues to develop. Conversely, children who possess relatively nonspecific motor signs during the first weeks or months of life may develop severe cases of cerebral palsy. Therefore, the diagnosis of cerebral palsy should be very tentative; a definitive diagnosis should be made only after the child's second birthday. Although a definitive diagnosis is not recommended until after the second year, early intervention in the child with cerebral palsy can reduce the effects of the disability. With this in mind, all parents should be aware of important growth and development landmarks in the lives of their children. Some conditions that may indicate the presence of cerebral palsy are as follows (Center for Disease Control (CDC), 2009).

After two months:

- Poor head control
- Stiffness in the legs, or legs that cross or scissors when picked-up
- Pushing away, arching back
- Failure to smile by 3 months

After 6 months:

- Continued difficulty controlling head when picked up
- Reach with one hand while the other hand is kept in a fist
- Floppy or limp posture
- Feeding difficulties—persistent gagging or choking when fed, tongue pushes soft food out of the mouth

After 10 months:

- Crawl by pushing off with one hand and leg while dragging opposite hand and leg
- Inability to sit unsupported

After 12 months:

- Inability to crawl
- Inability to stand without support

After 24 months:

- Inability to walk
- Inability to push toys with wheels

Children with cerebral palsy will encounter a lack of understanding related to their condition. Partial paralysis and facial or speech distortions may contribute to misconceptions that lead to social isolation. Although movement may be restricted in cerebral palsy, many children can function at levels that will meet the program goals of regular physical activity classes. It is the responsibility of teachers to adequately assess movement potential and provide movement experiences to promote independent functioning for children with cerebral palsy in a positive social environment. Children may also have other developmental problems, such as cognitive delays and perceptual difficulties, that will also limit skill development.

Etiology of Cerebral Palsy

Cerebral palsy results from a lesion in the brain that interferes with the development of the central nervous system. Although there are many possible causes, some of which cannot be traced, the major suggested cause during the prenatal period is anoxia in the fetus. Other suggested prenatal causes of cerebral palsy include maternal infection or disease, such as rubella; metabolic malfunctions; toxemia; and poor maternal care. Natal causes include premature birth, anoxia, trauma, breech birth, and prolonged labor. Postnatal complications include head injury or trauma, infections such as encephalitis (inflammation of the brain) or meningitis (inflammation of the brain and spinal cord), tumors, and toxic substances such as lead and arsenic.

Classifications and Types of Cerebral Palsy

It is sometimes difficult to determine the regions of the brain that are involved in cerebral palsy. The major areas of the brain that are affected are the cortex (pyramidal tracts), basal ganglia (extrapyramidal region), and the cerebellum (**Figure 15.1**).

The pyramidal tracts originate in the cerebral cortex and are responsible for voluntary control of the face, trunk, and limbs. Fibers from nerve cells that originate in the cerebral cortex descend to the spinal cord through the basal ganglia, enter the midbrain and hindbrain, and cross in these areas through the corticospinal tract. Fibers from the nerve cells of the right side of the cerebral cortex innervate the left side of the body, whereas fibers from the left side of the cortex innervate the right side of the body. Typically, the neurons of the cortex via the pyramidal tract provide a desired channel from the brain to the spinal neurons that transmit impulses that cause the muscle

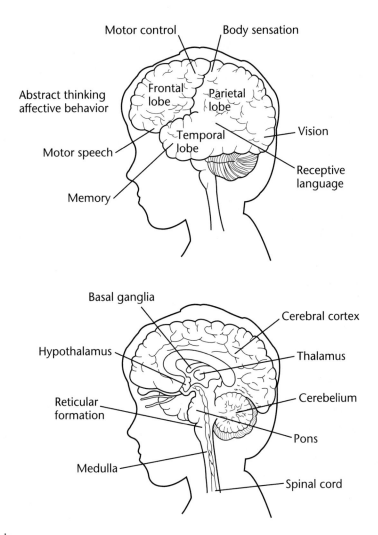

Figure 15.1 The brain.

to contract, relax, or initiate a movement. In addition, the corticospinal neurons also receive sensory information from the muscle that is essential for motor memory and control of movement. The cerebellum receives input from the motor areas of the cortex, brain stem, and sensory system, including the proprioceptor's; and consistently upgrades and monitors movement and feedback necessary for movement control. An injury to these nerve cells or fibers causes spasticity in the muscles innervated by these fibers in the right or left side of the body, depending on the location of the brain damage. In contrast, injuries in the basal ganglia or extrapyramidal system result in dyskinesia (uncoordinated or uncontrolled movement), as manifested by children with athetosis. This second motor pathway includes all motor axons not on the pyramidal systems. However these axons do not pass through the medullary pyramids and synapses in the basal ganglia, pons, medulla, and reticular formation. Rather, these axons descend through the internal capsule and laminate in subcortical structures to form a feedback loop. The function of the loop is to modify and adjust movements for postural and reflexive movements. Damage to the cerebellum area involves problems with coordination and balance generally seen in children with ataxia.

The complex pattern of these nerves and fibers makes it difficult to determine an exact classification of cerebral palsy. In fact, the traditional and prevalent classification is mixed cerebral palsy and reflects a combination of symptoms. The primary classifications of cerebral palsy are based on severity and movement characteristics. A more recent classification system developed by Palisano and colleagues (1997) has attempted to standardize gross motor function by levels of severity and age (Gross motor function classification system for cerebral palsy- GMFCS). For example, levels I and II are mild involvement, level III is moderate, and level IV and V are generally considered to be severe. These classifications are also divided into age groups before 2 years, second and fourth year, fourth year and sixth year, and sixth and twelfth year, to evaluate function through the developmental years.

The GMFCS has proved to be helpful in distinguishing motor functioning and present level of development. The descriptions are somewhat broad, but can be functionally based on the degree of motor involvement needed to develop a program plan including the following:

Mild Involvement

1. Movement potential for self-help, physical fitness, and motor skills

2. Response to training and intervention

3. Loss of functional capabilities without intervention

4. Little or no activity limitations

5. Control of head and movement functions, ambulation

Moderate Involvement

1. Variations of independent functioning in self-help and functional skills

2. Functional head control

3. Perceptual and sensory deficits that affect learning and motor skills, regardless of the type and severity of cerebral palsy present; delayed skill acquisition

4. Loss of motor function that affects speech and motor control

5. Utilization of assistive devices for ambulation

Severe Involvement

1. Poor head and movement control

2. Dependence in self-help skills and functional capabilities; reliance on assistive devices

3. Skeletal and postural deformities; muscle imbalance and tightness

4. Perceptual and sensory deficits that affect motor skill acquisition and learning

Another classification is based on the type of motor disability that is prevalent. These include spasticity, athetosis, ataxia, tremor, and rigidity, while mixed cerebral palsy commonly displays symptoms of each. The first three are the most common in a regular physical education setting, and a discussion of each follows.

Spastic Spastic cerebral palsy is present in 70 to 80 percent of all cases of cerebral palsy resulting from damage to the motor cortex where voluntary motor responses originate. Muscle movements are poorly coordinated and hypertonic with permanently increased muscle tone. Spasticity affects the flexor muscle groups that contribute to the maintenance of posture. The muscles in the lower limbs are rotated inward and flexed at the hip; the knees are flexed and abducted, while the heels are raised. The result is a forced crossing of the legs at the midline that is referred to as a scissors-type gait. In the upper limbs, the forearms are pronated with flexion at the elbows, wrists, and fingers.

Some muscles may function normally or fluctuate because of response in static strength or length of the muscle (United Cerebral Palsy (UCP), 2009). In normal functioning, a slight stretching of the muscle stimulates the muscle spindle of the stretched muscle, causing the muscle to contract appropriately, and is essential for maintaining muscle tone and maintenance of posture. In spasticity, the stretch reflex is exaggerated and causes muscle tightness and abnormal postures. Spastic muscles may also demonstrate a clasp-knife response, in which a sudden passive movement creates an initial buildup in resistance, followed by a sudden release of tension accompanied by a positive stretch reflex, similar to the action of opening a knife. Additionally, voluntary movements of spastic muscles tend to be slow and uncoordinated as children experience difficulty breaking free of stereotyped movements from their reflexes. Inadequate control of force may be observed at the beginning, middle, or end of a movement (Sugden & Keogh, 1990). As children mature and bones elongate, there is an increased amount of pull exerted by the muscles at the joint that exerts pressure on the muscles. This pressure causes tightening or contractures of muscles, such as the upward pull of the heel from a spastic gastrocnemius muscle. As a result, the child requires training programs to balance opposing muscle groups.

Children with mild spasticity will have a minimal loss of function caused by lack of coordination. Mild cases are usually characterized by hemiplegia. Most of these children should be able to walk and run but may have difficulty with refined tasks (Martin, 2006). A child with moderate spasticity will have varying degrees of functioning on one side of the body or minimal involvement in four limbs. Most children possess functional ability on the nonaffected side of the body and exhibit more purposeful movement if they are not stressed, fatigued, or overstimulated. Moderate spasticity also requires stretching activities to overcome the impaired range of motion caused by contractures.

Children with severe spasticity will be extremely limited in movement and muscle tone in all limbs. Voluntary movements are minimal and are often accompanied by the retention of primitive reflexes that interfere with purposeful movement. As the severity increases, the child tends to demonstrate one-sided postural control. They generally tend to prefer the unaffected side and are positioned with the head, neck, and trunk aligned inappropriately. The arms are not used to counterbalance their movements and are initiated by the unaffected side in stepping, crawling, or reaching activities. Severe involvement will require a specialized program of special physical education and physical therapy aimed at inhibiting reflexes, initiating movement, and improving physical fitness.

Athetoid Athetoid dyskinetic, or extrapyramidal cerebral palsy, results from a lesion in the basal ganglia that is located in the central portion of the cerebrum, which controls purposeful movement. Athetosid occurs in approximately 10 to 20 percent of all cases and is characterized by purposeless, involuntary, irregular movements in the extremities. Muscles of the head and upper limbs are mainly affected, with constant flexion in the upper limbs and extension of the fingers, wrists, and elbows while drawing the arms backward and palms downward.

Children with athetoid are constantly moving while demonstrating a lack of control and selectivity in movements. At times, movements are jerky and fast, while at other times movements may be slow and rhythmic. Contractures or increased muscle tension usually is not prevalent, because muscle tone is constantly changing. Generally, locomotion is uncoordinated, while protective and equilibrium reactions may still be present that interfere with development of purposeful movement. Children may also demonstrate a lack of head control, difficulty with speech, and facial contortions.

There are several forms of athetoid, the most common type of which is characterized by rotary movements. The amount of movement increases during periods of excitement or tension but can decline when children are in a calm and relaxed state. Mild to moderate athetosis includes movement in one or two limbs, whereas severe involvement entails three or four limbs. Another form of athetosis, called choreoathetosis, causes uncontrollable spasms that inhibit useful movement. Spasms in severe athetosis are more proximal and are characterized by flying arms and legs during movements. The distinguishing feature of athetoid is involuntary, uncontrollable movements of body parts. Although the reflexes are normal, performance of simple motor tasks may be difficult because of the uncontrollable, involuntary movements. It is also more noticeable during slow controlled movements, such as walking, as opposed to faster movements, such as running (UCP, 2009).

Ataxic Ataxic cerebral palsy is the result of a lesion in the cerebellum. The cerebellum organizes information to coordinate movement and is the feedback mechanism in the brain for muscular functioning. Ataxic occurs in fewer than 10 percent of all cases of cerebral palsy and is usually not congenital but acquired.

With ataxic, the amount of useful functioning varies, especially in children with mild involvement. Children will demonstrate a poor sense of balance, kinesthetic awareness, and uncoordinated movement. Ataxic is generally not diagnosed until the child begins to walk and demonstrates a lack of coordination. The child's gait will be disrupted by a lack of postural control and by inconsistent foot placement. Additionally, spatial awareness and coordination are affected by the disrupted feedback mechanism that causes children to overshoot or undershoot when reaching for objects and interferes with the dexterity needed for dribbling or catching a ball.

Influence of Primitive Reflexes and Other Characteristics

Reflexes are automatic responses of the nervous system that are present at birth and controlled by the primitive regions of the nervous system, spinal cord, labyrinth of the inner ear, and brain stem. They are responsible for changes in muscle tone and movement and gradually become integrated into voluntary movements as the higher center of the brain develops. Reflexes also aid children in assuming postures and controlling movement. During infancy, reflexes will dominate movement until 6 months of age. In children with cerebral palsy, reflexes may be stronger, persist longer, and may reemerge, especially after injury or trauma to the brain.

There are many reflexes that are prevalent in normal development. Three primary reflexes that affect postures and movement are the asymmetrical tonic neck reflex (ATNR), the tonic labyrinthine reflex (TLR), and the positive support reflex (PSR). Each reflex is elicited by a stimulus, and all three reflexes will affect movement.

The ATNR is elicited by either active or passive rotation of the head. When the head is rotated, the ATNR increases the extension of the arm and leg on the same side as the chin, while the arm and leg in opposition increase in flexion. Children will remain in this position until the head turns and releases the reflex. The presence of the ATNR causes an increase in muscle tone and may affect changes in posture.

For the TLR, the position of the labyrinth in the inner ear provides the stimulus. Extending the neck or lying on the back tilts the labyrinth and elicits the reflex, extending the legs and retracting the shoulders (**Figure 15.2**). Flexing the neck or lying on the stomach causes the hips and knees to flex and shoulders to protract (roll forward). When the TLR is present but not strong, changes in muscle tone may occur without any accompanying changes in position (Olney & Wright, 1994).

The PSR is stimulated, causing extension of the legs, when the balls of the feet touch a firm surface

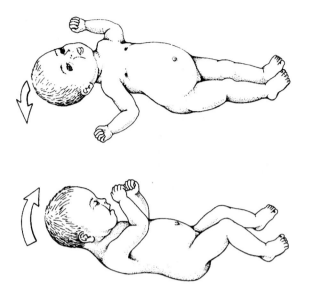

Figure 15.2 The tonic labyrinthine reflex.

(**Figure 15.3**). Normally this reflex contributes to supporting the child's weight while in the standing position. In cerebral palsy, this causes adduction and internal rotation of the hips, which interferes with standing and locomotion.

The persistence of undesirable reflexes and some developmental delay are characteristic of all types of cerebral palsy. For teachers it is important to understand the influence of these reflexes on normal motor development, muscle tone, and postures. For example, persistence of the TLR will interfere with postural control and mechanics, such as balance and tone needed for unsupported sitting or standing. The persistence of this reflex will not only disturb muscle tone and equilibrium in unsupported movements but also interfere with initiating purposeful movement. Many normal postural reactions may be totally lacking or

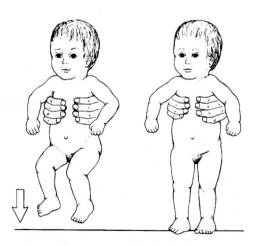

Figure 15.3 The positive support reflex.

incomplete. Movements that require constant changes in tone and equilibrium are then disrupted with the persistence of this primitive reflex. In addition, scissoring may occur because of the adduction and internal rotation of the hips. Toe walking may occur because of the tendency of a shortened gastrocnemius to lift the heel from the ground. Intervention should be aimed at inhibiting primitive reflexes and initiating purposeful and functional movements. It is important to enhance and sustain physical activity interventions to maintain function and avoid deterioration in performance (Bar-Or & Rowland, 2004).

Effect on Functional Development

Growth Poor growth has been well documented in children with cerebral palsy. The main variables causing poor growth have been classified as nutritional factors and neurological, or non-nutritional, factors. Stallings et al. (1996) stated that growth failure in individuals with cerebral palsy is often due to inadequate dietary intake. Non-nutritional factors causing poor growth have been classified as either direct, through a negative neurotrophic effect on linear growth; or indirect, through the endocrine system, immobility, or lack of weight bearing. Stevenson, Roberts, and Vogtle (1995) and Roberts, Vogtle, and Stevenson (1994) concluded that non-nutritional factors related to disease severity have a significant influence on the growth of children with cerebral palsy, even in the absence of malnutrition. Lin and Henderson (1996) supported these conclusions as they found that bone mineral content, bone mineral density, and lean muscle mass were all reduced in the affected versus the unaffected limb of hemiplegic individuals with cerebral palsy. They concluded that bone size and bone density decrease with increasing severity of the disability, thereby causing reductions in growth and maturation.

Locomotion The development of locomotion or gait patterns is often affected in children with cerebral palsy. According to Bar-Or and Rowland (2004), children with cerebral palsy become deconditioned and lose their mobility. The primary focus in the generation and control of locomotion has been the role of higher brain centers, such as the sensorimotor cortex. The deficits in locomotion in children with cerebral palsy have been ascribed to damage to the basic circuitry serving pattern generation, to failed maturation of spinal reflexes and/or the descending systems that control them, and to changes in the mechanical properties of muscles (Leonard, Hirschfield, & Forssberg, 1991). Leonard et al. (1991) also found that normal features of adult gait did not develop in children with severe cerebral palsy. These problems were

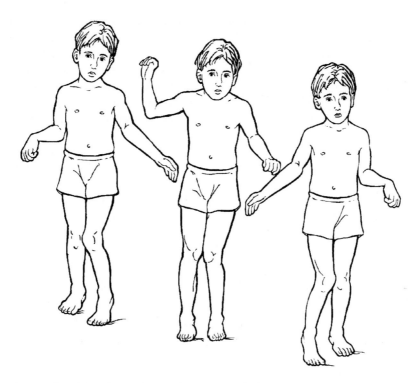

Figure 15.4 Typical gait of child with cerebral palsy, spastic diplegia, or paraplegia.

similar to those identified by Bar-Or (1983) and colleagues (Unnithan, Dowling, Frost & Bar-Or, 1996; Unnithan, Dowling, Frost, Volpe Ayub & Bar-Or, 1996). Bottos et al. (1995) also concluded that severe deformities, resulting from cerebral palsy affected the choice of locomotion pattern and indicated that locomotion pattern, age at onset, and even manner of execution all influenced prognosis for walking.

Weak muscles, rigid movements, and lack of stability are evident in most movements especially during gait (Unnithan & Maltais, 2004). The characteristic crouched gait pattern most evident in spasticity results from increased flexion in the hips and knees, and increased flexion in the ankles (see **Figure 15.4**). The inability to correctly sequence the contraction and relaxation of reciprocal muscle groups impedes the ability to lift and advance the leg in a forward motion. The restriction of the hips and knees limits the step length and compromises the ability to maintain stability. Movement is disrupted; synchronization of steps and balance are disrupted, causing the child to shorten their steps and crouch at the hip displacing the common gait characteristics. Recent studies have demonstrated the effectiveness of strengthening exercises in improving overall gait and specifically speed, stride length, and decrease of the double support phase of the gait cycle (Lee, Sung, and Yoo, 2008; Eek et al., 2008).

LEARNING ACTIVITY

What types of muscle contractions are used when walking up and down stairs? How do they relate to and impact a child with cerebral palsy? Consult the school physical therapist with regard to inhibiting persistent reflexes and encouraging range of motion in the extremities.

Planning the Physical Activity Program

Children with cerebral palsy have physical and motor limitations that are based on their predominant type of motor disability. Children with spasticity encounter difficulties in accomplishing activities that require muscular strength and/or endurance but are capable of more precise, fine motor movement than are children with athetoid. In contrast, children with athetoid are more proficient in performing locomotor activities than activities that require muscular strength.

A primary concern of teachers is the need to develop and maximize the movement potential of children. Early in the developmental process, the emphasis is on education, physical therapy, and surgery to enable children to function and develop appropriately. If the emphasis on movement is not continued, children will be at a disadvantage. The gains accrued from early emphasis on developing movement potential often dissipate without ongoing training. This will lead to a deterioration of movement and less ability to initiate movements, as well as increases in weight during the maturation process that are not accompanied by increases in strength and power (Bar-Or, 1983). Lack of physical training causes movement to become increasingly difficult, and children become less tolerant of the demands of activity as their cardiovascular functioning diminishes (Rose, Haskell, & Gamble, 1993). Furthermore, the lack of training is complicated by the increased reliance on electronic wheelchairs and devices that reduce the need for physical development.

Increasing the overall physical functioning of children with cerebral palsy is essential in developing a physical education program. Teachers should consider several factors in this program, including the team approach, movement efficiency, and motivation.

The Team Approach

The treatment of children with cerebral palsy requires the concerted effort of the collaborative team. To provide a comprehensive program for overall development, the following may be necessary:

- Surgery to stabilize muscular development and eliminate deformities
- Identification of primitive reflexes
- Therapy to achieve range of motion, and mastery of basic living skills
- Educational instruction to overcome learning problems and establish communication

Physical activity is especially important as a contributor to the total program and should be used extensively with those children whose disability is in the mild-to-moderate range. Activity can contribute to the functional independence of children by providing the opportunity to learn motor skills, develop fitness, and participate in leisure activities that are essential to their overall development.

Movement (Mechanical Efficiency)

The movement of children with cerebral palsy is low, especially in children with spasticity performing arm or leg movements because of wasteful contractions of the spastic, or dyskinetic, muscle (Bar-Or, 1983). For example, when children perform a rhythmic task such as walking, the agonist and antagonist muscles alternately contract and relax to permit efficient movement. In spasticity, these muscle groups may maintain increased tone in the arms and/or legs, leading to inefficient and wasteful motion. Furthermore, the amount of force exerted by the trunk muscles is difficult for

children to overcome, which significantly contributes to a lower efficiency of the working muscles. When assessing performance capabilities, Bar-Or (1983) indicated that such inefficiency not only is less economical for movement but also varied from one trial to another. Inefficiency may also be due to the child's attempt to compensate for gait deficiencies, thus exaggerating the movement further and leading to more wasteful motions. Bar-Or's work has been expanded to demonstrate how cocontraction compromises gait patterns and produces higher energy costs in children with cerebral palsy (Unnithan, Dowling, Frost & Bar-Or, 1996; Unnithan, Dowling, Frost, et al., 1996; Unnithan & Maltais, 2004).

Motivation

One aspect of a physical activity program that is often neglected is the motivation required to continue with a training regimen. Because a child with cerebral palsy needs to expend more effort to maintain an adequate level of physical functioning, it is essential for teachers to enhance the motivational aspects of participation. Teachers can utilize charts, contracts, and self-testing activities to increase motivation, as well as continually praise children for their effort and participation. Additionally, teachers can intersperse enjoyable or reinforcing activities into the teaching and conditioning process that enable children to continue their participation at a level designed to increase their overall functioning ability.

Implementing the Physical Activity Program

The selection of physical education activities should be based on the obvious motor characteristics of children within their classification system or the combination of motor characteristics from a mixed classification (**Table 15.1**). All children with cerebral palsy should be provided with opportunities to develop strength, endurance, and flexibility according to individual needs. It is evident that children with cerebral palsy will have deficiencies in strength, flexibility, coordination, and balance. In addition, children with spasticity may require stretching of flexor groups and strengthening of extensors, whereas children with athetoid and ataxic require relaxation, muscle stabilization, and coordination activities.

Because of the individualized level of functioning, it is necessary to progressively increase the child's tolerance for activity. Resistance exercises using wall pulleys, weights, surgical tubing, handling activities, and medicine balls can promote the development of strength and encourage socialization (Horvat, 1987; UCP, 2009). These activities also

Table 15.1 Classifications,* Motor Characteristics, and Appropriate Activities for Children with Cerebral Palsy

Classification	Motor Characteristics	Physical Education Activities
Spastic	Scissors gait resulting from the inward rotation of legs; hip flexion; knees and heels off the floor with toes pointing inward. Upper limb involves pronated forearms, which results in elbow, wrist, and finger flexion. Stereotypic movements from reflexes; increased muscle tone (hypertonicity) and possible clonus. Production of force is deficient with wasteful contractions. Lack of sensory information from muscle.	Aquatics, circuit and resistance training, walking stairs, hanging activities, slow stretching, flexibility exercises, yoga, relaxation activities, dance, rhythms, movement exploration activities to promote finger and wrist extension, body image and awareness using a mirror, jogging, track and field, and most ball sports (i.e., softball, volleyball, basketball), isometrics, pushing skills
Athetoid	Involuntary movements that are uncontrollable, unpredictable, and purposeless. Movements may be slow and rhythmic or jerky and fast. Also characterized by extra actions with voluntary movement. Unsteady and fluctuating muscle tone.	Aquatics, stretching, resistance, and flexibility exercises, rhythms, dance, movement exploration and body imagery with a mirror, low-organized games, badminton, table tennis, softball, basketball, bowling, track and field, volleyball, and walking stairs
Ataxic	Poor sense of balance and position of body. Uncoordinated and unsteady movements as child begins to sit, stand, and walk. Poor postural fixation with excessive righting reactions using arms to compensate.	Aquatics, balance activities, body awareness and movement exploration, flexibility and yoga exercises, stretching, rhythms, dance, bowling, golf, table tennis, most ball sports, track and field, tai-chi, and walking stairs

*Predominant classification. Often children will manifest mixed cerebral palsy, which includes motor characteristics from each classification.

develop both sides of the body, which aids in developing proper and symmetrical body mechanics. Dodd, Taylor, and Graham (2003) also indicated that home-based strengthening programs can be implemented to develop lower extremity strength and functional movement postural training. This has also been supported by several studies by Damiano and colleagues (1995) who support the use of exercise to promote functional ability in this population.

Cardiovascular endurance can be improved by jogging, cycling, arm ergometry, aerobic dance, riding, wheelchair rolling, swimming, or water exercises. Teachers should implement these activities in a noncompetitive atmosphere and provide rest intervals to postpone undue fatigue.

Some children may be apprehensive about the aquatic environment because of splashing or anxiety that may elicit abnormal muscle spasm. However, swimming is ideal because of the buoyancy provided by the water, lack of gravity, and the suspension of the entire body. Training can easily be implemented to promote fundamental movements, range of motion, and cardiovascular conditioning through water exercises.

By using the medium of the water, teachers can also incorporate games and water exercises to progressively increase endurance. The emphasis in the aquatic program should be on the integration of body parts and free movements rather than on implementing a stroke precisely. Proper breath control and flotation devices are also encouraged to provide intermittent training and a progressive endurance

program. Teachers should also provide warmer temperatures of water (85–88°) and air (85–90°) to protect children from undue cooling of the body. Aquatic activities in warm water may also aid in reducing tension, especially if the session does not exceed the child's comfort zone.

Dance activities can also promote fitness and are progressive in nature. Aerobics, line dances, folk dances, and other activities involve both sides of the body, use basic movements, and develop appropriate posture as well as provide an excellent social outlet for children.

Body image activities should be encouraged, such as body awareness and naming body parts. Movement exploration concepts are useful to stress movement of particular body parts as well as to improve balance and coordination. Laterality activities, especially in hemiplegia, can enable children to differentiate from the functional and affected side of the body.

Supplemental Activities

Children with cerebral palsy are generally less active than their peers and rely too much on mechanical devices for ambulation. Furthermore, the activity in regular physical education classes may not be rigorous enough to produce improvement in physical conditioning. The physical performance of children with cerebral palsy will decrease when an ongoing fitness program is not provided throughout the year (Lundberg, 1976; Sommer, 1971).

Obviously the motor functioning needs constant attention in order for the child to maintain overall functional ability. In providing an ongoing program, team members may consider the use of physical activity outside the school to provide an essential supplement to the physical education program. The potential benefits of physical activity in improving mobility have been well documented (Bar-Or & Rowland, 2004; Rotzinger & Stoboy, 1974; Dodd et al., 2003; Unnithan & Maltais, 2004; Martin, 2006). For example, a physical activity program outside the school led to improvements in walking speed, efficiency of movement, and some relief of spasms among severely involved individuals.

In order to avoid contraindicated activities, consultation with physicians and physical therapists is required. Children with spastic cerebal palsy should avoid activities that increase tension in already-tight muscles. For example, leg extensions may cause adduction in the lower extremities and would be contraindicated in some children. Likewise, children who experience grasping and releasing problems should not be evaluated for muscular strength using a hand-grip dynamometer.

For both spastic and athetoid cerebral palsy relaxation and tension-reduction activities can be beneficial. In spasticity, relaxation may counteract tight muscle groups, whereas in athetoid the constant muscle contractions may be controlled or quieted with stress-reduction and relaxation techniques.

To appropriately supplement the school physical education program, teachers can use sports and assign homework to improve mobility and increase physical functioning. Most children can tolerate intense activity for 15 to 20 minutes twice weekly, while less intense activity can be tolerated for longer periods (Bar-Or, 1983). Therefore, home-based activities can easily be implemented to provide additional opportunities for developing motor skills and physical conditioning if supervised properly within a medical margin of safety. For example, exercises developed by therapists and teachers, such as progressive resistance exercises, can be used to strengthen muscles, while relaxation techniques can aid in maintaining muscle balance and stability as well as facilitate reaching (Fetters & Kluzik, 1996).

Sports and leisure activities should also be encouraged for children (Jones, 1988; UCP, 2009). Since 1978, sporting events have been held for individuals with cerebral palsy to provide competition and socialization opportunities. These events include bowling, billiards, table tennis, archery, weight lifting, swimming, track and field, softball, cycling, and wheelchair slalom. The National Disability Sports Alliance (NDSA) and Blaze Sports uses the following eight-level classification system. Category A is (NDSA 2002) based on the functional level for individuals with cerebral palsy and head injuries. Currently Category B is being developed for individuals with muscular dystrophy and other physical disabilities.

Class 1: Severe involvement in all four limbs. Limited trunk control. Unable to grasp a softball. Poor functional strength in upper extremities, often necessitating the use of an electric wheelchair for independence.

Class 2: Severe to moderate quadriplegic, normally able to propel wheelchair very slowly with arms or by pushing with feet. Poor functional strength and severe control problems in the upper extremities.

Class 3: Moderate quadriplegic, fair functional strength and moderate control problems in upper extremities and torso. Uses wheelchair.

Class 4: Lower limbs have moderate to severe involvement. Good functional strength and minimal control problem in upper extremities and torso. Uses wheelchair.

Class 5: Good functional strength and minimal control problems in upper extremities. May walk with or without assistive devices for ambulatory support.

Class 6: Moderate to severe quadriplegic. Ambulates without walking aids. Less coordination. Balance problems when running or throwing. Has greater upper extremity involvement.

Class 7: Moderate to minimal hemiplegic. Good functional ability in nonaffected side. Walk/runs with noted limp.

Class 8: Minimally affected. May have minimal coordination problems. Able to run and jump freely. Has good balance.

Most children are capable not only of participating in sports but also of training in ways comparable to those of their able-bodied peers (Jones, 1988). Modifications of activity should be based on the child's functional ability, and training should be progressive and intensive enough to develop overall functional ability and sport-specific skill. In this manner, sports can contribute to increasing the functional ability of children while providing avenues for competition and leisure that contribute to the socialization process. Teachers should consider children and their motivation levels before modifying or substituting activities. All individuals respond differently to competition and training and should not be confined to limited activities, such as bowling and shuffleboard; rather, children should be allowed to participate in sports advocated by the NDSA, such as basketball, softball, weight training, and track.

Traumatic Brain Injury

Traumatic Brain Injuries (TBI) are characterized by a blow to the head or penetrating head injury that disrupts brain function. Children with TBI may demonstrate

CASE STUDY

Michelle suffered a brain injury during the second grade. Prior to her injury, she was an excellent student and gifted athlete. Physically, Michelle's strength and range of motion were restored during rehabilitation. However, she now experiences difficulty with open-ended tasks and games. For example, during physical education she performs all warm-up stretches and exercises; however, during games that require movement up and down the floor (e.g. basketball, frisbee, and soccer) she finds it difficult to keep-up with the group and to make decisions required to complete tasks. As a result, she becomes frustrated and wants to sit out during activity and has to be coaxed to participate.

Marty, her teacher, is very supportive and offers encouragement. He has assigned her to a smaller group to practice the skills before activities and games. Recently, prior to the floor hockey unit, he sent task cards home for Michelle to work on in hope that the anticipatory experience would lighten her processing load. Marty has also come to realize that Michelle has difficulty when the activity environment, for her, changes unpredictably and/or rapidly. To assist Michelle, he has created and implemented a communication strategy whereby classmates verbalize action cues for Michelle.

In the general school setting, Michelle continues to have issues with memory and keeping things in order. For example, sequential thinking becomes an issue when, in the restroom, she urinates prior to removing her pants. Understandably, this is embarrassing and frustrating. To assist Michelle, her teacher has developed written cue cards for restroom stall use, akin to task analysis, to help Michelle avoid further mishaps.

cognitive problems such as arousal, attention, concentration, memory, problem solving and decision-making (Katz et al., 2006; NIH, 2002). Likewise motor control, perceptual deficits, stability, social interactions, and control of behavior are linked with physical and cognitive functioning (Katz et al., 2006). According to the Center for Disease Control (2006), TBI affects nearly one million children annually. The leading causes of TBI are falls, motor vehicle accidents, assaults, and being struck by objects. In children, falls (42%) and motor vehicle accidents (34%) are the primary causes of injury among males and those in the age groups of 0–4 and 15–19 years of age (CDC, 2006).

The resultant complications may affect cognitive or physical functioning as well as social and emotional capabilities. Severe head trauma occurs in pediatric populations at a rate of 3 in 1,000. A loss of consciousness or coma is often used as an indicator of severe head trauma and is generally associated with a higher mortality rate. Medical treatment for postcoma children necessitates interventions that address any physical, cognitive, or accompanying deficits that are present. Primary physical concerns should emphasize muscle imbalances and skeletal and postural deformities that limit the child's functional development and self-sufficiency. Initial interventions may be hospital specific but should generalize to community and home-based functions. Recovery is based on the extent of injury, quality of medical services, and therapeutic intervention. Since TBI is so variable, each case should be treated separately. TBI is complex and functioning

will vary depending on the cause and location of the injury. Included in **Table 15.2** are some causative factors of TBI.

The prognosis and capabilities of the child's functioning will require extensive intervention as the child returns to school and home-based activities. Cognitive rehabilitation is essential for addressing primary defects in children with TBI. For children whose brains are still developing, new skills are learned by building on previous tasks. Injuries to the developing brain interfere with these cognitive functions, hindering the cognitive development of these children. Likewise, injuries to frontal-temporal regions affect new learning and may restrict the cognitive and behavioral function as the child develops physically. At best children will experience reduced cognition, inconsistency and difficulty with novel situations. Movement and exercise interventions should be specific movement sequences that lead to self-sufficiency. Acceptable levels of muscular strength and endurance are required to overcome postural deficiencies, while mastery of movement control systems are needed to manipulate objects as well as to develop movements required for ambulation. Because the attention span and motivation of the child with a head injury may be affected, specific behavior management procedures may also be required to promote exercise and movement behavior. Any insult to the development or functioning of the central nervous system affects physical functioning and cognition, as well as social or emotional behaviors.

Table 15.2   Types of Traumatic Brain Injury (TBI) (National Institute of Health, 2002)

Type	Severity	Description
Hematoma	Severe	Heavy bleeding in and around brain
Concussion	Minor	Loss of consciousness in response to head injury
Skull Fracture types		
• depressed	Severe	Pieces of skull press into brain tissue
• penetrating	Severe	Piercing of the skull to a localized area
• contusion	Severe	Bruising of brain tissue; shaking brain back and forth within skull (contrecoup)
• shearing	Severe	Diffuse axonal injury which damages individual neurons and loss of connection among neurons
Anoxia	Minor to severe	Absence of oxygen to tissues even with adequate blood flow
Hypoxia	Minor to severe	Decrease in oxygen supply causing cells to die in minutes

Only a fraction of children who survive severe head trauma recover completely and most may be totally dependent on medical and family intervention. For other children, adequate participation, self-sufficiency, and integration into community and school environments will require intervention from medical, community, and educational services (Ylvisaker, Todis, & Gland, 2001). Attention span, self-control, motivation, and short-term memory may be affected and require intervention strategies that may include behavior management, memory compensation, and functional skill development, as well as social and community-based participation skills (Katz et al., 2006).

Impact on Functional Development

Damage to the central nervous system may also contribute to a variety of physical problems associated with behavior. Depending on the severity of central nervous system dysfunction, individuals may have partial or little control of their extremities, spasticity, or even total paralysis. Movement-related disorders complicate the efficiency of movement as well as disrupt the development of functional movement and physical fitness. Inherent in disorders of this nature in children is the rapid development of the central nervous system, which accounts for the difficulty in diagnosing movement problems in pediatric populations. According to the Glasgow Coma Scale, head injuries can be classified into three categories: mild (13–15), moderate (9–12), or severe (3–8). The Glasgow Coma Scale grades an individual's level of consciousness on a scale of 3 to 15 based on their verbal, motor, or eye opening reactions (Koch & Narayan, 2007).

Several factors can contribute to developmental or acquired central nervous system damage, including birth disorders, trauma, infections, fevers, severe illness, brain tumors, head trauma, or injury. For example, the type of duration of the force as well as the direction and intensity of the force will impact function. When the head is struck, the impact can result in brain damage. Likewise, excessive shaking of an infant can cause damage to brain tissue. In other cases, TBI can occur from cumulative head trauma in children involved in sports.

In addition, the severity of involvement can affect treatment plans and functional capabilities. For example, the following classifications can affect the availability of physical and motor functioning in children with TBI.

Mild to Moderate Involvement

- Head control
- Independence in self-help skills
- Perceptual deficits
- Muscle imbalance
- Postural deformities
- Delayed movement and fitness responses to intervention
- Deficits in feedback mechanism

Severe to Profound Involvement

- Lack of head control
- Skeletal and postural deformities that limit movement
- Contractures and muscle imbalance
- Perceptual and sensory deficits in processing and feedback mechanisms
- Dependence on self-help skills
- Compromised movement potential and retention of functioning

LEARNING ACTIVITY

Discuss the functions of the brain and how they effect cognitive and motor behavior.

Planning the Physical Activity Program

Once a child has been formally diagnosed with a behavior problem that affects learning, specific evaluations in the major areas of service should be performed. These include the following:

1. a speech-language-communication evaluation by the speech and language pathologist to determine the level of receptive language and communication, expressive language and communication, and voice and speech production

2. a cognitive evaluation by either a clinical psychologist or a developmental pediatrician to determine the level of intellectual functioning

3. a neuropsychological and adaptive behavioral evaluation by a clinical psychologist or diagnostician to determine capability for self-sufficiency in activities of daily living and to establish a baseline of function in learning, performance, and socialization

4. a sensorimotor assessment by the adapted physical educator and/or occupational and physical therapist to detect potential deficiencies in physical and motor functioning.

Evaluation of sensorimotor performance is particularly important in situations where there is a question of motor delay or motor dysfunction, as well as to document areas of strengths and weakness for prognostic and intervention planning. Gross and fine motor functioning may be assessed through a variety of standardized assessment instruments appropriate for the developmental level of the child. Also, nonstandardized, more qualitative criterion-based observations of praxis (planning and sequencing of novel motor patterns and organization of goal-directed actions within the environment) are critical, because these capabilities are often deficient in the child with TBI.

Intervention (**Table 15.3**) should be aimed at developing functional skills and independence and requires extensive collaboration from various disciplines to foster behavioral, cognitive, communication, perceptual, physical, and social capabilities (Driver, 2006). For young children, control of the head and trunk should be established to initiate sitting and standing or functional ambulation. Because postural control includes balance and the ability to change positions, the versatility of movement may be limited. Balance and motor control must be achieved to facilitate movement. If accompanying control is affected by the competing actions of reciprocal muscle groups, mechanical efficiency is limited, and correct movement sequences are disrupted. Specific care is required to inhibit inappropriate reflexes that interfere with motor control and to avoid movements that may overstimulate the child. Specific interventions should attempt to establish appropriate developmental

sequences and control of movements that can be planned, replicated, and initiated independently (Diller & Ben-Yishay, 1989). After initial control is established, the coordination of specific movement patterns can be addressed to facilitate movement.

Traditional exercise programs can improve functioning in children that is conducive to mobility, movement development, perceptual development, and fitness development and that will generalize to overall functioning in tasks that are needed in home-based play, school, and social settings. Treatment should be based on a three-tiered approach that moves from dependent function to supported and independent function. An interdisciplinary approach should stress intervention in behavior management, cognition, and motor control focusing on the functional deficits that are reflective of the individual's behavior and cognition, as well as any accompanying physical dysfunctions (Phillips, 1994; Jaffe et al., 1992).

Behavior Management

Behavior management strategies should focus on appropriate behaviors at the child's stage of development including appropriate social interaction with peers in structured play settings. Strategies should aim to reduce manifestations of aggressive or passive behavior and impulsive responses to stimulation. Some behavior patterns may result from structural or neurological deficit and will be resistant to change. Careful management strategies must be maintained to ensure compliance with appropriate behaviors, such as active modeling and applying systematic consequences to eliminate inappropriate behaviors and to initiate and facilitate new behaviors. Physical activity responses generally respond well to behavior interventions and generalize to appropriate social interactions, such as play and activities of daily living.

Motivation is also an essential element of behavior that is important to restoration of functional capabilities. Children should not feel frustrated in their attempts to complete tasks, and in the early stages of learning they should receive appropriate rewards for initiating or attempting the task. Later, the criterion for the specific task can be altered to require a finer approximation of the task. Motivation is also essential for the child to exert sufficient effort to facilitate improvement in development and should be encouraged to ensure compliance. Rewarding appropriate behaviors will aid in developing new tasks and help eliminate unwanted behaviors. Likewise, the parent or teacher needs to structure the setting and behavior management system to ensure compliance for the treatment. Many children have a short attention span that is not conducive to a large number of trials or repetition of movements. Movement can be initiated and

Table 15.3 Physical Activity for Children with TBI

Behavior	Characteristics	Teaching Strategies	Physical Activity
Cognitive and perceptual disorders (motor control)	• Failure to retain information • Difficulty processing sensory stimuli/problem solving • Impaired memory functions • Difficulty with orientation	Determine level of functioning and most efficient modalities for learning. Enhance existing modality or compensate for a deficiency. Emphasize short- and long-term memory by structuring task, providing physical guidance, and prompting.	Good behavior game and social-sequence activities; praise for any accomplishment; program of aquatic fitness, motor skill development based on child needs and activities that can be sequenced.
Physical impairments	Muscle imbalances, skeletal and postural deformities • Spasticity • Fatigue	Develop strength to overcome postural deficiencies based on functional ability; develop movement control to manipulate objects and to develop ambulation.	Aquatics, progressive resistance exercises (surgical tubing and weights), flexibility, stationary cycling, walking, Tai Chi.
Hyperactivity and attention disorders	• Distractibility • Overactivity • Restlessness • Short attention span • Concentration • Perservation	Structure environment; use behavior strategies to strengthen or weaken behaviors.	Variety of gross motor skills, parachute, aquatics, dance, movement exploration activities that utilize simple terms, demonstrations, and concrete examples. Provide specific feedback. Demonstrate skills in a variety of settings.
Poor interpersonal relations	• Social detachment • Extreme sensitivity • Shyness • Inability to form close relationships	Foster teacher-child communication to strengthen, enhance, maintain, weaken, or eliminate certain behaviors. Provide clear directions and age-appropriate activities.	Social-sequence games and activities that require cooperation; movement education; activities that require two or more people; parachute activities; aquatics; physical fitness, including running and dance.
Anxiety reactions and frustrations	• Overanxiousness • Excessive fears • Impaired motivation • Agitation • Control of behavior • Depression	Structure environment and appropriate activities; foster teacher-child communication; use behavior strategies to emphasize behavior prompts.	Good-behavior game and social-sequence activities initially in a highly structured environment, and activities in which everyone is correct. Structured program with vigorous activities (parachute, running, jumping); movement exploration and dance therapy, acting out specific situations; relaxation training and activities emphasizing how slowly activity can be accomplished.

reinforced to gradually extend the time or number of trials the child can perform. Further, the environment can be structured to eliminate potential distractions in the early stages of learning and gradually reintroduce the child to situations where they must deal with multiple stimulation distinctions and vary their responses.

Implementing the Physical Activity Program

Cognitive Disorders

Primary cognitive deficits may be problems that require compensation if the behavior or development occurs at an age where neural plasticity does not allow

for other parts of the brain to assume functions. The type of injury, severity, and overall cognitive ability are often predicators of working memory (Conklin, Saloria, & Slomine, 2008). Memory deficits are common concerns that may be related to speed of processing or complexity of the task. Information that is missing or not recorded interferes with the acquisition and recall of important elements of the task. Generally, slowing the amount of information to be processed makes the skill easier to remember and perform.

Because children often lose a great deal of task-relevant information in processing information, it is important to cue relevant parts of the task that are essential to performance and rehearse the task in a variety of settings (Croce, Horvat, & Roswal, 1995). When the child learns a new task, it may be more beneficial to block practice trials so that the child can be reinforced immediately to establish an appropriate motor program of the desired response. Random trials can be applied later to ensure retention and adaptability to a variety of settings. Fatigue also affects memory functions and will degrade performance. Learning may still be occurring, but motivation and reinforcement may be delayed because the effects of fatigue are deleterious to performance.

Another aspect of memory and behavior is attention to the relevant components of the task. Children are normally less attentive to task-relevant information and crowd the system with irrelevant components of the task, resulting in faulty memory. Some attention may result from neurological deficits, whereas others can occur from a behavioral or motivational focus. The cause of the attention deficit should be determined in order to select the most appropriate method to present information. For example, the learning setting may not be conducive for focusing attention, requiring the teacher to minimize distractions within the environment or consistently employ their teaching and reinforcement strategies. Later, the child can gradually adjust to the environment by learning to deal with distractions or stimulation within the environment. The parent or teacher should also carefully structure their intervention to present instructions in a manner that the learner can assimilate and can appropriately and consistently apply behavior management strategies at the correct time (Martin, 1988). The greater the child's ability to maintain, increase, and focus attention, the more likely the child will be able to process the information presented and improve memory and subsequent cognitive functioning. Uomoto (1990) referred to two basic approaches for intervention. The first is a curriculum-based model to train areas that are impaired, for example, providing visual information to cue a movement. The other approach is a functional/goal-directed model that focuses on compensatory strategies to use with other intact modalities. The success of either strategy will encompass ongoing dialogue between the school, home, and community setting in order to provide as many opportunities as possible to facilitate learning.

Perceptual Disorders

The basic conception that the child is "hard-wired" and will respond to maturational constructs will not always apply to children with behavior and cognitive difficulties. Whether the brain has not developed appropriately or has sustained an injury, there is a remarkable ability or potential in the brain for recovery that was not originally apparent. Instead of being fixed and rigid, the brain may respond to intervention by reorganizing its ability to process information. Cope (1990) implied that the rehabilitation process

may facilitate reorganization and that recovery may depend on the amount of intervention. Reorganization may involve the development of new motor programs or schema that rely on a central mechanism and feedback to facilitate learning (Schmidt & Lee, 1999). This view would allow for retraining of previously learned skills or learning new skills that are developmentally appropriate. Tasks can be structured and reinforced at the child's level of functioning and gradually increase in complexity as the child develops cognitive and motivation skills.

Another approach to facilitate learning is the dynamical systems approach, in which control of coordinated movement deemphasizes the role of the brain and emphasizes the role of the environment and dynamic properties of the body and limbs (Magill, 2007). The coordinated structures of the muscles and joints will work in cooperative action to facilitate movement and will be developed through practice and experience. For children with TBI, the experience would be the rehabilitation process involving many disciplines. Muscles and joints can then act as a unit to achieve specific tasks, such as reaching for and grasping an object (Magill, 2007). Instead of a centrally stored mechanism that activates motor programs, commands are generated by a self-organized coordinative structure resulting from the child's intention to complete the action and environmental characteristics (Magill, 2007).

In contrast to closed-loop models of motor programming, commands are forwarded to the coordinative structures from the nervous system to initiate movement, not from a central mechanism but from internal and external sources. If available, feedback exists within components of the coordinative structures to compensate for nonfunctioning muscle units and does not need to be directed to a central mechanism.

One of the goals of intervention is to develop cognitive and motor functions through information processing. The child's brain is adaptable to learning new information, although learning strategies may be altered, requiring intervention, retraining, and behavior prompting. In some cases it may be neccessary to use information differently and to compensate to establish new behaviors (Cope, 1990).

As indicated earlier in the discussion on cognition, practice environments should be carefully structured to eliminate distractions and establish attention on the designated task. Physical guidance may be required to provide information relevant to positioning or feedback from the intended movement. As the child develops proficiency, augmented feedback concerning the consequences of a movement (KR) or the temporal, sequential, or force patterns of a movement (KP) can be utilized (Croce, Horvat, & Roswal, 1995).

The goals of treatment and specific functional objectives should be consistent with those of other behavioral or neurological disorders. For some children, the ability to function in school, home, and community settings may depend more on cognitive and behavior deficits than on physical functioning (Cope, 1990). Long-term planning should rely on integrating children into similar peer group activities. Once the child enters school, services should clearly focus on transitional services for community and home-based environments. This may encompass the interdisciplinary team framework of school and community agencies, as well as home interventions involving parents or siblings. Lehr (1989) indicated that the effects of injury on higher problem solving and on behavior may not be apparent until the child reaches the period during which development normally occurs. These delayed effects should be addressed because medical treatment has probably ended. Teachers and parents need to be aware of emerging deficits as children progress through their developmental stages, because expectations will change as the child grows and matures (Katz et al., 2006).

Physical Impairments

Early movements should emphasize stability, positioning, and proprioceptive information in a relatively closed, consistent environment until the child can learn to deal with more open or changing situations that require versatility of practice, sufficient motivation, or reinforcement. Likewise, the control of movement may depend on persistent patterns of neuromuscular dysfunction, such as hemiparesis, bilateral spasticity, ataxia, or dystonia (Molnar & Perrin, 1992). Because the variability of functioning will be apparent, motor skill acquisition needs to be stimulated to develop functionally appropriate developmental skills required to explore the environment. If function or, more specifically, functional skills are the primary goals of intervention, priorities should be established in conjunction with academic goals and objectives. For example, in some children diminishing muscle tone may not prove to be functional in stabilizing a position that is essential to developing motor skills such as sitting at a computer and visually processing tasks from left to right. Initial activities can be selected that are functional for movement such as strengthening the trunk for independent posture and tracking an object such as a ball, which is consistent with classroom activities. Decision-making components can be prompted, guided, and overlearned, especially if the learning environments and behavior strategies are consistent. Walking, stair climbing, aquatics, and cycling are simple maneuvers that require little instruction and can be controlled by the child and his or her rate of information processing.

Children with lower levels of cognitive functioning and motivation can learn these tasks, which should then be generalized and prompted in home and community settings.

Long-term effects of cognition and learning should be viewed as essential. Early in development, physical or social limitations may preclude appropriate play interactions that contribute to exploring the environment and learning new tasks. The child, because of his or her limitations or lack of appropriate responses, may not establish the basis for cognition and social interactions. Play, solitary or with others, can provide the necessary stimulation to establish and reinforce ongoing development in home and community settings. Children learn through the medium of play to socially interact with others as well as developing stability, reaching/grasping movements, and cognitive tasks, such as sorting and stacking. If the opportunity to develop these skills is lacking or motor development is deficient, the child is more likely to demonstrate cognitive and social interaction deficits.

For many children these skills are lacking and should be initiated as soon as possible. Ongoing stimulation from parents, peers, or others promotes the transition from school to home and community settings that are consistent with normal developmental principles. For some children, more active intervention by parents may be required to facilitate these sequences, especially in conjunction with the school intervention procedure. Further, tasks can be presented in a manner that is consistent and allows the child time to process information in a safe, secure environment that can be reinforced immediately. For school-aged children, the availability of services will vary according to states and school districts. Most schools and teachers probably will have minimal, if any, orientation to children with TBI. Because many children with mild dysfunctions will return to regular classroom settings (or, for more severely involved children, to special education classrooms), it is important to identify specific needs for successful school functioning. Although much of the school's function will focus on developing the child's cognition and behavior, it is vital to identify potential physical and motor needs that can aid in recovery and improve functioning (Fryer, 1989).

Activities that promote ambulation should be encouraged in schools, supplemented by community and home based programs that provide more opportunities for participation and aid in community integration. For example, a child who has overcome balance difficulties in school can progress to walking or riding bicycles with family or peers in community settings. Likewise, muscular strength and endurance can be developed in exercise programs, which enable the child to participate with peers in the neighborhood or community recreation settings. Further, processing and sequencing motor skills may generalize to activities of daily living (i.e., dressing) or may be used to promote the framework for developing cognition by encouraging attention and memory functions.

Older children should be encouraged to develop long-term regimens that foster mobility within the environment. Cardiovascular conditioning, muscular strength, and endurance will all contribute not only to overall physical functioning and fitness but also to the prerequisite skills for vocational training and to the physical skills needed in peer group interactions. It is apparent that most community-based and school-based programs are not sufficient to meet the diverse needs of children with TBI. As a result, additional services (including those that address physical and motor functioning) are needed, in particular those that relate to transitional services, recreation, and vocational training (Mills, 1988). Long-term planning should address the physical and motor needs across the developmental life span and contribute to the total intervention program.

Hyperactivity and Attention Disorders

For children who have difficulty focusing on activities for a specific length of time, the first step is to structure the environment in an attempt to eliminate the cause of the problem. Minor distractions may cause the child to lose attention and focus on a different task. By structuring the environment and reducing external stimuli, the teacher can help the child focus on completing the task or on increasing their time on task. For many fitness and movement sequences, such as riding a bicycle, simple movements can be gradually extended. Moderate activity may also increase the attention and focus of children while they are performing motor and cognitive tasks (Croce & Horvat, 1995). Other strategies, such as token or point systems, prompts, and group consequences, can also be used to help children concentrate and focus on a task. Furthermore, teachers may use goal setting for individual children as a method to gradually build upon a task.

Teachers should avoid long strings of verbal instruction, because many children have problems remembering sequences of words. Activities should be selected that accommodate simple terms or demonstrations that make it easier for the child to maintain attention. Written direction or visual cues may also be more helpful. Gross motor skills, parachute activities, aquatics, dance, fitness, and relaxation activities can aid in maintaining attention and eliminating hyperactivity.

Poor Interpersonal Relationships

Building interpersonal relationships is a goal of any activity setting and is evident in play activities in the preschool years. For children who shy away from an activity or from participating with others, teachers should establish specific causes for the problem. By structuring the environment and using social praise or point systems to involve the children gradually, the teacher usually can increase the probability of successful participation. Any activity that requires cooperation between two or more children can be used. For example, movement exploration activities can set the stage for social interaction by initially allowing children to perform in their own space and then gradually including others to complete a task. Likewise, parachute activities can be implemented to encourage movement initially at the child's pace and then be performed with others by having the children raise the parachute together or change places with other children. Play and recess activities also provide children the opportunity to participate alone or in small groups or games.

Many times, an unskilled child will shy away from activities until he or she can have some success. Fitness or movement activities can be provided initially until the child develops the necessary skill and confidence for group games. Other children respond to visual or tactile stimuli that aid in maintaining control. For the teacher, the key is to find the specific methods that open communication and responses within the child.

Anxiety and Frustration Reactions

Sometimes children are anxious about school or physical education activities and exhibit excessive fears about the nature of the activity. These fears may be unfounded but are real for the child. A fear of water is very real and frightening until the child can have some positive experiences. Ideally, teachers can control their environments and eliminate any problems that can cause anxiety or frustration.

Activities that involve a minimal amount of competition and provide immediate success can be initially performed. For example, children who are anxious about swimming can gradually be encouraged into the pool by using a series of steps, starting with feet in the water, to being supported by teachers, and then to entering the pool by themselves. Likewise, children afraid of hard objects can participate successfully with soft Nerf balls and playground balls before proceeding to larger and harder balls. In addition, teachers can select activities at the appropriate social-sequence level of functioning (such as throwing the ball against a wall before throwing to a partner) to gradually involve participation and help overcome anxiety or fear of the activity.

If children do not have pleasant experiences in school, they may feel rejected or become frustrated, Likewise, if they have difficulty accomplishing a task they may become anxious or frustrated, especially if other children are successful. Children may also react suddenly to loud noises or sounds that are seemingly benign to others. Positive communication and interaction with children and eliminating the sounds can alleviate their concerns. In addition, we should provide opportunities for children to achieve successes, and we should reinforce their efforts, especially because physical activity can positively influence mood (Driver & Alison, 2009).

Difficulty Controlling Behavior

Because aggressive behaviors may be harmful to other children, teachers should try to eliminate or weaken such behaviors as soon as possible. Punishment, contracting, and the Premack principle are behavior strategies that may eliminate inappropriate aggressive behavior. Teachers can also structure the environment to reduce stimuli or remove extraneous elements that may promote hostile behavior.

Consistent aggression may be an ongoing problem that requires communication, modeling, and contracting, whereas transient behavior problems can be overcome by structuring the environment, improving communication, and applying such techniques as modeling, contracting, punishment, prompting, and group consequences. Often, vigorous activities such as running or stationary cycling may be used at the beginning of class. In some instances, children can control their aggressiveness with physical activity. It should be noted that impaired safety and judgment are deficient and may result in making inappropriate decisions regarding their safety and participation.

Vigorous physical fitness, locomotor, and dance activities may be provided while the teacher or parents serve as active role models. In addition, other activities can be selected that emphasize control and incorporate relaxation training or visualization techniques. Relaxation activities are especially beneficial in helping the child regain and practice self-control. They also are helpful for hyperactivity and attentional disorders.

Seizure (Epilepsy) and Convulsive Disorders

A seizure or convulsive disorder is a neurological condition initiated by abnormal discharges in the brain (NIH, 2004). There are no specific causes for seizures; seizures are symptoms of a period when consciousness is impaired, which may or may not be accompanied by convulsive movements. Recently, terminology concerning epilepsy, which comes from the Greek word for *seizure*, has expanded to include convulsive and/or seizure disorders. Seizures may be misunderstood by educators and/or other children, causing a social stigma, depression, or a connotation of disease (de Souza & Salgado, 2006).

Approximately 30 percent of convulsive disorders occur in the period from birth to 5 years from problems in pregnancy, birth disorders, trauma, infections, and/or fevers, with the highest number of incidences occuring in children under 2 years of age (Epilepsy Foundation of America, 2009). In the early school years, 34 percent of these disorders are triggered by accidents and illness. Adolescent patterns include 13% of all cases and are due to severe illness, brain tumors, and head trauma, and 23 percent of the cases occur in adult years from brain injuries, brain tumors, and cardiovascular disease.

Heredity is usually not a direct cause of seizure disorders, although brain-wave patterns associated with seizures appear to run in families, and in males more than females. Also, there is a tendency for seizures to accompany other disorders that affect the neurological system, such as cerebral palsy, spina bifida, intellectual disabilities, head injuries, and learning disorders.

CASE STUDY

Billy is a 12 year old soccer player who has had seizures for several years. He wants desperately to play for his middle school team, but the coach is hesitant to let Billy participate.

Billy's parents and physician have indicated that his seizures are controlled by his medication, and that he has been seizure-free for two years. Billy has discussed his condition with his coach and the other players, in order for them to become more knowledgeable regarding seizures and his specific medications. His physician is an advocate of physical activity and supportive of Billy's participation in a supervised activity. The physician believes organized sport will be good for Billy's overall development: physical, social, and emotional. Reluctantly, the coach agrees to Billy's participation and contacts the local epilepsy foundation to become more familiar with epilepsy in general, and epilepsy-related safety concerns, including recommended first aid procedures.

Susceptibility

Several factors may cause a seizure or contribute to lowering the child's seizure threshold. For children who are susceptible to seizures, this necessitates an awareness of the potential factors that may trigger a seizure. Some of these triggers include:

- Chronic and recurrent head trauma
- Stressful conditions, including anger and fear
- Hyperventilation
- Alcoholic beverages
- Changes in the alkalinity of the blood, with low levels increasing susceptibility to seizures
- The menstrual period
- Changes in hormone levels
- Fatigue

Types of Seizures

There are several types of seizures that teachers should be able to recognize that are generalized or partial and further subdivided into more specific categories. Although these classifications are widely accepted, classification is extremely difficult considering the diversity of opinion and classifications worldwide. As our knowledge about seizures expands, future classifications may be based more on specific biochemical defects, lack of neurotransmitters, or genetic base rather than on clinical observation and electrographic presentations. Included in **Table 15.4** are characteristics of the more prevalent types of seizures and appropriate first-aid measures to be implemented by teachers (Epilepsy Foundation of America, 2009b; Freeman, Vinning & Pillas, 2002; Lesser, 1991).

Partial Seizures (Focal, Local)

There are several types of partial seizures. In one type of simple partial seizure, consciousness is not impaired; this type of seizure is also known as a sensory or motor seizure. The person may have a blank facial expression and experience psychic signs, such as the sensation of a smell or taste or unexplained emotions.

In another type of partial seizure, consciousness is not impaired but may be characterized by a jerking or twitching of the fingers or toes. This activity sometimes spreads throughout the body and becomes a convulsive seizure but sometimes remains localized to a certain part of the body. The person is awake and aware of his or her environment throughout the course of this type of seizure.

A complex partial seizure is the most common type of event and was formerly known as a temporal lobe or psychomotor seizure. This type of seizure involves an impairment of consciousness. The onset of this event is often preceded by an aura, and the abnormal activity is localized to a part of the brain. This type of seizure is characterized by loss of awareness of the environment and is very often associated with a blank facial expression and, possibly, semipurposeful movements. Seizures usually last from 1–5 minutes, and the person is often confused for a short period of time afterwards. Another type of partial seizure evolves to a secondary generalized seizure.

Generalized Seizures

Generalized seizures can be either convulsive or nonconvulsive. The type most people associate with epilepsy is the tonic-clonic seizure, formerly known as grand mal seizure. It involves the entire brain and is characterized by a sudden fall and rigid posture (tonic phase), which lasts approximately 10–20 seconds. This phase is followed by a rhythmic jerking of the limbs (clonic phase), or convulsing, and is often accompanied by frothy saliva on the lips and possible incontinence. Breathing is irregular during the seizure, and autonomic dysfunction is often prominent, resulting in cyanosis of the lips and fingers. The pH balance can be as low as 6.8, with a mixed metabolic and respiratory acidosis. The individual has no memory of the seizure itself. Afterwards the person is usually tired, may have a headache, and is confused (Gates & Spiegel, 1993). This type of seizure usually lasts about 2 minutes, although the person may still be unconscious after cessation of seizure activity.

Absence seizures, formerly known as petit mal seizures, are generally considered to be the second most common type of seizure. This type usually occurs during childhood and is "outgrown" by adulthood. Absences are characterized by a sudden interruption of activities accompanied by a blank stare and/or slurring of speech and, sometimes, eyelid flutter. Usually very brief, this type lasts an average of 3–10 seconds. The individual may not realize he or she has had a seizure or may be confused because of a perceived time lapse.

Atonic seizures, also called drop attacks, are another condition that is common during childhood, usually in children 2–5 years of age. The legs of these children suddenly collapse, causing them to fall to their knees, and recovery usually occurs after 10–60 seconds. Myoclonic seizures consist of sudden, powerful muscle jerks. They may occur in the whole body or only in certain body parts and are sometimes accompanied by a loss of consciousness.

Finally, infantile spasms, which can be caused by high fevers, usually begin between 3 months and 2 years of age. This type of activity is characterized by clusters of quick, sudden movements. The head falls forward, and the arms will flex forward if sitting. Legs will be drawn up if the child is lying down. Because

Table 15.4 First Aid for Seizure Disorders

Seizure Type	Characteristics	First Aid
Partial seizures		
A, Simple partial (consciousness not impaired)	Jerking begins in fingers or toes, and cannot be stopped by patient, but patient stays awake and aware. Jerking may proceed to involve hand, then arm, and sometimes spreads to whole body and becomes a convulsive seizure. Preoccupied or blank expression. Child experiences a distorted environment. May see or hear things that are not there, may feel unexplained fear, sadness, anger, or joy. May have nausea, experience odd smells, and have a generally "funny" feeling in the stomach.	Provide reassurance and emotional support; provide first aid if seizure becomes convulsive.
B, Complex partial (impaired consciousness)	Usually starts with blank stare, followed by chewing, followed by random activity. Children appear unaware of surroundings, may seem dazed and mumble. Unresponsive. Actions are clumsy and not directed. May pick at clothing, pick up objects, try to take clothes off. May run and appear afraid. May struggle or flail at restraint. Once pattern is established, some set of actions usually occurs with each seizure. Lasts a few minutes, but postseizure confusion can last substantially longer. No memory of what happened during seizure period	Speak calmly, and provide reassurance to child and others. Guide child gently away from obvious hazards, and stay with child until he or she is completely aware of environment. Provide assistance in getting home.
C, Partial seizures evolving to secondary generalized seizures *Generalized seizures* (convulsive or nonconvulsive); absence seizures	A blank stare lasting only a few seconds; most common in young children. May be accompanied by rapid blinking or chewing movements of the mouth. Children may be unaware of what's going on during the seizure but quickly return to full awareness once it has stopped. May result in learning difficulties if not recognized and treated.	Medical evaluation is recommended; first aid is not generally needed.
Primary generalized seizures	Sudden cry, fall, and rigidity, followed by muscle jerks, frothy saliva on lips, shallow breathing or temporarily suspended breathing, bluish skin, possible loss of bladder or bowel control. Usually lasts 2 to 5 minutes, followed by normal breathing. There may be fatigue, followed by a return to full consciousness. Often preceded by warning signal (aura) and characterized by tensing or static contraction (tonic phase) followed by spasmodic jerking (clonic phase).	Look for medical identification. Protect from nearby hazards. Loosen ties or shirt collars. Place folded jacket under head. Turn on side to keep airway clear. Reassure when consciousness returns. If seizure lasts more than 10 minutes or multiple seizures occur, obtain emergency medical care.
Atonic seizures (also called drop attacks)	The legs of children between 2 to 5 years of age suddenly collapse. After 10 seconds to 1 minute, child can recover, regain consciousness, and stand and walk again.	No first aid is generally needed.
Myoclonic seizures	Sudden, brief, massive muscle jerks that may involve the whole body or parts of the body. May cause children to spill what they are holding or fall off a chair.	A thorough medical evaluation should be performed; first aid is not generally needed.
Infantile spasms	Starts between 3 months and 2 years. If sitting up, the head will fall forward, and the arms will flex forward. If lying down, the knees will be drawn up, with arms and head flexed forward as if reaching for support.	Medical evaluation is required; first aid not generally required.

variability is so great among children with seizure disorders, parents and teachers should be aware of the following warning signs:

- Periods of blackout or confused memory
- Odd sounds, distorted perceptions, or episodic feelings of fear or apprehension that cannot be explained
- "Fainting spells" with incontinence or followed by excessive fatigue
- Episodes of staring or unexplained periods of unresponsiveness
- Episodes of blinking or chewing at inappropriate times
- Involuntary movements of arms or legs
- Any convulsion, with or without fever

LEARNING ACTIVITY

Describe what you would do if someone had a seizure in your presence. What should you not do?

Etiology

Epilepsy has a variable etiology, with concrete evidence to support some causes and mere speculation to sustain others; however, many seizures stem from still unknown causes. The relationship between epilepsy and previously sustained cranial trauma is extremely strong. This damage can occur in many different ways, including from external sources, such as hypoxia or hemorrhage at birth, or as a result of direct trauma to the brain. It can also arise from internal sources, such as infections, abscesses, strokes, toxic/metabolic entities, neoplasms, degenerative disorders, and developmental abnormalities.

There is much speculation throughout the medical and scientific communities around the possibility that a genetic factor could play a role in the development of epilepsy. This view stems from the discovery that there is sometimes a relatively high frequency of some specific types of epilepsy in one family and that the parents of a child with epilepsy often display abnormal electroencephalogram (EEG) readings. Nonetheless, a large portion of patients with epilepsy cannot attribute their condition to any identifiable cause.

Planning the Physical Activity Program

To develop an appropriate program for children with seizure disorders, teachers need a thorough understanding of medical considerations. Teachers can then develop the program based on relevant knowledge concerning fatigue, medication, diet, and physical activity in conjunction with the input from the educational programming team and can provide opportunities for social and physical development.

Fatigue

Fatigue is commonly identified as a trigger for seizures. However, most seizures seem to occur during rest periods or during sleep, not during periods of fatigue. Livingston (1971) indicated that more seizures occur while the individual is resting or idling and that physical and mental activity appear to inhibit seizures. Another misconception is that children with seizures require more sleep or rest than do their peers. But frequent rest periods are not needed beyond normal levels, and children should be encouraged to participate in the same manner as their peers. A regular sleep pattern is more advantageous than, for example, getting 6 hours one day and 12 the next.

The activity in physical education classes is seldom intense enough or of long enough duration to precipitate seizures. However, in cases where activities or the environment requires maximum physical exertion, periodic rest periods, based on the child's tolerance for activity, might be in order. As children adapt to these activity demands and increase their level of physical conditioning, fatigue can be delayed.

Medication

Anticonvulsant medication is effective in the treatment of 90% of all children with seizures. Children may receive medication throughout their lives or have their dosage reduced if seizures are controlled for 3 to 5 years (Bennett, 1995; Freeman et al., 2002; Chase, 1974). The common medications are anticonvulsants that counteract or stop the spread of abnormal electrical discharges in the brain. They are prescribed by the physician. Initially there may be a trial-and-error period in determining the type and dosage of medication required. At this time, teachers should be aware of conditions that should be avoided and provide feedback to physicians concerning the consequences of medication. Medication should be administered three to four times daily in individual doses. Most seizures occur only when the prescribed medication is not taken or the therapeutic range is not maintained.

It is also important for teachers to be informed of changes in dosage or type of medication to eliminate situations where the common side effects of medication could negatively influence performance. For example, children may not be able to participate in some gymnastic or bicycling activities if prescribed medications make them susceptible to dizziness and thus to injury. Several common medications used in the treatment of seizure disorders are included in **Table 15.5**, along with indications of specific seizures and common side effects (Bennett, 1995; Chusid,

Table 15.5 Common Medications Used in Seizure Disorders

Drug	Indications	Common Side Effects
Phenytoin (Dilantin)	Partial, tonic-clonic seizures	Fatigue, stomach upset, ataxia, drowsiness, nystagmus
Carbamazepine (Tegretol)	Partial, tonic-clonic seizures	Blurred vision, ataxia, low blood count
Phenobarbital (Luminal)	Partial, tonic-clonic seizures	Fatigue, skin rash, hyperactivity
Primidone (Mysoline)	Partial, tonic-clonic seizures	Drowsiness, hyperactivity, ataxia
Clorazepate (Tranxene)	Partial, absence, tonic-clonic	Ataxia, fatigue, nausea
Ethosuximide (Zarontin)	Absence seizures	Drowsiness, nausea, headache
Clonazepam (Klonopin)	Absence, myoclonic and akinetic seizures	Drowsiness, ataxia, drooling
Valproic acid (Depakene)	Partial, absence, and tonic-clonic seizures	Drowsiness, ataxia
Keppra (levetiracetain)	Partial onset seizures, myoclonic seizures for children over 12, primary generalized tonic-clonic seizures in children over 6	Dizziness, fatigue, insomnia, irritability
Lamictal (lamotrigine)	Controls many types of seizures and used as an add-on for partial seizures	Rash, dizziness, mild cognition and memory problems
Topamax (topiramate)	Total spectrum of seizures	Thinking, memory problems

1979; Jan, Ziegler & Erba, 1983; Freeman et al., 2002; Tettenborn & Kramer, 1992).

Diet

The physical health of children is directly related to their emotional health. Three nutritionally well-balanced meals should be consumed daily, especially when medication is administered three or four times daily. Fruit or other nutrious snacks can be used to enhance the student's energy level, although evenly spaced and well-balanced meals are the most important aspects of the diet. The diet becomes more important for children who are prone to seizures during periods of growth, when additional nutrients are needed, and during the teenage years, when children tend to skip meals or consume junk food.

A diet with high alkalinity or acidity may help to inhibits susceptibility to seizures. Acid-producing diets (ketogenic diets) with a high fat content, such as cream, butter, eggs, and meats, usually produce a quieting effect on electrical discharges and may be helpful in preventing seizures (Villeneuve et al., 2009; Epilepsy Foundation of America, 2009).

Physical Activity

In addition to rest and proper diet, regular physical activity should be encouraged. Most children with seizure disorders can participate in physical education and sports.

For those children whose seizures prevent regular participation, an exercise program designed within their abilities, such as walking or stationary cycling, should be encouraged until seizures are controlled. If children are multiply involved, regular activity is also important, especially manipulation of the limbs to prevent contractures and to increase functional capacity (Bauer, 1977).

Hyperventilation is generally thought to lower the threshold for seizures, and intense exertion usually is accompanied by hyperventilation. However, physical activity may have a suppressive effect on electrical wave abnormalities and seizures that may be induced by hyperventilation (Bar-Or & Rowland, 2004). Activities that improve physical conditioning are important for all children with a history of seizures because of the possibility of reducing the number of seizures (Gates & Spiegel, 1993).

Currently, it is still not apparent why physical activity raises the seizure threshold. Emotional stress, hyperventilation, and an increase in body temperature are the results of activity, yet activity still seems to inhibit seizures. Possible speculations concerning why physical activity can reduce seizures include the metabolic acidosis of exercise, which counteracts the alkalotic effect of hyperventilation, or the release of catecholamines during activity, which may elevate the seizure threshold (Korczyn, 1979).

Social Acceptance

A primary concern for teachers is to help children with seizures achieve a normal status within the school setting. The social consequences are sometimes more damaging to children than the apparent physical problems. To dispel myths, pity, and negative reactions, teachers must inform others that seizures are not a disease or contagious and strive to eliminate any misconceptions about this disorder. When others are aware of seizures and their frequency, they will understand the condition and be able to provide first aid when required. Sometimes the attitude of the teacher toward the child who is subject to seizures is important to successful participation. Usually open discussions of the conditions will resolve any misunderstanding and dispel myths concerning seizures.

Additionally, a common problem is that most children feel embarrassed after a seizure. Because they may lose consciousness and not recall the incident, the stares of their peers lead to uneasiness; they may also experience anxiety and depression (de Souza & Salgado, 2006). Parents and educators should also be supportive and understanding to remove the social stigma and help foster an appreciation of the medical nature of the disorder. Only through opportunities to participate and display their talents can children with seizures be supported and reinforced.

Implementing the Physical Activity Program

Developmental Physical Skills

Many children with seizure disorders can be delayed in academic progress. Moreover, other effects, such as deficits in memory, attention, and spatial abilities, may hinder the child's ability to perform physical activity. Although there are no direct effects on muscle function or cardiovascular development directly related to seizure disorders themselves, other than a sedentary lifestyle, seizure activity can impair gross motor control. Teachers should emphasize developing the large muscle groups and functional movement patterns as well as increasing muscular strength and endurance (Sillanpaa, 1995; Epilepsy Foundation of America, 2009).

In early adolescence, seizure disorders may also impair a child's sense of self-esteem and physical competence. The combination of puberty and the unpredictable nature of seizures can made adolescence a very awkward and unstable time for these children. Development of physical skills and the body's hormonal adjustments at this time can be further impaired by a lack of activity due to parental overprotection (Shinnar, Amir, & Branski, 1995).

Cognition and Motivation

The relationship between epilepsy and decreased cognitive function has been observed for years. The nature and the extent of the decline in cognition, however, have not been precisely classified. It is often unclear whether the decline is due directly to the epileptic condition or to the medication used in its treatment (Shinnar et al., 1995). It is also important to consider any behavior problems that may hinder a child's motivation or ability to function in group activities. Participation in physical activities and sports may foster the development of self-esteem and reduce any emotional problems that result from feelings of being different (Shinnar et al., 1995).

Community and Activities of Daily Living

Seizure disorders may disrupt daily living to the extent that some children may have difficulty in educational or work settings. In some cases, the disruption of the seizures themselves interferes with productivity or attending to school-related activities. Medication may also interfere with the child's ability to concentrate on physical functioning. Children may also feel self-conscious if others are present during a seizure. Any method that aids in reducing seizures or boosting self-esteem will improve the quality of life for these children. Physical and recreational activity should be emphasized to promote social interactions as well as to reduce seizure frequency and promote a healthy lifestyle.

Exercise and Activity

Activity should be encouraged for children with seizure disorders, especially during the early school years, by implementing programs similar to those of their peer groups. A statement from the United States Department of Health, Education, and Welfare's Commission for the Control of Epilepsy indicates that activity is important for children with seizures because evidence suggests that activity may reduce the likelihood of seizures (Bennett, 1995; Van Linschotten, Backx, Mulder & Meinardi, 1990; Epilepsy Foundation of America, 2009c).

It has been suggested that exercise programs progressively build stamina and help prevent children from reverting to a sedentary lifestyle. It is most important to promote endurance rather than necessarily strength or power. The primary goal is for the child to engage in physical activity, not only to reduce seizures but also to promote general health (Bar-Or & Rowland, 2004; Bennett, 1995).

When preparing an activity program, the teacher must notify health care providers (such as physicians and school nurses) of the child's condition. The child must agree to report any seizure immediately.

A few suggested cautions to keep in mind include the safety of the environment. As previously stated, activities such as swimming and high-altitude sports are generally avoided because of the possible danger if a seizure were to occur. For the same reason, playing surfaces and equipment must be considered. An especially hard surface, such as concrete, could become a hazard if the child were to fall into a seizure. Wrestling or tumbling rooms are often utilized for early activity, especially in young children with uncontrolled seizure frequency. Although these special safety considerations must be made, the exercise program for the child with a seizure disorder should not differ than those of other children. A gradual progression to increase any noted weaknesses or to improve general fitness levels should be employed. This will entail a combination of strength and cardiovascular workouts, as well as sports and skill development to improve function and social interaction.

Children with seizures may be comparable to their peer group in physical and motor performance. Bar-Or (1983) related the example of a 13-year-old girl with psychomotor seizures who participated in long-distance running to overcome her disability and completed several ultramarathons. Other seizure-disordered athletes have demonstrated similar performance in physical functioning. The extent to which children participate depends on the control of seizures, their ambitions, and how well they comply with a particular training regimen.

Enforced inactivity due to overprotection is often more detrimental than the risk of a seizure during activity. Livingston (1971) indicated that 15,000 individuals over a 34-year period of clinical supervision did not demonstrate a single case of seizures from athletics-related head trauma. The American Medical Association (1974) does not currently exclude children with seizures from participation in contact sports.

Most children can participate in activities such as cycling, horseback riding, climbing, skin diving, swimming, or sports that involve throwing or shooting if proper safety precautions are taken to reduce accidents. Children whose seizures are not controlled by medication or who manifest consistent seizures should be temporarily removed from those sports until their condition is controlled. Swimming and water activities should be supervised closely because of the potential danger inherent in the water environment. Laidlaw and Richens (1976) reported that seizures will seldom occur while swimming, but if a seizure does occur, the child should be supported by the pool deck. Other precautions in swimming activities may include the wearing of a brightly colored cap or use of a buddy system to aid in identification.

Children whose seizures are not under control may manifest a low level of physical and motor functioning if they are excluded from all physical activity. Participation of these children may be limited but still should be encouraged after consultation with the physician. Their cardiovascular efficiency can be improved through a gradual and progressive program to postpone fatigue and possibly elevate the seizure threshold, while other motor skills may be achieved through a developmental physical education program. To select appropriate physical education activities for these children, teachers should employ the following guidelines (Bar-Or & Rowland, 2004; Bower, 1969).

1. Encourage children to participate fully if their condition is under medical control.

2. Strenuous activity (e.g., long-distance running or a prolonged tennis match) is not contraindicated even if it causes marked fatigue.

3. Always supervise activities such as horseback riding, mountain climbing, swimming, or diving.

4. Limit bicycle riding if seizures are not well controlled by medication.

5. Collision sports (football, ice hockey, lacrosse, rugby) and contact sports (baseball, basketball, soccer, wrestling) can be practiced by medically controlled children. As in any athletic event, participants should be coached in the prevention of trauma.

6. Boxing, because of repeated impact on the head, is contraindicated.

7. For unexplained reasons, some activities may trigger seizures. When they are identified, they should be avoided.

8. Activities that provide hazards to peers or spectators are not allowed for uncontrolled children.

9. Individualized participation should be determined with the cooperation of the collaborative team, parent, and child.

Spina Bifida

Spina bifida is a condition that refers to a developmental defect of the spinal column in which the arches of one or more of the spinal vertebrae fail to fuse. The disorder occurs in 3 per 1,000 live births. Normal development of the central nervous system (CNS) in the fetus begins when a single sheet of cells (that is, the neural plate), enlarges and forms a symmetrical longitudinal groove. This groove deepens, and the sides fuse to form a hollow cylinder that eventually differentiates into the brain and spinal cord. During development, supportive and protective tissues, such as the meninges, will line the cord and finally be covered by the bony structure of the vertebral column.

In spina bifida or any neural tube defect, part of the nerve cord may fail to close or fuse. The nerve cord at that point remains immature and improperly formed. If the nerve cord fails to form properly, then the supporting tissues and structures, including the vertebral column and/or cranium, will be abnormal. In very severe conditions, portions of the brain may not develop.

Interference with the normal growth and development of the neural tube and closure during the early weeks of pregnancy is complex and probably is caused by genetic and environmental factors. However, the exact nature of the neural tube disorder depends on the part of the tube that fails to develop and the extent of normal growth achieved. If there is a failure of closure in the midline or lower end of the neural tube, the result is spina bifida; failure of the upper end or head of the tube results in cranium bifidum or anencephaly (Tarby, 1991; National Institute of Health, 2007).

Clinically, most dysfunctions in development are due to an abnormal closure of the neural groove. If the neural groove does not close properly at the cranial end, the whole forebrain, skull, and scalp will be missing. The child is stillborn, or death usually occurs within hours. This condition is termed *anencephaly* ("no brain").

A corresponding condition at the caudal end of the CNS (i.e., in the spinal cord) is spina bifida and usually occurs a the L_2–L_4 region of the spinal cord. There are three major types of spina bifida: (1) occulta (in which the abnormality is confined to the vertebrae only and is due to an unclosed posterior vertebral arch) and two types of spina bifida cystica, (2) meningocele (where the meninges protrude through the defect), and (3) myelomeningocele (where elements of the cord also protrude through the defect, resulting in severe neural deficits) (**Figure 15.5**). Myelomeningocele is often associated with the condition hydrocephalus, which results in severe mental retardation.

In spina bifida occulta, the malformation or lack of fusion usually is located in the lower spine of the vertebral arches. There is no distension or protrusion of the meninges, and the spinal cord and membranes are generally normal, with no accompanying loss of motor functioning. The site of the vertebral defect may be marked by slight swelling, dimple in the skin, or tuft of hair; or there may be no external evidence at all (Williamson, 1987).

In spina bifida cystica, some portion of the spinal cord or nerve roots are herniated through the vertebral arches into a sac-like cyst filled with cerebrospinal fluid (CSF). Of the two types of spina bifida cystica, meningocele is less debilitating and commonly affects 15–25% of all children with spina bifida cystica. In meningocele, the meninges protrude through the gap in the vertebral column to form a sac that is generally covered by the skin. Because the sac usually contains only the meninges and cerebrospinal fluid, the cord functions normally, and there is no significant loss of function. In many cases, surgery may remove the hernial protrusions.

In contrast, the other type of spina bifida cystica, myelomeningocele, results from the failure of the vertebral column to fuse. Distension of the meninges is accompanied by protrusion of the spinal cord into the sac. This results in permanent and irreversible neurological disability. Loss of function may not be confined to the lesion level and may affect normal functioning below the lesion and frequently several spinal segments above the lesion, with the possibility of autonomic abnormalities occurring at any point in the spine (Tarby, 1991). Many infants born with myelomeningocele have associated developmental abnormalities in the brain. The base of the brain (medulla) containing many of the cranial nerves and located within the skull may be present in the cervical vertebrae (in the neck region). This is commonly referred to as Arnold-Chiari malformation and affects up to 90% of children with myelomeningocele. It may obstruct the circulation of the CSF causing an accumulation of water in the cranial area (hydrocephalus).

Each child presents a unique set of clinical characteristics, with primary and secondary disabilities including the following:

Primary Disabilities	Secondary Complications
muscle paralysis	low self concept
skeletal deformities	low fitness
loss of sensation	obesity
hydrocephalus	poor functional strength
urinary and bowel incontinence	pressure sores
	respiratory difficulties
	learning and perceptual difficulties
	motor functioning
	seizures
	depression and axinety

CASE STUDY

Michael, a 12 year old with myleomeningocele, has just entered middle school. He uses a wheelchair for mobility; however, he still has some ability to ambulate with crutches and ankle braces. Frank, his physical education teacher, has worked with Michael to develop upper body strength, using hand weights. Also, Frank engages Michael in exercises designed to help him support his upper body, for example, seated pushups. Frank also works on maintaining Michael's upper body flexibility to facilitate his transfers and wheelchair maneuvering.

Michael's parents are concerned that he is putting on weight and want to be sure he maintains upper body function to facilitate his future vocational interest in computers. With the parents' concern in mind, Frank has developed a home exercise program for Michael to perform daily. To address his weight gain, he has encouraged Michael to participate in a community-based swim program, one that can provide him a social outlet and help maintain desired upper body function.

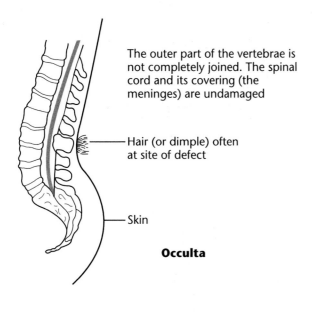

The outer part of the vertebrae is not completely joined. The spinal cord and its covering (the meninges) are undamaged

— Hair (or dimple) often at site of defect

— Skin

Occulta

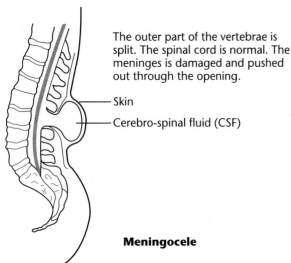

The outer part of the vertebrae is split. The spinal cord is normal. The meninges is damaged and pushed out through the opening.

— Skin
— Cerebro-spinal fluid (CSF)

Meningocele

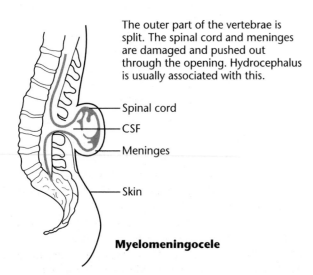

The outer part of the vertebrae is split. The spinal cord and meninges are damaged and pushed out through the opening. Hydrocephalus is usually associated with this.

— Spinal cord
— CSF
— Meninges

— Skin

Myelomeningocele

Figure 15.5 Abnormal development associated with spina bifida.

Planning the Physical Activity Program

Although multiple systems of the body may be involved in spina bifida, the leg muscles are most affected. The degree of muscular development and additional complications depend on the location of the lesion and the extent of the damage to the spinal cord.

Generally, individuals with spina bifida have bowel and bladder problems (incontinence), affected by the sacral nerves and level of the lesion. Difficulties with sensations result from dysfunction of the spinal cord. Paralysis in spina bifida occurs because of the lack of nerve innervation from the spinal cord to the working muscles (Tarby, 1991). However, some variation in functioning below the lesion is apparent. Spasticity and/or reflexive movement may be seen if the cord is not completely transected.

Hydrocephalus

Hydrocephalus refers to the buildup of CNS fluid inside the brain that occurs when normal circulation is obstructed because the open spine permits the lower portion of the brain to slip through the opening of the spinal cord (Spina Bifida Association, 2009). Hydrocephalus occurs when there is an imbalance between the amount of CSF produced and the rate at which it is absorbed. If hydrocephalus is unrestricted, the nerve cells are damaged as the skull stretches to accommodate the fluid buildup. The condition is characterized by an oversized head. As the child grows and the skull bones become set, the fluid pressure buildup may damage the developing brain unless the pressure is released. A balance between the amount of fluid formed and the amount absorbed decreases the abnormal rate of skull growth and is referred to as arrested hydrocephalus. There are no adverse effects of arrested hydrocephalus.

Unarrested or severe hydrocephalus may damage the cognitive areas of the brain as well as the motor areas that control movement of the limbs. The condition may predispose the child to ambulation with a wheelchair. Eyesight will deteriorate, and control of the respiratory and cardiac centers may also be adversely affected, resulting in complications in cardiorespiratory functioning. Severe cases are treated with the use of a shunt to channel excess CNS fluid from the cerebral cavity into either the heart or the abdomen, where it is absorbed by the body. The shunt is a flexible tube that is placed in the ventricular system of the brain to drain the excess flow of CSF (**Figure 15.6**).

Motor Function

The loss of motor function depends on the location, extent, and severity of the lesion (**Table 15.6**). Cervical lesions usually do not involve the spinal cord and

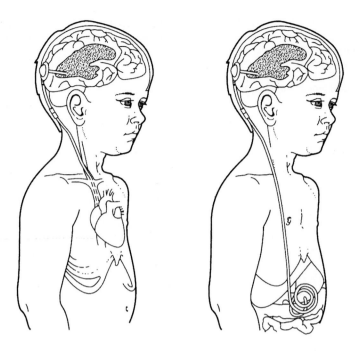

Figure 15.6 Ventriculoatrial shunt (left) and ventriculoperitoneal shunt (right).

rarely result in a loss of functional ability, whereas sacral lesions may result in a slight dysfunction.

Most individuals with myelomeningocele are affected at the lumbar and sacral regions because this is the last section of the neural tube to close. Approximately 30–50% of individuals with myelomeningocele are totally "flaccid" paraplegics, whereas most others have significant secondary problems that impair locomotion, including scoliosis, kyphosis, rib cage abnormalities, dislocation of the hips, and ankle or knee deformities (Tarby, 1991). An affected limb may be held in an abnormal position (i.e., contraction) because the antagonistic muscle pair is affected, resulting in flexion or contraction without reciprocal innervation of the corresponding muscle group. Additionally the hips may dislocate, and knees or ankle may become rigid, requiring bracing or additional support for ambulation. Ambulation is specially related to hip function and especially effected by range of motion, active muscle contraction across the hip joint, alignment and the effects of scoliosis/kyphosis, and the force needed to move forward (Spina Bifida Association, 2009). If these components are not functional, inefficient or cessation of ambulation will occur.

Intellectual Development

Children with spina bifida generally function within a range of normal intelligence, although this is not necessarily a fixed trait. These individuals are very verbal, which may give an initial impression of normal intelligence. Children with meningocele are likely to fall in the normal range of intelligence, whereas those with myelomeningocele demonstrate "low average" to reduced intellectual functioning (Dallyn & Garrison-Jones, 1991; Spina Bifida Association, 2009). Development depends largely on environmental factors and setbacks that may disrupt functioning, such as lengthy hospital stays, dependence, and poor self-esteem. The Spina Bifida Association (2009) advocates appropriate testing to determine the level of functioning and needs of the child. Variations may occur because of health problems, and learning difficulties are greater with more spinal cord damage and severe hydrocephalus (SBA, 2009). In addition, Gras, Berna, and Lopez (2009) indicate that thinking styles and coping strategies are needed for children with severe involvements in the intervention process. Additionally, sensory and perceptual defects from damage to the areas of the brain involved in perception may also induce learning disorders in children (McLane, 1994).

Incontinence

Incontinence is another problem for children with spina bifida. Incontinence is the inability to control the function of the bladder and/or bowels. Ninety-five percent of children with myelomeningocele do not have functioning nerves between the bladder and bowels and brain and are unable to perceive a distended bladder or to control bowel function. Those without control of the bladder have either a hypo or hyperactive bladder that causes difficulty in voiding.

Table 15.6 Motor Dysfunction and Suggested Physical Education Activities

Functional Levels	Physical and Motor Dysfunction	Impairment in Motor Function	Physical Education Activities
Thoracic (T_{12})	Lower limb paralysis; scoliosis; contractures	Standing brace and wheel-chair required for ambulation	Develop body awareness and upper limb function in young children; emphasize strengthening postural muscles for stability and transfers; encourage range-of-motion exercises; strength and aquatics to encourage movement and develop independent functions.
High lumbar (L_1–L_3)	Hip flexion and adduction; knee extension; scoliosis; hip dislocation	Crutches; long braces with hip support required for home community ambulation	
Low lumbar (L_4–S_1)	Knee flexors; ankle extensors; hip flexion and hamstring tightness; foot deformity	Short braces and crutches for home and community ambulation	
Sacral level (S_1–S_3)	Ankle flexors; inner and outer peroneal foot muscles; foot deformity	Supports in shoes for home and community ambulation	

For those with incontinence, catherization is performed, in which a tube is inserted into the bladder in order to drain the urine (Spina Bifida Association of America, 2009). Clean intermittent catheterization is necessary to avoid infections. For children with incontinence, a regular checkup by the physician is required to assess kidney function because the urine can back up into the kidneys and cause damage or infection. In addition, a carefully regulated diet is also necessary to aid in controlling bowel movements as well as obesity.

Implementing the Physical Activity Program

Motor Interventions

For young children, teachers should provide stimulation in the visual field and opportunities to fixate on and track objects and to manipulate objects. Eye-hand coordination can be improved by using toys of varying sizes and shapes so that they can be easily grasped and incorporated into activities that encourage movement. Teachers can promote tactile stimulation and eventually hand function by providing objects for the child to squeeze, grasp, wave, drop, and move. Teachers should also incorporate developmental tasks that stimulate upper and lower body movement.

Body awareness activities should include identifying body parts and encouraging movement within self-space of the environment. Group play activities should be encouraged to maximize movement

experiences as well as to stimulate social interaction and behavioral skills. Group play should be conducted in order to introduce activities that can also be used in home-based and community recreation activities.

Movement in the lower limbs should be encouraged to facilitate functional movement and to prevent contractures. Children should engage in appropriate developmental tasks that maximize upper body development, such as parachute activities to develop upper body strength, functional movement, and perception. They should also participate in games and dance activities (French & Horvat, 1983). For some children, parachute and other play activities may require some prompting to initiate movements actively.

Exercise Interventions

A child with spina bifida needs a comprehensive program of physical activity to maintain a healthy life. Intervention should occur as early as possible to facilitate functional movement. Early in development, home-based programs should be designed to teach parents how to exercise their baby's feet and legs in order for the child to be able to walk with crutches or leg braces or, for those without lower body functioning, to use a wheelchair for ambulation.

An exercise program for a child with spina bifida should involve a wide range of activities and exercises. (Horvat, 2007; Horvat, Mason, & Nocera, 2006). Flexibility training will help delay contractures that are due to muscle weakness, paralysis, and imbalance and should include stretching the hamstrings, heel cords, lower back, hip flexors, and shoulders.

Aerobic activity should be used to promote a healthy lifestyle and aid in weight management. During aerobic activity, the heart rate should be elevated gradually for 20 to 45 minutes. For children in wheelchairs, exercises such as arm ergometry, rapid wheelchair propulsion, wheelchair aerobics, and sports activities should be introduced to facilitate physical development and social outlets.

While aerobic training increases muscle endurance, resistance exercise increases functional strength. It is very important for children with spina bifida to strengthen all of their working muscles, particularly their triceps and shoulders. These are the major muscles that are used in transfers from wheelchairs and in walking with crutches. O'Connell, Barnhart, and Parks (1992) demonstrated that increased muscular endurance is highly correlated to wheelchair propulsion. Functional strength exercises include the overhead press, wheelchair pushups (grab arm rests and push body out of seat until elbows are straight), shoulder flies, tricep curls, and bicep curls (Lutkenhoff & Oppenheimer, 1997). Resistance training should begin at an appropriate age and concentrate on the muscles of the upper body to promote functional movements such as transfers and self-care activities. In conjunction with developing functional skill, a complete fitness program that includes stretching, aerobic exercise, and muscle strengthening may contribute to decreasing obesity, maintaining stronger bones, and better bowel function (Horvat, 2007; Horvat et al., 2006).

Special attention should be given to providing exercises to develop and maintain functional levels of physical fitness. Activities to strengthen the upper extremities that are used in transfers and propelling a wheelchair should be encouraged, as well as exercises designed to stabilize hip function for ambulation prevent contractures and increase range of motion. For example, the use of surgical hose, pulleys, hand weights, and dumbbells develops upper body strength that can be generalized to propelling a wheelchair (Shepherd, 1990; Horvat et al., 2006). Additional resistance exercises, such as arm cranking, promote aerobic endurance and cardiovascular conditioning that are needed for ambulation in community and vocational environments. Further, aquatic exercises and swimming skills should be emphasized, because buoyancy in the water offsets the child's weakness in lower extremities and can be used to accentuate upper body and cardiovascular development. Each activity, and the extent of the exercise, should be based on the abilities of the child and functional goals that promote self-sufficiency. Home and community programs can provide activities for additional stimulation, opportunities to practice, and social integration (Freed, 1990; Hinderer, Hinderer, & Shurtleff, 1994; Horvat, 2007).

Obesity is common in this population if activity is compromised. If the child continues to be inactive, the resulting weight gain adds an additional complication to an already low level of functional ability (Dixon & Rekate, 1991). Excessive weight gain in infancy may also affect metabolism and the distribution of fat cells (Dixon & Rekate, 1991). For these children, dietary care in conjunction with physical activity that maximizes skills necessary for functioning in the school, home, and community should be emphasized (Cusick, 1991; SBA, 2009).

Exercise interventions and motor programming for a child with spina bifida depend on the child's functional ability and complications associated with the disorder. The teacher should ascertain movement potential to develop a program based on the child's functional ability and programmatic goals that emphasize community and home participation as well as future vocational training goals. The nature of the child's disability should be recognized to ensure safe participation in light of medical contraindications. Because the child may have impaired mobility, teachers should promote strengthening muscle groups to aid in ambulation and self-sufficiency for activities of daily living. Appropriate social interactions should be encouraged to aid in overall development and social integration. Major goals of intervention should include the following:

1. Teaching gross motor and spatial skills to facilitate coordination

2. Developing and maintaining fitness and flexibility (i.e., developing strength in the shoulders, trunk, and arms; also cardiorespiratory endurance) to emphasize self-sufficiency

3. Encouraging movement and fitness to overcome susceptibility to obesity

4. Developing physical skills that generalize to activities of daily living and vocational skills

5. Promoting social development in recreational and group play activities, such as aquatics

6. Providing appropriate social outlets for enjoyment and self-satisfaction on an individual basis as well as with family or peers within the community

7. Develop muscle strength, flexibility, and power in hip to maintain ambulation

Although spina bifida is a birth defect for which there is no known cure, it is very important for teachers and parents to understand the disability and intervene at the earliest time possible to aid in the

LEARNING ACTIVITY

Discuss several techniques that can be used to develop Michael's upper body strength, including the muscles used in wheelchair ambulation and transfers.

child's development and self-esteem. The child will require assistance in learning how to care for himself or herself and become as independent as possible. Although some assistance may be required, most children with spina bifida can be independent and achieve functional skills necessary for a productive life.

CHAPTER SUMMARY

1. Children with neurological disorders are generally integrated into the regular physical education classes. Each disorder has its own unique characteristics that interfere with the learning of physical and motor skills. Because functional capacity varies according to the site and extent of injury to the nervous system, students should be treated individually and actively encouraged to participate.

2. Cerebral palsy can be described as a group of conditions that are manifested during infancy and are characterized by weakness, paralysis, poor muscle tone, and lack of coordination and motor functioning.

3. Cerebral palsy can be classified by degree of motor involvement, limbs involved, and/or motor disability.

4. Children with cerebral palsy have physical and motor limitations that are based on their predominant type of motor disability. Increasing overall physical functioning is the primary thrust in developing the physical education program.

5. The selection of appropriate physical education activities should be based on the obvious motor characteristics of children with cerebral palsy and Traumatic Brain Injury. These children need to develop optimal levels of muscular efficiency and physical fitness.

6. Primary physical concerns in head injuries should emphasize postural deformities that limit functional development and self-sufficiency.

7. Movement and exercise interventions should be designed to improve self-sufficiency.

8. Behavior approaches should be implemented to facilitate appropriate social interactions, compliance, and motivation to complete a task.

9. Primary cognitive deficits may require compensation or feedback strategies to facilitate learning.

10. Reorganization of the neurological system may require building motor schema by prompting and guiding children through a task.

11. Intervention should incorporate a multidimensional team that calls on parents, peers, teachers, and clinicians to promote functional skills that can be used in school, community, and home environments.

12. A seizure or convulsive disorder is a neurological condition initiated by abnormal discharges in the brain.

13. To develop an appropriate program for children with seizure disorders, the teacher needs a thorough understanding of medical considerations. The considerations include fatigue, medication, diet, and physical activity. Opportunities for social and physical development should be provided in the physical education program.

14. In planning the instructional program, the teacher should understand the use of anticonvulsant medications and their common side effects.

15. Physical activity is beneficial in elevating the child's seizure threshold and should be encouraged. For children whose seizures are not controlled, consultation with physicians is required.

16. Spina bifida refers to a developmental defect of the spinal column.

17. Primary disabilities in spina bifida include muscle paralysis, skeletal deformities, loss of sensation, hydrocephalus, and urinary and bowel incontinence.

18. Motor functions depend on the location, extent, and severity of the lesion.

19. Intervention should include providing activities that promote muscle strengthening, flexibility, and aerobic fitness to facilitate a healthy lifestyle.

REFERENCES

American Medical Association, Committee on the Medical Aspects of Sports Epileptics and Contact Sports. (1974). Position statement. *Journal of American Medical Association, 229,* 820–821.

Bar-Or, O. (1983). *Pediatric sports medicine for the practitioner.* New York: Springer-Verlag.

Bar-Or, O., & Rowland, T. (2004). *Pediatric exercise medicine.* Champaign, IL: Human Kinetics.

Bauer, E. W. (1977). *Thoughts on parenting the child with epilepsy.* Landover, MD: Epilepsy Foundation of America.

Bennett, D. R. (1995). Epilepsy. In B. Goldberg (Ed.) *Sports and exercise for children with chronic health conditions* (pp. 89–108). Champaign, IL: Human Kinetics.

Bottos, P., Puato, M. L., Vianello, A., & Facchin, P. (1995). Locomotion patterns in cerebral palsy syndromes. *Developmental Medicine and Child Neurology, 37,* 883–899.

Bower, B. D. (1969). Epilepsy and school athletics. *Developmental Medicine and Child Neurology, 11,* 244–245.

Center for Disease Control. (2006). *Facts about traumatic brain injury,* Atlanta, GA: CDC.

Center for Disease Control and Prevention. (2009). CDC Features, Atlanta: GA: CDC.

Chase, D. (1974). With epilepsy they take the medicine and play. *The Physician and Sports Medicine, 2,* 61.

Chusid, J. G. (1979). *Correlative neuroanatomy and functional neurology* (17th ed.). Lange.

Conklin, H. M., Saloria, C. F., & Slomine, B. S. (2008). Working memory performance following pediatric brain injury. *Brain Injury, 22,* 847–857.

Cope, D. N. (1990). The rehabilitation of traumatic brain injury. In Kottke, F. J., & Lehmann, J. F. (Eds.), *Krusen's handbook of physical medicine and rehabilitation* (4th ed.). (pp. 1217–1215). Philadelphia: Saunders.

Croce, R., & Horvat, M. (1995). Exercise-induced activation and cognitive processing in individuals with mental retardation. In Vermeer, A. (Ed.), *Medicine and sport science: Aspects of growth and development in mental retardation* 144–151. New York: Springer-Verla S.

Croce, R., Horvat, M., & Roswal, G. (1995). Coincident timing by nondisabled, mentally retarded, and traumatic brain-injured individuals under varying target exposure conditions. *Perceptual and Motor Skills, 80,* 487–496.

Cusick, B. (1991). Therapeutic management of sensorimotor and physical disabilities. In J. L. Bigge (Ed.), *Teaching individuals with physical and multiple disabilities* (3rd ed.). Columbus, OH: Merrill.

Dallyn, L., & Garrison-Jones, C. (1991). The long-term psychosocial adjustment of children with spina bifida. In H. L. Rekate (Ed.), *Comprehensive management of spina bifida.* (pp. 215–235). Boca Raton, FL: CRC Press.

Damiano, D. L., Vaughan C. L., & Abel, M. F. (1995). Muscle response to heavy resistance exercise in children with spastic cerebral palsy. *Developmental Medicine and Child Neurology, 37,* 731–739.

De Souza, E. A. P., & Salgado, P. C. B. (2006). A psychosocial view of anxiety and depression in epilepsy. *Epilepsy and Behavior, 8,* 232–238.

Diller, L., & Ben-Yishay, Y. (1989). Assessment in traumatic brain injury. In Bach-Y-Rita, P. (Ed.), Traumatic brain injury (pp. 161–174). New York: Demos Publications.

Dixon, M. S., & Rekate, H. L. (1991). Pediatric management of children with myelodysplasia. In H. L. Rekate (Ed.), *Comprehensive management of spina bifida.* (pp. 49–66). Boca Raton, FL: CRC Press.

Dodd, K. J., Taylor, N. F., & Graham, H. K. (2003). A randomized clinical trial of strength training in young people with cerebral palsy. *Developmental Medicine and Child Neurology, 45,* 652–657.

Driver, S., O'Connor, J., Lox, C., & Rees, K. (2004). Evaluation of an aquatics programme on fitness parameters of individuals with a brain injury. *Brain Injury, 18,* 847–859.

Driver, S. (2006). Applying physical activity motivation theories to people with brain injuries. *Adapted Physical Activity Quarterly, 23,* 148–162.

Driver, S., & Alison, E. (2009). Impact of physical activity on mood after TBI. *Brain Injury, 23,* 203–212.

Eek, M. N., Tranberg, R., Zugner, R., Alkema, K., & Beckang, E. (2008). Muscle strength training to improve gait function in children with cerebral palsy. *Developmental Medicine and Child Neurology, 50*(10), 759–764.

Epilepsy Foundation of America. (2009a). *About Epilepsy.* Landover, MD: Author.

Epilepsy Foundation of America. (2009b). *First aid for convulsive seizures.* Landover, MD: Author.

Epilepsy Foundation of America. (2009c). *Physical fitness and exercise.* Andover, MD: author.

Fetters, L., & Kluzik, J. (1996). The effects of neurodevelopmental treatment versus practice on the reaching of children with spastic cerebral palsy. *Physical Therapy, 74,* (4), 346–358.

Freed, M. M. (1990). Traumatic and congenital lesions of the spinal cord. In J. Kottke & J. F. Lehmann, *Krusen's handbook of physical medicine and rehabilitation* (4th ed.). (pp. 732–733).Philadelphia: Saunders.

Freeman, J. M., Vining, E. P. G., & Pillas, D. J. (2002). *Seizures and epilepsy in childhood: A guide,* 3rd edition. Baltimore: Johns Hopkins University Press.

French, R., & Horvat, M. (1983). *Parachute movement activities.* Bryon, CA: Front Row Experience.

Fryer, J. (1989). Adolescent community integration. In Bach-Y-Rita, P. (Ed.), Traumatic brain injury. (pp. 255–286). New York: Demos Publications.

Gates, J. R., & Spiegel, R. H. (1993). Epilepsy, sports and exercise. *Sports Medicine, 15*(1), 1–5.

Gras, R. M. L., Berna, J. C., & Lopez, D. S. (2009). Thinking styles and coping when caring for a child with severe spina bifida. *Journal of Developmental and Physical Disabilities.* 21(3), 169–183.

Hinderer, K. A., Hinderer, S. R., & Shurtleff, D. B. (1994). Myelodysplasia. In S. Campbell (Ed.), *Physical therapy for children* (pp. 571–619). Philadelphia: Saunders.

Horvat, M. (1987). Effects of a progressive resistance training program on an individual with spastic cerebral palsy. *American Corrective Therapy Journal*, 41, 7–11.

Horvat, M. (2007) Physical activity for children with spina bifida. *Insights Into Spina Bifida, 18,* 9.

Horvat, M., Mason, C., & Nocera, J. (June 27, 2006) The benefits of physical activity for children with spina bifida. Paper presentation at the Spina Bifida Association of America's national conference. Atlanta, GA.

Huberman, G. (1976). Organized sport activities with cerebral palsied adolescents. *Rehabilitation Literature*, 37, 103–107.

Jaffe, K. M., Fay, G. C., Polissar, N., Martin, K. M., Shurtleff, H., Rivara, J., & Winn, H. R. (1992). Severity of pediatric traumatic brain injury and early neurobehavioral outcome: A cohort study. Archives of Physical Medicine and Rehabilitation, 73, 540–547.

Jan, J. E., Ziegler, R. G., & Erba, G. (1983). *Does your child have epilepsy?* Austin, TX: Pro-Ed.

Jones, J. A. (1988). *Training guide to cerebral palsy sports* (3d ed.). Champaign, IL: Human Kinetics.

Katz, D. I., Ashley, M. J., O'Shanick, G. I., & Connors, S. H. (2006). *Cognitive rehabilitation: The evidence, funding, and case for advocacy in brain injury.* McLean, Va.: Brain Injury Association of America.

Koch, P. S. & Narayan, P. K. (2007). Traumatic brain injury. *International Anesthesiology Clinics ,* 45(3), 119–135.

Korczyn, A. D. (1979). Participation of epileptic patients in sports. *Journal of Sports Medicine*, 19, 195–198.

Laidlaw, J., & Richens, A. (Eds). (1976). *A textbook of epilepsy.* Edinburgh, Scotland: Churchill-Livingstone.

Lee, J. H., Sung, I. Y., & You, J. Y. (2008). Therapeutic effects of strength exercise on gait function of cerebral palsy. *Disability Rehabilitation, 30*(19). 1439–1444.

Lehr, E. (1989). Community integration after traumatic brain injury: Infants and children. In Bach-Y-Rita, P. (Ed.), Traumatic brain injury (pp. 233–254). New York: Demos Publications.

Leonard, C. T., Hirschfield, H., & Forssberg, H. (1991). The development of independent walking in children with cerebral palsy. *Developmental Medicine and Child Neurology*, 33, 567–577.

Lesser, R. P. (1991). *Diagnosis and management of seizure disorders.* New York: Demos Publications.

Lin, P. P., & Henderson, R. C. (1996). Bone mineralization in the affected extremities of children with spastic hemiplegia. *Developmental Medicine and Child Neurology*, 38, 782–786.

Livingston, S. (1971). Should physical activity of the epileptic child be restricted? *Clinical Pediatrics*, 10, 694–696.

Lundberg, A. (1976). Oxygen consumption in relation to work load in students with cerebral palsy. *Journal of Applied Physiology*, 40, 873–875.

Lutkenhoff, M., & Oppenheimer, S. (1997). *Spinabilities: A young persons guide to spina bifida.* Bethesda, MD: Woodbine House.

Magill, R. A. (2007). Motor learning: Concepts and applications (7th ed.). New York: McGraw-Hill.

Martin, D. A. (1988). Children and adolescents with traumatic brain injury: Impact on the family. Journal of Learning Disabilities, 21, 464–469.

Martin, S. (2006). *Teaching motor skills to children with cerebral palsy and similar movement disorders.* Bethesda, MD: Woodbine House, Inc.

McDonald, E. T. (1987). *Treating cerebral palsy: For clinicians by clinicians.* Austin, TX: Pro-Ed.

McLane, D. (1994). *An introduction to spina bifida.* Washington, DC: Spina Bifida Association of America.

Mills, V. M. (1988). Traumatic head injury. In O'Sullivan, S. B., & Schmitz, T. J. (Eds.), Physical rehabilitation: Assessment and treatment (2nd ed.) (pp. 495–513). Philadelphia: F. A. Davis.

Molnar, G. E., & Perrin, J. C. S. (1992). Head injury. In Molnar, G. E. Pediatric Rehabilitation. (2nd ed.) (pp. 254–292). Baltimore: Williams and Wilkins.

Mushett, C. A., Wyeth, D. O., & Richter, K. J. (1995). Cerebral palsy. In B. Goldberg (Ed.), *Sports and exercise for children with chronic health conditions.* (pp. 123–133). Champaign, IL: Human Kinetics.

National Disability Sports Alliance. (2002). Kingston, RI.

National Institute of Health. (2002). *Traumatic brain injury. Hope through research.* Bethada, MD: NIH.

National Institute of Neurological Disorders and Stroke. (2006). *Cerebral Palsy: Hope through research.* Bethesda, MD: NIH.

National Institute of Neurological Disorders and Stroke. (2004). *Seizures and epilepsy: Hope through research.* Bethesda, MD: NIH.

National Institute of Neurological Disorders and Stroke. (2007). Spina Bifida information sheet. Bethesda, MD: NIH

O'Connell, D. G., Barnhart, R., & Parks, L. (1992). Muscular endurance and wheelchair propulsion in children with cerebral palsy or myelomeningocele. *Archives of Physical Medicine and Rehabilitation*, 73, 709–711.

Olney, S. J., & Wright, M. J. (1994). Cerebral palsy. In S. Campbell (Ed.), *Physical therapy for children* (pp. 489–523). Philadelphia: Saunders.

Palisano, R., Rosenbaum, P., Walter, S., Russell, D., Wood, E., & Galupp, B. (1997). *Development and reliability of a system to classify gross motor function in children with cerebral palsy.* 39, 214–223.

Phillips, W. E. (1994). Brain tumors, traumatic head injuries, and near-drowning. In Campbell, S. (Ed.), Physical therapy for children. Philadelphia: Saunders.

Roberts, C. D., Vogtle, L., & Stevenson, R. D. (1994). Effect of hemiplegia on skeletal maturation. *The Journal of Pediatrics*, 125(5), 824–828.

Rose, J., Haskell, W. L., & Gamble, J. G. (1993). A comparison of oxygen pulse and respiratory exchange ratio in cerebral palsied and nondisabled children. *Archives of Physical Medicine and Rehabilitation*, 74, 702–705.

Rotzinger, H., & Stoboy, H. (1974). Comparison between clinical judgement and electromyographic investigations of the effect of a special training program for CP children. *Acta Pediatric Belgian Supplement*, 28, 121–128.

Schleichkorn, J. (1993). *Coping with cerebral palsy* (2nd ed.). Austin, TX: Pro-Ed.

Schmidt, R. A., & Lee, T. D. (1999). Motor control and learning: A behavioral emphasis (3rd ed.). Champaign, IL: Human Kinetics.

Shepherd, R. J. (1990). *Fitness in special populations.* Champaign, IL: Human Kinetics.

Shields, N., Taylor, N. F., & Dodd, K. J. (2008). Self-concept in children with spina bifida compared with typically developing children. *Developmental Medicine and Child Neurology, 50*(10), 733–743.

Shinnar, S., Amir, N., & Branski, D. (1995). *Childhood seizures.* New York: Karger.

Sillanpaa, M. (1995). Counseling and rehabilitation: The clinician point of view. In A. P. Aldenkamp, F. E. Dreifuss, W. O. Renier & T. Suurmeijer (Eds.), *Epilepsy in children and adolescents.* New York: CRC Press.

Sommer, M. (1971). Improvement of motor skills and adaptation of the circulatory system in wheelchair bound children with cerebral palsy. In U. Simiri (Ed.), *Sport as a means of rehabilitation.* Natanya: Wingate Institute.

Spina Bifida Association of America. (1997). *The teacher and child with spina bifida.* Rockville, MD: Author.

Spina Bifida Association. (2009a). *Fact sheets.* Washington, D.C.: Author.

Spina Bifida Association. (2009b). *Fitness strength and flexibility.* Washington, D.C.: Author.

Stallings, V. A., Zemel, B. S., Davies, J. C., Cronk, C. E., & Charney, E. B. (1996). Energy expenditures of children and adolescents with severe disabilities: A cerebral palsy model. *American Journal of Clinical Nutrition, 64,* 627–634.

Stevenson, R. D., Roberts, C. D., & Vogtle, L. (1995). The effects of non-nutritional factors on growth in cerebral palsy. *Developmental Medicine and Child Neurology, 37,* 124–130.

Sugden, D. A., & Keogh, J. F. (1990). *Problems in movement skill development.* Columbia, SC: USC Press.

Tarby, T. J. (1991). A clinical view of the embryology of myelomeningocele. In H. L. Rekate (Ed.), *Comprehensive management of spina bifida* (pp. 29–48). Boca Raton, FL: CRC Press.

Tettenborn, B., & Kramer, G. (1992). Total patient care in epilepsy. Epilepsia, 33(Suppl. 1), S28–S32.

United Cerebral Palsy. (2009). *Cerebral palsy— fact and figures.* Washington, D.C.: UCP.

United Cerebral Palsy. (2009). *Exercise principles and guidelines for persons with cerebral palsy and neuromuscular disorders.* Washington, D.C.: UCP.

Unnithan, V. B., & Maltais, D. (2004). *Pediatric cerebral palsy. Clinical exercise physiology,* 285–299, Philadelphia, PA: Lippencott Williams and Wikins.

Unnithan, V. B., Dowling, J. J., Frost, G., & Bar-Or, O. (1996). Role of concontration in the oxygen cost of walking in children with cerebral palsy. *Medicine and Science in Sports and Exercise,* 28(12), 1498–1504.

Unnithan, V. B., Dowling, J. J., Frost, G., Volpe Ayub, B., & Bar-Or, O. (1996). Cocontraction and phasic activity during GAIT in children with cerebral palsy. *Electromyography in Clinical Neurophysiology,* 36, 487–494.

Uomoto, J. M. (1990). Neuropsychological assessment and training in acute brain injury. In Kottke, F. J., & Lehmann, J. F. (Eds.), Krusen's handbook of physical medicine and rehabilitation (4th ed.). (pp. 1252–1272). Philadelphia: Saunders.

Van Linschotten, R., Backx, F. J. G., Mulder, O. G. M., & Meinardi, H. (1990). Epilepsy and sports. *Sports Medicine,* 10(1), 9–19.

Villeneuve, N., Pinton, F., Bahi-Buisson, N., Dulac, O., Chiron, C., & Nabbout, R. (2009). The ketogenic diet improves recently worsened focal epilepsy. *Developmental Medicine and Child Neurology, 51,* 252–253.

Wiley, M. E. & Damiano, D. L. (1998). Lower-extremity strength profiles in spastic cerebral palsy. *Developmental Medicine and Child Neurology, 40,* 100–107.

Williamson, G. G. (1987). *Children with spina bifida: Early intervention and preschool programming.* Baltimore: Paul H. Brooks.

Ylvisaker, M. Todis, B., & Gland, A. (2001). Educating students with TBI: Themes and recommendations. *Journal of Head Trauma Rehabilitation, 16,* 76–93.

Muscular Dystrophy and Arthritis

CASE STUDY

Tim was diagnosed with Duchenne muscular dystrophy at age five. He has difficulty managing stairs, walking, and falling. He enjoys activity, but tires easily and, as he tires, becomes noticeably frustrated. His parents note that he is continuing to lose muscular strength and range of motion.

At his IEP meeting, his physical education teacher recommended several activities to help maintain independent function by strengthening lesser affected muscle groups. He also recommended breathing and postural exercises to maintain lung function, stamina, and to prolong independent locomotion.

Further, the physical education teacher has provided Tim's parents with a series muscle strengthening exercises for Tim to perform at home, water exercises he can do assisted by his family outside of school, and has taken steps to help Tim become enrolled in a swimming program.

Skeletal neuromuscular disease is characterized by a persistent progressive deterioration of striated muscle tissue. Muscular dystrophy is distinguished from other neuromuscular diseases by four criteria: (1) a primary myopathy, (2) genetic base for the disorder, (3) progressive nature, and (4) degeneration of muscle fibers (Sarnac, 1992). In the disease, muscle cells degenerate, and fat and fibrous tissue emerge to replace the muscle tissue (Sarnac, 1992). Muscular dystrophies are a group of unrelated diseases transmitted by various genetic traits with varying clinical courses and characteristics.

Approximately 200,000 individuals in the United States have muscular dystrophy resulting from spontaneous changes in a gene (genetic mutations) or from idiopathic causes where there is no family history. According to the MDA (2009) muscular dystrophy can be inherited from autosomal dominant or a healthy gene from one parent and a defective gene from the other parent. Autosomal indicated that any of 22 non-sex chromosomes can cause a genetic mutation; autosomal recessive is when both parents have the gene and pass on the faulty gene to the child. Children have a 25 percent change of inheriting the faulty gene and a 50 percent chance of inheriting one gene and becoming a carrier. X-linked (sex linked) recessive is when the mother carries the affected gene on one of her two X-chromosomes and passes it on to a male child. Male children have a 50 percent chance of inheriting the disorder while daughters will have a 50 percent chance of inheriting the defective gene but are not affected by the gene. Although the muscular degeneration is debilitating and results in decreased functional ability, the specific cause of death results from complications involving cardiac and/or pulmonary failure.

The physical characteristics of the disease include muscular weakness, fatigue, and respiratory and/or heart complications. Individuals with muscular dystrophy commonly demonstrate low muscle endurance and fatigue quickly while walking and climbing stairs as the disease progresses. It is estimated that half of the individuals affected are children between the ages of 3 and 13. Major classifications (**Table 16.1**) that affect school age children include Duchenne,

Table 16.1   Types and Characteristics of Muscular Dystrophy

Type	Hereditary	Sex	Onset	Characteristics	Life Expectancy	Other
Duchenne, or progressive, MD	Sex-linked	90% male	2-6 years	Progression upwards from calf muscles—false enlargement of muscle (psuedohypertrophic). Pelvis, upper arms, legs are first affected. Progression is slow, sometimes with rapid bursts.	18 years	Heart involvement; intellectual involvement early in 30% of cases and not proportional to the severity of the disease
Becker MD	Sex-linked	Male	2–16 years	Nonprogressive scoliosis. Progression from pelvis, upper arms, and legs—less severe contractures and slower progression than Duchenne.	Middle age	Same as Duchenne with less involvement.
Facio-scapulo-humeral MD	Autosomal dominant	Male or female	Teens to early adulthood	Develops from face to shoulders to arms and then spreads to pelvic girdle area. Progression slow, sometimes with sports.	Middle to late age	Usually no cardiac or intellectual impairment
Limb-girdle MD	Primarily autosomal recessive	Male or female	Teens or early adulthood	Develops from shoulders to pelvis first, then spreads. Progression usually slow.	Approximately 50 years but may vary	Usually no cardiac or intellectual impairment
Myotonic	Autosomal dominant	Male or female	Early childhood to adulthood; newborn period for congenital form	Abnormalities in muscle contraction; myotonia; facial features and speech affected by disease progression and severity. Slow progression.	Adolescence to approximately 50 years, but may vary	Mild to severe intellectual involvement
Emery-Dreifuss MD	X-linked recessive; autosomal dominant	Male	10 years	Slow progression with progressive wasting of upper arm and lower leg; contractions in spine, ankles, knees, elbows, and neck.	Middle Age	Cardiac complications by age 30 requiring pacemaker.
Congenital MD	Autosomal recessive	Male or female	Birth to 2 years	Weakness and difficulty in meeting developmental landmarks and motor control; Unable to sit, stand, etc.; Contractures, scoliosis.	Infancy to adulthood	Some have no intellectual involvements; others are severely impaired. Weak diaphragm muscle and respiratory complications.
Distal MD	Autosomal dominant and recessive	Male or female	1 year to early adulthood	Six muscle diseases that affect distal muscles (forearms, hands, lower legs, and feet); progresses slowly and involves fewer muscles than other forms of MD.	Infancy to adult	Heart and respiratory muscle affected. Difficulty with hand movements and ambulation.

Becker, limb-girdle, facioscapulohumeral, congenital, Emery-Dreifuss, Distal MD, and myotonic muscular dystrophy (Blackman, 1997; Muscular Dystrophy Association, 2009; Sarnac, 1992.

Classification and Etiology

Duchenne Muscular Dystrophy

Duchenne muscular dystrophy (MD) is the most common childhood form of MD and is sometimes referred to as progressive or pseudohypertrophic muscular dystrophy. Duchenne is the most serious and debilitating of all the dystrophies. In approximately 90 percent of cases it can be traced to a sex-linked recessive trait characterized by the absence of the structural protein dystophin (Kilmer & MacDonald, 1995). This sex-linked genetic error occurs when a defective X (female) chromosome joins a normal Y (male) chromosome. The defective gene is carried by the mother and manifested in male offspring. The end result is a male with Duchenne MD (Kilmer & Mac-Donald, 1995) (**Figure 16.1**).

The remaining 10 percent of cases of Duchenne MD are *autosomal* (a chromosome other than sex chromosome) and not sex-linked. In these cases, both mother and father carry the recessive gene. A gene "mutation" may occasionally occur in conception, causing a dystrophic condition that may affect male and female offspring (Kilmer & MacDonald, 1995).

Early signs of MD include slow motor gains, low Apgar scores, and poor muscle tone. Changes in gait are evident during walking by 3 to 5 years of age, as well as evidence of clumsiness and frequent falls, wider base of support, waddling gait, and difficulty rising from the floor. Running and jumping are often affected by awkward movements and are characterized by lack of stability. Usually the disease progresses minimally until 7 years of age, when rapid decline in functioning is evident. A wheelchair is needed for ambulation by 10 to 13 years of age (NIH, 2006). Symptoms of both forms of Duchenne MD are similar. Slowness of gait, pseudohypertrophy of the calves (the calves appear muscular but in realty are weakening because the muscle tissue is replaced by fat, fibrous tissue), and Gowers' sign are the first noticeable characteristics of the disease. Gowers' sign is a characteristic of Duchenne MD that affects children while attempting to stand erect. While bending over, children place their hands on the knees and then move alternately up the thighs to achieve a standing position (**Figure 16.2**). Weakness is often observed proximally, with subtle changes in gait and initial difficulty in locomotor patterns and a tendency toward being clumsy. In addition, the neck flexors are weak, and children may demonstrate difficulties in lifting and controlling their head and neck.

The weaknesses of the hip flexor and extensors, as well as contractures, account for the deterioration of

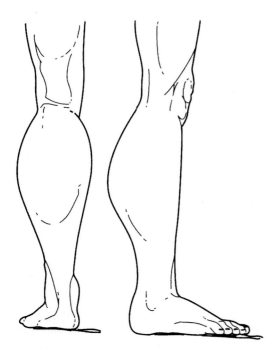

Figure 16.1 Calf manifesting pseudohypertrophy in Duchenne muscular dystrophy.

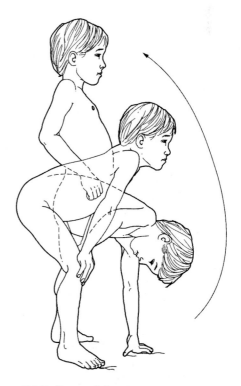

Figure 16.2 Gowers' sign.

gait and difficulty in functional tasks, such as stair climbing, locomotor activities, and rising from the floor (Kilmer & MacDonald, 1995). As the disease progresses, the muscles of the abdomen, pelvis, and hips weaken, lordosis develops (due to weakness of the abdominal and gluteus maximus muscle), the gait becomes waddling (due to gluteus weakness of the medius) (Adams & McCubbin, 1990). By the age of 6, children may have difficulty keeping up with peers and start to lose strength in a relatively linear fashion (Aitkens, McCrory, Kilmer & Bernauer, 1993). Contractures are noticeable as early as 3 to 4 years at the ankles and hip flexor, causing difficulties in pushing the heels to the floor. Contractures may also be noticeable at the hips, knees, and elbows during periods of immobilization or inactivity. The decrease in functional activity may exacerbate these contractures and is a rationale for intervention. In the final stages of the disease, scoliosis, or lateral curvatures of the spine, is prevalent, resulting in severe postural and structural deformities and compromising pulmonary abilities. Kilmer and MacDonald (1995) have indicated that spinal curves can develop rapidly and may exceed 100 degrees, necessitating spinal fixation. In addition, pulmonary functions and cardiac sufficiency are compromised by the progressive muscular weakness and spinal difficulties. The respiratory muscles may also be weakened, resulting in complications such as pneumonia and/or cardiomyopathy. Cardiomyopathy leads to ineffective systolic contractions and congestive heart failure, which is a common cause of death in this population.

The progressive loss of ambulation, muscular strength, and functional ability results in the use of a wheelchair. At this stage, maintaining existing muscular strength and restricting further atrophy is vital to preserving the child's ability to propel a wheelchair. Obesity becomes a problem at this stage as the child requires more force to move the body, and fat does not contribute to generating force. In conjunction with deteriorating strength and contractures, body fat compromises the child's ability to perform functional tasks. In later stages, the fat weight is lost as the disease progresses. Intellectual capabilities may vary; some learning problems occur in approximately 30 percent of cases.

Becker Muscular Dystrophy

Becker muscular dystrophy is similar to Duchenne muscular dystrophy but progresses more slowly and has a later onset, generally around 10 to 15 years of age. A greater percentage of the children are males, and the disease is sex-linked from a recessive X-linked chromosome caused by reduced amounts of dystrophin (NIH, 2006). Symptoms are similar to those of Duchenne muscular dystrophy. Children demonstrate a prolonged ambulatory capacity until 16 years or later, less severe contractures of the ankle and foot, and nonprogressive scoliosis and skeletal deformities (Bar-Or, 1983). Intellectual impairment generally is not evident in Becker's muscular dystrophy, although children may demonstrate varying learning disabilities (NIH, 2006).

Other characteristics include muscle weakness; wasting and contractures in the shoulder and pelvic muscles; pseudohypertrophy of the calves; loss of independent ambulation as disease progresses; and slow progressive weakness in the spine resulting in abnormal curvature of the spine that is not as severe as that seen in Duchenne muscular dystrophy. Respiratory failure is generally not significant, although heart abnormalities and cardiomyopathy may be present. Intervention should occur early in the course of the disease, when weakness and muscle fiber degeneration are minimal. Physical activity should be encouraged to maintain and maximize functional strength and range of motion for daily living skills and prolonging ambulation (Fowler & Taylor, 1982).

Facioscapulohumeral Muscular Dystrophy

Facioscapulohumeral MD is characterized by initial involvement of the face, shoulder, and upper extremities with moderate involvement of the pelvic girdle area that usually occurs in the teens to early adulthood. Pseudohypertrophy of the muscles is uncommon, and skeletal deformities, although lordosis is evident, and muscular contractures are rare. The disease can occur in either sex and is inherited by an autosomal dominant factor. Progression of the disease is slow, with ambulation remaining until middle age, and may be characterized by periods of remission.

The muscles most commonly involved are those that are associated with upper body function and object manipulation at the shoulders or above, including the trapezius, rhomboids, latissimi dorsi, and the pectoralis major, but not the deltoids. As the disease progresses, involvement and weakening occurs in the clavicular portions of the pectoralis, brachioradialis, biceps, wrist, and finger extensions. Involvement may also appear in the facial muscles, including the sphincter muscles of the mouth, buccinator muscles and the masseter muscles.

Limb-Girdle Muscular Dystrophy

Limb-Girdle Muscular Dystrophy refers to a dozen inherited conditions characterized by loss of muscle and weakening of voluntary muscles in the shoulders and hips (NIH, 2006). Limb-girdle MD is the least distinctive of the dystrophies, with symptoms usually occurring in the late teens to the third decade of life. The disease involves an autosomal recessive factor and is generally benign with great variations even within family members. Initial weakness occurs primarily in either the shoulder or pelvic girdle area but may extend to other muscle groups, such as the biceps, portions of the pectorals, brachioradialis, and the wrist and finger extensions. Weakness begins in the hip, quadriceps, and hamstrings, with evidence of waddling gait and Gowers' sign affecting walking and locomotor activities. Some pseudohypertrophy may occur in the calves, but most appears in the upper extremities. Muscle contractures and skeletal deformities appear in the latter stages of the disease. Life expectancy is approximately 50 years of age. It is not uncommon for the disease to be asymmetrical, resulting in one limb being much weaker than the other. Early bicep involvement is evident as well as deltoid weakness affecting functional tasks of the upper extremities. The muscles of the neck are also affected, although the facial muscles are not involved.

The muscles involved in the pelvic girdle area include a weakening of the sacrospinalis, iliopsoas, quadriceps, gluteus maximus, anterior tibial, abductors, and the peroneal muscles. The muscles weakened in the shoulder and arm areas include the serrati, the trapezius, latissimi dorsi, rhomboids, and the sternal portion of the pectoralis major.

Myotonic Muscular Dystrophy

Myotonic muscular dystrophy (Steinert's disease) is the second most common adult form of muscular dystrophy. It is autosomal dominant and characterized by abnormalities in muscle contraction (Jones, 1985). Myotonia, the primary characteristic of this disease, is usually not clinically or electromyographically evident until 5 years of age, unless it is the congenital form that is diagnosed at birth and results in severe cognitive deficits (Sarnac, 1992). Myotonia is the delay or inability to relax muscles after repetitive discharge, or contraction of a single muscle fiber after activation induced by the stretch reflex or electrical stimulation (Sarnac, 1992). Myotonia is commonly demonstrated in the hands and distal muscles. Speech is often affected because of involvement of the muscles of the face, tongue, and pharynx. Cardiac involvement is manifested by blocks in the Purkinje system and arrhythmias instead of cardiomyopathy present in other dystrophic conditions (Sarnac, 1992). Facial features include masseter muscle atrophy and inability to close the lips. The eye muscles are weak, affecting the ability to close the eyelashes. Neck muscles atrophy and are weak mainly in flexion, causing some cervical lordosis (Weisberg et al., 1989). Weakness in the extremities is present in distal muscles, characterized by weak hand muscles and foot drop. As with other types of muscular dystrophy, learning difficulties may occur, and no specific medical treatment can counteract these symptoms.

Emery-Dreifuss Muscular Dystrophy

Emery Dreifuss MD generally affects males and can be x-linked recessive or autosomal dominant (NIH, 2006). Onset occurs at approximately 10 years of age until 20 to 25 years. It is characterized by a slow progression with wasting in the upper arm and lower leg muscles. Contractures in the spine, ankles, knees, elbows, and neck promote muscle weakness and rigidity in the spine and toe walking (NIH, 2006). Weakness is also apparent in the facial muscles and shoulder; while heart complications are evident at 30 and often require a pacemaker (NIH, 2006).

Congenital MD

Congenital MD is a group of autosomal recessive dystrophies that affect males and females and are present at birth or before two years of age (NIH, 2006). Muscle weakness is evident as the child has difficulty achieving typical motor development landmarks such as sitting, standing, and ambulation. Muscle degeneration and weakness will vary with the type of disorder and may be mild to severe. The three groups of congenital MD are:

- Merosin-negative: protein merosin in connective tissue surrounding muscle is missing.
- Merosin-positive: merosin is present but other proteins are missing.
- Neuronal-migration disorders: migration of nerve cells to proper location is disrupted in fetal development.

Major complications of Congenital MD include contractions that impede movement of joints, scoliosis, and foot deformities. Children may also have difficulty with respiration, swallowing, vision, and speech problems. Because of the variability of congenital MD, intellectual functioning may range from appropriate to severe while the life span ranges from infancy to adulthood with minimal disability (MDA, 2009).

Distal Muscular Dystrophy

Distal MD or distal myopathy are six muscle diseases that affect the distal muscles or those farthest away from the shoulders, hips, hands, lower legs, or feet (NIH, 2006). Distal dystrophies involves fewer muscles, progresses at a slower rate, and is less severe. Children have difficulty with maintaining stability, and functional tasks such as walking and climbing stairs. Pulmonary and cardiac complications are also evident and onset is usually between 40 to 60 years of age; although autosomal recessive form may be evident at one year to young adulthood (NIH, 2006).

LEARNING ACTIVITY

Trace the progression of muscular dystrophy from its onset through progressive detriments in ability to function independently. Make a list of and discuss the benefits of water activity for a child with Duchenne muscular dystrophy.

Planning the Physical Activity Program

Children with muscular dystrophy battle several morphological constraints throughout the progression of the disease. The activity level of children should be encouraged to maintain the overall level of functioning. Depending on the progression of the disease, children progress through stages of functional ability (Bar-Or & Rowland, 2004; Kilmer & McDonald, 1995):

1. Low strength and endurance; normal ambulation with possible overwork weakness, slight deficiency in function

2. Reduction in activity; tendency to fatigue easily; reduced strength and endurance; habitual activity mild contractures and possible overwork weakness; ambulation with assistance

3. Poor strength and endurance; overwork weakness; contractures; limited ambulation and decrease in physical activity and standing

4. Ambulation significantly decreased; functional use of wheelchair; severe contractures and muscular weakness; pulmonary difficulties and cardiomyopathy

In order to postpone skeletal deformities and muscle deterioration, teachers should encourage increased activities at submaximals levels to promote ambulation. To promote physical activity, it is recommended that early intervention programs be implemented with the following guidelines:

1. *Medical Approval.* A physician's approval should be obtained prior to implementing a physical activity program. The physician will determine the type and stage of the disease and provide recommendations or contraindications to physical activities. Periodic evaluation will aid in determining progress or fluctuations in the child's functional ability.

2. *Assessment.* Initially, the individual's residual strength and endurance and flexibility in each affected area should be determined from medical reports, from parents, and from manual or quantitative strength tests by the clinician. The individual's overall ability to ambulate and the accompanying balance or gait disorders will determine the level and intensity of the training program. Strength,

flexibility, and functional capabilities should be periodically measured throughout the program to ensure proper daily management (Bar-Or & Rowland, 2004; MDA, 2009).

3. *Intensity.* Submaximal isotonic or isokinetic exercises should be used in the program. Strenuous, "all-out" bouts of exercise contribute to overworking weakened muscles and should be avoided with MD individuals (Croce, 1987; MDA, 2009). Submaximal exercises should be used to avoid muscle overloading. Teachers should select exercises with a high repetition maximum and low resistance in a manner that is consistent with untrained individuals. Alternative resistance exercise, such as exercises with surgical tubing or hand weights and water exercises, can also be used in weakened muscle groups. A mutual set of 12 exercises should be selected before multiple sets are allowed and used. Duration should be individualized and determined by the type and progression of the disease.

4. *Warm-up and cool-down.* To prepare the muscles before exercise, it is necessary to increase blood flow and body temperature in preparation for the more vigorous exercise. A gentle warm-up segment consisting of slow, static stretches should last approximately 6 to 8 minutes. In contrast, a cool-down phase should consist of 6 to 8 minutes of gentle, rhythmic stretching exercises to gradually control stimulated muscles and prevent contractures. The cool-down phase will not only enhance flexibility, but also aid in preventing injury and minimizing muscle soreness.

Primary areas of emphasis in both warm-up and cool-down include the hamstrings, iliotibial bands (groin and leg), heelcords, hip and knee extensions, elbow flexor, and hand flexor. The warm-up and cool-down not only prepare the body for exercise but also aid in combating contractures (Croce, 1987; Eng, 1992; MDA, 2004).

Implementing the Physical Activity Program

Early recognition of muscular dystrophy is essential for early intervention and acceptance of the disorder. Medication is ineffective in the progress of the disease, but early intervention will help maintain muscular strength and functional ability. Physical activity designed to promote range of motion aids in preventing contractures and tight muscles. The shortening of muscle groups has been recognized as being preventable in children with muscular dystrophy (Bar-Or & Rowland, 2004; MDA, 2004). Teachers should encourage activities that require using the limbs and implement muscular activity on a regular basis that is of short duration and does not push the child to exhaustion. Although overly vigorous and intense exercise may be harmful, inactivity will contribute to the deterioration of the functional ability and to the development contractures, atrophy, and spinal deformities (Eston et al., 1989; Lewis & Haller, 1992). Exercise should be encouraged to maintain posture in sitting and standing positions. Range-of-motion exercises can aid in delaying muscle tightness, which first appears in the hip flexor, hamstrings, triceps, toe flexor, forearm pronators, and wrist and finger flexor (Croce, 1987). Although programs that emphasize stretching in these muscle groups can delay contractures, the response of dystrophic muscles to exercise is still under speculation (Croce, 1987).

Resistive exercise programs for muscular dystrophy may be controversial because of concern regarding the efficiency of the programs. Johnson and Braddom (1971) recommended that heavy resistive exercise be avoided for weakened muscle because lifting heavy weights results in a marked loss of strength in the affected area and fatigues the involved muscles. In contrast, Milner-Brown, Mellenthin, and Miller (1986) concluded that muscle strength will increase with no evidence of overworked muscle weakness in submaximal long-term programs. Further, Fowler and Taylor (1982) indicated that submaximal exercise does not appear to be deleterious if initiated before pronounced muscle weakness and degeneration occur. To put theoretical research into perspective, it is obvious that several concerns are evident in developing exercise programs for individuals with muscular dystrophy:

- The extent of muscle weakness
- Progression of the disease
- Degree and intensity of the exercise
- Individual needs

The consensus of past research efforts seems to support the contention that unaffected muscle is trainable and can be strengthened, possibly aiding in slowing down the progression of the disease and deterioration of the muscles (Croce, 1987).

In addition, maximal aerobic power and muscular endurance is lower than in able-bodied individuals because of the smaller muscle mass and compromised cardiac and pulmonary functioning in individuals with muscular dystrophy. (Bar-Or, 1983, 1995; Bar-Or & Rowland, 2004). Decreases in exercise tolerance have been manifested by lower cardiopulmonary capacities and reduced endurance time. This decrease may be attributed to their decrease in leg strength as well as low aerobic power (Kilmer, Abresch & Fowler, 1993). Sockolov, Irwin, Dressendorfer, and Bernauer (1977) indicated that maximum heart rates in

dystrophic children were 30 percent lower than in able-bodied children, and maximal cardiac output was nearly 100 percent lower in the dystrophic children. Cardiomyopathy is detected as early as 10 to 12 years of age, with accompanying restrictions in pulmonary functioning (Eng, 1992). It is essential in the total treatment program to assess pulmonary capabilities and functioning because this is the most common cause of death in this population.

Individualized Program Approach

The components of an exercise program for children with MD should include muscular endurance, muscular strength, and maximal aerobic power (Bar-Or & Rowland, 2004). Muscular strength is essential for standing, walking, and performing other functional daily tasks (Bar-Or, & Rowland, 2004). It is apparent that healthy children will continue to increase their strength with age, whereas dystrophic children may display minimal increases or decreases in strength over a 10-year period beginning at 5 years of age. This nonprogression or deterioration in muscular strength has a definite effect on the child's functional ability and is a major concern in the development of the program. Other goals or concerns in developing programs include (1) self-help and ambulation, (2) anticipating prevention of complications, (3) recreational and vocational endeavors, and (4) counseling of children and family.

Factors to consider in the design of the program depend on the individual's age, the rate of progression, and the degree of muscular weakness (the extent of muscle fiber degeneration). A major consideration in establishing a program that contains submaximal strengthening exercises is the individual's tolerance level. Because the activity level of individuals with muscular dystrophy parallels the course of the disability, it is essential to facilitate development at their functional level. Bar-Or (1995) suggested that exercise programming follow these guidelines:

1. provide realistic short term goals for children and parents

2. focus on maintaining or reducing the rate of deterioration

3. focus on submaximal exercises and reducing intensity to avoid fatigue

4. prevent contractures and provide nutritional counseling in conjunction with training

5. provide activities in an enjoyable setting to facilitate compliance

The intent of the program should be to keep children at their highest functioning level. Decline in functioning is the result of a lack of residual muscle strength, especially in the knee and hip extensors; extent of contractures in the lower limbs; body weight and obesity; and psychological factors, such as fear of falling or withdrawal from social interactions and use of motorized devices (Bar-Or, 1983; Bar-Or & Rowland, 2004; MDA, 2009). As ambulation decreases, the exercise program can be altered to coincide with the functional ability of each ambulation stage. Adjustments in intensity or exercises may be needed to compensate for reduced functioning and are based on individual activity levels or periods of remission (Table 16.2).

Community and Home-Based Interventions

In order to facilitate the development of children with muscular dystrophy, teachers should encourage children to engage in alternate physical activities to maintain an active lifestyle. Cross-training principles can provide physical activity in another mode to alleviate stress on dystrophic muscles and avoid overuse or fatiguing of muscles (Horvat & Aufsesser, 1991). Swimming seems to be the preferred activity for children with muscular dystrophy (Muscular Dystrophy Association, 2004, 2009; NIH, 2006). For example, water exercises can provide muscular strength, endurance, and cardiovascular development while maximizing the benefits of water. Swimming can aid in mobility and maintain range of motion, respiratory exchange, and general conditioning in a program that can be continued after the child can no longer ambulate (Eng, 1992). Conditioning can proceed in the same manner by incorporating repeated movement at a designated

Table 16.2 Physical Activity Suggestions for Muscular Dystrophy

Type	Characteristics	Instructional Strategies	Physical Activity Suggestions
Duchenne	Muscle weakness, clumsiness, Gower's sign, contractures, scoliosis	Team approach to aid in ambulation and functional ability. Active participation and management of obesity and contractures. Cross-training applications for muscle strengthening.	Resistance exercises. Water exercises, stretching. Range of motion. Ambulation and stair climbing, parachute activities. Manipulative skills and recreational activities.
Becker	Same as Duchenne, with later onset and severity	Same as Duchenne.	Same as Duchenne.
Facioscapulo-humeral	Involvement of shoulder, chest, and face	Same as Duchenne, with emphasis on active participation and use of leisure skills.	Resistance exercises, parachute, aquatics and water exercises; manipulation activies that can be used in recreation, such as archery and bowling.
Limb-girdle	Involvements in shoulder or pelvic girdle; some pesudohyptropophy of calves but primary involvement in the upper extremities and pelvic girdle	Same as Duchenne, with emphasis on active participation and use of leisure skills.	Resistance exercises, parachute, water exercises, aquatics, lifetime sports and games.
Myotonic	Involvement in distal muscles; clumsy or slow in movement; inability to quickly relax muscle (myotonia)	Same as Duchenne, with activities that emphasize large muscle groups.	Resistance exercises; gentle flexibility and warm-up; aquatics, cycling.
Emery Dreifuss	Progressive wasting of upper arm, lower leg; contractures in ankle, knee joint, and neck	Promote functional ability. Active participation to manage obesity and release contractures; cross training for muscle strengthening.	Resistance exercises; gentle flexibility; passive stretching; aquatics; breathing exercises; relaxation training
Congenital MD	Inability to meet developmental landmarks and motor control; contractures; scoliosis	Active participation to manage obesity and contractures; muscle strengthening and developing motor skills.	Aquatics; relaxation exercises; resistance exercises; gait training and motor development program.
Distal MD	Weakness in forearms, hands, lower legs, feet; slow progression	Active participation; strengthening and stretching weakened muscles.	Resistance exercise; aquatics; gait training; manipulative skills; and recreational activities.

range of motion but using exercises and water as the resistance. In this manner, a total physical activity program may be utilized, as well as recreational activities that may be motivating to children to aid in retaining functional ability for as long as possible and generalize to community and home-based settings.

Used in conjunction with resistance exercises, cross-training can provide overall training benefits without undue fatigue in dystrophic muscles. Cross-training can also be used to facilitate functional movements such as transfers. Other activities that emphasize manipulation, object control, and stability should also be encouraged to maintain functional ability, including ambulation. For example, activities such as parachuting, bowling, and archery can help keep the child active while emphasizing flexion and extension movements and can be used over the life span in home and community settings. Likewise, play activities in young children should emphasize active movements that can help maximize functional development. In this context, basic locomotor activities are essential for motor development and achieving landmarks such as sitting, standing, and moving. Early diagnosis and intervention can also facilitate designing and implementing programs while children are functioning at their highest level. Because the work output of individuals with muscular dystrophy is markedly reduced, obesity is a common problem associated with lack of mobility. As the amount of weight increases, the strength required for ambulation increases, putting an already compromised muscular structure at risk. Proper dietary management should be implemented and monitored.

Daily activity can help children learn to control and use the muscles more efficiently, postpone some of the effects of a progressive disease, and allow them to participate with able-bodied peers and community and family-based activities. Psychologically there is considerable stress associated with the progressive nature of the diseases for the individual and family. Coping mechanisms may range from overprotection to denial of the disease (Eng, 1992). The frustrations associated with the disease, as well as social isolation and lack of self-concept and/or sexual expression, may result in attention and/or behavior problems. With proper medical supervision, trainable muscle should be maximized, and children should be encouraged to maintain their overall functioning physically as well as psychologically.

Juvenile Rheumatoid Arthritis (JRA)

Juvenile Rheumatoid Arthritis is a general term for all types of arthritis and related conditions occurring in children (Arthritis Foundation, 2009). The primary pathology of the chronic disease is inflammation of the connective tissues and is characterized by swelling, and pain. JRA or Juvenile Indiopathic Arthritis (JIA) is the most prevalent form and varies from the adult form. Subtypes are distinguished by number of joints involved within the first 6 months of the disease's onset:

- Systemic arthritis (Still's disease)
- Polyarticular arthritis
- Pauciarticular arthritis

Approximately 300,000 children, under 18 years of age, have some form of arthritis, and 8.4 million young adults between 18 and 44 have arthritis. Approximately 50,000 have juvenile rheumatoid arthritis (JRA). Arthritis affects girls twice as often as boys and may occur anytime from birth to 16 years of age (Arthritis Foundation, 2009).

Juvenile arthritis is characterized by major changes in the joints, including inflammation, contractures, and joint damage, all of which can affect mobility, strength, and endurance. Children may

CASE STUDY

Sue has severe juvenile rheumatoid arthritis (JRA), and has difficulty moving due to extensive, generalized pain. She ambulates effectively, but becomes frustrated by debilitating pain that affects her when she plays her favorite instrument, the organ. Although her hands and fingers are mildly affected, she can manage the keyboard in relative comfort; but, she cannot manipulate the foot pedals.

Fortunately, Sue's teacher is familiar with JRA and has suggested exercises to strengthen Sue's ankles and feet. Initial attempts to ride a stationary bike continued to cause pain. However, once the bike was adjusted to allow Sue to assume a recumbent position, she became able to pedal pain-free for five minutes, and has since gradually increased her pedaling both in frequency (consecutive days) as well as duration (60 minutes). Most importantly, her strength and range of motion in her feet and ankles have improved to the point where she is now able to play the organ without pain.

come to school with varying degrees of pain and stiffness or miss school entirely (Arthritis Foundation, 2009). Nearly all children with arthritis experience periods when symptoms reduce in severity or disappear, although they may go from being symptom free to experiencing extreme pain and swelling quickly. When the child is symptom free, or even relatively symptom free, the child should be encouraged to participate in most, if not all, developmentally appropriate physical activities. Developmental appropriateness is emphasized because many children with serious and prolonged involvement are smaller and less physically mature than their typically developing chronological age (CA) peers. Splinting is occasionally the procedure of choice when the purpose is to rest tender joints or prevent or minimize contractures. Typically, removable casts may be used at nights or for periods during the day. For example, a wrist splint worn during the day may permit active finger use while protecting the painful and possibly malformed wrist from unnecessary trauma.

The psychological and social impacts on a child with arthritis are multidimensional. Joint pain and stiffness may become an ongoing distraction for the child, which often mitigates against the child's ability to remain on task. To varying degrees, medication schedules can be disruptive and children may have side effects from the medication. Children may also feel embarrassed by the disease, isolated, inadequate, and angry about restriction resulting from the disease (Arthritis Foundation, 2009).

When children self-medicate, adults should take care to ensure that the children do, indeed, take their medications. Children sometimes simply forget to take their medications. Some children, however, may fail to take medications as a personal act of rebellion against the disease. Such children may perceive the disease as devaluing, and by opting not to medicate, the child demonstrates that he or she is no different from other children.

Children want to be perceived as being like other children. Taylor (1987) revealed several important differences of opinion regarding the consequences of JRA among children with the disease, their parents, and their teachers. The investigator found that both parents and teachers tended to focus on the physical symptoms of arthritis, whereas children reported that their major concerns centered on peer relationships and self-esteem. This finding suggests that from the child's perspective, the disease is secondary in importance to acceptance by others. In fact, children in the study were especially reluctant to allow teachers to inform classmates about the disease. Parents and teachers should try to foster an environment wherein the child is perceived by all as a person first. They should also encourage children to focus on strengths rather

than limitations; encourage decision making and responsibility; promote physical activity and developing skills and peer relationships that emphasize similarities rather than differences; and promote social interaction and extracurricular activities (Arthritis Foundation, 2009).

Systemic Arthritis

Systemic arthritis often is referred to as Still's disease. The condition is so named, because its symptoms were first described in 1897 by British physician George Still. Systemic arthritis occurs in approximately equal rates in both boys and girls and occurs in approximately 20 percent of children with JRA (Kock, 1992).

This particular form of the disease is termed systemic because the entire body (i.e., system) is affected. Among earliest symptoms of systemic arthritis is a high spiking fever. Fevers commonly reach 103 degrees. Within a few hours, temperature may return to normal. Fever spikes and remissions may occur as often as once or twice daily. During periods of fever, the child may experiences chills and feel very sick. When fever is gone, the child often feels quite well. The spiking fever condition can last weeks and may persist into months. A rheumatoid rash manifesting as pale red spots and covering various body parts often accompanies the fever.

Other manifestations of systemic arthritis include inflammation of the lining of the heart (pericarditis), the heart proper, or the lungs. Other characteristics may include swelling of the lymph nodes and enlargement of the liver and spleen. The red blood cell count may be depressed (anemia), and the white blood cell count may be elevated.

At the onset of systemic arthritis, arthritis and concomitant joint discomfort are often relatively minor manifestations of the illness and may not appear until months after heretofore mentioned symptoms have come and gone. Because joint discomfort is not an initial manifestation of systemic arthritis, the disease often is difficult to diagnose. Episodes of this disease may persist for months, disappear, and reappear months or even years later. Children may require hospitalization and be restricted in early participation in activity because of the general aches, pains, fatigue, and stiffness (Scull & Athreya, 1995). In time, about half the children with systemic-onset arthritis recover nearly completely, whereas the remaining half show progressive involvement of more joints that includes moderate to severe disability (Arthritis Foundation, 2009).

Polyarticular Arthritis

The term *poly* means "many." By definition, polyarticular arthritis means having arthritis in five or more joints. This form of the disease occurs in approximately 35% of children with JRA and is subdivided into two categories: rheumatoid factor positive (RF+) and rheumatoid factor negative (RF-) (Koch, 1992). The child's major symptom is the severity of pain in affected joints, including the knees, ankles, wrists, neck, fingers (**Figure 16.3**), elbows, and shoulders. Children with polyarticular arthritis live in constant pain. When polyarticular arthritis occurs in the jaw, bone growth may be retarded, resulting in a receding chin.

Given that pain is omnipresent in a child with polyarticular arthritis and that movement provokes pain, there is often a tendency for the child to avoid physical activity. The child's defense mechanism, in the face of pain, is often to sit motionless with joints flexed. Persistent flexion in affected joints, if not therapeutically managed, results in chronically disabling skeletal deformities and muscle contractures. The RF+ type will continue into adulthood, whereas the RF- may enter remission. The protracted nature of the disease typically results in the child's being small and sexually immature for chronological age.

Pauciarticular Arthritis

The term *pauci* means "few." By definition, pauciarticular arthritis means having arthritis in four or fewer joints within the first 6 months of the disease's onset. The large joints of the knee, ankle, elbow, or wrist are affected. This form of the disease most commonly

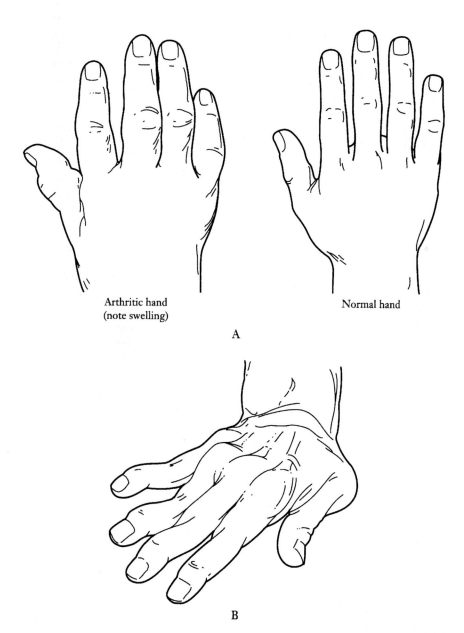

Arthritic hand
(note swelling)

Normal hand

A

B

Figure 16.3 (a) Arthritic hand compared with normal hand. (b) "Swan neck" deformity caused by arthritis.

occurs in young females but may affect either sex. Manifestations of this form of arthritis usually are limited to affected joints. Most commonly involved joints are the knee and ankle. Only one joint is involved in approximately 50 percent of cases. Joint pain and swelling often come on gradually when the child is between 2 and 4 years of age. The child with pauciarticular arthritis typically has no fever, does not have generalized symptoms, and does not appear sick. When compared with children who have polyarticular arthritis, children with pauciarticular arthritis seem quite well. The joint disease part of pauciarticular arthritis usually follows a benign course and may well resolve itself within a few years (Arthritis Foundation, 2009).

The most serious manifestation of pauciarticular arthritis often is not joint disease, but inflammation of the iris and muscles controlling the eye. This condition may develop unnoticed, because its onset and progression typically are insidious. Initial symptoms in such instances, because they are mild, may be dismissed as inconsequential. Children with red eyes, who rub their eyes often, and/or complain about bright lights should be referred to an ophthalmologist (a physician specializing in diseases of the eye). The condition develops in approximately one-fourth of children, mostly girls, who contract pauciarticular arthritis. Among children with the condition, approximately 60 percent recover completely, while approximately 25 percent may lose some vision. Early intervention eliminates or at least minimizes vision loss.

Planning the Physical Activity Program

Nonsteroidal anti-inflammatory drugs (NSAIDs) have become the preferred initial therapy in treating JRA. Within the NSAID family of medications, ibuprofen, naproxen (Naprosyn), and tolmetin sodium (Tolectin) have been approved for use in children 12 and under by the Food and Drug Administration (FDA). Six to 8 weeks often are required to fully determine NSAID efficacy, and laboratory tests should be administered to determine possible medication toxicity. Possible side effects of NSAID ingestion include stomach pain, nausea and vomiting, anemia, headache, blood in the urine, severe abdominal pain and peptic ulcer, fragility and scarring of the skin (especially with Naprosyn), and difficulty concentrating in school (Arthritis Foundation, 2009).

Aspirin may be prescribed for joint pain and inflammation and to reduce fever. Aspirin is often prescribed because of its effectiveness with relatively few side effects. Side effects do, however, occur. The child who takes aspirin in larger than typical doses may experience stomachaches, behavior changes, ringing in the ears, increased bruising following mild trauma,

and a sensation of having "stuffed-up" ears. It should be noted that aspirin taken by children has been linked with Reye's (pronounced "rise") syndrome. Reye's syndrome is an acute and sometimes fatal condition involving brain inflammation and liver enlargement. The teacher should be familiar with Reye's syndrome symptoms, including persistent vomiting and unusual irritability in the student. Continued reliance on aspirin as a medication of choice is founded on the assumption that, on a case-by-case basis, benefits outweigh risks.

Glucocorticoid Drugs

Steroids, including cortisone and prednisone, are among the most potent anti-inflammatory agents prescribed to treat joint inflammation, pain, and swelling. Glucocorticoid drugs act as immunosupressants. They are administered to desensitize the body's immune system response that causes joint disease. This family of anti-inflammatory agents typically is prescribed to therapeutically manage only those cases of joint disease that are most resistant to treatment. Glucocorticoid drugs must be prescribed with particular caution because of the potential for varied and serious side effects. They must be prescribed in the lowest effective dose and for the shortest possible time. Side effects can include high blood pressure, osteoporosis (softening of bones), slowing of growth and maturation rates, heightened susceptibility to infection, weight gain resulting from increased appetite, and increased risk of ulcers.

Exercise Considerations

Physical activity and exercise are mainstays in treatment and management of arthritis (**Table 16.3**). Although affected joints do require rest and need to be protected from undue trauma, exercise and physical activity help prevent or control joint deformities and muscle contractures. For children with arthritis, therapeutic exercise and active participation in recreation and sports is needed to maintain an active lifestyle (Arthritis Foundation, 2009; Scull & Athreya, 1995), which leads to the following benefits:

- Maintains joint flexibility
- Maintains muscle strength
- Regain lost motion or strength in a joint or muscle
- Makes functional activities, such as walking or dressing easier
- Improves general fitness and endurance
- Improves self-esteem
- Prevents deconditioning of the cardiopulmonary system
- Maintains bone density

Although children should be encouraged to actively participate, there are some potential adverse effects of

Table 16.3 Physical Activity Suggestions for Arthritis

Site	Characteristics	Physical Activity Suggestions
Joints	Pain; inflammation; stiffness; loss in range of motion	Avoid high-impact and contact sports. Emphasize range of motion and stretching; hot compresses, yoga, relaxation, and aerobic exercise; water exercise with a mild warm-up and strength exercises to stabilize joint at the child's comfort level. Aerobic activity for weight control.
Muscles	Weakness; contractures	Range-of-motion exercises (active or passive); isometric exercises. Water exercises, swimming in conducive environment (88–92°) using flotation devices, swim fins, etc. Stationary cycling, yoga, and relaxation activities. Emphasize ambulation and function.
Psychological functioning	Fatigue; pain; self-esteem problems	Reduce activity if child is fatigued, but emphasize that deconditioning can cause fatigue. Encourage activity that is conducive to developing physical functioning and social interaction with peers.

exercise on arthritis. Therefore, input from members of the collaborative team is required. Special care should be taken to avoid exacerbating symptoms of the disease. For example, excessive swelling, pain, or fatigue may signal that the child has exceeded the safety threshold of the activity. Likewise, a child with low muscular strength may compromise joint integrity and be at risk for further injury. In addition, joints without an appropriate range of motion or underlying osteoporosis may present risks for fracture (Scull & Athreya, 1995).

LEARNING ACTIVITY

Discuss a range of physical activities that can be used to help manage JRA. What treatment options in addition to strength and flexibility exercises may be indicated for JRA?

Implementing the Physical Activity Program

In addition to the input from the collaborative team on maximum joint protection and on the child's functioning, high-impact activities and contact sports should be avoided. Children should develop confidence in their physical abilities and be encouraged to pick a sport or activity of interest, while stressing activities that exercise the joints without eliciting too much stress on them (Arthritis Foundation, 2009). In preparation for activity, affected joints can be readied for movement by warm baths or layered warm paraffin applications. These preparations help reduce discomfort associated with motion and thereby may encourage child to "stick with" an exercise regimen and activity program. Hicks (1990) has recommended that children progress from range-of-motion and stretching exercises to isometric exercises to aerobic exercises to recreational activities.

The Arthritis Foundation (2009), recommends three types of exercise including:

- Flexibility exercises (stretching) for joint movement
- Strengthening exercises (resistance) including isometric and isotonic exercises to support and protect joints
- Cardiovascular (aerobic) exercises to control weight and maintain functional ability

Several programs including the Arthritis Foundation Aquatic Program, Arthritic Foundation Self-Help Program, People with Arthritis Foundation Exercise Program, and Walk with Ease are available from the Arthritis Foundation to help facilitate exercise programs. The Arthritis Foundation's Tai Chi program has also proven to facilitate mobility, breathing, and relaxation. The program consists of 12 movements, a warm-up, and cool-down phase. In addition, various yoga-based programs are also used for breathing, stretching, and strengthening. On a larger scale, The Center for Disease Control (CDC) has developed a National Arthritis Action Plan to facilitate self-management and improve physical, psychosocial, and work function for individuals with arthritis. Physical activity, The Arthritis Pain Reliever, is part of the overall campaign to facilitate and maintain function (CDC, 2008).

Mild exercise (i.e., warm-up) should precede more vigorous exercise. Muscle strengthening and flexibility exercises will help control pain and minimize joint deformity. Pain perception, of course, is in part subjective and varies among individuals. A good rule of thumb is that the teacher should know that exercise is important and encourage the individual child to exercise to, but never through, his or her threshold of discomfort. The point at which discomfort is perceived as pain is the point where exercise exercise intensity and/or duration should peak.

Isometric exercises may be particularly valuable adjuncts to strength maintenance or development programs, because they require muscle contraction while causing little or no movement at the joint. Isometric contractions may be held for 6 seconds at near-maximum effort several times daily. Isometric exercises can be performed with light weights or surgical tubing to the point of fatigue.

Range-of-motion exercises may be active, assistive, or passive, depending on individual need. Stretching should be steady and deliberate, not bouncy (i.e., ballistic). Depending on the individual child's exercise tolerance, a given stretch may persist for at least 6 seconds. Limb movement activities to maintain or rehabilitate range of motion often can be done by the child. Care must be taken in such instances to ensure the child does, indeed, carry out prescribed exercises. Children often do not appreciate the long-range value of prescribed activities and may be reluctant to inflict discomfort on themselves. Any program designed to minimize effects of arthritis will result in some discomfort to the child. The teacher must be patient in working with the child, to prevent the exercise regimen or activity from turning into a battle of wills.

The use of the aquatic environment is one of the best and safest exercise regimens to use for children. The total body can be exercised with minimal joint stress, and the child can develop flexibility as well as muscular strength. Water exercise, in which the child moves against the resistance of the water, can also be used. In addition, the pool environment can be used to develop aerobic conditioning and to help promote ambulation. For some children, personal floatation devices, swim fins, or kickboards may be needed to initiate movements and build functional strength prior to developing swimming skills. It is essential that the water and air be warm enough (88–92 degrees for water, 95–98 degrees for air) to avoid joint stiffness and pain (McNeal, 1990).

During acute stages of arthritis, activities that jar or otherwise traumatize affected joints (e.g., jumping, wrestling, catching heavy objects) are contraindicated. Ideal activities are those that encourage exercise through reasonable ranges of motion that do not traumatize joints. In addition to aquatics, cycling is an ideal exercise to promote muscular strength and flexibility. Because cycling is a low-impact activity, it does not compromise joint integrity but does allow the child to reap the physical and emotional benefits of activity.

Children with arthritis may also experience mood swings. These occur, in part, because symptoms of the disease vary in intensity. After a good night's sleep or during the course of days when symptoms moderate, the child's disposition often shifts toward the positive. Bouts of discomfort from joint pain, in contrast, may result in the child becoming fatigued or irritable.

Feelings of fatigue often accompany moderate and severe cases of arthritis. A response common among caregivers in such situations is to recommend reductions in activity, including rest. According to Ike, Lampman, and Castor (1989), fatigue results only in part from the disease. Unnecessary restriction of the child's activity plays a significant role in deconditioning, which in turn exacerbates the child's feelings of tiredness. Joint pain lasting longer than one hour after activity is an indication that the activity has been too strenuous. However, eliminating the child from participation may have adverse emotional effects. Activity should be encouraged that is beneficial to the child without triggering any of the side effects from their condition. Periodic assessment of physical functioning and constant monitoring of participation should provide the child with the opportunity to safely lead an active life.

CHAPTER SUMMARY

1. Muscular dystrophy is characterized by persistent deterioration of striated muscle tissue.

2. Primary characteristics of the disease are muscular weakness, fatigue, and respiratory and heart complications.

3. Major classifications include Duchenne, Becker, limb-girdle, Facioscapulohumeral, Emery-Dreifuss, Congenital, Distal, and myotonic muscular dystrophy.

4. Intervention activities should focus on maintaining muscular strength and functional ability.

5. Cross-training and home-based activities can be used to supplement the physical activity program.

6. Juvenile arthritis is characterized by joint inflammation, joint contracture, joint damage, and altered growth.

7. Three types of juvenile arthritis include systemic arthritis, polyarticular arthritis, and pauciarticular arthritis.

8. Activity is essential to develop strength, maintain flexibility and bone density, prevent deconditioning, and improve self-esteem.

9. Activity should be encouraged to support an active lifestyle, including isometric, isotonic, and flexibility exercises.

REFERENCES

Adams, R., & McCubbin, J. (1990). *Games sports, and exercises for the physically handicapped* (3rd ed.). Philadelphia: Lea and Febiger.

Aitkens, S. G., McCrory, M. M., Kilmer, D. L. & Bernauer, E. M. (1993). Moderate resistance exercise program: Its effect in slowly progressive neuromuscular disease. *Archives of Physical Medicine and Rehabilitation,* 74, 711–715.

Arthritis Foundation. (2009). *Arthritis answers: School success.* Atlanta: Author.

Bar-Or, O. (1983). *Pediatric sports medicine for the practitioner.* New York: Springer-Verlag.

Bar-Or, O. (1995). Muscular dystrophy. In American College of Sports Medicine, *Exercise Management for Persons with Chronic Diseases and Disabilities.* (pp. 180–188). Champaign, IL: Human Kinetics.

Bar-Or, O., & Rowland, T.W. (2004). *Pediatric exercise medicine.* Champaign: IL: Human Kinetics.

Blackman, J. A., (1997). *Medical aspects of developmental disabilities in children birth to three* (3rd ed.). Gaithersburg, MD: Aspen Publications.

Center for Disease Control. (2008). Physical activity. *The Arthritis Pain Reliever.* Atlanta, GA: CDC

Croce, R. (1987). Exercise and physical activity in managing progressive muscular dystrophy. *Palaestra,* 1, 9–15.

Eng, G. (1992). Diseases of the motor unit. In G. E. Molnar (Ed.), *Pediatric rehabilitation* (2nd ed.). (pp. 299–317). Baltimore: Williams & Wilkins.

Eston, R. G., et al. (1989). Metabolic cost of walking in boys with muscular dystrophy. In S. Oseid & K. Carlson (Eds.), *Children and exercise* XIII (pp. 405–414). Champaign, IL: Human Kinetics.

Fowler, W. M. (1982). Rehabilitation management of muscular dystrophy and related disorders. *Archives of Physical Medicine and Rehabilitation,* 63, 322–327.

Fowler, W. M., & Taylor, M. (1982). Rehabilitation management of muscular dystrophy and related disorders: The role of exercise. *Archives of Physical Medicine and Rehabilitation,* 63, 319–321.

Hicks, J. E. (1990). Exercises in patients with inflammatory arthritis. *Rheumatic Disease Clinics of North America,* 16, 845–870.

Horvat, M., & Aufsesser, P. (1991). The application of cross-training to the disabled. *Clinical Kinesiology,* 45(3), 18–23.

Ike, R. W., Lampman, R. M., & Castor, C. W. (1989). Arthritis and aerobic exercise: A review. *Physician and Sports Medicine,* 9, 51.

Johnson, E., & Braddom, R. (1971). Over-work weakness in facioscapulohumeral muscular dystrophy. *Archives of Physical Medicine and Rehabilitation,* 5, 333–336.

Jones, H. R. (1985). Diseases of the peripheral motor-sensory unit. *Clinical Symposia,* 37(2), 25–26.

Kilmer, D. D., & MacDonald, G. M. (1995). Childhood progressive neuromuscular disease. In B. Goldberg (Ed.), *Sports and exercise for children with chronic health conditions.* Champaign, IL: Human Kinetics.

Kilmer, D. D., Abresch, R. T., & Fowler, W. M. (1993). Serial manual muscle testing in Duchenne muscular dystrophy. *Archives of Physical Medicine and Rehabilitation,* 74, 1168–1171.

Kock, B. (1992). Rehabilitation of the child with joint disease. In G. E. Molnar (Ed.), *Pediatric rehabilitation* (2nd ed.) (pp. 293–333). Baltimore: Williams & Wilkins.

Lewis, S. F., & Haller, R. G. (1992). Skeletal muscle disorders and associated factors that limit exercise performance. In K. B. Pandolf (Ed.), *Exercise and sport sciences reviews.* (pp. 67–115). Baltimore: Williams & Wilkins.

McNeal, R. L. (1990). Aquatic therapy for patients with rheumatic disease. *Rheumatic Clinics of North America,* 16, 915–929.

Milner-Brown, H. S., Mellenthin, M., & Miller, R. G. (1986). Quantifying human muscle strength, endurance, and fatigue. *Archives of Physical Medicine and Rehabilitation,* 67, 530–535.

Muscular Dystrophy Association. (2009). *Facts about muscular dystrophy.* Tucson, AZ: Author.

Muscular Dystrophy Association. (2004). Making muscle, burning calories. *Quest,* 11, 1–3.

National Institute of Neurological Disorders and Stroke. (2006). *Muscular dystrophy: Hope through research.* Bethesda, MD: NIH.

Sarnac, H. B. (1992). Neuromuscular disorders. In R. E. Behrman et al. (Eds.), *Textbook of pediatrics* (14th ed.) (pp. 1539–1560). Philadelphia: Saunders.

Scull, S. A., & Athreya, B. H. (1995). Childhood arthritis. In B. Goldberg (Ed.), *Sport and exercise for children with chronic health conditions.* Champaign, IL: Human Kinetics.

Sockolov, R., Irwin, B., Dressendorfer, R., & Bernauer, E. (1977). Exercise performance in 6-to-11 year old boys with duchenne muscular dystrophy. *Archives of Physical Medicine and Rehabilitation,* 58, 195–201.

Taylor, J. (1987). School problems and teacher responsibilities in juvenile rheumatoic arthritis. *Journal of School Health,* 57, 186–190.

Weisberg, L., Strub, R. L., & Garcia, C. A. (1989). *Essentials of clinical neurology* (2nd ed.). Rockville, MD: Aspen Publishers.

Teaching Individuals With Health Impairments

Section V addresses the needs of children with disabilities that affect overall functioning. Respiratory disorders, diabetes, nutritional disorders, and cardiovascular disorders are all health related and interfere with the child's functional capabilities.

This section is designed to help you

1. recognize the characteristics of children whose health and overall functioning is compromised by impairment

2. understand the concerns, appropriate treatment, and medication that may be essential for these children

3. develop the expertise to design intervention programs that facilitate functional ability

4. incorporate information from the collaborative team to facilitate instruction in physical education

5. facilitate instruction and participation in physical education classes within a margin of safety

CHAPTER 17

Respiratory Disorders

CASE STUDY

Dave is an elementary school child with asthma. He enjoys physical education, but experiences difficulties with breathing during prolonged extended physical activity. His teacher is not certain how to respond when Dave experiences difficulty breathing. As a result, he generally requires Dave to sit out for part or all of the class period. Dave is not pleased with sitting and asks his parents to talk to the teacher about his asthma.

Dave and his parents explain to his teacher that Dave experiences exercise induced asthma brought on by *prolonged* physical activity. The teacher suggests that an asthma management plan be developed to identify triggers for Dave's asthma attacks, his medication and procedures such as a warm-up, breathing exercise and any pre-exercise medication that is required. The teacher also suggests ways to record and assess Dave's breathing over time, to determine the effectiveness of any forthcoming asthma management program. Dave's parents assure the teacher they are very supportive of his interest in and concern for effectively managing Dave's asthma. They reassert their commitment to the importance of regular physical activity in Dave's life and its role in the management of Dave's asthma.

The most common respiratory disorders in children are asthma and cystic fibrosis. Respiratory disorders contribute to school absence, decreased tolerance to physical exertion characterized by shortness of breath, and a lifestyle that interferes with active participation in physical and recreational activities. Children with respiratory disorders have traditionally been given a blanket excuse from participation in physical activity. This prevailing attitude by teachers and administrators has denied children the opportunity to develop age-appropriate physical fitness and motor skills and has kept them as spectators at a time when motor patterns are learned and incorporated into future learning experiences.

Because most children with respiratory disorders can be integrated into regular classes, it is essential to develop a familiarity with the functioning of the respiratory system, etiology and characteristics of respiratory disorder(s), medication that may be prescribed, and the development of a progressive program of physical activities based on the child's functional ability.

The Respiratory System

The lungs perform the most basic function involved in respiration, which is the exchange of oxygen (O_2) and carbon dioxide (CO_2) between the body and the external environment. The respiratory system is separated into upper and lower tracts; the upper track consists of the nose, pharynx, larynx, and trachea; the lower tract includes the bronchi and lungs (**Figure 17.1**). Each lung occupies half of the chest cavity and is primarily responsible for respiration and exchange of oxygen and carbon dioxide within the lobes while providing oxygen to and removing carbon dioxide from the blood. The right lung consists of three lobes (upper, middle, and lower), whereas the left lung contains two lobes (upper and lower).

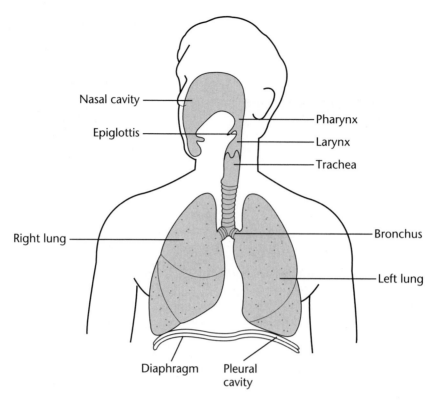

Figure 17.1 Respiratory system.

Air enters through the nasal cavity from the nose and/or mouth (which warms, filters, and humidifies the air) and then empties into the pharynx and trachea, or windpipe, before entering the lungs. The air enters the lungs through the primary bronchi, which branch into additional smaller passageways called bronchioles and finally into the alveoli, the tiny balloon-like air sacs in which oxygen and carbon dioxide are exchanged.

Ciliated mucous membranes line the nose, mouth, bronchi, and bronchioles and filter and warm the air in the lungs. If these inner membranes become irritated, mucus is secreted to protect the system and provide lubrication. In addition, the state of tension plays an important part in the diameter of the bronchioles (National Jewish Center for Immunology and Respiratory Medicine [NJCIRM], 2009). The smooth muscles of the bronchioles expand and contract during the breathing process. If the smooth muscles contract and swell, respiration become narrow and decreases the flow of oxygen into and out of the lungs. If the muscles operate properly, they will relax and allow the bronchial tubes to expand. The inflammatory component of respiratory disorders may also irritate the membranes and damage the elasticity of the bronchiole tubes. A stimulus may cause cells in the lining to release chemical substance mediators that lead to

inflammation (NJCIRM, 2009). The bronchiole tubes may also be predisposed to an increased sensitivity or hyperactivity that leads to muscle spasm and narrowing of the pulmonary pathways.

The diaphragm, a dome-shaped muscle separating the abdominal and chest cavities, is the primary muscle used in respiration. When the lungs expand, the diaphragm contracts, moving downward and increasing the chest cavity. When the diaphragm relaxes, it moves upward and decreases the chest cavity as air is being exhaled. Other muscles of the neck, chest, and abdomen (**Figure 17.2**) aid in the breathing process, although the diaphragm is primarily responsible for 65 percent of the respiration.

For children with respiratory disorders, the loss of elasticity in the pulmonary structures will ultimately weaken and depress the diaphragm, making it difficult to rise against the distended lungs. The other muscles used in respiration must then compensate for the diaphragm, resulting in shallow and labored breathing. When the breathing pattern is altered, the diaphragm may control only about 30 percent of the breathing process, while the neck, chest, and abdominal muscles must assume the remaining 70 percent of the breathing process.

In addition, obstruction of the airways prohibits the efficient removal of the air in the lungs and causes an

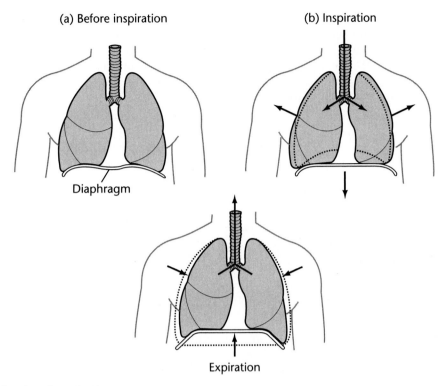

(a) Before inspiration

(b) Inspiration

Diaphragm

Expiration

Figure 17.2 Muscles of respiration.

increase in lung volume, thereby exerting more pressure on the diaphragm and again causing the diaphragm to flatten. In time, the muscle fibers in the diaphragm shorten and become virtually useless, while the muscles of the neck, chest, and abdomen gradually assume more functioning in the breathing process. The prevalence of obesity also contributes to reduced respiration. The obese abdomen adds pressure on the diaphragm, decreasing the abdomen's ability to rise efficiently and interfering with expiration.

The very structure of the respiratory system presents problems that may hinder breathing. Inflammation and swelling of the passageways will restrict the airways, while mucus may clog the air channels or the walls of the alveoli, causing air to become trapped in the lungs. Although asthma and cystic fibrosis are not synonymous, each affects pulmonary capacity and physical tolerance. This chapter discusses their common characteristics and effects on functional ability.

Asthma

Asthma is characterized by swelling of the mucus membrane lining the bronchial tubes, or excessive secretion of mucus and spasms of the air channels.

The major symptoms are a hacking cough, dyspnea (labored breathing or breathlessness) and wheezing, retraction, prolonged exhalation, rapid breathing, and constriction or tightness in the chest. In addition, an asthma attack may result in severe bronchiole obstruction with no passage of air.

The *hacking cough* constitutes the first indication of an impending asthma attack. Bronchiole tubes respond to irritants by secreting mucus, which in turn obstructs the flow of air into and out of the lungs. *Dyspnea* follows when the lining of the bronchiole tubes swells and constricts the airway further, diminishing the flow of air and causing difficulty in breathing. *Wheezing* occurs as a result of decreased air movement into and out of bronchiole tubes that have been constricted by the accumulated mucus. Because the air in the lungs is not completely expelled, the breathing pattern is altered. *Retraction* is evident as a sucking in of the chest or neck as the child exhales, while *prolonged exhalation* reflects a longer period to exhale than inhale because of the trapped air in the lungs. *Rapid breathing* may also be evident as the child tries to move the air into and out of their lungs.

Generally the reduction of breathing occurs during the expiration phase, when the airways are most restricted. The difficulty during expiration interferes with the entry of fresh air into the lungs as air passageways continue to swell and more mucus accumulates, further obstructing the breathing process. When the obstruction becomes severe, there is no wheezing or air movement. A *quiet chest* is symptomatic of a lack of air movement and is the most critical state of the attack.

Types of Asthma

Asthma is a chronic lung condition affecting approximately 6.8 million children under 18 years of age (American Lung Association, 2009). Asthma is classified according to type (such as extrinsic, intrinsic, or mixed) or severity (mild to severe). Whatever the type, asthma causes breathing problems such as coughing, wheezing, chest tightness, and shortness of breath (National Heart, Lung and Blood Institute [NHLBI], 2003b). Symptoms may occur from inflammation to the pulmonary pathways or exposure to triggers that exacerbate symptoms and cause an attack (NHLBI, 2003b). See the accompanying box.

One type of extrinsic asthma, allergic asthma, is caused by the reaction or hypersensitivity of an individual to the introduction of a normally harmless substance. These substances are called allergens and usually affect the child during the early school years, boys more often than girls by a 2:1 ratio. Allergens include pollens, dust, molds, animal fur, fumes, and smoke. Nonallergic asthma is not as prevalent as allergic asthma but is nevertheless often encountered by physical education teachers. At one time, nonallergic, or intrinsic, asthma was thought to be caused by emotional stress and/or fatigue. Emotions may exacerbate symptoms, but the symptoms generally disappear when the cause of the emotional tension is removed. Asthma can also be precipitated by physical activity. This type of asthma is commonly referred to as exercise-induced asthma (EIA) or exercise-induced bronchospasm (EIB). Mixed asthma is a combination of both intrinsic and extrinsic asthma, generally occurring in late childhood or adolescence and exhibiting itself more often in females than males.

Allergic Asthma The major causes of asthma are allergies to pollen, dust, molds, animal fur, smoke, dry cold air, and viral infections. Environmental allergies, such as grass, and unfavorable thermal conditions are more prevalent in outdoor settings. Pollens from flowers, shrubs, trees, and grass in the spring and summer to early fall contribute to reducing forced expiratory capacity. In indoor settings, such as the gymnasium, dust can accumulate and affect the individual year-round. Molds are more prevalent in damp weather or in the cool part of the day, with seasonal peaks in the winter and fall. Animal fur and smog are the worst offenders because of continued exposure throughout the year.

Exercise-Induced Asthma Another contributing cause of asthma is physical activity. Exercise may induce bronchospasm in children 6 to 8 minutes after maximal

---

Asthma Triggers

- Exercise—running or playing hard, especially in cold weather
- Upper respiratory infections—colds or flu
- Allergens
  - Pollens from trees, plants, and grasses, including freshly cut grass
  - Animal dander from pets with fur or feathers
  - Dust and dust mites in carpeting, pillows, and upholstery
  - Cockroach droppings
  - Indoor and outdoor molds
- Irritants
  - Cold air
  - Strong smells and chemical sprays, including perfumes, paint and cleaning solutions, chalk dust, lawn and turf treatments
  - Weather changes
  - Cigarette and other tobacco smoke

Source: National Heart, Lung, and Blood Institute (2003b, 2007).

work of approximately 170–180 beats per minute, or in people of any age whose heart rate reaches about 50 beats per minute below the estimated maximum for at least 5 minutes—in other words, whenever exertion demands about 70 percent of the body's aerobic power. Exercise-induced asthma (EIA) may occur in approximately 75 percent of all individuals with asthma, beginning with the constriction of the muscles surrounding the bronchial tubes. The severity of EIA can be mild or intense and is characterized by dyspnea and wheezing. The airway increases in size during the initial stages of exercise (bronchodilation) and then contracts, restricting the passage of air. In addition, a late-phase or late-onset asthma can be noted hours later as a secondary response to the initial exercise and release of chemical mediators (Katz & Pierson, 1988; Gong, 1992).

Figure 17.3 illustrates the drop in expiration that occurs approximately 8 to 10 minutes after exercise. Recovery will generally occur 15 to 60 minutes after cessation of activity. Late-phase asthma occurs several hours after the initial exercise, although this period of bronchi constriction is not as severe as the original effects. The physiological causes of EIA are relatively unclear (NHLBI, 2003b). The activation of receptors in the cell membrane may result in the discharge of chemicals that tighten

the bronchiole muscles and result in bronchospasm; defective metabolism of chemicals and psychological factors all may contribute to bronchospasm. Other theories relate to the loss of heat or water in the bronchiole pathways and the cooling of intrathoracic airways by incompletely conditioned air, which precipitates the liberation of bronchoconstrictive mediators (Cypear & Lemanske, 1995). In addition, it is apparent that a period of immunity from bronchospasm occurs if strenuous exercise is introduced within 40 minutes. If introduced within 40 minutes of initial exercise, additional exercise seems to diminish EIA with the same workload, although activity at 120 minutes reproduces EIA (Cypear & Lemanske, 1995; Katz & Pierson, 1988). This provides evidence that the introduction of medication may alleviate some of the symptoms that may be exacerbated by activity (NHLBI, 2003b).

Psychosocial Considerations

Other causes of asthma involve psychosocial considerations. Excitement, fear, and stress can affect the production of adrenalin and the balance of the mechanisms required to maintain functional breathing. Although asthma is a medical and not a psychological malady, it may be a product of psychological factors accompanied by chemical changes in the body. More important, emotional problems and feelings of being different from one's peer group may develop because of the child's condition, exacerbating asthmatic symptoms.

Children with asthma often have difficulty coping with their illness and may experience feelings of fear and helplessness during attacks. Their overall ability is hampered by respiratory distress, which may contribute

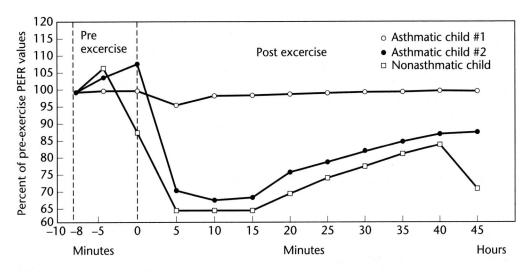

Figure 17.3 Exercise-induced asthma.

Asthma Management Plan Contents

- Brief history of child's asthma
- Asthma symptoms
- Information on how to contact the child's health care provider and parent or guardian
- Signature from physician and parent or guardian
- List of factors that make the child's asthma worse
- The child's personal best peak flow reading, if the child uses peak flow monitoring
- List of the child's asthma medications
- A description of the child's treatment plan, based on symptoms or peak flow readings, including recommended actions for school personnel to help handle asthma episodes

Source: National Heart, Lung, and Blood Institute (2003b).

---

to depression and seclusion because of their activity limitations. Many children also possess a poor self-image or a negative attitude toward physical activity because they fear provoking an attack. The uncertainty of feeling tightness in their chest or shortness of breath may promote a negative concept toward activity. Parents and teachers often contribute to anxiety and a negative attitude by overprotecting children because they lack sufficient knowledge related to asthma and the benefits of physical activity (Butterfield, 1993).

Planning the Physical Activity Program

When planning the physical education program for children with asthma, the teacher must have a thorough knowledge of the child's needs, including medication needs. Proper training methods and the specific needs of the individual should be emphasized in the development of the asthma management plan. See the accompanying box.

Breathing is generally too shallow in children with asthma. Using the upper chest muscles inefficiently and contracting the abdomen while inhaling restrict the amount of air channeled to the lungs. Respiratory muscles may be developed through a proper training program as well as through teaching the proper use of these muscles during respiration. Ideally the diaphragm will be the major respiration muscle used in normal breathing and will help the child remove trapped air and breathe more efficiently. Children who use only the muscles of the

shoulders and chest to breathe are not in a relaxed state and keep filling and emptying only the top part of their lungs.

If the diaphragm is relaxed, it will move downward and outward during inspiration, then proceed upward in expiration. The phrenic nerve, which innervates the diaphragm, is susceptible to tension and will restrict the movement of the diaphragm as well as the pectoral, intercostal, levatores costarum, serratus, transversus thoracis, abdominal, scalene, and erector spinae muscles.

To improve endurance and use respiratory muscles efficiently, breathing exercises may be introduced by teachers and practiced by children in school or at home. In this manner, appropriate breathing techniques can be implemented to prevent the shortening of chest muscles used in respiration, increase the diameter of the chest, and strengthen the diaphragm. Before beginning a session of breathing exercises, teachers should emphasize proper breathing techniques, contracting the diaphragm downward and pushing the abdomen outward during inspiration. They should also demonstrate relaxed breathing with a short inspiration followed by a longer exhalation through pursed lips.

Children should then be placed in a relaxed position (lying, sitting, or standing). The easiest method to teach diaphragmatic breathing is to place children in a supine position with flexed legs and with hands on their abdomen to feel the motion of breathing (**Figure 17.4**). Children can focus on relaxed breathing and calmly inhale and exhale (Hogshead & Couzens, 1990). It is

Inhale   Exhale   Inhale

Figure 17.4 Diaphragmatic breathing exercises.

important for the children to feel they have control of their breathing. The teacher should emphasize slowly breathing in and out to regulate respiration. Children can also visualize emptying and filling their lungs and relaxing tight muscles as they seek to manage their breathing.

During an asthma attack, breathing and imagery should be utilized for 5 minutes or until wheezing has subsided. In addition, children can perform breathing exercises at home on a daily basis to promote deeper and more efficient inhalation and exhalation.

Diaphragmatic breathing can also be encouraged by vigorous games, such as raising a parachute, tumbling, or bouncing on a trampoline. Other activities that are appropriate for children with asthma (e.g., water exercises) also can be paired with diaphragmatic breathing techniques. Because swimming generally does not provoke symptoms in children with asthma, the natural inclusion of water exercises as a warm-up or conditioner will supplement a total conditioning program.

Medication

Medication is beneficial in preventing asthma attacks, relieving bronchospasm, and allowing children to train and lead a more normal lifestyle. Both quick-relief and long-term medications can be used. It should be noted that medication can be taken daily to prevent symptoms or prior to exercise to alleviate EIA. Many symptoms of an impending attack are prevented through medication administered either orally or by aerosol. Each is effective, though aerosol medication may act more quickly with a reduced dosage. Most inhaled medications are available in metered-dose inhalers (RMDI or puffers) to ensure appropriate delivery of the prescribed medication (Fitch, 1986; NJCIRM, 2009). **Table 17.1** includes common medications used in the treatment of children with asthma (Cypear & Lemanske, 1995; NHLBI, 2007).

Implementing the Physical Activity Program

Before children with asthma are exposed to a physical activity, teachers should accumulate information that will be useful in providing an appropriate program and will contribute to awareness of the functioning, desire, activity, and history of the individual. In developing the asthma management plan, teachers should be aware of such factors as age, type of respiratory disorder, and the conditions that may trigger an attack. For example, cold air or allergic conditions from the environment may provide complications for the child. If physical education is carried out on a year-round basis, scheduling may be modified when pollen count is lowest or during the colder months, when sessions should be scheduled in the afternoon to take advantage of higher temperatures. Indoor participation may also be an alternative.

The degree of severity and the frequency of attacks are also important considerations. It is recommended that children with severe asthma not participate in sports that require activity for long duration, such as basketball and soccer, but instead in intermittent-duration sports, such as tennis and gymnastics. The biggest concern is to provide as few restrictions as possible for children based on their level of functioning and their desires.

Another consideration is the medication that is needed to alleviate symptoms of the respiratory disorder, especially in running sports and in cold weather (Hogshead & Couzens, 1990). Exercise is generally prescribed by physicians, and all medical information should be taken into account when the planning team considers possible contraindications and plans substitution of appropriate activities. Pulmonary efficiency can be measured by the physician through forced expiratory volume (FEV), which is the amount of air forcefully exhaled in 1 second after inhalation, or through the

Table 17.1 Asthma Medication and Treatment

Medication	Treatment
Theophylline	May inhibit EIA in oral dose at full therapeutic dosage. Short-acting is effective for 2–4 hours taken 30 minutes before exercise; long-acting is effective for 4–6 hours taken 60 minutes before exercise and is beneficial for night-time asthma.
Cromolyn/sodium	Nonsteroidal anti-inflammatory therapy; may be more effective as aerosol in providing protection against EIA for 1–2 hours when taken 20–30 minutes before exercise; stabilize cells that release inflammatory chemicals; both are preventive medications and need to be taken regularly to be effective.
Beta-2 agonists	May be valuable and effective bronchodilators to aid asthmatics before physical activity. Albuterol should be taken 20 minutes before exercise and is effective for 4–6 hours; terbutaline and metaproterenol are taken 10 minutes before exercise and are effective for 1–2 hours; fenoterol inhibits EIA and rapidly reverses acute symptoms and is taken 15 minutes before activity. Aerosols are preferred because of superior protection, rapid action after inhalation, and fewer side effects.
Leukotriene modifiers	Newer class of long-term control medicines that block the action of chemicals in the airways and block leukotrienes that increase inflammation.

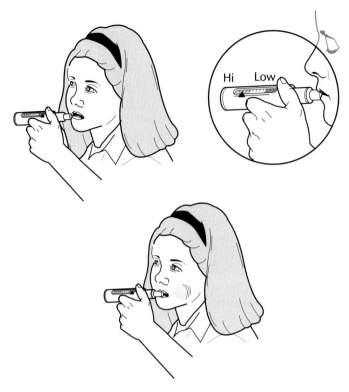

Figure 17.5 Peak flow meter.

number of liters per minute children can move when asked to breathe as deeply as possible. A peak flow meter (**Figure 17.5**) can be used to measure the movement of air into and out of the lungs, aid in monitoring changes in asthma, and provide an indicator of potential problems, especially if the reading is below 80 percent of the child's normal reading (NHLBI, 2007). **Table 17.2** provides physical activity guideline for peak flow meter readings. Peak flow meter reading should be taken prior to participation in physical activity.

Safety during respiratory distress must also be emphasized. Educators and children should be taught to recognize the warning signs of an attack and to administer appropriate self-care procedures. During coughing and wheezing spells, exercise should be stopped, and children should assume a relaxed position to concentrate on total relaxation of the entire body. If discomfort continues, children should practice relaxation exercises to remove trapped air from the lungs. For persistent wheezing, warm, moist air or

Table 17.2 Peak Flow Meter Readings & Physical Activity Notes

Color	Peak Flow Reading	Physical Activity Notes
Green	80–100%	Full participation
Yellow	50–80%	• Child should take rescue inhaler as prescribed
		• Modified participation
		• Inquire about pre-medication
		• Increase warm-up and cool-down periods, etc., per child's Asthma Action Plan
Red	less than 50%	Medical Alert
		• Child should take rescue inhaler as prescribed
		• May require emergency protocol
		• Check child's Asthma Action Plan
		• No physical activity
		• If child improves after taking medication as prescribed, include child in activities such as time- or scorekeeper

Source: American Lung Association (2009).

warm water (e.g., tea, soup broth) should be administered, and relaxation and proper breathing stressed. Medication should then be provided if the preceding steps are not effective. As an attack subsides, children should return to class and proceed with the normal schedule of activities. This will enable them to assume self-control as well as allow other peers or teachers to understand that asthma is not a debilitating disease (NHLBI, 2003a, b).

Although medication and breathing exercises help increase breathing capacity, physical education programs should also be designed to increase work tolerance by improving cardiovascular and musculoskeletal function, thus reducing the demands of physical exertion (Cypear & Lemanske, 1995; Bundgaard, 1985). It is extremely important for teachers to provide a well-rounded program, including physical fitness, motor skills, recreational skills, and relaxation activities, based on the asthma management plan. Teachers and coaches can follow the guidelines of the National Heart, Lung and Blood Institute (2003b) included in the accompanying box. For example, a sprint in track or swimming will require a short burst of activity that commonly will not induce bronchospasm. However, if children do not adequately prepare for the demands of daily activity, their performance and condition may deteriorate if the activity is repeated over several days. This is also apparent in athletes who run or swim in several qualifying races before their final event.

In the past children with asthma have been restricted from participating in physical education. As a result, some children may possess extremely low cardiovascular efficiency. In some children the slightest exertion may cause heavy breathing, similar to that of individuals who are not physically fit, while strenuous exercise beyond 8 to 10 minutes usually elicits exercise-induced bronchospasm. It will be necessary for children, parents, and teachers to consult the asthma management plan, recognize the signs of an attack, and initiate proper safety procedures while the episode is still mild. When children become aware of an attack, they can slow their pace or stop the activity for a brief period. Additionally, with a well-controlled, progressive program, teachers may terminate exercise for the day, recording the child's performance as a goal to surpass the next day. For example, if children suffer distress while walking or jogging, teachers can record a distance ($3^1/2$ laps) and time (3:15), which may become the next day's goal or even the next day's time for a rest interval.

The potential for EIA is an obvious concern. If children become fatigued or dehydrated or are inadvertently pushed to exertion, some symptoms may develop. However, with medication, interval activity, and submaximal exercise, EIA will generally not be induced. Teachers should gradually increase the activity until mild exercise can be tolerated and sustained for 15 minutes, four times per week. One should remember that with severe asthma, this objective may take several years to reach and should be attempted only in consultation with the physician.

Actions for the Physical Education Teacher/Coach

- Follow the action plan. If indicated, follow premedication procedures before exercise; know how to access the plan and consult with the school nurse.

- Appreciate that exercise can cause acute episodes for many children with asthma. Exercise in cold, dry air and activities that require extended running appear to trigger asthma more readily than other forms of exercise. However, medication can be taken before exertion to help avoid an episode. This preventative medicine enables most children with exercise-induced asthma to participate in any sport they choose.

- Warm-up and cool-down activities appropriate for any exercise will also help the child with asthma.

- Keep medications available for activities that take place away from school or after regular school hours.

- Keep relief medication readily available. Learn signs of distress and allergic reactions. Have an emergency plan.

- Encourage exercise and participation in sports for children with asthma. When asthma is under good control, children with the disease are able to play most sports. A number of Olympic medalists have asthma.

- Encourage children with asthma to participate actively in sports, but also recognize and respect their limits. Permit less strenuous activities if a recent illness precludes full participation.

- Maximize communication with parents, health care providers, and school staff. Learn about triggers and medication plans.

Source: National Heart, Lung, and Blood Institute (2003a).

Guidelines for Activity

Generally, with proper medication and training, participation in physical education, sports, and recreational activities is within the realm of children with asthma. Once teachers are prepared to manage the program, the following guidelines should be followed when implementing the activity program:

- Children should take medication as prescribed.
- Monitor with a peak flow meter.
- Recognize the warning signs of asthma.
- Avoid triggers.
- Intervene with proper treatment.
- Work with school team to treat symptoms.

Warm-up and Cool-down Exercises

A gentle warm-up consisting of flexibility exercises and stretching, mild cardiovascular activity (walking), and muscular strength and endurance activities (push-ups and sit-ups) will aid in bronchodilation and the breathing process (Berman & Sutton, 1986; Hogshead & Couzens, 1990). Warm-up exercises should accompany each activity session for approximately 6 to 10 minutes, not raising the heart rate to more than 150 beats per minute (Bar-Or, 1983).

Progressive Exercise Activities

Initially, teachers should select activities that require the child to work for 5 minutes and then rest for 5 minutes, gradually increasing the duration and intensity (Katz, 1987; Gong, 1992). Swimming is probably the ideal activity for children with asthma. Fewer attacks occur during swimming, even in a competitive atmosphere. Also, children manifest fewer breathing problems in a horizontal position, although on land the horizontal position does not alleviate breathing difficulty. Forced and coordinated breathing in the front crawl also has positive benefits because of the proper diaphragmatic breathing techniques used in the stroke. Swimming is also ideal for a progressive endurance program, because children can stop when fatigued, rest at the end of a lap, and use kickboards and flotation devices to keep the activity submaximal. As muscular strength, cardiovascular conditioning, and swimming techniques improve, children will be more apt to increase endurance levels for the activity as well as postpone fatigue and possibly reduce their reliance on medication (Fitch, Morton, & Blanksby, 1976).

Traditionally, running has been contraindicated for children because of EIA, especially in cold weather. However, if running events are of short duration, they should not induce bronchospasm. Because most bronchospasm will subside in approximately 20 minutes, children may "run through" the condition after initially feeling some discomfort (Fitch, Blitvich, & Morton, 1986; Hogshead & Couzens, 1990). Generally, rather than run through periods of discomfort, it is more beneficial to utilize combinations of walk/jog/run and long and slow distances. In this manner exercise can be initiated at a submaximal level and increased based on the child's tolerance level for activity. Programs for children with asthma may vary, and activities can be modified or substituted to take into account atmospheric conditions and/or match the child's specific needs. For example, stationary cycling and walking are activities that are appropriate for developing a progressive exercise program. Hiking and cross-country skiing, even with thermal problems, may also contribute to increased functional ability.

Muscular Strength and Endurance

Resistance training may be utilized in a progressive strength program, especially if the exercises used to strengthen the respiratory muscles are implemented in a circuit training program (Bar-Or, 1983). By using low resistance with a progressive number of repetitions, children can stretch and increase the endurance of muscles in respiration. Teachers should also stress appropriate breathing and lifting techniques, because proper breathing while moving resistance is actually a form of diaphragmatic breathing and is required in a weight-training program. One precaution with progressive resistance exercises is that children should not move weights overhead because the increased stress of the overhead position may cause irritations of the lining of the lungs and bronchiole tubes.

Pre-exercise Medication

To stabilize the pulmonary structures, medication may be used prior to activity or in conjunction with the warm-up procedure. Especially in the case of EIA, medication should be taken approximately 30 minutes prior to activity. Medication, especially aerosols, may also be taken during activity to alleviate asthma symptoms.

Sports and Games

Most activities that are intermittent in nature are appropriate for the child with asthma. It is important for teachers to emphasize correct technique in tennis, golf, baseball, basketball, and skiing to minimize the amount of effort required to perform the activity. Teachers should have children perform at submaximal levels when learning the skill, gradually increasing the duration and intensity of the activity.

Adaptation may be necessary for individuals in some activities. For example, teachers may substitute more frequently in basketball, gradually increasing the playing time based on the student's tolerance. The child may not want to leave the activity, however, so it is essential to teach the warning signals of an impending attack and to stress increasing the tolerance and duration of activity. Additionally, activities such as the trampoline, gymnastics, and jump rope have been successful because they are intermittent-type activities and help dislodge mucus from the breathing pathways.

Relaxation

Relaxation activities should be used to stretch and relax the muscles of the diaphragm. In addition, relaxation is appropriate for relieving stress and controlling emotions that may precipitate an attack. Relaxation also promotes efficient breathing and can be used to forestall an attack once coughing has begun (Lehrer, Hochron, McCann, Swartzmann & Reba, 1986). Progressive relaxation may help children control wheezing and relax the diaphragm, as may a cool-down exercise after strenuous activity (Freeberg, Hoffman, Light & Krebs, 1987; Hogshead & Couzens, 1990). Another method of promoting relaxation and learning to recognize an impending attack is to develop home-based materials, including charts, activities, and motivational devices, for children and parents to learn about asthma and to take the appropriate steps when confronted with stressful situations or warm-up before activity. Many of these materials are available to teachers from the American Lung Association and the National Heart, Lung and Blood Institute.

Cystic Fibrosis

Cystic fibrosis is a genetic life-threatening disease with an incidence of 1 per 2,500 live births. The disease is inherited as a autosomal recessive trait carried by both parents and is primarily confined to Caucasians. Cystic fibrosis is assumed to be an abnormality or inadequacy of the hormones or enzymes of the body that involve the respiratory track, gastrointestinal tract, and sweat glands.

The child's physical appearance depends on the severity and clinical state of the disease. Because of hyperinflated lungs, the chest will have a large, rounded appearance, while the abdomen will be distended due to gas from poor digestion and frequent passage of a large quantity of stools. The limbs are thin, and children have a frail appearance. Puberty may be delayed as a consequence of chronic illness and motivation (Orenstein, 2003). The prognosis of the disease varies; approximately 60 to 75 percent of children die before 18 years of age. However, with an increase in early diagnosis and treatment intervention, the life expectancy of individuals with cystic fibrosis has increased dramatically with a better quality of life (Cystic Fibrosis Foundation, 2009).

In cystic fibrosis, the membranes that line the organs produce an abnormally thick and sticky mucus that clogs the bronchiole tubes and interferes with the breathing process. Additionally, the pancreatic ducts are obstructed, preventing digestive enzymes from reaching the small intestine and resulting in malnutrition. Furthermore, the diseased pancreas contains cysts, and fibrous scarring can occur in advanced stages of the disease.

Although the lungs, pancreas, and intestinal mucus and sweat glands are affected, the clogging and obstruction of the bronchiole tubes and lower respiratory tract is the most serious problem of cystic fibrosis. More than 90 percent of all deaths result from progressive obstruction of the bronchiole tube resulting in infection (Nixon, 1997; Orenstein, Henks, & Cerney, 1983). The sputum that clogs these tubes allows for colonization of bacteria that cannot be eradicated, causing a low degree of pulmonary function. Because the mucus secreted by the bronchiole tubes is not easily expelled, the lungs are not cleared, the breathing passageways are obstructed, and the respiratory process is decreased. As in asthma, children with cystic fibrosis can inhale more easily because the bronchiole tubes will dilate,

CASE STUDY

Bradley is an elementary student with a pulmonary problem different from asthma. Bradley's cystic fibrosis affects his breathing from the accumulation of a sticky mucus that clogs pulmonary structures and restricts breathing. He misses class often due to pulmonary infections and has difficulty keeping up with his classmates during activity. Bradley is a little small for his age but wants to participate with his peers. His teacher, Mr. Croce, is very supportive of Bradley and tries to involve him during all activities and allows him to participate at his own rate. Mr. Croce has also developed some home-based exercises for Bradley to do when he misses school. He encourages Bradley to utilize exercises that help with pulmonary clearance and strengthen the muscles used in respiration.

whereas clogged bronchiole tubes become smaller and more restricted during exhalation. Perhaps even more threatening to the progressive deterioration of the condition is the prevalence of infection in the bronchiole tubes, which is due to poor clearance of inhaled materials, inadequate removal of sputum, and damage to the tissues in the lungs. Infection and inflammation also may interfere with lung defenses. Tissue damage results from the release of toxins from inflammation and infection (Orenstein, 2003). According to Orenstein (2003), the rate and intensity of progressive deterioration varies; some younger children have several complications, whereas young adults may demonstrate only mild pulmonary problems.

Another concern for children with cystic fibrosis is the deficit in the reabsorption of sodium, which leads to an increased level of sodium and chloride concentrations in perspiration. Because of this, children may be at risk of injuries resulting from heat and/or humidity. In addition, the presence of cystic fibrosis is determined by analyzing perspiration for abnormal sodium and chloride concentrations.

The treatment of cystic fibrosis has developed to overcome some of the problems indicated by the disease. The pancreatic insufficiency necessitates synthetic pancreatic extracts to aid in the digestive process. Vitamin supplements (A, D, E, K) are utilized, because children may demonstrate malnutrition and have difficulty absorbing nutrients directly from food. Salt is given freely, especially after periods of physical activity, and fluid replacements are encouraged for children. The congestion in the lungs is treated primarily through the use of antibiotics, which work to decrease the production of sputum and the colonization of bacteria. Daily pulmonary therapy, including postural drainage, aerosol therapy, and mist tents to dilute the secretions in the lungs, is used outside school to aid in the ejection of mucus.

LEARNING ACTIVITY

Compare and contrast the differences in pulmonary function between asthma and cystic fibrosis. What exercises and medications are appropriate for each disorder?

The primary responsibility of teachers should be to help children clear pulmonary secretions and to increase their tolerance for exercise. The use of activity as therapy for cystic fibrosis has only recently been advocated and includes the following beneficial effects (Bar-Or & Rowland, 2004):

- Improved clearance of mucus
- Increased endurance and strength of respiratory muscles
- Reduced airway resistance
- Improved exercise tolerance
- Improved sense of well-being

Increased activity will aid in preventing the accumulation of sputum and possibly deter the progressive condition of the disease (Canny & Levison, 1987; Nixon, 1997). Because many individuals may be overprotected at home, it is necessary to encourage activity and allow participation with peers. Participation will not only increase tolerance to activity, but also promote the development of a positive body image and self-esteem (Edlund et al., 1986; Horvat & Carlile, 1991).

When selecting activities for children with cystic fibrosis, teachers should encourage individuals to cough freely and expel excess mucus and allow them to go to the bathroom often, take the appropriate medication, supplement salt, and base the program on their exercise tolerance to increase participation gradually. Activities should be selected to strengthen abdominal muscles, chest, and shoulders to overcome deformities associated with posture and the hyperinflation of the lungs. Activities such as tennis, canoeing, golf, skiing, horseback riding, and weight training utilize the respiratory muscles of the upper body and are ideal in helping to improve the exercise performance of students with cystic fibrosis (Horvat & Carlile, 1991; Keens et al., 1977; Strauss et al., 1987).

Active sports such as running, cycling, and swimming require short bursts of energy and help create coughing, expelling sputum and increasing endurance (Zach, Purrer, & Oberwaldner, 1981). Individuals should be excused periodically to expel mucus, and any social stigma attached to this occurrence should be discouraged and, ideally, eliminated.

Orenstein and others (1981, 1995, 2003) have suggested a program consisting of warm-up, walking, jogging, cool-down, and games as appropriate for children with cystic fibrosis to increase their pulmonary function and exercise tolerance. Wilbourn (1978) has also advocated running to increase tolerance, while Schleichkorn (1977) has encouraged children with cystic fibrosis to participate in any form of exercise in which they feel capable, including football, basketball, skating, dancing, tennis, roller-skating, gymnastics, tumbling, and badminton. Scheiderman-Walker et al., (2009) utilized a home-based exercise program and stressed variations to facilitate compliance. Orenstein (1995) has recommended games such as tennis, where skill is more essential than strength or endurance but encourages children to participate as fully as possible. Because the program and activities are similar to those of children with other pulmonary disorders, most activities may be used for either disorder. It is of primary importance to encourage active participation rather than exclusion from physical activity and focus on several aspects of fitness including aerobic endurance, balance, flexibility, and motor skills (Gruber et al., 2008).

For children with cystic fibrosis, physical activity such as running, swimming, and upper body exercises may be used in conjunction with pulmonary therapy and may serve as an alternative to tedious chest therapy sessions. By working in conjunction with physicians, teachers can develop a program based on the child's needs that will increase his or her tolerance level, remove excess sputum, and consist of activities that are not injurious to the lungs (Edlund et al., 1986; Stanghelle et al., 1986; Stanghelle, Michalsen, & Skyberg, 1988).

CHAPTER SUMMARY

1. Two of the more common respiratory disorders in children are asthma and cystic fibrosis. Both disorders contribute to school absenteeism and a decreased exercise tolerance, which may interfere with active participation in physical and recreational activities and with quality of life.

2. Because most children with respiratory disorders are educated in a regular class setting, it is necessary that the teacher be familiar with the etiology and characteristics of respiratory disorders as well as the general functioning of the respiratory system.

3. The major symptoms of asthma are a hacking cough, wheezing, dyspnea, and a feeling of constriction in the chest. An asthma attack may result in severe bronchiole obstruction with no passage of air.

4. Asthma may be caused by allergies, exercise, the environment, or psychological factors.

5. Because breathing is affected by asthma, the muscles used in respiration need to be developed. Breathing exercises should constitute an integral part of the physical activity program for children with asthma.

6. Asthma is generally controlled through medication that aids in bronchodilation. The most common and fast-acting types of bronchodilators are the aerosols.

7. Activities should be selected that gradually increase work tolerance by improving cardiovascular and musculoskeletal functioning, thus reducing the demands for physical exertion.

8. Many activities need not be modified or adapted for children with mild cases of asthma; however, for those children who are more severely involved, activities that are intermittent in nature are advisable.

9. Cystic fibrosis is a life-threatening condition involving excessive secretion of mucus, saliva, and perspiration. Physical appearance depends on the severity and clinical state of the disease.

10. In cystic fibrosis the membranes that line the organs produce an abnormally thick and sticky mucus, which clogs the bronchiole tubes and interferes with the breathing process.

11. Physical activity has recently been advocated as therapy for children with cystic fibrosis and includes the following benefits: improved clearance of mucus, increased endurance of respiratory muscles, reduced airway resistance, and improved exercise performance.

REFERENCES

American Lung Association. (2009). *Asthma friendly schools initiative toolkit*. Washington, D.C.: Author.

Bar-Or, O., & Rowland, T.W. (2004). *Pediatric exercise medicine*. Champagne, IL: Human Kinetics

Bar-Or, O. (1983). *Pediatric sports medicine for the practitioner*. New York: Springer-Verlag.

Berman, L. B., & Sutton, J. R. (1986). Exercise for the pulmonary patient. *Journal of Cardiopulmonary Rehabilitation, 6*, 52–61.

Bundgaard, A. (1985). Exercise and the asthmatic. *Sports Medicine, 2*, 254–266.

Butterfield, S. A. (1993). Exercise-induced asthma—A manageable problem. *Journal of Physical Education, Recreation and Dance, 64*, 15–18.

Canny, G. J., & Levison, H. (1987). Exercise response and rehabilitation in cystic fibrosis. *Sports Medicine, 4*, 143–152.

Cypear, D., & Lemanske, R. F. (1995). Exercise-induced asthma. In B. Goldberg (Ed.), *Sports and exercise for children with chronic health conditions* (pp. 149–165). Champaign, IL: Human Kinetics.

Cystic Fibrosis Foundation. (2009). Living with cystic fibrosis. Bethesda, MD: Author.

Edlund, L., French, R., Herbts, T., Ruttenberg, H., Ruhling, R., & Adams, T. (1986). Effects of a swimming program on children with cystic fibrosis. *American Journal of Diseases in Children, 140,* 80–88.

Fitch, K. D. (1986). The use of anti-asthmatic drugs: Do they affect sports performance? *Sports Medicine, 3,* 136–150.

Fitch, K. D., Blitvich, J. D., & Morton, A. R. (1986). The effect of running training in exercise induced asthma. *Annals of Allergy, 57,* 90–94.

Fitch, K. D., Morton, A. R., & Blanksby, B. A. (1976). Effects of swimming training on children with asthma. *Archives of Disease in Childhood, 51,* 190–194.

Freeberg, P. D., Hoffman, L. A., Light, W., & Krebs, M. K. (1987). Effect of progressive muscle relaxation on the objective symptoms and subjective responses associated with asthma. *Heart and Lung, 16,* 24–30.

Gong, H. (1992). Breathing easy: Exercise despite asthma. *The Physician and Sports Medicine, 20,* 159–167.

Gruber, W., Orenstein, D. M., Braumann, K. M., & Huls, G. (2008). Health-related fitness and trainability in children with cystic fibrosis. *Pediatric Pulmonology 43,* 953–964.

Hogshead, N., & Couzens, G. S. (1990). *Asthma and exercise.* New York: Holt.

Horvat, M., & Carlile, J. R. (1991). Effects of progressive resistance exercise on physical functioning and self concept in cystic fibrosis. *Clinical Kinesiology, 45,* 18–23.

Katz, R. M. (1986). Prevention with and without the use of medications for exercise induced asthma. *Medicine and Science in Sports and Exercise, 18,* 331–333.

Katz, R. M. (1987). Coping with exercise-induced asthma in sports. *The Physician and Sports Medicine, 15,* 101–108.

Katz, R. M., & Pierson, W.E. (1988). *Exercise induced asthma: Current perspective.* In advances in sports medicine and fitness. W. A. Grana, J. A. Lombardo, B. J. Sharkey, & J. A. Stone (Eds.), Chicago: Year Book Medical Publishers.

Keens, T. G., Krastins, I., Wannamaker, E. M., Levison, H., Crozier, D. N., & Bryan, A. C. (1977). Ventilatory muscle endurance training in normal subjects and patients with cystic fibrosis. *American Review of Respiratory Disease, 116,* 853–860.

Lehrer, P., Hochron, S., McCann, B., Swartzman, L., & Reba, P. (1986). Relaxation decreases large airway but not small airway asthma. *Journal of Psychosomatic Research, 30,* 13–25.

National Heart, Lung and Blood Institute. (2003a). *Managing asthma: A guide for schools.* Bethesda, MD: Author.

National Heart, Lung and Blood Institute. (2003b). *Asthma and physical activity in the school.* Bethesda, MD: Author.

National Heart, Lung, and Blood Institute. (2007). *So you have asthma.* Bethesda, MD: Author.

National Jewish Center for Immunology and Respiratory Medicine. (2009). *Understanding your child and asthma.* Denver: Author.

Nixon, P. A. (1997). Cystic fibrosis. In American College of Sports Medicine, *Exercise management for persons with chronic diseases and disabilities.* (pp. 81–86). Champaign, IL: Human Kinetics.

Orenstein, D.M. (2003). *Cystic fibrosis: A guide for parent and family.* Philadelphia, PA: Lippincott Williams and Wilkins.

Orenstein, D. M. (1995). Cystic fibrosis. In B. Goldberg (Ed.), *Sports and exercise for children with chronic health conditions.* (pp. 167–186). Champaign, IL: Human Kinetics.

Orenstein, D. M., Franklin, B. A., Doershuk, D. F., Hellerstein, H. K., German, K. J., Horowitz, J. C., & Stern, R. C. (1981). Exercise conditioning and cardiopulmonary fitness in cystic fibrosis. *Chest, 80,* 392–98.

Orenstein, D. M., Henks, K. G., & Cerney, F. C. (1983). Exercise and cystic fibrosis. *The Physician and Sports Medicine, 12,* 59–77.

Schleichkorn, J. (1977). Physical activity for the child with cystic fibrosis. *Journal of Physical Education and Recreation, 48,* 50.

Schneiderman-Walker, J., Pollock, S. L., Corey, M., Wilkes, D. D., Canny, G. J., Pedder, L., & Reisman, J.J. (2009). A randomized controlled trial of a 3-year home exercise program in cystic fibrosis. *Journal of Pediatrics*: 136, 273–275.

Stanghelle, J. K., Hjeltnes, N., Michalsen, H., Bangstand, H. J., & Skyberg, D. (1986). Pulmonary function and oxygen uptake during exercise in 11-year-old patients with cystic fibrosis. *Acta Paediatricia Scandanavia, 75,* 651–61.

Stanghelle, J. K., Michalsen, H., & Skyberg, D. (1988). Five-year follow-up of pulmonary function and peak oxygen uptake in 16-year-old boys with cystic fibrosis with special regard to the influence of regular exercise. *International Journal of Sports Medicine, 8,* 19–24.

Strauss, G. D., Osher, A., Wang, C., Goodrich, E., Gold, F., Colman, W., Stabile, M., Dobrenchuk, A., & Keens, T. (1987). Variable weight training in cystic fibrosis. *Chest, 92,* 273–276.

Wilbourn, K. (1978). The long distance runner. *Runner's World, 8,* 62–65.

Zach, M. S., Purrer, B., & Oberwaldner, B. (1981). Effect of swimming on expiration and sputum clearance in cystic fibrosis. *Lancet, 11,* 1201–1203.

CHAPTER 18

Diabetes

CASE STUDY

Ian is a senior in high school who has diabetes. He takes physical education first period every morning and participates in baseball after school. He always eats a good prepractice meal consisting of cereal, fruit, bread, and juice. He finds, however that he becomes fatigued some days and not others. He also reports a lack of energy during practices and games, although he takes insulin every day.

Although Ian takes insulin as prescribed, it would appear his diabetes is not under control. Initially, he needs to monitor and record his blood sugars in the morning before and after breakfast. If his pre-breakfast blood sugar is low (less than 75), the ingestion of carbohydrates would ideally increase his blood glucose to a range of 150–175.

Because Ian is active during first period his blood sugars might well drop to within normal parameters without insulin or a reduced dose of insulin. However, the physical education activities in which he participates from day to day generally vary in intensity and duration and this complicates how much insulin may be required. His physical education teacher and coach have suggested that he test his blood sugars routinely before and after activity. By so doing, he can adjust the insulin or use quick acting sugars accordingly to ensure he does not experience dramatic ups and downs in blood glucose. This maintenance protocol could help Ian perform consistently at higher levels, because it would better accommodate daily fluctuations in diet and levels of physical activity.

With proper planning, an appropriate physical activity program can be designed for children with diabetes. When the disorder is managed properly, individuals with diabetes are usually normal in appearance and not limited in motor functioning. In fact, some individuals with diabetes have had successful careers in professional sports. Many times the management aspects of their disorder prohibit individuals with diabetes from participating in physical activity programs. However, diabetes is not an excuse to avoid exercise but is in fact a reason to engage in activity. While diabetes may present management problems, an understanding of characteristics, safety procedures, treatment, diet, and appropriate exercise can facilitate active participation in physical activity programs. In this context, it is essential that school personnel be aware of diabetes treatment and care required in a school setting (American Diabetes Association, 2008).

Diabetes is a complex metabolic disorder that affects approximately 151,000 children from birth to 20 years of age (National Institutes of Health, 2003). Peak incidence will occur around puberty, with males showing a later peak than females. The ability of the body in the person with diabetes to adequately produce and use insulin is affected, and the individual is unable to utilize sugar properly. There are two types of diabetes, both of which are characterized by metabolic disorders of carbohydrates, fats, and proteins. The current terms used to describe these two types of diabetes are Type I, or insulin-dependent, diabetes; and Type II, or non–insulin-dependent, diabetes. Type II diabetes is adult-onset diabetes and is usually treated with diet and/or medication to regulate blood sugar levels rather than with insulin injections. This type of diabetes is becoming more common in children and is associated with obesity, inactivity, and ethnicity (ADA, 2008). This chapter discusses Type I, or insulin-dependent diabetes, which primarily affects school-aged individuals and is treated with insulin injections because of an inadequate production of insulin.

Characteristics of Diabetes

The majority of children with Type I, or insulin-dependent, diabetes are identified during the school years and constitute approximately 10 to 15 percent of all individuals with diabetes. The advent of diabetes will commonly occur during puberty, although it may develop earlier and sometimes develops in the 20s. Type I is the most common type of diabetes in children and adolescents (ADA, 2008). When diabetes is controlled, the child's height and weight will be similar to those of others of his or her peer group. Type I diabetes is characterized by the sudden appearance of frequent urination, increased thirst, unusual hunger, weight loss, weakness and fatigue, blurred vision, skin disorders and infections, nausea, and vomiting. Diabetes also affects the production of hemoglobin and oxygen transport capabilities by the prolonged elevation of blood glucose levels and affects the endurance capabilities of the uncontrolled diabetic (Berg, 1986). There is also a failure to note increased capillary density with exercise in Type I diabetes (Horton, 1989). The onset of the disease may be recognized immediately or may become evident over a period of several months. Most people with Type I diabetes are not obese or overweight at the onset of the disease, in contrast to people with Type II diabetes (Horton, 1995).

Because children with Type I diabetes may be deficient in insulin production and in their ability to use insulin, it is necessary for teachers and school personnel to understand the metabolic process involved in the disease. Diabetes involves the metabolism of carbohydrates, which are the main source of energy for the body. During this process the body breaks down consumed food and converts it into elements essential for sustaining life, enabling the cells to build and repair tissue (**Figure 18.1**). This substance produced by the body from the breakdown of carbohydrates is called *glucose*. Glucose is then transported to the working muscles and utilized for energy, while the remaining blood sugar is stored as glycogen in the liver, and as fat in adipose tissue, for future activity. In diabetes, the body is unable to use food and glucose properly because of deficient insulin production.

Insulin is a hormone produced by the beta cells in the islets of Langerhans in the pancreas. The pancreas is located adjacent to the stomach and spleen in the abdomen and involves both exocrine or nutritive functions (production of digestive enzymes) and endocrine functions (production of hormones). The body requires insulin in the digestive process to regulate the amount of glucose for use by the cells of the body. Through the action of insulin, the glucose derived from the digestive process will be utilized as energy for the cells as it is transported in the bloodstream and made available for use by body tissues. Insulin dosages should be noted in the Diabetes Medical Management Plan and school procedures should be followed (ADA, 2008).

This process can be explained by comparison with a lock-and-key scenario. In order to open a door, the key must fit a specific lock; for glucose to enter the cell, insulin must open the cell membrane to allow transport to occur. When insulin binds with the cell-receptor site, glucose can enter. When it is not used properly, too much glucose will remain in the bloodstream instead of being used by the cells to produce energy. This deprives the body of energy, while excess glucose builds up in the bloodstream and finally spills into the urine. If insulin is not available to transport the glucose, muscular functioning will be impaired, energy levels will be low, and dehydration and other complications will occur.

Insulin is, then, responsible for making glucose available for muscular action during the consumption of food and making possible the storage of glucose as glycogen in the muscle and liver, and as fat in adipose tissue, for periods of fasting and/or future muscular activity. Insulin will also restrict the burning of body fat. People without diabetes have the innate capacity to regulate glucose levels via insulin, whereas people with diabetes must be cognizant of blood glucose and ingest insulin accordingly. For example, during the nondiabetic's sleep, insulin will circulate through the bloodstream, maintaining an adequate level of glucose in the blood and regulating the release of glucose from the storage deposits in the liver, fat, and muscle in a process called *gluconeogenesis*. In gluconeogenesis,

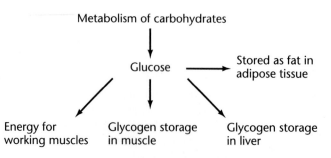

Figure 18.1 Metabolism of carbohydrates.

when the body stores of carbohydrate are low (below normal), moderate quantities of glucose can be formed from amino acids and glycerol portion of fat (Horton, 1989). Approximately 60 percent of amino acids are converted to carbohydrates. Further, new glucose is formed and hepatic stores of glycogen are broken down to re-form glucose in cells by *glycogenolysis*. During this period of inactivity and lack of food, the blood sugar will remain in a relatively narrow range of approximately 60 mg/dl; when the person is awake and functioning, the blood sugar range is approximately 100 mg/dl, and 150 mg/dl following the consumption of calories. In the nondiabetic, amounts of insulin and glucose are regulated automatically, but in the diabetic the beta cells in the pancreas are not able to produce or secrete insulin. Because of the lack of production of insulin, the ability to make glucose available to the cells is affected, causing the blood glucose level to rise. This causes a stimulation of the pancreas to meet the need for insulin that it is unable to produce.

When the body is unable to control high glucose levels, the kidney releases glucose into the urine to decrease the level of sugar in the blood. This is a function of the kidney in terms of reabsorbing glucose. Glucose is spilled into the urine when the ability to reabsorb glucose is exceeded, at 175–200 mg/dl. When the capacity to reabsorb glucose is reached, glucose will be present in the urine. Unfortunately, the elimination of glucose is accompanied by large amounts of water to prevent the urine from becoming thick and resembling maple syrup, and the rapid water loss can lead to dehydration. In order to prevent dehydration, people with diabetes will exhibit excessive thirst.

In addition to excessive thirst (polydipsia) and excessive urination, excessive eating is also directly attributable to the lack of insulin. Children lose a large number of calories in the urine, often as much as three-fourths of the calories ingested, leaving only a small portion available in the blood that can be used to initiate muscular action. Additionally, glycogen cannot be transported to the bloodstream, thus depriving the cells of the glucose needed to produce energy. As a result, the person with diabetes consumes more calories to alleviate this deficiency. All of these are the "textbook" symptoms associated with diabetes and should be used strictly for identifying uncontrolled diabetics.

Children with Type I diabetes have poorly functioning beta cells to produce the amount of insulin that is required for controlling glucose metabolism. Low concentrations of insulin in the bloodstream then affect the regulation of the release of stored glycogen from the body to maintain an adequate blood sugar level. As a result, the large quantity of glucose produced by the body compounds the problem of already high blood sugar levels and the resulting failure of transporting glycogen to the cells. Insulin regulates glucose levels not only by entering muscle and fat cells but also by preventing stored glycogen from exiting muscle and liver cells by inhibitory responses. Glucose and fatty acids are the major metabolic fuels for muscle and are released into circulation by the liver and adipose tissue, and amino acids are available from the muscle (Horton, 1995). According to the ADA (2008), a target range of insulin will be developed by the child's health care team. Basal insulin (background insulin) works throughout the day while Bolus insulin is given when food is ingested or when blood glucose is too high (correction Bolus) to lower the blood glucose (ADA, 2008). The ADA specifies the insulin to carbohydrate ratio as 1:10 or one-unit of insulin for every 10 grams of ingested carbohydrate.

The alpha cells produce and secrete a hormone called *glucagon*, which raises the blood sugar level by changing the stored glycogen in the liver to glucose, which is transported to the cells by insulin (**Figure 18.2**). Glucagon is a hormone secreted when the blood glucose concentration is low, primarily to convert liver glycogen into glucose to elevate blood glucose (Horton, 1989). In reality, glucagon actually helps increase the uptake of amino acids and stimulate gluconeogenesis. It also has glycogenolytic properties in the liver and, with epinephrine, is a major glucose counter-regulatory hormone during exercise (Horton, 1989). A balance is maintained, with the glucagon keeping the blood glucose from becoming too low while the insulin keeps it from becoming too high. If this does not occur and the balance is distorted, the body cannot use the available sugar to supply its own energy requirement and relies on the energy in fat stored in the body. This occurs in normal metabolism.

For some individuals, glucagon can be injected to raise blood glucose levels by stimulating the liver to

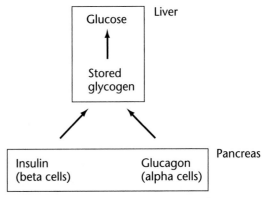

Figure 18.2 Regulation of insulin and glucose.

release stored glucose and is a treatment for severe hypoglycemia (ADA, 2008). The recovery time from hypoglycemia will vary according to the blood glucose level and the duration before the treatment (ADA, 2008). Trained individuals performing at higher intensities (VO$_2$ max) will use less carbohydrate and more free fatty acids (FFA) than untrained individuals. In this context, the trained individual will have a slower rate of decline of muscle and liver glycogen stores, a trait commonly associated with greater endurance (Horton, 1989). The problem in diabetes is that instead of glucose metabolism, there is excessive fat metabolism and increased ketone production, which leads to ketoacidosis.

Ketones form when the body cannot utilize glucose to supply energy. Although the presence of low levels of ketones is not dangerous when glucose levels are normal, when fewer calories are consumed the body breaks down excess stored fat. The production of ketones (ketosis) alters the acid base (pH) chemistry when the body cannot eliminate these by-products rapidly enough or when too many are produced, resulting in a high-acid state called *ketoacidosis*. Ketosis is the accumulation of ketones in the body from the incomplete metabolism of fatty acids. It is generally caused by carbohydrate deficiency or inadequate utilization and an abnormal state of acidity due to rapid and incomplete breakdown of fat (Campaigne & Lampman, 1994). The presence of ketones is a sign that diabetes is poorly controlled, requiring prompt attention. This is a life-threatening situation that calls for immediate medical attention and the administration of insulin to restore proper chemistry, regulating the amount of glucose and insulin in the blood. When the chemistry of the body is affected by the production of ketones, the blood sugar level is dangerously high, and dehydration occurs. A medical emergency called *hyperglycemia* occurs, which may lead to diabetic coma. Hyperglycemia, excess sugar in the blood, usually develops gradually over a longer period of time. A diabetic coma will occur when too much sugar remains in the blood because there is insufficient insulin to use it properly (NIH, 2003). The detection of hyperglycemia is quite difficult but is usually characterized by fatigue and lethargy. The most prevalent sign may be the "fruity" odor of the diabetic's breath. Individuals with diabetes are especially prone to hyperglycemia when insulin is omitted, during infections, in periods of stress, and when there is a minimal compliance to diet.

Immediate action is necessary to prevent diabetics from lapsing into a coma. Children should be taken to a physician or hospital for the injection of insulin. Physical education teachers do not administer insulin but must recognize these symptoms in order to circumvent emergency situations and provide prompt medical attention.

Hypoglycemia is the other reaction that results when insulin and glucose are not maintained in a proper balance. In hypoglycemia due to excess blood insulin, blood sugar is too low to sustain muscular action, and fainting occurs. Children and teachers should recognize that in strenuous physical activity extra sugar is required to balance what is burned during active participation. More energy is required for physical activity, illness, infection, periods of growth, fatigue, excitement, and anxiety that may adversely affect the balance between sugar and insulin. Individuals with diabetes must always be prepared to treat insulin reaction by taking quick-acting sugars to maintain this balance. Hypoglycemia may also occur when too much insulin is administered, meals are skipped or delayed, not eating as prescribed in the management plan, exercising too long or intensely, or a combination of these factors (NIH, 2003).

The hypoglycemic reaction (**Table 18.1**) is characterized by a confused mental state, lack of coordination, impaired movement, and finally a loss of consciousness. The onset of hypoglycemia varies in most individuals but is generally quite rapid. It is important, there-fore, for teachers and children to recognize any warning signs or symptoms to prevent a life-threatening situation.

Evaluation of Blood Sugar

In the past, urine tests have been implemented to record the sugar level in the diabetic's urine at periodic daily intervals to maintain essential blood sugar levels. These tests involved dipping treated paper into the urine. The color of the paper then indicated the amount of sugar present in the urine. Diabetics usually tested their urine three or four times a day with a tape corresponding to specific colors to determine the level of sugar in the urine. However, the accuracy of these tests in identifying blood glucose levels is poor, and the process is now obsolete.

Recently, several home tests have been developed to measure blood sugar by reading a single drop of blood. Self-monitoring devices can be used to measure more specific levels of blood sugar to determine how much sugar is needed to normalize the blood glucose level.

Former athletes have credited the monitoring of blood sugar as a precise method of monitoring insulin requirements and ability to improve performance. When the child's blood sugar is excessively high or dangerously low, he or she will tire easily and lack energy. By monitoring blood sugar levels

Table 18.1 Comparison of Hypoglycemia and Hyperglycemia

Symptom*	Hypoglycemia (Insulin Reaction)	Hyperglycemia (Diabetic Coma)
Onset	Symptoms appear rapidly	Symptoms are gradual
Skin	Pale, moist	Dry, hot skin
Behavior	Confused, irritable	Drowsy, lethargic
Breath	Normal	Fruity odor (acetone)
Breathing	Normal to rapid	Heavy, labored breathing
Sugar in urine	Absent or slight	Large amounts
Hunger	Present	Absent
Thirst	Absent	Extreme thirst
Performance	Decreased	Decreased

*Symptoms may be present and vary according to degree of reaction and the individual's response.

with self-monitoring devices, the athlete can achieve more exact and quicker results than by using urine tests. The athlete will know immediately what remedy is required to reverse his or her current status—either eat more carbohydrates, or add more insulin to resolve their diabetic problem. Consistent monitoring will allow children to feel better and to postpone fatigue (Schechter, 1985; ADA, 2008).

Planning the Physical Activity Program

Children with diabetes will present unique problems for teachers. Although these children will require special assistance to manage their problems, teachers should not call attention to the disorder or cause children to feel different from their classmates. Children with diabetes may encounter difficulties in balancing their diet and partaking in physical activity but should function appropriately if communication is maintained among the health care team members to alleviate anxiety and confusion concerning diabetes. Shared knowledge and cooperation among parents, teachers, and medical and school personnel will contribute to accomplishing specific tasks in the management plan for diabetes. The Diabetes Medical Management Plan (DMMP) may contain specific content information, health care providers, insulin, and blood glucose monitoring including insulin pumps, meals and snack information, exercise and treatment for hypoglycemic/hyperglycemic. This document is completed by the parent and health care team and is kept at the school to facilitate diabetes management (NIH, 2003). The DMMP should include:

- Emergency contact information
- Level of self-care

- Blood glucose monitoring
- Insulin/medication administration
- Glucagon administration
- Meal and snack schedule
- Physical activity and sport
- Recognition and treatment of hypoglycemia and hyperglycemia.

Initially it is helpful for teachers to gather information before the school year begins to determine the child's routine and specific needs. Teachers should be aware of the following guidelines when developing the physical activity program for children with diabetes (American Diabetes Association, 2008):

- Do not assign vigorous physical exercise before lunch.
- Allow a midmorning or afternoon snack if this is part of the dietary plan.
- Allow children an inconspicuous place for snacking and urine/blood testing.
- Have sugar readily available.
- Encourage children to carry some form of sugar and to recognize their own reactions.
- Encourage children to consume extra calories prior to strenuous exercise.
- Be aware of symptoms of hyperglycemia and hypoglycemia, and inform teachers and coaches.
- Administer safety and treatment procedures consistent with school and medical policies.

Treatment for Hypoglycemia and Hyperglycemia

Although the proper management of diabetes should prevent any medical complications, teachers should be able to implement certain procedures that may be required in physical activity programs. An individualized Diabetes Medical Management Plan should be developed with input from parents, the diabetes care team, and school personnel. This plan can be used in conjunction with the IEP to address the heath care needs of the child (ADA, 2008). Hypoglycemic reactions cause a rapid falling of blood sugar that necessitates immediate treatment and generally occurs before meals and during or after exercise. Mild symptoms include trembling, shaking, rapid heart rate, palpitations, increased sweating, and excessive hunger. Moderate symptoms may include irritability, and impaired concentration and attention. Severe reactions may result in the inability to swallow, unresponsiveness, and convulsions (NIH, 2003).

The following treatment for hypoglycemic reactions is recommended by the ADA (2008): *Provide sugar immediately.* This can take the form of a liquid fruit juice or one-half cup of carbonated soda pop (not diet), which can be absorbed more quickly than hard candies without the chance of choking. Children may need coaxing to eat. Within 10 minutes improvement should be evident, at which point additional food should be ingested and the normal school routine resumed. If improvement is not noted in 10 to 15 minutes, parents and/or physicians should be notified. If children are unable to swallow, nothing should be given orally, and medical attention is required. Children should carry edibles with them for emergencies

Teachers should also recognize the symptoms leading to hypoglycemic reaction and be aware of the balance between activity, diet, and/or insulin. If the balance has been altered or activity increased, proper management will include increasing food intake prior to exercise or decreasing the amount of insulin to maintain this balance. Insulin may be required at meals or require ratio dose and correction dose (ADA, 2008).

For hyperglycemia, immediate action is necessary to prevent children from lapsing into a diabetic coma. Children with diabetes should be taken to a physician or hospital immediately for an injection of insulin, though all parties involved should remember that the situation is not easily reversed and resolved with insulin. If symptoms approach a diabetic coma, there is a severe problem in management of this disease and in recognition of the condition. In this instance the DMMP should be followed stringently. In addition, the Quick Reference Emergency Plan in **Figure 18.3** can provide school personnel with specific directions for treatment (NIH, 2003).

Insulin is injected for absorption into the bloodstream because an oral dosage may be destroyed by the oral enzymes that digest or break down protein. Various insulins will be utilized for specific purposes. Short-term or rapid-acting insulin and intermediate-acting insulin work faster and last briefly but are useful in situations in which the quickest entry into the blood is required, whereas long-term insulin is used to provide insulin throughout the day. With monitoring and the use of multiple-dose insulin, children should be able to manage their own diabetes (Horton, 1995).

Insulin is commonly injected into the subcutaneous fat above the muscle and not directly into an exercising muscle. Care must be taken against injection into active muscles because of the rapid absorption into the bloodstream at the injection site and the subsequent drop in blood sugar level. Most injections should be in areas not heavily used, such as the abdomen, gluteal area, deltoid, or thigh area. The site of injection depends on the activity, that is, on the nonexercising muscles (e.g., in the arm when the child is running or in the leg when the child is swimming).

Insulin injections include a combination of rapid-acting insulin, peaking in 1 hour; short-acting insulin, peaking in 2 hours; intermediate insulin, peaking in 4 to 6 hours; and a long-lasting insulin, which peaks in 7 to 8 hours. Insulin pump therapy may also be used to provide short-acting insulin at a continuous rate or at times when blood sugar is too high or prior to a meal. The number, choice, or combination of insulins is selected by the physician and health care team and is based on the nature of the diabetes, age, size, diet, and activity patterns. Many children will require multiple injections, or a split or correction dose of approximately two-thirds the daily dosage in the morning and one-third prior to the evening meal or bedtime. Teachers must be cautioned that insulin in not a cure-all for the individuals with diabetes. Children should not rely primarily on insulin to manage diabetes but should stringently maintain a balance among insulin, diet, and exercise.

LEARNING ACTIVITY

Visit a local pharmacy or the American Diabetes Association website, and identify various types of available insulin. Discuss how various insulin types are used in the successful management of diabetes.

Diet

For insulin-dependent children, diet can contribute to the maintenance of daily living by lowering blood sugar and avoiding problems associated with insulin reactions. When used in conjunction with exercise, diet may aid in reducing dependence on insulin and avoiding complications associated with diabetes, such as blindness, kidney failure, and coronary disease.

Quick Reference Emergency Plan
for a Student with Diabetes
Hyperglycemia
(High Blood Sugar)

Photo

Student's Name

Grade/Teacher   Date of Plan
Emergency Contact Information:

Mother/Guardian   **Father/Guardian**

Home phone   Work phone   Cell   Home phone   Work phone   Cell

School Nurse/Trained Diabetes Personnel

Contact Number(s)

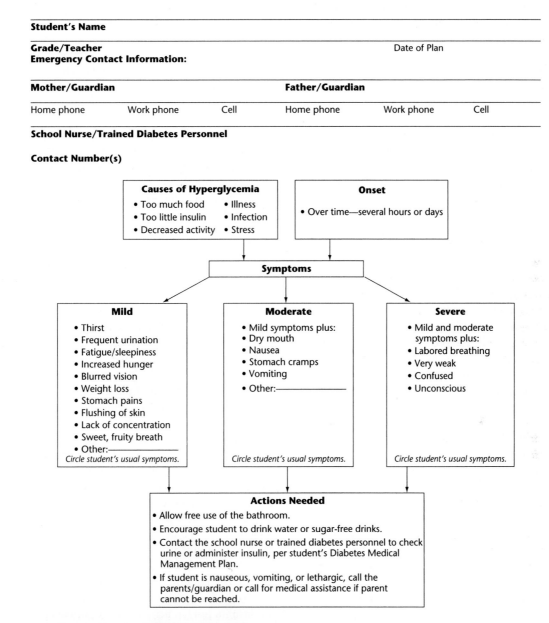

Causes of Hyperglycemia
- Too much food   • Illness
- Too little insulin   • Infection
- Decreased activity • Stress

Onset
- Over time—several hours or days

Symptoms

Mild
- Thirst
- Frequent urination
- Fatigue/sleepiness
- Increased hunger
- Blurred vision
- Weight loss
- Stomach pains
- Flushing of skin
- Lack of concentration
- Sweet, fruity breath
- Other:————
Circle student's usual symptoms.

Moderate
- Mild symptoms plus:
- Dry mouth
- Nausea
- Stomach cramps
- Vomiting
- Other:————
Circle student's usual symptoms.

Severe
- Mild and moderate symptoms plus:
- Labored breathing
- Very weak
- Confused
- Unconscious
Circle student's usual symptoms.

Actions Needed
- Allow free use of the bathroom.
- Encourage student to drink water or sugar-free drinks.
- Contact the school nurse or trained diabetes personnel to check urine or administer insulin, per student's Diabetes Medical Management Plan.
- If student is nauseous, vomiting, or lethargic, call the parents/guardian or call for medical assistance if parent cannot be reached.

Written Plans for Diabetes Management

Plan	What it covers	Who writes it
DMMP	*"Doctors Orders"* - details all aspects of routine and emergency diabetes care	Personal health care team
504 Plan IEP	*Education plans* - details both health care and educated related aids, services, accommodations, and special education services the student needs.	504 team IEP team
IHP	*School nursing care plan* - specifies how diabetes care as prescribed in the DMMP will be delivered in the school	School nurse
Quick Reference Emergency	*Tool for school staff* - how to recognize and treat hypoglycemia or hyperglycemia	School nurse

Figure 18.3 Quick Reference Emergency Plan.

Source: National Institute of Health (2003).

Individuals with diabetes should strive for a balance of calories consumed and expended. Traditionally, the American Diabetes Association has recommended diabetic diets consisting of 60% carbohydrate, 30% protein, and 10% fat. Insulin secretion must be matched with dietary intake to maintain normal blood glucose levels, which should remain constant from day to day. When too many calories are consumed, the blood glucose will rise, so it is essential to keep and maintain this balance.

Children who exercise will find a greater demand for carbohydrates in their diets and should remember that exercise generally will decrease the level of blood sugar; therefore, it is necessary to plan accordingly to maintain this balance. Blood glucose will also continue to decrease after exercise, necessitating testing after exercise and several hours later to document a latent drop (Horton, 1988). The implementation of a diet is often restrictive and discouraging for individuals with diabetes. Each diet should be adapted for individual needs. For example, obese individuals with diabetes, who typically have Type II diabetes, will have an additional complication: Their beta cells are extinct and lose their sensitivity to insulin, and the body will require more insulin to absorb the glucose in the bloodstream and to maintain glycogen storage. This will require obese individuals to implement a weight-reduction program as well as plan a structured diet for their diabetes.

According to the ADA (2008) nutrition planning is essential and should

- Maintain blood glucose in the target range
- Prevent or delay complications
- Facilitate growth and development
- Maintain a healthy weight
- Facilitate learning

Most diets are planned according to the child's size and energy expenditure and should be planned in conjunction with insulin usage to promote adherence. The following guidelines should be used in selection of foods for the individual with diabetes (ADA, 2008):

1. Develop an individualized meal plan. Insulin to carbohydrate ratio varies by child.

2. Time meals and snacks to balance physical activity and insulin.

3. Encourage a sound nutritional plan for all children and a family diet plan.

4. Motivation for compliance to the diet can be encouraged by allowing occasional deviations from the diet and does not always limit the child.

5. Diets should be selected in which the six food groups (grains, vegetables, fruits, milk, meat/lean protein, and fat) can allow for substitutions with other foods in the same group under the auspices of a physician.

6. When exercising add food to the exchange.

7. Nutrient types affect glucose differently; carbohydrates have the biggest effect on blood glucose.

8. The total amount of carbohydrates is more important than the source (sugar or starch).

Exercise

During muscular activity or exercise, the primary fuel for the working muscles is glucose. To sustain exercise, more glucose is required, necessitating the release of glycogen from the liver and resulting in an increase of blood flow and glucose uptake to meet the increased energy demands. As exercise continues, the level of glucose falls, and body fat becomes the major source of energy. In a trained individual, glucose sparing occurs with use of FFA as the major source of energy. Plasma glucagon also rises during exercise, stimulating glycogen breakdown in the liver and maintenance of blood glucose. The decline in insulin and increase in plasma glucagon function together to maintain a constant glucose supply (Horton, 1989). This will occur when glucose levels are near normal prior to exercise. If glucose is 250 mg/dl, glucose will either level out or increase due to increased production of glucose from the liver, with no corresponding increase in use by the muscles, resulting in poorly regulated diabetes. Most physicians recommend a blood glucose level between 100 and 250 mg/dl prior to exercise and caution participants to snack prior to exercise if blood sugar is below 100 mg/dl. In contrast, when the blood sugar level reaches about 250 mg/dl and ketones are present, exercise should be delayed. During activity, the uptake of glucose by the working muscles increases, while the level of insulin that is needed decreases. This is potentially significant for individuals with diabetes because these working muscles will not require increased levels of insulin during activity; thus, the person can rely less on insulin. In fact, activity may improve glucose tolerance as long as 24 to 48 hours after exercise (Landt et al., 1985). At the completion of exercise, blood flow to the muscle decreases, although the uptake of glucose will remain three to four times higher than the resting level for approximately one hour in order to replenish the glucose level in the muscles (Berg, 1986; Campaigne & Lampman, 1994).

The lack of glucose output in diabetics may advance the onset of hypoglycemia unless individuals decrease the amount of insulin or increase the amount of carbohydrates consumed. Exercise allows for this reduction in insulin, while an increased consumption of carbohydrates allows for normal glucose metabolism and reduced insulin (Horton, 1995). A precisely managed exercise program will provide the benefits of reducing the blood sugar level by (1) enhancing the muscle glucose uptake, (2) increasing the sensitivity of the insulin receptors, and (3) increasing utilization of glucose, as well as free fatty acids, by the working muscles (Franz, 1984).

Because activity patterns, and demands of the activity, among children with diabetes may vary according to growth, weather, time of year, and temperature, as well as intensity of exercise, it is essential to coordinate activity with diet and insulin. Previous experiences with activity in conjunction with diet and insulin can be helpful in selecting initial tolerance levels and intensity of physical activities. Most authorities suggest that individuals with diabetes eat before exercise and take a glucose supplement hourly to prevent hypoglycemia, to improve performance, and to maintain blood glucose levels (Horton, 1995). In most instances activity will lower blood glucose; however if insulin is not available, blood glucose can be higher requiring adjustments in monitoring medication and food (ADA, 2008). In this manner, individuals will not be required to increase their insulin and should be able

to reduce their reliance on insulin by proper balance of insulin, diet, and exercise (Berg, 1986).

Implementing the Physical Activity Program

The benefits of physical activity have already been discussed as they relate to maintaining a balance between insulin and blood sugar. However, the physiological and social aspects of physical education and sport must not be neglected. By excluding children with diabetes from participation, teachers hinder the acceptance of their condition by their peers (Engerbretson, 1977). Bierman and Toohey (1977) have also indicated that activity should be practiced in conjunction with medication and diet, with emphasis on health and enjoyment.

No physical or recreational activity is outside the realm of children with diabetes if proper control is maintained (Colberg, 2001; Horton, 1995; Stratton, Wilson, & Endres, 1988; Murphy, 1987). Activities with predictable energy expenditures such as cycling, running, and swimming are recommended over intense activities that are difficult to standardize because of unpredictable

Sample Exercise Session

Preactivity Meal	Glucose Monitoring	Warm-Up	Exercise Session	Cool-Down	Glucose Monitoring
3 hours before	Prior to exercise	5 min.	20–60 min.	5 min.	After exercise

Monitor glucose

Glucose Monitoring:	• Before and after activity.
	• Record information: Adjust and fine-tune insulin/ medication and food.
Warm-up:	• Stretching.
	• Full range of motion.
Exercise:	• Hydrate during activity; ingest extra carbohydrate if needed.
	• Evaluate intensity a few minutes after starting and a few minutes before stopping. Adjust speed if necessary.
	• Monitor blood glucose or insulin.
Cool down:	• Gradually decrease intensity.
	• Stretch muscles used in exercise.
Glucose Monitoring:	• After activity ingest carbohydrates as needed.
	• Hydrate.

energy expenditures (Riddell & Bar-Or, 2002). The activity should be selected on the basis of its ability to help maintain a proper balance between insulin and blood sugar. An evaluation of the child's functional capacity should give teachers an entry point for beginning a program (Fremion, Marrero, & Golden, 1987). The level at which children are able to swim or run should dictate the level of their participation and can be a measure for maintaining the balance between insulin and blood sugar. More intense participation or training for specific sports will require adjustments according to the child's potential and his or her management of diabetes (Blackett, 1988; Riddell & Bar-Or, 2002). The box on page 277 includes a sample exercise session for an athlete with diabetes (Colberg, 2001; Riddell & Bar-Or, 2002).

In physical activity, teachers sometimes do not allow individuals with diabetes to participate because of possible reactions and because of their "delicate" condition. This practice not only is based on false assumptions but also may cause children to hide their condition from teachers and coaches. Clearly teachers must recognize the problems and considerations required to develop and implement an appropriate program; however, educators who take on too much responsibility may also provide a disservice for children with diabetes. Children must learn to manage their diabetes, and teachers should learn not to segregate children from their classmates.

The participation of children with diabetes should not extend beyond their limits or through periods of distress. Children should use these "down" times to sit, conserve energy, and take additional supplements. In addition, teachers must be aware that children with diabetes may use the disease to avoid activities. The best possible approach is for teachers to recognize the importance of activity, be prepared for reactions by keeping fast-acting sugars on hand, and encourage children to participate in as many physical education and sports activities as possible. By being knowledgeable, teachers and school personnel can develop a DMMP and will feel secure in classes, children will feel at ease with their classmates and with physical activity, and the benefits of physical activity are more likely to be achieved.

CHAPTER SUMMARY

1. Diabetes is a complex metabolic disorder that affects the body's ability to produce and/or use insulin.

2. Because diabetes may present a management problem for the teacher, several factors are essential in planning and implementing a physical activity program. These factors include the recognition of the characteristics of diabetes, safety procedures, treatment, diet, and exercise.

3. Type I, or juvenile-onset, diabetes is characterized by an insulin dependence due to inadequate production of insulin. Characteristics include frequent urination, increased thirst, unusual hunger, weight loss, weakness, fatigue, blurred vision, nausea, and skin disorders and infections.

4. Insulin is used to regulate the amount of glucose used by the working muscles. When insulin is not available to transport glucose, muscle functioning will be impaired.

5. Glucagon is a hormone produced by the alpha cells that raises the blood sugar level by changing stored glycogen in the liver to glucose, which is then transported to the cells by insulin.

6. Ketoacidosis is a high-acid and life-threatening state that calls for immediate insulin to regulate the balance of glucose and insulin in the body.

7. Hyperglycemia results when too much blood sugar remains in the blood or there is insufficient insulin to use it properly. Hyperglycemia can lead to diabetic coma.

8. Hypoglycemia is due to excess blood insulin and blood sugar that is too low to sustain muscular action. Quick-action sugar is required to maintain the balance.

9. Insulin injections may be rapid-acting, peaking in 1 hour; short acting, peaking in 2 hours; intermediate, peaking in 4 to 6 hours; or long-lasting, peaking in 7 to 8 hours.

10. During activity, the uptake of glucose by the working muscle is increased, while the amount of insulin needed is decreased. Activity also improves the muscle's uptake of glucose after the termination of exercise.

11. Physical and recreational activities are appropriate for children with diabetes if proper control is maintained.

12. Management of diabetes should rest with diabetics, not teachers. However, educators must recognize management problems and program considerations of children with diabetes.

REFERENCES

American Diabetes Association. (2008). *Diabetes care at school: What key personnel need to know.* Alexandria, VA: Author.

Berg, K. E. (1986). *Diabetic's guide to health and fitness.* Champaign, IL: Human Kinetics.

Bierman, J., & Toohey, B. (1977). *The diabetic's sports and exercise book.* Philadelphia: Lippincott.

Blackett, P. R. (1988). Child and adolescent athletes with diabetes. *The Physician and Sports Medicine, 16,* 133–149.

Campaigne, B. N., & Lampman, R. M. (1994). *Exercise in the clinical management of diabetes.* Champaign, IL: Human Kinetics.

Center for Disease Control and Prevention. (2003). *Take charge of your diabetes,* 3rd edition. Atlanta, GA: Department of Health and Human Services.

Colberg, S. (2001). *The Diabetic Athlete.* Champaign, IL: Human Kinetics.

Engerbretson, D. L. (1977). The diabetic in physical education recreation and athletics. *Journal of Physical Education and Recreation, 48,* 18–21.

Franz, M. J. (1984). *Diabetes and exercise: How to get started.* Minneapolis: International Diabetes Center.

Fremion, A. S., Marrero, D. G., & Golden, M. P. (1987). Maximum oxygen uptake determination in insulin dependent diabetes mellitus. *The Physician and Sports Medicine, 15,* 119–126.

Gordon, N. F. (1993). *Diabetes: Your complete exercise guide.* Champaign, IL: Human Kinetics.

Horton, E. S. (1989). Exercise and diabetes in youth. In C. V. Gisolfl & D. R. Lamb (Eds.), (vol. 2) *Youth, exercise and sports* (pp. 539–570). Dubuque, IA: Benchmark Press.

Horton, E. S. (1995). Diabetes mellitus. In B. Goldberg (Ed.), *Sports and exercise for children with chronic health conditions.* (pp. 355–373). Champaign, IL: Human Kinetics.

Horton, E. S. (1988). Role and management of exercise in diabetes mellitus. *Diabetes Care, 11,* 201–211.

Juvenile Diabetes Foundation International. (1996). *What you should know about diabetes.* New York: Author.

Landt, K., Campaigne, B., James, F., & Sperling, M. (1985). Effects of exercise training on insulin sensitivity in adolescents with type I diabetes. *Diabetes Care, 8*(5), 461–465.

Murphy, P. (1987). Children with medical conditions can go to summer camp. *The Physician and Sports Medicine, 15*(7), 177–183.

National Institutes of Health. (1986). *Diabetes in America.* Washington, DC: United States Department of Health and Human Services.

National Institute of Health. (2003). National Diabetes Education Program. Washington D.C.: United States Department of Health and Human Services.

Riddell, M.C., & Bar-Or, O. (2002). *Children and adolescents: Handbook of exercise in diabetes.* Alexandria, VA: American Diabetes Association 547–565.

Schechter, A. (1985). The diabetic athlete: His toughest opponent is his own metabolism. *Sports Illustrated, 62,* 10–13.

Stratton, R., Wilson, D. P., & Endres, R. K. (1988). Acute glycemic effects of exercise in adolescents with insulin dependent diabetes. *The Physician and Sports Medicine, 16*(3), 150–157.

19

Nutritional Disorders

CASE STUDY

Ron has several children in his class who exceed the recommended BMI or weight for their frame and age. To complicate matters, one child has diabetes, another has severe asthma, while another child is trying to lose weight for an athletic competition. Ron decides to implement a walking/running program that can be modified to accommodate children with individual differences and children who have mobility issues. He teaches the class how to monitor heart rate as well as use heart rate monitors to meet their target heart rate. Ron also has the children record caloric intake (as best they can), and monitor their calorie expenditure versus consumption.

Ron consults with the educational team to establish an individualized program for specific children who want to lose or gain weight, or who want to lead a healthier lifestyle (e.g. the child with diabetes is counseled with regard to diet, exercise, and insulin). Next, Ron has each student categorize what he/she has eaten and determine the number of calories associated with this food group. Additionally, Ron has each student take home and share his/her program with parents so that the family might become a partner in the health intervention.

Nutritional disorders most often encountered in the school setting are obesity, anorexia nervosa, and bulimia nervosa. Each disorder contributes to a decrease in functional ability and presents problems in maintaining a healthy lifestyle. To counteract these problems, teachers must understand the bases of these disorders and implement sound nutritional and exercise alternatives in an appropriate setting.

Obesity

Obesity is rapidly being recognized as a serious health problem for children and is commonly associated with individuals with disabilities because of their relatively nonactive lifestyles. No longer is obesity confined to the adult population—it is presenting a genuine hazard for children. Even with variations in assessment procedures, the prevalence of American adults who were over-weight (≥85 percent of BMI) rose from 25.49 percent in 1976–1980 to 34.70 percent in 1988–1994 the prevalence nearly doubled in children ages 6–11 years from 7.6 percent to 13.7 percent; and rose from 5.7 percent to 11.5 percent among adolescents. According to the Centers for Disease Control (CDC) (2008), the prevalence of obesity (above 30 BMI) increased from 12 percent to 18 percent from 1991 to 1998 (Nestle & Jacobson, 2000). In a recent analysis the prevalence of children and adolescents (6–19 years) at risk for overweight ranges from 19 percent to 35 percent (Henley et al., 2004). Henley et al. (2004) also reported that by their calculations the prevalence of overweight or obesity in American adults approached 65 percent. Although individuals may lose weight, they cannot reduce the number of fat cells accumulated during the developmental years.

Fat cells may shrink during weight reduction, but if the person gains weight they become bigger and often create more fat cells to store the additional calories.

Obesity is highly correlated with risk factors for hypertension, atherosclerosis, heart disease, non-insulin dependent diabetes mellitus, and particularly in young adults psychosocial problems (Bar-Or & Rowland, 2004). However, an even greater concern from a public health point of view is that juvenile obesity will likely result in adult obesity. After adjustment for parental obesity, the ratios for obesity in adulthood with early childhood obesity and adolescent obesity are 1:3 and 17:5, respectively. Furthermore, after adjustment for the child's obesity status, the ratio for obesity in adulthood associated with having one obese parent is significantly greater (Whitaker et al., 1997).

Obesity also affects functional ability as individuals require more effort to initiate and sustain movement. Most children possess the ability to learn a motor skill; however, obesity may directly contribute to a lack of physical fitness and result in awkward movements. Children who are obese often encounter problems with a poor body image and self-concept and frequently become the target of jokes by their classmates. Children may have problems from excessive fat accumulation that restrict their ability to bend and move the trunk and limbs; the insulating effect of fat will cause children to perspire more freely and increase their susceptibility to rapid increases in body temperature; sores and chafing will develop between the legs and under the arms, and the skin will become irritated and inflamed during activity. Finally, excessive weight contributes to postural faults, such as kyphosis, lordosis, flat feet, and general susceptibility to injury.

There are many definitions for overweight and obesity among children and adolescents. Most however are based on weight for age or weight for height. According to Bar-Or and Rowland (2004), the commonly used threshold for being overweight in preschoolers is weight for height at the 95th percentile. In older children and adolescents, the more common criteria is based on body mass index (BMI). Body mass index is the ratio of body weight in kilograms to body weight squared (m^2). The threshold for being overweight using BMI is 85 percent; for being obese using BMI the 95 percent is used. The major drawback for using either of these methods is that they both ignore the contribution of fat mass to total body mass (Bar-Or & Rowland, 2004). For that reason skin folds are often used to measure percent of body fat and obesity.

Obesity is generally defined in the educational setting in relation to the expected weight for a particular height and body type. Children who are *overweight* are 10 to 20 percent above their expected weight, whereas children 20 to 50 percent above their ideal weight are termed *obese,* and above 50 percent, *severely obese.* These definitions are complicated by what actually constitutes ideal body weight and methods for assessing body composition. Other factors, including body type, height, and the distribution of fat, all contribute to the determination of a judgmental ideal weight. Further complicating the determination of an ideal weight are changes reflected in the maturation process that affect the relationship of skinfold fat to body fat. For example, girls at 9 years of age may have a skinfold thickness of 24 millimeters, which may be normal at the 25th percentile for that age group, whereas the same percentage at 14 years of age may place them at the 50th percentile. Hence, the determination of body fat varies across age ranges as during development. As mentioned previously, in absence of what constitutes a standard for normal, the National Heart, Lung, and Blood Institute (NHLBI, 1998), recommends using a body mass index (BMI) that is based on the 85th percentile values for age and gender. The CDC (2008) offers a simple BMI percentile calculator for children and adolescents. This calculator provides BMI and the corresponding BMI-for-age percentile on a CDC BMI-for-age growth chart. This calculator can be used for children 2 through 19 years old.

Dietz (1995), and the NHLBI (1998), indicate that the prevalence of obesity varies by age, sex, ethnicity, and regions of the country. More specifically, obesity increased in children 6 to 11 years by 54 percent and in adolescents 12 to 17 years by 39 percent, using the 85th percentile of the triceps skinfold as a reference point. Dietz (1995) also indicated that the largest increase in obesity occurred in African American children and in boys from 6 to 11 years of age of all races. Obesity is also more prevalent in the northeast, followed by the midwest, south, and west. It is more prevalent in winter and spring.

Biological, psychological, and sociological factors have also been attributed to obesity. Approximately 90 percent of children are overweight because they consume more calories than they are able to expend, with between-meal snacks accounting for 25 to 40 percent of daily caloric intake. The remaining 10 percent are obese because of conditions relating to improper functioning of the endocrine glands. However, the extra accumulation of calories does not always imply overeating and may result from a variety of factors (Bar-Or & Rowland, 2004; Nestle & Jacobson, 2000; NHLBI, 1998). Some of the specific factors that contribute to an increase in the number of calories consumed and resultant obesity include the following:

1. *Overeating.* An excess of caloric intake over the normal expenditure will lead to an accumulation of fat. Overeating may mean extra portions at mealtime or eating between-meal snacks that are

high in calories and low in vitamins and minerals. This problem may be the result of a physiological need but generally develops into a habit rather than hunger.

2. *Inactivity.* An imbalance may also be caused by not expending enough calories to balance the amount of consumed calories. Inactivity is probably the most prominent factor in obesity. Children who are inactive may become even more sedentary because of their obesity. Children with disabilities are generally inactive and overprotected because of their condition; limiting opportunities to participate greatly restricts their activity levels. Television viewing, computer games, and general time on the computer are major causes of inactivity. Based on 1990 data, the odds of being overweight at ages 10 to 15, increased five fold among children watching television more than 5 hours a day, compared to children who only watch television 0 to 2 hours per day. Also, activity patterns appear to aggregate within families. Parental obesity and activity patterns affect a child's activity patterns. Peer relationships also influence a child's level of activity, especially during adolescence.

3. *Psychological problems.* When children are not able to cope with school, stress, social problems, and parents, they may overeat to cope with their problems or depression. Although there is no physiological need for food, the consumption of food initially fills the need caused by problem situations. This can lead to a vicious cycle if the child becomes more obese and insecure about his or her body image, thereby repeating the cycle by eating more.

4. *Genetic patterns.* It is interesting to note that fewer than 10 percent of children who are obese have parents who are not obese, whereas 40 percent have one parent who is obese, and 80 percent have two obese parents. Genetic patterns also contribute to the accumulation of fat in certain areas of the body, such as the hips, thighs, abdomen, and chest. Specific body types are also determined by genetic background, and children should understand that weight loss may be evident in some areas of the body, while weight gain may accumulate in other areas.

5. *Family eating patterns.* Eating habits that are learned in infancy are passed down, as well as attitudes toward activity. For the family who snacks constantly and eats fast foods and desserts, the tendency to put on and retain weight is greater than for the family who plans sensible and nutritious meals.

6. *Endocrine disorders.* Disorders affecting one or more of the endocrine glands can contribute to obesity and generally include the following disorders:

   a. *Thyroid gland.* Malfunctioning results in puffiness and swelling of tissue, but not accumulation of fat.

   b. *Pituitary gland.* Malfunctioning is accompanied by excess hair growth, menstrual irregularities, deposits of fatty tissue around breasts, abdomen, face, and neck.

   c. *Hypothalamus.* Overreaction can cause a signal for hunger when calories are not required. Located in the brain, the hypothalamus regulates the neural input for hunger.

   d. *Adrenal cortex.* Overstimulation of the outer covering of adrenal glands embedded in perineal fat above each kidney is characterized by early development of secondary sex characteristics.

   e. *Iatrogenic obesity.* This kind of obesity results from long-term administration of cortisone or adrenocortical steroids to control asthma, allergies, arthritis, kidney disorders, or leukemia.

Planning the Physical Activity Program

To develop an appropriate program for children who are overweight, it is essential to establish communication among the parent, health educator, nurse, classroom teacher, and the child. Classroom teachers should refer children who are overweight for a fitness and nutritional program while providing encouragement for adherence and monitoring the success of the program.

If children have little or no concern with their physical appearance or are resistant to weight-reduction programs, the likelihood of success will be marginal. Physical education teachers in conjunction with classroom teachers should attempt to create situations that develop an awareness of obesity and discuss factors that can contribute to a successful intervention program. These factors should include diet and nutrition education, self-confidence, parental involvement, modified lunch, behavior modification, attitude about physical activity, and the classroom teacher's availability for assistance in the program (Bar-Or, 1995; Sallis, Chen, & Castro, 1995).

Many times this communication can be established by a letter outlining the proposed program for classroom teachers and parents. In addition, physical education teachers can discuss the program at the parent-teacher meeting or parent education and training seminars. The cooperation of teachers and parents is necessary to ensure success of the program.

The incorporation of every available resource will provide the support and monitoring that is required for effective intervention. In this manner all of those involved can best determine the activities and motivational procedures necessary to meet the child's needs.

Evaluation of Obesity

To properly determine body weight, percentage of body fat, and the overall physical functioning of the child prior to a weight reduction program, the following characteristics should be assessed (Sallis et al., 1995).

1. *Height and weight.* A determination of the height and weight of children may be helpful for future comparison. In addition, height and weight can be used to determine BMI and percentile ranking of individuals.

2. *Attitude and self-concept.* An appraisal of attitudes toward physical activity and self-concept can and should be conducted prior to an activity program to ensure the probability of success in the weight-reduction program. An informal observation by classroom teachers or by parents can provide useful information about the child's interest or lack of interest in physical activity. In addition, teachers or school psychologists can administer an attitude or self-concept inventory to determine interest, self-concept, and body image as an aid in determining the effectiveness of the program.

3. *Physical fitness.* Teachers should determine the physical fitness levels of children, including strength and perceived exertion for activity (Bar-Or, 1995). Body composition measurements or BMI can be determined to evaluate the child prior to activity and during the program. Using Lohman's equation for children, the calf and or subscapular skinfold can be used because of the relative ease of measurement and the high correlation to total body fat (Lohman, 1987, 1992).

The triceps skinfold can be measured over the right arm midway between the elbow and acromion process of the scapula, while keeping the skinfold parallel to the humerus in the upper arm (**Figure 19.1**). Measure the subscapular skinfold on the right side of the body approximately 1 centimeter (½ inch) above the inferior angle of the scapula in line with the natural curve of the skin.

The following procedure is recommended for administering skinfold tests (Lohman, 1987; Rimmer, 1994):

1. Firmly grasp the skin between the thumb and forefinger, and lift the skinfold.

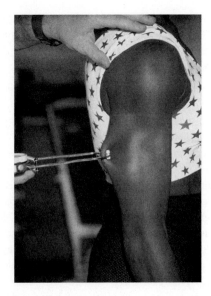

Figure 19.1 Triceps skinfold.

2. Place the contact surfaces of the caliper 1 centimeter, or ½ inch, above or below the finger.

3. Slowly release the grip on the calipers, enabling them to exert tension of the skinfold.

4. Read the skinfold to the nearest 0.5 millimeter after the needle stops, 1 to 2 seconds after releasing the grip on the caliper.

5. Take the measurements three consecutive times, and record the middle score to the nearest millimeter.

In addition, it is useful to practice the testing procedure to become more experienced and accurate in the measurement. Furthermore, the subscapular skinfold should be administered to females while they are wearing a two-piece swimsuit or loose-fitting shirt. To determine percentage of body fat, the results of skinfold measurements can be compared to charts for boys and girls of all ages (**Table 19.1**). The specific skinfold measurements define risks of fatness for boys and girls (Lohman, 1992). For example, a boy whose sum of triceps plus subscapular skinfolds is 21 millimeters is located at optimal range or approximately 15 to 18 percent body fat. Measurement of skinfold thickness can determine the percentage of body fat and risk for fatness. The higher the skinfold, the higher the level of body fat.

Skinfold thickness between 10 and 25 mm in boys and between 15 and 25 mm in girls generally indicates an acceptable level of body fat. Scores in the high to very high range will indicate the necessity for a weight-reduction program, while children in the very low range probably have too little body fat. A scarcity of body fat may also be detrimental because it is indicative of a loss of lean muscle tissue that may contribute to health-related and growth problems. In addition, if

Table 19.1 Percentage of Body Fat in Children

BOYS

Triceps plus calf skinfolds

Range	Skinfold Measurement (mm)	Percentage of Body Fat
Very low	0–5	0–6%
Low	5–10	6–10%
Optimal	10–20	10–20%
Moderately high	25–32	20–25%
High	32–40	25–30%
Very high	40 or above	30% or higher

Triceps plus subscapular skinfolds

Very low	0–9	0–6%
Low	5–13	6–10%
Optimal	13–22	10–20%
Moderately high	22–29	20–25%
High	29–39	25–30%
Very high	39 or above	30% or higher

GIRLS

Triceps plus calf skinfolds

Range	Skinfold Measurement (mm)	Percentage of Body Fat
Very low	0–11	0–12%
Low	11–17	12–15%
Optimal	17–30	15–25%
Moderately high	30–36	25–30%
High	36–45	30–36%
Very high	45 or above	36% or higher

Triceps plus subscapular skinfolds

Very low	0–11	0–11%
Low	11–15	11–15%
Optimal	15–27	15–25%
Moderately high	27–35	25–30%
High	35–45	30–35.5%
Very high	45 or above	35.5% or higher

Source: Data from *Measuring Body Fat Using Skinfolds* [videotape] by T. G. Lohman, 1987, Champaign, IL: Human Kinetics. Copyright 1987 by Human Kinetics Publishers. Used with permission.

medical supervision and evaluation are required, a more specific evaluation may be required before the teacher can develop reasonable training goals for the child with weight problems.

Implementing the Physical Activity Program

Children require opportunities to lose weight. By incorporating opportunities for weight reduction into physical activity programs, teachers can help children lose weight and, more important, maintain the weight loss. Teachers should work within the auspices of the educational team for advice on dietary, emotional, and exercise needs while children are engaged in the program.

To implement a program, it is essential to recognize that calories are the specific amounts of energy that activity will require. Physical activities will burn various amounts of calories, and foods contain a specific caloric content.

For a clear picture of body weight and weight reduction, consideration should be given to caloric intake, caloric content of food, energy expenditure, and calorie cost of activities (Katch & McArdle, 1996). If children maintain a balance between the number of calories consumed and the number expended, they will acheive a constant body weight. By consuming more calories than expected, children will store extra calories in the fat cells, causing a change in body composition and increasing total body fat. If physical activity decreases while more calories are consumed, there is a tendency for the muscles to atrophy while the amount of body fat increases. If children consume more while they maintain the same level of physical activity, both body weight and fat will increase. However, if the amount of calories is reduced while exercise also is restricted, the gain of body fat is negated. Although weight loss is desirable, the decrease in physical activity may result in losing lean body tissue (Eisenman, Johnson, & Benson, 1990).

The best method for children to lose body fat is to reduce the number of consumed calories and increase the level of physical activity. This will ensure that weight loss will occur from the loss of body fat and not from loss of lean muscle tissue (Clark, 2008). A low consumption of calories also initiates metabolic changes, such as a drop in the blood sugar level, that aid in burning stored glycogen and fat and releasing glucose from the liver for activity. Many physiological factors contribute to a weight loss program besides simply caloric intake and the burning of calories. The teacher should consider exercise, nutrition, behavior management, emotional support, and the kind and amount of homework assigned when designing the physical education program.

Exercise

The activity levels of children with weight problems are often low, creating the imbalance of caloric intake that results in increased weight gain and a high percentage of body fat. Often this lack of activity is exacerbated by a fascination with television and video games. In January 2000, the U.S. Department of Health and Human Services launched its Healthy People 2010 initiative and lists physical exercise as its first priority for behavior change and improving the overall health of Americans. Based on this report, participation in regular physical activity is essential for maintaining a healthy body, enhancing psychological wellbeing, and preventing premature death. It also listed objectives for promoting physical education in schools and communities.

Exercise expends a specific number of calories and may also help reduce the size of fat cells and prevent obesity (Epstein, 1995). However, exercise is a slow process, and it is difficult to maintain motivation. Often exercise alone is not effective for weight reduction (Snetselaar, 1997). According to Votruba et al. (2000), exercise is beneficial in weight-reducing programs because of its positive impact on body composition (i.e. increasing fat-free mass), and its role in enhancing weight loss, albeit the effect is small in most instances. Depending on body type and amount of excess weight, the child may not be proficient in moving. Teachers should consider the following approaches for an activity program that is recommended by Bar-Or (1995):

1. Emphasize large muscle groups.
2. Move the entire body over distance.
3. Deemphasize intensity and emphasize duration.
4. Raise daily energy expenditure by 10 to 15 percent.
5. Include muscle strength activities.
6. Use daily or near daily activity, and gradually increase the frequency and volume.
7. Select activities the child enjoys, and solicit parental and group involvement.
8. Provide reinforcement and token remuneration.

To select the appropriate exercises, teachers should develop reasonable exercise goals that are not overly strenuous or painful. As children lose weight and increase their physical proficiency, the program can be modified to accommodate increased performance levels. Selected activities should emphasize aerobic activities that start slowly and can be increased gradually in duration and intensity. Walking, jogging, cycling, swimming, water exercises, aerobic dance, and cross-country skiing are appropriate activities that can be used by children during and after school to aid in weight reduction (Hoerr, 1984). It is important to note that although school-based physical education interventions only have a modest impact on improving BMI and/or skin fold measures in children and adolescents, they have many other beneficial health effects (e.g. improved blood lipid profiles and cardiovascular functioning) (Council on Sports Medicine and Fitness, 2006; Harris et al., 2009).

Of particular importance is the acquisition of gross motor skill activities that are required for participation. If these fundamental skills are not mastered, obese children will be more likely to withdraw and avoid participation in any activity, because these skills are the basic component of games and sports. Although weight may restrict performance, the more successful children become in their performance, the more they will be reinforced for participation and will increase their activity levels.

Diet and Nutrition

Diet and nutrition are important factors, with an emphasis on reducing the number of calories consumed. In a school setting this may be accomplished by offering a nutritionally balanced diet that includes the four basic food groups. To lose one pound requires a deficit of 3,500 calories, so the selection of low-calorie foods may contribute to losing weight because it decreases the number of calories consumed. Teachers can assist with the development of a sound nutritional program without prescribing a diet and reducing dietary fat and excessive calories.

Epstein, Masek, and Marshall (1978) implemented a traffic-light program for children to reduce the amount of calories they consumed. By using a color-coded, calorie-based program, they increased the child's knowledge of the amount of calories in specific foods. Green-light foods, such as celery and carrots, contained less than 20 calories per serving and were encouraged. Yellow-light foods included staples such as meats and potatoes from the basic food groups, averaging about 20 calories per serving. Red-light foods, such as candy, cake, and soft drinks, had more than 20 calories per serving. These were the foods that children were encouraged to avoid. By learning the caloric content of specific foods and food groups and limiting themselves to only four red-light foods per week, these children clearly demonstrated the ability to avoid high-calorie foods, select nutritionally sound foods, and lose weight. The food groups were also helpful for parents in designing meal plans for children while they were in the program. *The Stop-Light Diet for Children* is now available for teachers, parents, and children (Epstein & Squires, 1988).

The appropriate calorie limit will vary according to the child's age and activity level. In general, the guidelines in **Table 19.2** can be used to help children meet the amount of calories required for healthful living and create an imbalance necessary for weight loss to occur (Eisenman et al., 1990). These guidelines adhere to the weight-loss provisions that are recommended by most experts, which advocate a nutritionally balanced diet in conjunction with exercise and behavior management as the proper method to lose and control weight.

Snetselaar (1997) also advocated mild calorie reduction (of 500 to 1,000 calories) resulting in a gradual weight loss without outstanding side effects. Because an energy deficit of 3,500 calories is needed to lose a pound of body fat, eliminating 500 calories a day (3,500 a week) will result in a loss of one pound without the side effects (dehydration; loss of electrolytes, minerals, and glucogen stores; and lean body tissue) that are prevalent in more extreme weight-loss programs. Children should not lose more than 1 or 2 lb a week and should avoid extreme diets that may disrupt the metabolism of waste materials and growth of muscles, organs, and bones. In addition, any limitation of fat or growth-restrictive diets should not be implemented for children under 2 years of age (Dietz, 1995).

Overall, it would appear the best method for improving BMI and body composition profiles in children and adolescents is a program of diet therapy and physical activity in combination (Bo et al., 2008). According to the NHLBI (1998), a diet individually planned should take into account the individual's overweight status to create a deficit of between 500 to 1,000 kcal/day. Besides decreasing levels of saturated fat in the diet, total fat ingested should be 30 percent or less

of total calories. Reducing dietary fat, in addition to reducing dietary carbohydrates, is often required for acceptable weigh reduction. In so far as physical activity is concerned, increased levels of physical activity is an important component of any weight-loss program; although a much greater component of the lost weight occurs because of caloric restrictions. However, as mentioned previously, sustained physical activity is important for its other benefits, as well as being integral in preventing weight regain.

Behavior Management

Although weight loss will occur with caloric restrictions and exercise, it is often difficult for children to initiate and maintain a weight reduction program. To achieve long-term weight loss and increase motivation, behavioral interventions are required. Several examples of appropriate weight loss and behavior management incentives follow.

1. *Self-monitoring.* Children or parents can chart and record the food consumed, caloric cost of the food, exercise, and weight on a daily basis. This information can be used as a personal recording to chart weight loss (Brown, 1997).

2. *Social reinforcements and prompts.* Another technique to provide incentives is the use of social reinforcement and prompts to praise appropriate behaviors. Teachers or parents can also provide additional praise for maintaining appropriate habits. In the traffic-light program, Epstein and Squires (1988) incorporated a lifestyle approach for the entire family to burn extra calories. For example, instead of riding to the store, children and parents might walk; instead of watching television after dinner, the family might ride bicycles or take a short walk to burn extra calories, thus promoting a generally more active lifestyle.

3. *Contracting.* Another method of encouraging weight loss is to develop a contract outlining a realistic program to help children lose weight and maintain weight reduction. Care must be taken to observe the rules of the contract and to select a reasonable weight loss time line (Brown, 1997).

4. *Activity reinforcers.* Activity can be a powerful reinforcer in a physical education class. By partaking in enjoyable activities, children can be encouraged to reduce their calorie intake and increase their activity. Dietz (1995) has recommended focusing on behaviors that reduce energy expenditure, such as limiting television viewing to increase time for more active participation. Reinforcement can also be provided for exercising 5 days a week or increasing level of performance and can easily be used during every class period or at home. Activity reinforcers

Table 19.2 Calorie Levels for Children

	Age	Number of Calories (kcal)
Boys and girls	1–3	1,300
	3–6	1,600
	6–9	2,100
Boys	9–12	2,400
	12–15	3,000
	15–18	3,400
Girls	9–12	2,200
	12–15	2,500
	15–18	2,300

also may enhance the child's attitude toward exercise and promote positive aspects of activity, much more so than using exercise as a punishment. The more children increase their activity, the greater the success of a weight reduction program.

Emotional Support

Many children suffer from a poor self-image and feel insecure about themselves. Losing weight is extremely difficult, and teachers or nurses can provide the emotional support that may be needed. Another supportive measure may be to establish a school health club, in which children meet periodically to create a learning environment for nutrition and a sounding board for problems. Teachers, parents, and school nurses can serve as consultants to the club and help arrange learning activities and provide guidance for children (Little, 1983). The club can also arrange an exercise and/or recreational outlets for children in order to change sedentary habits and encourage more active lifestyles.

Homework and School-Based Interventions

A homework program can also be devised to aid children in weight reduction and in increasing physical activity outside the school setting. Homework may involve a series of learning experiences about the body, diet, and nutrition that contain readings on a specific topic and a self-testing quiz. In addition, a home exercise program may be devised by the teacher to be used in conjunction with the school physical education program. Teachers can also allow children to accumulate points for a variety of additional activities performed outside the school or with the family.

The school provides the most important variable in the success of a weight reduction program. The Committed to Kids Pediatric Weight Management Program described by Brown (1997) incorporated lifestyle management exercise and behavioral intervention for children. Brownell (1992) also detailed strategies to support long-term weight loss that emphasized exercise, social support, and cognitive restructuring to understand overeating and adherence to a weight loss program. Sallis (1993) indicated that educational approaches to diet and exercise have short-term effects and instead recommended programs to teach children how to change their behaviors and create a supportive environment to facilitate exercise and a healthy diet.

Combining the Treatment Factors

A reasonable method of attaining calorie deficits, and thus weight loss, is to educate children at an early age in the benefits of nutrition and exercise. Because most parents will not be able to afford expensive clinical treatments, the school can effectively educate and treat factors related to obesity or coordinate programs between home and school (NHLBI, 1998; Sallis, 1993).

The team approach is the most effective and the safest way to lose weight and maintain the loss. A program emphasizing a weight loss of 1½ pounds per week (one pound lost by dieting and a half pound by exercise) will result in a safe, gradual weight reduction primarily of body fat and very little of lean body tissue.

The combination of proper nutrition and exercise on a gradual basis is the safest method of conducting a weight reduction program. In addition, physical educators have an excellent opportunity to change attitudes and habits toward exercise. By offering emotional support, and sound nutritional and exercise programs as motivational techniques, teachers can safely implement and continue a weight reduction program for children with weight problems.

Eating Disorders

The eating disorders anorexia nervosa and bulimia nervosa have become increasingly important over the past two decades as their prevalence and the difficulties associated with their treatment have become focal points of educators and clinicians. Chronic forms of eating disorders develop in about 25 percent of patients, and between 5 to 20 percent of such patients are unresponsive to therapeutic interventions. Those individuals who are unresponsive to therapy die as a result of this disorder (Abraham & Llewellyn-Jones, 2001; Garfinkel, 1995; NIMH, 2007).

Chronic forms of eating disorders are due, in part, to society's view of the ideal body (Abraham & Llewellyn-Jones, 2001; Barber, 1998; Williamson et al., 1995). In today's society, thinness is seen as a way of achieving acceptance. Teen magazines continually focus on women's figures, and dieting, and a majority of articles contained in these magazines emphasize ways of dieting and exercising for thinness instead of for health. Fitness videos offered in stores are routinely focused on appearance instead of health. Hence, individuals with either anorexia or bulimia nervosa are pathologically preoccupied with weight and body shape and have a very strong desire for a thinner physique. Unfortunately, for many adolescents, expectations for body shape and size are unrealistic, as are their approaches for attaining their desired body shapes. The ability to recognize when an individual's desire for improving body shape through exercise and diet is dangerous to health and what to do about it is a critical component of your job as a physical educator.

According to Abraham and Llewellyn-Jones (2001), no single explanation sufficiently details why eating disorders occur. The question of whether a defective gene causes eating disorders is currently being researched, but at best accounts for only a few sufferers.

The developmental, learning, and social theories offer possible reasons as to why eating disorders occur more often in women with an onset more likely to occur in the late teens and early 20s; however, these theories do not adequately explain why only some individuals develop eating disorders while others do not, or why these disorders persist in some individuals and not others. Because of these inconsistencies a model that incorporates a more global viewpoint of the disorder has been advanced (Abraham & Llewellyn, 2001). This multidisciplinary explanation for the development of eating disorders incorporates a wide range of issues, which are often interactive. Some of these categories include:

- Psychological—Is the individual obsessive and a perfectionist? Does the individual have socially anxious issues with control?

- Social and Cultural—Does the individual display body image and self-esteem issues? Are family issues present?

- Mental Disorders—Does the individual possess aspects of depression, alcohol or drug dependency, obsessive-compulsive disorder, or manic depressive disorder?

- Biological—Is there a family history or predisposition to eating disorders or some other medical condition (e.g. diabetes) that could predispose the individual to eating restraints?

The two most common forms of eating disorders are anorexia nervosa and bulimia nervosa. Anorexia nervosa ("self-starvation disorder") is characterized by "a deliberate, self-imposed starvation owing to a relentless pursuit of thinness and fear of fatness" (Garfinkel, 1995). The most evident signs of anorexia nervosa include a distorted body image, rapid decrease in weight, preoccupation with food and its fat and calorie content, and the loss of hair from the head.

Bulimia nervosa ("binge and purge disorder") is characterized by "episodic patterns of binge eating accompanied by a sense of loss of control, and efforts to control body weight such as through self-induced vomiting or use of laxative" (Garfinkel, 1995). Individuals with bulimia are preoccupied with the fat and calorie content of foods. They have very unusual eating habits that consist of strict dieting, even fasting, followed by frequent episodes of binge eating. People with bulimia fear rejection and disapproval. They need the reassurance and approval; without it, their self-esteem drops.

In truth, individuals may exhibit symptoms associated with more than one type, and many individuals alternate between the features of both anorexia and bulimia nervosa. Hence, in addition to self-starvation, the person with anorexia may in some instances resort to purging when forced to eat; conversely, the person with bulimia may fast occasionally after a major binge episode to limit the amount of weight gained.

There are many misconceptions regarding what type of individual has an eating disorder. A major misconception is that eating disorders are found only in the young adult population, predominantly middle-class, Caucasian females. Contrary to this popular belief, eating disorders are usually first evident in infancy, childhood, or adolescence, and anyone—regardless of race, ethnicity, or social position—can suffer from an eating disorder. Although females constitute the majority of all people with eating disorders (NIMH, 2007), between 10–15 percent are male, and the incidence of eating disorders in males has increased conspicuously over the past decade. Although the data on females and eating disorders are incomplete, even less is known regarding eating disorders in the male population. Based on the available data, experts believe that the reasons for disordered eating in males is similar to that found among females: that is, body dissatisfaction and attaining the "ideal body" (Keel, Klump, Leon, & Fulkerson, 1998).

Recognizing the warning signs of eating disorders is the first step in helping the individual recover. Along with amenorrhea (lack of menstruation) in females, individuals with anorexia or bulimia may also suffer from the following (Williamson et al., 1995):

1. Gastrointestinal problems, such as chronic stomach pain, bloating, constipation, diarrhea, and cramping

2. Dental and gum disease

3. Cardiac arrhythmias, hypotension, and hypothermia, which are related to dehydration and malnutrition, which in turn lead to decreased heart rate, decreased blood pressure, electrolyte abnormalities, and decreased cardiac output

4. Mineral disturbances, which ultimately lead to a reduction in bone density and bone mineral content and, often, to osteoporosis later in life

It should be noted that excessive and compulsive exercising might also be considered a "red flag" of an eating disorder. What constitutes excessive exercising, however, is a gray area. As a general rule, motivation and attitude about exercise are what separate a compulsive exerciser from a normal exerciser. If the person does not view exercise as enjoyable and practices it only to burn calories and to relieve the guilt associated with eating too much, then that person may be a compulsive exerciser.

Excessive weight loss may lead to physical damage to the growth process and disturb the chemical balance of the body, contributing to depression, feelings of guilt, anxiety, and a sense of hopelessness. Frequently the child's emotional state is disturbed; she will appear scrawny or sickly and demonstrate a poor performance in school. Approximately 15 percent of all serious cases will manifest health conditions that result in death.

Individuals with anorexia are characterized as overachievers and perfectionists, and they generally manifest low personal esteem and a fear of not achieving parental expectations. They choose to lose weight through dieting as a method of achieving recognition, which leads to an obsession with losing weight. Compounding this cycle are parents who may become overprotective and less demanding, leaving the child to control things. The longer a person loses weight, the more recognition and reinforcement that person will receive for dieting.

Eating disorders are also on the rise in the athletic population, especially with the female athlete (Dosil, 2008). Athletes are predisposed to eating disorders because of the pressures that surround them. Athletes strive for perfection. The goals of an athlete are strength, power, and endurance. Athletes feel that if they reduce their body fat percentage, they can improve not only their appearance, but also their performance. Athletes receive a lot of pressure from coaches, parents, and friends to strive for greatness, and the last thing that athletes want to do is to disappoint their coaches or families; consequently, they may go to extremes.

Specific sports are associated with a higher prevalence of eating disorders. In females, gymnastics, figure skating, cheerleading, and long-distance running have a high incidence of eating disorders. Competitors in these sports depend on and are judged by appearance as much as talent. Cheerleaders and figure skaters are lifted by partners, so it is imperative that they maintain a low body weight. Male athletes, especially in wrestling and distance running, are often susceptible to eating disorders because a low body weight is essential for performance. Other than starvation, wrestlers also engage in diuretic and laxative use, excessive exercise with the use of rubber suits, and saunas. Because of engaging in the aforementioned regimens, wrestlers often suffer from intense dehydration, which can result in death.

Options available to help these individuals are limited. Probably the most important advice for dealing with a child suspected of having an eating disorder is to proceed carefully and always be nonjudgmental in approach. Most important, these individuals need to be referred to competent professionals. For some children, the access to a teacher or coach can provide the essential information on appropriate weight gain and loss. Often a good first step is to call local hospital and mental health facilities for a referral to names of qualified professionals who deal with eating disorders. Another contact point is the American Dietetic Association, who can help you find a dietitian in your area who is expert in treating eating disorders. Having this information for parents of children with eating disorders can be a positive first step along the road to treatment (Salomon, 1999).

Some individuals recovering from an eating disorder may choose exercise as a compensatory behavior or replacement for restricting calories or purging behaviors. If this be the case, model healthy behaviors and avoid focusing on the child's weight and body shape. Emphasize instead that exercise is important for health and important for improving strength and stamina. Above all else, stress the importance of regular eating to maintain strength and stamina (Solomon, 1999).

Implementing the Physical Activity Program

The role of teachers who have children with anorexia or bulimia in their charge is dramatically different from the role they are expected to take on when developing a program for children who are obese. Focusing on reducing calories or increasing activity is not appropriate for a child with anorexia. Consequently, the collaborative programming team must work in unison to prevent severe problems. Physical educators, through the assessment of percentage of body fat, can ascertain the possible onset of the anorexic condition and can alert children, parents, and teachers to potential problems of excessive dieting and nutrition. For instance, children with too little body fat may lose too much lean body tissue or be at risk in the growth and development stage of life (Williams, 1993). Recognition of potential symptoms of anorexia nervosa should lead to appropriate consultation and treatment programs.

Teacher awareness and recognition of symptoms may also aid in providing the potential anorexic with information related to the hazards of dieting and dangers of losing weight rapidly. Teachers can also help provide the emotional support and reinforcement that are needed for these students. Anorexia nervosa will demand teacher awareness and a thorough understanding of the problem. Additionally, the role of educators working with children will include the following (Solomon, 1999):

- Knowing their roles and limitations
- Recognizing signs and symptoms of anorexia nervosa
- Being supportive and avoiding judgments
- Being understanding of parents
- Acknowledging the psychologist's role as primary in the treatment process

Most of the treatment procedures for the child with anorexia revolve around the family and individual therapy, as well as appropriate behavior management techniques that can be developed with the support of the educational programming team. Teachers can provide expertise in the area of growth and development, exercise, relaxation training, body image activities, and appropriate behavior management strategies. In this manner teachers can provide an important link with the physician, psychologist, parents, clinician, and school personnel to aid in the treatment of eating disorders.

CHAPTER SUMMARY

1. Nutritional disorders that are often encountered in the school setting are obesity, anorexia nervosa, and bulinia nervosa. All contribute to a decrease in functional ability and present problems in maintaining a healthy lifestyle.

2. Obesity is a common problem for children with disabilities because of their relatively nonactive lifestyles. Other health problems associated with obesity include high blood pressure, high cholesterol, cardiovascular problems, and diabetes.

3. Intervention for children should incorporate every available resource that can provide support and monitoring. The teacher should work within the auspices of the educational programming team for advice on dietary, emotional, and physical activity needs while students are engaged in the program.

4. Whether or not children lose weight depends on a simple energy balance concept. If more calories are consumed than expended, the child will gain weight. Conversely, if more calories are expended than consumed, the child will lose weight.

5. In selecting appropriate exercises, teachers should develop reasonable exercise goals that are not overly strenuous or painful. As children lose weight and increase their physical performance, the program can be modified to accommodate increased performance levels.

6. Activities selected should be aerobic in nature; duration and intensity can be increased as needed.

7. A combined approach that utilizes sound nutritional and exercise habits, as well as behavior management techniques, is the treatment of choice.

8. Anorexia nervosa is a common eating disorder affecting mostly females. It is characterized by loss of weight due to a reduction in food intake and loss of appetite.

9. Signs and symptoms of anorexia and bulimia include exaggerated interest in food, with refusal to eat; denial of hunger; excessive exercise; eating binges followed by vomiting; utilizing diet pills and laxatives to reduce weight; and distorted body image.

10. Excessive weight loss may lead to physical damage to the growth process and disturb the chemical balance of the body, contributing to depression, guilt, and anxiety.

11. Teacher awareness and recognition of symptoms may aid in providing the potential anorexic with information related to the potential hazards of dieting and dangers of losing weight rapidly.

12. Most treatment procedures revolve around the family and individual therapy as well as appropriate behavior management techniques developed by the multidisciplinary team. Physical education teachers can provide an important link with professionals to aid in the treatment of anorexia nervosa by providing information on growth and development, exercise, body image activities, and appropriate behavior management techniques.

REFERENCES

Abraham, S., & Llewellyn-Jones, D. (2001). *Eating Disorders: the Facts* (5th ed.). NY: Oxford Press.

Barber, N. (1998). The slender ideal and eating disorders: An interdisciplinary "telescope" model. *International Journal of Eating Disorders, 23,* 295–307.

Bar-Or, O. (1995). Obesity. In B. Goldberg (Ed.), *Sports and exercise for children with chronic health conditions* (pp. 335–353). Champaign, IL: Human Kinetics.

Bar-Or, O., & Rowland, T. (2004). *Pediatric Exercise Medicine form Physiological Principles to Health Care Application.* Champaign, IL: Human Kinetics.

Bo, S., Ciccone, G., Guidi, S., Gambino, R., Durazzo, M., Gentile, L., Cassader, M., Cavallo-Perin, P., & Pagano, G. (2008). Diet or exercise: What is more effective in preventing or reducing metabolic alterations? *European Journal of Endocrinology, 159,* 685–691.

Brown, D. K. (1997). Childhood and adolescence weight management. In S. Dalton (Ed.), *Overweight and weight management.* Gaithersburg, MD: Aspen Publications.

Brownell, K. D. (1992). *The Learn Program for weight control.* Dallas, TX: American Health Publication Company.

Center for Disease Control and Prevention. (2008). *BMI Percentile Calculations for Child and Teen English Version.* http://apps.nccd.cdc.gov/dnpabmi/

Clark, N. (2008). *Sports nutrition cookbook.* Champaign, IL: Leisure Press.

Council on Sports Medicine and Fitness. (2006). Council on school health. Active healthy living: Prevention of childhood obesity through increased physical activity. *Pediatrics*, 117, 1834–1842.

Dietz, W. H. (1995). Childhood Obesity. In L. W. Y. Cheung & J. B. Richmond (Eds.), *Child health, nutrition and physical activity* (pp. 155–169). Champaign, IL: Human Kinetics.

Dosil, J. (2008). *Eating Disorders in Athletes*. West Sussex, England: John Wiley and Sons.

Ebbeling, C. B., & Rodriguez, N. R. (1997). Anthropometric techniques for identification of obese children: Perspectives for the practitioner. In S. Dalton (Ed.), *Overweight and weight management* (pp. 486–496). Gaithersburg, MD: Aspen Publishers.

Eisenman, P., Johnson, S, & Benson, J. E. (1990). *Coaches' guide to nutrition and weight control* (2nd ed.). Champaign, IL: Human Kinetics.

Epstein, L. H. (1995). Exercise in the treatment of childhood obesity. *International Journal of Obesity*, 19, 117–121.

Epstein, L. H., Masek, B., & Marshall, W. (1978). A nutritionally based school program for control of eating in obese children. *Behavior Therapy*, 9, 766–788.

Epstein, L. H., & Squires, S. (1988). *The stop-light diet for children: An eight-week program for parents and children*. Boston: Little, Brown.

Garfinkel, P. E. (1995). Eating disorders. In H. I. Kaplan & B. J. Sadock (Eds.), *Comprehensive textbook of psychiatry/VI* (vol. 2, 6th ed.). Baltimore: Williams & Wilkins.

Harris, K., Kuramoto, L., & Schulzer, J. (2009). Effects of school-based physical activity interventions on body mass index in children: A meta-analysis. *Canadian Medical Association Journal*, 180(7), 719–726.

Henley, A., Ogden, C., Johnson, C., Carrol, M., Curtin, L., & Flegal, M. (2004). Prevalence of overweight and obesity among U.S. children, adolescents, and adults, 1999–2002. *JAMA*, 29(23), 2847–2850.

Hoerr, S. L. (1984). Exercise: An alternative to fad diets for adolescent girls. *The Physician and Sports Medicine*, 12, 76–83.

Katch, F., & McArdle, W. (1996). *Nutrition, weight control and exercise* (4th ed.). Philadelphia: Lea and Febiger.

Keel, P. K., Klump, K. L., Leon, G. R., & Fulkerson, J. A. (1998). Disordered eating in adolescent males form a school-based sample. *International Journal of Eating Disorders*, 23, 125–132.

Little, J. (1983). Management of the obese child in the school. *Journal of School Health*, 53, 440–441.

Lohman, T. G. (1987). *Measuring body fat using skinfolds*.

(Videotape). Champaign, IL: Human Kinetics.

Lohman, T. G. (1992). *Advances in body composition assessment*. Champaign, IL: Human Kinetics.

Mayer, J. (1968). *Overweight: Causes, cost, and control*. Englewood Cliffs, NJ: Prentice Hall.

National Heart, Lung, and Blood Institute. (1998). *Clinical guidelines on the identification, evaluation, and treatment of overweight and obesity in adults*. NIH Publication # 98-4083.

National Institute of Mental Health. (2007). *Eating Disorders*. NIH Publication # 07-4901.

Nestle, M. & Jacobson, M. (2000). Halting the obesity epidemic: A public health approach. *Public Health Reports*, 115, 12–24.

Rimmer, J. H. (1994). *Fitness and Rehabilitation Programs for Special Populations*. Dubuque, IA: Brown and Benchmark.

Sallis, J. F., Chen, A. H., & Castro, C. M. (1995). School-based intervention for childhood obesity. In L. W. Y. Cheung & J. B. Richmond (Eds.), *Child health, nutrition, and physical activity*. (pp. 179–204). Champaign, IL: Human Kinetics.

Sallis, J. F. (1993). Promoting healthful diet and physical activity. In Millstein, S. G., Peterson, A. C., & Nightingale, E. O. (Eds.), *Promoting the health of adolescents: New directions for the diversity-first century* (pp. 209–241). New York: Oxford University.

Salomon, S. (1999, May–June). Identify the eating disordered client. *Personal Fitness Professional*, 39–41.

Snetselaar, L. B. (1997). *Nutrition counseling skills*. Gaithersburg, MD: Aspen Publishers.

U.S. Department of Health and Human Services. (2000). *Healthy people 2000: National health promotion and disease prevention objectives*. (DHHS Publication No. 91-50212). Washington, DC: U.S. Government Printing Office.

Votruba, S., Micah, B., Horvatz, B., & Schoeller, D. (2000). The role of exercise in the treatment of obesity. *Nutrition*, 16, 179–188.

Whitaker, R.C., Wright, J.A., Pepe, M.S., Seidel, K.D., & Dietz, W.H. (1997). Predicting obesity in young adulthood from childhood and parental obesity. *The New England Journal of Medicine*, 337(3), 869–873.

Williams M. W. (1993). *Nutrition for Fitness and Sport* (2nd ed). Dubuque, IA: William C. Brown.

Williamson, D. A., Netemeyer, R. G., Jackman, L. P., Anderson, D. A., Funsch, C. L., & Rabalais, J. Y. (1995). Structural equation model of risk factors for the development of eating disorders in female athletes. *International Journal of Eating Disorders*, 17, 387–393.

CHAPTER 20

Cardiovascular Disorders and Hypertension

Maria had a heart transplant when she was six years old. She is doing well, but is behind her first-grade classmates in motor skills and physical functioning. Maria's teacher, Mrs. Robles, isn't sure what activities Maria can participate in during physical education and recess so she contacts Maria's parents and physician to determine the best course of action. Maria's physician helps Mrs. Robles plan some activities that don't overtax Maria physically but allows her to develop her motor skills and cardiovascular endurance. Maria's program commences with a minimal level of activity, slowly adding time and intensity to the program. Over the course of the semester, Maria becomes more physically fit and gains more confidence in her ability to perform a variety of physical skills.

In another class, Sam has had an aortic valve transplant. He wants to be active, but tires easily. Sam's doctor has only advised him to not overdo it. Sam's teacher is confused as to what activities Sam can partake in, so Sam's physician is contacted to quantify what overdoing it means, and to discuss some recommendations on activities that can be used to improve Sam's physical functioning. Based on the physician's input, Sam's teacher sets up a program of walking and cycling, being sure to carefully monitor that Sam's heart rate stays within the recommended target heart rate guidelines. Sam and his teacher chart Sam's progress and vary the exercise protocol as Sam adjusts to the activity.

Cardiovascular disorders can take many forms, including high blood pressure, coronary heart disease, heart-valve defects, or rheumatic fever/rheumatic heart disease. According to the World Health Organization (2007), cardiovascular disease causes 17.5 million deaths in the world each year and is responsible for nearly half of all deaths in the United States and other developed countries. Overall, it is the leading cause of death in adults. In the United States alone, more than 80 million American have some form of cardiovascular disease, leading to just about 2400 deaths every day. To put this number in perspective, cancer, which is the second largest killer, accounts for about half as many deaths (World Health Organization, 2007).

Most people only think of middle-aged and older adults as being affected by cardiovascular disease, whereas children are usually thought of as having healthy hearts. Yet, nine out of every 1,000 babies born in the U.S. have some type of congenital heart abnormality. It is estimated that almost one million people living in the U.S. were born with a congenital heart defect.

Moreover, pathological studies have shown the presence of atherosclerosis at autopsy after death of children and adolescence and that these atherosclerotic lesions correlate highly with known risk facts for such lesions, specifically low-density lipoprotein cholesterol, triglycerides, blood pressure, body mass index, presence of obesity, and presence of cigarette smoking. Therefore, existing evidence suggests that the development of atherosclerotic disease begins as early as childhood and that primary intervention of this disease ought to commence at this time as well (Kavey, Lauer, & Hayman, 2003).

Cardiovascular problems are categorized as either congenital or acquired disorders that occur before or after birth and are the direct result of damage to the heart and/or blood vessels, septal defects, or valvular heart dysfunctions. Most causes of congenital defects are unknown, although some are genetically linked to or result from an injury to the fetus during pregnancy.

Because the severity of congenital defects usually requires surgery or medication to correct the defect, most children have received treatment by the time they enter school and therefore have few symptoms associated with their particular problem. Those children with severe congenital problems will require extensive medical supervision or treatment and may be confined to the hospital, home, or special school.

Primary concerns for teachers are acquired cardiovascular disorders among children in the school setting that may present a potential health hazard. Rheumatic heart disease, heart murmurs, arrhythmias, and hypertension are disorders that affect children and are the focus of this chapter. These conditions are often prevalent in the integrated setting or may be associated with other disabilities.

Children with existing cardiovascular disabilities and those who suddenly acquire a cardiovascular disability may manifest emotional frustrations because of their forced inactivity. They may withdraw from activity and feel inferior to peers in physical fitness and motor development because of their inability to fully participate in age-related activities. This may lead to social rejection that may be as damaging psychologically as it is physically.

For children with cardiac disorders, appropriate physical and motor fitness activities are needed. The cooperation of the collaborative programming team, including the physician, nurse, physical educator, health educator, and special educator, is needed to develop appropriate goals to initiate a comprehensive physical activity program. Teachers can also incorporate a well-rounded program of nutrition, exercise, and education for the elimination of cardiac risk factors to safely incorporate children into a physical activity program and contribute to a healthy lifestyle. Another concern for teachers is to determine the degree of participation in activities that will be needed to maintain physical fitness and promote total body development. Opportunities to relieve anxiety and depression through physical activity and relaxation training also can be implemented as a means of integrating children into regular physical education classes.

Rheumatic Heart Disease

Rheumatic heart disease can occur at any age, but usually occurs in children between 6 and 12 years of age who have had rheumatic fever. Rheumatic fever develops as a reaction to antibodies formed as a defense against streptococcal bacteria. Damage to the heart

may often occur from inflammation, which causes scarring that most notably appears in the heart valves over a period of years. After children have contracted rheumatic fever, they are susceptible to repeated attacks, further increasing the probability of inflammation and scarring that may damage the heart. Rheumatic fever may be identified by symptoms such as pain in joints and muscles, poor appetite, uncontrolled movements of arms, legs, or face (twitching of muscles), frequent nosebleeds, fever, streptococcal infection, sore throat, weakness and shortness of breath, and difficulty in swallowing (World Health Organization, 2001). Penicillin and other antibiotics can usually treat strep throat and prevent acute rheumatic fever from developing. Antibiotic therapy has significantly reduced the incidence and mortality rate of rheumatic fever/rheumatic disease. Despite current therapies available, rheumatic heart disease killed nearly 3,500 people in the United States in 2005–2006.

When the inflammation caused by rheumatic fever leaves one or more of the heart valves scarred, the end result is rheumatic heart disease. Because the buildup of scar tissue reduces the effectiveness of the heart and valves, the supply of blood is decreased throughout the body. Deterioration of the valves may result in the inability to open and close effectively. A leaky or constricted valve will affect the child's cardiac efficiency and ability to perform physical activities, because the blood supply to the working muscles is inadequate.

As a result of one or more attacks of rheumatic fever, the valves of the heart will suffer permanent damage. The mitral and aortic valves allow the blood to pass in one direction. Consequently, if the valves become inflamed, resulting in the development of scar tissue in the leaflets, the valve may become fused, restricting the movement and narrowing the opening of the valve. The result is a constricted, or *stenotic*, valve. Conversely, valves may atrophy and prohibit proper closure. This *regurgitant* valve allows the blood to flow back into the atrium or ventricle. **Figure 20.1** depicts the fetal heart.

Recent medical advances have reduced some of the problems associated with rheumatic heart disease. Surgery can be performed to remove scar tissue, to repair damaged valves, or to implant artificial valves. Medication has also been used in rheumatic fever to treat symptoms and possibly prevent more serious heart damage or recurring attacks.

Heart Murmurs and Arrhythmias

A variation from the normal sounds of the heart may be audible during the school years. These sounds are referred to as *murmurs* and are not necessarily pathological. There are two types of heart murmurs, innocent

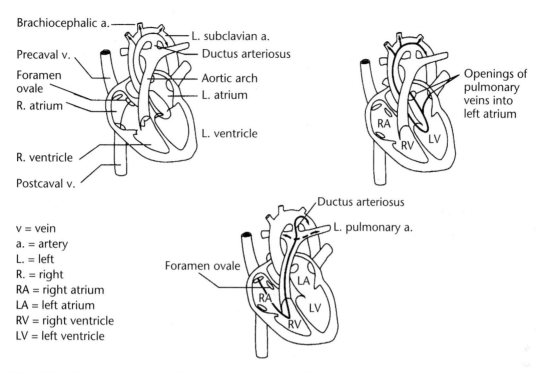

Figure 20.1 Chambers, openings, and circulation in the fetal heart.

murmurs and abnormal murmurs. An individual with an innocent murmur has a normal heart and need not worry. On the other hand, an abnormal murmur is a much more serious matter. More than half the children in the U.S. have had heart murmurs at one time or another. Luckily, most of these murmurs are innocent murmurs and are harmless.

Although heart murmurs are innocent and not serious, some may be the result of an underlying heart problem. The most common type of abnormal heart murmur in children is congenital heart disease, where babies are born with some type of structural heart defect. Common congenital defects that cause heart murmurs include: (1) holes in the walls between heart chambers (known as septal defects); (2) heart valve abnormalities, including valves that do not allow enough blood to flow through them (stenosis) or those that do not close properly causing leaking or regurgitation. Other causes of abnormal heart murmurs in children include infections that damage the heart muscle (Shafler & Rose, 1974).

A concern for teachers is the adaptability of children with a heart murmur to physical activity and sports programs. The Fourth Report on High Blood Pressure in Children and Adolescents (2004) has recommended a thorough cardiac screening to eliminate suspected causes of heart murmur, including assessment of resting heart rate, respiration, and blood pressure, and palpation between the femoral and brachial arteries to determine extra sounds, clicks, or splitting of sounds. If a defect is suspected, children can then be referred for

a more extensive evaluation, including an electrocardiogram. If no defect is evident, children will be able to participate in a physical activity program based on consultations with a cardiologist and the guidelines for participation presented later in this chapter.

Arrhythmias are changes in the regular beat of the heart and may occur from extra or ectopic beats of atrial, junctional, or ventricular origin (Fourth Report on High Blood Pressure in Children and Adolescents, 2004). Most ectopic beats are benign and will not be dangerous to children and often disappear with low-intensity exercise. However, ectopic beats that persist require a more extensive evaluation to determine the specific cause of the defect and, more important, whether to curtail participation in physical activity and sports.

Teachers of children with cardiac disorders must be aware of how their performance may be affected. Active participation need not be eliminated and, as mentioned earlier, is an essential social and emotional outlet for children. With proper supervision, children should be able to engage in an activity program and eliminate or decrease cardiac risk factors that may impede physical functioning.

Hypertension

Another concern for parents and educators is hypertension in the school-aged population. Hypertension is also one kind of cardiovascular deficit that teachers and school personnel can help identify and incorporate into a treatment program. Because children with disabilities may be susceptible to high blood pressure, it is essential to remediate the problem before a more serious consequence, such as a stroke, might occur.

Hypertension, or high blood pressure, is a common threat to the health of many Americans. Essential or primary hypertension is usually prevalent in adults but is being discovered more frequently in school-aged children. Therefore, there is a need to understand the disease and to include blood pressure measurements as part of the school physical examination.

With high blood pressure, the risk of cardiovascular disease increases. Hypertension is a contributor to heart disease, kidney disease, stroke, and loss of vision. The major abnormality appears to be increased vascular resistance, which causes the heart and blood vessels to work harder to transport blood to the body (Subramaniam & Lip, 2009). Many cases of school-aged hypertension may be explained by an underlying disorder. Causes of this type of hypertension, called secondary hypertension, include kidney disease, coarctation of the aorta, and neurological or hormonal disorders. However, numerous authorities have reported an alarming increase in cases of primary hypertension being diagnosed during the school years (Brady, et al., 2008; Loggie, 1992; National Heart, Lung, & Blood Institute, 2005).

It is important to identify children with hypertension and begin treatment as soon as possible. Children with primary hypertension may be asymptomatic or may complain of frontal headaches, dizziness, fatigue, nosebleeds, anxiety, and nervousness. Causes of hypertension may include inactivity, genetic predisposition, stress, and diet. Any or all of the following risk factors may contribute to primary hypertension, which is no longer considered an adult problem and has been reported in children as early as 3 years of age (Brady & Feld, 2009; Londe, 1983):

- *Genetic predisposition.* Inheritance, or genetic predisposition, is an indicator of similar blood pressure levels in parents and children, but it has not been demonstrated to be a true predictor of future hypertension. Early reports indicated that about 28 percent of children with one hypertensive parent were also hypertensive, while the incidence increased to 65 percent if both parents were hypertensive. Current information indicates that the incidence of hypertension among children with one hypertensive parent is 51 percent. A family history of complications is usually apparent in 50 percent of all school-aged children with hypertension. A strong relationship in blood pressure levels exists between twins and siblings, while a weaker relationship is apparent in half siblings and in parents and offspring. Blood

pressure in both females and males is the same until adolescence; after 14 years of age, males demonstrate higher normal standards of measurement (McCrory, 1982).

- *Obesity.* The incidence of childhood and adolescent obesity has been on the rise over the past decade throughout developing countries (World Health Organization, 1997). In the United States alone, nearly one in four children and adolescents is considered overweight or obese. Moreover, this increase is particularly evident among Hispanics and African Americans (Bar-Or & Rowland, 2004). Obesity strongly predisposes children to increased rates of hypertension, and childhood obesity plays a critical pathogenic role in increased rates of hypertension in adults (Viridis, et al., 2009).

- *Race.* As a group, African American children usually demonstrate a higher blood pressure reading. The Centers for Disease Control (2009) also indicated that hypertensive African American children exhibited a high sodium excretion and a tendency for obesity, which may contribute to increased levels of hypertension. Hohn, Dwyer, & Dwyer (1994) also reported increased blood pressure levels in African American and Asian children in comparison to white children.

- *Sodium.* There is a general agreement that increased levels of sodium contribute to hypertension. For example, primitive tribes in various parts of the world manifest no primary hypertension because their diet is low in sodium, whereas in northeastern Japan, where salt intake is high, hypertension is 40 to 50 percent higher than in other parts of the world. In a clinical setting, the reduction of salt has been shown to lower the blood pressure of hypertensive individuals, whereas increased consumption of salt increased the blood pressure readings (CDC, 2009).

- *Salt sensitivity.* Some individuals may also possess a genetically determined sensitivity to salt. Blood pressure in these individuals will increase when sodium consumption increases, whereas non-salt-sensitive individuals who increase their sodium intake will excrete more sodium and display no deleterious side effects (Weinberger, 2004). The American Heart Association (1999) recommended a low salt intake for children at risk for hypertension as a preventive measure. Keeping a balance of sodium and potassium may also contribute to the absence of hypertension. Recommendations from the National Heart, Lung, and Blood Institute (2008) emphasize limiting sodium intake to no more than 2,400 mg. or approximately 1 teaspoon each day, and to avoid fast foods that are high in salt and sodium.

- *Stress.* Temporary stress may result in an increased blood pressure reading. Children who are predisposed to stress or who live in a stressful home environment may be susceptible to higher blood pressure levels (Gasperin et al., 2009). Additionally, children with disabilities often encounter frustrations from their conditions that evoke stress and may contribute to hypertension.

Implications of High Blood Pressure

To adequately diagnose and prevent hypertension in school-aged children, blood pressure measurements should be incorporated into the pediatric physical examination for early detection. A primary source of information for screening children is available from the medical history and a limited number of laboratory studies, including a physical examination, urinalysis, and chemical analysis of renal function.

Secondary causes of hypertension can also be detected from the medical history and routine laboratory information. The previous history should be examined to determine the presence of hypertension and any contributing factors: the use of hormones (i.e., oral contraceptives, corticosteriods); indications of cardiac, vascular, or renal disease; diabetes; excessive dieting; and excessive sodium intake. The development of blood pressure distributions by age and sex have now made it possible to compare high blood pressure values.

The Fourth Report on High Blood Pressure in Children and Adolescents (2004) suggested that three elevated readings on separate occasions be obtained before diagnosing hypertension in an individual. The initial reading should be plotted on a measurement grid, and if that value exceeds the 95th percentile for systolic and diastolic blood pressure, the measurement should be repeated. Consistently elevated readings would then be indicative of high blood pressure, whereas a transitory high reading may be attributed to illness or environmental factors that influence blood pressure. In addition, the National Heart, Lung and Blood Institute (NHLBI, 2005) recently updated its blood pressure standards for children 1–17 years of age that are adjusted for height. According to the NHLBI (2005), the upper limits for normal blood pressure (that is, the 90th and 95th percentiles for blood pressure readings) are lower for shorter children than are blood pressure standards based on age and gender alone. In contrast, the upper limites for normal blood pressure are greater for taller children (NHLBI, 2005). **Table 20.1** and **Table 20.2** contain condensed versions of the standards for boys and girls 6–14 years of age (NHLBI, 2005).

Some children may also demonstrate "tracking" or consistently high blood pressure throughout their school career. It is not known whether the "tracking" pattern will continue into adulthood or whether that

value at or above the 95th percentile is predictive of future problems. More research is needed to determine specific levels of blood pressure in children, because values for adolescents may vary. Although information is needed on hypertension in children and a blood pressure examination is recommended, it is necessary to be aware that blood pressure varies and not wrongly classify children as hypertensive and thus subject them to needless medical treatment.

The Fourth Report on High Blood Pressure in Children and Adolescents (2004) recommended that children who exhibit sustained elevations in blood pressure be evaluated in the following areas before classifying them as hypertensive: (1) family history; (2) blood pressure of parents and siblings; (3) medical history citing complications or symptoms such as headaches, nosebleeds, dizziness, blurred vision; and (4) a physical examination. After the diagnosis of hypertension is confirmed, steps can be implemented to circumvent the potentially dangerous effects of hypertension. Lieberman (1978) has recommended counseling children and families concerning weight reduction, avoidance of salt, eliminating stress, not smoking, and participating in a physical activity program as essential for treating school-aged children with hypertension.

Monitoring Blood Pressure

Blood pressure may be monitored with a pressure cuff placed around the biceps of the arms. Pressure is applied to the brachial artery until the pressure inside the cuff approximates the blood pressure. Then the pressure on the arm is released, allowing the blood to flow. Measurements of the systolic and diastolic pressure are made by auscultation with a stethoscope (**Figure 20.2**). The more difficult it is for the blood to flow through the body, the higher the values that will be recorded.

Blood pressure is recorded in two numbers (e.g., 140/90). The upper pressure, or the systolic blood pressure, is the force generated within the arteries during contraction of the heart. When the heart fills with blood, it contracts, pushing the blood through the arteries; the systolic blood pressure is represented as the force exerted against the arteries by the blood as it is pumped through the vessels (**Figure 20.3**). The lower number, or diastolic blood pressure, is the pressure that occurs after contraction, when the heart is recovering and is beginning to refill before the next contraction (Brady et al., 2008).

An elevated diastolic reading should be more cause for concern because the heart is between contractions and should be in a relaxed state. Consistently high diastolic readings may be indicative of serious heart disease, such as a narrowing, or constriction, of the arteries. Readings for a normal blood pressure are usually 120/80, with 140/90 considered an elevated reading in adults and adolescents. However, blood pressure

Table 20.1 Blood Pressure Levels for the 90th and 95th Percentiles of Blood Pressure for Boys by Percentages of Height

		Systolic BP (MM HG) by Height Percentiles							Diastolic BP (MM HG) by Height Percentiles						
Age	BP Percentiles	5th	10th	25th	50th	75th	90th	95th	5th	10th	25th	50th	75th	90th	95th
6	90th	105	106	108	110	111	113	113	68	68	69	70	71	72	72
	95th	109	110	112	114	115	117	117	72	72	73	74	75	76	76
7	90th	106	107	109	111	113	114	115	70	70	71	72	73	74	74
	95th	110	111	113	115	117	118	119	74	74	75	76	77	78	78
8	90th	107	109	110	112	114	115	116	71	72	72	73	74	75	76
	95th	111	112	114	116	118	119	120	75	76	77	78	79	79	80
9	90th	109	110	112	114	115	117	118	72	73	74	75	76	76	77
	95th	113	114	116	118	119	121	121	76	77	78	79	80	81	81
10	90th	111	112	114	115	117	119	119	73	73	74	75	76	77	78
	95th	115	116	117	119	121	122	123	77	78	79	80	81	81	82
11	90th	113	114	115	117	119	120	121	74	74	75	76	77	78	78
	95th	117	118	119	121	123	124	125	78	78	79	80	81	82	82
12	90th	115	116	118	120	121	123	123	74	75	75	76	77	78	79
	95th	119	120	122	123	125	127	127	78	79	80	81	82	82	83
13	90th	117	118	120	122	124	125	126	75	75	76	77	78	79	79
	95th	121	122	124	126	128	129	130	79	79	80	81	82	83	83
14	90th	120	121	123	125	126	128	128	75	76	77	78	79	79	80
	95th	124	125	127	128	130	132	132	80	80	81	82	83	84	84

*Height percentile determined by standard growth curves.
†Blood pressure percentile determined by a single measurement.

Adapted from the National High Blood Pressure Education Program—Courtesy of the National Heart, Lung and Blood Institute (NHLBI, 2005).

Table 20.2 Blood Pressure Levels for the 90th and 95th Percentiles of Blood Pressure for Girls by Percentages of Height

		Systolic BP (MM HG) by Height Percentiles							Diastolic BP (MM HG) by Height Percentiles						
Age	BP Percentiles	5th	10th	25th	50th	75th	90th	95th	5th	10th	25th	50th	75th	90th	95th
6	90th	104	105	106	108	109	110	11	68	68	69	70	70	71	72
	95th	108	109	11	111	113	114	115	72	72	73	74	74	75	76
7	90th	106	107	108	109	111	112	113	69	70	70	74	72	72	73
	95th	110	111	112	113	115	116	116	73	74	74	75	76	76	77
8	90th	108	109	11	111	113	114	114	71	71	71	72	73	74	74
	95th	112	112	114	115	116	118	118	75	75	75	76	77	78	78
9	90th	110	110	112	113	114	116	116	72	72	72	73	74	75	75
	95th	114	114	115	117	118	119	120	76	76	76	77	78	79	79
10	90th	112	112	114	115	116	118	118	73	73	73	74	75	76	76
	95th	116	116	117	119	120	121	122	77	77	77	78	79	80	80
11	90th	114	114	116	117	118	119	120	74	74	74	75	76	77	77
	95th	118	118	119	121	122	123	124	78	78	78	79	80	81	81
12	90th	116	116	117	119	120	121	122	75	75	75	76	77	78	78
	95th	119	120	121	123	124	125	126	79	79	79	80	81	82	82
13	90th	117	118	119	121	122	123	124	76	76	76	77	78	79	79
	95th	121	122	123	124	126	127	128	80	80	80	81	82	83	83
14	90th	119	120	121	122	124	125	125	77	77	77	78	79	80	80
	95th	123	123	125	126	127	129	129	81	81	81	82	83	84	84

*Height percentile determined by standard growth curves.
†Blood pressure percentile determined by a single measurement.

Adapted from the National High Blood Pressure Education Program—Courtesy of the National Heart, Lung and Blood Institute (NHLBI, 2005).

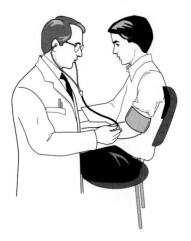

Figure 20.2 Blood pressure cuff and stethoscope.

continuously rises from birth to adolescence and after age 14 may be higher in males than in females.

The difficulty is to determine normal limits of blood pressure in children. The Fourth Report on High Blood Pressure in Children and Adolescents (2004) considered blood pressure exceeding two standard deviations above the mean by age group as indicative of hypertension. By these older standards, the upper limits for blood pressure in boys 9 years old were approximately 121/81, and 140/89 for boys 15 years old. Persistent supine readings of above the 95th percentile for systolic or diastolic pressure were used to define school-aged hypertension, with readings between the 90th and 95th percentiles considered high-normal. Although various values are used in determining blood pressure in children, it is now recommended that blood pressure values be compared

to the percentile indicated not only by age and gender but also by height (NHLBI, 2005). Consistent readings at the 95th percentile are cause for further examination and possible treatment of the problem.

LEARNING ACTIVITY

Analyze the activity restrictions of various cardiovascular disorders and plan activities that are best suited to meet the needs of children with cardiovascular disorders.

Planning the Physical Activity Program

The identification of cardiovascular problems and hypertension should focus on educating parents and children concerning the effects of the disorder. Teachers, either at a parent education meeting or with appropriate medical personnel, can discuss blood pressure, its fluctuations, complications, readings, and possible abnormalities in the heart. Several materials are available from the American Heart Association (AHA) that can be used in this education program, such as *Abnormal Heart Rhythms: What Parents Should Know, Congenital Heart Disease; Physiological and Functional Heart Mummers*, and *Children and Heart Defects*. Another source of educational material is the American Alliance for Health, Physical Education, Recreation and Dance, which offers *Heart Power* (a school program from preschool to grade 8), *Jump Rope for Heart, Hoops for Heart*, and *Heart Partners*. In addition, most physicians recognize the benefits of physical activity and adhere to

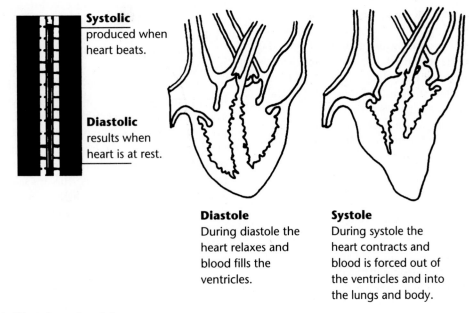

Systolic produced when heart beats.

Diastolic results when heart is at rest.

Diastole During diastole the heart relaxes and blood fills the ventricles.

Systole During systole the heart contracts and blood is forced out of the ventricles and into the lungs and body.

Figure 20.3 Diastole and systole.

the the updated guidelines established by the American College of Sports medicine (ACSM) and the AHA (Haskell, et al., 2007), which cite physical inactivity as a risk factor for coronary artery disease, obesity, high blood pressure, and cholesterol. The AHA (2004) scientific position statement includes the following guidelines:

- Do moderately intense cardio 30 minutes a day, five days a week. Moderate-intense physical activity can be accumulated throughout the day in 10-minute bouts, which can be as effective as exercising for 30 minutes continuously.

- Combination of moderate- and vigorous-intensity physical activity can be used to meet guidelines.

- To promote optimal health, individuals benefit from performing activities that maintain or increase strength. To maximize strength development, resistance training is highly recommended. It is recommended that between eight to ten strength-training exercises, 10–15 repetitions of each exercise, two to three times a week should be performed.

- More is better—the new guidelines emphasize that physical activity above recommended minimum levels produce even greater health benefits.

To develop a program for individuals with cardiovascular problems, the teacher should, at the least, be able to identify and provide education in specific factors that contribute to the abnormality. To effectively plan and implement an appropriate program for children, the educator should also consider the effects of weight reduction, sodium intake, the kidneys, potassium and magnesium intake, medication, and exercise.

Weight Reduction

Obesity, especially in individuals who are more than 20 pounds over the ideal body weight and who possess a high percentage of body fat, is a major cardiovascular risk factor. Decreasing the amount of body fat not only is important in itself, but also usually entails other behaviors that help reduce cardiovascular risk factors: reducing fat, sodium, and total calorie intake in the diet, and increasing physical activity.

Dietary guidelines recommended by the National Heart, Lung and Blood Institute (2003) to be used for weight reduction include the following:

1. Eat a nutritionally sound diet encompassing all food groups.

2. Base caloric intake on growth rate, activity level, and percentage of body fat.

3. Keep total fat intake to approximately 30% of calories: 10% or less from saturated fat, 10% from monosaturated fat, and less than 10% from polyunsaturated fat. Emphasize reducing total fat and saturated fat.

4. Keep daily cholesterol intake to approximately 100 milligrams of cholesterol per 1,000 calories, not to exceed 300 milligrams (to allow for differences in caloric intake per age group).

5. Eat protein from a variety of sources, keeping total protein intake to about 15% of all calories.

6. Consume carbohydrates from complex carbohydrate sources that are high in starch and fiber and provide necessary vitamins and minerals. Carbohydrate intake should total about 55% of caloric intake.

7. Limit consumption of foods with excessive amounts of salt, especially processed meats and condiments with a high sodium content.

8. Limit serving sizes, and increase physical activity.

Sodium

Sodium intake for Americans is ten times the needed daily requirement. The reason for restricting sodium is to reduce the excess fluid in the vascular system, which contributes to high blood pressure. An individual's capacity to excrete salt, rather than the amount of salt he or she consumes, is what contributes to hypertension (Weinberger, 2004). This is demonstrated in older individuals, in whom impaired excretion of salt is often accompanied by a decrease in kidney function and, in turn, by hypertension.

The Kidneys

Some children may have a genetic sensitivity to salt and be unable to handle salt effectively. The retention of salt leads to increased fluid and pressure as well as an increase in the volume of blood flowing through the vascular system (Weinberger, 2004). When excess fluid is eliminated, blood pressure is lowered because of improved runoff of the blood from the smaller vessels to the tissues.

Table salt is 40% sodium. Salt intake should be limited to 5 grams per day, or 2 grams of sodium per day. Canned foods, baby formula, pretzels, pickles, bacon, and any other foods that contain a large amount of sodium should be avoided. Many dairy products and processed foods contain sodium. Because many parents and children may be unaware of the sodium content of foods, they must be taught how to restrict salt intake. Students who are salt sensitive and accustomed to eating foods high in salt must eliminate these foods gradually, which will necessitate a change in individual and family eating habits.

Potassium and Magnesium

A deficiency in potassium may also contribute to hypertension, whereas high intake of potassium may counteract the effects of high blood pressure and aid the kidneys in excreting sodium (Londe, 1983). In addition, an increased potassium intake may also protect against the onset of hypertension. Foods with a high content of potassium include fat-free milk, bananas, apricots, grapefruit, orange juice, carrots, cauliflower, corn, oranges, brussels sprouts, potatoes, mushrooms, and spinach.

Magnesium may also contribute to the control of high blood pressure by regulating heartbeat as well as helping the muscles of the arteries relax and contract. The correct magnesium intake may be met by a well-balanced diet including almonds, beans, peanuts, walnuts, whole-rye flour, whole-wheat flour, oats, bran, rice, and lentils.

Medication

Medication can also be effective in controlling hypertension but should be used only for severe cases. Most authorities contend that medication is dispensed too easily, especially in students with borderline hypertension (NHLBI, 2005). Because hypertension is a physical symptom of a possible serious future disease, physicians must balance the risks of medication and any possible side effects against mild elevations of blood pressure, which may be effectively reduced by dietary or exercise prescriptions implemented early in the treatment phase.

The National Heart, Lung, and Blood Institute (2005) recommends medication if the condition is severe or resistant to other preventive measures, with a periodic evaluation of the effectiveness of these prescribed drugs. Common medications include diuretics, such as cholorothiazide, hydrochlorothiazide, and furosemide; vasodilators, such as hydralazine; and agents that affect the actions of the autonomic nervous system, such as metoprolol and propranolol. The teacher should be aware of the potential side effects of medication on the exercising child. Gordon (1997) indicated that Beta blockers and calcium antagonists (diltiazem and verapamil) will decrease heart rate to both submaximal and maximal exercise, while dihydropyridine-derivative calcium antagonists and direct vasodilators may increase heart rate responses to submaximal exercise. Further, antihypertensive medications may predispose the exercising child to postexercise hypotension (Gordon, 1997).

Exercise

Often overlooked by the medical community is the value of physical activity in controlling hypertension. The ACSM and AHA (Haskell et al., 2007) both strongly support physical activity as a means of increasing overall physical fitness and lowering the risk factors of coronary artery disease. Myers (2003) also advocate exercise as means of controlling coronary heart disease, while Mark and Janssen (2008) extol the benefits of exercise in reducing blood pressure in youth.

Myers (2003) indicates that a sedentary lifestyle is one of the five major risk factors (in addition to high blood lipid values, high blood pressure, obesity, and smoking) for cardiovascular disease and stroke, and that regular exercise has a positive effect on many of the established risk factors for cardiovascular disease and stroke. When combined with other lifestyle changes (e.g. improved diet), the impact of exercise can be dramatic. The benefits of regular exercise on cardiovascular risk factors include: (1) increase in exercise tolerance; (2) reduction of body weight; (3) reduction in blood pressure; (4) reduction in bad cholesterol (LDL levels); (5) increase in good cholesterol (HDL levels); and (6) increase in insulin sensitivity. Bar-Or & Rowland, (2004), also advocate endurance-type conditioning activities to improve resting blood pressure values and overall physical functioning. In addition, aerobic conditioning may decrease resting peripheral resistance, submaximal systolic arterial pressure, heart rate, and pulmonary functions.

The Fourth Report on High Blood Pressure in Children and Adolescents (2004) recommends intense exertion in adolescents with hypertension for improving cardiovascular fitness, suggesting such activities as swimming, running, baseball, and basketball, as opposed to static exercises such as isometrics and weight training. More recently, the American Heart Association and the American College of Sports Medicine (Haskell et al., 2007) have endorsed exercise to overcome heart disease, and the AHA implemented *Jump Rope for Heart* and other programs designed to enhance cardiovascular conditioning in the school. The AHA also has provided funding for the state heart associations and the American Alliance for Health, Physical Education, Recreation and Dance to implement and expand this program to encourage all children to participate (AAHPERD, 2008).

Implementing the Physical Activity Program

Physical activity programs that address cardiac impairments or hypertension should be implemented for children recovering from temporary defects, rheumatic heart disease, and hypertension who may be participating in regular physical education classes. Most medical and support personnel agree that eliminating an individual from participation will be more harmful than helpful. Specific tolerance for activity is based on the child's functional ability and desire to participate. For example, at the University of Georgia, a member of the golf team originally learned golf to remain active after extensive heart surgery as a child. From his initial participation to promote activity, he developed his skill sufficiently to compete in college, along with enhancing his physical functioning.

Initially, when children return to school after rheumatic fever, they may be limited in their activity levels. Most children, after a three-month recuperation period, should gradually increase their participation in fitness activities and avoid contact sports, activities requiring maximal effort, or isometric activities. If valvular involvement is present, exercise may be contraindicated, and the physical activities should not focus on cardiovascular conditioning but on increasing tolerance for lifetime sports. Examples of these activities include leisurely hikes, golf, stationary cycling, and archery.

Teachers must use their professional judgment and work closely with physicians and appropriate school personnel in recommending guidelines for cardiac patients. Activities should be based on the AHA (1999; 2004) guidelines and include activities with mild, moderate, and marked restrictions. These activities should be used as guidelines for the teacher and be implemented in conjunction with the recommendation of the educational programming team. Some general recommendations follow.

Mild Restrictions

Most individuals with mild restrictions will have little, if any, activity limitations. Activities appropriate for children with mild restrictions include: swimming, aerobics, jogging, softball, cycling, walking, dance, and stationary cycling. Competitive sports may be included unless the atmosphere is highly competitive. However, isometric-type activities and activities involving maximal effort should be avoided.

Moderate Restrictions

Activities can be adapted for children with moderate restrictions by eliminating competition, reducing boundaries or height (e.g., lowering a volleyball net), or focusing on relaxation and progressive reconditioning activities, such as golf, bowling, volleyball, archery, walking, stationary cycling, flexibility exercises, relaxation exercises, table tennis, lead-up games, aerobic dance, and social dance.

Severe Restrictions

For children who are just returning to school and need severe restrictions, the teacher should include activities that involve a low expenditure of energy and that increase tolerance to activity. These activities include leisurely hikes, walking, bicycling, shuffleboard, archery, bowling, horseshoes, social dancing, and fly casting.

Graded Exercise Program

A graded exercise program should be based on the tolerance of an individual for physical activity. By gradually increasing the workload on the heart, physicians can determine the heart's functional capacity and reaction to work by the number of beats per minute.

To determine functionally the energy cost of an activity, METS, or metabolic equivalents, can be used. One MET is equivalent to the resting oxygen consumption per kilogram of body weight and can be used to measure the intensity of the activity. Most activities have a determined MET value and will allow teachers and physicians to control the intensity of the activity program. For example, individuals who are limited to a MET energy cost of 7 would participate in walking, social dancing, and other recreational activities below the intensity of 7 METS. This will then allow teachers and physicians to set a target heart rate and control the intensity of the program while providing for safe and active participation.

It is also critical to specify the duration and frequency of the activity. Most children will have little or no exercise restrictions. For exercise to be beneficial, it is recommended that it be conducted three times weekly for 20 minutes (vigorous-intensity exercise) or five times weekly for 30 minutes (moderate-intensity exercise) (Haskell, et al., 2007). Vigorous-intensity exercise is exemplified by jogging, and causes rapid breathing and significant increase in heart rate. Naturally, all exercise programs with cardiovascular compromised children must be under the guidelines of appropriate medical personnel. In this manner children can participate safely, and the amount of future activity can be determined within a medical margin of safety.

Participation may be guided by several other factors that will be useful for teachers in implementing the program, including the following:

1. Develop diversified program by seeking input from the collaborative programming team, including parents, children, physical educators, and appropriate medical personnel. Base the program goals on the child's functional level and interest.

2. Implement relaxation exercises as a warm-up and cool-down after every activity session.

3. Examine children periodically for stress by checking pulse rate or blood pressure before or after exercise to determine tolerance and adaptability to activity.

4. Encourage children to follow an appropriate weight control and dietary program (eliminating salt, reducing caloric intake, and encouraging potassium intake).

5. Be aware that if adverse environmental factors, such as cold, heat, improper ventilation, humidity,

or smog, are present, activities may need to be modified or decreased.

6. Reduce strain on the cardiovascular system by eliminating isometric exercises and teaching appropriate breathing techniques, such as exhaling in the effort phase of weight lifting or swimming.

7. Alternate periods of rest and activity, starting with a low number of repetitions and short time periods and gradually increasing the duration of the activity.

8. Avoid competitive or stressful situations by using relaxation or stress-reduction techniques.

9. If children have just returned to school, have them perform exercises in a back-lying position; have them gradually change positions to allow the cardiovascular system to adjust to a new position.

CHAPTER SUMMARY

1. Cardiovascular disorders are categorized as congenital or acquired. Congenital heart problems develop at birth, and the causes are generally unknown. Acquired heart problems include rheumatic heart disease, heart murmurs, arrhythmias, and hypertension.

2. Appropriate physical and motor fitness activities should be an integral part of the physical education program, as should appropriate nutrition and exercise habits. These program goals are to be developed with input from the educational programming team.

3. Rheumatic heart disease results from rheumatic fever. Damage to the heart occurs from inflammation, causing scarring to the heart.

4. Heart murmurs and arrhythmias are common disorders in the school-aged population. A child's participation in physical education should be determined in consultation with a cardiologist.

5. Hypertension, or high blood pressure, is increasing among school-aged children. Other health problems are associated with hypertension, and children should be monitored regularly.

6. Physicians often recommend regular monitoring, a detailed medical history, decreased salt intake, weight reduction, medication, and increased exercise for the management of hypertension.

7. Specific recommendations and activities that are appropriate for the implementation of an activity program should be based on a graded response to the student's tolerance for activity. The frequency, intensity, and duration of activities are of particular importance in designing and implementing an appropriate physical education program for the child with cardiovascular problems.

REFERENCES

AHA Scientific Statement. (2004). Recommendations for physical activity and recreational sports participation for young patients with genetic cardiovascular diseases. *Circulation, 109*, 2807–2816.

American Alliance for Health, Physical Education, Recreation and Dance. (2008). *Jump Rope for Heart.* www.aahperd.org/Jump/ (accessed on September 3, 2009).

Bar-Or, O., & Rowland, T. (2004). *Pediatric Sports Medicine: From Physiological Principles to Health Care Application.* Champaign, IL: Human Kinetics.

Brady, T., & Feld, L. (2009). Pediatric approach to hypertension. *Seminars in Nephrology, 29*(4), 379–388.

Brady, T., Siberry, G. & Solomon, B. (2008). Pediatric hypertension: A review of proper screening diagnosis, evaluation, and treatment. *Contemporary Pediatrics,* November 46–56.

Centers for Disease Control. (2009). Application of Lower Sodium Intake Recommendations to Adults—United States, 1999–2006. *MMWR Morbidity and Mortality Weekly Report, 58*(1), 281–283.

Gasperin, D., Netuveli, G., Dias-da-Costa, & Pattussi, M. (2009). Effect of physiological stress on blood pressure increases: A meta-analysis of cohart studies. *Medline-NLM,* ID#: 8901573.

Gordon, N. F. (1997). Hypertension In *ACSM's exercise management for chronic diseases and disabilities.* Champaign, IL: Human Kinetics.

Haskell, W., Lee, I. M., Pafe, R., Powell, K., Blair, S., Franklin, B., Macera, C., Heath, G., Thompson, P., & Bauman, A. (2007). Physical activity and public health: Updated recommendations for adults from the American College of Sports Medicine and the American Heart Association. *Medicine and Science in Sports and Exercises, 39*, 1423–1434.

Hohn, A. R., Dwyer, K. M., & Dwyer, J. H. (1994). Blood pressure in youth from four ethnic groups:

the Pasadena Prevention Project. *Journal of Pediatrics, 125,* 368–373.

Kavey, R. E., Laurer, R. M., & Hayman, L. L. (2003). American heart association guidelines for primary prevention of atherosclerotic cardiovascular disease beginning in childhood. *Circulation, 107,* 1562–1566.

Lieberman, E. (1978). Hypertension in childhood and adolescence. *Clinical Symposia, 30,* 1–43.

Loggie, J. (1992). *Pediatric Hypertension.* Boston: Blackwell Scientific Publications.

Londe, S. (1983). Epidemiology of essential hypertension in children. In S. Blumenthal (Ed.), *Hypertension: Prevention, diet, and treatment in infancy and childhood symposium proceedings.* New York: Biomedical Information Corporation.

Mark, A. & Janssen, I. (2008). Dose-response relation between physical activity and blood pressure. *Medicine and Science in Sports and Exercise, 40*(6), 1007–1012.

McCrory, W. W. (1982). What should blood pressure be in healthy children? *Pediatrics, 70,* 143–145.

Myers, J. (2003). Exercise and Cardiovascular Health. *Circulation,* e2–e5.

National Heart, Lung, and Blood Institute. (2008). *Prevent and Control Blood Pressure: Mission Possible.* http://hp2010.nhlbihn.net/mission/partner/should_know.pdf.

National Heart, Lung, and Blood Institute, (2005). *The 4th report on the diagnosis, evaluation, and treatment of high blood pressure in children and adolescents.* Publication # 05-5264.

National Heart, Lung, and Blood Institute. (2003). *Your Guide to Lowering Blood Pressure.* Publication # 03-4082.

Shaffer, T. E., & Rose, K. (1974). Cardiac evaluation for participation in school sports. *Journal of American Medical Association, 228,* 398.

Subramaniam, V., & Lip, G. (2009). Hypertension to heart failure: A pathophysiological spectrum relating blood pressure, drug treatments, and stroke. *Expert Review of Cardiovascular Therapy, 7*(6), 703–713.

The fourth report on the diagnosis and treatment of high blood pressure in children and adolescents. (2004). *Pediatrics, 114*(2), 555–576.

Virdis, A., Ghiadoni, L., Masi, S., Versari, D., Daghini, E. Giannarelli, C., Salvetti, A., & Taddei, S. (2009). Obesity in childhood: A link to adult hypertension. *Current Pharmaceutical Design, 15*(10), 1063–1071.

Weinberger, M. (2004). Sodium and blood pressure. *Current Opinions in Cardiology, 19,* 353–356.

World Health Organization. (1997). *Obesity: Preventing and managing the global epidemic.* Report of a WHO consultation on obesity. Geneva: World Health Organization.

World Health Organization. (2001). *Rheumatic Fever and Rheumatic Heart Disease.* Report of a WHO expert consultation. Geneva: World Health Organization.

World Health Organization. (2007). *Cardiovascular Diseases- Fact Sheet #317.* http://www.who.int/mediacentre/factsheets/fs317/en/index.html.

Developing and Implementing the Physical Activity Program

Physical education specialists need to design and deliver activity curriculums so that all students come to appreciate the value of lifelong physical fitness and activity. Thoughtfully conceived and enthusiastically taught, physical education, with emphasis on fitness and skill development, can help instill and reinforce a commitment among all students that the pursuit of health promoting physical activity should be central to one's value system.

Throughout Section VI, students are introduced to pedagogy representative of today's best practices in physical education. After having studied this section's content, and under supervision, practiced strategies recommended herein, you will have begun to lay a solid foundation for the effective teaching of health-related physical fitness and health promoting lifetime activity skills.

CHAPTER 21

Teaching Physical Fitness

CASE STUDY

Ann and Louie go to the same school. Ann is an active child who enjoys the outdoors. She enjoys playing with neighborhood friends in group pick-up games and participates in a number of organized sports. Ann is successful in a range of activity settings and loves a physical challenge. When tested for fitness in school, Ann, who is fit and in shape, "gives it her all," and does not mind performing in front of other students.

Louie, on the other hand, prefers to stay inside. Louie, who uses a wheelchair for many life activities, walks; but does so with recognizable difficulty. He rarely takes part in activities and games and does not participate in organized sports. When tested for fitness in school, Louie has been found unable to perform one push-up and has difficulty with sit-ups. He is embarrassed when asked to perform fitness activities in the presence of peers.

The goal of teaching fitness to all children, gifted, typical, and challenged alike, is to have each child acquire a constellation of knowledge, skills, and attitudes that will undergird individual commitments to wholesome, health promoting physical activity across the lifespan. The purpose of this chapter is to provide knowledge and present strategies to help physical educators, generalist and adapted specialist alike, teach physical fitness lessons to students with disabilities.

Given the above scenario, one could reasonably deduce that Louie has *learned* to avoid, whereas Ann has *learned* to enjoy and value, a variety of health promoting physical and leisure activities. For Ann, physical activity has become gratifying. Given continuing encouragement and barring unforeseen circumstances, she is likely well on her way to a lifetime where physical activity is central to her identify. At this time, Louie's prognosis for a lifetime of physical activity appears, at best, uncertain.

Physical educators must recognize that the delivery of developmentally appropriate physical education is essential to fitness improvement and maintenance in the present as well as over the course of a lifespan for *all* children. This is no less true for Louie. Your obligation to all students, including Louie, is to build-in opportunity for positive physical education experiences among all students and, thereby, create the conditions for everyone's success.

What is Physical Fitness?

One is physically fit when one is able "to perform daily tasks vigorously and alertly, with energy left over for enjoying leisure time activities and meeting emergency demands." (Presidents Council on Physical Fitness and Sports, www.fitness.gov/fitness.htm)

Physical fitness is a multi-faceted phenomenon. Physical fitness components, of which there are generally believed to be 10, tend to exist mutually exclusive of one another; meaning that good fitness with respect to one component does not necessarily ensure or promote fitness with respect to other components. For example, one may enjoy excellent cardiovascular fitness, while, at the same time, not have a health promoting level of muscular strength.

Each of the 10 components of physical fitness falls under one of two umbrella categories. Categories are termed *skill-* and *health-related*.

Skill-related fitness includes:

- Agility (Example: changing directions rapidly in tennis)
- Power (Example: making a jump shot in basketball)
- Speed (Example: throwing a ball forcefully)
- Balance (Example: standing on a step ladder and reaching to change a light bulb)
- Coordination (Example: juggling scarves)
- Reaction time (Example: stopping/starting, as instructed, immediately upon hearing the whistle blow)

Skill-related fitness development requires practice (i.e., learning) in very much the same way that skill development on a musical instrument requires practice. Potential for skill-related fitness development, like potential for skill development on a musical instrument, is determined significantly by genetics (i.e., natural ability). Some people simply have more natural ability to develop skill in specific areas than others. While everyone does not have the skill-related fitness potential to become a standout athlete like Tiger Woods, most possess more than sufficient sport-related skill development potential to support enjoyable, active, healthy lifestyles over the course of a lifetime (e.g., the avid recreational swimmer, tennis player, golfer).

While the commitment to develop skill-related fitness enjoys wide support among physical educators, development of health-related fitness, to be addressed below, generally is found to be even more highly prioritized.

Health-related fitness includes:

- Cardiovascular (aerobic) endurance
- Body composition
- Muscular strength
- Muscular endurance
- Flexibility

Cardiovascular Fitness

Cardiovascular (aerobic) fitness is often regarded as the most critical health promoting component of health-related fitness. Cardiovascular fitness is related to the capacity of the cardiovascular system and lungs to deliver oxygen to muscles and tissues. It is achieved by moderate intensity, high duration exercising of large muscle groups, examples of which include walking, jogging, cycling, dancing, and swimming.

Teaching Strategy: Given the goal to improve cardiovascular endurance: design a curriculum, including teaching strategies, that provides opportunity for students to participate in moderate to vigorous activity a minimum of three times per week. The duration of exercise should gradually be increased to between 20 and 30 minutes. Vary exercise duration according to each individual's level of function and type of fitness activity. Louie, with whom we are now

Figure 21.1 Cardiovascular fitness is the most critical health-promoting component of physical fitness.

acquainted, may need to start with a walking program; for example, two minutes walking, followed by two minutes resting. **Teaching Tip:** The heart and lungs do not know what kind of activity is producing the exertion; so, have fun!

Flexibility

Flexibility is the ability to move the body through ranges of motion sufficient to support active living and to protect against injury. Flexibility is essential in routine daily living (e.g., reaching to a high shelf, getting into and out of confining spaces) as well as in leisure (i.e., back swinging and following through with a golf club). Flexibility is important for all children (**Figure 21.2**); but can be especially important among students with disabilities whose conditions heighten risk for inflexibility, muscle strains, and contractures (e.g., juvenile rheumatoid arthritis, spastic cerebral palsy, spina bifida, congenital hip dislocation).

Teaching Strategy: Exercise to improve flexibility should include static stretches held for at least 15 seconds. Flexibility exercises should be included in *every* fitness-specific activity lesson to help prevent injuries, improve range-of-motion, reduce contractures, and to prepare muscles for range-of-motion challenging activities (e.g., gymnastics). Students with a range of flexibility-limiting conditions may need to stretch as a routine component of all daily lessons, including lessons not specifically fitness-centered.

Muscular Strength

Muscular Strength, in its purest form, is the amount of force that a muscle or muscle group is able to exert in one maximum effort. When teaching for muscular strength, the goal should be to develop strength sufficient for daily living activity, employment requirements, and/or leisure pursuits (**Figure 21.3**). Among persons with disabilities who disproportionately present with low fitness, attention to improving muscular strength can become an important consideration in promoting independent living. Inadequate strength, as in Louie's case, would potentially limit his ability to function independently with regard to daily activities; and, no less important, to experience success in health- and socialization-enriching leisure pursuits (i.e., golf, archery, wheelchair basketball).

Teaching Strategy: Be creative; search out a range of relatively high resistance, low repetition strength-building activities that your students are likely to enjoy. Example exercises include pulling and pushing one's own body while seated/lying prone on a gym scooter, pulling oneself through water by practicing swimming strokes; use of hand and wrist free weights, surgical tubing, training machines, and ropes, and climbing courses. The above activities are offered primarily as springboards for your imagination.

Muscular Endurance

Muscular Endurance is the ability to work individual muscles or localized muscle groups against resistance

Figure 21.2 Measuring hip and back flexibility.

Figure 21.3 Activities that require students to lift, push, or pull their own body weight help develop muscular strength.

for a prolonged period of time. An example of muscular endurance would be the lifting of objects (e.g., bagging groceries) or using a tool (e.g., a hammer to pound nails) numerous times in succession. Louie would need to work on upper-arm muscular endurance if his goal is to be able to perform more than one push-up.

Teaching Strategy: To improve muscular endurance, try relatively light weights that can be lifted across an extended number of repetitions. **Teaching Tip:** Muscular strength exercises can become muscular endurance exercises. Simply, decrease the resistance or

the amount of weight used in strength development exercises, thereby enabling the number of repetitions maximum to be increased.

Body Composition

Body Composition is about the relationship of body fat to lean body weight. Lean body weight is the nonfat body weight composed primarily of bone and muscle mass. The authors' intent, for fitness development purposes, is to *not* focus on weight or raw body mass index; but, rather to focus on the promotion of active student lifestyles, the goals of which are to reduce the risks associated with becoming overweight.

Teaching Strategy: Emphasis on low intensity, high duration activity that calls into play many or all of the body's large muscle groups simultaneously not only improves cardiovascular endurance; at the same time, it helps reduce excess body fat. Louie, and students whose circumstances are similar to Louie's, especially students from homes where active lifestyles may not be the norm, will need a gentle transition into activity designed to promote and maintain healthy body composition.

Guidelines and Strategies for Developing Your Physical Fitness Curriculum

To the end that physical education curricula achieve their potential to promote health-related fitness, the National Association for Sport and Physical Education, Council on Physical Education for Children (2004) recommends:

> Children should accumulate at least 60 minutes, and up to several hours, of age-appropriate physical activity on most days of the week. This daily accumulation should include moderate and vigorous physical activity, with the majority of the time being spent in activity that is intermittent in nature.

When developing curriculums, including accompanying teaching strategies designed to improve physical fitness among students with disabilities, one needs to take into consideration the fundamental principles of exercise physiology including; (1) overload and adaptation, (2) progression, and (3) specificity (McArdle, Katch, & Katch, 2006; Wilmore & Costill, 1999).

Overload and Adaptation

The body's cardiovascular, pulmonary, and muscular systems will adapt to exercise *when they are overloaded.* A body system experiences overload when it is made to work harder than it is normally used to working. The process whereby overload leads to increased capacity to function is known as *adaptation.* When the overloading of a body system ceases to be overloaded (due to adaptation); that system will no longer continue to improve. For continued improvement beyond the initial overload, a new level of overload will need to be established.

Overload generally is achieved by working or exercising:

- More often (increased frequency)
- Harder (greater intensity)
- For a longer period of time (increased duration).

Depending on the fitness component targeted for improvement, overload can be achieved by:

- Adding resistance
- Adding repetitions
- Increasing duration of work periods
- Calling upon muscles to move through greater ranges of motion.

Teaching Strategy: Patience is the key! Adaptation takes time. Begin instruction with light workloads based on current, individual fitness levels. Then, gradually increase overload until the fitness target has been achieved. If one of Louie's fitness goals is to perform one push-up, his teacher may have him begin his strength training program with modified push-ups and upper body endurance-related activities (e.g., pulling himself along the gym floor while lying in a prone position on a gym scooter).

Progression

Progression refers to the gradual increase of overload. Rates of progression need be tailored to individual needs. The goal is to achieve desired progress, while avoiding too aggressively increased workloads likely to result in otherwise avoidable injury and/or cumulative fatigue. A gradual, systematic approach to increasing exercise difficulty avoids exacerbation of pre-existing conditions, minimizes muscle soreness and unnecessary injuries, and, as a result, helps encourage active, enjoyable participation.

Teaching Strategy: Start exercising the student based upon where the student *is;* not where you would like the student to be. Structure fitness lessons such that they are progressive: that is, increase activity stressfulness in small increments so as to ensure improvements, while avoiding setbacks. Recognize that individual student circumstances (e.g., asthma, cardiac insufficiency, muscular dystrophy) may call for reduced exercise intensity at the program's onset; followed by gradually increased intensity in accordance with the individual student's adaptation to overload. Louie's disability makes walking difficult; therefore, Louie's daily fitness program may begin with a short lesson that focuses on improving walking mechanics; followed by rowing, biking, swimming, or any activity of a fitness nature that he is known to enjoy. **Teaching Tip:** To encourage fitness improvement beyond class time, consider activities in which Louie can participate beyond school hours with family and/or friends.

Specificity

Engaging in exercise to improve one component of fitness generally will not improve fitness with regard to another, *untargeted* fitness component. For example, targeting flexibility development can not be expected to improve strength. By way of another example, if one's goal is to improve strength, one must engage in activity specifically designed for strength development (i.e., high resistance, low duration). If improvement in cardiovascular endurance is the goal, one must perform activities specifically designed to involve large muscle groups that, in turn, tax the heart and lungs for extended periods of time.

Teaching Strategy: Be sure to address each fitness component within your library of fitness lessons. There is no need to include all or even most fitness components in any single lesson. Write into each lesson the *specific* fitness area(s) intended to be the focus of any given class period.

LEARNING ACTIVITY

Develop a list of activities enjoyed by one student, a friend, or yourself, and determine which fitness components are likely to improve by participating in each activity. Is there a component of fitness missing? Might some components have been overly emphasized? Which area(s) perhaps need more/less attention?

Research has demonstrated that children's potential for improving fitness varies from component to component. For example, a well-constructed training program (i.e., one that adheres to the principles of gradual overload/adaptation, progression, and specificity) will significantly improve strength and muscular endurance in children. However, cardiovascular endurance training improvements in children, as measured increases in VO2 max in controlled pediatric exercise studies, have been shown to trail those of similarly trained adults by a margin of two-thirds (Rowland, 2005).

How Do I Teach Fitness to Students with Various Abilities; Including Children with Disabilities, and Varying Levels of Fitness?

To begin with, quite generally, fitness *is* fitness and teaching fitness *is* teaching fitness. Children with a wide range of disabilities, except for notable extremes, are more like their classmates without disabilities than different.

Fitness may be thought of as a continuum, and children, regardless of ability/disability, may be identified at points along the entire continuum. The challenge, then, for adapted physical educators is *not* to

develop fitness programs "for the disabled," but rather to develop programs according to exercise physiology principles for children *who happen to have* one or more disabilities.

The four steps below are designed to assist in setting up a quality fitness program:

1. Assess each student's current fitness weaknesses and strengths

Select assessments according to the assessment tool's potential to measure what it purports to measure. (Considerations include: does the child understand what is expected? Do test items fall reasonably within the child's present range of ability and tolerance for activity? In other words, does it discriminate?) Then, collect and evaluate data to establish an informed starting point for fitness development and maintenance.

Steps need be taken to ensure that the testing experience does not become an ordeal for the child. Rather, it should be designed to be perceived as positive and educational from the child's perspective. Pangrazi (2007), in support, observes, "Students can learn about their personal fitness and how to develop a lifestyle that maintains good health without being turned off by the testing experience."

Fitness assessments should never be allowed to become embarrassing and, as a direct result, destructive of student self-esteem. Arguably, marginalized self-esteem and, likely, the student's marginalized attitude toward physical education that follows, will have a more lasting impact on the child's active lifestyle choices than will any given assessment instrument on any given day.

Fitnessgram is one example of a currently accepted fitness assessment instrument potentially effective for use with children, including children with disabilities, who present with wide range of abilities (Cooper Institute, 2004). Fitnessgram items classify fitness performances according to two categories: "needs improvement" and "healthy." Fitnessgram's goal is for all students to have personal performances that rise to and/or remain in the "healthy" zone. For more information, refer to the Cooper Institute's website at www.cooperinst.org and/or www.fitnessgram.net. Additional fitness assessments for consideration may be found in Chapter 3, Table 3.2.

Teaching Strategy: Teach to the child's current fitness level (i.e., first walk, then jog... slowly.), not where you would like the child to be. Do *not* administer the mile run simply to test! For example, when assessing cardiovascular fitness, as needed, begin with an assessment such as the Fitnessgram's Pacer item; and, then, do so only when your student is age-appropriate and otherwise ready to run.

Assess a child (or yourself) using Fitnessgram. According to each of the five health-related fitness components, do your student's (or your) results fall into the "healthy" or "need improvement" zone? Write specific goals for your student (or yourself) designed to improve fitness as needed to achieve the "healthy" zone or to maintain fitness in the "healthy" zone according to criteria established for each item measured.

2. Target specific areas for improvement when developing your fitness program

Chart the specific fitness areas, by child, where need for improvement is indicated (e.g., upper body strength, flexibility), and set goals to be accomplished according to individual student need. Whenever possible, give students a variety of activities to choose from to develop specific fitness goals.

When developing any fitness program, including development of individual-specific fitness goals; the teacher should take into full consideration psychological characteristics of the children whom she/he will teach. Children unaccustomed to exercise, often including children with disabilities more than children without, will be observed to reach psychological limits before reaching physiological limits (somewhat akin to the thinking of the beginning jogger versus the seasoned marathoner). Often, children with disabilities more than children without, before they arrive for the first day of class, will already have become products of well-intentioned; however, in the end, debilitating; over protection. The physical educator, whether teaching fitness or teaching skills, will find himself/herself challenged to help instill in the unnecessarily sheltered child an "I can" frame of mind. Helpful tips to facilitate attitude adjustments may be found in the Behavior Management section of Chapter 4.

Teaching Strategy: When age and developmentally appropriate, afford each student opportunity to create her/his own unique program. Students able to understand and afforded opportunity for goal input, no matter what the age, often adhere to self-developed programs more readily than to programs externally imposed. For example, one of the goals set for Louie, in collaboration with his teacher, might be to swim the length of the pool and back in seven minutes or less, using the back crawl. Louie's teacher will provide skill instruction, modified according to Louie's unique needs, on how to efficiently perform the back stroke. Given time and opportunity to practice, Louie, in pursuit of his self-set goal, may be likely to work harder than he otherwise might if he had been working to achieve a goal imposed solely by the teacher.

3. Offer clear and specific instruction; teach to the goals

Establish specific, attainable goals and take steps to ensure that every student experiences success (however large or small). Master physical education teachers develop the ability to continually monitor and adapt their instruction to ensure that exercise programs, individually tailored, remain appropriate and safe for every student.

The manner in which fitness is taught determines how students feel about making fitness a part of their lifestyle (Pangrazi, 2010). Whenever possible, teach students how to self-design and self-direct workouts within a specified period of time; one mutually determined by student and teacher.

Teaching Strategy: Teach fitness by example; demonstrate setting personal fitness goals, according to age developmental appropriateness of students: including the steps you use to improve or maintain your own fitness level. Be creative when thinking of ways to motivate your students to follow your good example.

Log your personal physical activity types and levels both at school and at home for one week. Are you, as a pre- or in-service physical educator, moderately to vigorously physically active at levels for durations of 20 to 30 minutes three or more times per week?

4. Periodically reassess progress and adapt individual programs as fitness improves

Acknowledge genuine improvement, however modest. Among some students with disabilities, it may be necessary to measure improvement (including sincere effort in absence of improvement) in proverbial feet rather than miles. Be ready to provide *immediate* and *daily* feedback for success. Offer positive encouragement and cues in areas where expectations for improvement persist.

When feasible, emphasize self-testing activities to help children learn to evaluate their personal fitness levels. Allow students to self-check fitness levels throughout the school year, rather than just at the beginning and/or end of the year.

Teaching Strategy: Get to know your students as individuals. Create the conditions for children to work at levels where you and (more importantly *they*) believe they will succeed.

Fitness and the Prevention of Lifestyle-Related Disability

Research spanning recent decades has consistently revealed that physical activity and musculoskeletal stress are important for promoting bone and soft tissue growth in children. Children's involvement in physical activity and/or sport training can provide long-term health benefits, including timely stimulation of bone growth and an accumulation of bone density that reduces the risk of osteoporosis in later adult years (Rowland, 2005).

Further, research has demonstrated that physical activity, for purposes of developing and maintaining fitness levels that lower risk for disability later in life, need not be strenuous to the point of having to endure major discomfort (U.S. Department of Health and Human Services, 1996). What is important, according to the report, is that people who enjoy physical activity, especially at an early age, become predisposed to continued participation in health promoting physical activity throughout the lifespan.

The 1996 surgeon general's report confirmed the importance of regular moderate physical activity in reducing the risk of acquiring lifestyle-related chronic diseases such as hypertension, diabetes, heart disease, stroke, and colon cancer. The report recommends people select activities that they enjoy and can fit into their daily lives. It confirms that significant health benefits can be obtained from wheeling one self or walking briskly for 30–40 minutes per day. Well-designed school physical education programs, according to the report, can be effective in reducing the prospect of acquiring numerous lifestyle-related conditions later in life. For further information on the first surgeon general's report on physical activity go to www.cdc.gov/nccdphp/sgr/sgr.htm

Critical Thinking and Discussion

What instructional strategies could be used to improve fitness in the following students?

1. Maria has reduced muscular function and her overall fitness levels are low due to moderate to severe juvenile rheumatoid arthritis. She experiences contractures, particularly in flexor muscle groups, and has difficulty with her walking gait. What role can physical education play in management of Maria's fitness, contractures, and mobility issues?

2. Jared is seven years old and lacks motivation in fitness-related activity. He appears to have issues with understanding directions, staying on task, and completing tasks. It has yet to be determined whether Jared's difficulties are of organic or situational origin. What steps would you take to help get to the root of Jared's motivation issues, and, subsequently, to help pique his interest in the fitness curriculum?

CHAPTER SUMMARY

1. Development of health-related fitness should be accorded high priority status in developmental adapted physical education, given the common and unnecessary reality of low fitness in the community of people of all ages who have disabilities.

2. Components of health-related physical fitness include cardiovascular endurance, body composition, muscular strength, muscular endurance, and flexibility.

3. Cardiovascular fitness development calls for a moderate-intensity activity involving one or more of the body's large muscle groups. Activity duration is critical to cardiovascular fitness development. Exercising major muscle groups, in addition to promoting cardiovascular fitness development, increases caloric expenditure and, thereby, helps promote healthy body composition.

4. Flexibility exercise should be static in nature and incorporated into regular activity sessions to eliminate injuries, improve range-of-motion, prevent contractures, and prepare the muscles for a range of physical activities.

5. Relatively high resistance, low repetition activity is most suitable for strength development purposes.

6. Muscular endurance involves the ability to execute one movement repeatedly. One helpful strategy to achieve muscular endurance overload involves decreasing in resistance in exercises otherwise designated to develop strength; thereby allowing the maximum number of repetitions in such exercises to increase.

7. Exercise physiology principles that inform development of fitness curriculums, irrespective of ability/disability, include principles of overload and adaptation, progression, and specificity.

8. Children with disabilities, given overrepresentation in the population of persons who present with low fitness, generally may benefit from participation in health-related fitness curriculums designed to promote independence associated with tasks of daily living, eventual employment, and worthy use of leisure time.

9. Successful fitness activity teaching among students of varying abilities calls for:

   a. Assessment of each student's current fitness weaknesses and strengths

   b. Development of fitness curricula designed to improve or maintain individual student fitness levels

   c. Implementation of instruction specific to fitness development, as needed, in each of the five areas of health-related fitness

   d. Reassessment (throughout the year) to determine progress and adapt the curriculum as fitness improves

SELECTED FITNESS AND FITNESS TEACHING RESOURCES FOR CONSIDERATION:

National Center on Physical Activity and Disability: **www.ncpad.org/**

Sports n' Spokes Magazine: Published six times a year, and focuses on wheelchair sports and recreational activities **www.pvamagazines.com/sns/**

Special Olympics Coaching Guides (Nutrition, Safety, & Fitness): **http://info.specialolympics.org/**

PE Central: **www.pecentral.org**

PE Central-Adapted Physical Education: **www.pecentral.org/adapted/adaptedmenu.html**

The President's Council on Physical Fitness and Sports: **www.fitness.gov/fitness.htm**

Palaestra: A quarterly publication featuring physical education, recreation, and sport for persons with disabilities **www.palaestra.com**

REFERENCES

American College of Sports Medicine. (2010). *ACSM's health-related physical fitness assessment manual* (3rd ed.). Philadelphia: Lippincott, Williams & Wilkins.

Cooper Institute. (2004). *Fitnessgram/activitygram test administration manual.* (4th ed.). NY: Cooper Institute.

Council on Physical Education for Children (COPEC). (2004). Physical activity for children: A statement of guidelines for children ages 5–12. Reston, VA: National Association for Sport and Physical Education, an association of the American Alliance for Health, Physical Education, Recreation, and Dance.

Horvat, M. & Croce, R. (1995). Physical rehabilitation of individuals with mental retardation: Physical fitness and information processing. *Critical Reviews in Physical and Rehabilitation Medicine,* 1(3), 233–252.

McArdle, W. D., Katch, F. L., & Katch, V. L. (2006). *Essentials of exercise physiology* (3rd ed.). Philadelphia: Lippincott, Williams & Wilkins.

National Association for Sport and Physical Education. (2005). *Physical best activity guide: Middle and high school levels.* (2nd ed.). Champaign, IL: Human Kinetics.

Pangrazi, R. P. (2010). *Dynamic physical education for elementary school children* (16th ed.). San Francisco: Benjamin Cummings.

Rowland, T. A. (2005). *Children's exercise physiology* (2nd ed.). Champaign, IL: Human Kinetics.

Seaman, J. A., Corbin, C., & Pangrazi, R. P. (1999). Physical activity and fitness for persons with disabilities. *Research Digest Series* 3(5): 2–12.

U.S. Department of Health and Human Services (USDHHS). (1996). Physical activity and health: A report of the surgeon general. Atlanta: USDHHS, Centers for Disease Control and Prevention, National Center for Chronic Disease Prevention and Health Promotion.

Wilmore, J. H., & Costill, D. L. (1999). *Physiology of sport and exercise* (2nd ed.). Champaign, IL: Human Kinetics.

CHAPTER 22

Teaching Motor Skills

Jerry is generally a happy eight year old child without discipline issues. He can walk and run with modest proficiency, but has noticeable difficulty galloping and sliding. Jerry's legs are not strong enough to support hopping on either foot. Therefore, he is unable to skip. His balance due to lack of leg strength also is shaky. Despite that Jerry tries hard in physical education, he remains uncoordinated, and games of skill continue to be difficult for him. Jerry benefits from a positive attitude toward school in general. He is improving academically and currently tests in the low-average range on core academic assessments.

Most often, motor skills, particularly skills termed *phylogenetic* that appear throughout the human species, emerge and require little instruction for achievement. Jerry, however, presents as an exception to that rule. Given Jerry's young age and the relative mildness of his apparent delays in motor development, there is reasonable cause not to rush to label him. Many child development professionals believe that labels, hastily or misapplied, have potential to do more harm than good.

While we do not yet know precise reasons beyond apparent low strength for Jerry's lagging fundamental motor skills development, we do know that he needs individual attention and ample opportunity to work on his fundamental motor skills. Individual attention and opportunity to practice should, at the very least, help ensure that Jerry does not fall further behind. Ideally, through individual attention, he will close the gap.

The fundamental skills Jerry currently lacks are analogous to building blocks that comprise the foundation upon which a sturdy house is built. Just as strong houses cannot be built on shaky foundations; neither can active lifestyles be built on absent or inadequate, foundationally prerequisite fundamental motor skills.

Once we have helped Jerry acquire functional levels of locomotor, non-locomotor, manipulative, and rhythmic skill (i.e., provided a firm foundation), we can begin to weave these new skills into motor patterns that will better enable him to become successful in, and enjoy a wide variety of, lifetime physical activities, games, and sports.

This chapter presents information on motor skill development strategies to help physical educators, generalists, and adapted specialists alike, teach motor skills to children with disabilities. This chapter focuses predominately on the acquisition of fundamental motor skills considered foundationally prerequisite to success in activities ranging from basic play through serious sport. Fundamental motor skill development progressions are described throughout the chapter and accompanied by teaching cues and pointers designed to facilitate successful teaching and learning.

Fundamental motor skills well taught and well learned are important for their own sake. However, they are no less important, because they help motivate children to want to continue on to develop more specialized activity skills and to remain physically active in school, after school, and beyond school years.

Factors Influencing the Acquisition of Fundamental Motor Skills

The successful teaching of fundamental motor skills calls for a practical understanding of a multitude of factors that affect skill acquisition processes. These individual factors can singularly affect learning; however, more often, these factors affect learning in combinations unique to the child's circumstances. As you consider the factors below, think about the different combinations, and how recognition of such combinations can inform the development of teaching strategies tailored to meet the needs of the child.

Movement Responses

In human motor development, movement responses to stimuli progress from total body undifferentiated movement observed in infancy to controlled movement by individual body parts observed in adulthood. For example, when an infant becomes excited and responds to various stimuli (e.g., auditory, visual, kinesthetic, tactile) her/his whole body responds. Gradually, as the child matures, one may notice how she/he progressively gains control of muscles appropriate to the stimulus (e.g., 'wave bye-bye,' 'so big;' to, eventually, as an adult, pressing the elevator button with a single finger tip).

Gross Motor to Fine Motor Progression

Seminal work during the early–mid 20th century by child development icon Arnold Lucius Gesell, MD (1880–1961) detailed much of what we know about and apply in the field of child motor development today. Gesell, ahead of his time, studied development of infants and children both with and without disabilities (Gesell, 1928, 1954). Gesell was among the first, if not the first, to chronicle how children gain control over the body's larger muscles before gaining control over smaller muscles. Because larger muscles tend to be predominately responsible for larger gross motor skill performances, proficiency in gross motor skills (e.g., running, jumping) tend to precede proficiency in fine motor skills (e.g., keyboarding, threading a needle). He also cited through his maturationist theory how infants and young children's central nervous systems mature in two orderly directions (see the following). His work has left a lasting mark on child development theory and practice to this date.

Central Nervous System (CNS) Maturation

Infants are born with central nervous systems that are far less mature than are those of adults. The central nervous system typically undergoes an orderly maturation process that continues at least through middle childhood. The practical significance of this understanding is that the CNS controls the actions of muscles necessary for the execution of motor skills; that skills attempted to be taught in advance of adequate CNS maturation, will become a source of frustration for both teacher and child. This is not necessarily because the child is not trying or the teacher is not teaching, but because the child's CNS is not neurologically ready. While environmental factors (nurture as opposed to nature) can and do affect skill acquisition processes, quite generally the more mature the CNS, the greater the potential to acquire and execute movements with skill.

The orderly maturation of the CNS progresses in two directions. These directions are termed *progressions*. The progressions are termed *cephalocaudal* and *proximo-distal*. Each is important to your practical understanding of human motor skill acquisition processes.

Cephalocaudal Progression

The term in Greek, literally means head-tail. It describes the direction of CNS maturation beginning with head control and culminating with gaining control over the farthest reaches of the lower extremities. As the cephalocaudal progression progresses in an infant and young child, she/he progressively develops increased potential for purposeful control of skeletal muscle (Berk, 2008). The practical application of this understanding is that children, in a generally orderly manner, acquire skill in upper body region muscle groups before lower body region muscle groups. An example derives from the observation that infants are able to control eye, head, and neck movements before they acquire control of torso muscles that support sitting posture. The practical application of this understanding is that children, in the midst of cephalocaudal progression development, generally execute motor skills in upper body regions *with precision* before they can execute similarly complex skills with similar precision in lower body regions. Equally important is the practical understanding that skills introduced in advance of sufficient cephalocaudal progression progress will not accelerate cephalocaudal progression progress.

Cephalocaudal progression in action

Note that four distinct stages (**Figure 22.1a–d**) appear in the development of overhand throwing skill:

1. Arm action only

2. Arm action, followed by body rotation

3. All of step two, followed by a step forward with the right foot (assuming right-handed thrower)

(a)

(b)

(c)

(d)

Figure 22.1 The four stages of the cephalocaudal progression.

4. All of step three, preceded by a preparatory step forward (i.e., a wind-up) with the left foot.

Now, observe how the child, as she/he moves successively through stages one through four, is able to call into play controlled movements from successively lower body region muscle groups. This phenomenon occurs largely because cephalocaudal progression development, as it moves successively into lower body regions, enables muscle groups at successively lower body regions to come under the child's voluntary control.

LEARNING ACTIVITY

Given your understanding of the cephalocaudal progression, as explained above, how might that understanding inform your decision of which fundamental motor skills should be introduced first? Can you offer specific examples?

Proximo-distal Progression

Conceptually, the proximo-distal progression operates in a manner very similar to that of the cephalocaudal progression. The difference being that, with the proximo-distal progression, the CNS's direction of maturation begins at the body's midline and progresses out through the extremities (Berk, 2008). A practical application example of this understanding is that children generally acquire control of shoulder girdle muscles before they acquire a similar quality of control over muscles that cross the elbow. The introduction of fine motor coordination activities involving hands and fingers should wait until there is adequate proximo-distal progression development to control fine motor manipulative activity at the outer reaches of the upper extremities. This, in part, explains why children are taught and learn to print in advance of being taught to write in cursive.

The proximo-distal progression in action   Note that three distinct stages (**Figure 22.2a–c**) appear in the development of catching skill:

1. Stage one: Arms reach forward at approximately shoulder height and shoulder's width apart. Purposeful muscle contraction to affect the catch occurs only at the shoulder joint. Extended arms, then, come together in anticipation of the ball's arrival. As yet, little or no purposeful muscle activity occurs at the elbows, shoulders, wrists, hands, and fingers.

2. Stage two: Arms reach forward in anticipation of the ball, as in stage one. However, in stage two, the child, in anticipation of the oncoming ball, flexes at both shoulders and elbows to 'scoop' the ball into and trap it against the wall of the chest. In the stage two trapping response, flexed elbows come to rest against the rib cage. As yet, little or no purposeful muscle activity occurs at wrists, hands, and fingers.

3. Stage three: Arms reach forward in anticipation of the oncoming ball. As the ball arrives, shoulders and elbows flex to absorb the ball's impact. Simultaneously, hands with extended fingers bi-laterally clasp the ball (Wild, 1938).

Now, observe how the child, as she/he moves successively through stages one through three of learning to catch, is able to call into play controlled movements from muscle groups successively distant from the body's midline. This phenomenon occurs largely because proximo-distal progression development, as it moves outward toward the hands and fingers, enables muscle groups successively distant from the midline to come under the child's voluntary control.

LEARNING ACTIVITY

Given your understanding of the proximo-distal progression, as explained above, in which sequence should fundamental motor skills be introduced? Can you offer specific examples?

Possible impact of disability on the rate of CNS maturation

According to Hoffman, Rice, and Sung (1996), as cited by Tice and Travers (2005), "About six to 15 percent of children have a chronic condition that affects their physical health and potentially their developmental trajectory as well." Often, children with disabilities are found to be physiologically less mature for their chronological age than are same chronological age children who do not have disabilities. This phenomenon can occur for a range of reasons whose explanations transcend the scope of this chapter. The critical knowledge to take away at this point is that delayed maturation in general, for whatever reason, can be expected to manifest itself in delayed cephalocaudal and proximo-distal progression development.

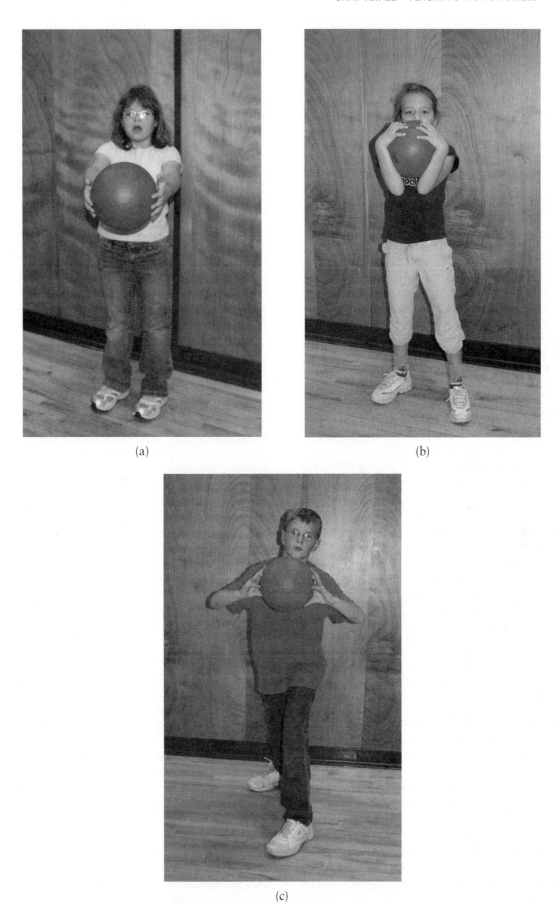

(a)

(b)

(c)

Figure 22.2 The proximo-distal progression in the development of catching skill.

✔ TEACHING TIPS

Become familiar with developmental stages through which children pass as they move from immature to mature motor performance in fundamental motor skills. For any given skill, identify and reinforce performance at the child's present level.

Most children who are given encouragement and opportunity will progress naturally to the next stage of skill performance. At the first sign of a subsequent stage's emergence, begin to provide reinforcement and ensure opportunity for the child to perform at that stage. Continue in this manner from stage to stage until the child has achieved what you believe to be his/her potential with regard to that given skill.

Note that when teaching children who have disabilities, some may not naturally progress from one developmental stage to the next. This may occur due to a specific central nervous system deficit or, more simply, because physical and motor activity has been significantly absent in the child's life experience. Here, formal prompting from the teacher or helping adult may be necessary. Where performance delays persist in the absence of reasonable explanation; and, particularly, where gaps between performance expectations and actual performances become part of a larger pattern; medical evaluation of the child may be indicated.

Fundamental Motor Skill Development

Development of fundamental motor skills is influenced by intricate interaction between nature (i.e., heredity and maturation) and environment/opportunity (i.e., nurture). Apropos to the nature versus nurture argument, noted Canadian psychologist Donald Olding Hebb, when once asked, which contributes more to who we become, 'nature or nurture,' he allegedly responded, "Which contributes more to a rectangle, its length or its width?" (Scott, 1995; Meany, 2001, 2004; Herschkowitz & Herschkowitz, 2002). In effect, nature (i.e., our heredity) and nurture (i.e., our environment) are interwoven into the fabric of who we become.

The challenge for all physical educators, (1) is to understand how the child's biological attributes and prior experiences combined have brought the child to where she/he is today and; (2) subsequently, to design and deliver lessons that hold promise for helping each child achieve his/her unique potential. The likelihood of the child achieving fundamental motor proficiencies in accordance with potential; low, modest, or extraordinary, will be directly related to the quality and quantity

of instruction received through the physical education curriculum.

When we teach motor skills to children with disabilities, it is helpful to think of the child's achieving progressively more sophisticated motor skills as being analogous to climbing up successive rungs of a developmental ladder. The adapted physical education teacher need understand that there is not a separate developmental ladder for children who happen to have disabilities. The ladder of human motor development is universal. For example, given there are three developmental stages in learning to catch, children, given the potential, will achieve catching skill in the same one, two, three-stage order irrespective of ability/disability. *The challenge for adapted physical educators is not to imagine and invent new developmental ladders, but, rather, to design individually tailored lessons that minimize the impact a disability may have on the climb up the ladder that is, indeed, universal.*

Fundamental Motor Skills: The Building Blocks

While fundamental motor skills generally do not need to be formally taught, because they are phylogenetic; they cannot be expected to naturally emerge or be perfected if the environment (nurture) does not present adequate opportunity.

With regard to opportunity, physical education teachers must recognize the importance of what are called 'windows of opportunity' in acquisition of all phylogenetic motor skills. With skills judged to be phylogenetic, there appear to be finite periods of ripeness when children are most ready to learn. The windows generally open and close variously during early and middle childhood, depending upon the individual child's rate and level of CNS maturation. With specific regard to skills of a phylogenetic nature; opportunity lost, including attempts at remedial instruction once windows have begun to close, may be tantamount to having tried to do too little too late (Gabbard & Rodriguez, 2002).

Teaching cues and pointers have been embedded into this chapter's fundamental skill descriptions to assist in developing your own strategies for effective instruction of fundamental (largely phylogenetic) motor skills. Consider cues and pointers to be *examples only*; as springboards for your professional imagination that support experimentation with your own ideas.

Fundamental locomotor skills

Fundamental locomotor skills are those that propel the mover (bipedal human) through three-dimensional space. There are just eight ways humans move on two feet (some suggest only seven, because the skip, generally the last of the fundamental locomotor skills to emerge and be perfected, combines walking and hopping). Eight fundamental locomotor skills are as follows:

- Walk
- Run
- Gallop
- Slide
- Jump
- Hop
- Leap
- Skip

Walking   Walking is the most basic of bipedal locomotor skills. It is perhaps the most recognizable milestone in the human motor development experience. Walking involves the transfer of weight from one foot to the other while, at all times, maintaining contact with the ground with at least one foot. The entire developmental process of learning to walk, on average, takes about five years. Thus, a child who begins to walk, usually at age one, generally does not achieve a mature, adult pattern walking until approximately age six (Gallahue & Donnelly, 2003).

Mechanically efficient walking begins with good posture. Good posture, whether walking or standing is not necessarily characterized by ramrod straightness. Rather, spinal curves (thoracic in the upper spine; lumbar in the lower spine) should be present, but moderate. An excessive thoracic curve often results in a compensatory excessive curve in the lumbar spine. Where thoracic curves are exaggerated, head and neck tend to protrude forward. In posture exhibiting proper lumbar curve, one should be able to stand with back, hips, and heels touching the wall; while snugly fitting the hand (palm of the hand flat against the wall) between the mid-lumbar spine and the wall.

Excessive spinal curves can place undue stress on posture muscles and ligaments that maintain the spinal column in an erect position. Excessive curve in the lumbar spine can be the cause of low back pain. Excessive curve in the thoracic spine is often accompanied by a sunken chest which, if sufficiently sunken, can mechanically impede breathing.

Characteristics of the earliest stages of walking are as follows:

- Flat back
- Noticeable flexion of hips and knees
- Arms held high and to the sides
- No purposeful reciprocal arm movement
- Forward tilted pelvis
- Feet at approximately shoulder's width apart
- Feet turned outward
- Steps are flat-footed

As walking matures:

- Gravity produces spinal curves
- Pelvic tilt diminishes, because hips become more flexible; thus minimizing pelvic tilt and obligatory abdomen protrusion
- As hips become more flexible, knees are able to straighten
- With improved balance, arms lower to sides and begin to move in opposition to feet
- With improved balance, step width narrows
- Steps become more uniform in both width and length
- Flat-footed walking gives way to heel-toe walking

Children, in the midst of learning-to-walk, are impressionable, therefore, model and teach for the *joy* of walking and moving. Children's walking paces will be individual, but should rise to the level of exercise for health and skill building's sake. Pace in walking activities should not rise to a level beyond which the child is able to carry on comfortable conversations.

TEACHING TIPS

Afford immature beginning walkers (i.e., generally, but not always, toddlers) ample opportunity to walk. As children begin to appear ready, have them practice walking on rough, uneven, and slanted surfaces (upward, downward, slant right, slant left).

As the child becomes able to understand directions, she/he may be prompted to walk on lines or down lanes that are straight, circular, and/or random shaped. Wheelchair users, likewise, can strive to move straight down lines or between lanes. For children who are blind or visually impaired, lines can become lanes when parallel ropes are strung at approximate waist height between sets of posts. Streamers suspended near the end of and above the lane, in addition to teacher cueing, can signal to the child when she/he should stop.

Running   Running is the most rapid form of locomotion and is integral to a wide range of physical education, recreational, and sport activities. By definition, a walk becomes a run only when the child becomes momentarily airborne as the trailing foot leaves the ground before the lead foot re-establishes contact (Gallahue & Ozmun, 2006). Speed alone does not differentiate between walking and running. A fast walk can be faster than a slow run.

The child who learns to run well can enjoy success in a wide range of games and activities. In contrast, inability to run well virtually ensures frustration and failure. Repeated failure, in turn, becomes a disincentive to want to be active.

Because the point of running often is to get from one point to another as quickly as possible, skilled running generally implies the ability to run in a straight line. It also implies, however, the ability to weave and dodge if the quickest way from point A to point B is something other than a straight line; as is often the case of active play, recreational sports, and games.

In skilled running, feet should point straight ahead. Some of the most successful runners actually toe-in a bit. Toeing-in places the big toe in its most advantageous position to exert force in the thrust from one step to the next.

Arm swing should be in the forward-backward plane in opposition to the feet. To the extent arms thrust, each should thrust forward in coordination with the opposite thrusting foot.

The head should remain stable and be pointed in the direction of travel. Left and right head rotation can be uncomfortable and make staying on course difficult. Rotation of the head back and forth becomes evident when children try to run as fast as they can.

Running requires forward lean to maintain speed and momentum. Generally, the faster the run, the greater will be the need for forward lean. When jogging comfortably, forward lean may be barely discernable. At all times, children, whether running very fast or comfortably jogging, should be prompted to remain relaxed. Tense muscles inhibit freedom of movement and hasten the onset of undue fatigue.

There are occasions in physical education, recreation, and sport activities when running backward is required. This warrants some practice of backward running activities.

Activity Cues: When teaching running, children should be prompted to lean the trunk forward slightly, move flexed arms forward and backward in opposition to legs, lift knees high, and bring heels close to seat. Emphasize looking forward, perhaps at some object in the distance, and take big steps.

 TEACHING TIPS

In the best (i.e., mature) runs, steps are of consistent length and width, arms move in precise opposition to feet (hands tend to be held lower to ground than elbows). Generally, the most efficient run is the one that minimizes time being airborne. To help teach proper foot placement in running, have the child run in loose or soft dirt. Where soft dirt is not available, a bit of chalk dust on shoes will leave foot strike marks on hard running surfaces.

A line drawn in the dirt will help the child self-evaluate the straightness of her/his run. If lines for running on or between cannot be drawn on hard activity surfaces, masking tape will suffice. Wheelchair runners and children who use a range of assistive devices for ambulation, like stand up runners, can strive to move straight down lines or between lanes.

For children who are blind or visually impaired, lines can become lanes when parallel ropes are strung at approximate waist height between sets of posts. Streamers suspended near the end of and above the lane, in addition to teacher cueing, can signal to the child when she/he should stop.

Emphasize relaxation during running. Relaxation is indicated when jaw, hands, and fingers wobble loosely during the run. Also, in relaxed running, wrists generally are held lower than elbows as arms swing in opposition to the feet. Encourage older children to self-evaluate relaxation while running.

Jumping Jumping is defined as taking off on either or both feet and landing on two feet. Vertical jumping may be developmentally less complex than horizontal jumping (Horvat, Kelly, & Block, 2007). The relative complexity of horizontal jumping over vertical jumping may, in part, explain why vertical jumps often appear first.

Jumping can occur from a stationary position or from a walk or run. Although a jump can occur in any direction, most jumps are vertical, straight ahead, or nearly straight ahead. Often, first, rudimentary jumps in young children fail, because, as the child thrusts arms upward, she/he often simultaneously flexes at the hips (Cratty, 1994). The result is that one motion (hip flexion) cancels out the other (upward arm thrust), and the child fails to leave the ground. Power necessary for a successful jump comes from vigorous extension of the hips and knees and plantar flexion of the feet. Arms assist in the jump by swinging upward or upward and forward to the desired direction. (**Figure 22.3a–c**).

When landing, the lower extremities should be relaxed to avoid jarring. Balls of the feet and knees and ankles should flex to absorb the force of impact. Particularly in forward jumping, arms may assist in balancing the body as legs are brought forward during the jump to maximize distance; and, then, flexed in advance of the body's center of gravity direction of travel to absorb the impact of landing.

The earliest vertical and horizontal jumps typically occur from a standing position. As children gain confidence in jumping horizontally, the horizontal jump usually, and without prompting, becomes initiated from a walk and then a run. Children who jump horizontally from the walk or run, to be successful, must be able to take off on one foot. For one-foot takeoff jumps to become fully utilitarian, the child should strive to take off from either foot with equal facility.

Activity Cues: Prompt younger children to bend knees; swing arms backward, then forward and upward, and reach for the stars.

(a)

(b)

(c)

Figure 22.3 Mature jump.

✔ TEACHING TIPS

When you believe a child might be ready to attempt his/her very first jump, place the child on the lowest step on a group of stairs. Hold the child's hand, and ask the child to jump to the floor immediately below. Often the child's first efforts will resemble a step rather than a jump to the floor. However, with encouragement, steps will develop into jumps. If steps can be approached from the sides of stairs, allowing the child to jump from the side of steps to the ground, the child, in due time, holding the teacher's hand, may jump to the ground from the second step.

To motivate children to jump vertically for height, suspend a brightly colored object directly above the practice spot. If the object is a star, for example, the child can 'reach for the stars.' Where children of varying jumping abilities in the same setting are asked to jump for height, suspend colorful ribbons in a row, each of which is successively higher from the ground than the preceding one. Ask children to jump for the ribbons they believe they can reach. When a child consistently reaches one ribbon, she/he may then be prompted to reach for the next higher ribbon. Remember to reinforce successful efforts as well as successful jumps.

When teaching horizontal jumping, taking off of one or two feet, tape a line across a gymnastics mat. Ask the child to jump over the line. When success comes, add another line a few inches ahead of and parallel to the first and ask the child to jump perhaps 'across the river.' As success continues gradually widen the river, or among older students, a measured distance.

Consider using a gymnastics mat for the jumping surface. Mats help ensure jumper safety should the child fall upon landing.

Leaping Leaping is similar to running. Where running accentuates forward motion; leaping accentuates upward motion. In leaping as in running, the child takes off on one foot, becomes airborne, and lands on the opposite foot. Although there is no hard fast rule, a run generally becomes a leap when more effort is expended to go upward than forward.

During takeoff and landing, weight should be concentrated on the balls of the feet. This provides for maximum spring on takeoff and maximum cushion on landing. The knee that bears weight on impact should be flexed slightly in anticipation of landing to avoid jarring on impact.

Leaps can be used to surmount small obstacles in the path of a runner. In a game setting, one might need to leap over a fallen player. Players in ball games will sometimes need to leap into the air to catch a ball. For leaping to become truly functional, a child should strive to become able to take off and land on either foot with equal facility.

Activity Cues: Model and say to the child, "lean your upper body forward into the leap. Extend your lead leg into the air. At the same time, reach forward with the opposite arm in the direction of the extended lead leg. Be sure to bend the knee you are landing on so that you land softly."

✔ TEACHING TIPS

Leaping, at least in its earliest stages, for safety, should occur on gymnastics mats. Earliest leaps should be from the standing position, as if the child were leaping from one stone to the next when trying to get across a stream without getting her/his shoes wet (can use rubber bases to simulate stones). Be sure to have children leap with both left and right feet leading. Subsequent leaps can be initiated from walks and runs.

Be sure to emphasize leaping height, because things above the ground need to be reached or, in the case of obstacles on the ground, cleared. Likewise, emphasize leaping for distance, because obstacles on the ground, like creeks or small streams need to be gotten across. Again, emphasize leaps both for height and distance that originate on both the left and right. In due time, add to the above challenges, that of continuing the walk or run upon landing without a break in stride.

Hopping Hopping, by definition, is rising from the ground on one foot and landing on the same foot. For hopping to have full utility, the child should strive to hop effectively on either foot and in virtually any direction.

According to Cratty (1994):

Three year olds may hop once, but by the beginning of the fourth year, most children can hop on the preferred foot, three or four times in succession, taking off and landing on the same foot.

Hopping is an important motor skill for safety's sake. When a child is pushed or falls off balance in any direction except directly forward or backward where a step will suffice, hopping is the skill that most makes sense for regaining balance. The push or fall transfers weight onto one foot. Before balance is irretrievably lost, the weighted food and leg thrust the body momentarily into the air. While the body is airborne, the same leg becomes aligned with the direction of travel, and upon landing on that leg, balance is restored. (**Figure 22.4a** and **b**).

Figure 22.4a Immature hop.

Figure 22.4b Mature hop.

Hopping, from the perspective of strength required, is the most physically demanding of the fundamental locomotor skills, because it requires total body weight to be carried on one leg throughout. For this reason, hopping is also most demanding with respect to balance.

Activity Cues: lean body forward slightly, move arms forward and upward to help lift body from the ground, lift (non-support) thigh upward.

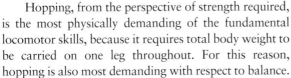 **TEACHING TIPS**

Until the child can effectively stand on one foot, she/he has not yet achieved readiness to hop. One should be able to hop on either foot in any direction with equal facility. While hopping is immature, the knee generally is held forward, while the thigh assumes a horizontal to the ground position. As hopping becomes more mature, the knee begins to point downward and the thigh becomes relatively more perpendicular to the ground. For hopping to be truly functional, one should be able to hop forward, backward and diagonally on either the left or right foot.

Initially, children will hop vertically on the preferred foot. Do not expect travel at this point. Eventually, the best hoppers are the ones who

can hop rhythmically and repeatedly on either foot. To encourage children to try to hop repeatedly, and eventually rhythmically, use percussion such as a drum or tambourine. Alternately, play slow to moderately paced music with a heavy beat.

Once hopping on the preferred foot has become reasonably established, switch attention to developing hopping skill on the non-preferred foot. Be sure to return to the preferred foot often to maintain preferred foot hopping skill.

Place six to eight inch diameter circles relatively close together on the floor. Engage children to hop from circle to circle. In time, have children hop from circle to circle on both the preferred and non-preferred foot. Later, move circles to varying distances apart, some relatively close to and others relatively far from one another.

As appropriate, involve all children in hopping and hopscotch-type activities. Understand that some boys may not be motivated to hop, because they (including some adults) may perceive hopping to be a 'girl's' skill. Hopping, nonetheless, is important for all children irrespective of perception, because of its unique asset as a safety skill.

Sliding Sliding is the most effective locomotor skill for rapid lateral (i.e., side-to-side) movement. It enables quick movement to the right/left; followed by a quick stop and quick movement in the opposite direction to the left/right. The advantage sliding skill offers in active play and game situations is that it enables quick changes in left-right direction without the child having to commit to that direction.

Sliding skill is effective in tag-type activities where one is 'it' and trying to tag another player. Likewise it is effective when one is not 'it' and trying to avoid being tagged. It is effective in shadowing an opponent when the objective is to prevent the opponent from going around and reaching a goal. It is effective when a ball must be fielded; but, first will require quick movement to the right or left. The fielder need only execute a couple of quick slide steps to the right/left to successfully catch the ball.

Activity Cue: The movement in sliding is 'step-close step.' In a slide to the right, the first move is a step to the right with the right foot; followed by an immediate close step that draws the left foot back in proximity to the right foot. The exact opposite occurs in a slide to the left.

 TEACHING TIPS

When teaching the slide one-on-one or helping a child in the group who is experiencing particular difficulty, face the child and hold outstretched hands. Ask the child to be your mirror. When you step to the side with your left foot, the child who is facing you will step to the side with his/her right foot, thus mirroring you. The same will be true, next, for the close step motion. Practice a single step-close step in one direction; then repeat in the opposite direction. Once the above has been achieved, try step-close stepping repeatedly in one direction; followed by step-close step in the other direction. Once this has been accomplished, have the child try to mirror your movements without holding hands.

Note, that for recreational game and sport purposes, the slide step from an athletic stance is most effective. In an athletic stance, the child flexes at the hips and knees, and concentrates weight on the balls of the feet. This has the effect of lowering center of mass so that movements to left and right can be more quickly made.

Galloping Galloping is a first cousin to sliding. It, too, calls for a step-close step motion, and is important for all the same reasons as is sliding. The gallop is characterized by any step-close step motion going directly forward or backward or any diagonal motion either forward or backward while going either to the left or right. When galloping in any direction, either foot may lead depending upon what the situation calls for. For this reason, galloping is most useful when children are able to gallop in all directions alternately with the right or left foot in the lead, as needed.

Activity Cues: Cues are essentially the same for galloping as for sliding. The step sequence and rhythm remains 'step-close step.'

 TEACHING TIPS

An effective way to teach beginning galloping is to have the child imitate walking with a limp. Ask the child to begin limping faster. A limp is essentially a step-close step motion. At some point, a rapid limp becomes a slow gallop. Try it!

Skipping Skipping, because it alternately combines walking and hopping, is the most complex of all locomotor skills. It involves the alternation of feet and a combination of one walking step forward followed by an immediate hop on the same foot.

Skipping, unlike each of the foregoing fundamental locomotor skills, seems to offer little in the way of enhancing survival potential. Few, if any, emergency situations or traditional game/sport activities call for a skipping response. However, skipping can reasonably be considered an essential social/locomotor skill, when one enjoys expression through rhythm and dance.

Activity Cues: The pattern for the skip is right foot step, hop; left foot step, hop. In practice, the verbal cue 'step-hop, step-hop' is an effective strategy for teaching the rhythm of skipping.

TEACHING TIPS

The arm swing in skipping is similar to the alternate arm swing used in walking and running. Arms also assist in mediating balance and in attaining skipping height or increasing stride, whichever is appropriate. For skipping to produce the often desired effect of being springy and rhythmic, center of mass should be forward such that most takeoff and landing weight is on the balls of the feet.

Once skipping steps can be chained, emphasize arm swing in opposition to the feet. Have children skip to the rhythm of a percussion instrument (e.g., drum) or appropriately metered (not too fast, not too slow) music with a heavy beat.

Non-Locomotor Skills

Non-locomotor (also called 'axial') skills are defined as movements that are stationary. Skills listed as non-locomotor or axial vary from source to source (Pangrazzi, 2007; Gallahue & Ozman, 2006; Humphrey & Yow, 2002). The following is a representative sample:

- Push
- Pull
- Twist
- Bend
- Stretch
- Rise
- Swing
- Sway
- Dodge
- Balance
- Turn
- Spin

Little is known about the developmental sequence of axial skills; very few observational studies have been conducted on children (Gallahue & Ozmun, 2006). However, axial skills are ubiquitous in motor activity games and sports. Unlike bipedal locomotor skills that favor children who ambulate without assistive devices (e.g., crutches, canes, walkers, wheelchairs), axial skills can and should become central to the motor skills repertories of all children who have potential for these movements. Depending on individual situations, most children, irrespective of ambulation mode, quite often do participate meaningfully in inclusion class settings. Characteristically, axial skills are used in concert and combination with other movements, locomotor and manipulative, and the variations are endless.

Teaching tips for non-locomotor skills

Push Whether the child is standing or sitting, call attention to the importance of relationship between points of support and the object to be pushed. Have children experiment with body positions/alignments for pushing various objects, light and heavy, high and low. Activities: push against a wall, gently against a partner; transfer from wheelchair to conventional chair; perform a modified push-up.

Pull Call attention to the importance of the relationship between points of support and the object to be pulled. Have children experiment with best body positions/alignments for pulling various objects, light and heavy, high and low. Activities: Grasp hands

with partner. Pull against partner as partner resists. Pull on winter boots. From wheel chair, pull doors open. Reach for ball with extended leg and foot. Pull beanbag to within reach. Play tug-of-war. From floor, pull self into wheelchair.

Twist Emphasize that when twisting, a firm base of support is important for maintaining balance. As appropriate, ask children to slowly and deliberately twist head/neck left and right (carefully); upper arms and forearms inward and outward; legs inward and outward, ankles inward and outward. Activities: Play the game Twister. Do the dance, the Twist. Twist the entire body to the left and right. Twist upper body in combination with spinning (see spinning below).

Bend Bend (i.e., flexing and extending) each body segment that is able to bend in one or more directions (e.g., neck; forward, backward, side-to-side [carefully], elbows, fingers, wrists, knees, hips, back, ankles). Emphasize bending slowly and deliberately and only as far as comfortably possible. Bend only to the beginning of discomfort so as to avoid injury. Activities: Bend to go beneath objects. Play Limbo. How many body parts can you bend at one time? Throw a three foot length of rope into the air; when it lands, lie on the floor, and try to bend your body in a way that looks like the rope. Do a backbend.

Stretch Stretch as many body segments as possible; stretch only as far as is comfortably possible. Then, gradually stretch farther as range of motion improves; stretch slowly and deliberately (don't bounce) and hold for a few seconds. Activities: How many ways can you stretch? Jump and stretch to reach for the stars. Stretch like the 7th inning stretch in baseball.

Rise Emphasize ways to get up from squatting, kneeling or lying (i.e., prone, supine, on side [left and right] positions). Activities: Practice rising from each position. Push against wheel chair armrests to transfer from wheel chair to conventional chair.

Swing Involves pendulum- or rotary-type action essentially confined to arms and legs. Activities: Swing to slow to moderate tempo music. Swing (rotate) arms like the blades of a windmill. Swing arms and legs left and right to a rhythmic drum beat, like a clock's pendulum.

Sway Involves shifting weight from side-to-side, right to left, as the torso rhythmically bends in an arc. Sways may also move diagonally from front to back. Backward to forward swaying calls for weight to remain essentially equally distributed on both feet. Backward to forward sway motion causes weight to shift alternately from heels to balls of feet. Activity: Mimic a willow tree swaying in the wind.

Dodge   Weight shifts with torso motions as in swaying, except dodging actions occur more quickly (e.g., dodging to keep from being struck by a projectile. Activity: Have children work as partners. One lightly tosses/lobs a non-threatening projectile (e.g., a nerf ball or bean bag), and the other dodges the ball. Emphasize that the nerf ball/bean bag travel in an arc to ensure it is lightly tossed/lobbed rather than thrown.

Balance   Balance is the functional relationship between body's points of support and center of gravity. Balance may be static or dynamic. An alternate form of dynamic balance involves balance where the medium upon which the child attempts to balance is moving. Activities: stork stand (static); walk on balance beam (dynamic); walk bounce on mini-tramp (balance where medium is moving).

Turn   Involves rotation along the body's long axis. Activities: step to quarter turns, half turns to left and right. Jump to quarter and half turns to left and right. Activity cue: head leads, looking in the direction of the turn.

Spin   Involves a motion similar to turning; however, much more rapid. Spinning can be complemented by spine rotation (twisting) in the direction of the spin. Activities: step to quarter, half, and full turns to left and right. Jump to quarter, half, and full turns to left and right. Activity cue: Head leads looking in the direction of the turn.

Manipulative skills

Manipulative skills are those in which a child handles objects with hands, feet, or other body parts. Manipulative skills are foundationally prerequisite to success in a broad spectrum of physical activities, game and sports. Children encouraged to develop manipulative skills during their younger years are usually more successful in game situations later in life (Kovar et al., 2007).

Manipulative skills can be divided into two general categories; *receipt* and *propulsion*. Examples of manipulative skills include rolling, throwing, catching, kicking, striking; serial ball bouncing as in basketball, dribbling as in soccer, passing, and volleying.

Throwing

Depending on age, ability, and age appropriateness; children can throw underhand, overhand, or side arm (a variation of the overhand throw). Depending on age, ability, and age appropriateness, projectiles may include balloons, whiffle balls, nerf balls, kush balls, yarn balls, golf-and baseball-sized balls. When helping young children learn to throw, the ball's size should fit comfortably in the child's hand. For this reason, larger playground balls, for purposes of teaching throwing, are not included in the list.

The first throw   Very young children's first throws quite generally are underarm and unintentional. What often happens is that the child is holding a projectile in her/his hand. Partially due to gravity, the hand is at the side. The child, for whatever reason, begins swinging the hand back and forth in pendulum fashion, and the projectile accidently becomes launched into the air. Any combination of the following three things immediately happens; each of which is positively reinforcing to the child: (1) she/he receives praise, (2) the projectile makes for visual stimulation as in flies through the air, and (3) the projectile makes an attention getting sound when it strikes whatever surface it might land on. Accidental releases continue to happen. The three reinforcers continue to be forthcoming, and the child, one day in anticipation of praise and visual and auditory stimulation, premeditates and releases the projectile voluntarily.

Underhand throw   In voluntary throwing, the underhand throw developmentally appears before the overhand throw. The earliest underhand throw involves arm action only, with both feet remaining firmly on the ground. The second stage (assuming a right-handed throw) involves a follow through motion with the right foot as the ball is tossed. In the third stage, all of stage two occurs, preceded by an anticipatory (wind up) step forward with the left foot. Common variations of the underhand throw include bowling, serving a volley ball, and pitching horseshoes.

Activity Cues for the earliest underhand throw: For a right handed throw, put left foot forward, swing right hand back, and throw ball and thumb at target.

Overhand throw   Of all ways to throw, the overhand throw has been studied most extensively by far. Generally, of all ways to throw, the over hand throw is the most versatile. The most definitive study of overhand throwing skill development remains that undertaken by Wild (1938). Wild determined that throwing develops in four distinct, objectively observable stages:

- Stage one: Arm action only. (**Figure 22.5a**). Both feet firmly planted on the ground throughout. No body rotation whatsoever.
- Stage two: Arm action with body rotation. (**Figure 22.5b**). Both feet still firmly planted on the ground.

- Stage three: Arm action, body rotation, followed by a follow through step forward with right foot (assuming a right handed thrower) (**Figure 22.5c**).
- Stage four: All of stage three above, but proceeded by a (wind-up) step forward with the left foot (**Figure 22.5d**).

Results of Wild's investigation revealed that, by age six, the majority of boys had achieved throwing proficiency at the stage four (mature) level. However, the majority of girls, irrespective of age, were found not to have progressed beyond stage three. Wild posited that low throwing skills, as observed among young female subjects in her study, was driven predominately by lack of reinforcement, low expectations, and inopportunity. Wild's positing has been reiterated by Thomas and Marzke (1992) who suggest that the sociocultural importance of throwing well for males creates an atmosphere in which girls who throw poorly are allowed to continue throwing poorly and boys are trained until they throw well. Given remarkable

(a)

(b)

(c)

(d)

Figure 22.5 The four stages of the overhand throw.

advances in girls' and women's sports opportunities and achievements in recent years, one can reasonably conclude Wild's and Thomas' and Marzke's explanations to have been accurate.

Regarding which to teach first when teaching throwing, speed or accuracy, Haubenstricker and Seefeldt (1986) recommend teaching first for speed. Accuracy comes somewhat naturally as throwing skill matures (note Wild's four stages above). As throwing skill matures, more body segments are brought into motion in proper sequence such that the principle of summation of forces maximizes velocity of the ball at the moment of release. In effect, what Haubenstricker and Seefeldt suggest is that function (i.e., accuracy) follows form (i.e., speed that results from achieving a mature throwing pattern).

Activity Cues for stage one overhand throw: Prompt children to "pick a spot, bring the ball (object) back by your ear, elbow out, throw the ball (and hand) at the spot".

Big ball versus small ball, which should come first?

Often, when one inspects the equipment room in a facility where physical education is taught to young children, one will find an assortment of balls disproportionately large compared to the size of the child and, specifically, the child's hand. Rationale for presentation of the 'big ball first' historically has been that children who have yet to develop fine motor skills ought to be given somewhat oversized objects to grasp and manipulate.

Although provision of reasonably oversized objects may be helpful for children first learning to catch, presenting the big ball first tends not to be helpful in learning to throw. When learning to throw, an oversized ball, compared to the child's small hand, becomes unnecessarily awkward for the child to manipulate and control (**Figure 22.6a**). Often the throwing pattern that results is little more than one that makes best of a bad situation. Should you question the above premise, try throwing a basketball overhand with your preferred hand as you would otherwise a baseball. Do so both for speed and for accuracy. If the size of the basketball makes overhand throwing awkward, imagine the awkwardness a small child experiences when she/he is first given a basketball-sized ball or even an eight inch playground ball with which to learn to throw. The awkwardness that you felt only becomes exaggerated for the child. Therefore, when teaching children to throw, especially when the object is to develop progressively more functional throwing patterns for both speed and accuracy, favor a ball whose diameter fits comfortably into the child's hand (**Figure 22.6b**).

(a)

(b)

Figure 22.6 Big ball vs. small ball.

LEARNING ACTIVITY

> If possible, in a supervised environment, work with one or more children aged 3 to 5 with throwing larger, then progressively smaller balls, both for speed and accuracy. For speed say, "Try to throw hard as you can." For accuracy, say, "Try to hit the target."
>
> Consider the results of your trials. Did you observe differences in distance and/or accuracy as a function of the size of the ball thrown? If and when 'yes,' why? If and when 'no,' why not?

Catching

Unlike learning to throw, when teaching catching, presenting a bigger ball (within reason) in the beginning tends to be more effective (Thomas, Lee, & Thomas, 2008). The relatively bigger ball hastens success, because it affords an as yet imprecise catching response more surface area to grasp onto. Also, the ball's larger size affords it greater stimulus value (i.e., it is easier to see and focus on). The value of increasing ball size does, however, reach diminishing returns when the ball becomes so large that the child's arms and hands can no longer effectively enclose around it.

Children learning to catch progress through three stages:

- Stage one: Arm action at the shoulder only. Here, there is no purposeful elbow or wrist/hand action (except for grasping the ball). Arms are held at about shoulder's width apart. Arms come together when child senses the incoming ball.

- Stage two: The 'scooping' or 'trapping' response. Here, there *is* purposeful shoulder and elbow action. Still, there is no purposeful grasping from hands and wrists. As the ball comes over the top of the outstretched arms, the shoulders and elbows flex, with elbows coming to touch the lower ribs, to trap the ball against the chest.

- Stage three (mature, adult catching): In anticipation of the arriving ball, shoulders and arms flex to 'give' with the oncoming ball. When the ball arrives, wrists, hands, fingers close around the ball. Elbows, now, extend out to the side.

Catching is developmentally more complex and appears later in children than throwing. Therefore, concentrate only on throwing when teaching immature throwers. In place of catching, ask children to retrieve balls they have thrown or let thrown balls rebound from a wall.

Activity Cues: Prompt children to keep eyes focused on the oncoming object and "grab the ball with both hands." Be sure to model and reinforce the catching response that reflects the child's present catching development stage.

 TEACHING TIPS

Be patient. Maturation can seldom be rushed. Understand that predominately maturation, but in the presence of encouragement and opportunity, will largely determine when the next stage of catching development replaces the present stage.

When children are first learning to catch, the easiest ball to catch is the ball rolled to the child who is sitting, facing the ball, with legs straddled. Otherwise, the easiest *airborne* ball to catch, by far, is the one that the child him/herself drops and catches on the rebound and or tosses directly above into the air.

LEARNING ACTIVITY

> Experiment with bouncing the ball; then, lightly tossing the ball underhand to a child. Which presentation of the ball, if any, appears easier/more difficult to catch? Why? Why not? Now, try lightly tossing the ball with no bounce, first underhand; then over hand, to the child. Which presentation of the ball, if any, appears easier/more difficult to catch? Why? Why not?

Coincidence Anticipation Coincidence anticipation research applicable to the teaching of catching offers potential insights as to why children in early stages of learning to catch may or may not be successful (Stadulis, 1971). Coincidence anticipation, for this discussion's purposes, is defined as anticipating the coincidence of a thrown object arriving between the child's hands at precisely the moment when the child executes her/his catching response.

Contrary to popular belief that, among young catchers, 'the slower the ball is coming the easier it will be to catch,' Stadulis' research suggests that (1) each child has his/her own unique catching response time, (2) some children's catching response times are slower/faster than others, and (3) regardless of whether the individual child's catching response is fast or slow, his/her response remains quite consistent from one time to the next, at least during earliest stages of learning to catch. To facilitate success during early stages of learning to catch, try to determine each individual child's, as yet inflexible, catching response time. Anticipate the coincidence of each child's hands coming together at precisely the moment when the ball will arrive. Now, toss the ball such that it arrives at the precise moment when the catching response time draws the hands together (**Figure 22.7a–d**).

Whenever coincidence anticipation positively affects catching success, need for insight and skill on the thrower's part becomes paramount. When coincidence anticipation results in a catch, the successful catch should no less be acknowledged as a successful throw.

LEARNING ACTIVITY

Toss a ball at various velocities to a child in order to determine consistency in the child's catching response time. Now, adjust your throw (which is flexible, because you're the adult) to the child's catching response time. To the extent coincidence anticipation works, the ball will be more consistently caught. Because successful catches are positively reinforcing, the child is likely to learn to catch sooner and to persist in wanting to catch.

Further considerations to help ensure catching success among young children and older children whose catching development is delayed are as follows:

- Ball should have high stimulus value (i.e., its color should contrast with whatever colors appear in the background out of which the ball is coming).

- Background from which the ball needs to be picked-out should not be cluttered. The child should as easily as possible be able to discriminate the ball from the background out of which it is coming. A plain colored background, one that contrasts with the color of the ball, is ideal.

- Ball should have a rough surface; one that reduces slipperiness and maximizes interaction between hand/finger surfaces and the ball's surface.

- Ball should be relatively light, so it does not hurt child when child misses. Hurt leads to fear. Fear leads to avoidance responses to catching and avoidance to wanting to try to catch altogether.

- Ball should be soft and malleable, so that fingers will dig in. Again, this maximizes interaction between hands/fingers and ball surface. Also, this reduces the likelihood of hurt when the child misses the catch.

(a)

(b)

(c)

(d)

Figure 22.7 Coincidence anticipation.

- Partially deflate an inflatable ball. The partially deflated ball better conforms to the child's grasp configuration and hurts less when child misses.
- Kush balls, because they are light and easily conform to virtually any grasp, are among the easiest balls for a beginner to catch.

Striking and Kicking

Striking and kicking occur when an object (e.g., ball, badminton bird) is hit with a body part (e.g., hand) or a striking implement (e.g., bat, club, mallet, paddle, racquet). Kicking is essentially striking with the feet.

Striking Striking with an implement presents a greater challenge to the child than does either catching, throwing, or striking with the hand, because striking implements effectively cause the wrist lever to become longer and, thus, more tricky to control.

Two-handed strikes are more difficult for young or developmentally immature children than are one-handed strikes, (**Figure 22.8a–c**) because the former require bilateral hand/arm coordination including, of course, use of the non-preferred hand. Whereas, one-handed strikes allow use of the preferred hand only; thus, essentially eliminating any requirement for hand/arm coordination (Cratty, 1986). Given, two-handed strikes are developmentally more complex; it is generally advisable to introduce the one-hand strike first.

(b)

(c)

(a)

Figure 22.8 Beginning one-handed strike.

Among beginning strikers, a striking implement's striking surface should be somewhat on the large side to help ensure early striking success. The striking instrument, however, must not be overweight. The handle of the striking implement should be of a diameter such that its gripping surface fits comfortably within the child's enclosing grasp. It should not be too large; nor too small. Just as it is helpful for striking surfaces to be somewhat oversized to ensure success, the object to be struck (e.g., ball) may likewise be somewhat oversized. While the object being struck may be oversized, it, too, like the striking implement, must not be overweight.

To improve the likelihood of success with early one-handed strikes, the object to be struck should be suspended from a heavy string, twine, or light rope. (This applies, of course, only to objects that eventually fly through the air before being struck.) When the time comes for the first two-handed strikes, the object to be struck, generally a ball, may be placed on a tee. As appropriate, gradually progress from striking a suspended or teed ball to striking one that has been lightly pitched.

Kicking   A ball can be kicked from a stand, walk, or run. Depending upon the ball's position in relation to the child, the ball may be kicked by making contact with the instep, top/outside of the foot, or toe.

With immature kickers, the kicker stands directly in front of the ball. The knee tends to be held straight, and only the hip flexes. As the kicker matures in skill, the knee will flex as the thigh comes forward. Just prior to foot contact with the ball, the knee extends; thus giving the ball additional velocity. Eventually, the kicker assumes a sideward orientation to the ball. This allows for hip and spine rotation, along with hip flexion and knee extension. Together, the combined forces maximize the speed of foot contact with the ball (**Figure 22.9a–c**).

As appropriate, the kick may in due time be approached either from a walk or run. For kicking to become fully utilitarian, the child should strive to kick with facility with either foot and with the ball approaching from a variety of directions.

Controlling the ball is most difficult when contact is with the toe. The small contact surface of the shoe's toe box makes the ball's direction unpredictable, particularly among unskilled kickers. The height of a kicked ball is determined by placement of the non-kicking (supporting) foot in relation to the ball. When the supporting foot is placed beside the ball, it will soar upward as well as forward. When the supporting foot is placed behind the ball, it will follow a low trajectory.

Once the child moves beyond kicking the ball from a straight forward, standing position that involves only flexion at the hip; introduce the ball such that the child, still from a stationary position, kicks with the instep; and, then, with the outside/top of the foot. In due time, repeat the above; but, now, with the child approaching the ball from a walk, possibly a run.

Whether walking or standing, have the child kick the ball toward a wall. In this way, because the ball rebounds, little time is lost retrieving balls. Have the child strive to kick the ball straight ahead into the wall. If the ball rebounds back to the child, she/he will know the straight ahead kick has been accurately placed.

Dribbling   A series of short kicks to move the ball from part of the play area to another distinguishes foot dribbling from the singular act of kicking the ball

(a)

Figure 22.9 Proper kicking.

(b)

(c)

Figure 22.9 *(continued)*

just one time. In dribbling, it is important to try to keep the ball close to the feet such that it remains under control. Successful dribbling calls for being able to move the ball with either foot.

Activity Cue: "Gently tap the ball with the inside of your foot."

 TEACHING TIPS

Dribble the ball, first walking; then, as appropriate, gradually transition to running. Have the child/children dribble the ball to a predetermined point and back. Children who walk with crutches can dribble using either a foot or crutch, as needed. Wheelchair soccer players can use footrests in place of feet to propel the ball.

Ball bouncing Ball bouncing, or dribbling with the hands, plays a major role in many physical education, recreation, and sport activities. It requires at the very least concentration, visual tracking, and hand-eye coordination. The child, while hand dribbling in a range of activity situations, can be standing, walking, running, galloping, and/or sliding.

Activity Cues: With earliest dribbles, children tend to use a flat hand. To help children dribble with better control, ***demonstrate*** how to bounce the ball,

touching it only with the thumb and fingertips. Use the word "push."

TEACHING TIPS

Children who first try to bounce a ball in series, as in dribbling, often tend to slap at the ball. This causes the ball to bounce out of control. When this happens, instruct the child to 'pet,' not slap, the ball. Ask children, "Who has a pet dog or cat?" If one or more children raise their hands, you are in luck. Suggest that if you pet your dog or cat nicely, it will want to stay with you. If you pet your dog or cat too hard, it will want to run away. The ball acts the same way.

Ensure that when the child dribbles the ball that it comfortably rebounds to approximately waist height. A ball that rebounds higher or lower will become unnecessarily difficult to control. Height of the ball's bounce can be varied by inflating/deflating the ball.

Dribbling may be taught with the aid of a heavy, rhythmic beat. A recorded drum beat will suffice. Accompanying the beat, the teacher, too, may dribble, thereby affording the child simultaneous visual and auditory cues. For dribbling to be as versatile as possible, encourage the child to dribble with each hand.

Teaching for Rhythm

Any motor skill that can be executed serially is potentially a rhythm skill. Hence, all fundamental locomotor and non-locomotor skills have potential to become rhythmic. Even throwing becomes rhythmic if one becomes able to juggle. With skills that can be performed serially; quite generally, the more rhythmically they can be performed, the more skillful the performer. When serial skills are performed rhythmically, typically, the end of one repetition of the skill simultaneously marks the beginning of the next. The more quickly the repetitions simultaneously follow one another, the more rapid the rhythm.

While all children may not have potential to perform all motor skills rhythmically, all children should have opportunity to come as close to rhythm performance in as many motor skills as possible.

Specificity

The principle of specificity in motor learning, Henry (1968), fittingly acknowledged as the father of motor behavior research in physical education (Schmidt & Lee, 2005), essentially states that individuals generally learn only the specific motor skills that they practice. For example, throwing a ball overhand cannot be expected to produce improved performance when batting from a tee. Learning to throw an over-sized playground ball first should not be expected to help the child effectively learn to throw a more reasonably sized ball; one which fits comfortably into the child's hand. Throwing experience in the absence of later catching cannot be expected to improve catching. A guiding principle should be that, whenever possible, the ultimate skill to be learned is the one that should be practiced. The practical application of this understanding is that the teacher must teach, reinforce, and provide opportunity for the child to practice the specific skill(s) the teacher wants the child to learn.

The Role of Play in Motor Skills Development

> "It is paradoxical that many educators and parents differentiate between a time for learning and a time for play without seeing the vital connection between them."
>
> —Leo Buscaglia, author; professor, Department of Special Education, University of Southern California
> "You can learn more about a person in an hour of play than in a year of conversation."
>
> —Plato

When children move purely for enjoyment, when activity serves as an end in itself; we call such activity 'play.' Children are motivated to play when it is fun, because it is fun. Play is fun for children when they possess skills for successful play, the majority of which are motor skills, and, more specifically, fundamental motor skills.

In the play lives of children, play skills are *social* skills. Children have both physiological and psychological needs for play, because play in large measure is the way children learn, physically and intellectually, about the world in which they live. Said another way; children first learn to play so that they might then play to learn.

Children may learn fundamental skills in physical education; but it is in active play where these skills (skills that should be used over the lifespan) are afforded opportunity to be perfected. Unfortunately, for a range of reasons in recent decades (witness the ongoing obesity epidemic in the US alone), there has been a trend toward less and less active play among children and youth (and, indeed, in adults).

Opportunities for movement-based play (e.g., toys, bicycles, tricycles, handcycles, scooters, swing sets, chairs to wheel, ramps to ascend/descend, stairs to climb), although certainly not found everywhere, can be found in many children's play environments. Where circumstances including locale and/or economics preclude access to more sophisticated play modalities; trees can replace jungle gyms; tires tied to ropes suspended from tree limbs can replace swings in the park; a tightly wadded section of the newspaper wrapped with duct tape can become a ball; an "X" taped or chalked onto a wall can become the target; a fallen tree log can become a balance beam. Economics and locale need not materially impact children's opportunities to play, and children of all abilities need be afforded developmentally appropriate opportunities to play for its own sake and to learn through play.

Many children with disabilities, for reasons that include well-intentioned, overprotective, and misguided under expectations, do not have ample opportunity to participate in and learn through active play. Among our top priority goals as adapted physical educators should be the enrichment of play opportunities for all children, and particularly for children who too often are disenfranchised from play for no reason other than disability. We make giant leaps toward the achievement of physical education skill teaching and learning goals when we sensitively (not to be confused with meekly) challenge preconceived notions about the essential role of activity and play in the lives of children who happen to have disabilities, when children in adapted physical education learn fundamental motor skills that become pillars in the platform upon which lifetimes of active play, recreation, and sport are built.

Adapted Physical Education National Standards

Adapted Physical Education National Standards (APENS) (2006) requires adapted physical educators to have knowledge of typical motor development as well as understanding of the influence of developmental delays on these processes (Standard #2). Besides understanding human motor development, a master teacher will work to understand individual differences that may prevent the learning of a skill and make adjustments in teaching methods and instructions. Be creative, and modify, modify, modify until there is success! Strive for zero reject; zero fail.

Depending on the unique abilities of each child you may need to implement programs that include one or more of the following:

- Provide sensory integration (different objects), cognition (presenting information so the child understands), and conceptual (the big picture) components of movement.

- Provide *time to process* information and avoid overstimulating children with vast amounts of sensory stimuli.

- *Practice over time* to learn the skill; provide opportunities for retention.

- Practice in a *variety of environments* (e.g., gym, field, track, court) and situations— games usually are dynamic.

- *Build on success and previous learning*; use progression and add "parts" to the skill when appropriate. For some children, using the entire skill may be easier than breaking the skill into sub-skills.

- Implement multi-faceted instruction: visual demonstration of skills; auditory cues (very limited-one word if possible); and kinesthetic orientation, for some children there is a need to physically assist the child to move through the motor pattern—to recognize where body parts are in relation to one another and the body's position in space.

Critical Thinking Activities

1. Jerry can walk and run, but has difficulty galloping or sliding. Jerry's legs are not strong enough to hop and his balance is shaky. Though he works hard when in physical education class, he is not very well coordinated and some games are difficult for him. What role can physical education play in improving Jerry's motor skills and improve self esteem and athletic performance?

2. Design a motor development program for Jerry. Assume you have tested him for fundamental non-locomotor skill development, and have discovered delays in three skills (you choose the skills and delays). Share your program design and reasons therefore with the class.

3. Assess all eight locomotor skills of an elementary child. Which of the child's locomotor skills appear mature/immature for age? Write specific teaching cues that can be used to assist development of locomotor skills found to be immature for the child's age.

4. Assess the throwing, catching, and striking skills of two children with very different abilities. Use balls of different size, shape, color, and texture. How do ball characteristics appear to affect catching in each child? How different are their catching response times?

CHAPTER SUMMARY

1. The ability to acquire efficient motor skills and patterns, irrespective of the child's ability level, is directly related to the quality and quantity of opportunity, practice, and instructional experiences afforded the student. Although a specific disability may impede or alter the development process, most children can achieve age level skills with proper instruction, repetition, and practice.

2. Motor skill development progresses from total body undifferentiated movement to controlled movement by individual body parts; from gross to fine; head to toe; and body midline out to extremities. All of the above occurs as it does because of how the central nervous system develops.

3. Balance, leg strength, and neurological development influence the development of locomotor skills. The eight basic locomotor skills are walk, run, gallop, slide, jump, hop, leap and skip.

4. Non-locomotor skills (i.e., push, pull, twist, bend, stretch, rise, swing, sway, dodge, shake, balance,

turn, collapse, spin) are defined as movements that are stationary and usually are in combination with other movements.

5. Manipulative and rhythmic skills, in conjunction with locomotor and non-locomotor skills, form the foundation for a variety of game and sport skills. Examples of manipulative skills include rolling, throwing, catching, kicking, striking, dribbling, passing, and volleying.

6. A master teacher will work to understand individual differences that may prevent the learning of a skill, and make adjustments in teaching methods and instructions.

REFERENCES

Adapted physical education national standards/ national consortium for physical education and recreation for individuals with disabilities. (2006). Kelly, L. E., editor. (2nd ed.). Champaign, IL: Human Kinetics.

Berk, L. E. (2008). *Infants, children, and adolescents* (6th ed.). Boston: Pearson Education, Inc.

Cratty, B. J. (1986). *Perceptual and motor development in infants and children* (3rd ed.). Englewood Cliffs, NJ: Prentice-Hall.

Cratty, B. J. (1994). *Clumsy child syndromes: Descriptions, evaluation, and remediation.* Chur, Switzerland: Harwood Academic Publishers.

Gabbard, C., & Rodriguez, L. (2002). *Optimizing early brain and motor development through movement.* Monterey: Excellence Learning Corporation.

Gallahue, D. L., & Ozmun J. C. (2006). *Understanding motor development: Infants, children, adolescents, Adults* (6th ed.). New York: McGraw-Hill.

Gallahue, D. L., & Donnelly, F. C. (2003). *Developmental physical education for all children* (4th ed.). Champaign, IL: Human Kinetics.

Gesell, A. L. (1928). *Infancy and human growth.* Boston: The Macmillan Company, Inc.

Gesell, A. L. (1954). *The embryology of behavior* L. Carmichael, (Ed.) 2nd ed. New York: Wiley.

Haubenstricker, J., & Seefeldt, V. (1986). Acquisition of motor skills during childhood. In V. Seefeldt (Ed.). *Physical activity and well-being.* Reston, VA: AAHPERD.

Henry, F. M. (1968). Specificity vs. generality in learning motor skill. In R. C. Brown & G. S. Kenyon (Eds.). *Classical studies on physical activity.* Englewood Cliffs, NJ: Prentice Hall.

Herschkowitz, N., & Herschkowitz, E. C. (2002). *A good start in life: Understanding your child's brain and behavior.* Washington, D.C: Joseph Henry Press (an imprint of the National Academy of Sciences).

Horvat, M., Kelly, L. E., & Block, M. E. (2007). *Developmental and adapted physical activity assessment.* Champaign, IL: Human Kinetics.

Humphrey, J. H., & Yow, D. A. (2002). *Adult guide to children's team sports.* Hauppauge, NY: Nova Science Publishers, Inc.

Kovar, S.K., et al. (2007). *Elementary classroom teachers as movement educators.* (2nd ed.). NY: McGraw-Hill.

Meaney, M. J. (2001). Nature, nurture, and the disunity of knowledge. *Annals of the New York Academy of Sciences,* 935:50–61.

Meaney M. J. (2004). The nature of nurture: maternal effects and chromatin remodeling, in Cacioppo, J.T., & Berntson, G.G. (Eds). Essays in Social Neuroscience. Cambridge, MA: MIT Press.

Pangrazi, R. P. (2010). *Dynamic physical education for elementary school children* (16th ed.). San Francisco: Benjamin Cummings.

Schmidt, R. A., & Lee, T. D. (2005). *Motor control and learning: A behavioral emphasis.* Champaign, IL: Human Kinetics.

Scott, A. (1995). *Stairway to the mind: The controversial new science of consciousness.* New York: Springer.

Stadulis, R.E. (1971). Thesis (Ed. D.). Teachers College, Columbia University.

Tice, K. M., & Travers, J. F. (2005). *Handbook of human development for health care professionals.* Mississauga, Ontario, CA: Jones and Bartlett Publishers.

Thomas, J. R., & Marzke, M. (1992). The development of gender differences in throwing: Is human evolution a factor? *The academy papers—enhancing human performance in sport,* edited by R. Christiana and H. Eckert, 60–76, Champaign, IL: Human Kinetics.

Thomas, K. T., Lee, A. M., & Thomas, J. R. (2008). *Physical education methods for elementary teachers* (3rd ed.). Champaign, IL: Human Kinetics.

Wild, M. (1938). The behavior patterns of throwing and some observations concerning its course of development. *Research Quarterly,* 9, 20–24.

CHAPTER 23

Teaching Adapted Aquatics

I will never forget the time, some years ago, when a little guy with cerebral palsy looked up at me ... from where he was resting, propped up in the corner of the pool, and said, "you know something, Louise! This is the only place in the world where I can walk!" ... It just tore me up! But it was true; for him, with his disability, walking was impossible on land, but the water provided the support, lessened the need for weight bearing and balance, and made it possible for him to have independent mobility. It was the freedom from disability, a time to achieve. Looking from his perspective, there was no question about why he should be in the water. (Priest, 1982)

CASE STUDY

Selena is an eight year old child who has been diagnosed with juvenile rheumatoid arthritis (JRA). Her form of JRA has been specifically diagnosed as polyarticular (poly meaning 'many;' articular meaning 'joints'). Selena's case is reasonably typical in that pain and swelling is occurring in the small joints of the hands and weight bearing joints including hips, knees, ankles and feet.

Selena's doctor, a specialist in pediatric rheumatology, has recommended that she remain physically active throughout the course of her disease; but that she must avoid activity that will jar affected joints. Her doctor advises that inactivity, which often occurs among children with JRA, may result in osteoporosis, loss of strength and endurance, and in inflexibility.

Selena's doctor highly recommends pool exercise as being ideal, because it can be vigorous; yet, at the same time, it need not be jarring to joints. Exercise in the pool has been recommended specifically to help Selena avoid osteoporosis and to develop, or at least maintain muscular strength and endurance. Pool activity, likewise, has been recommended for flexibility maintenance, because water-supported limbs are able to move relatively pain-free through complete or near complete ranges of motion.

Defining moments in life for both child and teacher have a way of remaining enduringly poignant. Aquatic activities provide all students, with and without disability, opportunity to enjoy mobility freedom often not attainable in any other environment. The value of freedom derived from the simple joy of learning to swim and "play" in the water can sometimes simply be lost in the shuffle of life that goes on in a typical school day. This chapter strives to help recover that loss. It is designed to introduce the reader to aquatics skills teaching, and present strategies to help the physical educator, generalist, and adapted specialist alike, teach swimming and related water activities safely and successfully to students with disabilities.

Benefits of Swimming and Related Water Activity

Swimming and water safety instruction is valuable for its own sake. Among children with disabilities swimming further provides unique opportunities to develop fitness, motor fitness, social skills, and self-confidence (Lepore, Gayle, & Stevens, 2007).

An extraordinary benefit of participation in adapted aquatics derives from water's wonderful potential to minimize the impact many disabilities have on mobility. In the water; children, especially children with mobility disabilities, can become free to move without having to manage the likes of wheelchairs, walkers, crutches, and braces. Water environments afford opportunity for children, with a range of developmental motor delays, opportunity to perform fundamental motor skills and patterns in the water environment that otherwise would not be possible on land.

Pools offer great potential to become fitness playgrounds for students. Aquatic environments are rich in potential for children with disabilities to develop cardiovascular fitness, flexibility, muscular strength, muscular endurance, balance, and coordination.

For children with disabilities, swimming skills can be considered as much social skills as they are motor skills. As swimming skills develop they open doors to opportunity for positive social contact with peers. Positive interactions with peers, in turn offer excellent potential for improvement of self-esteem.

Swimming and related water activity can stimulate learning often associated with the traditional classroom environment. A range of academics can be embedded in aquatic lessons whereby cognitive concepts associated with reading, spelling, or math can be reinforced. For example, students may locate, identify, and dive for objects submerged in the pool (e.g., plastic letters, placards bearing student's names, triangles that are red, rubberized weights, pennies), read lessons for the day from a wall poster, or count laps (Lepore 2005).

Safety in and Around Water

Drowning is the second leading cause of unintentional injury-related death among children ages 1 through 14. Drowning usually happens quickly and silently; many children who drown in home pools are known to have been out of parents' sight for less than five minutes (Centers for Disease Control and Prevention, 2009). According to an American Red Cross survey (2009), approximately half of adults responding to the survey report having personally experienced near drowning; while one in four report having known someone who actually drowned.

In a world with few absolutes, safety is absolutely the first factor to address in teaching swimming and related water activity; including that of the student, swimming assistants, and, you, the teacher. Every effort must be made to prevent accidents through constant awareness of potential hazards and consistent enforcement of stringent safety standards. While the teacher may direct attention to an individual student or group

of students, she/he or the lifeguard on duty, must be in a position to observe the safety of *each* swimmer at *all* times. Both teacher and lifeguard must be aware of all children's safety-related medical conditions, including how to properly respond in case of an emergency.

Children with disabilities often pose unique safety challenges beyond those encountered in general aquatics instruction settings. The ubiquitous slippery pool deck offers but one example:

- Children with visual impairment may not notice a slippery spot.
- Children with hearing loss may not hear; and therefore, are unable to heed warnings.
- Children with cognitive impairment may not understand "slippery when wet."
- Children with attention deficits simply may not be on task.
- Children with muscular weakness, upon slipping, may not have strength to regain balance.
- Children with neurological impairments, upon slipping, may not regain balance in time to avoid a fall.

For your safety (including liability) and the safety of your students, *insist* that there be a *certified* lifeguard on the pool deck whenever children are in or around the pool. Post pool rules and safety procedures in prominent places (doors through which students regularly pass are ideal). Be sure that all safety precautions are consistently enforced. Call upon children to verbalize in their own words pool rules and safety precautions. Understand that you, the teacher, are the professional in charge, and given that responsibility, ultimately you will be held answerable for all that occurs.

Facilities

Many pools, especially older ones, were not built with children in mind. Certainly, older pools were not built with children who have disabilities in mind. Such pools, absent of retrofitting, may not be suitable for student use regardless of whether students do or do not have disabilities. Indeed, older pools will require adaptations prior to becoming acceptable for use with young children; especially children who have disabilities.

Although many children who have disabilities will not require special pool accommodations, circumstances unique to individual students generally will require that the pool area be made fully disability accessible. The following architectural structures must be assessed and, as needed, corrected as each relates to pool area accessibility and safety:

- Entrances and doorways
- Restrooms and showers
- Wheelchair access routes

- Deck conditions
- Water depth and condition
- Lockers and changing rooms
- Ladders, steps, stairs, ramps, lifts
- Water and air temperature
- Lighting

Be certain you thoroughly understand the pool's emergency response plan, and know the specific protocol for signaling an emergency within the facility. Predetermine who will be responsible for implementing emergency protocols. Ensure that a certified lifeguard is on duty at all times to assist with emergencies. While lifeguards are on duty, they are to have no other duties. Lifeguards must be expected to monitor all pool-related activity from the lesson's beginning to end.

Many pools are kept at water temperatures more conducive to swimming competition than aquatic instruction. Water temperatures conducive to competition are, by far, too cold for children who are learning to swim. Establish positive working relationships with the swim coach and custodian to maximize potential for optimum pool water temperature when your students arrive. Be prepared to have to advocate for your students' water temperature needs.

When water temperatures can be regulated, they should be adjusted to accommodate the anticipated activity levels of your children. Greenshaw and Sadler (1988) report that children with disabilities between the ages of birth and six years generally respond best when water temperatures are between 90 and 95 degrees Fahrenheit.

Teaching and Learning

In preparation for adapted aquatic unit planning and instruction, the instructor, in the following order, must:

1. Assess individual student abilities

2. Determine individual student goals

3. Develop individualized plans to meet individual student needs.

The above actions may already have been taken, and, if so, results should appear on the child's individualized education plan (IEP). Ideally, the teacher who teaches adapted aquatics to the child will have been the person responsible for steps 1 through 3 above.

Assessing Individual Students

Regular assessment resources for children without disabilities often can be used as guides with little or no modification when assessing children with disabilities. Regular checklists are useful, because children,

irrespective of ability/disability, generally progress developmentally from one swimming skill to another in like order. Disability *alone* generally does not alter the order in which swimming skills are achieved. What will differ, however, is the pace at which individual students learn.

Developmental checklists typically list skills in order from beginning to advanced. The development of fundamental swimming skills, similar to fundamental skills development on dry land, tends to be hierarchical. Because fundamental skills tend to develop hierarchically, a fundamental skill missing at any given level will likely impede the swimmer's ability to develop related skills at subsequently higher levels. The appropriate analogy on dry land is that a child must first learn to walk before she/he can learn to run. One example of a developmental skills checklist suitable for use in adapted aquatics appears in **Table 23.1**.

In addition to fundamental skill assessment, the teacher should:

1. Depending on developmental level, encourage the child to talk about his/her capabilities (swimming and non-swimming), past experiences, successes, fears, and interests.

2. Read and fully understand the child's medical clearance form. Ensure that the physician's recommendations are addressed in development of the student's individualized curriculum and IEP. A consultation is in order when physician's recommendations are vague, unclear, or you are in doubt regarding appropriateness of recommendations.

3. Consult with parents. They were, after all, their child's first teacher. Be sure not to dominate conversations. Be prepared to listen.

4. Consult with teacher, colleagues, and allied professionals (e.g., physical therapist, orientation and mobility specialist, speech therapist, occupational therapist, school nurse, school psychologist) who know the child from the perspectives of their own disciplines. Use what you learn to determine student's strengths as you set goals and develop the curriculum. Likewise, consider limitations unique to each child. Determine how each child's unique circumstances are likely to impact adoption of safety strategies and/or present obstacles to achieving swimming skills.

A number of good resources are available to help the teacher assess individual student aquatic skill levels. Such resources, in addition to providing assessment tools, also offer curriculums into which children are placed according to assessment results. Examples include:

- Learn to Swim Program. A program presently used by Special Olympic teachers and coaches to assess

Table 23.1 Learning Survival Swimming Skills

Name of Student: _____

Check off (i.e., date) when student has accomplished each task

Independence

_____ Sits on pool edge

_____ Sits on pool edge and kicks

_____ Enters water with assistance

_____ Enters water independently

_____ Stands in water with assistance

_____ Stands in water independently

_____ Walks across pool in shallow water (waist deep) with assistance

_____ Walks across pool independently

_____ Exits water with assistance

_____ Exits water independently

Breathing

_____ Blows into water

_____ Places face in the water (add counting!)

_____ Demonstrates continuous rhythmic breathing (turning head to side for breath)

_____ Submerges in chest-deep water with assistance

_____ Submerges in chest-deep water independently

_____ Opens eyes underwater (can use goggles)

_____ Touches pool bottom in waist-deep water

_____ Sits on pool bottom in chest-deep water

_____ Bobs in chest-deep water

Entry

_____ Jumps into shallow water with assistance

_____ Jumps into shallow water independently

Front Float (Prone Float)

_____ Floats on front with assistance (prone float)

_____ Floats on front independently (prone float)

_____ Pushes and glides on front with assistance

_____ Pushes and glides on front independently, recover to standing

_____ Performs front float with a flutter kick

_____ Performs front float using kickboard and flutter kick with assistance

_____ Performs front float using kickboard and flutter kick independently

Back Float

_____ Floats on back with assistance

_____ Floats on back independently

_____ Push and glide on back with assistance

_____ Pushes and glide on back independently, recover to standing

_____ Performs back float with a scull

_____ Performs back float with a scull and flutter kick

Combinations

_____ Moves from front float to back float with assistance

_____ Moves from front float to back float independently

_____ Moves from back float to front and return with assistance

_____ Moves from back float to front and return independently

_____ Front survival float (face down)

_____ From back float, turns to front survival float and recovers to stand

and instruct participants at every stage of aquatics skills development (non-swimmer through competitive athlete). This program is available free of charge from Special Olympics at: www.specialolympics.org.

- The Lone Star Adapted Aquatics Assessment Inventory and Curriculum is designed for use with students, age 3–21 who present with the full range of IDEA recognized disabilities. It serves both as an assessment tool and curriculum. The program is presented in seven levels, beginning at level one with the student sitting at pool's edge and culminating at the conclusion of level seven with student swimming extended laps using the backstroke. In addition to the seven assessment and curriculum levels, the program offers a component for initial screening (to facilitate placement) and one that specifically addresses the learner's safety knowledge and skills (Apache, Hisey, & Blanchard, 2005).

- The Conaster Adapted Aquatics Screening Test (Conastar, 1995) "provides adapted physical education teachers, regular P. E. teachers, adapted aquatics teachers, or related personnel in aquatics with a norm based swimming assessment." Norms are available for males and females age 5–21 who present with three categories of disability: intellectual disability (IQ range: 36–70); cerebral palsy (spastic, athetoid, and ataxic), and autism spectrum disorders. Screening item categories include:

  - Psychological/Physical Adjustment Skills
  - Entering and Exiting the Pool
  - Range of Motion (ROM) in Water
  - Breath Control/Respiratory Skills
  - Balance and Floatation
  - Active Movement in Water

- American Red Cross (ARC) learn to swim program (American Red Cross, 2004). This program is taught according to six levels, ranging from absolute beginner to the highly skilled swimmer:

  - Level 1: Introduction to water skills [ages four and up] (*e.g., enter and exit water safely, submerge mouth, open eyes under water*).
  - Level 2: Fundamental aquatic skills (*e.g., jump from pool edge into waist deep water, submerge head for five seconds, front and back float unsupported*).
  - Level 3: Stroke development (*e.g., jump into deep water, submerge and retrieve an object; perform front/back crawl, 15 yards*).
  - Level 4: Stroke improvement (*e.g., swim underwater three body lengths, perform feet-first surface dive, perform front/back crawl 25 yards*).
  - Level 5: Stroke refinement (*e.g., survival floating two minutes, tread water using two different kicks for two minutes, front/back crawl 50 yards*).
  - Level 6: Swimming and skill proficiency (*e.g., personal water safety, fundamentals of diving, fitness swimmer*).

Although the ARC six-level system has not been designed specifically to accommodate swimmers with disabilities, skill progressions, irrespective of ability/disability, tend to remain fixed. Therefore, progressions and curriculums developed for general populations usually are applicable to students who have disabilities provided, of course, they are developmentally appropriate. In this case, instructors accustomed to teaching adapted aquatics should be able to adapt the ARC model, on a case by case basis, to accommodate learners who present with unique needs.

Setting Goals

Safety in and around water, above all else, remains the first goal in all aquatics instruction. Students who learn, and who are expected to remain mindful of basic personal safety practices, will have taken the critical first step toward becoming comfortable during aquatic activities (Lepore, Gayle, & Stevens, 2007). Poolside and in-water safety skills and basic survival skills should be stressed during every lesson. Examples of pool safety and water survival skills include:

- Knowing not to run on the pool deck
- Knowing where and how to safely enter the pool
- Mouth closure while underwater
- Rolling over from front to back
- Treading water
- Bobbing to get a breath of air
- Recovering from a fall into the pool
- Use of reaching assists and floatation devices
- No tolerance for horseplay

A second important goal, especially when teaching young and/or inexperienced swimmers, is to strive for an environment which is nonthreatening; but also, fun and enjoyable. To ensure that the learning environment is non-threatening, teach for self-confidence first. Then, teach for skill. Teaching for self-confidence can occur, at first, away from the pool. It can even occur in a regular class setting. Then, gradually students may transition to outside-of-water poolside activity. The most basic out-of-water activities are:

- 'Washing' one's face with a wet wash rag or sponge
- Blowing bubbles with a straw into a water-filled bucket
- Blowing bubbles directly into a large (e.g., 32 ounce) cup without a straw
- Having students become accustomed to the feel and fit of life vests well in advance of first entry into the water
- Playing with swim aids on dry land that subsequently will be used in aquatic instruction (e.g., inflatable balls, kickboards, noodles)
- Creating a 'water table' on top of which are kitchen sink-size plastic pans of the sort used for hand-washing dishes and, perhaps, a 10 gallon

aquarium. Fill containers with water. then place retrievable objects in each container. Objects can be anything that will not float (e.g., small stones, placards upon which each each student's name is printed, pennies). Ask each student individually to retrieve his/her name; the brown stone; or five pennies; or "See how many things you can pull out of the water before I say 'stop.'"

- At poolside, have children engage in play-type activities in water-filled kiddie pools. At some point, place objects into the pools previously used in water table games, and repeat the water table games.

An important third goal, this one long range, is to teach swimming skills from the perspective that they are for lifetime fitness and recreation. Cardiovascular fitness (See Chapter 21, Teaching Physical Fitness) is often regarded as the most critical health promoting component of health-related fitness. Cardiovascular fitness is achieved through the moderate intensity-high duration exercising of large muscle groups. Swimming is an ideal cardiovascular activity because it does not stress joints and does not require on land locomotor mobility. As cardiovascular fitness improves, swimming is more likely to become a long term recreational activity of choice. If one cannot yet swim, one can walk in water or kick and tread water while wearing a life vest.

Given the goal to improve cardiovascular endurance through water activity, units should be planned that provide opportunity for children to participate in moderate to vigorous aquatic activity a minimum of three times per week. Gradually, as appropriate, activity durations may be increased to between 20 and 30 minutes.

LEARNING ACTIVITY

Create a series of pool exercises specifically designed to preserve Selena's overall bone density. Develop a list of pool activities designed to help ensure Selena maintains muscular strength, endurance, and flexibility in each affected joint.

Developing an instructional plan

Considerations in designing an aquatics instructional plan are similar in theory and practice to plans developed for dry-land instruction. Take into consideration the following:

- General functional level of the child
- Goals to be achieved
- Skills to be taught

- Skill level of the swimmer
- Time allocated for the unit and individual lesson
- Availability of teaching assistants
- Size, shape, and accessibility of the facility
- Extent to which shallow and deep water areas are available for lessons
- Whether instruction will be one-on-one, small group, or with peers who do not have disabilities (inclusion)

LEARNING ACTIVITY

What indicators and/or criteria would you use to evaluate the effectiveness of the program you have designed to meet Selena's individual needs?

Presenting the Actual Lesson

Time devoted to each lesson element will depend on the goal of the lesson, nature of the activity to be taught, water tolerance of the child, and the amount of teaching time available. The typical lesson should include a pre-lesson checklist; followed by warm-up, skill development, fitness activity, and a cool-down activity or game. Refer to **Table 23.2** for an example of an adapted aquatics lesson plan.

Pre-Lesson Checklist

Always:

- Make sure that a lifeguard is on duty.
- Take a head count of swimmers and record their attendance.
- Provide lifeguard and assistants with safety information that includes emergency contingency plans, swimmer medical and/or behavioral issues.
- Establish expectations with children before the lesson begins; ensure that swimmers know their boundaries.
- Ensure that swimmers know the specific signals to be used in the event of an emergency.
- Remind children of proper ways to enter and exit the water.
- Prepare all necessary equipment prior to the lesson.

Entering and Exiting the Pool Transferring into the pool can be accomplished in a variety of ways that ensure safety for each child. Children may enter the water independently, with manual assistance from the teacher at poolside, or from an assistant already in the water. When a child enters or exits the pool, it is important that teacher/assistant and child (to the extent possible)

Table 23.2 Sample Adapted Aquatics Lesson Plan

Name: Selena

Date: January 22, 2010

Medical Concerns: Juvenile Rheumatoid Arthritis. Pain and swelling in small joints of the hands and weight-bearing joints; including hips, knees, ankles, and feet.

Objectives of Lesson	Equipment
Safety: Demonstrate proper use of lifejacket. Perform back float with use of a lifejacket.	Life jacket
Skill: Hold breath underwater for three seconds.	
Fitness: Walk unassisted two widths of the pool.	

Activity	Cues	Formation	Time
Warm-up: Adjustment to water.			
1. Sit on edge of pool, splash water with feet and hands.	"Kick and splash."	One-on-one	1 min.
2. Enter pool with assistance.			1 min.
3. Submerge to chest/shoulders/neck.	"Hide your neck."		1 min.
4. Move in place for 2 minutes.	"Try to jump or run."		2 min.
Skills: Breathing.			
1. Blow bubbles.	"Blow as many bubbles as you can."		1 min.
2. Blow to move a floating object.	"How can you move an object?"		2 min.
3. Take 10 breaths above water.	"Breathe in and out 10 times."		1 min.
4. Place chin, then mouth in water.	"Hide your chin."		1 min.
5. Place mouth underwater, hold breath.	(Demonstrate)		1 min
6. Place mouth underwater, 3 seconds.	"Count to three!"		3 sec.
7. Place mouth underwater, blow bubbles.	"How long can you blow bubbles?"		1 min.
Skills: Buoyancy and fitness.			
1. Perform the flutter kick while holding onto side of pool.	(Teacher demonstrate)		2 min
2. With (or without) holding onto side of pool, walk one width and back.			3 min.
Safety:			
1. Demonstrate how to put on a lifejacket.	(Demonstrate)		3 min.
2. Perform back float with lifejacket (with assistance).	"Can you touch the back of your head to the water?"		1 min.
3. Move in lifejacket around shallow end of pool (with assistance).	"How can you move with your hands and feet?"		3 min.
4. Add flutter kick, arm movements to #3	Say, "flutter kick."		2 min.
Cool Down:			
1. Remove lifejacket and place it where it belongs.			2 min.
2. Gently stretch arms, shoulders, and ankles in water.			2 min.

mutually understand the entry/exit strategy. Communicate ahead of time to minimize any misunderstanding or anxiety the child or assistant(s) might have. Use of a shower chair designed to be wet or prosthesis designed for water use, when available, can maximize exit independence for children with certain mobility impairments and amputations. To facilitate entering and exiting, pools where adapted aquatics is taught may be equipped with in-water movable floors adjacent to the pool's edge. These have the effect of raising the bottom of the pool for children and adults whose feet might not otherwise touch the bottom (see **Figure 23.1**).

Pool lifts may be operated independently, as appropriate, by participants or, otherwise, by the teacher or assistant. Newer or retrofitted older pools may have wet ramps for entering and exiting the water. Proper training in use of lifts must be completed by anyone who personally uses the lift. The same holds true for all persons who assist swimmers using lifts to enter and exit the water.

LEARNING ACTIVITY

What consideration, if any, will you give to water temperature? What criteria might you rely upon to determine whether a pool facility's design is compatible with the program you would create specifically for Selena?

Figure 23.1 Type of raised pool floors.

Warm Up (5 to 10 minutes) Warming up with light activity for five or more minutes prior to instruction best prepares children for each lesson element that follows. Select activities that systematically and gradually involve all muscles and body parts. Include body stretches, stationary swim strokes, calisthenics (in or out of the water), and walking/running (in the water) to help prepare both mind and body for swimming.

Skill and Fitness Development (15 to 20 minutes) These elements can be taught separately or together depending on the goals of the lesson. If a child's program calls for mastery of swimming strokes, the child can work to improve skill and fitness simultaneously during the entire course of the lesson.

Cool-Down (5 to 10 minutes) Cooling-down is as important as warming-up. Age appropriate water games and activities are fine for cooling down as long as they have the effect of reducing the body temperature (if appropriate) and lowering heart rate to near pre-activity levels.

When pool water has been inordinately cold that day, the need to warm-up will be more immediate than the need to cool-down. Children who need warming to regain a comfortable body temperature will still need to have heart rates gradually returned to near pre-activity levels. A well constructed cool-down ensures an uneventful

recovery from effects of exertion. An abrupt cessation of activity can provoke cramps, cause muscle soreness, and/or prolong residual fatigue long after the lesson has ended. Cool-down also provides time for the teacher to bring closure to the class through discussion of learning that has just taken place.

Teaching Tips

Spend as much time as necessary with each skill, working at the child's comfort level and pace. Make accommodations as the child may not learn skills precisely in the order presented. For example, if a child is unable to blow bubbles into the water, continue to teach the activity, but also introduce other skills. Once a child begins bobbing and breathing, blowing bubbles may come naturally.

For many beginning swimmers, putting the face underwater for the first time will prove to be challenging. Be patient. Through play, demonstration, and the teacher gaining the child's confidence, the child will little-by-little begin to submerge parts of the face (e.g., "Hide your chin, nose, cheek.").

When a new or non-swimmer is anxious about entering the water, sit quietly with the swimmer at poolside. Talk about something unrelated to swimming and/or look together at things around the pool. Sometimes, blocking off a section of the pool with lane buoys, rather than exposing student to the entire large pool space, will help him/her feel more at ease. Pool familiarization activity for the child who is anxious may initially include touching the water, splashing water on oneself, walking or crawling down the wet ramp, and, finally, gradually, movement into shallow water (Special Olympics Aquatics, 2004).

As appropriate, make the pool environment visually stimulating. Scatter quantities of swimming equipment (e.g., plastic bottles, sponges, fun floatable objects) throughout the pool; thus requiring the child to move objects out of the way in order to move from place to place. Or, see how quickly the child can safely collect the objects from the pool and, then, place them on the deck. As an exception to the stimulating pool environment rule, note that for some students with disabilities (e.g., ADD, ADHD, autism spectrum, EBD), a visually stimulating pool environment risks the potential to become an unwelcome distraction.

Children who are unsure of the water often tend to close their eyes until they gain confidence. To build the child's confidence, demonstrate that water does not hurt the eyes. Submerge yourself and come up with eyes open. Be sure to come up smiling!

Practice walking in water while blowing ping-pong balls (or eggs!) across the surface. Begin early on by working with the student to exhale through the nose. Example activities: "See if you can blow bubbles with your mouth." "See if you can blow bubbles with your nose." "See if you can blow bubbles with your mouth *and* nose." Ability to blow bubbles through mouth and nose helps children progress toward developing breathing techniques to be used with the basic strokes.

Types of Swim Aids and Their Uses

Adapted aquatic instructors rely on a range of equipment to support the instruction of differently abled learners. According to individual learner need, the instructor may use:

- Foam mats placed on the pool deck, to be used by children for warm-ups and practicing swimming strokes.
- Foam mats floating on the pool's surface provide children sitting or lying on the mat with a softer entry point into the water.
- Kickboards to provide upper body support in the water. Inflatable tubes, inflatable doughnuts, inflatable balls, and noodles serve the same purpose (**Figure 23.2a** and **23.2b**).
- Pull buoys (floatation devices for legs) affixed to legs can help keep lower extremities from sinking into the water.
- Aqua vests can be used for in-water jogging.
- 'Swimmies/floaties' can be used to support upper arm floatation. Floatation swimwear is available in sizes ranging from infant to adult.
- Small buckets can be used to scoop water from the pool and pour it over one's head. Flower sprinkler pails can serve the same purpose.

Used correctly and according to individual learner needs, swim aids help:

- Ensure pool area safety and comfort in general.
- Free the teacher, who may need hands free to instruct, from having to physically buoy the student.
- Afford variety for the child; thereby, helping make learning more enjoyable and fun.
- Help enable the child to assume and maintain correct swimming body positions.
- Minimize apprehension that often results, especially among children who cannot or who are as yet unable to swim.

When using any floatation device, the teacher must be certain the device fits and is secured properly *every* time it is used. This is particularly important when such

(a)

(b)

Figure 23.2 Two types of swim aids.

devices are used with young children and persons who do not understand how to or cannot put on their own secure floatation devices correctly. Even when children are able to help don their own floatation devices, responsibility remains fully with the teacher to ensure that each child's floatation aid is fully functional.

Children with severe impairments are of particular concern and must be observed very closely whenever a floatation device is in use. Understand that children with severe disabilities may not comprehend or be able to communicate when something with the floatation device is amiss. Children with severe disabilities, therefore, must be observed constantly by a responsible adult to ensure they do not become entrapped in or completely slip out of the device (Gross, 1987).

Floatation devices, quite generally, should be considered means to ends, not ends in themselves. Certain children with severe disabilities, however, may benefit from use of swim aids indefinitely and, swim aids not unlike wheelchairs, canes, crutches, and walkers, promote independence. Over time and across the spectrum of potential for swimmer development, the majority may be expected to achieve confidence and skill such that swim aids eventually outlive their usefulness.

Green and Miles (1987) strongly encourage use of masks, fins, and snorkels in teaching basic swimming skills to children with disabilities. Swim fins can be used to advantage by swimmers with lower extremity impairments to develop stronger dolphin and flutter kicks (e.g., amputation, spasticity). Swim fins also help swimmers to remain horizontal to the direction of travel and increase speed with minimum effort.

A diving mask that enables the swimmer to see underwater can be a great motivator. For young and inexperienced swimmers, seeing underwater can be a new and exciting experience. For swimmers afraid of water, being able to see both above and below the surface can be calming. The snorkel can be used to aid the swimmer who, as yet, is unable to consistently bring his/her face above water to breathe.

LEARNING ACTIVITY

How might an assortment of rubberized weights, life vests, and improvised flotation devices (e.g., swimmies/floaties; plastic jugs with handles filled with varying amounts of water) be used progressively to exercise each of Selena's affected joints?

Multisensory Approaches to Aquatic Instruction

Human sensory modalities are somewhat like radio TV antennae that receive signals. Human sensory modalities, like antennae, receive and deliver sensory signals to the brain. Proponents of multisensory approaches to learning generally believe that when sensory modalities are stimulated simultaneously, there is greater likelihood the student will understand more precisely what sort of response is expected. For example, the teacher *simultaneously* can:

- Visually demonstrate and verbally explain a skill (e.g., "Watch me. Watch how my legs kick up and down. Now, let's do it together.").

- Verbally instruct the student and touch a body segment to be moved (e.g., tell the student to raise his/her arm out of the water, and, at the same time, touch the arm to be raised).

- Verbally instruct the student and kinesthetically position student's body (**Figure 23.3a** and **23.3b**) through water (e.g., say, "Move your arms like a windmill." At the same time, grasp student's arms and kinesthetically pattern student's arms through the windmill-like motion of the front crawl.)

(a)

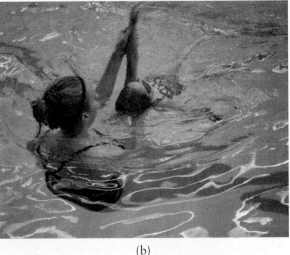

(b)

Figure 23.3 Kinesthetic patterning of a kindergarten-age non-swimmer.

While all children rely on sensory modalities for learning, all children do not learn equally through the same sensory modalities. Visual learners prefer demonstrations. Auditory learners prefer verbal instructions. Tactile learners respond well to touch, and kinesthetic learners tend to think on their feet. The teacher should strive to determine each child's preferred sensory modalities and present lessons accordingly.

While learning through one sensory modality can be relatively concrete, learning through another can be relatively abstract (e.g., cueing through kinesthetic patterning is concrete; cueing via auditory instruction is abstract). Whenever a student appears not to understand instruction via relatively abstract verbal or visual instructions, try pairing such instruction with tactile stimulation and kinesthetic patterning.

Aquatic Games

Aquatic games can be used to introduce skills through activity perceived as play and to reinforce skills taught earlier in the present or previous lesson. Through potential for focus on fun, aquatic games help reduce the anxiety that some children experience when confronted with newness and uncertainty. This is especially true with children for whom newness is equated with feelings of ineptness. Many traditional dry land and water games are easily modified for use in adapted aquatics (i.e., volleyball, basketball, and water polo; all in the shallow end). Be sure to consider the information processing and mobility characteristics of each

as games are modified, and re-modify as needed. Modification has been successful when everyone has had fair opportunity to safely and successfully participate.

Competitive Swimming

Competitive swimming events for children with disabilities, depending upon locale, are held at the local, state, regional, national, and international level. Competition opportunities range from entry level to world class elite.

Competitive swimmers with disabilities do not always compete directly against other swimmers with disabilities. When a swimmer with a disability is able to compete meaningfully, including safely, against athletes without disabilities, she/he should be considered a viable candidate for such opportunity. In fact, such opportunity has now achieved the level of civil right. However, the right to participate is not absolute. When a teacher/coach or administrator determines whether participation is likely to be safe, she/he must equally consider safety needs of participants who do not have disabilities.

Many local and international sport organizations that offer competitive swimming, likewise offer skill development opportunities for people who desire to improve swimming skills only for recreational purposes. Specific information regarding where adapted sports programs may be found, including specific sports sanctioned by each organization, is included in Chapter 24, Sport for Persons with Disabilities.

SUMMARY

1. Priority one in teaching swimming to students with disabilities is to create and maintain a teaching/learning environment that ensures safe and successful participation for all students and staff.

2. Two-thirds of the Earth's surface is covered with water. Perhaps for this reason alone, aquatics should be a significant component of virtually every adapted physical education program where opportunity for pool access exists.

3. Aquatic activities provide children both with and without disabilities opportunity to experience freedom of movement unencumbered by gravity;

an experience that can not be replicated in any other environment.

4. Teaching swimming skills to children with disabilities affords remarkable potential to improve motor fitness, physical fitness, social/recreational skills, survival potential, self-confidence, and self-esteem.

5. The aquatics instructor must assess individual student's abilities before establishing individual student goals. Assessment and goal setting needs to be completed before meaningful instruction can begin.

6. Developmental stages though which students progress while learning to swim, irrespective of ability/disability, remain quite stable and fixed. However, rates at which individual students acquire skills may be expected to vary widely.

7. Time devoted to each element of any lesson will depend on; (1) the goal of the lesson, (2) characteristics unique to the student being taught, (3) the nature of the activity to be taught, (4) water tolerance of the student(s), and (5) total time allocated for teaching and learning.

8. The typical aquatic lesson should include; (1) pre-lesson check list to ensure student, teacher, and pool readiness for the lesson, (2) warm-up in and/or out of the pool, (3) lesson for the day (i.e., skill teaching/learning time), (4) time dedicated to fitness maintenance/development, and (5) cool-down activity or game time to restore near pre-activity temperature and heart rate.

REFERENCES

American Red Cross. (2004). *Water safety instructor manual.* Yardley, PA: Stay Well.

American Red Cross Survey (May, 2009) www.redcross.org http://www.redcross.org/portal/site/en/menuitem.94aae 335470e233f6cf911df43181aa0/?vgnextoid=3781a934e 1e51210VgnVCM10000089f0870aRCRD

Apache, R. R., Hisey, P., & Blanchard, L. (2005). An adapted aquatics assessment inventory and curriculum. *Palaestra, 21*(2), 32–37.

Centers for Disease Control and Prevention. (cited September 15, 2009). http://www.cdc.gov/ HomeandRecreationalSafety/Water-Safety/waterinjuries-factsheet.htm

Conatser, P. (2006). Inclusive activities for individuals with disabilities. PELINKS4U Promoting Active & Healthy Lifestyles, section: Adapted Physical Education 8(8). Retrieved from http://www.pelinks4u.org/archives/ adapted/100106.htm

Conatser, P. (1995). *Adapted aquatics swimming screening test.* Lubbock, TX: Author

Gallahue, D. L. & Ozmun J. C. (2006). *Understanding motor development: Infants, children, adolescents, adults* (6th ed.). New York: McGraw-Hill.

Green, J. S., & Miles, B. H. (1987). Use of mask, fins, snorkel, and SCUBA equipment in aquatics for the disabled. *Palaestra, 3*(4), 12–17.

Greenshaw, A. & Sadler, B. (1988). Whale . . . wet happenings and learning experiences. *Palaestra, 5*(1), 10–11.

Gross, S. (1987). Use and misuse of flotation devices in adapted aquatics. *Palaestra, 4*(1), 31–33, 56–57.

Lepore, M., Gayle, G. W., & Stevens, S. F. (2007). *Adapted aquatics programming: A professional guide* (2nd Ed.). Champaign, IL: Human Kinetics.

Priest, L. (1982). *Adapted aquatics teaching methods* (p. 2). Indianapolis: Council for National Cooperation in Aquatics.

Special Olympic Aquatics. 2004. Special Olympics Quick Start Coaching Guide. cited on September 10, 2009 http://www.specialolympics.org/uploadedFiles/Aquatics+ Quick+Start+Guide.pdf http://www.specialolympics.org/ aquatics.aspx

Winnick, J. P. (2005). *Adapted physical education and sport* (4th ed.). Champaign, IL: Human Kinetics.

CHAPTER 24

Sport for Persons with Disabilities

CASE STUDY

Danny is a 14 year old high school freshman. He loves football and has always aspired to play on his high school football team. This semester, Danny is trying out to play on his high school's junior varsity team.

Danny's has only one kidney. While his single kidney enables renal functions within normal parameters; the coach, high school principal, and a school board believe that Danny should not be allowed to participate in any heavy contact sport given the possibility of serious injury to his remaining kidney.

The school offers a range of sports in which Danny can compete; sports that offer virtually no prospect of kidney injury. School officials insist that they are not denying Danny opportunity to participate in athletics; but, rather, just football. They argue that they are exercising their legal obligation to reasonably protect Danny from an avoidable accident that could change his life forever.

Danny's parents, however, disagree. They support Danny's desire to play football, and argue that he has demonstrated more than adequate athletic ability to earn a spot on the team. He is likewise a very good student. Danny's parents claim that, in light of Danny's athletic and academic prowess, the *only* reason he is being denied football is because of his single kidney; a condition that, apparently according to his school, is disabling. To support their argument that he cannot legally be denied opportunity to participate *purely* on the basis of disability, Danny's parents cite Section 504 of the Rehabilitation act of 1973. If unresolved at the local level, Danny's parents intend to take their case to the State High School League and, if necessary, to court.

Tribute to Sir Ludwig Guttman ('Father Ludwig')

Activity opportunities widely acknowledged to be sport or sport-like have been in existence for people with disabilities for perhaps 100 years. Formal, organized competition of sport for persons who are deaf, termed Silent Games, first took place in Paris in 1924 (www.deaflympics.com). One can only speculate that activity opportunities leading to recognized need for formal games predated the first formal contests.

While not in any way to diminish the range of early sport and physical activity initiatives for persons with a range of disabilities, the *beginnings* of what might fairly be called *the movement* occurred with the rehabilitation of soldiers having sustained spinal cord injuries during WWII. And, the person widely considered the movement's inspiration, one who remains singularly legendary in the sport for persons with disabilities community today, is Sir Ludwig Guttmann, MD (1899–1980).

Ludwig Guttman, respectfully and affectionately know as 'pappa' or 'father' Ludwig, is often regarded as the father of wheelchair sports. Guttman, a neurologist, became affiliated with the Stoke Mandeville Hospital, Aylsbury, England in 1944. Then and there, the British government commissioned Guttmann to establish and direct a spinal injuries care unit for the large number of veterans having incurred spinal cord injuries during WWII combat.

Guttmann summarily dismissed the, then, commonly accepted notion that the prognosis for persons with spinal cord injuries was hopeless. He believed and went on to demonstrate that conditions complicated by spinal cord injury (medical, physical, psychological, and social) could be ameliorated significantly by engaging patients in a range of therapeutic physical activities. Early activities included punch ball, darts, archery, and table tennis. Later, he instituted wheelchair polo and basketball. An associate of Guttmann, Joan Scruton, recalls,

> One of the main treatments (for patients) was sport, even when they were lying in bed. We had a quartermaster sergeant who was seconded from the army to do sport with the patients. When they were lying in bed he would throw a medicine ball to them and they would throw it back to get the strength in their arms . . . Sport was of course critical to get their strength; their future depended on being able to lift themselves into the chair. The second point was psychological because when patients came in, they stayed sometimes three or four years to get over their sores and kidney infections and to rehabilitate. (Steadward & Peterson, 1997)

Sport, according to Sir Ludwig, was a requirement for soldiers in rehabilitation. Scruton further recalls:

> They had to do a sport. It was part of the treatment. It was not a question of would you like to do archery; no, it was part of the treatment, like taking their medicine, or doing physiotherapy. And Sir Ludwig would make sure that they did it.

Guttmann's successes became legendary. When spinal cord injured veterans arrived at Stoke Mandeville Hospital in the early to mid 1940s, the odds of living more than three years post-injury were a meager 20 percent. Today, in no small measure due to the groundbreaking and inspirational work and philosophy of Sir Ludwig, a person with a spinal cord injury now has an 80 percent likelihood of living a full life expectancy (Godfrey & Weisman).

Guttmann went on to establish the Stoke Mandeville Games, athletic contests for spinal cord injured veterans in 1948. He prophesied and hoped the Stoke Mandeville games would someday achieve fame worldwide as the Olympics for persons with disabilities. Guttman worked to formally connect international wheelchair athletic competition with the Olympics. He succeeded in helping to establish the first Paralympic Games in 1960. Predominately, athletes using wheelchairs competed in the first few Paralympic Games. Today, the Paralympic Games (**Figure 24.1a–f**) include

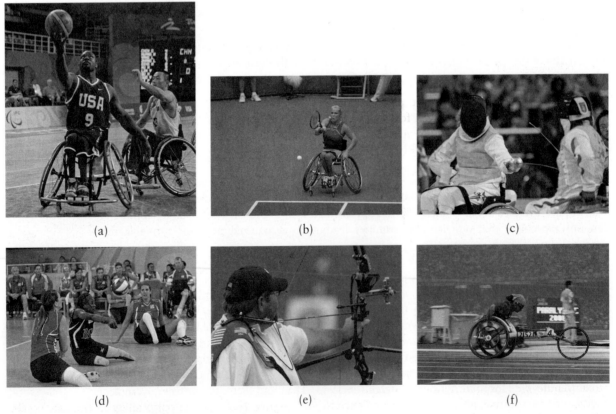

(a)

(b)

(c)

(d)

(e)

(f)

Figure 24.1 U.S. Paralympic athletes in action.

athletes with the following disabilities (www.paralympic.org):

Amputation: Athletes with a partial or total loss of at least one limb.

Cerebral palsy: Athletes with a brain-affected disorder resulting in problems with movement and posture.

Intellectual disability: As determined by IQ assessment, adaptive behavior assessment, and age of onset.

Spinal cord injuries: Athletes with at least a 10 percent loss of function of the lower limbs.

Visually impaired: Athletes who are affected by disorders of vision ranging from partial sight through total blindness.

Les autres: French for "the others." Athletes who are affected by a range of conditions that fall into the categories mentioned above (e.g. multiple sclerosis, dwarfism).

While Sir Ludwig's legacy is most prominently associated with early wheelchair sports (informal and organized), his philosophy from some 70 years ago that physical, athletic, and sport activity are invaluable in the social, emotional, and physical habilitation/rehabilitation of persons with disabilities, continues to inspire athletes and advocates alike. Pappa Ludwig's thinking continues to thrive in the sports for persons with disabilities community.

Evolution in "Why sport for persons with disabilities?"

Historically, participation in sport among persons with disabilities has been promoted for, at minimum, three important and enduringly valuable reasons. They include:

- Sport as habilitation/rehabilitation/therapy
- Sport as opportunity to have and socialize through normalizing life experiences
- Sport for sport's sake (i.e. because I am an athlete)

Sport as habilitation/rehabilitation/therapy

Given recognition that physical activity and exercise has potential to promote physical, mental, and emotional health; it has become and remains a staple prescription in the habilitation and rehabilitation of persons both with and without disabilities. From a therapeutic perspective, physical activity and exercise offer potential for habilitation and rehabilitation

among persons with conditions that disable including, by way of example only:

- Arthritis (e.g. contracture prevention)
- Cerebral palsy (e.g. helps maintain range of motion in muscle flexor and inward rotator groups)
- Chronic pulmonary obstructive disease (e.g. helps improve circulation and endurance)
- Heart disease (e.g. helps safely maximize cardiac function)
- Muscular dystrophy (e.g. helps manage contractures and maintain strength)
- Amputations (e.g. helps develop strength and maintain/improve ranges-of-motion for managing prostheses)
- Multiple sclerosis (e.g. helps maintain muscle function, range-of-motion)
- Diabetes (e.g. helps maintain blood sugar within normal parameters
- Depression (e.g. mood elevation)
- Behavior disorders (e.g. positive behavior modification).

Because sport enjoys near universal approval as a positive institution in society; sport, as therapy, offers potential to be perceived as meaningful activity, something to which to look forward; (**Figure 24.2**) while other forms of therapy, no matter how efficacious, may be dismissed, however unfairly, as drudgery or hard work.

Sport as opportunity to have and learn from normalizing life experiences

Quite typically, a person with disability does *not* want his/her disability to become central to her/his identity. Neither does she/he wish to be perceived as being sick and, as a result; treated differently from persons without disabilities. Too often, however, the person's

Figure 24.2 Sport as opportunity for normalizing life experience.

disability becomes central to her/his identity. The end result, often, is differential treatment based on disability label alone, including disenfranchisement, solely by virtue of disability label, from a range of normalizing life experiences throughout life (Taub & Greer, 2000).

Sport is potentially normalizing for a range of reasons. It teaches about competition. It teaches cooperation in a world that values people coming together to achieve common goals. It teaches that following mutually agreed upon rules is about fairness for all. It teaches that an ethical person and a good sport quite generally are one and the same. It teaches leadership and teamwork, including when each is called for. It teaches the setting of and striving to achieve worthwhile goals. It is a place where common interests are shared and, out of common interests, friendships made. Sport, precisely because it is so universally accepted as a normal childhood (and beyond) life experience, is excellently positioned to become normalizing for children (and adults) with disabilities, many of whom historically have been disenfranchised from a spectrum of normalizing and socializing life experiences.

Sport for sport's sake

Certainly, physical activity, exercise, and sport will continue to have enduring value for their critical roles in habilitation, rehabilitation, and normalizing. There, however, will come a time when a person who has a disability ceases to pursue sport for purposes founded in habilitation, rehabilitation, or normalizing life experiences. Such a person sees her/himself first and foremost and is seen by others as an athlete pursuing athletic excellence. The fact that the person, as an athlete, has a disability becomes relegated to the status of coincidence (e.g. some athletes are bald). The sport experience is no longer about therapy. It is about sport for sport's sake, "Sport, because I am an athlete." At this level, the pursuit of athletic excellence, bound only by potential to achieve, becomes the primary driving motivation to participate.

Sport Development and Competition Opportunities

To risk a cliché, the time to bend the twig is while it is young (i.e., pliable). The 'twig' cliché speaks volumes regarding the perpetuating value of active lifestyles in the lives of young people as they evolve through childhood, adolescence, adulthood, and into what are euphemistically called 'the golden years.'

Regarding sport and health-promoting physical activity, may we accept as givens that:

- Sport well-played is a metaphor for a life well-lived?

- A good sport and an ethical person are one and the same?
- Interest in sport (both as participant and spectator) is woven into the mainstream of life's social dynamics?
- Activity across the lifespan, sensibly approached, is enduringly, and holistically physical, and emotionally health-promoting?

To the extent answers to the above are 'yes,' as they impact children without disabilities; would not those same answers easily, arguably be 'yes' for children who have disabilities? After all, children are children first. Disability or not, children are more alike than different.

According to Hilgers (2006), 41 million American children and youth play in competitive sports, and this number has risen significantly over the last 10 to 20 years. Bear in mind, the 41 million include children overwhelmingly without disabilities. Children with disabilities are overwhelmingly underrepresented in the world of youth sport, regular or adapted. This continuing reality begs the question, why?

Regarding the potential for sport participation as value adding in the lives of children with disabilities, Fitzgerald (2009) writes:

Sport has, and will undoubtedly continue to be, an important part of the fabric of society. Whatever a person's disposition and response toward sport, we should be mindful that initial sports experiences provide the platform from which thinking about sport is molded and this subsequently influences future choices and engagement in sport . . . I make this important point, because there should be recognition that as scholars, students, and practitioners we have a responsibility not only to advocate for young disabled people in sport but also need to do this in the broader dimensions of life. After all, sport is inextricably connected to wider social practices and norms and we need to engage in these debates if we are serious about enhancing the sporting opportunities and experiences of young disabled people. (p. 1)

Participation in youth sport and physical activities can become enduringly beneficial across the lifespan for children with and without disabilities. Participation models are abundant for children without disabilities; where are the models of opportunity for children with disabilities; particularly children with disabilities for whom participation in traditional programs may not be equitable?

Sport organizations

Each organization below is cited because it offers skill development and competition opportunities for children and youth who have disabilities. This section emphasizes programs that provide opportunity for children and youth who might not otherwise participate meaningfully in traditional programs. The list is reasonably comprehensive, but certainly not exhaustive. It should be noted that each organization also offers skill development and competition opportunities for adults.

BlazeSports offers youth development programs for persons with a range of physical, neurological, sensory, and orthopedic disabilities. BlazeSports, whose mission is to "advance the lives of youth and adults with physical disability through sport and healthy lifestyles" operates in 50 U.S. communities and in the District of Columbia. The organization provides "sports training, competitions, summer camps and other sports and recreational opportunities for youth and adults with spinal cord injury, spina bifida, cerebral palsy, traumatic brain injury, muscular dystrophy, amputation, visual impairment or blindness as well as other physical disabilities" (www.blazesports.org). BlazeSports operates in partnership with the National Recreation and Park Association (NRPA), and, among other programs and services, offers youth sport training camps for participants at three levels ranging from novice participants to high performance athletes in training.

Wheelchair Sports USA's (WSUSA) mission is to "provide sports and recreation opportunities for people with physical and visual disabilities by facilitating, advocating, and developing a national community-based outreach program, providing resources and education, conducting regional and national competitions, and providing access to international competitions." Founded in 1956 as the National Wheelchair Athletic Association, WSUSA moved in 1982 from its original home in New York to Colorado Springs, CO to join other athletic associations that make up the US Olympic Committee. WSUSA sponsors the following sports:

- Archery
- Track and field
- Billiards
- Shooting
- Swimming
- Table tennis
- Weightlifting

Commitment to youth sport development is central to WSUSA's mission. Junior athletes comprise 30 percent of WSUSA's total membership, and regional associations affiliated with WSUSA conduct annual competitions for youths age 5–18 (http://www.wsusa.org/).

Disabled Sports/USA (DS/USA) was founded by Vietnam War veterans with disabilities in 1967. DS/USA originated as the National Amputee Skiers Association, but over the years has grown to achieve global recognition in a range of sports for persons with disabilities communities. The organization's participation base has expanded dramatically over its 40 year history. Today, participants include persons with visual impairments, amputations, spinal cord injury, dwarfism, multiple sclerosis, head injury, cerebral palsy, and a range of neuromuscular and orthopedic conditions. Today, DS/USA is a Disabled Sports Organization(DSO) member of the U. S. Olympic Committee. DS/USA sponsors the following sports:

- Golf
- Hiking
- Hunting and fishing
- Nordic skiing
- Water sports
- Running
- Sailing
- Snowboarding
- Strength straining
- Surfing
- T'ai chi
- Tennis
- Waterskiing
- Yoga

DS/USA sponsors a youth mentoring program whose purpose is to, "increase youth sports involvement and to foster social interaction between people of all abilities through mentoring." Quoting DS/USA's mission statement, in part, "Youth sports mentoring…provide(s) opportunities for youth with disabilities to develop greater self-confidence, independence and a healthier, more physically active lifestyle by developing effective mentoring relationships using sport and recreation activities as the basis." A downloadable brochure describing DS/USA youth mentoring programs, offered to children through young adults 3–21, may be retrieved at http://www.dsusa.org/.

The National Wheelchair Basketball Association (NWBA): Founded in 1948, predominately by veterans who had sustained spinal cord injuries during WWII, the NWBA includes more than 200 teams from across the US and Canada that compete in 22 leagues and seven divisions (www.nwba.org).

Originally, spinal cord injury was the common denominator disability that qualified a player to compete in a wheelchair basketball event. Today, athletes with a range of physical and orthopedic disabilities are candidates for NWBA competition. Generally, athletes become eligible to compete when the nature of the athlete's disability, irrespective of diagnosis, is such that it prevents him/her from meaningful participation in stand-up basketball. Competitions include women's, men's, and junior teams.

University of Illinois summer sport camps offer sport instruction in track and field and basketball for youth using wheelchairs, either beginners or somewhat more experienced, who wish to fine tune fundamental and advanced wheelchair basketball skills.

Additionally, elite athlete camps are offered on a 'by invitation only' basis. The University of Illinois wheelchair sports program is particularly noteworthy for numerous accomplishments spanning 60 years, among them being a precursor influence for founding the National Wheelchair Basketball Association. For further information regarding wheelchair sports, coaching clinics, and youth athlete camps, go to: http://www.disability.uiuc.edu/athletics/.

Special Olympics: While Special Olympics is not the oldest sport organization for persons who have disabilities, it remains the organization most widely known. Special Olympics was founded in 1968, under auspices of the Joseph P. Kennedy Jr. Foundation, and predominately under leadership of the late Eunice Kennedy Schriver (1921–2009). What began as a summer games for athletes whose primary diagnosis was intellectual disability (initially from 28 states and Canada) has grown into a worldwide international athletic event.

Today, there are more than 2.5 million Special Olympics athletes, with a goal of 3 million by 2010. Athletes hail from more than 180 countries. Summer and winter international games are held alternately every two years.

Special Olympics currently offers participation opportunities in 34 sports. Participants may begin at age eight, and there is no upper end age limit. A young athletes program is available for children ages two through seven. Opportunities are offered in all 50 US states and most US protectorates (http://www.specialolympics.org).

For persons who coach or otherwise assist in teaching sports to children and youth with intellectual disabilities, Special Olympics offers *free of charge* on its website 34 teaching/coaching guides downloadable in PDF format. http://specialolympics.org.

It is noteworthy to mention that 'Special Olympics' must by no means be considered the generic term for all sports for persons who have disabilities. This misunderstanding, however naive and innocent, remains a source of frustration among athletes, coaches, and fans in the sport for persons with disabilities who have no connection whatsoever with the Special Olympics organization.

Courage Center: Located in Golden Valley, MN, Courage Center has, for decades, been an international leader in providing sport development opportunities for children, youth, and adults with disabilities (**Figure 24.3a** and **b**). Minnesota is a four-season state, and, in response, Courage Center offers participation opportunities, indoors and outdoors, year around. Courage Center, through its Camp Courage, offers a range of youth sport development during summer months. Youth sport development camps include: (1) recreational sports session, (2) power soccer camp, and (3) Paralympics sports session. All sessions are offered to beginner through experienced participants. Opportunities by season, are as follows (http://www.couragecenter.org/):

Fall/Winter

- Alpine skiing
- Nordic skiing
- Archery
- Basketball
- Curling
- Dog sledding

(a)

(b)

Figure 24.3 Courage Center athletes participate in sports including golf and baseball.

- Fitness training
- Ice fishing
- Martial arts
- Quad rugby
- Sled hockey
- Skating
- Mono-ski camp
- Tennis

Spring/Summer

- Archery
- Golf
- Biking
- Handcycling
- Horseback riding
- Kyaking
- Paralympic academy sports camp
- Rock climbing
- Sailing
- Scuba
- Softball
- Swim team
- Tennis
- Track and field
- Waterskiing

United States Association for Blind Athletes (USABA), member of US Olympic Committee, has reached more than 100,000 blind individuals through its range of programs and services (http://www.usaba.org/). The USABA has among its goals to provide more than 3,000 youth with the skills needed to participate in not only their PE classes, but on sports teams alongside sighted youth. Explicitly, USABA supports participation both in regular and adapted sport. USABA members range from children who are blind developing sports skills to elite athletes who train for competitions, including the Paralympic Games. USABA offers opportunities for development and competitions in the following sports:

- Track and field
- Cycling
- Goalball
- Judo
- Powerlifting
- Showdown
- Skiing
- Swimming
- Tenpin bowling
- Wrestling
- 5-a-side football

National Beep Baseball Association (NBBA): Beep baseball is played by athletes who are blind. In beep baseball the ball beeps and the bases to which batters run buzz. Games typically last six innings, unless more are needed to break a tie. There are two bases in beep baseball (each cone shaped and four feet tall). One base is placed approximately where one traditionally finds first base and the other where one traditionally finds third base. Pitchers and catchers on beep baseball teams are sighted. In beep baseball, pitchers and catchers pitch and catch *for their own teams*. A pitcher in beep baseball earns a reputation by how many hits she/he *gives up*. The pitcher says, "ready' and upon releasing the ball says "pitch." The pitcher's goal is to consistently place the pitched ball at a spot where the batter, if she/he consistently swings the bat, is likely to strike the ball. When a fair ball is hit, one of the two bases, randomly selected by the umpire, begins to buzz. The object of the game is for the batter to run to and contact the buzzing base before an opposing team fielder can cleanly field the beeping ball. Beep baseball spectator etiquette requires that spectators remain quiet whenever the ball is in play, so that the beeping ball and buzzing base can be heard by players. Cheering may occur only after the ball is declared dead. For in depth information about the sport, go to: http://www.nbba.org/.

National Sports Center for the Disabled (NSCD) began in 1970 as a one-time ski lesson for children with amputations from the Children's Hospital of Denver. Today, NSCD serves persons with a wide range of disabilities including, but not limited to:

- Attention deficit disorder
- Amputation
- Autism
- Bone Disorder
- Brain injury, cerebral palsy
- Deafness
- Developmental disabilities
- Diabetes
- Epilepsy, Fragile X
- Hemophilia
- Little People
- Multiple Sclerosis
- Muscular Disorder
- Nerve Disorders
- Paraplegia
- Post-Polio
- Respiratory disorder
- Spina Bifida
- Spinal Cord Injury
- Stroke
- Vision Loss/Blindness

NSCD offers a winter and summer sport and outdoor adventure learning and participation programs for persons ages 5 and older. Summer activities include canoeing, horseback riding, fishing, rafting, kayaking, and rock climbing, and ability league soccer camps. Winter activities include alpine skiing (sit and standup), snowboarding, ski biking, and cross-country skiing (sit and standup). Both segregated and integrated participation programs, as well as family plans, are offered. For current information go to: http://www.nscd.org/.

Dwarf Athletic Association of America (DAAA): Dwarfism is a general descriptor for a range of conditions that result in dwarfed stature. Persons who compete in DAAA events are classified according to body proportions and height. Classification is designed to promote fair competition based on an athlete's technique and ability, rather than mechanical advantage. Events are offered in four divisions beginning 'Future' (six years and under) through 'Master' (40 and above). Events include (http://www.daaa.org/):

- Track and field
- Swimming
- Boccia
- Soccer
- Basketball
- Volleyball
- Table tennis
- Powerlifting

Athlete classification systems

Classification systems become common throughout sport once participation becomes competitive. Classification systems are designed to ensure that competition is equitable; that participants in a given sport compete on a 'level playing field.' In traditional, able-bodied sport; classification systems typically include weight, gender, age, and level of success previously achieved (e.g. belt color in the martial arts). Sport classification systems for persons who have disabilities likewise rely on the above categorizers to ensure that competition at the starting point is fair; however, in addition, rely on classifications termed *medical* and *functional*.

Medical classification systems measure the affect a given disability has on the individual's mobility (http://www.wsusa.org/). Medical classification does not take into consideration functional skills required for individual sports. In effect, medical classification is designed to help determine residual mobility.

Functional classification systems tend to be sport specific. They are less concerned with the condition causing disability and more concerned, irrespective of disability type, with how much functional physical ability the participant is likely to be able to bring to

the task at hand (Wheelchair Sports, USA.; International Paralympic Committee, 2008).

Both medical and functional classification systems continue to be in use, although there appears to be a trend among adapted sports organizations toward relatively greater reliance on functional classification systems. According to the International Wheelchair Rugby Association (www.iwrf.com/):

> Classification systems have been in use in sport for persons with disabilities since the mid-1940s. The early classification systems were based on medical diagnoses, such as spinal cord injury, and were not specific for the unique functional demands of each sport. However, more recent transitions from medical classification to sport-specific classification systems have resulted in functional classification, where class is based on an athlete's functional abilities (rather than medical diagnosis) specific to the physical demands of each unique sport.

Classification system examples: Medical and functional

Medical classification systems generally are designed to determine the degree to which a *medical* condition that causes disability (e.g. spinal cord injury) is likely to impact the individual's potential to perform. Examples of medical classification systems are those that classify athletes who are blind or visually impaired (**Table 24.1**) and athletes in wheelchair basketball (**Table 24.2**). Classification systems variously can be complex, and listing of specifics of classification systems across the sport for persons with disabilities spectrum transcends the scope of this chapter. For further classification information, contact the appropriate sports organization or association.

Functional classification systems differ from medical classification systems in that their foci, rather than on the medical conditions that cause disability, are on what observable functional physical abilities the participant has/does not have that are likely to impact the individual's potential to participate equitably in a given sport. For example, when classifying athletes for Paralympic swimming, the athlete's functional ability to swim, over medical diagnosis, determines the athlete's participation class. Swimmers in Paralympic competition, irrespective of disability type, are classed for competition according to abilities that affect success specific to swimming, namely joint mobility, coordination, strength, and swimming skill. Generally, functional classification evaluations are made collaboratively by one with expert knowledge in the sport for which classification is being made, along with one who has expert knowledge of the disability manifested by the athlete being classified (Disability Sports Classification Skills, 2007).

Two distinct benefits of functional classification are: (1) within any given disability category (e.g. cerebral palsy/spina bifida), same disability category athletes can

Table 24.1 Medical classification United States Association of Blind Athletes (USABA) Visual Classification

Competition shall be divided into four classifications:

Class B1

No light perception in either eye up to light perception, but inability to recognize the shape of a hand at any distance or in any direction.

Class B2

From ability to recognize the shape of a hand up to visual acuity of 20/600 and/or a visual field of less than 5 degrees in the best eye with the best practical eye correction.

Class B3

From visual acuity above 20/600 and up to visual acuity of 20/200 and/or a visual field of less than 20 degrees and more than 5 degrees in the best eye with the best practical eye correction.

Class B4

From visual acuity above 20/200 and up to visual acuity of 20/70 and a visual field larger than 20 degrees in the best eye with the best practical eye correction.

Source: USABA, 2009.

be grouped according to available physical function that is germane to a specific sport rather than by specific disability type (similar to the functional handicapping system in regular golf) and (2) individual participants who present with different disabilities or multiple disabilities, provided their sport-specific ability and skill levels are closely matched, can compete equitably irrespective of disability type. "(Functional) classification system(s) can be used both for single disability and cross-disability competitions. In other words, function is primary and medical is secondary" (Pacieorek, 2005).

Participation: Integrated or Separated?

Until quite recently opportunities for persons with disabilities to participate in organized sport; integrated or segregated, school- or community-based, was the exception to the rule. However, beginning in the last

quarter of the 20th century, legislation began to be enacted at the federal level that rendered illegal the exclusion of persons with disabilities from opportunities to participate in athletics based solely on disability alone.

Most notably, in the 1970s, regulations implementing the Federal Rehabilitation Act of 1973, Section 504, applicable to public schools and public community-based organizations (i.e., recipients) read, in part:

> A recipient to which this subpart applies shall provide ... extracurricular services and activities in such manner as is necessary to afford handicapped students an equal opportunity for participation in such services and activities.... In providing ... athletics ... to any of its students, a recipient to which this subpart applies may not discriminate on the basis of handicap. A recipient that ... operates or sponsors interscholastic, club, or intramural athletics shall provide to qualified handicapped students an equal opportunity for participation.

Table 24.2 Medical classification National Wheelchair Basketball Association

Each classification will be given a numerical value or factor as follows:

Player Classification

Class I - Complete motor loss at T*-7 or above or comparable disability where there is total loss of muscle function originating at or above T-7.

Class II - Complete motor loss originating at T-8 and descending through and including L**-2 where there may be motor power of hips and thighs. Also included in this class are amputees with bilateral hip disarticulation.

Class III - All other physical disabilities as related to lower extremity paralysis or paresis originating at or below L-3. All lower extremity amputees are included in this class except those with bilateral hip disarticulation.

Team balance

Class I = 1 value point

Class II = 2 value points

Class III = 3 value points

Women shall be allowed to roster and participate on a men's team one class level below their actual medical classification level. No player shall drop below the Class I level. At no time in a game shall a team have players participating with a total of value points greater than twelve or more than three Class III players playing together at the same time.

*T = thoracic vertebrae
**L = lumbar vertebrae

Source: Modified from NWBA Official Rules Case Book, 2007–2008.

Regarding whether a student's athletic participation should be integrated or separated, the US Code of Federal Regulations, Title 45, Volume 1, Section 84.47 (Nonacademic services), revised January 1, 2008, read as follows:

> A recipient to which this subpart applies shall provide . . . extracurricular services and activities in such a manner as is necessary to afford handicapped students an equal opportunity in such . . . activities . . . A recipient may offer to handicapped students . . . athletic activities that are separate or different only if separation or differentiation is consistent with the requirements of Sec. 84.43(d) and only if no qualified handicapped student is denied opportunity to compete for teams . . . that are not separate or different.

Further, Sec. 84.43(d) of the above regulation states, "A recipient . . . shall operate its program or activity in the most integrated setting appropriate."

Clearly, the above federal regulations require that (1) students with disabilities cannot be denied opportunity to participate in regular athletic programs based on disability alone and (2) segregated programs may be offered to athletes with disabilities only when lack of ability to safely and successfully participate in a regular sports program (i.e., talent) or a legitimately disqualifying medical condition, *not simply disability label alone*, disqualifies her/him from integration into the regular program.

Participation: Integrated or Separated? Interpreting the Laws

A cursory glance at the previously outlined laws might lead to the presumption that determination as to whether disability alone has qualified/disqualified an athlete from regular sport participation might be rather clear cut. After all, the athlete either has the skills and abilities to make the team or he/she does not. However, the issues sometimes are not that simple. Examples:

- An athlete who is deaf and who otherwise has excellent football knowledge and skills may not be able to hear the coach's verbal instructions or quarterback's signals called. Should this athlete be considered ineligible to participate?
- An athlete with a below the elbow prosthesis possesses skills and knowledge sufficient to earn her a spot on the school's basketball team. However, there is concern that the hardness of her prosthesis, unlike a biological forearm and hand, could put other players at risk both on the court and in practice. Should this athlete be considered ineligible to participate in regular basketball?

- An athlete with excellent sport skills and knowledge is otherwise qualified to participate in a range of sports with potential for more than incidental physical contact. However, the athlete has only one kidney, a vital organ. Should the school deny this athlete opportunity to participate in sports of a contact nature ostensibly 'for his own good'?
- An athlete with intellectual disability has the skill and knowledge to successfully participate on her school's swim team, but she does not meet the school's academic eligibility requirements. Should she be disqualified on the basis of academic performance as measured against the school's academic eligibility requirements applicable to students without intellectual disabilities?

With regard to the examples listed, if you were the parent, coach, principal, or school board member, how would you decide? What factors might influence your decision? As you consider your decision, recall federal (P. L. 93-112 (1993), Americans with Disabilities Act) and anti-discrimination laws require reasonable accommodations be made for persons with disabilities such that sport placement decisions are equitable and safe for participants with and without disabilities alike.

While many cases regarding proper placement of athletes with disabilities are not potentially as 'grey area' ones cited above; understand, however, that such cases, when agreement cannot be reached between parents and school, have potential to be decided by courts of law.

Adapted Athletics and State High School Leagues

In the early-mid 1990s, state high school leagues, through committees of the National Federation of State High School Associations, began to discuss responsibility to sanction competitive sport opportunities for students with disabilities (Huber, 1994). Given the date of the foregoing reference and the number of state high school leagues yet to sanction competitive athletics for students with disabilities, there is yet to occur what might fairly be considered a trend to 'get onboard.' While community-based competitive athletic competitions for athletes with disabilities are offered in a number of states, relatively few opportunities presently are offered under the auspices of state high school leagues.

Minnesota remains a leader in state high school league sponsorship of adapted athletics. In 1992, following two decades of grassroots advocacy and lobbying, the community-based Minnesota Adapted Athletic Association, formed in 1975, became fully embraced by the Minnesota State High School League

(MSHSL). MSHSL athletes who participate in adapted events participate in one of two divisions: physically impaired (P.I.) or cognitively impaired (C.I.). Sports in each division include bowling, floor hockey, soccer, and softball.

These MSHSL sanctioned sports, including both the P.I. and D.I. divisions, accommodate some 3,000 participants per school year. For further information regarding; rules and policies, adapted athletic eligibility requirements, and supplemental rules specific to each sport, go to http://www.mshsl.org. These resources are recommended for use for comparison purposes or, as models where programs remain yet to be developed.

In 1996, in Georgia, the American Association of Adapted Sports Programs (AAASP) was founded as a 501(c) (3) non-profit whose stated mission is "to oversee the partnership of leaders in education and community to lay the foundation for a national network of interscholastic adapted athletic programs" (http://www.adaptedsports.org/). AAASP strives to promote interscholastic competition for athletes who use wheelchairs and athletes who are blind or visually impaired. AASAP sports, include wheelchair handball, wheelchair basketball, power soccer, wheelchair football and beep baseball for athletes who are blind or visually impaired.

In 2001, AAASP formed an alliance with the Georgia High School Association; resulting in AAASP becoming the official sanctioning and governing body for Georgia interscholastic adapted athletics. In 2006, AAASP entered into a similar partnership with the Alabama High School Athletic Association.

State high school athletic associations considering development of competitive sport opportunities for athletes with disabilities may wish to examine the AAASP model now in use. Also, available from AAASP are a range of instructional videos, rule books, and training manuals appropriate for use by both coaches and athletes and model forms and documents designed for coaches and program coordinators.

The above organizations can be considered examples of models for promoting school sanctioned sports programs for athletes who have disabilities. Teachers, coaches, students, parents, and community advocates of school-based sport opportunity for students with disabilities should contact the state high school athletic association in their respective states to determine the status of and advocate for adapted sport.

LEARNING ACTIVITY

Find out where adapted athletic activities are offered in your area. Ask your instructor, contact athletic directors in nearby school districts, or contact your state department of education's physical and/or adapted physical education consultant to find out where adapted athletic events are held. Select an athletic activity to attend; if possible, attend adapted athletic events for children, adolescents, and adults. Write a brief synopsis of the event. Did the event meet or exceed your expectations? What did you learn from the event?

Once you have attended a few events, consider volunteering to help out at events. Volunteering can become the vehicle for invaluable hands-on experience. If that were not incentive enough, volunteering at worthwhile community sport and recreation events, especially for preservice physical educators (regular and adapted), is an excellent resume builder.

CHAPTER SUMMARY

1. Sir Ludwig Guttman (1899–1980) is widely regarded as the father of wheelchair sports. In 1948, he founded the Stoke Mandeville games for athletes with spinal cord injuries, an event that he hoped one day would become equivalent of the Olympics for wheelchair athletes. He succeeded in helping establish the first Paralympic Games in 1960. Today, the Paralympics, which he was instrumental in inaugurating, offers world class competition opportunity for athletes with a full range of disabilities.

2. Historically, sport for persons with disabilities has been endorsed for, at minimum, three reasons: (1) as habilitation/rehabilitation/therapy, (2) as opportunity for normalizing life experience, and (3) sport for sport's own sake (i.e., "because I am an athlete"). This 1, 2, 3 numbering is not intended to imply a hierarchy. Certainly, anyone can participate in sport for one or all of the above reasons at the same time.

3. Initiatives to provide active lifestyle, including sport opportunities for persons with disabilities

should occur as early in life as is reasonably possible. Positive activity experiences early in life offer greatest potential for physical activity and sport to become and remain healthy lifestyle behavior choices for persons with and without disabilities throughout a lifetime.

4. Sports organizations cited in this chapter are exemplary of what is happening in sports for persons with disabilities communities today. Readers should become familiar with these organizations if they are reasonably nearby. When these organizations are not nearby, four alternatives exist: (1) Learn more about the organization by visiting its web site. (2) Contact local educators, regular and adapted, to find out the kinds of adapted sports opportunities that exist in your area, (3) Consult local directories to locate recreation service providers that offer recreational sport experiences for persons with disabilities (e.g. adapted bowling, skiing). (4) Contact your state department of education's physical education consultant (regular and/or adapted) for local as well as statewide information regarding adapted physical education and/or sport participation opportunities.

5. Organizations that sponsor adapted sport competitions use classification systems to ensure that competition among athletes is equitable (i.e., that all competitors, by virtue of classification according to ability are fairly matched). There are two

classification systems used: *medical* and *functional*. Often both systems are called upon to classify athletes for competition.

6. Athletes with disabilities must not, purely on the basis of disability, automatically be considered ineligible to participate in regular sports programs and on regular sports teams. A range of civil rights laws require that disability alone cannot be used arbitrarily to disqualify an athlete from participation in a regular sports program or on a regular sports team. Adapted athletics, of equal quality to regular programs, should become the alternative only when the athlete's disability legitimately renders her/him not able to meaningfully participate in a regular sports program.

7. State high school leagues are beginning to come on board with regard to sanctioning adapted athletics in manners similar to their sponsorships of regular, non-adapted athletics. However, state high school leagues that fully endorse adapted athletics remain exceptions to the rule.

8. The most valuable supplement to your classroom and book learning about adapted athletics is to proactively seek out hands on experience. Find an adapted physical activity program. Volunteer. Better yet, volunteer with an adapted physical education classmate for mutual support. Quite generally, adapted physical activity programs are virtually always in search of volunteers with a sincere desire to make a positive difference.

CHAPTER REFERENCES

http://www.adaptedsports.org/adaptedsports/about/about_mission.

Camp (n.a.): Youth Sessions. (2009). Golden Valley, MN: Courage Center.

Classification. (August 2008) (n.a.). Bonn Germany: International Paralympic Committee).

www.couragecenter.org/sports

www.daaa.org/DAAA_activities.html

www.deafalympics.com/about/

Disability Sports Classification Skills. (2007). Singapore: Singapore Disability Sports Council.

American Association of Adapted sports Programs. (n.d.). Retrieved September 3, 2009., from http://www.adaptedsports.org/

Blaze Sports (n.d.). Retrieved September 3, 2009, from www.blazesports.org

Camp (n.a.): Youth Sessions. (2009). Golden Valley, MN: Courage Center.

Classification. (August 2008) (n.a.). Bonn Germany: International Paralympic Committee).

Courage Center (n.d.). Retrieved September 3, 2009, from www.couragecenter.org/sports

Deaflympics (n.d.). Mission Statement. Retrieved on September 3, 2009, from www.deaflympics.com/about/

Disability Sports Classification Skills. (2007). Singapore: Singapore Disability Sports Council.

Disabled Sports USA (n.d.). Youth Sports Mentoring Program. Retrieved on September 3, 2009, from http://www.dsusa.org/MentoringProg/MetPDF/DSUSA%20Youth%20Sports%20Mentoring%20Brochure.pdf.

Dwarf Athletic Association of America (n.d.). Sports Rules. Retrieved on September 3, 2009, from www.daaa.org/DAAA_activities.html

Fitzgerald, H. (2009). [Text editor and Chapter 1 author]. Chapter 1: Disability and Youth Sport. Page 1. New York: Routledge.

Godfrey & Weisman, (n.d.). A History of Wheelchair Sports. Retrieved on September 3, 2009, from http://www.spitfirechallenge.ca/Sir%20Ludwig%20Guttmann%20early%20history.htm)

Hilgers, L. (07/05/2006). Youth Sports Drawing More Than Ever. Retrieved on August 31, 2009, from (http://www.cnn.com/2006/US/07/03/rise.kids.sports/index.html).

Huber, J. H. (1994). Minnesota high school league incorporates Minnesota Association for Adapted Athletics into league structure. *Palaestra*, September 22.

International Wheelchair Rugby Federation (n.d.). Classification. Retrieved on September 3, 2009, from www.iwrf.com/classification.htm

Minnesota State High School League (n.d.). Retrieved on September 3, 2009, from www.mshsl.org

National Beep Baseball Association (n.d.). About Us. Retrieved on September 3, 2009, from http://www.nbba.org/info.htm

National Sports Center for the Disabled (n.d.) Retrieved on September 3, 2009, from http://www.nscd.org/

National Wheelchair Basketball Association (n.d.) About Us. Retrieved on September 3, 2009, from www.nwba.org/index.php?option=com_content&view=article&id=5&Itemid=118

Official Website of the Paralympic Movement (n.d.). Retrieved on September 3, 2009, from www.Paralympic.org

Pacieorek, M. J. (2005). (Editor: Winnick, J. P.). *Adapted Physical Education and Sport* (4th ed.). Champaign, IL: Human Kinetics.

Public Law 93–112. (1973). Americans with Disabilities Act.

Rehabilitation Act of 1973, Section 504. US Code of Federal Regulations, Title 45, Volume 1, Section 84.47 (Nonacademic services). Revised January 1, 2008.

Special Olympics (n.d.). Sports Info, Rules, and Coaching Guides. Retrieved on September 3, 2009, from www.specialolympics.org/sports.aspx.

Steadward, R. & Peterson, C. (1997). *Paralympics: Where heroes come.* Edmonton, Alberta: One Shot Holdings Ltd.

Taub, Diane E. and Kimberly R. Greer. 2000. "Physical Activity as a Normalizing Experience for School-Age Children with Physical Disabilities: Implications for Legitimation of Social Identity and Enhancement of Social Ties." *Journal of Sport & Social Issues* 24:395–414.

The Division of Disability Resources and Educational Services, University of Illinois at Urbana-Champaign (March 15, 2008). Adapted Athletics. Retrieved on September 3, 2009, from www.disability.uiuc.edu/athletics/

United States Association of Blind Athletes (n.d.). About Us. Retrieved on September 3, 2009, from http://www.usaba.org/Pages/usabainformation/aboutus.html

What is Classification, (n.a.) (n.d.) St. Peters, MO: Wheelchair Sports, USA

Wheelchair Sports USA (n.d.). About Wheelchair Sports, USA. Retrieved on September 3, 2009, from www.wsusa.org/index.php?option=com_content&task=view&id=1&Itemid=439

Index

AAASP. *See* American Association of Adapted Sports Programs

AAHPERD, 20

acceptance, 43

accommodation, 154–155

acquired amputations, 195–196, 196*fig*

acquired disabilities, 6, 43–44

acute exercise, 101

AD. *See* Asperger's Disorder

ADA. *See* Americans with Disabilities Act

adaptation, 311, 314

adapted athletics, 362

    See also sports, disability and

adapted physical education, 7, 50

    See also physical education

Adapted Physical Education National Standards (APENS), 339

ADD. *See* attention deficit disorder

Adderall, 130

ADHD. *See* attention deficit hyperactive disorder

adipose tissue, 107

administrators, 55*t*, 57–58

advocacy organizations, 11

aerobic capacity, 101–103

air conduction testing, 175

airway obstruction, 256–257

albinism, 156

allergic asthma, 258

alpha motor neurons, 91, 91*fig*, 92*fig*

amblyopia, 156

American Association of Adapted Sports Programs (AAASP), 194

American Association of Health, Physical Education, Recreation and Dance (AAHPERD), 20

American Association on Intellectual and Developmental Disabilities (AAIDD), 115–116

Americans with Disabilities Act (ADA), 15–16

amphetamine (Adderall), 130

amplification, for deaf, 173–175

amputations, 200

    acquired, 195–196, 196*fig*

    by age, 196*fig*

    classification of, 197*fig*

    congenital, 195, 196*fig*

    physical limitations/concerns and, 196–198

    self-concept and, 198

    skin care for, 198

    strength training for, 199*t*

    See also limb deficiency

anaerobic capacity, 101–103

anencephaly, 227

ankle deviations, 188–189

anorexia nervosa, 288–291

anterior pelvic tilt, 188

anxiety, TBI and, 219–220

APENS. *See* Adapted Physical Education National Standards

aphasia, 125

aquatic activity. *See* swimming

arrhythmias, 295–296, 303

arteriovenous oxygen difference (AVD-O_2), 103

arthritis. *See* juvenile idiopathic arthritis; juvenile rheumatoid arthritis; pauciarticular arthritis; polyarticular arthritis; systemic arthritis

ASD. *See* autism spectrum disorders

Asperger's Disorder (AD), 143–142, 145, 149

    ASD and, 143

    diagnostic criteria for, 143*t*

aspirin, 248

assessments, 26–27

    authentic, 28, 29*t*, 39

    for consideration, 30–31*t*

    instruments for, 28–29

asthma, 255, 257

    causes of, 267

    management of, 260

    medication for, 261, 261*t*, 267

    physical activity for, 260–265, 267

    psychosocial considerations of, 259–260

    relaxation for, 265

    severity of, 261

    tolerance level for, 264

    triggers, 258

    types of, 258–260

    See also exercise-induced asthma

astigmatism, 155

asymmetrical tonic neck reflex (ATNR), 71*t*, 72–73, 73*fig*, 207

ataxic cerebral palsy, 207, 211*t*

atherosclerosis, 293

athetosid idyskinetic cerebral palsy, 207, 211*t*, 212

athletes, 360–361

    eating disorders and, 290

    See also adapted athletics

athletic coach, 56*t*, 59

ATNR. *See* asymmetrical tonic neck reflex

attention deficit disorder (ADD), 126

    physical activity and, 128–131

attention deficit hyperactive disorder (ADHD), 126–127

    diagnostic criteria for, 128

    physical activity and, 128–131

attention disorders, 134*t*–135*t*, 136–137, 139

auditory acuity, 88*t*, 89, 97

auditory brain stem response, 175

auditory discrimination, 88*t*

auditory figure-ground, 88*t*, 89

auditory perception, 163

auditory-perceptual development, 88*t*, 89

auditory-tactile/kinesthetic integration, 95*t*

auditory training, 173–175

authentic assessment, 28, 29*t*, 39

autism

    diagnostic criteria for, 142*t*

    high functioning, 145

    physical education and, 148*fig*

autism spectrum disorders (ASD), 4

    AD and, 143

    assessment of, 146–147

    causes of, 144–145

    characterization of, 142

    classification of, 141–144

    diagnosis of, 141–144

    DSM-IV-TR and, 142

    epidemiology of, 144–145

    motor characteristics of, 145–146

    motor learning/educational approaches and, 146–149

    physical education and, 147, 149

    sensory-motor interventions and, 146

Daily Book Cutting Log

Name: Andres Perez   Date: 11/25/24

BIN #	BOOKS COMPLETED	BIN #	BOOKS COMPLETED
Bin 1	22	Bin 41	
Bin 2	22	Bin 42	
Bin 3		Bin 43	
Bin 4		Bin 44	
Bin 5		Bin 45	
Bin 6		Bin 46	
Bin 7		Bin 47	
Bin 8		Bin 48	
Bin 9		Bin 49	
Bin 10		Bin 50	
Bin 11		Bin 51	
Bin 12		Bin 52	
Bin 13		Bin 53	
Bin 14		Bin 54	
Bin 15		Bin 55	
Bin 16		Bin 56	
Bin 17		Bin 57	
Bin 18		Bin 58	
Bin 19		Bin 59	
Bin 20		Bin 60	
Bin 21		Bin 61	
Bin 22		Bin 62	
Bin 23		Bin 63	
Bin 24		Bin 64	
Bin 25		Bin 65	
Bin 26		Bin 66	
Bin 27		Bin 67	
Bin 28		Bin 68	
Bin 29		Bin 69	
Bin 30		Bin 70	
Bin 31		Bin 71	
Bin 32		Bin 72	
Bin 33		Bin 73	
Bin 34		Bin 74	
Bin 35		Bin 75	
Bin 36		Bin 76	
Bin 37		Bin 77	
Bin 38		Bin 78	
Bin 39		Bin 79	
Bin 40		Bin 80	

TOTAL:_____/ 600

SHIFT:_____   STATION #:_____